The Land That I Show You

STANLEY FELDSTEIN received his Ph.D. from New York University and is a member of the faculty at the New School for Social Research, where he teaches American Jewish history. He has written reviews for the New York *Times,* the *Journal of Southern History,* and the *Journal of Negro History.* He is author of *Once a Slave* and *The Poisoned Tongue,* a documentary history of American racism, as well as the Anchor Press book *Ordeal of Assimilation.* Dr. Feldstein lives in Brooklyn, New York, with his wife and two children.

THE LAND
THAT I SHOW YOU

Three Centuries of Jewish Life in America

STANLEY FELDSTEIN

ANCHOR BOOKS
Anchor Press/Doubleday
Garden City, New York

1979

The Land That I Show You was originally published in hardcover by Anchor Press/Doubleday in 1978.

Grateful acknowledgment is made to the following sources:

Excerpt from *Born a Jew,* by Boris Bogen. Published by The Macmillan Company, 1930.

Excerpt from *As I Know Them: Some Jews and a Few Gentiles,* by Rebekah Kohut. Published by Doubleday & Company, Inc., 1929.

Excerpt from *My First Eighty Years,* by Bernard Horwich. Published by Argus Books, Inc., 1939, Chicago.

Excerpt from *Is Curly Jewish?* by Paul Jacobs. Copyright © 1965 by Paul Jacobs. Reprinted by permission of Atheneum Publishers.

Excerpt from *Impresario,* by Sol Hurok and Ruth Goode. Reprinted by permission of Random House, Inc.

Excerpt from *Take My Life,* by Eddie Cantor. Copyright © 1957 by Eddie Cantor and Jane Kesner Ardmore. Published by Doubleday & Company, Inc. By permission of McIntosh & Otis, Inc.

Excerpt from *Groucho and Me,* by Groucho Marx. Copyright © 1959 by Groucho Marx. Reprinted by permission of the publisher, Bernard Geis Associates, Inc.

Excerpt from "Recollections of a Student," by Moses Soyer, in *The Educational Alliance: Restrospective Art Exhibit,* April 29–May 18, 1963. Reprinted by permission of David Soyer.

Excerpt from *A Child of the Century,* by Ben Hecht. Copyright 1954 by Ben Hecht. Reprinted by permission of Simon & Schuster, a Division of Gulf & Western Corporation.

Excerpt from Rabbi Martin Siegel, "Diary of a Suburban Rabbi," edited by Mel Ziegler, *New York* Magazine, January 18, 1971. Copyright © 1971 by New York Magazine Corp. Reprinted by permission of *New York* Magazine.

Excerpt from "The New Suburbanites of the 50's," by Harry Gersh, *Commentary,* March 1954. Copyright 1954 by the American Jewish Committee. Reprinted from *Commentary* by permission.

Excerpt from "New Jewish Community in Formation; A Conservative Center Catering to Present-Day Needs," by Morris Freedman, *Commentary,* January 1955. Copyright © 1955 by the American Jewish Committee. Reprinted from *Commentary* by permission.

Excerpt from "Uncle Tom and Other Such Jews," by M. Jay Rosenberg, *The Village Voice,* February 13, 1969. Copyright © The Village Voice, Inc., 1969. Reprinted by permission of *The Village Voice.*

Excerpts from *Some of These Days,* by Sophie Tucker. Copyright 1945 by Sophie Tucker. Reprinted by permission of Bert Tucker.

Excerpts from "You're in the Army Now," by Henry U. Ribalow, *Contemporary*

FOR MY FAMILY
Susan, Eileen & Louis

Acknowledgments

WITHOUT the assistance of many people, this book never could have been written. I am most grateful to Loretta Barrett, editorial director of Anchor Press, for her advice, patience, and encouragement. She suggested the project and helped me find my way through the maze of material.

My special thanks to Rabbi David M. Posner, of New York's Temple Emanu-El, for his valuable suggestions on the religious aspects of American Jewish life and to Sylvia Smialy Posner, of Hebrew Union College, who took an active part in my research.

Thanks are also due to Mark Sufrin, whose advice, observations, and interpretations at various stages of the manuscript proved most helpful, and to my sister Thelma Feldstein Rahinsky for her translations of the Yiddish material and her warm support.

My friends at Doubleday—Angela Cox and Harriet Rubin—and my students at the New School for Social Research gave me useful comments and editorial help.

Many institutions and organizations assisted me in collecting material for the book. Most of all, I want to express gratitude to Mr. Phillip Miller, librarian of the New York school of Hebrew Union College—Jewish Institute of Religion, and his staff, and to Dr. Abraham Peck, assistant to the Director of the American Jewish Archives at the Cincinnati school of Hebrew Union College.

Stanley Feldstein
Brooklyn, New York
July 1977.

Contents

CHAPTER VIII

NO LONGER STRANGERS

CHAPTER IX

INTO THE PRESENT

LIST OF ILLUSTRATIONS

(following page 102)

(following page 222)

"Go forth from your native land . . .
to the land that I show you."

GENESIS, 12

CHAPTER I

Sephardim, the First to Come

JEWISH COLONIAL LIFE 1654–1776

And it came to pass in the year 5414 [1654] that the Portuguese came back to Brazil, and from the Hollanders took their land by force. And God had compassion on his people, granted them favor and grace. . . . And all our people went down to the sea in . . . ships, and spread sail, and God led them to their destination to this land, and they . . . reached the end of the inhabited earth called New Holland.

—David Franco-Mendes, *History of the Great Men of Israel* (1784)

IN 1654, Brazil was reoccupied by the victorious forces of a Portuguese liberation army, and the small Jewish community, fearing a return of the Inquisition, hastily made plans to seek refuge elsewhere. As Portuguese troops approached Pernambuco, a band of twenty-three Jews, who had courageously joined their neighbors in defense of the colony, sought the assistance of several families boarding a ship for New Amsterdam. They pleaded to be taken along, but the French barque *Sainte Catherine* was small, dangerously overcrowded, and commanded by Captain Jacques de la Mothe, a man who made no secret of his dislike for Jews. Money, however, and the promise of additional payment on arrival were enough to secure passage.

As penniless refugees, the Jews who disembarked at New Amsterdam were unwanted and, for the Dutch, their presence at the primitive outpost at the mouth of the Hudson River was a calamity. "The Jews who arrive here," wrote an angry Peter Stuyvesant in a letter to the settlement's directors in Holland, "would nearly all like to remain . . . but with their customary usury and deceitful trading with Christians are very repugnant. . . ." They are a very "crafty and generally treacherous people . . . and owing to their indigence . . . might become a charge in the coming winter . . . such hateful enemies of the name of Christ [should] be not allowed further to infect and trouble this new colony."

Before the ink on the letter dried, Stuyvesant ordered that "the Jews who came from the West Indies and now from the Fatherland must prepare to depart. . . ."

Johann Megapolensis, the Catholic-born zealot of the Reformed Church, echoed the same sentiment. In the past he had opposed separate worship by Lutherans and Quakers; now he fought any progress by Jews. In a letter to his archbishop in Holland, he wrote:

> Some Jews came from Holland last summer in order to trade . . . they were healthy, but poor. . . . They came several times to my house, weeping and bemoaning their misery. Some more have come from Holland this spring. They report that many more of the same lot would follow, and that they would build here a synagogue. This causes among the congregation here a great deal of complaint and murmuring. These people have no other God than the Mammon of unrighteousness, and no other aim than to get possession of Christian property. . . . Therefore, we request your Reverences to obtain from the Messrs. Directors, that these Godless rascals, who are of no benefit to the country but look at everything from their own profit, may be sent away from here.

While the colony's rulers demanded the removal of the newcomers, Holland's Jewish leaders took steps to remind the Dutch West India Company that deporting the Jews from the colony could "be of no advantage to the Company but rather damaging. . . . There are many of the [Jewish] nation," they pleaded, "who have lost their possessions" in defense of Dutch interests in Brazil "and have arrived from there in great poverty."

> It is well known to your Honors that the Jewish nation in Brazil have at all times been faithful and have striven to guard and maintain that place, risking for that purpose their possessions and their blood. . . .
> Your Honors should also please consider that many of the Jewish nation are principal shareholders in the Company.

The decision to allow the Jews to remain further incensed Stuyvesant. "Giving them liberty," he argued, "we cannot refuse the Luthers and Papists." To quell the bitter governor, the directors assured him that Jewish settlement did not imply "civil and religious liberties" and certainly not "license to exercise and carry on their religion in synagogues and gatherings."

With permission to settle, the tiny band of Jews waged an aggressive fight to win acceptance: they paid their taxes and worked toward the growth of the city. When the city's defenses were strengthened against Indian attack, several Jewish donors voluntarily contributed one hundred guilders each, a sum exceeded only by Stuyvesant and four others. And when an ordinance was passed disqualifying Jews from standing guard but forcing them instead to pay a special tax, Jacob Barsimson and Asser Levy demanded the right "to keep guard with other burghers, or be free from the tax. . . ." Their petition, however, was rejected, and the sardonic Stuyvesant, at a meeting of the New Amsterdam Council, told them "to depart whenever and whither it pleases them." Nothing was further from their minds, and in their persistence they eventually secured permission to stand guard like any other citizens.

Levy's determined efforts to secure greater liberties for himself and his coreligionists were rewarded with success. To the astonishment of officials, he requested burgher rights (citizenship), claiming that "such ought not be refused him as he keeps watch and ward like other burghers," and submitted a burgher certificate from the City of Amsterdam "proving that the Jew is a burgher there." Unwilling to make this crucial decision, the burgomasters placed the burden with Stuyvesant and his council. Fortunately, the governor was in ill favor in Holland and, recognizing that it was not the time to further anger his superiors, ordered the determined Levy to be admitted as a burgher.

Though plagued by restrictions, "the Jews," wrote Hendrik Van Loon, "continued to come to Nieuw Amsterdam in ever increasing numbers, and the people . . . continued to resent their presence, to bombard the magistrates with complaints whenever a Jew kept open shop on the Sabbath day, whenever another tried to enter a trade which was held to be an exclusively Christian occupation, whenever a few Jews tried to mount guard with the rest of the citizens, whenever fresh shiploads from Brazil arrived and dumped a few dozen more hungry-faced Jewish children on the wharves of the Company."

The Jewish fight for equality continued for the ten years of their residence in New Amsterdam. In 1664, an English man-of-war appeared off the coast, its cannon trained on the heart of the city. In the future, the struggle would be waged against a new, and somewhat more enlightened, colonial ruler.

In the seventeenth century, prospects for European Jewry were bleak. In Eastern Europe, they were victims of savage pogroms and in the Austrian Empire were subjected to medieval restraints and economic distress. France barely tolerated them, and on the Iberian Peninsula inquisitional courts were sentencing marranos* to be burned at the stake. Jews from these regions, bold enough to seek a new life, looked to the commercially emerging nations of the west—England and Holland—for refuge.

In these two nations, Jews were, in varying degrees, made to feel comparatively welcome. Attracted by a growing mercantile economy and religious tolerance, they settled and prospered as merchants and businessmen. Seventeenth-century London and Amsterdam became the home of a mixed Sephardic (of the Iberian Peninsula) and Ashkenazic (of Eastern and Central Europe) Jewish community.

While most newcomers found life good and remained in their new homelands, some, encouraged by tales of economic success, chose to resettle in England's overseas possessions. Boarding the ships, many thought of the dangers, but their dream of greater religious freedom and a chance to live as full citizens of a country gave them courage.

There were few Jews in Puritan New England. Even Boston, the largest and most influential settlement in British North America, had no Jewish community until the 1840s, particularly ironic in view of the keen interest that Puritans displayed in the Jews.

Puritan concern with Jews, however, was purely academic, never coupled with religious toleration or the call for Jewish settlement. In fact, the earliest reference to a Jew living in Massachusetts was accompanied by a notice warning "him out of the colony." Puritan sentiment is strikingly evident in a letter written by Winslow of Plymouth to Governor Winthrop of Massachusetts, explaining that his colony was opposed to the settlement of ". . . Jew, Papist or any other."

The pattern was the same in New Hampshire, Connecticut, and

---

* Jews who converted to Christianity during the Spanish Inquisition, many of whom practiced Judaism in secret.

Maine. Again Jews tried to settle, but no community was ever established, as they sought other areas with greater economic opportunity and more hospitable political environments.

In Newport, a community free of Puritan hostility, Jews managed to carve out their New England enclave. The original Jewish community of Newport was West Indian in origin. Attracted to the settlement in the 1650s by its commercial possibilities, they settled, and called on their West Indian brethren to follow. Newport, described by Cotton Mather as a "receptacle of the convicts of Jerusalem and the outcasts of the land," was a happy contrast to the other New England settlements. It gave Jews far greater opportunities than any of the other colonies, and quickly emerged as the most important Jewish settlement. George Mason, in his *Reminiscenses of Newport,* described the Jewish element:

> The Jews . . . were not only noted for their knowledge of mercantile and commercial affairs, but also for their industry, enterprise, and probity. . . . They were neither good sailors nor good soldiers; nor did they appear to be very fond of books. Moses Lopez and Jacob Joseph, it is true, were numbered among the founders of the Redwood Library, and . . . Jacob Rodriguez Rivera was a stockholder in that institution; but this may be taken as one of many evidences of their desire to promote whatever promised to be a public benefit.

Like Newport, the commercial possibilities of New York and the governor's welcome to dissenters attracted Jewish settlers. In 1730 the survivors of New Amsterdam established Shearith Israel (Remnant of Israel) Synagogue and opened the doors to a congregational school. Peter Kalm, a Christian visitor to New York in 1748, sketched the Jewish community:

> . . . there are many Jews settled in New York, who possess great privileges. They have a synagogue and houses, and great country seats of their own property, and are allowed to keep shop in town. They have likewise several ships, which they freight, and send out with their own goods. . . . they enjoy all the privileges common to other inhabitants of this town. . . .
> . . . I was frequently in company with Jews. I was informed . . . that these people never boiled any meat for themselves on Saturday, but . . . always did it the day before; and that in winter they kept a fire during the whole Saturday. They commonly eat no pork; yet I have been told by several men of credit, that many of them (especially among the young Jews) when traveling, did not make

the least difficulty about eating this, or any other meat that was put before them; even though they were in company with Christians.

He went on to discuss Jewish religious observance:

> I was in their synagogue . . . and each time I was put in a particular seat, which was set apart for strangers or Christians. Both men and women were dressed entirely in the *English* fashion; the former had all of them hats on, and did not once take them off during the service. The galleries, I observed, were appropriated to the ladies, while the men sat below. During prayers the men spread a white cloth over their heads; which perhaps is to represent sackcloth. But I observed that the wealthier sort of people had a much richer cloth than the poorer ones. Many of the men had Hebrew books, in which they sang and read alternately.

Striking out from New York, Jews moved south along the Delaware River and settled Philadelphia, but well into the eighteenth century they still were hesitant about migrating to the Quaker colony. Though Pennsylvania had no established church and offered as much freedom as New York and Newport, there was still the question of economic opportunity. Jews waited to see if Philadelphia would have a bright commercial future, and those anxious to relocate avoided permanent settlement in the area until the 1730s.

By this time, colonial Jewry saw the rise of commercial Philadelphia. Anticipating its becoming the mercantile center of North America, they began to arrive in numbers, deserting New York, Newport, and other surrounding areas.

Dissatisfied with the opportunities they found, a handful pushed west to the frontier, helping lay the foundation for the development of Pennsylvania. Very soon, these adventurous Jews practiced their professions, plied their wares, and tilled the soil in the frontier settlements of Schaefferstown, Lancaster, Easton, Reading, and Pittsburgh.

In the eighteenth century, the area between Philadelphia and Charleston contained few Jewish pioneers. This vast territory, which included Maryland, Virginia, and North Carolina, would not attract Jews until the end of the American Revolution. At no time prior to the outbreak of war did any of these colonies house a substantial bourgeoisie or boast of large cities offering commercial enterprises. Most Jews, accustomed to urban life and not wishing to engage in agriculture, saw little future in the plantation economy of these colonies.

There were, however, reasons other than economic which kept Jews away. In Virginia the population was not as religiously mixed as other colonial settlements, consisting almost entirely of staunch Church of Englanders who wanted to keep the province Anglican.

As late as 1791, Jews were still wary of the colony. Rebecca Samuels, wife of a Petersburg silversmith, described conditions in a letter to her parents:

> When the Jews of Philadelphia or New York hear the name Virginia, they get nasty. And they are not wrong! It won't do for a Jew. In the first place it is an unhealthy district, and we are only human. God forbid, if anything should happen to us, where would we be thrown? There is no cemetery in the whole of Virginia. . . . You cannot imagine what kind of Jews they have here. They were all German itinerants who made a living by begging in Germany. They came to America during the war, as soldiers [Hessians], and now they can't recognize themselves. . . . The whole reason why we are leaving this place is because of [the absence of] *Yehudishkeit* [Jewishness].

"Dear Parents," she continued,

> I know quite well you will not want me to bring up my children like Gentiles. Here they cannot become anything else. Jewishness is pushed aside here. There are here [in Petersburg] ten or twelve Jews, and they are not worthy of being called Jews. We have a shohet [ritual slaughterer] here who goes to market and buys terefah [non-kosher] meat and brings it home. On Rosh Ha-Shanah and on Yom Kippur the people worshipped here without one sefer torah, and not one of them wore the tallit . . .
>
> You can believe me that I crave to see a synagogue to which I can go. The way we live now is no life at all. We do not know what the Sabbath and the holidays are. On the Sabbath all the Jewish shops are open; and they do business on that day as they do throughout the whole week. But ours we do not allow to open. With us there is still some Sabbath. You must believe me that in our house we all live as Jews as much as we can.

South Carolina was more favorable to Jewish settlement, because its initial colonization took place under a charter embodying John Locke's liberal political ideas. Jews started to arrive and, by 1710, formed a large enough group to hold their first religious service. Responding to Charleston's growth as a large commercial center, by mid-century they made their way to the colony from London, New York, Georgia, and the West Indies. By the outbreak of the Revolution, in 1775, the little synagogue community of the 1750s grew to fifty families, about two hundred people, and took its place as the capital of southern Jewry. Almost immediately, some Jews moved out of South Carolina's coastal tidewater and settled parts of the interior.

In the charter granted by George II to the trustees of the colony of Georgia, freedom of religion was guaranteed to all, and Governor James Oglethorpe demonstrated no prejudice toward anyone of any religion. Oglethorpe, however, met resistance from both trustees and settlers who were anxious to keep Jews out of the colony. "I beg leave to say something of the Jews," wrote Thomas Coram, a resident of the colony, "who, to the number of between forty and fifty, have procured themselves to be already settled there contrary to the will and without the consent of the trustees, and there are more of their nation now going over to them. I humbly conceive these shocking matters require your most serious attention; for unless you speedily take some vigorous resolutions to suppress effectually the two great evils aforesaid, Georgia will soon become a Jewish colony. . . ." But the governor persisted and created a favorable climate for Jewish settlement.

Georgia, geographically situated between England's prize possession of South Carolina and the hostile territory of Spanish Florida, was established to create a buffer zone against Spanish and French intrusion. To protect its southern frontier through the establishment of this colony, Parliament advanced funds for the venture. In addition to the government subsidy, some of the money was raised through public subscription. Among those empowered to solicit contributions were three influential members of London's Shephardic community: Alvaro Lopez Suasso, Francis Salvador, and Anthony Da Costa.

Under the authority of their commission, the three secured a considerable amount of money, but instead of giving it to the trustees, as they were instructed, used the funds to help poor London Jews migrate to Georgia. Informed that the three Jewish commissioners had exceeded their authority, the trustees demanded the surrender of the commissions and the return of the money. The trio refused and proceeded with their plans. On July 11, 1733, a ready-made Jewish community set foot in the port of Savannah: thirty-two Sephardim and nine Ashkenazim—fifteen of them females.

Oglethorpe, surprised by their arrival, considered rejecting their entry. But the charter guaranteed freedom of religion to all but Catholics and he admitted them. Reasoning that they would be helpful due to their experience as traders and merchants, he notified London of his decision.

Outraged by Oglethorpe's action, the trustees ordered him to "use his best endeavors that [the Jews] be allowed no kind of settlement with any of the [religious] guarantees," expressing fear that the Jewish presence would prove detrimental. Ignoring London's instructions, the governor encouraged the Jews to remain and notified his superiors that his action "has not proved a detriment to the colony."

Jewish settlement in British North America thrived, their presence grew, and they went on to become industrious, influential citizens of the new land.

Colonial rights granted the Jews had their roots in the England of Cromwell. Exiled in 1290 by Edward I, Jews trickled back to the kingdom during the Cromwellian era. Influenced by wealthy Dutch Sephardim, Oliver Cromwell was convinced that Jewish mercantile skills would be valuable in England's quest to dominate the Atlantic trade. Cromwell, however, faced strong opposition to the Jewish influx. Compelled by his opponents to openly deny the legislative right of return, he still permitted Jewish settlement, without legally authorizing it. Cromwell's policy of "toleration by oversight" benefited the Jewish community: it was almost certain that any legislation governing Jewish resettlement would have been accompanied by severe restrictions. Instead, Jews found themselves in a nation whose laws ignored their existence.

Not long after, Britain granted Jews full economic equality, some civil freedoms, and religious liberty. More important, Jews were not forced to dwell in ghettos. Granted the privilege of free choice of settlement, they were able to enter the body politic and to a limited degree attain the rights that all Englishmen possessed.

After success at home, some Jews sought opportunities in the overseas possessions. But those who ventured across the Atlantic—with the anticipation of transplanting their rights granted by the Crown— discovered that their hope of civil equality would not fully materialize.

Upon arrival in America, Jewish immigrants learned that all colonies were not held directly by the Crown but were controlled by proprietors who legislated their own regulations with regard to settlement. In this fashion William Penn established his colony for Quakers, the Calverts planned Maryland for Catholics, the London Company of Virginia favored members of the Anglican Church, and the Puritans, while proclaiming Massachusetts Bay and Plymouth as their own, discouraged other non-conformists from settlement.

Nevertheless, some provinces deviated from a religious orientation—perhaps the best example being the Carolinas. The proprietors of these colonies were not interested in perpetuating a specific religious belief or in politically limiting its Dissenters; rather, they were primarily concerned with economic development and making a profit from their investment. Realizing that increased population was the key to financial success, the Carolina leadership sought a new and different attraction to induce farmers, skilled craftsmen, artisans, and merchants to settle. In order to compete with the well-established colonies to the north, they did what most others refused to do—open the territory with the full guarantee of civil freedom to "healthens, Jews, and other Dissenters."

Still, most colonies did not follow the Carolina example and placed strong emphasis on religious objectives. Jews and Christian Dissenters were confronted with severe religious and political restrictions throughout British North America. Due to their insignificant numbers and low visibility, however, Jews were not the primary targets of the repressive legislation. At no time during the colonial era was there ever enacted any law whose purpose was to restrict Jewish rights. Rather, the legal disabilities were directed against Protestant non-conformists and Catholics. But in the interpretation and enforcement of these restrictive codes, the Jew—not of the majority religion—was obliged to share the fate of the Dissenter: New York levied taxes in support of an established church; Massachusetts reserved the franchise to Trinitarians; Pennsylvania permitted only Christians the right to hold office and vote; Virginia forbade Jews to employ Christian domestics; Georgia granted Jews the right to hold office only if they abandoned certain religious beliefs; and Maryland enacted a law that permitted blacks (bond and free) to testify against Jews but not against other whites. All colonies had an established church, and in most only that institution could hold public services.

Prominent among these restrictions were the Sunday laws. These statutes, designed to force everyone to respect the Christian Sabbath, became a major hindrance to Jews. Though never expected to attend church services, Jews were compelled to absent themselves from work, refrain from travel, forgo recreational activities, and stay off the public streets. Since Jews were the only group that respected Saturday as the Sabbath, this restriction caused severe hardship. The law could have caused more than mere financial loss, for if a Jew was found guilty of violating the Lord's Day statute, he was threatened with punishments that ranged from fine and imprisonment to flogging and death.

There were also blasphemy laws. Enacted by almost every colony, these statutes made it illegal for anyone to deny the doctrine of the Trinity. If a Jew, in the act of explaining the nature of his faith to a Christian, denied the New Testament or spoke of the coming of the Messiah or rejected Christ, he could be subjected to arrest and severe penalties—in some colonies, death.

In the summer of 1658, Jacob Lumbrozo, a Portuguese Jew living in Maryland, was denounced by several pious Puritans and Quakers "for uttering words of blasphemy against our Blessed Saviour Jesus Christ." In February 1659, he was arrested and charged with denying the divinity of Christ. Lumbrozo explained to the court that as a Jew he could not accept the resurrection of Jesus but had certainly not intended to degrade the Christian Messiah.

Lumbrozo, the only colonial Jew ever to be brought to court for the crime of blasphemy, was mysteriously released after the preliminary investigation. "It may be," wrote historian Jacob Marcus, "that the Calverts, restored to power after the Puritan interregnum, freed him, or he possibly benefited from the generous terms of the amnesty proclaimed in Maryland in March 1659 to celebrate Richard Cromwell's assumption of the Lord Protectorate after the death of his father, Oliver. It is more probable, though not documented, that Lumbrozo saved his life, as many Jews had done before in Europe, by submitting to baptism. At any rate, by September 10, 1663, John Lumbrozo, as he then called himself, had taken the oath of allegiance and become endenizened. The following year found him serving as a juryman, a privilege reserved to Christians."

Along with religious repression, there were laws against office holding and the vote. In the colonies, these political privileges were tied to property qualifications, religious affiliation, and special oaths. Though Jews could have satisfied the financial requirements, they were nevertheless barred from political participation, because they would not utter the religious oath containing the words "faith in God Jesus Christ."

Denied the political privileges of freeholders, Jews waited until the English Parliament passed the Plantation Act of 1740, which abolished this oath. The act naturalized foreign Protestants and others who "settled . . . in any of His Majesty's Colonies in America."

All eligible petitioners, except Catholics, had to have lived in the colonies for seven years, with only two months absence during that period. Also, an oath of Abjuration had to be taken. However, should those who qualified for citizenship omit parts of the oath, they were simply fined ten British pounds for each omission. The terms of the Plantation Act were greeted with jubilation by the Jewish community. Jews were no longer required to bare their heads while taking the oath or forced to profess faith in "God Jesus Christ" or recite the phrase "upon the true faith of a Christian." Jews were now permitted to read from the Old Testament rather than from an Anglican prayer book when participating in this ceremony.

Although taking the oath of citizenship was a solemn affair, involving the rite of sacrament, this was not required of the Jew. He merely signed his name on the court clerk's register and was sworn in. The newly granted political right was not taken lightly by Jews who qualified for citizenship. Rather, the Oath of Abjuration was read from a scroll with great ceremony by the Jewish petitioner.

When naturalized, Jews were included in the colonial body politic and began, for the first time in their painful history, a journey that eventually led to full emancipation. Yet even with the passage of the Plantation Act, Jews still were confronted by political disabilities: the law prohibited the newly naturalized subject from serving in Parliament, the Privy Council, and in high civil and military capacities. Also, Jews were excluded from receiving grants of property from the Crown, and despite the new law, certain colonies placed barriers, however temporary.

Jews were severely restricted for most of their colonial experience, but most recognized that they enjoyed more freedom in America than anywhere else in the world. They also recognized that they enjoyed a wider range of freedom than Catholics and Protestant non-conformists. With the exception of the infamous Lumbrozo blasphemy case, no Jew was ever arrested, imprisoned, or harmed because he was a Jew.

The American colonies were primarily a land of farmers, and as late as the mid-eighteenth century, nine tenths of the inhabitants made their living from the soil. Yet, in the midst of this overwhelmingly agricultural society, one distinct group—the Jews—did not become farmers but, rather, devoted their energy and skills to trade, shopkeeping, and international and intercolonial trade. Jews, however, had a token representation on the farms and plantations of the seaboard provinces.

Along with the handful of Jewish yeoman farmers were some who purchased land to improve the acreage and sell it at a profit, others who acquired land upon the foreclosure of a mortgage, and those who received land grants—a practice common to the early settlement of the Carolinas and Georgia. Samuel Judah tilled a homestead in Vermont, Jacob Lumbrozo grew tobacco in seventeenth-century Maryland, Naphtali and Isaac Hart cultivated their New England property with hired hands and slaves, Simon Valentine operated a five-hundred-acre plantation on the outskirts of Charleston, and Francis Salvador, the South Carolina planter, grew indigo on six thousand acres tilled by more than two dozen slaves.

The primary commercial center for the American colonies was the British West Indies, the very area where Jews were firmly established and where Jewish mercantile influence was extremely important. America's Jewish merchants, using their religio-commercial connections, enjoyed a competitive advantage over many non-Jews engaged in that same lucrative intercolonial trade. Since the West Indian trade was a necessity to America's economy and since this trade was, in varying degrees, controlled by Jewish mercantile houses, American Jewry was influential in the commercial destiny of Britain's overseas empire.

In time, American trade with the West Indies boomed. Jewish merchant shippers, in addition to their tobacco and sugar imports, advertised commodities such as "White [indentured] servants, sundry sorts of earthen ware in casks and crates, Cheshire cheese, loaf sugar, cutlery ware, pewter, grindstones, coals and sundry other goods. . . ." Other merchants placed ads that offered the colonials more luxurious products: "pins and needles, scotch snuff, oil-cloth umbrellas, fine writing paper, indigo, Geneva, and other goods exceedingly cheap for ready cash."

As the profits from overseas trade soared, Jewish merchants outfitted ships for India, Malabar, and China. Abraham deLucena and Luis Gomez, two New York Sephardim, exported large amounts of wheat to Lisbon—their ships returning with Portuguese wines or often with new Jewish settlers. As a consequence of this trade, colonial newspapers advertised for sale "Callicoes, Chintz, Bombazeens, Sattins, Blunderbuses, Cannon Balls, Regimental Shoe Buckles, Buttons and Perfumery." On March 3, 1729, Luis Gomez called the public's attention to a "parcel of very fine glasses with fine brass arms." In the New York *Mercury* of August 1, 1761, Jonas Phillips offered "sundry European and India goods, likewise wines, brandies, tea, raisins, Florence Oyl and biscuits."

Along with the consumer goods, some merchants carried another type of cargo: African slaves. Jews entered the slave traffic long after it was established, when Jacob Rivera imported several Africans for sale to the highest bidder; some years after this venture, Isaac Elizar and Samuel Moses outfitted a ship for the same purpose. The most influential merchant to enter the slave trade was Aaron Lopez, who began his career as a slaver in 1764.

So profitable was his first voyage that by the 1770s Lopez was sending three ships a year, each returning with eighty to one hundred slaves destined for the West Indies. Lopez also sent some of his human cargo to Charleston, where Solomon Isaacs and the firm of DaCosta and Farr were acting as import agents. After glancing at the advertisements for "needles and pins," one might turn the page of the New York *Gazette* to an item declaring that Abraham Mendes was offering "a Parcel of Likely young Negroes."

In addition to the overseas trade, Jews engaged in a variety of regional enterprises. Aaron Lopez of Newport supplemented his mercantile activities by investing in fishing and whaling and the manufacture of candles. In time, his activities touched such diverse fields as the production of rum, the construction of houses, and the supply of prefabricated houses for the West Indies. At the peak of his commercial empire, his ships carried fish, livestock, and lumber from New England, iron from Rhode Island, flour and wheat from New York, naval stores from Pennsylvania, and rice from South Carolina. In return for these products, Lopez brought to the colonies sugar and molasses from the West Indies and textiles and hardware from Great Britain, employing a new form of marketing: the use of a business agent, or factor. "Dealing with the West Indian planters," wrote Bruce Bigelow, "was always a ticklish problem for a northern merchant, and Lopez knew that a good bargain could be struck more quickly by a shrewd factor than a stupid captain. The wise policy was to have one's own man on the spot to make acquaintances among the leading planters and merchants, sell the cargoes of livestock, provisions, and lumber direct, and secure early return shipments of sugar and molasses."

On eastern Long Island, Aaron Isaacs traded in real estate, operated a windmill, and supplied New England with beef. The Louzada brothers, of New Jersey, merchandised their goods out of a general store; Myer Hart, of Easton, Pennsylvania, sold liquor, was an innkeeper, traded in real estate, and shipped grain overseas. In Philadelphia, David Franks made his fortune in mercantile shipping, fur trading, and especially supplying troops during the French and Indian War. So lucrative was this military business that others became involved in ventures of their own to provision the British and colonial militias. "The colonial wars," noted a Jewish visitor from England, "afforded Jews the opportunity to become commercially active in the western trade and the military operations of the British, the French, and the Indians."

In addition to these commercial pursuits, Jews were active in other areas of economic enterprise. They worked as ranchers, craftsmen, peddlers; became apprentices and clerks, commercial agents for shippers, brokers, and factors; dabbled in insurance brokerage and finance; and in a few cases, took part in smuggling and privateering.

During the French and Indian War, Jewish merchants were granted commissions to prey on French commerce: Sampson Simon's *Hardy, Sampson, Union,* and *Polly,* Hayman Levy's *Dreadnought,* and Judah Hay's *Duke of Cumberland* struck at enemy shipping. Levy also supplied the army with "Camp Equipages of all sorts . . . Knee and Stock Buckles, Hair Cockades, Scarlet Broad Cloths. . . ."

Jews contributed heavily to colonial industrial development: Abraham DeLyon helped develop Georgia's wine industry; Moses Lindo, of Charleston, utilized his skills in the manufacture of indigo; and Joseph Ottolenghe set out to make Georgia a major silk producer; Joseph Simon, of Lancaster, Pennsylvania, manufactured guns; the Gratz brothers, of Philadelphia, invested in mines in western Connecticut; Myer Myers manufactured jewelry; and Solomon Marache produced some of the finest earthenware and glassware in the colonies.

Moses Lopez acquired control of Newport's potash industry in 1753, James Lucena was granted a monopoly to manufacture Castile soap, Mordecai Sheftall of Georgia engaged in the lumber business, the Gratz brothers manufactured masts for the British Navy, and Naphtali Hart and Company operated as builders. In time, Jewish industrial enterprises were so widespread that they varied from the construction and sale of new and reconditioned ships to the ownership and operation of distilleries.

Perhaps the most significant industrial undertaking of the Jewish industrialists was the production of spermaceti candles. Made from the oil of sperm whales, these were introduced into America by Portuguese Jews who came to monopolize the industry. In order to solidify and control this particular industry, the Jewish "candle giants" united in 1761 to form the United Company of Spermaceti Candles—the first legal monopoly in North America. According to the agreement, each candle manufacturer pledged to do all within his power that was "fair and honorable" to prevent the establishment of any new spermaceti candle works. In time this unique method of production became one of the prime forces behind the whaling industry, for over a century one of New England's main industries.

Philadelphia Jews were particularly interested in western trade and colonization, among them Joseph Simon, whose commercial interests extended beyond Pennsylvania to the Ohio Valley and the banks of the Mississippi River, and David Franks, who sought to establish a colony in the Illinois country. The most important Jewish merchants in the western trade, however, were the Gratz brothers. Though they were primarily engaged in overseas trade, the brothers saw the need for western development, and after the signing of the anti-British Non-Importation Agreements, in 1765, they turned their attention to the interior. By 1778, they were doing business in territories that eventually became West Virginia, Ohio, Indiana, Kentucky, Illinois, and Missouri, then the farthermost points of the frontier.

The Gratz brothers were not the only Jews interested in opening the West. In 1763 the company of Ezekiel and Levy Solomons moved into the western trade, and in that same year Levy Andrew Levy established a fur-trading business in the lands surrounding Lake Erie. In time, others joined the western commercial movement to the frontier wilderness. Among these pioneers were Chapman Abram, who traded around Detroit; Simon, Trent, Levy and Company, whose trade reached Illinois; and Levy Franks, who serviced the Indians, the French, the British, and the colonials on the Mississippi frontier.

Despite their small number, Jews made a significant contribution to colonial economic development. They helped build the cities, civilize the frontier, and provide the commercial means to unite the provinces. Indeed, Joseph Addison was correct, in 1712, when he spoke of colonial Jewry as "the pegs and nails in a great building, which, though they are but little value in themselves, are absolutely necessary to keep the whole frame together."

The synagogue-centered community that Jews established in colonial America had its origin in the older Jewish communities of Europe. In order to appreciate the religio-communal life of early American Jewry, one must briefly consider the framework of the European *kahal* (Jewish community organization), the inherent values that prevailed within its structure, and the needs these values satisfied.

The *kahal* was a comprehensive organization that incorporated the Jewish population of a particular area (city, town, village). It controlled all Jewish institutions within its affixed geographical boundaries and exercised an authority over the synagogues, religious schools, ritual baths, medical facilities, mutual-aid societies, and rabbinic courts. Authorized and backed by the power of the state, it collected taxes, settled civil disputes, and functioned as an instrument by which Jewish leaders held sway over the members of their community. Significantly, this self-contained communal life was vital to the survival of European Jewry as a distinct religious and cultural society.

The *kahal,* which functioned as the most influential agency of Jewish group survival, provided a common meeting ground for Jew to meet and marry Jew, fostered group identity, and maintained institutions that transmitted the culture and values of Judaism. It also served as the central institution to which Jews could rally for protection against periodic anti-Semitic outbursts and provided charity for the unfortunate. In addition, it furnished the Jew with the psychological security necessary to live among people who were raised on anti-Semitism.

Unlike European Jews, those who settled in the British colonies were without the authority or corporate status to establish kahalic structure, much less their own judicial system. Nevertheless, in an effort to re-create and utilize what had worked so well for them in Europe, they organized a de facto *kahal* in America. First to be established was the synagogue—the core of the colonial Jewish community—then burial grounds, religious schools, and philanthropic agencies.

From their first days in America, the synagogue became the most important unifying force in the Jewish community. Services were conducted regularly, marriage within the group was encouraged, *kosher* food and *matzoth* were made available, and in some areas, religious courts were established to settle civil disputes among Jews. Every synagogue furnished the community with a meeting ground where Jews could mingle without distinction as to wealth or social standing.

The synagogue-centered community was responsible to those in need and helpless. With money provided by synagogue budgets, funds raised on the High Holy Days, and contributions solicited at weddings and funerals, the synagogue provided free religious instruction for the children of the poor, interest-free loans, pensions for widows, medical care for the disabled, burial for the dead, and redemption of debtors from prison. As was the tradition of Jewish *tsedakah* (charity) in Europe, the needy were given free seats to the synagogue, *matzoth* for Passover, and fuel during the winter.

Synagogue minute books of that time indicated the nature of colonial charity: ". . . it is unanimously agreed to allow Rachel Campenel the sum of Twenty Pounds Current money pr. annum in consideration of her age and infermities." A widow was given "Six Shillings per week in case there is any surplus after the officers are paid . . . it was also agreed that Mrs. Louzada should be sent into the Jerseys, dispatcht by Sedaka [charity] and that the debts of hers . . . should also be paid out of the publick moneys."

Wandering beggers pleaded for assistance, not so much for their love of travel but because they were driven from place to place. "That three Corse Shirts be made and sent to Aaron Pinto as he is almost naked," read one minute book, "and that he is to be dispatcht by first oppty to Newport in order to take passage for Surinam and if he will not go is to remain at his own expense."

Jews also recognized their obligation to the ancient homeland, Palestine. Throughout the colonial era, *meshullahim* (emissaries) from the Holy Land visited the colonial Jewish communities in search of funds for poor Palestinian Jews. They traveled from town to town soliciting contributions for their own disapora communities. Sometimes they preached in the synagogues and often settled questions of religious law and interpretation. Their mission over, they returned to Palestine with the spiritual and financial support of American Jews.

Though the organization of the modified *kahal* was successfully transplanted to the American colonies, adherence to synagogue dictates was voluntary rather than compulsory. Despite the security provided by the synagogue-centered community, by the close of the eighteenth century voluntary religious affiliation was to dominate American Jewry. It was the spiritual as well as the geographic distance of America from the center of the flourishing Jewish culture in Europe that diluted the orthodox tradition. Lacking a religious hierarchy for guidance and pressured by the personal freedom that America afforded, colonial Jewry witnessed the disintegration of the synagogue-centered community. No longer would the synagogue have monopolistic control over charity, *kosher* meat, and Jewish burial grounds. Jews now sought the services of commercial agencies for these essentials. The concept of the *kahal* became obsolete in America.

The first European immigrants to America brought with them negative stereotypes about Jews derived from the Middle Ages. Though the anti-Jewish image was altered when transplanted across the Atlantic and tempered by conditions of their new environment, many of the medieval concepts were retained and nurtured.

Medieval Europeans characterized Jews as a "people hidden within the walls of their separate ghettos," possessing "some fearful demonic powers that enabled them to persist and survive." To compound this image, the literature of the period convinced Europeans that Jews were Christ killers and the slayers of Christian children.

Stage productions portrayed Jews as "sinful," "detestable," and "accursed" people. In fifteenth-century England, for example, the *Play of Corpus Christi* said Jews were a people "selling, kissing, and betraying Jesus." One can imagine the frenzy of anti-Jewish feeling after witnessing "Jesus, covered with blood, bearing His cross to Calvary" while "four Jews [were] scourging and dragging Him with ropes."

European literature portrayed the Jew as a slaughterer and parasite. In the works of Chaucer, Jews were accused of blood sacrifices, mutilation, kidnaping, and ritual murder of Christian children. Shakespeare created Shylock, whose "crime" of usury was soon equated with ritual murder and physical mutilation. Marlowe's *The Jew of Malta* accused Jews of spreading the Black Plague by poisoning the wells, while Robert Daborne's *A Christian Turn'd Turk* alluded to Jewish cannibalism.

In an appeal to the throne against the naturalization of Jews, an anonymous pamphleteer wrote one of the worst vilifications of Jews in colonial times:

> The Jews are a . . . covenant-breaking nation of people; a set of evil-doers, a generation of vipers, doing evil with both hands, according to all nations around them; as bad, nay worse, than Sodom and Gommorrah, casting all God's laws and ordinances behind them, trampling them under their feet, rejecting, forsaking, and despising God Himself; provoking Him continually to His face, grieving Him to His heart, forgetting Him days without number, always erring in their hearts and disobeying His voice.

The anti-Jewish image soon reached the American colonies. In 1752, *The Merchant of Venice* was produced in Virginia, Charleston, Philadelphia, and New York; other productions, such as Richard Cumberland's *Fashionable Lover,* which exploited the theme of the Jew/villain, made the circuit of the major cities. The plays and literature contributed to the anti-Jewish image in the colonies. The Newport synagogue was described as the "synagogue of Satan," and it was not uncommon to hear expressions such as "Jew merchant," "rich as a Jew," "honest Jew," and "worthy Jew." The most direct example of anti-Jewish sentiment was expressed in verse by John Malcolm, who when writing to General Horatio Gates in 1790 on the funding of the national debt wrote:

> Tax on tax young Belcour cries,
> More imposts, and a new excise.
> A Public debt's, a public blessing
> Which 'tis of course a crime to lessen.
> Each day a fresh report he broaches,
> That Spies and Jews may ride in coaches.
> Soldiers and Farmers dont despair,
> Untax'd as yet are Earth and Air.

Though principally confined to verbal assaults, anti-Jewish sentiment also manifested itself in physical deed. In 1668, Balthazar D'Haert of New York defended himself in court against the charge of cheating a Jewish merchant by stating that the plantiff was a "devilish Jew." The jury found D'Haert not guilty. But more serious were the physical attacks on Jews and Jewish institutions. In 1743 a mob attacked a funeral procession from New York's Shearith Israel, and three years later, Philadelphia's Jewish community witnessed the desecration of its burial grounds.

The living as well as the dead were abused. According to the British Trade and Navigation Acts, aliens were not permitted to trade in the colonies. It was therefore essential for merchants to become naturalized. Several Newport residents, Abraham Rodriguez, Solomon Hart, Moses Lopez, and Jacob Rivera, were naturalized in New York before settling in Newport. But when Aaron Lopez and Isaac Elizar, two Newport Jews, applied for naturalization they were denied, because "no person who does not profess the Christian religion can be admitted free of this colony." The court added that Newport was crowded and that their petition was "wholly inconsistent with the first principles upon which the colony was founded. . . ." Immediately after being rejected, both men went to other colonies, where they were naturalized with no difficulty under the same Act of Parliament. There could be no doubt that the Rhode Island decision was based only on the fact that they were Jews.

During the Revolution, Jews were victims of attacks on their loyalty and faith. In 1776 the *Pennsylvania Evening Post* demanded that Jews be denied the right to own property or serve as government officials. If this action was not taken, the editors asserted, the new nation would be subjected to a "national slavery," which would make America "unsafe for Christians." Several days later, the same newspaper warned that the erection of new synagogues would turn America into an asylum for the "outcasts of Europe."

Though anti-Jewish prejudice was part of the American scene, Jews nevertheless managed to establish themselves in colonial society. A significant aspect of Jewish acceptance was found in the Christian theological interest in Jews and Judaism. Among the first to demonstrate this concern were the Puritans, who promoted the study of Hebrew, "God's chosen tongue." Such Puritan scholars as John Harvard, Michael Wigglesworth, and Henry Dunster, the first president of Harvard, acquired a knowledge of the language. The Puritans also favored Hebrew names for their children and closely followed the news of European Jewry. The first book published by the Puritans was the *Bay Psalm Book,* a metrical translation of the Psalms rendered directly from the Hebrew text. The study of Hebrew was required at Harvard College, Hebrew passages were read daily at the school, and until 1819 the graduation exercises included an oration in the ancient tongue.

Beyond their academic interest in Jews, the Puritans wanted to convert them. Cotton Mather, accepting the biblical prophecy that there was to be a calling and conversion of the Jewish nation, dreamed of his chance to convert a Jew. So obsessed was he that in 1696 he wrote:

> This day, from the dust, where I lay prostrate, before my lord, I lifted up my cries, for the conversion of the Jewish nation, and for my own having the happiness, at some time or other, to baptize a Jew. . . .

Roger Williams shared the same obsession. Though he believed that all men, including Jews, were entitled to worship as they pleased, he supported those Christian zealots who advocated Jewish conversion. There were others—Samuel Sewall, Chief Justice of the Massachusetts Bay Colony; Anne Bradstreet, the poet; and William Penn, governor of Pennsylvania—all expressing a theological interest in Jews. Their concerns, however, centered more on the American Indians, who they believed were the descendants of the ten lost tribes of Israel. According to Sewall, Indian conversion was soon to come. Bradstreet was also convinced that the Indians "shall return to see Zion with bliss."

Theological interest in Jews remained strong beyond the Revolutionary decades. Numerous tracts discussing Jewish conversion were published, among them *Faith Encouraged, Some Thoughts on Christianity,* and *An Account of the Remarkable Conversion of Jachiel Hirshel.* The Revolution and the decade that followed were also marked by an interest in America's Jews: the Old Testament was used by some to justify the break with England, and when discussing the nature of the seal of the new United States, Benjamin Franklin proposed it show Moses parting the Red Sea. Thomas Jefferson suggested that the seal display the people of Israel being led out of the land of Egypt. Even in secular matters, colonial interest in Jews remained strong. The colonial press reported Jewish business transactions in Europe, the amount of charity bequeathed to Jewish welfare agencies, treatment of Jews in European ghettos, accounts of inquisitional trials, and events surrounding the British "Jew Bill."

The American stage, though limited in scope, gave many performances of plays with Jewish characters or Jewish themes. The first to reach the colonial stage was an English production of *The Merchant of Venice,* performed in Yorktown, Virginia, in 1752. In the following years, thirty more plays with Jewish themes were brought to the American stage, each giving colonial audiences a glimpse of the European conception of Jewish life.

Among these plays were Hannah Cowley's *The Belle's Stratagem,* the first production in America in which a Christian disguised himself as a Jew for some evil purpose, and John O'Keeffe's *The Young Quaker,* whose Jewish character, Shadrach Boaz, was described as "the most repugnant stage Jew of the century." According to historian J. M. Landa, Boaz was "without a redeeming feature . . . a comic, cowardly villain who epitomized what had gone before, standardized it afresh, and fashioned an 'improved type' for subsequent dramatists to copy slavishly." Though most of this literature had little to do with the real life of Jews, colonial society believed what they saw.

The intellectual fascination of many Christian leaders with the Jews was another element that thrust the Jew into prominence in the colonies. Ezra Stiles, a Newport clergyman, was engaged in missionary activity, and his interest in Jewish conversion and the ten lost tribes subsequently turned to an academic pursuit of Judaism. While minister of his own congregation, he became a frequent visitor to the Newport synagogue, and in time his association with Hazzan Touro and Rabbi Raphael Carigal led to his study of Hebrew. The Congregationalist minister was soon translating the Psalms and studying the Pentateuch. By the 1770s, Stiles was immersed in Adrian Reland's *Introduction to the Rabbinical Literature* and Basnage's *History of the Jews,* and his desire for more knowledge about the Jews led him to an investigation of Hebrew mysticism.

The basic reason for acceptance of the Jew was economic. But colonial society also sought out Jews to convert them, to learn about Judaism, and to develop mutual intellectual relationships. Moreover, migration to the colonies was sparse and additions to the population were necessary and welcome.

Equally significant was the fact that Jews never constituted a threat to the Protestant majority. They had the advantage of not being black, and due to their experience with the Inquisition could hardly be considered sympathetic to Catholicism. In a nation one fifth black and which preferred not to be inundated by "papists," Jews were accorded total or nearly total equality. Under these circumstances, the practical pressures of colonial life ultimately determined the acceptance of the Jewish citizen.

Perhaps as important were the humanitarian principles of tolerance. As the eighteenth century advanced, many colonials became less concerned with religious differences. The separation of church and state widened as religious monopoly dwindled and as people came under the influence of European humanism and the Enlightenment. In turn, those who advocated the revolutionary ideology that gripped America in the 1770s rose to challenge both political and religious oppression. No doubt, the radical concepts echoed at the Continental Congresses affected all people with dissenting religious beliefs—including Jews.

With the outbreak of the American Revolution, colonial Jewry— never subjected to anti-Jewish statutes, ghettos, repressive legislation, or restrictive guilds—was on its way to complete acceptance. America had finally come to the realization that Jews, like others, could contribute more than mere economic skills to the new nation.

If colonial society was ready to accept its Jewish citizens, Jews wanted to embrace America. Some refused to compromise their religous fervor or alter their European life-styles, but others did not hesitate to exchange European orthodoxy for a place in Christian America; they abandoned the synagogue, Anglicized their names, intermarried, or converted to Christianity.

Perhaps the most significant factors that enabled Jews to deculturate as easily as they did were the lack of institutional and legislative restrictions in America. Contrary to European practice, the colonial provinces were without a *kahal,* ghettos, or medieval legislation that forbade Jews to socialize with Christians. Colonial Jews shaved their beards, cut their earlocks, dressed in the latest fashions, purchased land, socialized with Christians, and participated in all forms of community activity. Above all, though devoted to a specific Jewish life-style, they developed no all-embracing Jewish culture. Under these circumstances, American Jewry was free to modify or exchange the European modes for American manners and mobility.

Jewish acculturation manifested itself in a variety of ways. The noun "Jew," which colonial Jews considered a pejorative term, was replaced by "Hebrew," "Israelite," or "follower of Judaism." Also, the adjective "Jewish" was replaced with "Mosaic." Thus, one might have described himself as a Pennsylvania Israelite who followed the Mosaic tradition.

Jews also anglicized their names: Jacob became John, Hannah became Grace, Hirsh was changed to Henry, Phoebus to Phillips, Kalman to Coleman, Sampsons to Simons, and Lieba to Love. Children born on this side of the Atlantic did not escape the quest for Americanization: synagogue schools had students with such unlikely Jewish names as Priscilla, Frances, Betsy, Eliza, and Edward.

In addition to changing their names, some ate non-kosher food, worked on the Sabbath, and occasionally attended the local church to listen to a Sunday sermon. Upon observing the transformation of the Jewish life-style, one Hessian soldier on duty in revolutionary New York wrote his family in Germany that

> the Jews cannot be told, like in our country, by their beards and costume, but are dressed like other citizens, shave regularly, and also eat pork, although their religion forbids it. Jews and Christians, moreover, do not hesitate to intermarry. The Jewish women have their hair dressed and wear French finery like the women of other faiths.

Another aspect of assimilation was the zeal to participate in the activities of the Christian community. In education, for example, some Jewish youths received their secular training in private Christian grammar schools, while others attended colleges that were established "for

Church and Christ." It was not unusual to find Newport Jewry uniting with their Christian neighbors to build a college or a hospital. Jews gave freely of their time and money to erect libraries in New York, maintain militias and fire companies in Pennsylvania, and promote public works in Delaware.

In addition to their concern for civic improvements, Jews demonstrated their eagerness to "belong" through philanthropic activities. They contributed to Benjamin Franklin's Pennsylvania hospital, donated funds to the College of Philadelphia, provided money for the erection of a Lutheran sanctuary in New York, and aided in the construction of Manhattan's Trinity Church. Significantly, the Jewish philanthropic effort was hardly isolated or exceptional, but part of a pattern.

TOGETHER IN FREEDOM—1776–1840

In July 1775, when the Provincial Congress of Georgia was in debate over relations with England, the Reverend John J. Zubly delivered a sermon that rejected all forms of submission to the Crown. Addressing the delegates, the influential Protestant clergyman declared: "As to the Jewish religion, it cannot be charged with favoring despotism. The whole system of that religion is so replete with laws against injustice and oppression; and by one of its express rites it proclaimed liberty throughout the land to all inhabitants."

Perhaps these remarks explain why the vast majority of the three thousand Jews threw caution to the wind and joined the patriot cause. One must, however, look beyond the principles of The Enlightenment to the practical considerations that encouraged Jewish "radicalism." The Declaration of Independence promised equality before the law— and Jews were highly conscious that the promise included themselves. Jews were Americans and wished to remain citizens of the new nation even if still hampered by discriminatory statutes.

The ideological divisions among Jews cut through families and communities. As Benjamin Franklin's son remained loyal to the Crown, so did Alexander Zuntz, commissary to Hessian mercenaries in New York; David Franks, royal purveyor and commissary-general of British troops; Myer Hart, supplier to British troops in Pennsylvania; Moses Nunes, searcher of the port of Savannah; and Myer Pollock, who supported the British war effort in Newport.

The contributions to the revolution of those siding with the patriots were many. In addition to those who served as soldiers and sailors, brokers helped establish the government's credit, purveyors supplied the Continental Army with weapons, gunpowder, clothing, and food, and merchants signed the Non-Importation Agreements. "The conduct of the people here," complained Governor James Wright of Georgia in a letter to England, "is infamous. One Sheftall, a Jew, is chairman of the Parochial Committee . . . and this fellow issues orders to captains of vessels to depart the king's port without landing any of their cargoes. . . ."

The first of many Jewish soldiers to fall in battle was the South Carolinian Francis Salvador. In July 1776, Salvador, along with several hundred men, fought a band of Cherokee Indians organized and equipped by the British. In addition to those who died in the Revolution, many suffered injuries and imprisonment. Solomon Buch, wounded at Philadelphia in 1777, wrote to a friend expressing the desire "to be able to get satisfaction and revenge the wrongs of [his] injured country."

Philip Moses Russell froze at Valley Forge. Mordecai Sheftall was imprisoned after the British captured Savannah; Colonel Sheftall, a deputy commissary general to the Continental forces in South Carolina and Georgia, described his ordeal.

"On our way to the office where I used to issue provisions," he wrote, "I was ordered to give information of what stores I had in town and what I sent out of town, and where. This I declined doing, which made [my captors] angry." The British then asked Sheftall if he knew that Charleston was taken. "No," answered the prisoner.

"Poor, deluded wretches," exclaimed one officer. "Good God! how you are deluded by your leaders!"

Sheftall refused to believe the story and asked who had taken it, and when.

The officer boastfully told his prisoner that "General James Grant, with 10,000 men, [had] taken the city eight or ten days ago." The patriot smiled and answered that "it [was] not so, as I had a letter in my pocket that was wrote in Charleston but three days ago by my brother."

He replied we had been misinformed. I then retorted that I found they could be misinformed by their leaders, as well as we could be deluded by ours. This made him so angry that when he returned me to the guardhouse, he ordered me to be confined amongst the drunken soldiers and negroes, where I suffered a great deal of abuse and was threatened to be run through the body or, as they termed it, "skivered" by one of the York Volunteers, which threat he attempted to put into execution three times during the night, but was prevented by one Sergeant Campbell.

Colonel Natham Bush describes action at the battle of Long Island:

. . . Thursday evening late, the Regulars landed on Long Island, ten thousand men, within two miles of our line. About midnight our advanced guard descried two men in a watermelon patch, which they fired on, when a number of the men who lay concealed returned the fire. . . . they [the British] made great havoc among our men, and after taking General Sterling and the Colonels Miles and Atlee prisoners, put our men to flight, when many of the men and officers were killed. I am told the loss on our side is between eight and nine hundred, but the loss on their side is much greater.

Many Jews also served the government in non-military capacities. Robert Morris, Superintendent of Finance, had three Jewish aides: Haym Salomon of Philadelphia, Jacob Hart of Baltimore, and Isaac Levy of New York. Benjamin Levy and Benjamin Jacobs signed currency bills, and Joseph Simons, Bernard Gratz, and Aaron Levy supplied Pennsylvania troops with everything from gunpowder to clothing. The Sheftalls were fiscal officers for South Carolina; Isaac Levy and Myer Michaels provided financial aid to the Virginia cause; and Mannuel Josephson of New York equipped the Continental armies with a variety of weapons.

Perhaps the best-known Jewish patriot is Haym Salomon. After the British captured New York, this Polish-born Jew remained in the enemy camp to act as an interpreter for the Hessians—and spy for the Americans. After two years of clandestine activities, he was discovered and sentenced to death. He escaped, however, and upon arrival in Philadelphia offered his talents to the Continental Congress. So outstanding were his services that Robert Morris considered him indispensable in maintaining the credit of the new nation.

Joining Salomon in the war effort were others, who outfitted ships with cannon and took to the high seas as privateers. Challenging the British merchant fleet were Moses Michael Hays of Boston, Isaac Moses, and Benjamin Seixas of Pennsylvania and Aaron Lopez of Newport.

In New York, those Jews who sided with the Revolution were uprooted by the British occupation. Not wishing to remain while the city was occupied by English troops, Gershom Mendez Seixas, *hazzan* of Shearith Israel, led the rebel congregation first to Stratford, Connecticut, and then to Philadelphia. Only in 1784, when the English had withdrawn, did New York's Jews return home.

Similarly, the city of Newport was occupied. Eight thousand British troops sacked the city and imprisoned those who supported the rebel cause. The Jewish community, overwhelmingly patriot, fled to areas controlled by the Continental Army. However, unlike New York, Newport Jewry never recovered from their exodus. Though some Jews returned to the city, most resettled in other areas. No longer would Newport be the capital of the American Jewish community.

As some established communities faded, new ones were born. With the conclusion of the war, Jewish settlements increased in Delaware, New Jersey, and throughout New England. Now no longer hindered by the Proclamation of 1763 which restricted westward expansion, Jewish pioneers on the Atlantic seaboard looked to the West and the land beyond the Allegheny Mountains—though, this time, their settlement would not be made as British colonists but as American citizens.

America's independence did not radically alter the political or legal status of Jews in American society. What was achieved, through the adoption of the Constitution, was political equality on the national level. For the first time, separation of church and state, freedom of conscience, and abolition of religious tests for federal officials became the law of the land.

Mindful that their political future was at stake at the federal convention in 1787, American Jewry followed the proceedings with keen interest. One Philadelphia observer, Jonas Phillips, was aware that the concept of state sovereignty enabled eleven states to adopt constitutions compromising the rights of Jews.† South Carolina required voters and officeholders to be Protestants, New Jersey restricted full political participation to "persons . . . of any Protestant sect," Delaware established a religious test for public office, Maryland declared that "any person, appointed to any office . . . subscribe a declaration of his belief in the Christian religion," and Pennsylvania decreed that its public officials "acknowledge the Scriptures of the Old and New Testament."

American Jews were disheartened; they had fought too hard and sacrificed too much to allow their rights to be circumscribed without protest. In Philadelphia, Jewish leaders presented a petition to the

† Only New York and Massachusetts provided full equality.

Council of Censors asserting that the state's "religious test deprives the Jews of the most eminent rights of freemen" and represents "a stigma upon their nation and religion."

The Pennsylvania legislators read the petition and ordered it tabled. Several years later, Jonas Phillips sent a similar petition to the Constitutional Convention. In an attempt to gain for all Jews what had been denied by Pennsylvania, he requested that the federal convention incorporate into the new Constitution the principles contained in the Declaration of Independence. In a letter to the delegates, he asserted that Pennsylvania's religious oath conflicted with one's freedom of conscience, that "to swear and believe that the New Testament was given by divine inspiration is absolutely against the Religious principles of a Jew," concluding, "if the [federal] Convention shall in wisdom think fit and alter the said oath . . . the Israelites will think themselves happy to live under a government where all Religious societies are on an Equal footage."

Phillips delivered his petition two weeks after a secret session of the convention enacted Article Six, which stated that "no religious test shall ever be required as a qualification to any [federal] office or public trust." For the first time in history, a nation passed into law a principle of religious freedom.

American Jewry was fully aware of the political importance of the new federal Constitution, and joined with Christian neighbors to celebrate. In Philadelphia the parade was led by government officials and the clergy of various Christian denominations and a rabbi marching arm in arm. Naphtali Phillips, a young observer, described the event:

> . . . in an open carriage drawn by elegant horses sat Chief Justice McKane with other judges of the [Pennsylvania] Supreme Court, holding in his hand the new [United States] Constitution in a frame. This was received by the populace with great rejoicing.
>
> . . . the procession then proceeded from about Third Street near Spruce, northward towards Callowhill Street, then wheeled towards Bush Hill, where there was a number of long tables loaded with all kinds of provisions, with a separate table for Jews, who could not partake of the meals from the other tables; but they had a full supply of soused [pickled] salmon, bread and crackers, almonds, raisins, etc. This table was under the charge of an old cobbler named Isaac Moses, well-known Philadelphian at that time.

Benjamin Rush also commented on the ecumenical character of the celebration:

. . . Pains were taken to connect ministers of the most dissimilar religious principles together, thereby to show the influence of a free government in promoting Christian charity. The Rabbi of the Jews locked in the arms of two ministers of the gospel, was a most delightful sight. There could not have been a more happy emblem contrived, of that section of the new constitution, which opens all its powers and offices alike, not only to every sect of Christians, but to worthy men of every religion.

As Dr. Rush so wisely concluded, in the new constitutional republic the Jew was now accepted as a citizen instead of a tolerated outsider.

From the inception of the constitutional republic, the federal government's attitude toward religion was one of neutrality. Thus, it was no wonder that the various Jewish communities entered the portals of American history by paying homage to the first President of *their* United States. Savannah Jewry expressed its "unbounded confidence in [Washington's] integrity" and praised his "unexampled liberality," which, they declared, dispelled the cloud of religious bigotry and superstition.

The Newport congregation also pledged their loyalty to the government, "which to bigotry gives no sanction, to persecution no assistance." Washington, who was familiar with the travail of the Jews, responded with affection and eloquence:

> The citizens of the United States of America have a right to applaud themselves for having given to mankind examples of an enlarged and liberal policy; a policy worthy of imitation. All possess alike liberty of conscience and immunities of citizenship. It is now no more that toleration is spoken of, as it was by the indulgence of one class of people, that another enjoyed the exercise of their inherent natural rights. For happily the government of the United States, which gives to bigotry no sanction, to persecution no assistance requires only that they who live under its protection should demean themselves as good citizens, in giving it on all occasions their effectual support.

Others who served as President during the Federal Period (1787–1840) wholeheartedly supported the concepts proclaimed by Washington. In a letter to Mordecai M. Noah, John Adams wrote:

> I wish your nation may be admitted to all the privileges of citizenship in every country of the world. This country has done much. I wish it may do more; and annul every narrow idea in religion, gov-

ernment, and commerce. Let the wits joke; the philosophers sneer! What then? It has pleased the Providence of the "first cause," the universal cause, that Abraham should give religion, not only to Hebrews, but to Christians and Mahometans.

Like Washington and Adams, Thomas Jefferson, on the occasion of the consecration of the synagogue of Savannah, wrote "[I am] happy in the restoration of the Jews, particularly, to their social rights, and [hope] they will be seen taking their seats on the benches of science as preparatory to their doing the same at the board of government." Supporting this point of view was Jefferson's Virginia colleague James Madison. In a letter to Dr. Jacob De La Motta, of Savannah, he declared:

> Equal laws protecting equal rights, are found as they ought to be presumed, the best guarantee of loyalty, and love of country; as well as best calculated to cherish that mutual respect and good will among citizens of every religious denomination which are necessary to social harmony and most favorable to the advancement of truth.

And these equalitarian principles were expressed with action. The practice of issuing Thanksgiving Day proclamations frequently led government officials to use sectarian language. After the adoption of the Constitution, however, Washington, who delivered his first Thanksgiving address in 1789, avoided mentioning Jesus or Christianity. Rather, he addressed his remarks to "All Religious Societies and Denominations, and to All Persons whomsoever within the United States." Jefferson, on the other hand, not only avoided issuing a religious proclamation but went on record opposing such statements as a violation of church and state.

As a consequence of this libertarian environment, Jews pursued public office, engaged in politics, exercised their franchise, and were candid in their political sympathies. Reuben Etting, for example, was appointed federal marshal for Maryland, Nathan Levy and Benjamin Nones served as consuls in South America, Isaac Harby edited a pro-Jefferson newspaper in Charleston, Alfred Mordecai of Virginia attended West Point, Uriah P. Levy rose to the rank of commodore in the Navy, and Mordecai Noah, who held the first major diplomatic post awarded to a Jew, served as American consul in Tunis.

Though Jews generally fared well on the federal level, there were a few whose First-Amendment Rights were violated. In 1815, Secretary of State James Monroe ordered the recall of Mordecai Noah from his diplomatic post because Noah used embassy funds to rescue several French-speaking hostages, who claimed to be American citizens, from Moroccan pirates. More important, however, were remarks in Monroe's letter of dismissal: "At the time of your appointment, as Consul at Tunis, it was not known that the Religion you profess would form any obstacle to the exercise of your Consular function."

Upon his return to the United States, Noah answered his critics in a pamphlet entitled *Correspondence and Documents Relative to the Attempt to Negotiate for the Release of American Captives at Algiers.* Quickly, Isaac Harby of Charleston and Naphtali Phillips of New York joined the protest. Phillips, president of Congregation Shearith Israel, charged that the dismissal was motivated by Noah's religion, and Harby, a well-known playwright and editor of the *Southern Patriot,* demanded an inquiry "into the nature of the causes why [Noah] was so abruptly recalled." In reference to Monroe's anti-Jewish remarks, he wrote:

> It was this sentiment, Sir, which immediately fixed and riveted my attention, my astonishment. I would ask, since it was not *then* known, whether it has been since discovered that religion disqualifies a man from the exercise of his political functions? Or has this doctrine *ever* been known, since the hour of the establishment of our invaluable Constitution?

In his forceful protest, he lectured Monroe on the nature of a free society:

> It is upon the principle, not of *toleration* (for man has no power to tolerate religion—that is a concern between man and his maker) but upon the principle of equal, inalienable, *constitutional rights,* that we see Jews appointed to office, that we see them elected in our state representation, and that, in proportion as their talents and their influence can bear them through, we see them mingling in the honours of their country. They are by no means to be considered as a *religious sect,* tolerated by the government; they constitute a portion of the people. They are, in every respect, woven in and compacted with the citizens of the republic. Quakers and Catholics, Episcopalians and Presbyterians, Baptists and Jews, all constitute one great political family. *Simplex, duntaxat, et unam.* ["One and only one."] In this light, every wise statesman must regard them.

Harby concluded his protest with an appeal to Monroe to erase the discriminatory sentence that appeared in the letter. "Strike it from the records of your office," he wrote, because it can "only remain to your injury, and to the reproach of the liberal character of [this nation's] institutions."

The Noah affair notwithstanding, as far as the federal government was concerned, religious liberty was to characterize its philosophy and action. Several years after the signing of the Declaration of Independence, American Jewry felt secure in their status as first-class citizens of the United States.

Though Jews were granted full equality on the federal level, they did not enjoy the same treatment in the states. Apparently, the framers of the state constitutions failed to consider the freedom implied in the Declaration of Independence or the First Amendment (forbidding "the establishment of religion"); eleven states effectively denied what the constitutional framers in Philadelphia had expressly granted. Indeed, not until these "sovereign" states provided full religious freedom would Jews enjoy their birthright as Americans.

Delaware, while not disenfranchising its Jewish citizens, established religious qualifications for public office. Its constitution stipulated that all officials subscribe to the following oath: "I do profess faith in God the Father and in Jesus Christ His only Son, and in the Holy Ghost." New York and Massachusetts, on the other hand, managed to break the chains of colonial tradition. Written in 1777, the New York Constitution guarantees "the free exercise and enjoyment of religious freedom and worship, without discrimination or preference [to] all mankind." Further, it declared all previous legislation "construed to establish or maintain any particular denomination of Christian [to be] repugnant to this constitution . . . and they hereby are, abrogated and rejected."

In addition to religious oaths, several states had local ordinances designed to retain the Christian character of America, the most striking example being the Sabbath law. In 1793, Jonas Phillips refused to testify in a Pennsylvania court on the Jewish Sabbath. The court refused to acknowledge his religious convictions and fined him ten pounds. Similarly, in 1816, Abraham Wolff of Philadelphia was convicted for "performing worldly employment on the Lord's Day, commonly called Sunday." Wolff's attorney claimed that his client was a Jew and therefore not "within the meaning of the act inflicting the penalty." Needless to say, the claim was denied and the conviction upheld.

Though Jews were disabled by Sabbath legislation and judicial interpretations, they nevertheless did not falter in their demand for equal justice. In North Carolina, for instance, Jacob Henry was elected to the House of Commons in 1809. Shortly after he took his seat in the legislative body, a motion was made to remove him because he denied "the divine authority of the New Testament, and refused to take the oath prescribed by law for his qualification." After debate on the question, Henry rose to defend his religious convictions:

> The religion I profess inculcates every duty which man owes to his fellow men; it enjoins upon its votaries the practice of every virtue, and the detection of every vice, it teaches them to hope for the favor of heaven exactly in proportion as their lives have been directed by just, honorable, and beneficent maxims. This then, gentlemen, is my creed . . . at any rate, I am sure that you cannot see anything in this religion to deprive me of my seat in this house.

The speech made an indelible impression, even outside of North Carolina, and the subsequent victory was used in the struggle for equality in other states. In spite of his triumph, Henry's success was in form, not substance. Though he retained his seat, the decision was based on a constitutional provision that prohibited non-Protestants from occupying a position in "any civil department." Accordingly, the interpretation made did not prohibit such persons from serving in the legislature but barred those same individuals from civil office. In effect, Jews could enact laws but could not execute them.

In Maryland, attempts to remove religious oaths from the constitution led to a struggle in the legislature. In 1797, Solomon Etting of Baltimore began a determined effort to have the constitutional provision against Jews rescinded. However, his repeated petitions were met with repeated rejections. Discouraged by the "unfeeling" attitude of the lawmakers, he gave up his annual petitioning. In 1818, however, long after Etting abandoned his efforts, Thomas Kennedy‡ took up the fight. Written by a committee of three, the "Jew bill," which was introduced to the legislature by Kennedy, called for the abolition of religious oaths. Further, it declared that if a test oath was to be required for Jews, it should "be administered on the five books of Moses."

Though the original bill was defeated, the publicity it received during the debate caused pressure to swell not only in Maryland but in other states as well. The *Maryland Censor* remarked that "we are truly mortified that a bill extending to the Jews, civil rights enjoyed by other citizens of the state, has been rejected." Two Philadelphia journals echoed similar sentiments: "If the legislature of Maryland have the

‡ A Catholic.

right to disfranchise any portion of the freemen of that state, because
they believe in the God of Abraham, Isaac, and Jacob," wrote the
Aurora, "they may next decide which of the various sects are the *true*
Christians, and disfranchise all the rest."

The *Freedman's Journal* commented:

> It is with much regret we observe the illiberal principles which
> have pervaded the legislature of Maryland, in rejecting the bill,
> commonly called the Jew bill, which went to put the descendants of
> Abraham, as regarded their civil rights, on the same footing with
> those who go under the name *Christian.* In Maryland, a Jew can-
> not hold office whatever. These things ought not to be in this coun-
> try, the asylum of the oppressed.

The Charleston *Southern Patriot* joined the protest:

> But it may be said that when we speak of distinction we should
> turn our attention home, and look at the conduct of Maryland,
> who appears to have caught the spirit of the German governments.
> Yes, it may be said, as a reproach to our country, the people of
> Maryland permits civil proscription to stand in their constitution to
> the dishonour of our age—to the disgrace of their state.

The bill, with Catholic support, was finally enacted into law on February 26, 1825, twenty-eight years after Etting sent his first petition. The
final version, however, was not as liberal as Kennedy's original proposal. Henceforth, it declared, Jews elected to public office were compelled to "subscribe a declaration of [their] belief in a future state of
rewards and punishments [hereafter]." In addition, citizens of Maryland who were non-conforming Christians, deists, atheists, Moslems,
and Buddhists were excluded from public trust. Interestingly, Thomas
Jefferson, a deist, would not have been eligible to serve in the Maryland
state government.

State constitutional disabilities notwithstanding, Jews occupied a
more privileged position in America than in any other country in the
world. In time the laws and ordinances of the states would be eliminated or modified, and they, too, would accommodate their Jewish citizens.

Jews were highly conscious of the favorable treatment they received
in America, and consequently, throughout the Federal Period, their
spokesmen pledged fidelity to the nation that provided them untold opportunities. Gershom Mendez Seixas commented to his Shearith Israel

congregation in 1789 that it pleased "God to have established [the Jews] in this country where [they] possess every advantage." Mordecai Manuel Noah, delivering his first important address on the future of American Jewry, in 1818, spoke of an America where Jews live "secure in person and property, protected from tyranny and oppression. Forty years of experience have tested the wisdom of our institutions, and they will only be surrendered with the [non-] existence of the nation." Noah, a pioneer of American Zionism, discussed the eventual return to the Holy Land: "Until Jews can recover their ancient rights and dominions, and take their rank among the governments of the earth, this is their chosen country."

In 1821, Dr. Jacob De La Motta contrasted the American Jewish experience to the condition of Jews "in foreign lands, [who were] writhing under the shackles of odious persecution, and wild fanaticism." Not mentioning a future exodus to Palestine, he spoke instead of conditions in America. *"Here,"* he declared:

> a liberal and tolerant spirit, pervades every individual. *Here,* unbiased protection, and friendly co-operation, are alike extended, without consideration or reference to public view, and guards its preponderance from the touch of illiberality. *Here,* a union of friendship and fellowship is promoted and encouraged. . . . It is *here,* that we are reasonably to expect the enjoyment of the rewards for our consistency and sufferings, as promised by the word of God, when he declared he would not forsake us.

In the United States, according to De La Motta, Jews would find their refuge. Indeed, the Jew remained in America to participate in its physical expansion, raise families, establish synagogues and mutual aid societies, promote their culture, encourage education, and confront the fortuities of life.

By the early-nineteenth century, Jews were merging into the general American society, bolstered by self-respect, pride, and friendly relations with the Christian community.

In the colonial decades, the predominant Christian attitude toward the Jew was one of intellectual curiosity and practical interest. Hannah Adams, America's first woman historian, examined the Jewish experience because of her curiosity and determination to "investigate the fate of this wonderful people." Adams, who abhorred "the imperfection of prejudice," produced the finest contemporary examination of the Jew in

America, *History of the Jews* (1812), written with sympathy and compassion, with insight and deep understanding.

"Mrs. Crawford"* expressed an intellectual interest in the Jewish female, through poetry. Her objectivity, however, is open to question. In the poem *The Crusader's Song to the Hebrew Maiden,* the heroine accepted Christianity for the sake of her lover:

> Christian soldier, must we sever?
> Does thy creed our fates divide?
> Must we part, and part forever?
> Shall another be thy bride?
> Spirits of my fathers sleeping;
> Ye, who once Zion trod,
> Heaven's mysterious council keeping,
> *Tell me of the Christian's God!*

Other intellectuals, notably Ralph Waldo Emerson, Henry Wadsworth Longfellow, Nathaniel Hawthorne, and Orestes A. Brownson, recorded their reactions to the Jewish experience. In 1832, Emerson wrote of the ghetto in Ferrano, Italy, where he witnessed three thousand Jews "shut [in] every night, as in Rome, like dogs." Orestes A. Brownson was equally interested. In the *Boston Quarterly Review* of July 1842 he paid tribute "to the Jew [for] having originated. . . . his own literature, and . . . [for] having become the chosen of God to instruct the nations in the deepest principles of philosophy, of jurisprudence, and theology. . . ."

Longfellow wrote *The Jewish Cemetery* at Newport:

> How strange it seems: These Hebrews in their graves,
>   Close by the street of this fair seaport town. . . .
> The very names recorded here are strange,
>   Of foreign accent, and of different climes;
> Alvares and Rivera interchange
>   With Abraham and Jacob of old times. . . .
> Closed are the portals of their Synagogue,
>   No Psalms of David now the silence break,
> No Rabbi reads the ancient Decalogue
>   In the grand dialect the Prophets spake.
> Gone are the living, but the dead remain. . . .

Christians displayed a practical as well as intellectual interest. In 1819, W. D. Robinson called on Europe's Jews to consider settlement

---

* The author is not otherwise identified.

in the United States. In a display of brotherhood, he assured them that the nation's religious fanatics were "harmless, and [that] their influence [was] felt in a very limited sphere." The New York *Commercial Advertiser* also encouraged Jewish immigration. In 1822, it told Christian readers that the Jews would be a valuable addition to the commercial, manufacturing, and agricultural interests of the country. Appealing to the Jewish sense of security, it declared that in America

> a new generation, born in more enlightened times, and having the benefit of education, would be free from those errors generally imputed to the Jews, and [Jews] would have every inducement to become valuable members of society—That toleration and mildness upon which the Christian religion is founded, will lend its influence to the neglected children of Israel, who, in the United States, can find a home undisturbed.

The *North American Review,* gave a detailed account of the Charleston Reform Movement, and *Niles' Weekly Register,* one of the nation's most influential journals, reported on a variety of domestic and foreign "Jewish events." From its inception, in 1811, to its termination, in 1849, the *Register* informed the public of anti-Semitism in Russia, rabbinic meetings in Poland, desecration of synagogues in Germany, and Jewish philanthropic activities in America. On March 13, 1847, the *Register* published an account of "a large and respectable assembly of the Congregation Shearith Israel . . . in New York for the purpose of taking measures for the relief of the famishing thousands of their fellow mortals in that unfortunate and destitute country Ireland . . . a large collection was taken up."

Not all press coverage was favorable. In Charleston, South Carolina, Christian politicians charged that there was a "Jewish vote." Immediately, Jewish spokesmen rallied to "disclaim any . . . intention to be represented [by the press] as a peculiar community," and on October 1, 1832, the Charleston *Courier* published a letter signed by "eighty-four Israelites" which declared: "We will not support any man for office who is not selected by the public for himself, his character, and his talents."

Because of the interest Christians had in their Jewish neighbors, a high degree of social intercourse developed. Often, this activity was manifested through interreligious courtesies: in 1802 General Christopher Gadsden presented the Charleston Congregation five valuable books as a gift; in 1823 the Episcopal bishop of New York was given a letter of introduction to London's chief rabbi by Congregation Shearith Israel; and in 1836 Congregation Anshe Chesed erected its *sukkah* in the yard of the New York Dispensary. When Congregation Mikve Israel of Savannah received a gift of land from the city to erect its synagogue, its officers invited the mayor and city aldermen to take a prominent place in the reviewing stand when the building's cornerstone was laid.

Many Christians and Jews exchanged letters that talked of their friendship: Writing to Maria Elizabeth Fenno, a Christian friend, Rebecca Gratz cautioned her companion against having a love affair with a married man. Realizing that the nature of the letter might upset her sensitive friend, she qualified her remarks: "If I had loved you but a little, I should not have hazarded your displeasure, but as I love you with sincerest affection and proudly aspire to be called your friend, I must try to deserve that title by preferring your future welfare even to your present gratification."

In the spring of 1832 James J. Stark, a Georgia legislator, called Dr. Philip Minis "a damned Jew [who] ought to be pissed on." Following tradition, Minis demanded satisfaction in the form of a duel, then the socially acceptable way to settle disputes of honor. "Stark and Minis met at City Hotel," reported an observer, "where Minis pronounced Stark a coward. Stark advanced and put his hand in his pocket and drew a gun . . . Minis drew and shot Stark through the throat." Though Minis killed a Christian, his victory was accepted by the community because his actions were socially acceptable. Jews could now be like other men.

Because of increased socializing with Christians, the Jewish community faced serious problems: intermarriage and conversion. By the 1840s, the number of Jewish women in proportion to eligible males was quite low, and some men married Christians. Of the 699 Jewish marriages in the period between 1776 and 1840, 28.7 per cent were with Christians. "Of mixed marriages," wrote one investigator, "six were cases of miscegenation—three with mulattoes, two with Indians, and one with a Negro."

But, ironically, it was this very intermingling that made these marriages more acceptable to Christian and Jew, despite negative opinions by both. Sara Hall, a Christian, wrote that while Jews mixed with Christians freely, intermarriage should be discouraged:

In all the various intercourse of social life, we know of no uncharitable barriers between Jews and Christians in our happy country. Talents and virtues are alike honored in both; but in the view of a more intimate connection, many a youth enchained by the charms of a lovely Jewess, has breathed the vain aspiration of Paul to Agrippa, "I would thou wert not only almost, but altogether such as I am," *not expecting these bonds.*

Rebecca Gratz agreed:

I believe it is impossible to reconcile a matrimonial engagement between persons of so different a creed, without requiring one or the other to yield. In all instances we have heard of in real life, this has been the case and where a family of children are to be brought up, it appears necessary that parents should agree on so important a subject.

Intermarriage was one expression of social interaction that neither community advocated or fully accepted, but American Jewry of the early-nineteenth century appears to have tolerated those who took Christian mates. It was the apostate, however, who was always branded a traitor to the faith and excluded from the community.

The attempt by Christian missionaries to convert Jews was not inspired by hatred but, rather, by the desire to show Jews the way to salvation through Jesus. Nevertheless, when Joseph Frey published *Israel's Advocate,* a journal that sought to convert Jews, S. H. Jackson responded with a vitriolic attack in his own publication, *The Jew; being a Defense of Judaism against all Adversaries, and Particularly against the Insidious Attacks of Israel's Advocate.*

Frey's activities were not aimed at American Jewry but, rather, at European Jews. He was primarily interested in bringing converts to the United States to settle in "ghettoized" agricultural communities, but his efforts failed. Fearing conversion, however, some Jewish spokesmen launched a tenacious defense of their religion and questioned the tenability of Christianity. A Jewish response of such ferocity would never have been whispered, let alone published, just a few decades earlier. Such was the new-found confidence of the American Jew, battles won, preparing the soil for the immigrants that followed.

CHAPTER II

Continued Migration

NEW FRONTIERS IN AMERICA: ARRIVAL AND ADJUSTMENT

UNTIL the 1830s the emigration of Jews to America consisted of individuals and isolated families. In 1836, however, economic and political conditions for Jews in Central Europe deteriorated, and what had been a mere trickle of emigrants in the eighteenth century became the mass migration of entire Jewish communities.

German statesmen, swept by Europe's reactionary ideology, deprived Jews of civil rights, consigning them to a place of permanent inferiority. Students rioted in the streets of Baden, Frankfurt, and Munich, where Jewish homes were burned and Jewish shops looted. In Bavaria, authorities stemmed the growing Jewish population by limiting the number of marriages. Thousands came down with "emigration fever." The *Allgemeine Zeitung des Judentums,* expressing the mood of German Jewry, called on its readers "to seek a new Fatherland, where they [could] exercise the professions they learned, [and] show off their wares, their knowledge and their learning."

Such editorial comment influenced whole communities to depart. The *Israelitische Annalen* reported:

> From Swabia, February, 1840. . . . The emigration fever has steadily increased among the Israelites of our district and seems about to reach its high point. In nearly every community there are numerous individuals who are preparing to leave the Fatherland

early next year and to seek their fortune on the other side of the ocean.

Those lucky enough to escape to America wrote letters to family and friends. "When I look at America," wrote one newcomer, "there is no difference in the civic relations between Christians and Jews and everybody can do what he wishes, but what is more, everybody who is ready to exert himself only a little can easily find work and his efforts in every trade are rewarded . . . no craftsman who is ready to work will have anything to regret if he comes to America."

Leopold Kompert, the prominent Bohemian novelist, also urged his brethren to go "on to America. Because servile hordes and sordid-minded people have not understood and do not understand the spirit of liberty, we have to suffer . . . there is no other desire among us than to get away. . . . Our goal must, therefore, be emigration, the founding of a new fatherland, the immediate achievement. . . . Let us go to America!"

In 1840, the American-Jewish community numbered approximately 15,000, ten years later 50,000, and by the outbreak of the Civil War 150,000. On the eve of the great Russian invasion, in 1880, the total had grown to 250,000. By the time the second migration subsided, American Jewry was transformed into a German community.

The migratory waves that flooded the interior of the United States in the nineteenth century passed over the mountains and along the rivers in a relentless movement of people toward the Pacific coast. These migrants were mostly Americans, but as the mid-1800s approached, thousands of uprooted foreigners, essentially from Western Europe, committed themselves to populating the American frontier. This was also a period of expansion for American Jewry, as the decades of the German Jewish emigration (1830–70) paralleled the establishment of vast numbers of American towns and the founding of most of the nation's Jewish communities.

Both native-born and immigrant Jews spread across the country in search of economic opportunity. If fortunate, their journey led them to busy crossroads or active frontier towns. They established themselves as peddlers, merchants, storekeepers, farmers, and professionals. If economic conditions were not favorable, they again took to the rivers, highways, and railroads to further penetrate the frontier.

The American pioneer was attracted to towns and cities situated on rivers, territorial roads, canals, and railroads. At such commercial crossroads, Jewish merchants became involved in the marketing of food stuffs, the distribution of cotton, or the manufacture of finished products.

The discovery of mineral deposits also drew Jews to virgin territory. The settlement of the mining frontier, however, altered the traditional modes of transportation as prospectors and merchants sought the fastest route to the mineral-rich regions. To get to California, many cut new trails across the wilderness, sailed around Cape Horn, or crossed the Isthmus of Panama to board ships bound for hastily erected boom towns. Soon, Jews established communal life along the entire length of the West Coast.

Within a decade after the 1848 California gold rush, similar mineral strikes encouraged Jewish settlement in the remote areas of Colorado, New Mexico, Nevada, and Utah. In these territories, Jewish merchants supplied the swelling populations with everything from household utensils to pickaxes and ready-made clothing. In Utah, the Salt Lake City *Telegraph* noted Jewish commercial success:

> *July 16, 1864.*
>
> The changes in Main Street have been going on with great rapidity; every foot of ground seems to be claimed for commercial purposes. The sound of the chisel and hammer falls upon the ear from every direction. In a few weeks that street will be crowded with merchandise and will present an appearance of a metropolitan mart. The Ransohoffs are expecting a rich and heavy stock. Siegel & Co., a new house, has got an early advance and are opening up to the wholesale trade. When Bodenberg and Kahn . . . , who are yet to make their names familiar to the people . . . come in with their huge piles, we will most assuredly have enough [goods] to last a while.

By the outbreak of the Civil War, the network of Jewish settlements spread throughout every territory and state in the Union. Reports confirming the development of communal life on the frontier appeared regularly in the American press. In 1846, Louisville and Cleveland saw the erection of synagogues and the formation of "Israelite societies." Ten years later, Madison, Wisconsin, advertised for a rabbi, and Houston, Texas, announced the chartering of its first Hebrew congregation.

Reports of a frontier presence also appeared in the Jewish press. In 1860, the *Israelite* reported that the twelve Jewish families at St. Joseph, Missouri, had acquired burial grounds and "broached the subject of forming a congregation." From the Rocky Mountains, the same journal published a communication that encouraged emigration to the Southwest:

> *Jefferson Territory, January 5, 1860:*
>
> I presume your readers will not object to hear a word from me in relation to what everyone calls "Pike's Peak." But having the interest at heart of Judaism I avail myself of the opportunity to inform our brethren who intend emigrating to this wild western country, known as the Rocky Mountains, what we intend and are doing to advance the cause of Judaism, in this far western country. . . . We are now here, altogether, some fifteen Israelites. We, thinking it best to provide for our brethren who intend coming here next Summer with their families have organized ourselves into a Congregation under the name Beth Elohim Batmidbar, "The House of the Lord in the Wilderness," for the purpose of promoting Judaism in the country; our action upon this was not intended for our purpose entirely but for those who intend coming and who intend to follow the Jewish rites as they were taught. We have secured ten good city lots of considerable value as a donation from the town company, for the purpose of building a House of Worship. We have also secured ten acres of good land about two miles from the city limits for a burial ground, which we will hold in trust for the benefit of those who may come.

The *Jewish Messenger* in 1861 noted that Los Angeles Jewry organized Congregation Beth El and a Hebrew Benevolent Society. In the Pacific Northwest, the *Journal* accounted for Portland, Oregon:

> The [Jewish] holidays were observed in a more than usually solemn manner by our Portland brethren, they having inaugurated their new synagogue, by a renewed determination to adhere to their holy religion "after the customs of their forefathers." The place of worship was well attended, the stores of all Hebrew merchants being closed; and the streets wore a dull appearance in consequence, the Jewish merchants being among the most prominent citizens of Portland.

From these detailed newspaper accounts, it is evident that by the second half of the nineteenth century, Jewish communities were well established throughout the United States.

Jewish penetration of the frontier began in regions bordering the Ohio River, the first establishment being in Cincinnati. As the migration continued southwest, communities sprang up in West Virginia, Indiana, and Kentucky. The construction of roads and canals carried these pioneers to the remotest corners of the Ohio Valley. Michigan, whose settlement was dependent on overland travel, was penetrated when the Michigan-Chicago Road enabled Jews to take up residence at Ann Arbor, Ypsilanti, and Marshall. They soon reached western Kentucky and, with the completion of the National Road, marched into western Maryland and Indiana. Making use of the network of canals, Jewish settlement continued into Cleveland, Akron, Dayton, and Toledo, and by 1856, with the opening of the Wabash-Erie Canal, their presence was felt throughout Illinois.

Though Jews settled along the entire frontier of the old Northwest, Cincinnati became the most important community west of the Alleghenies. The first Jew to enter the "Queen City of the West" was Joseph Jonas, a native of England who arrived in 1817. Known and respected as an Israelite, he was, nevertheless, looked upon as a curiosity, being the first Jew seen by many. People came from miles around to gaze upon this "Jewish watchmaker." In one instance, an old Quakeress, unable to contain her curiosity, approached him and asked: "Art thou a Jew? Thou are one of God's chosen people? Wilt thou let me examine thee?" She walked around him for several minutes and finally exclaimed, "Well, thou are no different to other people!"

For two years, Jonas remained Cincinnati's only Jew. He was mindful, however, of a promise made to his Philadelphia friends that "he might be a nucleus around which the first congregation might be formed to worship the God of Israel in the great western country." In 1819, his dream came true and he was joined by three others: Lewis Cohen of London, Barnet Levi of Liverpool, and Jonas Levy of Exeter.

Joseph Jonas, who had not attended religious services since his arrival, took the opportunity to pray to the God of Abraham. Together with David I. Johnson, a Jewish resident from neighboring Brookville, the four Cincinnati Jews held Ohio's first service of worship, in the fall of 1819, departing from the tradition that required a *minyan* of ten adult males because of their intense desire to participate in such a service. This tiny group formed the nucleus of a community, and by 1824 attracted enough Jews to organize the first congregation west of the mountains. By 1836, Jonas' promise made to his Philadelphia brethren was fulfilled as Cincinnati Jewry erected a synagogue and proclaimed the practice of Judaism "according to the form and mode of worship of the Polish and German Jews."

Jonas Simson Thomas, a Bavarian immigrant, settled in Cleveland in 1837. Two years after his arrival, the city of six thousand had twenty

Jews, including enough adult males to hold services, organize Congregation Anshe Chesed, and purchase burial grounds.

Chicago, on the shores of Lake Michigan, lay to the west. Though Jews arrived there in the 1820s and '30s, it was not until 1849, when the Illinois & Michigan canal and the Galena & Chicago railroad were completed, that their community grew. The city became a center of trade, attracting Jews as permanent settlers. While Chicago expanded, William Renau, an original founder of the Order of B'nai B'rith, sought to promote Jewish agricultural colonies in the area.

He traveled around the country promoting the settlement of Jewish immigrants in agricultural communities. The idea of Jewish communal agriculture came to fruition with the establishment of the Jewish Agricultural Society and the appointment of Henry Meyer as its western agent. Meyer, in search of a proper site for the colony, came to Chicago and purchased 160 acres in the town of Shaumburg, Cook County. He informed his superiors that he "had found the right place" and urged the society to direct Jewish immigrants to the area. "Chicago," he said, "opens a vista into a large commercial future, and the land around it, which is flowing with milk and honey, is particularly adapted for tillers of the soil."

A number of Jews came to the Chicago area, but only two settled as farmers in the Shaumburg region. Most remained in the city and drifted into a variety of commercial enterprises. With this influx of Jews, the need for a permanent congregation became apparent, and on November 3, 1847, twenty people meeting at the dry-goods store of Rosenfeld and Rosenberg formed Kehilath Anshe Mayriv—"Congregation of the People of the West." In a decade, Chicago Jewry established its second congregation—B'nai Sholom—the Hebrew Benevolent Society, and the Ladies' Relief Society. By 1867, ground was broken for the city's first Jewish hospital.

Striking out from the Chicago region, Jews migrated to the surrounding areas. In Indiana they formed communities at Fort Wayne, Lafayette, and Indianapolis, and after penetrating Iowa, peddled their wares on the fringes of the Louisiana Territory.

To the north was Minnesota, where in the decades before the Civil War Jewish Indian traders were conducting business at Taylor Falls and St. Croix. As the territory opened for settlement, this tiny band of Jewish traders were joined by others, and soon Jewish communities were established at St. Paul, Minneapolis, and Duluth.

Jewish pioneers entered Michigan by water, road, and rail. Settling the Ann Arbor-Ypsilanti region were a mixture of Bavarian, Bohemian, Hungarian, and Silesian immigrants, who by 1850 had developed thriving communities along the route of the Michigan Central Railroad. In this area they were pleased to find among the non-Jewish German farmers their own language and familiar traditions.

Detroit, however, became the chief commercial center of the region attracting Jewish settlers. Detroit Jewry, noted one observer, grew "like the wheat grains on a sultan's chessboard so that within a very short time after 1850, Detroit's first Jewish arrivals had ample company."

As in the case of Detroit, the settlement of Milwaukee and the surrounding Wisconsin territory was motivated by economics and dependent upon convenient transportation. Though the community had its origins with the arrival of the Meyer brothers, Moses Weil, Isaac Neustadt, and Solomon Adler, it was not until the 1850s that Milwaukee Jewry began to blossom. By 1856, the community of two hundred families supported three synagogues, several parochial schools, and numerous fraternal and cultural organizations and benevolent societies. As participants in the city's commercial life, Jews became prominent as grain dealers, shippers, peddlers, merchants, and clothing manufacturers.

Jews owned five of the city's fourteen most important clothing firms and were in control of most of the city's retail dry-goods trade. Among those responsible for this achievement were the firms of Solomon Adler and Bros., whose gross sales from clothing reached $600,000 annually, and Zellner and Bonns, who manufactured civilian and military uniforms. Also prosperous in the wholesale clothing industry were Friend & Bros., Shakman Bros., and E. Silverman & Co.

As dry-goods dealers, the Mack Bros., Adler, Newbouer & Co., and H. Stern & Bros. offered the public the most varied assortment of dry goods and notions in town. Similar success stories are contained in the commercial operations of Marcus Heinmann, a millinery dealer; Joseph Bremer and Moritz L. Morawetz, the city's largest wholesale grocers; and Bernhard Leidersdorf, owner of the Western Steam Tobacco Works.

South of Wisconsin, the river arteries carried the Jewish community to St. Louis. Few Jews settled in this Mississippi town in the early-nineteenth century, and it was not until 1841 that the United Hebrew Congregation was established. St. Louis Jewry boasted a thriving community, yet faced numerous problems: "One," noted an observer, "was that many [Jews] remained in the city for only a short time before proceeding further west or south." Since its location made the city a natural jump-off point, many Jews departed east to Louisville, west to the California gold fields, or south toward the Gulf states.

Even with the constant loss of Jews attracted to other areas, the community flourished. Henry Meyers, secretary of the United Hebrew Congregation, described the growth of the St. Louis community:

> The congregation to which I belong, and to which I have the honor of being secretary, has increased so rapidly within the last twelve months (so much beyond our most sanguine expectations) that I am sure you will participate with us in our exultations. At our last holy days our synagogue was crowded to almost suffocation, not less than from five to six hundred persons being present, when but a few years ago we could boast of fifty or sixty, and it is still increasing.
>
> There is also a new German synagogue started, which in a little time will become of importance. We have also two benefit societies, both flourishing, and we are about organizing a Benevolent Society for the relief of our less fortunate Brethren, the progress of which I will inform you of at some future day.

While St. Louis was experiencing this growth, Jews traveled downstream to seek their fortunes in the lower Mississippi Valley, settling at the site of the great cotton market at Memphis; the oil and seed-mill towns of Natchez, Vicksburg, and Shreveport; the cotton-shipping center of Baton Rouge; the geographically strategic Mobile; and the busy port of New Orleans.

From the lower Mississippi Valley and Louisiana, Jews advanced into Arkansas and Texas. At the time of its admission into the Union, in 1836, Arkansas housed Jewish communities at Little Rock, Arkadelphia, Arkansas Post, and Pine Bluff. Not until after the Civil War, however, did the state witness a respectable immigration of Jewish settlers. In an attempt to limit the swelling number of East European Jews settling in the urban centers of the post-Civil War East, the Alliance Emigration Society sought to relocate the newcomers in the South and Southwest. Solomon Franklin, of Pine Bluff offered the society his own land:

> I shall furnish land, houses, leaseholds; in short, everything required for the organization of a settlement. All this I shall furnish free, except for food and clothing, . . . the settlers will receive one half of the produce, consisting mainly of grain and hemp. Should they prefer to work for monthly wages, if they sign up for at least

three years, I offer them fifty [dollars] per month, in addition to lodging, food, water, and medical care.

In Texas, Jewish pioneers from the eastern seaboard and the lower Mississippi Valley organized communal life at Galveston, Houston, San Antonio, Austin, and Dallas. First to arrive in the Texas region was Solomon Parr, who opened a general store in Bolivar in 1832. The Massina family of New Orleans, the Dyers of Baltimore, and the Ostermans, Gottschalks, Seeligmans, Polocks, and DeCordovas of Philadelphia followed, all making significant economic and political contributions to the state.

Settled by Jews from Baltimore and Philadelphia, Galveston became an early center of Jewish life in Texas. Here they formed the nucleus that established the first communal institution in the territory: the Galveston Jewish Cemetery. Observing the growth of Texas Jewry, the Galveston *News* commented: "We anticipate the organization of a Jewish Congregation and the addition of a synagogue to the number of our places of worship."

Moving west, Jews pushed beyond the Mississippi Valley to the open spaces of the Great Plains. Traveling twenty-three hundred miles along the Missouri, Platte, Yellowstone, and Snake rivers, they established communities in western Missouri, Kansas, Nebraska, the Dakotas, Wyoming, and Montana.

The comforts and commercial opportunities of St. Louis were not enough to keep Missouri Jewry from looking elsewhere. Many left this thriving crossroad of business and followed the Missouri River inland to the farthest corner of the state to settle at Kansas City. Others chose the more commercially attractive areas of the Pacific coast. Herman Ganz, however, made Kansas City his home in 1856, joined by his brother Benjamin, Henry Miller, and Louis Hammerslough—all Germans, all bachelors, and all permanent settlers. From this seed the community grew and with the improvement in transcontinental transportation, Kansas City Jewry soon stood second in the state only to the thriving settlement at St. Louis.

Rather than the lure of commercial opportunity, many emigrants were attracted to the Kansas Territory because of the intense struggle between pro- and anti-slavery factions. It appears that settlement in the area was prompted in 1854, when Congress repealed the Missouri Compromise and replaced it with the Kansas-Nebraska Act, which opened the territory to slavery. Thousands of settlers flocked to Kansas in order to take their place among the contending groups. Once settled, free-soilers, abolitionists, and proslavery groups engaged in both verbal and violent protest. Among those who arrived to fight the injustice of slavery were August Bondi, the Wiener brothers, and Jacob Benjamin —all Jews and all supporters of the abolitionist John Brown.

As a youth, Bondi had fought in the Austro-Hungarian Revolution. The decline of Europe's liberalism motivated Bondi and thousands like him to emigrate to the United States, and it was his deep passion for justice that brought him into the Kansas anti-slavery struggle. Theodore Wiener, Bondi's partner in several commercial ventures, was a proslavery man. He had lived in Texas and Louisiana, and came to Kansas to seek his fortune rather than to fight for humanity. But in time Wiener reversed his position and threw himself into the anti-slavery movement.

There were also those who came to Kansas in search of commercial opportunity, among them Samuel and Hester Rosenberg, who came from Kentucky by wagon and opened a furniture store at Fort Leavenworth in the 1850s. Bernard Korman established a tin shop, and Philip Rothschild, who was one of the town's most successful businessmen, was the proud owner of that city's first brick building. Rothschild is better remembered for organizing the first B'nai B'rith lodge, in 1866, for establishing the Ft. Leavenworth Literary Society, and for his charitable activities.

Kansas Jewry took an active part in the state's political life. August Bondi, after the Civil War, became postmaster of Salina; Jews were elected as mayors of Rosedale, Wichita, and Dodge City; and Adolph Gluck, while a Dodge City councilman, appointed Wyatt Earp to enforce the law in that wild frontier town.

The settlement of Nebraska began with the passage of the Kansas-Nebraska Act, in 1854. Following the Missouri River north, or going overland by foot and wagon, Jews reached Omaha, "the gateway to the Far West." The first Jew to take up residence was Leopold May, a young German bachelor whose mercantile business served the needs of the city's three hundred residents. According to the *Rocky Mountain News* of April 23, 1859, the company of May & Weil, of Omaha and Council Bluffs, carried "ready-made clothing, boots and shoes, hats and caps, India rubber goods, blankets, buffalo robes and overshirts, revolvers and knives." Fortunately, competition did not drive the Jewish community apart, and soon its members co-operated in organizing a variety of communal organizations.

By 1858, the discovery of gold at Pike's Peak made Omaha a prosperous city, as it served the needs of those bound for the mining camps to the south. The economic progress of the city attracted others, and by the outbreak of the Civil War, Omaha housed a large Jewish community.

Max Meyer, hearing of Omaha's commercial success, arrived in 1866 to open a tobacco business. Soon he and his brother were selling jewelry and musical instruments throughout the territory. Meyer's firm, the first to install a telephone, branched out to Cheyenne, Wyoming, and hired five salesmen to canvass the territory to the west.

Julius Meyer, who also arrived in 1866, operated a successful trade with the Indians. Buying a variety of items from the neighboring tribes and selling them to the locals, he learned to speak several Indian languages and came to be regarded by the tribes as so trustworthy that the chiefs agreed to use him as their interpreter. Known by the tribes as the "curly-haired white chief," he was frequently visited by such Indian notables as Sitting Bull, Spotted Tail, Red Cloud, and Swift Bear. On one occasion, Spotted Tail, a Sioux chief, was so taken with Meyer's sincerity, that he offered the merchant his own pipe and tobacco pouch, a gesture that was considered the warmest expression of friendship an Indian could make. On another occasion, Meyer was the guest of honor at an Indian dog feast (a favorite meal of the tribes). Meyer explained to the Indians that, although he was honored by the feast, he could not partake, as dog meat is not kosher. Because Jewish Indian traders and peddlers were frequently feted by the Indians, who had to substitute hard-boiled eggs, the Indians dubbed the Jews "eggeaters."

To the north and the west, Jews continued to establish settlement points: in the Dakotas they were attracted by the Black Hills gold rush of 1875; Wyoming in 1878 housed a Jewish community of forty at Cheyenne, attracted by the commercial activities associated with the search for mineral wealth; in Idaho and Montana they again were drawn by the discovery of gold.

In their haste to reach the Montana gold fields, Jewish prospectors and merchants crossed the Great Plains from St. Louis and Fort Leavenworth and made their way along the Missouri River. Isadore Strasburger abandoned diggings in Colorado and made the trek north with the hope of being among the first to stake a claim. Like Strasburger, however, who opened a general store, most were forced to surrender dreams of riches as their diggings proved as empty as their dreams. Jews appeared at settlements dotting the Montana countryside, among them the city of Helena, named for a Jewess and housing enough Jews to warrant the establishment of a Hebrew Benevolent Association in 1866 to "relieve the distressed and support the afflicted." The association had sixty-four members and was the first Jewish communal organization in the territory. Yet Montana Jewry was slow to increase. In 1873, the *Israelite* reported that there were a mere twelve families among Helena's 3,500 residents. In 1880 the number of Jews rose to 112, and nineteen years later, when Montana was admitted as a state, the Jewish population state-wide had climbed to 2,500.

Though these regions owed their initial development to the presence of gold, the 1848 California strike was the most important event on the mining frontier. Within a few years after the discovery at Sutter's Mill, Jewish merchants furnished the hastily erected mining camps with a variety of supplies and at the same time established permanent settlements in Sacramento, San Diego, San Francisco, Sonora, Los Angeles, San Bernardino, and San Jose.

Most Jews did not join the search for gold, but instead concentrated their efforts on commerce. Polish-born Morris Shloss came to San Francisco in September 1849. He brought with him a wagon packed in a large crate and, at the pier, was approached by a stranger who asked what was in the huge box. Informed that it contained a wagon, the man offered Shloss one hundred dollars. Shloss, who had paid only fifteen dollars for the wagon, quickly accepted.

The new owner of the package carefully opened the crate and, after removing the wagon, turned to Shloss and said: "Stranger, you may keep the wagon, for I only want the box. I am a cobbler, and in the daytime it will be my shop, and at night, my residence." The box measured seven feet high, four feet wide, and fifteen feet long.

Others who came to the gold-rich areas of California realized that fortunes could be made by catering to the needs of the community. In Sacramento, Louis Sloss and Simon Greenewald established a mercantile exchange, Moses Hyman operated a thriving jewelry business, and Joseph Haines opened a store that sold ". . . brandy, gin, wines, cigars, tobacco, brogans, boots, clothing, counter scales, [and] medicines adapted to [the California] climate."

One of the most successful of all the merchants was Levi Strauss. Traveling around the mining camps, he often heard complaints about the poor quality of work pants. Quick to take advantage of an opportunity, Strauss started to manufacture overalls made from a heavy tent material he had in his stock. The results were more than satisfactory: the material stood up under heavy wear. He had discovered his own "gold mine."

He informed his brothers in the East of his success and instructed them to buy all the denim and heavy duck available and produce pants and overalls for the California market. At twenty-three years of age, Strauss, prospering with his new product, established Levi Strauss & Co. in New York and San Francisco.

Strauss was joined by other merchants, who, in their desire to seek new and larger markets, expanded their operations to include commercial ventures other than with the mining trade. Among those now doing business in California were Levy & Co., selling luxury goods imported from Europe; the Hecht Brothers, offering dry goods; and the Goldstones, who became leaders in the ready-made clothing industry.

As the Jewish population increased, their economic interests widened. Ben Davidson, the Abrams brothers, Leopold Lowenberg, and Jesse Seligman engaged in banking. The most successful of these men was Seligman, who soon played a prominent role in international finance. The Dreyfus family controlled the largest vineyards in the state, and the Castle, Guggenheim, and Rosenberg brothers were among the most successful fruit producers. The best summary of California Jewry's economic success was to be found in an editorial in the *Jewish Chronicle:* "The Hebrew is not a nomad. When once he settles in California he becomes a resident, identified with and aiding its progress. Take Hebrew energy and capital from California and the state would be bankrupt."

As an overflow from the California settlement, Jewish emigrants entered Oregon in 1849, and went southeast to Arizona, New Mexico, Nevada, Utah, and Colorado. The Colorado gold rush of the 1850s and the discovery of silver, lead, and copper were responsible for the permanent settlement of Jews in the territory. Motivated by dreams of riches, they came to this western wilderness in the decade prior to the Civil War. Settled by even greater numbers after the war, the region prospered.

When railroads connected the territory with the East, Jewish emigrants made their way to Denver and soon were holding services in the Pike's Peak region. Despite the influx of Jews to the territory, it was not until the mid-1870s that Denver Jewry built Congregation Emanuel or developed a tightly knit community. By the late '70s and early '80s, Denver Jewry ranked high among the more important Jewish communities of the West. Colorado Jewry spread throughout the region and founded settlement points in Boulder, Black Hawk, Greeley, San Luis, and Central City.

While Colorado was witnessing an increase in its Jewish population, in Philadelphia a youthful Jewish immigrant from Switzerland was embarking on a peddling career that would lead him to great financial success. Wandering the Pennsylvania countryside laden with goods, Solomon Guggenheim hardly looked like a man who one day would make a major contribution to the development of American industry.

Guggenheim quickly rose to join the ranks of the wealthy, expanding his economic interests in several directions. One area in which he invested his capital was a flooded Colorado mine that he hoped to turn into a productive business. Soon after his investment was made, he questioned the soundness of this venture. He went to Leadville in 1881 and while investigating his holding realized that the commercial establishments surrounding the mining industry were an untapped source of wealth.

Guggenheim's plunge into the mining business proved to be the wisest financial move of his brief business career. Realizing that the greatest profits were to be made in smelting and not mining, he purchased eighty thousand dollars worth of Globe Smelting stock, instructed his son to learn all he could about smelting ore, and established the Philadelphia Smelting and Refining Company. After he built his first smelter, at Pueblo, Colorado, his economic interests spread throughout the state. From an investment in a flooded mine, Guggenheim emerged as one of the most successful and important financial giants in the United States.

Communal action characterized many activities of Colorado Jewry. For example, many Jews who migrated to the region did so not for financial reasons but to benefit from the dry climate—which was the only cure for those with tuberculosis. But the cost of medical treatment and relocation was beyond the means of hundreds of the sick, and they were forced to settle in the slums, where the air they breathed was fouled by soot and smoke from the smelters. To help these people, Denver Jewry acted as a unified group. The city's first hospital was built, staffed, and maintained with funds contributed by the Jewish community. The Jewish philanthropic tradition prevailed from its inception: the facility was non-sectarian and always lived up to its motto: "None may enter who can pay—none can pay who enter."

Like those who settled in Colorado, the pioneer Jews of Utah first tried to make their fortunes in other western regions. In time, however, for a variety of reasons, they made their way to the region of the Great Salt Lake. Salt Lake City soon became known for its hospitality as a halfway station between the Missouri River and California and became an important western Jewish settlement point.

Once established at Salt Lake City, permanent Jewish residents played host to "wandering Jews," who, making the journey to the Pacific coast, interrupted their march to "break bread" with their Utah brothers. Many of the Jewish adventurers who laid over were either sick with fever or destitute, unable to continue their journey; they accepted what was offered by the Jewish aid societies, in some cases remaining to become part of the permanent community.

As with all Jewish communities in nineteenth-century America, the Salt Lake City synagogue, the benevolent societies, and the burial grounds formed the nucleus of communal life. In 1866, Salt Lake City established the Hebrew Benevolent Society to aid distressed Jews and organized a burial society on a plot of land donated by the Mormon leader Brigham Young.

In neighboring Nevada, Jews were found only in sparse numbers, C. H. Meyer, one of Carson City's few Jewish residents, described the condition of Nevada Jewry:

> *Carson City, Nevada Territory, November 13, 1862.*
>
> Only a very small number of our persuasion reside in this city. Aside from a Jewish benevolent association, no other Jewish society exists here. This benevolent association had $157.50, funds which they entirely donated to the committee of the Sanitary Fund, to be applied to the sick and wounded soldiers [Civil War] who fought for the preservation of this Union.
>
> Virginia City, situated sixteen miles from this place, has already a larger population of Israelites. On the approach of Yom Kippur last they formed a congregation to observe that holy day and the succeeding festive days. Thus, you will see that although silver mine speculation and thoughts to win fortunes in this new country almost exclusively fill the human mind, still Israelites forget not, in this distant country, on their God or on their duties as the descendants of their forefathers. This last-mentioned place, Virginia City, is surrounded by silver mines. It is the most important place in the whole territory. Some of those mines are very rich and yield immense fortunes to their lucky owners.
>
> I hardly expect that you would find much interest in affairs of this country aside from religious affairs. I think, however, the time is not distant when the growth of our Jewish population will require the organizing of congregations and other religious institutions. There exists too much wealth in the silver mines of the territory to

deny the expectation of a very rapid increase of our population, for it is a known fact that our people are found to reside where money can be made.

In 1846, as a result of the Mexican War and the philosophy of "manifest destiny," Americans drove southwest. Prominent among this group was Solomon Spiegelberg, who pushed his ox train over the Santa Fe Trail toward New Mexico. Upon arrival at Santa Fe, he joined Colonel Alexander Doniphan's military venture into Mexico as an army provisioner. Within two years after his arrival, Mexico was defeated, the Treaty of Guadalupe-Hidalgo (1848) ceded the territory to the United States, and Spiegelberg was fast becoming a rich merchant. He was joined by his four brothers and several other Jewish newcomers who found employment at the growing firm of Spiegelberg & Bros.—the major supplier of the United States Army in the New Mexico Territory.

New Mexico developed rapidly and with it the commercial enterprises of the Spiegelberg family. On July 9, 1868, the first issue of the *Daily New Mexican* printed the following announcement:

> Spiegelberg Brothers, Importers, and Wholesale and Retail Dealers in Foreign and Domestic Dry Goods—Clothing, Boots, Shoes, Hardware, Queensware, Liquors, Groceries, etc. . . .
>
> Merchants will find it to their advantage to call on us before going East, as we keep on hand an assortment of goods especially adapted to this market and of the adjoining territories. Two of our firms are permanently in the New York market, purchasing goods. Those who deal with us can rely upon our stock being of the best quality and at the lowest prices.

Also attracted to the former territories of Mexico was Herman Ehrenberg, the first Jew to settle in Arizona. He went to the region to develop its mineral resources, but in order to supplement his income from mining, he established a general store with Michael Goldwasser—later changed to Goldwater—a Jewish immigrant from Russia-Poland. In 1866, Ehrenberg was killed en route from San Francisco. After his death, Goldwater founded on the Colorado River the town of Ehrenberg in memory of his partner, renamed the store Goldwater & Brother, and built the business into one of the most important financial institutions in Arizona. In time, the small general store became the civic and mercantile center of the entire region.

From profits made as army suppliers, the Goldwaters entered the freighting business, carrying supplies from the Pacific coast to Arizona and New Mexico. However, the mines surrounding the Goldwater enterprises gave out and the region quickly diminished as a commercial center. Goldwater & Brother relocated to other parts of Arizona and quickly extended their financial and political influence to all sections of the territory.

Michael Goldwater was not the only immigrant Jew to seek commercial success in the Arizona Territory. Sol Barth came in 1862, settled in La Paz, and soon was guiding others through the dangerous Indian Territory. From his profits as a sutler (civilian army supplier) and guide, Barth opened a general store and became an important commercial figure. The Prescott *Miner* noted his activities:

> Sol Barth, of St. Johns, Little Colorado, came in this morning with 90,000 lbs. of barley for C. P. Herd & Co. This barley is raised at Stinson's ranch, and is said to be an excellent quality. Sol and his brothers are in the stock and freighting business on the Little Colorado, where they have been for several years.

Isador Solomon, an immigrant from Posen, came to the territory in 1876. Once settled in Pueblo Viejo, he opened a mercantile exchange supplying the settlers, native Mexicans, and Indians with a variety of goods. Solomon's establishment became the post office and official trading center for the area, and the name of this southwestern outpost was changed to Solomonville for its first postmaster.

Dividing his time between family business and civic matters, Solomon was forced to travel frequently. On one trip through the Arizona "badlands"—where there was ever-present danger of attack by Indians or bandits—his stage coach was held up. In the course of the robbery, he thanked the bandits for not harming anyone and only taking their valuables. The bandits seemed pleased with this attitude and talked with their victim. Solomon asked that his watch, a family heirloom, be returned. To his surprise, the hold-up men returned it and apologized. Encouraged by the positive response of his captors, Solomon again made a very unusual request: could the victims have some money for food for the remainder of their trip? To Solomon's astonishment, the bandits provided funds and sent the coach on its way.

Isador Solomon, like most other Jews who crossed the nation, displayed courage and fortitude. Because of these characteristics, American Jewry, which numbered five substantial communities during the co-

lonial period, grew to about two hundred settlements by the eve of the
great Russian Jewish immigration.

RETURN TO THE SOIL

In the first half of the nineteenth century there were several efforts to
encourage Jewish immigrants to settle in agricultural co-operatives. The
movement was motivated by the need to draw from the urban areas the
rapidly increasing number of Jews who were dependent on the funds
provided by philanthropic agencies. Though the concept of co-operative
agriculture appeared to be the best solution for urban overcrowding, almost all of these agrarian experiments were "paper" projects, with little
more than discussion as their result.

Coupled with the need to draw people from an overpopulated urban
environment, "Jewish agricultural colonization" served a second, and
perhaps more noble, purpose: that of Zionism. Lastly, early-nineteenth-
century America was characterized by the romantic mystique of the as-
sociative colony, as some Jews, as well as the Shakers and Owenites,
sought to establish their "Zion in the wilderness." Jewish colonization
was not only an attempt to relieve the burgeoning Jewish urban masses
or simply land-speculation schemes, but a combination of American
romanticism and a kind of Jewish Messianism that lasted throughout
the nineteenth century.

The first proposal to organize Jews in a co-operative colony was
made by William Davis Robinson, a land speculator who in 1819 published a pamphlet addressed to the . . . *Jewish religion in Europe, on
the Subject of Emigration to, and Settlement in, One of the Most Eligible Parts of the United States of North America.* The Robinson plan
advanced the idea that wealthy European Jews should buy vast tracts of
land in the upper Mississippi Valley for the re-establishment of those
less fortunate. According to the proposal, each Jewish settler would receive a tract of land on credit, funds for transportation, and capital for
the necessary farming tools. Robinson, a Christian, believed his proposal would benefit both European Jewry and American economic development. Though he was sincere in his efforts, his plan failed to elicit
a favorable response from European or American Jewry.

The following year, Moses Elias Levy, whose son David Levy Yulee
was to become Florida's first United States senator, proposed the creation of a communal settlement in Alachua County, Florida. Levy wrote
to the officials of New York's Shearith Israel Synagogue and proposed

the establishment of a theological seminary. He suggested the development of a Jewish agricultural community, and to display his faith in such a project, pledged a tract of land for the planned community. His proposal for a community and his offer of land, however, received little enthusiasm from New York Jewry.

Despite the lack of response, Levy managed to bring several families from New York, New Jersey, and Europe to his Alachua colony. He built homes, cleared land, and furnished the newcomers with provisions and tools. By 1823 there were fifty people at Alachua, "all of whom were brought there . . . at [Levy's] own expense for the purpose of forming a settlement."

The next year, hoping to induce others to make the Florida community their home, Levy and his agents publicized the project. Quickly, twenty-five houses were built, forty-five miles of road were completed, plans were drawn for a sawmill, and three plantations were established on three hundred acres of cultivated land. Though Levy's advertising extolled "the fertility of the soil, salubrity of its air, sublimity of its scenery, [and] abundant supply of cattle and stock," the colony, open to all, including non-Jews, failed to attract more than a handful of people.

Unlike Levy's settlement, Joseph Frey's project was aimed at Jews *only*—converts to Christianity. Joseph Christian Frederick Frey, a converted Jew, and the American Society for Meliorating the Condition of the Jews, a missionary organization, set about to establish an agricultural co-operative for converted European Jews. In 1824 the society planned to buy land, build a community, and supply Jewish converts with tools so that they could "be principally employed in agricultural and mechanical operation."

Within a year, the society purchased a farm in Westchester County, New York, placed Frey in charge of its operation, and braced itself in anticipation of the influx of converted Hebrews. To the disappointment of the directors, the Jews did not come, and recognizing their failure, the society withdrew from the project. Another colonization venture had died in infancy.

To this same decade belongs Mordecai M. Noah's projected colonization scheme: Ararat. This project, unlike the colony of Frey's society, was to be "a city of refuge for the Jews [only]." In this respect, Noah's call for the establishment of a Jewish state made him America's first Zionist and a forerunner of Theodor Herzl.

In 1825, Noah announced to the world a plan for the establishment of a Jewish state under the protection of the American Constitution. On the Niagara River, close to the city of Buffalo, New York, was wooded

Grand Island, which Noah wanted as the center of a Jewish republic. With several associates, most of whom were Christians, he acquired a section of land and an option to purchase more and, appropriately, named the colony for the mountain on which Noah's Ark had rested as the flood subsided: Ararat.

Noah announced his intentions in a *Proclamation to the Jews:*

> In His name do I revive, renew and re-establish the government of the Jewish nation, under the auspices and protection of the constitution and laws of the United States; confirming and perpetuating all our rights and privileges, our name, our rank, and our power among the nations of the earth, as they existed and were recognized under the government of the Judges.

To accomplish his goal, Noah invited world Jewry to come to America and become citizens of Ararat. To assist in the organization of the project, he asked Abraham de Cologna, Chief Rabbi of France; Rabbis Solomon Herschell and Raphael Meldola of Great Britain; and several prominent American and European laymen.

Before receiving a response from this distinguished group of leaders as to their willingness to co-operate, Noah made plans for the dedication of Ararat's cornerstone. On September 2, 1825, the pageantry began with a Masonic and military parade through the streets of Buffalo to the entrance of the Episcopal church, where the leaders gathered, and in full Masonic and military dress paraded down the aisles to the music of the Grand March from "Judas Maccabaeus." The Reverend Mr. Addison Searle presided, the choir sang, the organ played, and the lengthy orations filled the air. After the completion of the preliminary events, the cornerstone was laid. Its inscription read:

ARARAT
A City of Refuge for the Jews,
Founded by Mordecai Manuel Noah *in the Month of Tizri*
Sept. 1825 & *in the* 50th *year of* American Independence.

Reaction to the project, however, was less than favorable. The European religious and lay leaders promptly disassociated themselves from the scheme, while only Gabriel Riesser, a prominent defender of Jewish rights in Europe, commented favorably on the plan. To Noah's disappointment, European Jewry did not flock to Grand Island. It seems that the written text of the proposal was suppressed by the Russian and Austro-Hungarian empires and Jews living under these monarchies never heard of the project. Indeed, even the West European press aided in bringing about its failure, as editorial comment was almost always negative.

In the United States, the press joined the written attack. *Niles' Weekly Register,* for instance, portrayed Ararat as a scheme of "some foreign speculators—Jews themselves, . . . who have no sort of objection to advance their own wealth at the cost of their fellows—and to get money, honestly if they can, *but to get money.*" Noah's City of Refuge, like all previous colonization projects failed, and all that is left to remind us of the city is the cornerstone, housed in a Buffalo museum.

Visions of creating a Jewish agricultural community, however, did not fade from the American scene. In 1837, there arose another organization seeking to settle in co-operative colonies. The movement, led by the society of Zeire Hazon (The Tender Sheep), was organized in New York City by German Jewish emigrants. The group, which sought the creation of a settlement on the Great Plains, hoped to solve the problem of urban overcrowding and their own economic distress. In an appeal to other Jews, the society declared that their members, all recent arrivals, "have endeavored to gain a livelihood by pursuing their different occupations, but owing to the difficulties with which they have had to contend, . . . [were] unable to lay up anything for their future support." Thus, they asserted, "[we] have organized [ourselves] into an association, for the purpose of removing West, and settling on some part of the Public Lands, suitable for the agricultural purposes."

Unfortunately, the year 1837 was one of nationwide financial panic. The Tender Sheep, who so much wanted to join America's farmers, were forced to remain in New York and join the pool of workers and peddlers that made up the immigrant labor force.

The initial attempts to create Jewish co-operatives in the United States were all failures. American Jewry was not ready to support such experiments, and European Jewish emigrants were equally not anxious to till the soil. The "Jewish agrarian movement," however, prepared the way for more successful endeavors in the latter part of the nineteenth century.

PEDDLERS AND MERCHANTS

Rabbi Isaac Meyer Wise, the most influential American Jewish leader in the latter half of the nineteenth century, saw a man with a straw hat pulled down on his face. He wore an oversized coat stained with perspiration, carried two large bundles on his shoulders, and "dragged himself along with painful effort." As the stranger came closer, Wise realized that hidden behind the odd clothing was his friend Stein. As though he had read the rabbi's mind, Stein looked Wise squarely in the face and with a smile on his lips said, "Most of the German and Polish Jews in America look like this." Wise walked his friend home, accepted an invitation to rest in his living room, and waited while Stein changed his garments.

"A quarter of an hour later," remarked Wise, "Stein emerged completely metamorphosed. He looked genteel again." Stein, now in proper attire, turned to his wife and laughingly explained to her that the rabbi had "met him in his peddler's costume." Wise, still puzzled by Stein's dress, asked his friend to explain the phenomenon of the Jewish peddler. What followed was Stein's description of the stages by which the peddler rose to commercial success:

> Our people in this country, said [Stein], may be divided into the following classes: (1) the basket peddler, he is as yet altogether dumb and homeless; (2) the trunk-carrier, who stammers some little English, and hopes for better times; (3) the pack-carrier, who carries from 100–150 pounds upon his back, and indulges the thought that he will become a businessman someday.

"In addition to these" said Stein, "there is an aristocracy, which may be divided into three classes:

> (1) The wagon-baron, who peddles through the country with a one- or two-horse team; (2) the jewelry-count, who carries a stock of watches and jewelry in a small trunk, and is considered a rich man even now; (3) the store-prince, who has a shop and sells goods in it.

The "first one," he asserted, "is the slave of the basket and pack, then the lackey of the horse, in order to become, finally, the servant of the shop." "But what about the people of intelligence?" protested Wise. "In America," answered Stein, "a man must be either all head or all back. Those who are in this country must be all back, and forgo all intellectual pursuits . . . the foreigner must either become rich, or go to the wall; he has no alternative. The end and aim of all striving in this country is to become rich; everything else is secondary."

In this simplistic explanation of the *raison d'être* of American Jewry, Stein described the mode and in some cases the motivations that permeated the life of the itinerant Jewish peddler.

Peddling has been portrayed as a Jewish innovation by which "greenhorn" Jews sought, almost rapaciously, to earn a livelihood. But there is little truth in this assertion. The peddler was not peculiarly Jewish, but rather a vocational "hand-me-down" from the non-Jewish Yankee of an earlier period. No longer needing the opportunity provided by the career of door-to-door salesman, the New England peddler was replaced by the "Jew peddler."

Most nineteenth-century Jewish emigrants came with little capital and rarely had business connections awaiting them in the United States. In the decade of the 1850s, as many as 20 per cent of those who settled in New York City required the assistance of Jewish charitable agencies. Arriving with little, and in a land where the language and customs were strange, the immigrant Jew had to face the basic problem of resettlement: how to support the family.

For some, the simplest mode of self-employment was peddling. Jews knew of its existence in Europe, knew it required little capital to start, and were willing to endure the hardships of the peddler's life. Initially, the peddler sold to other immigrants, who spoke his language and were familiar with this type of transaction. He knew that many of his potential customers, unfamiliar with American ways, were unwilling to purchase from established, single-price retail stores. He had a ready-made market in the ghettos of immigrant society. If he was successful, the peddler's business grew and he was soon able to expand his trade from the "greenhorn" sections to other areas of the city and countryside, and carried his *pak tsores* (bag of troubles) into familiar and unfamiliar surroundings, sometimes taunted and stoned, and always shunning houses with the sign NO BEGGARS OR PEDDLERS ALLOWED.

Perhaps half of the Germans who arrived in New York City in the 1840s took up the trade. A familiar advertisement was that of Grossheim, Schreiber & Co., announcing to the trade that "German [Jewish] peddlers will find a complete and varied assortment of supplies at the undersigned." The Jewish peddler, who introduced the practice of installment buying, became more and more visible, and the stereotype of the "Jew peddler" emerged. A popular verse, *A Day on Coney Island*, celebrated his increasing numbers:

> On ev'ry path, by almost every tune,
> Industrious Israelites a living "earn,"
> By selling colored specs to screen the eyes,
> Which would not serve an idiot in disguise,
> Purchase by all means—yellow, green or blue—

You will aid one member of a useful crew;
He *will not work;* he neither starves, nor begs,
But peddles healing-salve for wooden legs.

The stereotype did not discourage William Frank, who peddled in Philadelphia and in the Pennsylvania countryside. Frank came to New York on November 1, 1840, borrowed thirty dollars and headed for Philadelphia, where he accumulated enough money to purchase goods and begin to peddle. During his stay in the city, he was introduced to Blum and Simpson, dealers in dry goods who provided him a stock of quality merchandise on credit. Within one year, Frank was successful enough to enter the ranks of the store princes.

Others followed Frank's example and bought goods on credit and took to the countryside. In the rural areas far from the convenient stores of the urban centers, farmers with cash and little opportunity to spend it welcomed the peddler. The itinerant peddler became a vital link connecting the rural settler to the urban manufacturer.

For some, peddling was a temporary vocation. As soon as they accumulated the necessary capital, they turned from wandering salesman to "respected" retail-store owner. Adam Gimbel was one who made this transition. He came from Bavaria to New Orleans in 1835 and, like many before him, peddled his wares along the length of the Mississippi River. Successful, he opened a dry-goods store in Vincennes, Indiana, and with the aid of his sons expanded the business to Danville, Milwaukee, Philadelphia, and New York City. Gimbel the peddler was the beginning of what would become one of the most successful retail establishments in the United States.

Benjamin Bloomingdale also came from Bavaria. He peddled in Kansas and across the Great Plains and accumulated enough money to enable him and his son, Lyman, to establish a hoop-skirt factory in New York City. In 1872, Lyman and his younger brother Joseph founded a retail dry-goods business in Manhattan, and within one year after the end of the Civil War opened Bloomingdale Brothers Department Store.

Few peddlers were as successful in their transition to store prince as the Gimbels and the Bloomingdales. As Stein had described to Rabbi Wise, most remained "pack-carrier[s], who [carried] from 100–150 pounds upon [their] back, and [indulged] the thought that [they] would become a businessman someday." Peddling was a difficult, often dangerous life, lived on the edge of failure.

Abraham Kohn, a peddler, described the hardships:

Winter has come . . . not far from here we were forced to stop on Wednesday because of the heavy snow. We sought to spend the night with . . . a Mr. Spaulding, but his wife did not wish to take us in. She was afraid of strangers, she might not sleep well, we should go on our way. And outside there raged the worst blizzard I have ever seen. Oh, God, I thought, is this the land of liberty and hospitality and tolerance? Why have I been led here? After we had talked to this woman for half an hour, after repeatedly pointing out that to turn us both into the blizzard would be sinful, we were allowed to stay.

Not all of the difficulties were with the weather. Local legislation, often passed to protect village merchants, required fees from peddlers. Peddlers unable to pay sometimes found themselves in jail. The peddler also had a language barrier, often could not obtain kosher food, was unable to attend religious services, and had to face anti-Jewish discrimination, rough treatment from local bigots, and crude jokes. They were robbed and murdered, their bodies often found along some rural road.

In 1873, a Jewish peddler was murdered in Louisiana. *Die Deborah,* which reported the incident, expressed an opinion about the lynching of the accused felons:

We reported last week that a German peddler has been robbed and murdered by a company of negroes [in] Baton Rouge. The victim was a Jew, and burial rights were accorded him by the local Jewish welfare organization. The perpetrators of the crime did not long enjoy their loot. The very next morning, four negroes were detained on suspicion. After a brief investigation, one of them was released. The three others, however, still in possession of the plunder, were hanged in short order by outraged citizens, who strung them up on the nearest tree. Such occurrences, to be sure, transcend the bounds of law. When it is observed, however, that murderers delivered to justice are permitted to go scot-free after a mere day's detention, it is perhaps permissible, in the interests of personal security, even to prefer lynching.

The religious plight of the wandering peddler proved a real hardship. Abraham Kohn notes in his diary:

. . . leading a [peddler's] life, none of us is able to observe the smallest commandment.

Thousands of peddlers wander about America; young, strong men, they waste in the summer's heat; they lose their health in the icy cold of winter. And thus they forget completely their creator. They no longer put on phylacteries; they pray neither on the working day nor on the Sabbath. In truth they have given up their religion for the pack which is on their back.

Not all who joined the ranks of store princes spent an apprenticeship as basket peddlers or trunk carriers. Many with capital avoided the life of the peddler and went directly into merchandising. Abraham Abraham, an American-born Jew of Bavarian parents, served as an apprentice retail clerk in Newark, New Jersey, where he worked with Benjamin Altman, also of retail fame, and a son of Benjamin Bloomingdale. Using the experience he gained as an apprentice, Abraham went into partnership with Isidore and Nathan Straus and opened what was to become one of the most successful retail operations in the nation, Brooklyn's A. & S. Department Store.

A similar success story is the establishment of the Mark I. Jacobs Co. of Tucson, Arizona. In 1867, Jacobs learned that the U. S. Army was locating its Arizona headquarters in Tucson. He recognized that the town of just under three thousand people would one day be a bustling mercantile center and sent his two sons, Lionel and Barron, to open a store. Upon arrival, the two boys were disappointed to discover that Tucson was only a small, sleepy place of low houses on the bank of the Santa Cruz River.

They spent the next two months importing everything from "hairpins to harmonicas," and from their rented quarters, sold food, dry goods, clothing, and such unusual frontier items as mirrors, violins, sheet music, and glass. The Jacobs Company grew rapidly. Military forts dotted the territory, and Tucson emerged, as Jacobs anticipated, as the distribution center for the troops. By 1875, the Mark I. Jacobs Co. was the fifth-largest retail house in the city, and in time the family enterprises became influential in the economic growth not only of Arizona but of the entire Southwest.

The plunge into business, which would characterize Jewish enterprise for the next century, paid handsome dividends for the Jacobs family. Within several decades, the family established additional stores and added banking to their holdings. In 1882, the Jacobs family controlled Arizona's First National Bank.

Like Abraham, Straus, and Jacobs, German-American Jewry in the nineteenth century began to enter a variety of economic fields. More Jewish store owners appeared, Jewish workers became businessmen, and kosher butchers became meat packers. Significantly, the Jewish economic experience was characterized by movement from one business to another: Joseph Newhouse moved from notions to clothing and petroleum in Cincinnati; David Teller went from dry goods in North Carolina to tobacco manufacturing in Philadelphia; Abraham Jacobs from retail clerking in Louisville to liquor, groceries, and real estate in Colorado; and Isaac Neustadt from a Milwaukee retail grocery to insurance.

In addition to the rise of peddler to merchant, some Jews entered areas that brought them to the top of American industry and finance: Solomon Guggenheim became the "copper king," and the Zellerbach family joined the ranks of the nation's most successful industrialists. Anthony Zellerbach was born in Bavaria in 1832 and emigrated to Philadelphia in 1846. Within two decades, he and his two brothers had established one of the nation's most successful paper-and-pulp businesses. He brought his family to San Francisco and with the aid of his sons, Jacob and Isidore, laid the foundation for what is now the internationally known firm of Crown Zellerbach.

Isaac Friedlander, the "Grain King of California," also gained a national reputation. Born in Oldenburg, Germany, he was attracted to San Francisco during the gold rush. While in California, he set about not to prospect but to make the area a major wheat producer, seeking to establish himself as a major exporter of the grain to Great Britain and Australia. Twenty-three years after he arrived, Friedlander was exporting three fourths of the state's wheat crop.

In finance, too, Jews began to emerge as influential leaders. August Belmont, born August Schonberg, acted as agent for the Rothschilds in all of their financial matters in the Western Hemisphere; Benjamin Davidson, of Davidson, May & Co., a California firm, also represented the House of Rothschild; and in a smaller way, Edward Kanter established the German-American Bank of Detroit. In time, America would witness the emergence of the Seligmans, Lehmans, and Loebs, the giants of Jewish finance.

Joseph Seligman emigrated to America in 1837, and until the late 1840s he and his family peddled throughout the South. Business was good and the family turned to textiles in New York and Connecticut. Like the peddling venture, textiles were good to the Seligmans and they used their profits to form the investment firm of J. & W. Seligman & Co. In 1869 they bought seats on the New York Stock Exchange, used their offices to act as fiscal agents for the United States Government, and by the late 1870s were participating with the House of Morgan and the House of Rothschild in multimillion-dollar loans.

Similarly, Henry Lehman, a Bavarian emigrant and Alabama peddler,

became a significant figure in American finance. After carrying a peddler's pack for a year, Lehman established a notions shop in Montgomery, Alabama. The firm of H. Lehman & Bro. was soon dealing in
commodities and in 1858 expanded operations to New York City. By
1870, H. Lehman & Bro., one of the most successful houses in the nation, was instrumental in the creation of the New York Cotton Exchange.

The last of the trio was Solomon Loeb—like the others, from Bavaria
and a dry-goods merchant. After a number of years in retail dry goods,
Loeb joined in partnership with Abraham Kuhn, a Cincinnati clothing
dealer, and founded the investment-banking firm of Kuhn, Loeb & Co.
In time, Jacob H. Schiff, Loeb's son-in-law, would make the firm one of
the nation's leading financial institutions.

But few Jews who sought refuge in America during the German mi-
gration achieved this degree of fame and fortune. More typical of most
American Jews was their participation in the development of New York
City's men's clothing industry.

At the start of the Civil War, New York City had emerged as the nation's leading center for the production and distribution of men's clothing. Though their population was extremely high in the city, Jews
played little part in the early growth of the industry. In time they did
enter the trade, not as partners with Brooks Brothers, but as retailers
and wholesalers of secondhand and cheaply manufactured items commonly called "slops."

William Bobo, a visitor to New York City, described Chatham
Square, the center of the secondhand trade, as "Jerusalem, from the
fact that the Jews do most, if not all the business on this street." Another observer described the secondhand market place:

> In front of each [clothing store], from sunrise to sundown, stands
> the natty, blackbearded and fiercely-moustached proprietor; every
> now and then venturing when a countryman passes, to tap him del-
> icately on the arm, and invite him to look at the magnificent assort-
> ment of wares and wearables within. Stooping, as you enter the
> low, dark doorway, you find yourself in the midst of a primitive
> formation of rags, carefully classified into vests, coats, and panta-
> loons.

Attractive or not, secondhand clothing was a growing and important
business. Throughout the latter half of the nineteenth century, Jewish
entrepreneurs made their living dressing the American people with

"slops." From this enterprise, another and perhaps as important a vocation emerged: the cleaning business. Since the garments had already been worn, it was reasonable that their repair and cleaning would lead to a good business, accounting for the large representation of Jews in the modern dry-cleaning industry.

Though few in number, Jews joined the retail "firsthand" clothing industry. Selling quality garments, their names appeared on the signs of retail shops and wholesale firms from coast to coast. Among the hundreds who later ventured into this industry were J. L. Back & Co., establishing outlets in the cities of the Great Plains; William Seligman, who supplied St. Louis with the latest fashions; Levi Strauss, who satisfied the demands of the miners and cowboys by producing sturdy pants; and Levy and Wolfe, who established the New York Shirt Depot for San Francisco residents who wished to dress in the latest New York styles.

The average German-Jewish immigrant was not as successful as Seligman or as unlucky as the Louisiana peddler found face down in a pool of blood. He was, rather, like most other newcomers, a poor man with few skills, seeking to enter the mainstream of American life. In some cases he found the opportunity in one of the occupations open to greenhorns. In others, he was forced to join the thousands who, in order to survive, relied on Jewish philanthropy. Yet, as a group, German-American Jewry went on to become an important economic force in nineteenth-century America.

THIS IS YOUR HOME

At the beginning of the nineteenth century, European Jews, still living under the oppression of medieval laws and customs, were not considered members of the body politic. Rather, they existed as separate communities within their host countries and ruled themselves, to the degree permitted by their respective governments, by the law as set down in the Talmud. Indeed, Napoleon, who by virtue of his victories had acquired a vast Jewish population, was perplexed by the peculiar status of the Jews of Western Europe.

In order to define the civil status of his Jewish subjects, he met with several spokesmen from west of the Elbe River and inquired as to the effect of the revocation of the specific disabilities imposed on their communities. He wanted to know if the newly emancipated West European

Jew was willing to become part of the national community of his respective nation or retain the non-status of the prerevolutionary period. Those present at this audience were not particularly devoted to the concept of the *kahal* or to the *Talmudic* laws that governed them. They reassured the enlightened French ruler that their people would accept the responsibilities and privileges of full citizenship. As a result, West European Jews were permitted to enter the mainstream and lead lives not as Jews living at the sufferance of France, Germany, Italy, or Austria but as Frenchmen, Germans, Italians, and Austrians who practiced Judaism.

Influenced by the effects of emancipation and wishing a greater identification with their Christian fellow citizens, West European Jewry, particularly in Germany, sought to change the mode and manner of the Jewish religion. In particular, their rebellion, more commonly known as the Reform Movement, was aimed at the lack of decorum during the orthodox service, the wearing of the traditional hat and prayer shawl, the un-Western manner of Hebrew chanting, and the absence of a sermon during the service. In their attempts to modify the orthodox ritual, a number of German rabbis introduced several innovations: hymns were sung in German rather than Hebrew, sermons were preached, the length of the service was shortened, organ music was played, Protestant-type Sunday schools were established, and the traditional *bar mitzvah* was replaced with a confirmation service characteristically Christian.

As a result of the Reform Movement, the waves of Germans who emigrated to American shores brought with them this modern spirit. Thus, it fell to hazzan Isaac Lesser,* in the first half of the century the most influential Orthodox leader, to contend with the reform activities of Leo Merzbacher, Isaac Mayer Wise, and David Einhorn.

Though Lesser was the foremost spokesman for tradition, he recognized the need for some change. Lamenting the decline in synagogue attendance and the lack of decorum during services, he advocated several modifications. For instance, he sought to change the *minhag* (ritual), provided it did not compromise traditional theology; advanced the need for decorum and aesthetics during the service; and, in order to "reach and teach" the congregants, promoted the concept that a sermon be delivered in English.

* Lesser, later a newspaper publisher and prominent in Jewish education, was one of the first Jewish leaders to call for "a return to Zion" and was an outspoken foe of anti-Semitism.

In his effort to narrow the gap that separated orthodoxy from the American religious environment, he further suggested the elimination of money offerings during the reading of the Torah and opposed those traditions whose beginnings were based on superstition. Lesser, noted Herbert Parzen, historian of Conservative Judaism, became "the principal protagonist of Orthodoxy as well as the foremost antagonist of Reform." Though his ideas displeased a few, they did sway many, and in his attempt to retain and make relevant the traditional, Lesser perhaps sowed the seed of reform in America.

In the midst of Lesser's activities, German Jewry arrived and established the "reform Vereine" (reform societies, which soon became "temples," the name given to reform synagogues). The advocates of change came to the temples, and with time orthodox Jewry witnessed the emergence of such reform institutions as Har Sinai of Baltimore (1842), Emanu-El of New York (1845), and Sinai of Chicago (1858). These temples soon became the outposts from which reform launched its attack on American orthodoxy: they installed organs, utilized mixed choirs of men and women, translated Hebrew prayer into English, reduced the length of the service, and permitted male and female to pray side by side. Indeed, these innovations caused such turmoil among members of some congregations that warring factions often challenged the outcome of synagogue elections in civil courts.

Though reform was a German import, there was some movement in this direction among native American Jewry. The initial signs of reform Judiasm appeared in Charleston in 1824. Ironically, it was in a traditional Sephardic congregation, Beth Elohim, and not a German congregation that reform was first suggested in America. A gathering of forty-seven members, led by Isaac Harby and David N. Carvallo, both influenced by developments in Germany, revolted against what they considered meaningless forms of worship. In their petition requesting modification of the service, they asked the Charleston congregation for a shorter, more intelligible, and more decorous ceremony. They insisted not upon a change in theology but, rather, a significant change in religious practice: the recitation of the basic prayers in English rather than Hebrew, the introduction of a sermon, the elimination of unintelligible benedictions in Spanish, and finally, the abolition of the practice of offering money during the service.

Their demands, stated a petition written by Harby, were not designed "to *overthrow,* but to rebuild. . . . We wish not to destroy," they insisted, "but to *reform* and *revise* the evils complained of . . . not to abandon the institutions of *Moses,* but to *understand and observe them* . . . to worship God, not as *slaves of bigotry and priest craft,* but as enlightened descendants of that chosen race, whose blessings have scattered throughout the land of Abraham, Isaac and Jacob."

The petition was quickly rejected by the Beth Elohim leadership, and in protest twelve of the more resolute reformers left the congregation and founded the Reformed Society of Israelites. In November 1825, the first anniversary of the society was celebrated. Isaac Harby, in an anniversary discourse, upheld the principles of Charleston reform:

> What is it, then, we ask of the Hebrew vestry? The abolition of the ancient language and form of Jewish worship? Far from it . . . our desire is to yield everything to the feeling of the truly pious Israelite; but to take away everything that might excite the disgust of the well-informed Israelite. To throw away rabbinical interpolations; to avoid useless repetitions; to read or chant with solemnity; to recite such portions of the pentateuch and the prophet, as custom and practice have appointed to be read in the *original Hebrew;* but to follow such selections with a translation in English, and a lecture or discourse upon the law, explanatory of its meaning, edifying to the young, gratifying to the old, and instructive to every age and class of society. Is this abolishing our mode of sacred worship? Is this sapping the foundations of our venerable faith? No, my friends, this is stripping it of foreign and unseemly ceremonies, divesting it of rubbish, and beautifying that simple Doric column, that primeval order of architecture, which raises its plain but massy head amid the ruins of time and the desolation of empires!

Within two years, membership in Harby's society reached fifty. They produced a new prayer book, introduced the use of the organ, and advocated a variety of other reforms to accommodate Judaism to "the situation of an enlightened world." Nevertheless, the immediate results of the Reformed Society of Israelites were negligible. On May 2, 1833, the project collapsed and the funds collected for the planned synagogue were returned to the membership with interest. Significantly, the demands for reform within Beth Elohim were led by laymen, not rabbis. No doubt, some American Jews were coming to grips with a rigid orthodoxy they felt was no longer meeting their needs.

In the 1840s, the makeup of American Jewry changed considerably. Approximately fifteen thousand Jews were settled throughout the nation, and of this number, a substantial portion were from Germany.

Among those recent German emigrants was Isaac Mayer Wise, who was to become the most influential of all rabbis to advocate changes within the synagogue. He came from Bohemia in 1846 and, soon after his arrival, joined Lesser's call for the unification of all American synagogues. In spite of their efforts, however, this was never realized.

Wise also advocated the adoption of a modern Hebrew prayer book to replace the traditional Sephardic *minhag,* and the establishment of an American rabbinic institution. In order to fulfill these objectives, he resigned from his Albany, New York, pulpit, and in 1854 was elected rabbi of the Reform Congregation Bene Yeshurun in Cincinnati, a position he held until his death. There he established the *American Israelite,* an English-language periodical that opposed Lesser's *Occident,* and in time added the German-language newspaper *Die Deborah.* For the remainder of his career, both journals carried his message of reform throughout the Jewish community.

By 1857, his concept of a modern Hebrew prayer book reached fruition. The first edition of *Minhag America* (the American Ritual), though it enraged Lesser and the more conservative adherents of Judaism, was adopted by a number of congregations. In 1873, he established the Union of American Hebrew Congregations, the unifying force of the Reform Movement, and two years later opened the doors of Hebrew Union College in Cincinnati, the first successful institution of Jewish higher learning in America.†

The only man to rival the influence of Rabbi Wise in the Reform Movement was David Einhorn. He arrived in the United States in 1855 and brought with him a reputation as an outstanding leader of German reform. Installed as rabbi of Har Sinai in Baltimore, he gained control of the eastern, more radical reformers, who opposed the moderate, midwestern leadership of Wise. Indeed, even the reformers had to contend with a split in their ranks.

Under Einhorn's leadership, the philosophical position of American Reform Judaism was established. By 1885 the movement had grown so rapidly that its leaders called a rabbinical conference to establish a unified program. Consequently, Kaufmann Kohler, Einhorn's son-in-law, issued a call to "all . . . American rabbis [who] advocate reform and [who are] in favor of *united action* in all matters pertaining to the welfare of American Judaism." Fifteen rabbis attended and, under the leadership of Kohler, drafted the Pittsburgh Platform—a statement that

† Maimonides College, established by Isaac Lesser in Philadelphia in 1867, was forced to close in 1873.

embodied the philosophy of Einhorn and summarized the aims and objectives of the Reform Movement.

In a time of dramatic and rapid social change in America, Jews demonstrated the depth of their assimilation by the acceptance of the platform. It marked the culmination of decades of struggle for reform of traditional Jewish religious laws and customs, and for the first time in history, Jews became a modern people, adapting to the imperatives of a world in flux.

The statement asserted that Judaism was "a progressive religion," and repudiated the Mosaic laws, which were "not adapted to the views and habits of modern civilization." More important, it denied the national character of the Jewish people: "We consider ourselves no longer a nation," said the rabbis at Pittsburgh, "but a religious community, and therefore expect neither a return to Palestine . . . nor the restoration of any of the laws concerning the Jewish state."

As a result of the influence of reform, some Jews borrowed many of the better elements of the Protestant form of worship, and some synagogues took on the atmosphere of a Protestant church.‡ The service, now almost all in English, was read and sung mostly by the rabbi and not the congregation, *yarmulkes* (skull caps) and *tallitot* (prayer shawls) were no longer worn, the music of an organ and the voices of a choir filled the air, and men and women, contrary to orthodox practice, prayed side by side. In addition, there were Sunday services at some temples, the sermon became a key part of the service, and religious education was modeled after the Protestant Sunday school.

Together with the principles espoused at Pittsburgh and the later innovations, there was another significant event that led to the religious counter-revolution of Conservative Judaism: the infamous *trefa** banquet. In July 1883, several hundred distinguished Jewish and Christian leaders attended a dinner at Cincinnati's Highland House Restaurant. The event, held to honor the Union of American Hebrew Congregations and celebrate the first graduation of Hebrew Union College, would traumatize both orthodox and moderate factions within the American Jewish community.

According to the eyewitness account of Rabbi David Philipson, as the first course was served, "terrific excitement" filled the room: "Two rabbis rose from their seats and rushed from the room. Shrimp [some

‡ This formulation is based on extensive discussions with Rabbi David M. Posner of Temple Emanu-El in New York City.
* Non-kosher.

have claimed that they were clams on the half shell] had been placed before them as the opening course." Indeed, there are those who insist that this incident, which took place two years before the Pittsburgh meeting, was the catalyst for the Conservative Movement. The orthodox press had a field day as they splashed their accounts of the *trefa* banquet across their front pages. In many Jewish homes and in most synagogues the reaction was shock: "My God! the reformers have gone too far!"

In time, the combined effect of the activities and objectives of reform led to the religious countermeasures of Sabato Morais. Under his leadership and with the aid of a dozen Sephardic and Ashkenazic congregations the Conservative Movement was born. In 1885, seeking a religious middle ground, Morais and Rabbi Henry Mendes of New York's Shearith Israel, founded the Jewish Theological Seminary Association. The association's constitution summed up the need for a halfway point between orthodoxy and reform:

> The necessity has been made manifest for associated and organized effort on the part of the Jews of America faithful to Mosaic Law and ancestral traditions, for the purpose of keeping alive the true Judaic spirit; in particular by the establishment of a seminary where the Bible shall be impartially taught and rabbinical literature faithfully expounded, and more especially where youths, desirous of entering the ministry, may be thoroughly grounded in Jewish knowledge and inspired by the precept and example of their instructors with the love of the Hebrew language and a spirit of devotion and fidelity to the Jewish law.

The battle between the two new religious philosophies would rage well into the twentieth century. However, there was on the horizon yet another belligerent: renewed orthodoxy, brought by millions of East Europeans fleeing czarist oppression. In the twentieth century, American Jewry would witness its most significant intrareligious struggles.

Just as the Sephardim of an earlier migration banded together to form a homogeneous community, so the German immigrants of the mid-1800s sought the companionship of their own. It was not unusual for these newcomers to found institutions to serve human needs or to display a desire to organize fraternal societies. A multitude of agencies were established which provided fellowship, cultural activities, and above all philanthropy, an explicit obligation of every Jewish community.

In the first two centuries of Jewish settlement, charity was largely an unorganized effort carried out by the synagogues. Most congregations, as was the custom in Europe, maintained special funds for the needy, and rarely was a destitute Jew turned away empty-handed. The vast increase of those who needed assistance, however, dictated a change in the methods by which aid was dispensed, and by the mid-1800s, a variety of private philanthropic agencies were established to supplant the older and more informal acts of generosity. Apparently, the old ways were ineffective and inefficient, for, too often, new immigrants unknown to the congregations went unnoticed. Consequently, Hebrew benevolent societies appeared and proliferated throughout the Jewish community.

In addition to the benevolent societies, special agencies were established for specific purposes. Shearith Israel organized the first family welfare agency, in 1828; the Society for the Education of Poor Children offered education and vocational training "to the children of indigent Jews" in 1843; the Hebrew Widows' and Orphans' Association was formed in Milwaukee in 1863; and the New York community opened the first Home for the Aged in 1872. Medical facilities were also made available to those in need: Cincinnati Jewry built their first Jewish hospital in 1850; in New York City the first Jewish hospital, later called Mt. Sinai, was opened in 1855; and in Philadelphia the Jewish Hospital Association was established in 1865.

Due to the increase in the number of agencies, attempts at charitable co-operation were made on the local level. In Cincinnati, Dr. Max Lilienthal organized an agency in 1856 to co-ordinate all relief work; in Chicago the United Hebrew Relief Association (1859) was designated the parent body of a variety of philanthropic societies, and in Philadelphia a General Relief Association directed all charitable efforts.

Jewish philanthropic activities reached across the seas and touched the less fortunate Jews of the Holy Land. Just as they had come during the colonial period, Palestine "messengers" in search of funds continued to arrive throughout the nineteenth century. Isaac Lesser, who supported the concept of restoration of the Holy Land, saw in the messenger system vast disorganization, and he set about modernizing the meager Palestine effort. In October 1849 he proposed a plan calling on all of America's Jewish communities to contribute regularly to Palestine relief. In this manner, he asserted, the funds spent to transport the messengers could be better utilized in the Holy Land. In response to Lesser's suggestion, Shearith Israel pledged twenty-five dollars, and the Mobile, Alabama, congregation offered the same amount, but the two contributions were not enough to convince the American Jewish community that the plan was sound.

Lesser was untiring in his agitation for a unified Palestine effort, and in 1853 he joined several influential New York Jews to establish the North American Relief Society, "for the sole purpose . . . of affording permanent aid to poor [Palestine] Israelites." He hoped this was the beginning of a national organization. Indeed, in 1853–54 the society collected five thousand dollars for distribution to the needy Jews of Palestine.†

American Jewry was not totally committed to Palestine relief. Though they did continue to contribute to the messengers, they would leave for the 20th century the concept of total commitment to Palestine Jewry. In all other aspects of assistance, the 19th century Jewish community met its charitable obligations.

In addition to involvement in benevolent societies, German-American Jewry moved toward the establishment of a variety of fraternal organizations. The first was the Independent Order of B'nai B'rith (Sons of the Covenant), established by twelve German immigrants in New York City in 1843. They met originally to discuss the lack of Jewish unity (outside the synagogue community), the limited amount of Jewish social life, and the anti-Jewish discrimination of the Masons and the Odd Fellows. Consequently, B'nai B'rith was formed, and the aims of the society, both fraternal and benevolent, were clearly stated in the preamble to its constitution:

> B'nai B'rith has taken upon itself the mission of uniting Israelites in the work of promoting their highest interests and those of humanity; of developing and elevating the mental and moral character of the people of our faith; of inculcating the purest principles of philanthropy, honor and patriotism; of supporting science and art; alleviating victims of persecution; providing for, protecting and assisting the widow and orphan on the broadest principles of humanity.

B'nai B'rith became the largest and most influential Jewish fraternity in the United States. By the last quarter of the nineteenth century it not only contained a Jewish membership of all geocultural backgrounds but also provided an assortment of cultural and social events. Significantly, the "broadest principles of humanity" were expressed through its creation of such divergent institutions as Maimonides Library (1850), the Hebrew Agricultural Society (1851), and numerous national and local agencies for the aged, the sick, and the orphaned.

† In 1853–54 famine gripped Palestine, and the five thousand dollars was collected only after an appeal from Sir Moses Montefiore, of Great Britain.

The pattern set by B'nai B'rith was followed by others. In the next three decades, American Jewry established the United Order True Sisters (1846); the Independent Free Sons of Israel (1849); Order Brith Abraham (1859); Order Kesher shel Bazel (1860); and the Independent Order Sons of Benjamin (1877). While none of these organizations were as successful as B'nai B'rith, they did represent the fraternal orientation of a segment of nineteenth-century American Jewry. Above all, they helped to bring about the national unity of the American Jew, which became vital to the survival of the Jewish people in the twentieth century.

The cultural manifestations of nineteenth-century American Jewry were by no means a simple echo of European forms but, rather, a response to the new environment. Immigration created a hunger for an enlarged cultural life, and one such need was filled by the Jewish newspaper. In the sphere of journalism, together with Mordecai M. Noah and Isaac Harby, there was Isaac Lesser, the father of the American Jewish press. In 1843 Lesser published the *Occident,* the first successful Jewish monthly in America.‡ In its first issue, he set forth a policy "to give circulation to everything which can be interesting to the Jewish inhabitants in the western hemisphere."

Despite the *Occident*'s lackluster quality, the paper was the mainstay of Jewish journalism for twenty-six years. In that span it took part in every religious and literary controversy of interest to the Jewish community. Its pages reflected Jewish life and were used as a platform by such notables as David Einhorn, Isidor Busch, and Max Lilienthal. Editorially it advocated orthodox religious unity, upheld traditional Judaism, and condemned those who turned toward Reform or Christianity. Most important, the *Occident,* until its last issue, in 1868, remained an influential literary vehicle that united the far-flung Jewish communities in the United States.

In 1849, two additional periodicals appeared, both weeklies and published in New York City. The first, *Israels Herold,* was written in German and edited by the abolitionist Isidor Busch (later Bush). The primary aim of Bush's journal was "to bring about unity among [America's] Jews." In its short life the paper promoted Reform Judaism, campaigned for more efficient immigrant aid, and reported on

‡ In 1824, S. H. Jackson published *The Jew.* The primary purpose of this periodical was to make the Jewish community aware of the conversion activities of Joseph Frey (see pages 40, 59) and the American Society for Meliorating the Condition of the Jew. It was published for two years.

agricultural and industrial pursuits among Jews. Lacking support, it ceased publication after three months.

Another weekly, this one in English, was soon offered to the Jewish community. On October 19, 1849, six months after *Israels Herold* stopped printing, Robert Lyon, an English-born Jew, founded the *Asmonean*. This first successful weekly, whose editorial policy reflected a position of neutrality in the clash between reform and orthodox, was well received by its readers. In its nine years of publication, its editorial page advanced the concept of religious unity and provided a platform for the differing views of Jewish leaders. Among its more important achievements, the paper gained the reputation as the standard New York periodical read by those who wished to be informed of current trends in Jewish cultural and social life.

In the mid-1850s the *Asmonean* reached the peak of its popularity, but with the establishment of several competing periodicals the paper lost circulation. Filling the void left by the *Asmonean* were Wise's *Israelite* and the German-Language *Die Deborah* (Cincinnati); Einhorn's *Sinai* (Baltimore); and Samuel Isaac's *Jewish Messenger* (New York).

The *Israelite* and *Sinai* promoted Reform Judaism, and the *Messenger* was the spokesman for Orthodox Judaism. Yet the *Messenger* gave space to lighter content and regularly published fiction and poetry. It printed articles that reflected concern for the welfare of the Jewish community: establishing an orphanage, advancing the idea of a board of delegates of American Israelites, supporting the unification of all New York charities, and promoting the Jewish Free School. Following in the footsteps of the *Asmonean,* the *Messenger* led the struggle to eliminate the inequities that existed in the Jewish community.

Though several Anglo-Jewish newspapers (i.e., the Jewish press in English) were read nationwide, regional journals began to appear in most large Jewish communities. In San Francisco two newspapers were established before the Civil War. Herman Bien and Henry Labatt organized the *Voice of Israel* in 1856, and Julius Eckman published the *Weekly Gleaner* in 1857. As a result, the Anglo-Jewish press in the decades before and after the Civil War was present throughout the United States. These journals not only brought news to isolated Jews but provided a cultural outlet and served as a vital force that helped unite the national Jewish community.

In addition to the press as an intellectual stimulus, nineteenth-century American Jewry, specifically the Germans, participated in a variety of cultural activities and supported several of their own cultural organizations. The German immigrants transplanted to the new land several institutions they admired in their old home and gave root to German culture in the United States.

Thus, in the years following the mass migration of the 1830s and '40s, America witnessed the growth of the German Jewish periodical, German Jewish schools, and the German language. Moreover, many German cultural institutions were organized and maintained by the Jewish community, among them glee clubs, reading and dramatic societies, the German-language theater, amateur theatrical groups, opera, and literary associations.

One organization dominated by German Jews was the Young Men's Hebrew Literary Association, or Y.M.H.A. Organized in the 1850s in Philadelphia, these literary societies were the beginning of the Jewish "Y" movement. By late in the decade, these organizations had been so well received that they were founded in New York (1851), Baltimore (1854), New Orleans (1855), Richmond (1856), Augusta (1857), and Louisville (1862). The "Y" movement rapidly spread across the nation to such other principal Jewish communities as Chicago, Cleveland, St. Louis, and San Francisco.

Most of the "Y's" supported libraries, reading rooms, and meeting halls, and their activities included lectures, debates, drama, youth programs, and a wide assortment of social events. They were not social clubs, however, for they prohibited card playing, gambling, and drinking. In time, the "Y" became one of the principal Jewish cultural institutions in the United States. Noteworthy is the fact that the first professional to be hired was a librarian.

By the middle of the nineteenth-century, enrollment in Jewish religious schools had declined, probably the result of the growth of public education.

In the decades prior to 1860, American Jewry maintained a variety of educational institutions. These facilities, all associated with synagogues, offered both religious and secular studies. Yet schools administered by the clergy lost their appeal, and as midcentury approached, scores of Jewish parents turned toward public institutions. The high cost of tuition might have influenced their decision, but a more important reason was the changing character of the public school. In 1855 public education shed its Protestant orientation, and with this turn of events Jews entered the tax-supported system in increasing numbers.*

* However, not until well into the twentieth century was religion separated from the nation's public schools.

The result: many full-time religious schools closed, and religious instruction became a supplement provided by the synagogue.

For this reason, a number of Jewish communities, wishing to maintain a religious atmosphere for their children, revitalized the Jewish day-school program and attempted to compete with public education. Added to the already established Jewish educational system, day schools were founded in Cincinnati, Boston, Baltimore, and Philadelphia. In New York City, agencies of this type provided instruction to more than eight hundred students. The *Asmonean,* a vigorous supporter of traditional Jewish education, promoted the values inherent in the day-school program. In 1851 its editors reported on the necessity of full-time religious schools and warned against sending children to "schools where [it was] an impossibility . . . to be present at the reading of prayers . . . without . . . being infected by the [religious] doctrine[s] inculcated."

Isaac Lesser also expressed doubts about public education and was also impressed by the first-rate education obtainable at a day school. In 1853 he visited a New York religious school:

> We witnessed a partial examination of the school under the care of the Rev. Herman Felsenheld, attached to the Henry Street Synagogue. Whilst we were there, the scholars, both male and female, probably near 100 in number, were examined in English by the teacher of that branch of education, and considering that nearly all the children are those of German immigrants, and that they hear seldom any other language than that spoken at home, and in view that many of the pupils themselves are only lately in this country, they acquitted themselves remarkably well. We could not stay to hear their examination in Hebrew, but the well-known ability of the learned teacher leaves us no doubt that they are proficient in what they have learned.

Lesser and Dr. Max Lilienthal also visited the Union School, on Ludlow Street, and observed classes in Hebrew, geography, English, and German. "We must acknowledge," he wrote, "that the proficiency displayed was excellent." After witnessing the educational quality of the two schools, Lesser concluded that

> both schools are an evidence of progress, and we confidently look forward to a greater extension of the course of education under our own teachers. . . . The [Jewish] people are just awakening; and so soon as they understand their wants, the necessary step will be taken to remedy the existing defects [in Jewish education].

Due to serious handicaps, however, Jewish educational institutions could not compete with public education. The tuition was expensive, the more qualified teachers sought careers in public education, and most important, the day school lacked the outside contacts that were helpful in securing the better economic and social positions in American society. For some pupils, a sectarian education was a disadvantage rather than an advantage.

Furthermore, there were influential Jewish personalities who actively promoted the use of public education. Isidor Bush urged St. Louis Jewry to utilize public education:

> Religious, or rather Christian, instruction has been kept out of [the public school] system by its wise founders, and I believe I have some reason to believe that this has been done partly with regard to our confession. . . . And *why* should we refuse to participate in the blessings of this grand institution, towards whose support we contribute our mite, and to the benefits of which we are fully entitled?

Bush concluded:

> . . . that a Jewish school, embracing all branches of instruction, could not exist for one year in St. Louis, and would at the same time be prejudicial, in many respects, to our children; that it would be resorted to but by a very small number, and would thus leave by far the greater number of our sons and daughters without religious instruction. And I believe, on the other hand, that by devoting our zeal, means and energy to an exclusively religious school, in the same way we have proposed, sending our children at the same time to our public schools for the acquirement of other branches of learning, the result would exceed our most sanguine expectations: —that thus our children will become good pious Israelites, and worthy American citizens, our pleasure in life, our support and pride in the eve of our days.

Say you will try it, and let us join hand in hand.

Isaac M. Wise, the midwestern reform leader, also endorsed public education. In 1870, he declared that "our settled opinion here [in Cincinnati is] that the education of the young is the business of the State, and the religious instruction, to which we add Hebrew, is the duty of religious bodies. The secular branches belong to the public schools, religion in the Sabbath schools, exclusively."

The attempt by the Jewish day school to compete with public education met with failure. Saturday (the Jewish Sabbath) instruction was eliminated by the public schools, and the reading of dogmatic biblical passages came to an end. In 1853, the City of New York took control of public education and upheld a state statute of 1842 prohibiting religious instruction. The struggle in most states, however, to eliminate religion from tax-supported institutions was not that simple. In the last half of the nineteenth century, religious teaching via public education was still a serious matter.

One of the most important legal battles in the separation of religion from public education occurred in Cincinnati in 1869. The Ohio Supreme Court upheld a Cincinnati Board of Education decision to discard the daily reading from the King James version of the Bible. Though only two members of the school board were Jewish,† the majority recognized that Jews "have equal civil rights with orthodox Christians, [and] the Bible must of necessity be excluded from the State schools. . . ."

Justice John Welch wrote the opinion for the high court:

> . . . true Christianity asks no aid from the sword of civil authority. It began without the sword, and wherever it has taken the sword it has perished by the sword. To depend on civil authority for its enforcement is to acknowledge its own weakness, which it can never afford to do.

Though an important victory for Ohio Jewry, it was only temporary. In 1859, Bible reading was reintroduced into the Ohio school system, and it was not until well into the twentieth century that all states enforced the First Amendment to the federal Constitution.

In spite of the long and often painful struggle to separate religion from public education, Jews recognized the value of tax-supported schools. Accordingly, the Jewish turn toward public education had a significant impact on their acculturation and Americanization. The public school would be a major avenue by which Jews entered the mainstream of American society.

NATIVIST CALL TO ARMS

Isaac Mayer Wise arrived in New York with little money and a great deal of luggage. At the dock, he approached a German driver and

† One Jewish member, Henry Mack, voted for retention of Bible reading.

asked the charge for transportation to his lodgings. The price seemed too high, so the rabbi turned to another, this time an Irishman, and negotiated a more reasonable charge for the service. Wise made similar arrangements for several others and this irritated the German drivers, who expressed contempt for "the Jew [who was taking] bread out of their mouths." As Wise and his companions boarded the Irishman's wagon, the Germans showered him, "with all possible abjurations against the Jews." "Aha!" said Wise, "you left home . . . in order to get away from the disgusting Judaeophobia, and here the first German greeting that sounds in your ear is *'Hepp, hepp!'* "‡

But these anti-Jewish cries were by no means representative of American society. Jews were generally welcomed by most of the Christian community. European anti-Semitism had not crossed the ocean to taint American thought; also, the Jewish community was very small and possessed few special interests, so Christians seeking economic and social dominance had little reason to object to Jewish settlement.

But if there was no established pattern of anti-Semitism, Jews did experience a certain discrimination. In the 1840s, some were denied equal opportunity in employment and others were excluded from burial grounds. The New York *Times* protested against German-Americans who prevented Brooklyn Jewry from burying its dead:

> There are some 12,000 or 14,000 persons of Jewish persuasion in this city, and finding it difficult to obtain burial grounds within the city limits, they have purchased land on Long Island and other places. A German [Jewish] congregation purchased a burying ground near East New York, and one day last week, having the occasion to bury an aged member, the German [Christian] population of that place, with stones, guns, and clubs, dispersed the members, ordered them off, wounded several persons severely, and compelled them to deposit the body in the Cypress Hills Cemetery . . . these German immigrants imagine that a free country means the privilege of doing what they please, and violating law and order whenever it suits their purpose. A lesson or two will let them understand in what their rights consist.

In Ohio, Louis Stix, a storekeeper, went one evening with his Christian friend McCullough to a masked ball. As they entered the room someone said, "what business have you here? We do not want Jews." McCullough knocked the man down and advised Stix to leave, knowing

‡ A nineteenth-century German anti-Semitic slogan meaning "down with the Jews."

that trouble was brewing. On his way home, Stix lamented that he "had no idea that in free America such narrow-minded prejudices had been imported from the mother country. . . ."

The next day, the anti-Semite came to Stix's store and announced that he was going to sue for damages. The Jewish merchant smiled when he heard the threat of legal action, for McCullough had told him, wrote Stix in his autobiography, "that nothing would please me better than to be sued in such a cause, for that would have meant ruin to the prejudiced German's business, as his drugstore was right in the Jewish quarter, and fully half of his patrons . . . were of the Jewish faith."

Though incidents like these occurred, the Jew was often defended. In the 1850s, for example, the Washington, D.C., *Sentinel* wrote that among Jews there were "fewer paupers and fewer criminals than any other race. . . . A Jewish beggar is a thing almost unknown." Nevertheless, not every periodical expressed such a favorable view. The Sacramento, California, *Transcript* printed an anti-Jewish story that followed the classic medieval pattern: Jew and non-Jew in a commercial transaction; Jew attempts to outwit non-Jew; non-Jew defeats Jew by threat. Simply, it was a modern rendition of Christ driving the money-changers out of the Temple:

> Slippery Gentlemen—the other day a miner entered one of our Jew stores . . . and purchased several articles, for which he paid [gold] dust. The Jew remarking the cleanliness of the gold, offered $16.25 per ounce, for all in the bag. The owner consenting, the Jew tumbled it into the scales, threw in his weights hastily, and then placed the gold with another lot in his possession, remarking that there was just $443. The miner was wide awake, however, having had it previously weighed, and told Mr. Jew that he had just $500, and the quicker he forked up the coin the better it would be for him. The Jew parleyed, when the miner drew one of Colt's revolvers, which had an electric power in convincing the Jew of his mistake, and forthwith he paid the miner the whole of his demand, remarking that he believed he was mistaken.

Some stories characterized the Jew as a criminal. In 1858, the Milwaukee *Daily News* described "anxious Jews" at a police station. Annoyed with this description, one Milwaukee citizen wrote to ask "what [the writer meant] by saying a lot of anxious Jews." Angrily he protested:

> Does he wonder so much at seeing a Jew at the Police Station? (a thing which indeed so rarely occurs that the editor of the *News*

thinks it is a treat for his readers, to inform them that for once they have found a Jew before the Police Court), or do we live in the fifteenth century yet, to throw a stigma of hatred on the Jews? Are the "Jews" not as good a law-abiding body of citizens as the Gentiles? And why when you try a drunken Irishman or German, does it not say, a squad of "anxious Catholics or Protestants" was found yesterday?

In New York City the *Police Gazette* regularly described German Jews as receivers of stolen goods. "Many of them," declared the editor, "are professional lifters, burglars, and swindlers."

Accounts portraying a negative Jewish image sometimes led to violence. In 1850, the *Allgemeine Zeitung des Judentums* (New York City) described the final product of anti-Jewish literature:

> [On] the eve of the great day of Atonement . . . a rumor spread that the Jews had murdered a Gentile girl for holiday. About 10:30 a crowd of some 500 men [mostly Irish] burst into [a building occupied by Jews], broke down the doors, and literally pulled from their beds sleeping women. . . . A most shocking riot ensued; everyone who resisted was knocked down, a little box of jewelry to the amount of 63 dollars was stolen from a peddler. The remarkable thing about this affair is that three Irish policemen were the leaders of this raging riot, and the tumult thereby acquired a sort of official character. . . .

Anti-Jewish prejudice also reached into agencies of the federal government. The case of Captain Uriah P. Levy of the United States Navy is an outstanding example of this phenomenon. In 1857, in an attempt to be reactivated to service, Levy went before a naval board of inquiry to plead his case. He was certain that his dismissal from service was because of his religion. The testimony of Commodore Isaac Mayo exposed the prejudice of Levy's fellow officers:

> I [Mayo] returned from my recruiting, and upon rejoining the ship . . . some of the junior officers of the ward mess asked me if I knew that Levy had been ordered to take passage in the ship . . . and the object of some of them was to keep him out of the ward room mess. I asked them if there was anything particular against Levy, any particular reason why he should not be admitted in the mess. They said he was a damned Jew. . . .

Levy's counsel convinced the naval board that his client was dismissed because he was a Jew, and as a result, Levy was reactivated to duty; in time he rose to the rank of commodore, commanding the Mediterranean Fleet.

In the 1860s, anti-Jewish sentiment, though still not guided by an ideology, again made itself felt.* Aaron Hirsch discussed in his autobiography the anti-Semitic sentiments of Union soldiers during the Civil War. Hirsch, an Arkansas merchant and pro-Confederate, was standing in front of his store as a Union cavalry troop, made up of German immigrants, galloped through the main street. When they saw his sign, HIRSCH AND ADLER, they yelled: "Zudesh, Secesh [Jewish secessionist]," and fifty of them dismounted, entered his store, and packed up everything in it. According to the merchant, the troopers were particularly unfavorable to him because he was a Jew. When he complained to the federal provost marshal, the officer replied that *Zudesh Secesh* was not entitled to any consideration.

The attitude toward Hirsch was not confined to Confederates but spread across the nation to affect those who were loyal Unionists. In San Bernardino, California, Dick Cole walked into a store operated by Wolf Cohn. The two men talked, an argument developed, and after calling Cohn "a damned Jew son of a bitch," Cole fired his pistol. Cohn's brother Isaac, seeing the murder, drew his revolver and shot Cole dead. The story quickly spread, and drunk locals gathered in the saloon to make plans to "burn out the Jews." Frightened of the possibility of an American pogrom, Jews boarded up their stores, others fled their homes, and a few armed themselves. Fortunately, cool heads prevailed. Isaac Cohn was arrested for murder but never tried, and bloodshed was averted as both factions worked to restore harmony to the community.

Though most of these anti-Jewish incidents were not protested, some felt a Jewish defense was in order. One was Simon Wolf, a Washington, D.C., lawyer who was the unofficial representative of American Jewry to American Presidents. In a letter to William Cullen Bryant,† Wolf decried the "unjust attacks made upon American citizens of the Jewish faith.

"I am not," he wrote, "one of those who have raised an immediate outcry if perchance a criminal was called a Jew, nor have I assumed

---

* During this decade, the most infamous case of anti-Semitism was General Ulysses S. Grant's Order No. 11. This communication, issued during the Civil War, ordered all Jews out of the regions of northern Mississippi, Kentucky, and Tennessee. The incident will be discussed in the section on the Civil War.
† Editor of the New York *Evening Post*.

that because some subservient, pliant editor launched forth his slimy vituperations, they were the opinion of the American press; nor do I claim to be a religious Israelite, but I do claim to be an Israelite and American."

He spoke of the treatment of Jews in the Press:

Has the [civil] war now raging been inaugurated or fostered by Jews exclusively? Is the late Democratic Party composed entirely of Israelites? Are all blockade-runners and refugees descendants of Abraham? Are there no native Americans engaged in rebellion? No Christians running the blockade, or meek followers of Christ within the folds of Tammany?

In conclusion, Wolf asserted:

. . . that some of the grandest acts of heroism performed during the war were done by Jews. That more than a thousand commissioned and non-commissioned officers and thousands of privates are serving in the Union Army, whose faith is in God and their country. Who was it that on the banks of the Green River, in the Spring of 1862, when a company of the Thirty-second Indiana Volunteers were attacked and surrounded by thousands of Texans, stood single-handed and alone against fearful odds, scorning to surrender, killing and wounding eight of his assailants, and at last yielding his life a sacrifice to duty, and thus saving his scattered regiment? Lieutenant Sachs, a Jew!

. . . Was your own brave citizen, Lieutenant Colonel Newman, who offered his life as a sacrifice, and who upon his dying bed received the promotion of a brigadier generalship, ever mentioned as a Jew?

. . . Is Moses A. Dropsie, Esq., one of Philadelphia's most gifted and talented lawyers, and who has been ever an active abolitionist, a traitor because he is a Jew?

Civil War anti-Jewish prejudice subsided with the Union victory. However, in the decades of the Gilded Age, though still not guided by an ideology, discrimination aimed at Jews became more intense.

By the late 1870s, the Jewish community had grown to 250,000, new immigrants making up the bulk. For the most part, they were poor, uneducated, and culturally deprived. According to both Jewish and Christian observers, the "new Jew," as opposed to native American Jews, displayed "irritable qualities."

What emerged was a new stereotype: Jews were vulgar, loud, ill-mannered, pushy, and ostentatious. It prompted a more vicious campaign of social discrimination. In 1872, B. F. Waterman was denied the right to serve in the New York Militia, and several years later, Joseph Seligman, a leading New York banker, was refused accommodations at the fashionable Grand Hotel in Saratoga, New York.

The "Seligman Affair" captured the attention of the American Jewish community. In 1877, the Saratoga resort instituted a policy of "No Jews or Dogs Admitted Here." This vacation spot was the scene of a pitched battle between angry Jews and bigoted hotel owners. The struggle intensified and, rather than accept the shabby treatment, several Jewish millionaires counterattacked and bought a number of the better hotels, turning Saratoga into a popular Jewish resort. This "Battle of Saratoga" was a Jewish victory, but the Jews did not win the war. By the 1880s, similar policies were instituted in other resort areas; the word *restriction* would have a new meaning for American Jewry.

Another incident in the anti-Jewish pattern emerged when Austin Corbin, President of the Manhattan Beach Company of Brooklyn, New York, refused to admit Jews to his beach or hotel. According to the New York *Herald,* Corbin "would rather sink the two millions [he invested in the railroad] and hotel than have a single Israelite take advantage of its attraction."

"You see," said Corbin, "[the Jews] are a pretentious class, who expect three times as much for their money as other people. They give us more trouble on our [rail] road and in our hotel than we can stand. Another thing is, that they are driving away the class of people who are beginning to make Coney Island the most fashionable and magnificent watering place in the world."

"I'll tell you," he concluded, "if I had my way and there was no one to consult [his partners] in the matter but myself, I would have stopped the Jews from coming long ago." Ironically, Corbin ended the interview by telling the reporter not to give the impression that he was "warring against the Jewish people"; yet he willfully stigmatized the Jews as "having no place in first-class society."

In addition to overt acts of discrimination from resorts, there was prejudice in other areas of American life. Jews found themselves shut out of exclusive private schools and prominent social organizations. In Cincinnati the University Club was disbanded when its sole Jewish member nominated another for membership, and in New York the Union Club refused to admit Theodore Seligman, though his father was an original founder. The foundation was being laid for twentieth-century American anti-Semitism.

The efforts of nineteenth-century Jewish leaders to bring about religious unity were a failure. Yet, in spite of the religious divisions there were common concerns, specifically the defense of civil liberties at home and the protection of Jews elsewhere, which motivated the community to form a united front. American Jewry realized that anti-Semitism could rise at the slightest provocation, recalling the Damascus Blood Libel in 1840, Swiss discrimination in 1850, the Mortara Affair in 1858, and the plight of Russian and Romanian Jewry in the 1860s and 1870s.

The first international incident pulling American Jews together occurred in 1840, when the Syrian authorities imprisoned thirteen Damascus Jews for ritual murder.‡ Shocked by the medieval accusation and distraught by reports of torture, Jews throughout the Western world sought the aid of sympathetic governments. The London Board of Deputies sent Sir Moses Montefiore and Isaac Adolphe Crémieux to the Pasha of Egypt to ask him to intervene on behalf of those who survived the Syrian scourge.

In America, protest meetings took place in New York, Philadelphia, Richmond, Charleston, Cincinnati, and Savannah. In New York, a committee of prominent Jews appealed to President Martin Van Buren to "direct the Consuls of the United States, in the Dominions of the Pasha of Egypt, . . . to obtain a fair and impartial trial for [the Jews] at Damascus."

In response to the petition, Secretary of State John Forsyth informed the committee "that the heart-rending scenes which took place at Damascus had . . . been brought to the notice of the President" and that the American "Chargé d'Affairs at Constantinople, was instructed to interpose his good offices in behalf of the oppressed and persecuted race of Jews in the Ottoman Dominions. . . ."

A large segment of the Protestant community lodged similar objections to the Syrian persecution. Henry W. Ducachet, the Episcopalian rector of St. Stephen's Church of Philadelphia, wrote Hyman Gratz:

> that the Christian community generally, and the Christian clergy especially, will gladly and generously co-operate with you [the Philadelphia committee] in any plan you may adopt for [Damascas Jewry's] relief. As it regards myself, allow me to say, that if it should be thought by you necessary to resort to any . . . aid beyond what you yourselves can give, I will most cheerfully bring the case before my congregation, plead their cause . . . and obtain from

‡ The myth that Jews killed Christians in order to obtain blood for the Passover ritual was still being circulated in Europe, the Middle East, and America.

them all the assistance which they can give. . . . it is not, sir, the cause of the Jews only you are about to espouse: it is the cause of humanity.

Neither the demonstration of national Jewish unity, the intervention of the American Government, nor the support of the Protestant community stopped the Syrian massacre. However, the events of 1840 did have far-reaching repercussions on American Jewry; it disclosed the need for a national self-defense organization to meet future crises. The Damascus emergency also marked the decline of Sephardic dominance in the United States. Though the Sephardic trustees of Shearith Israel* condemned the Syrian libel, they refused to permit a protest meeting in their building; this action not only represented the abdication of Sephardic leadership but signaled the rise of German Jewry in America.

In the next decade Jews again came together to protect their civil rights. This time it was not due to the medieval practices of the Middle East but because of the actions of the Swiss Confederation. In 1850 a commercial agreement was negotiated at Berne by the United States and Switzerland. The treaty was submitted by President Fillmore, with certain reservations, for Senate ratification. Apparently the President objected to the treaty's first article, which stated that because "of the Federal Constitution of Switzerland, Christians alone are entitled to the enjoyment of the privileges guaranteed by the present articles in the Swiss Cantons." Simply, the rights of American Jewish citizens were not protected while in Switzerland.

Individual Jewish leaders decried the discriminatory tone of the treaty and urged their representatives in the Senate to register a "no" vote. Similar to their reaction to the Damascus incident, the Jewish community held mass meetings and flooded the Congress with petitions demanding protection for *all* American citizens. The Cincinnati community wrote Secretary of State Daniel Webster and informed him that

> the Amendment to the [United States] Constitution . . . part of which is as follows "Congress shall make no law respecting an establishment of religion or prohibiting the free exercise thereof" would appear to exclude the right or power of the Senate to ratify any treaty conferring exclusive rights to any religious denomination, apart from this it is contrary to the whole spirit of our institutions.

Webster replied that the committee did him "no more than justice in expressing the belief, that [he] would not approve of any measure,

---

* The mother synagogue of American Sephardim.

which might infringe the rights . . . of any class of [his] fellow citizens." Not satisfied with platitudes, Alexander Kursheedt, leader of the New York protest group, petitioned the Senate to induce the Swiss Confederation "to concede to our citizens of all denominations . . . that full enjoyment of religious liberty, which is accorded to their respective subjects on our soil."

Because no American was directly affected by the agreement, little was done to pressure the Swiss Government for change. In 1853, however, A. H. Gootman, an American Jew, was ordered by the Swiss authorities to leave their country. Again American Jewry united to protest.

Moved to action on behalf of Gootman, the leadership in 1857 called a national convention to discuss strategy. The first of its kind, the Baltimore gathering appointed Isaac M. Wise as chairman and petitioned President James Buchanan for an opportunity to present grievances before him. Soon after the appeal was delivered, the President called some of the delegates to Washington, and after hearing their arguments pledged his support to the Jewish cause. Nevertheless, Buchanan did little. Though he committed himself verbally, he remained inactive, and because of his lack of concern the Jewish community had to wait until 1874, when the Swiss Constitution extended equal rights to all.

In the same decade, American Jewry turned its attention to Italy, where Edgar Mortara, the Jewish child of Girolamo Mortara Levi was kidnaped and secretly baptized. News of the incident, highlighted by the involvement of the Catholic Church, reached the United States. Immediately, Jews sprang into action to protest the forced conversion and to condemn the Catholic Church for sanctioning the theft of a child from its parents.

In Philadelphia, Isaac Lesser recognized the need for unified action and called for a national convention; Cincinnati Jewry petitioned the Pope for a redress of the situation; and Milwaukee Jews summoned a gathering of "men of all creeds and political opinions." America took sides on the issue. Jews and Protestants joined forces, while the Catholic community either defended the action or remained silent. Rabbi Isidor Kalisch, a prominent Milwaukee religious leader, condemned the Jesuits of the Catholic Milwaukee *Seebote* who defended the kidnaping of the Mortara child.

Protestants, too, saw in the incident a threat to their interests. Rev. Matthew R. Miller, in the Cincinnati *Presbyter,* asserted that "unquestionably the little Hebrew boy Edgar Mortara has *passively* given the world one of the best arguments of all the nineteenth century against Popery."

Unanimously opposed to the kidnaping, an outraged secular press joined the battle. *Harper's Weekly* commented that "any church [which claims] the right of physical appropriation of anybody is absurd."

For the most part, the Catholic community supported the Pope's position. After all, they reasoned, the Jews were "Christ killers" and the Protestant majority were still their "wicked enemies." The New York *Freeman's Journal and Catholic Register* dismissed the abduction as a "bug-a-boo" story circulated at the "expense of Catholicity." Similarly, the United States *Catholic Miscellany* wrote:

> There is no more disgusting chapter, we make bold to say, in the whole annals of religious hypocrisy, than the conduct of the anti-Catholic press, secular and religious, both in Europe and the United States, in relation to the so-called "abduction" of the child Mortara.

Another Catholic response, which appeared in the Washington, D.C., *States*, characterized the protest as "the old Jewish hatred of Christianity":

> A Jewish child had been made a Christian. There's the rub. It would not do for the Jews to make open war against Christianity in Christian countries. They are too shrewd to do that. But they well know that the Papacy is the great bulwark of Christendom, and hence they boldly hurl their missiles against it, calculating that many Protestants will be silly enough to aid them in that impotent undertaking. . . . I cannot but regret that such liberal feelings did not actuate their co-religionists in the days of Jesus of Nazareth, the proto-martyr, Stephen, and Saul of Tarsus.

By no means were Jews absent from the war. Isaac Lesser in an appeal to all Americans condemned the Church for making "any act of barbarity legal," and Penina Moise, the foremost Jewish poet, expressed her thoughts in verse:

> Oh! every chord of sympathy vibrated in my breast,
> When o'er the broad Atlantic came the news of that arrest;
> Which breaking through each ordinance of Heaven and of Earth,
> Has torn a helpless infant from the authors of its birth
> Consigning to a stranger's care, and to a bigots creed
> A child of Abraham's covenant—one of his chosen seed.

In spite of the strong united front presented by the Jewish community, their efforts to have Edgar Mortara returned to his parents failed.

However, the activities surrounding this international incident had an important and positive result: the creation of the Board of Delegates of American Israelites. If similar incidents were to happen again, the Jewish community was prepared to deal with the problem with a strong organization. The establishment of the Board of Delegates was a significant step toward Jewish unity and Jewish self-defense.

In the decades after its establishment, the Board concerned itself with the Swiss treaty, persecution of Moroccan and East European Jewry, and Civil War anti-Semitism. As a watchdog of Jewish interests, it was ever-present when the civil rights of American Jews were threatened. By the time of the massive Russian emigration in the 1880s, fifty-four of the 185 congregations were active members.†

In addition to conflicts with Syria, Switzerland, and the Catholic Church, American Jewry also challenged the long-standing anti-Semitic tradition of czarist Russia. During the presidency of Andrew Jackson, the United States negotiated a treaty of commerce with the czar's representatives. Though the final agreement, at the insistence of Russia, denied American Jews their full civil rights while resident in Russia, Jackson, on April 18, 1833, signed the treaty.

For the next three decades, because no American Jew was affected by the disabling anti-Semitic clause of the treaty, no occasion arose to protest the agreement. America seemed satisfied that its citizens were protected and chose to let things remain as they were. However, in 1864, Bernard Bernstein, a Polish Jew and naturalized American, was imprisoned by Russian authorities. Apparently Bernstein had still had an unfulfilled military obligation to the czarist regime when he emigrated, in 1845. With the aid of Secretary of State William H. Seward, Bernstein was released, but to the anger of the Jewish community, the incident was not pursued by the State Department, which chose to accept the Russian interpretation of citizenship and the discriminatory treatment of its Jewish citizens.

After the Bernstein case, the State Department did make inquiries into the nature of the Russian interpretation of the treaty, but their efforts were feeble. America, it seemed, was still agreeable to the Russian position: refusal to treat American Jews any differently from its own Jewish subjects.

For the next thirty years, the problem was negotiated and renegotiated by the two nations. Not until 1911 did the Congress, under pres-

---

† Due to its anti-Reform orientation, leaders such as Isaac M. Wise, Max Lilienthal, and David Einhorn were opposed to its activities.

sure from the American Jewish Committee,‡ demand a final adjudication of the problem. After eighty years of Russian refusal to treat all Americans equally, President William Howard Taft ordered the abrogation of the Russian-American Treaty of 1832.

This was not the only time the United States came into conflict with Russia over the treatment of Jews. In 1869, Jews were stunned by news that their coreligionists were being subjected to inhuman treatment by the czar. In an appeal for aid, the Washington, D.C., chapter of B'nai B'rith informed President Ulysses S. Grant that "by the enforcement of a harsh law, some two thousand Jewish families [were] expatriated from their homes into the interior of primitive Russia."

After being asked "to plead the cause of these unfortunates," the President responded that he "would take great pleasure in being the medium to cause the revocation of the ukase, and would lay the appeal before [his] Cabinet." According to Simon Wolf, the unofficial Jewish representative to the White House, Grant did more in behalf of Jews "at home and abroad, than all the presidents of the United States prior thereto and since."* Though Grant's directive to the State Department to intervene on behalf of Russian Jewry did little to change Russian policy, his sympathetic response has been noted as a legitimate expression of his friendship for American Jewry.†

From the 1840s until the advent of mass Russian Jewish immigration, anti-Semitic incidents helped unify the American Jewish community. Though many of these events took place in foreign lands, American Jews recognized their obligation to support their brothers elsewhere. They understood all too well that an attack on one was an attack on all. Their unique brand of collective security, though not termed such in the nineteenth century, was vital to their survival as a religious and cultural community.

The Civil War's Opposing Views

When the American and Foreign Anti-Slavery Society met on May 31, 1853, its annual report contained an evaluation of the abolitionist activities of American Jewry. The conclusions reached by the society

‡ Established in 1906.
* Wolf's reflections took place forty years after the event.
† Some historians claim that Grant's action was an apology for the infamous Order No. 11, to be discussed in the next section.

were disappointing, indicating that "the Jews of the United States have never taken any steps whatever with regard to the Slavery question."‡

> As citizens . . . deem it their policy "to have every one choose which ever side he may deem best to promote his own interests and the welfare of his country." *They have no organization of an ecclesiastical body to represent their general views; no General Assembly, or its equivalent.** . . . It cannot be said that the Jews have formed any denominational opinion on the subject of American slavery. Some of the Jews, who reside in the slave states, have refused to have property in man, or even to have any slaves about them. They do not believe that any thing analogous to slavery, as it exists in this country, ever prevailed among the ancient Israelites. But they profess to believe that "the belief of Abraham, enlarged by Moses, and now acknowledged by the Jews, is one of purity and morality, and one which represents the strongest possible supports for civil society, *especially a government based upon principles of equality and liberty of the person!* . . . The objects of so much mean prejudice and unrighteous oppression as the Jews have been for ages, surely they, it would seem, more than any other denomination, ought to be the enemies of *Caste*, and the Friends of *Universal Freedom*.

For the most part, the statement was correct. Individual Jews took part in the growth of the institution as well as in the debate over its morality: Newport Jewry engaged in the Atlantic slave trade in the mid-eighteenth century; the Rivera family carried "black cargoe" in the 1750s; and in 1762, Isaac Elizer and Samuel Moses outfitted an African slaver in anticipation of acquiring "as many good mercantable young slaves as [possible]. . . ."

Similar participation existed in the South in the nineteenth century. A small number of Jews engaged in the domestic slave trade, bought and hired slaves to be used on their farms, and treated their chattels in the same manner as their Christian neighbors. One wonders if Benjamin Davis, who in 1838 placed an ad in the Columbus (Georgia) *Enquirer* offering for sale "sixty likely Virginia negroes" was reminded of the

---

‡ While the Protestant denominations were divided, most synagogues maintained a neutral posture or took little action in the struggle to eliminate or retain slavery. This situation may be attributed to the absence of any central synagogue hierarchy. The lack of such an institution led to the independence of local congregations and the freedom of Rabbis to determine their own policies. However, Jews as individuals took stands on both sides of the slavery issue. Yet, as with most Americans, the greater number remained neutral.
* Italics mine.

similar plight of his own people who were enslaved by the Egyptian Pharaohs.

At the same time, Jews gave voice to a variety of pro- and anti-slavery opinions. The best-known rabbinical justification of the institution was voiced by Rabbi Morris J. Raphall of Congregation B'nai Jeshurun in New York City. On January 4, 1861, Raphall delivered a treatise on "The Bible View of Slavery" to a synagogue packed with worshipers. In his sermon he insisted that the Old Testament sanctioned the institution and that the abolitionists twisted biblical interpretation for their own ends. According to the rabbi, ". . . the property in slaves is placed under the same protection as any other species of lawful property, when it is said, *Thou shalt not covet thy neighbor's house, or his field, or his male slave, or his female slave, or his ass, or aught that belongeth to thy neighbor.* That the male slave and female slave here spoken of do not designate the Hebrew bondman, but the heathen slave. . . . That the Ten Commandments are the word of God, and as such, of the very highest authority, is acknowledged by Christians as well as Jews."

Not satisfied with defending the institution, he also assaulted the abolitionists:

> I would therefore ask the reverend gentleman of Brooklyn [Henry Ward Beecher] and his compeers—How dare you, in the face of the sanction and protection afforded to slave property in the Ten Commandments—how dare you denounce slaveholding as a sin? When you remember that Abraham, Isaac, Jacob, Job—these men with whom the Almighty conversed . . . that all these men were slaveholders, does it not strike you that you are guilty of something very little of blasphemy? And if you answer me. "Oh, in their time slaveholding was lawful, but now it has become a sin," I in my turn ask you, "When and by what authority you draw the line? Tell us the precise time when slaveholding ceased to be permitted, and became sinful? When we remember the mischief which this inventing a new sin, not known to the Bible, is causing; how it has exasperated the feelings of the South, and alarmed the conscience of the North, to a degree that men who should be brothers are on the point of embruing their hands in each other's blood, are we not entitled to ask the reverend preacher from Brooklyn, "What right have you to insult and exasperate thousands of God-fearing, law-abiding citizens, whose moral worth and patriotism, whose purity of conscience and of life, are fully equal to your own . . . ?

The response to Raphall was immediate. The pro-slave Richmond *Daily Examiner* called it the "most powerful [religious defense of slavery ever] declared," and the Memphis *Commercial Appeal* hailed the pronouncement as "the most thorough refutation of the rabid, abolition views of Henry Ward Beecher." At the same time, however, the anti-slavery faction within the Jewish community rose to challenge what they feared would be interpreted as an official "Jewish position." Michael Heilprin, a Polish emigrant and editor of the New American Cyclopaedia, condemned the rabbi for promoting "a Divine sanction of falsehood and barbarism." In a point-by-point examination of "The Bible View of Slavery," he refuted each of Raphall's arguments. Heilprin asserted that a "general refutation of our Rabbi's view can be found in the history of the Hebrews as a nation, a history of fifteen centuries, full of wars, revolutions, civil strifes, and catastrophes, but without mention of slave risings, or a single similar event." Indeed, those who read the blistering anti-slave argument in the pages of the New York *Tribune* were reminded that American history "has scarcely a page on which is not written the black word *slavery*."

Prior to Heilprin's response, individual Jews had both rejected the proslave argument and disobeyed federal law protecting the "peculiar institution." In 1851, though the *Asmonean* supported the Fugitive Slave Law of 1850 and "the principle of reclaiming the absconded slave," Michael Greenbaum, a Chicago abolitionist, led an anti-slavery crowd and freed a fugitive who had been arrested by federal officials.

Others, such as Louis Stix, expressed sympathy for the plight of blacks but did nothing to promote their liberation. Though he classified himself as an "outspoken" opponent of all involuntary servitude, he still advocated *gradual* emancipation and a government indemnity for "[his] southern neighbors for their pecuniary losses in parting with their slaves." Ironically, though Stix frequently expressed sympathy for the slaveholders' economic position, he still managed to enrage his "southern neighbors." He told the following story:

> In a general conversation, a co-religionist and brother merchant living in the South . . . remarked [to me] that Southerners could not live without slaves. I replied to this by a very uncalled for remark not at all flattering to our own race living in the South. As this was at the dinner table, the Southerner . . . drew his pistol to compel me to take back my words. A gentleman from Cincinnati [also a Jew], who was at the table, also drew his pistol and

offered to meet the Southerner in any way he desired. The latter was only too glad to get away, and I hope has since learned to do without slaves, or has returned to the place from which he came, where he was almost a slave himself.

The attitude and inaction of Louis Stix represents the neutral position of the average non-slaveholding Jew. Though few joined the radical abolition cause, there did emerge in the 1840s and 1850s a vociferous Jewish group that committed itself to immediate emancipation. In the main these people were all recent immigrants.

Ernestine Rose came to the United States in 1836 and immediately acquired a reputation as an ardent feminist and radical abolitionist. From the inception of her anti-slavery activities, the Polish-born daughter of a rabbi had no patience for those who characterized the slave's life as "happy and carefree." Angry with this false portrayal, she once told a crowd of anti-slavery enthusiasts that

> even if slaveholders treated their slaves with the utmost kindness and charity; if I were told they kept them sitting on a sofa all day, and fed them with the best of the land, it is none the less slavery; for what does slavery mean? To work hard, to fare ill, to suffer hardships, that is not slavery; for many of us white men and women have to work hard, have to fare ill, have to suffer hardship, and yet we are not slaves. Slavery is, not to belong to yourself—to be robbed of yourself.

Others joined the anti-slavery crusade, among them many who fought in the European revolutions of 1848 and had to flee the continent. August Bondi, Jacob Benjamin, and Theodore Weiner fought with John Brown in 1856, and Isidor Buch and Moritz Pinner led the fight for emancipation in Missouri.

Rabbi David Einhorn, editor of the German-language *Sinai,* consistently reminded his Baltimore readers of an institution designed "to reduce defenseless human beings to a condition of merchandise [which] relentlessly [tore] them away from the hearts of husbands, wives, parents, and children. . . ." As a result of his activities, he was forced to flee the city in 1861, amid riots between rival factions.

One of the most interesting abolitionists was August Bondi, a veteran of the 1848 Revolution whose radical idealism motivated him to join John Brown in 1856. While in Texas, Bondi's radicalism was stirred as he witnessed a slaveholder "deliberately [empty a shotgun] load into the shoulder of [a] colored boy." He condemned the cruelty and "put into [his] remarks all the vinegar of an eighteen [year-old] smart aleck." As Bondi watched, Reverend Roach of the Southern Methodist Church stepped in front of him with a warning to keep out of his master-slave disputes: "We have no use for northern abolitionists," said the minister, "and only your age protects you from deserved punishment."

While in St. Louis, Bondi read an article in the New York *Tribune* that called on all freedom-loving men "to rush to Kansas and save the Territory from the curse of slavery." That same day, he packed his saddlebags and boarded a steamer to fight for freedom and justice. A week later, "light with only [his] Colts, [he] struck out for the Kansas territory." Shortly thereafter, with two Jewish companions, Jacob Benjamin and Theodore Weiner, he found John Brown's guerrillas and, in time, saw action in the Blackjack Border War and at Osawatomie and Pottawatomie.

The fighting over, he looked back with affection on "old Capt. Brown . . . a man steadfast to principles which [were] just and righteous." Bondi said that the violence at Harpers Ferry would never have happened had not Brown witnessed the "tiger-like inhumanity" of the proslavery "border ruffians."

With the outbreak of the Civil War, Bondi once again found himself fighting to rid the nation of slavery. "My mother said," he wrote, "that as a *Jehudi* [Jew] I had the duty to perform, to defend the institutions which gave equal rights to all beliefs." On November 26, 1861, he went off to war:

> I saddled my half-breed mare . . . embraced and kissed all, and slowly rode on, a half mile south, towards the hill where John Gerth, on his black Canadian, waited for me. . . . I turned towards my beloved ones who stood before their door in the valley, my dear wife with the six-month baby in her arms. The sun had risen. I waved adieu to wife and child, father and mother, and rode on south with the young man, John Gerth, who from that morning, remained my chum till he was killed at Mark's Mills, Ark., April 25th, 1864.

If the Jews of the anti-slavery movement were committed to immediate abolition, their coreligionists in the slave states displayed equal enthusiasm in support of the institution. Rabbi J. M. Michaelbacher of Richmond noted that enslavement and the prison-like atmosphere of the slave states were the only means to prevent a repetition of the Santo Domingo massacre of the 1790s: †

> [The abolitionists] invite our man-servants to insurrection, and they place weapons of death and fire of desolation in their hands that we may become an easy prey unto them; they beguile them from the path of duty that they may waylay their masters, to assassinate and to slay the men, women and children of the people that only trust in thee.

Political spokesmen such as David Levy Yulee of Florida, David Kaufman of Texas, and Judah P. Benjamin of Louisiana also defended the institution. Edwin DeLeon, the Charleston-born diplomat and journalist, also expressed "opposition to [the] mistaken philanthropy [emancipation], which, in [his] judgement . . . wherever triumphant, has brought forth weeds, ashes, and blood as its only fruits; as witness the emancipation of St. Domingo. . . ."

In addition to those who held political, diplomatic, and journalistic positions, there were ordinary citizens who also objected to emancipation. Emma Mordecai believed "that the institution of slavery was refining and civilizing to the whites . . . and at the same time the only known institution that could elevate the Negro from barbarism and develop the small amount of intellect with which he is endowed." In the same vein but more to the point, Aaron Hirsch, an Arkansas merchant, declared that "slavery as it existed in the South was not so great a wrong as people believe. The Negroes were brought here in a savage state; they captured and ate each other in their African home. Here they were instructed to work, were civilized and got religion, and were perfectly happy."

The Jewish defense of slavery paralleled the thoughts and opinions of their Christian neighbors. Like non-Jewish slaveholders, Jews in small numbers bought and sold slaves and made use of their labor. Those who were members of the slaveocracy participated in every aspect of the system. Thus one finds "kindly" David Brandon of Charleston requesting in his will that his daughter take his "faithful servant and friend Juellit" under her "protection to treat him as well as [she] would do me . . . and never forsake him being the best friend I ever had." On the other hand, Jews also engaged in the dehumanization process—the

† The blacks on the island of Santo Domingo, influenced by French revolutionary doctrines, rose against the whites, and the ensuing massacre sent a shock of fear through the slaveholding regions of the United States.

making of a thing of a human being. No doubt, slave trader Abraham Seixas broke up slave families when he advertised his merchandise in the South Carolina *Gazette:*

> He has for sale
> Some Negroes, male,
> Will suit full well grooms,
> He has likewise
> Some of their wives
> Can make clean, dirty rooms.
>
> For planting, too
> He has a few
> To sell, all for the cash,
> Of various price,
> To work the rice
> Or bring the lash.

It was not as Jews, but as individuals, that men held slaves, espoused the proslavery cause, or joined the abolitionist camp; the American Jewish community, as such, took no position. However, many Jews gathered at both extremes—from self-sacrificing abolitionists to die-hard defenders of the practice.

Shortly after a Confederate bombardment forced the surrender of Fort Sumter, the *Jewish Messenger,* perhaps the only Anglo-Jewish newspaper to wholeheartedly champion the Union cause, urged its readers to "stand by the flag!" Unlike the editorial neutrality of Wise's *Israelite* (Cincinnati) or Lesser's *Occident* (Philadelphia), the *Jewish Messenger* called on the Jewish people to be true to the Union and the Constitution.

> What death can be so glorious as that of the patriot, surrendering up life in defense of his country,—pouring forth his blood on the battlefield—to live for ever in the hearts of a grateful people? Stand by the flag! Whether native or foreign born, Christian or Israelite, stand by it, and you are doing your duty, and acting well on your part on the side of liberty and justice!
> STAND BY THE FLAG!

Over six thousand Jews rallied to the defense of the Union. In Chicago an enthusiastic meeting of "patriotic Israelites" was held to raise a company of volunteers, encouraging every Jew to assist "the government in its efforts to maintain the integrity of the Union and the crushing out of the rebellion." As a result the "Israelite Company" of

Colonel Isaac Franks, a New York patriot who served with George Washington's Continental Army at the Battle of Long Island. About the Declaration of Independence he said, "We would support the same with our lives and fortunes." Portrait by Gilbert Stuart (American Jewish Archives)

Seventeenth-century sea trader Michael Gratz, from Philadelphia; helped open the Allegheny Mountains to settlement and trade. Portrait by Thomas Sully (American Jewish Archives)

Rebecca Gratz (1781–1869). Model for Sir Walter Scott's Rebecca, in *Ivanhoe*, founded the first Hebrew Sunday School Society in America. Portrait by Thomas Sully (American Jewish Archives)

Uriah Phillips Levy (1792–1862), Commodore, United States Navy. Commander of the Mediterranean Fleet; abolished corporal punishment in the Navy. Restored Thomas Jefferson's estate and willed it to the federal government. (American Jewish Archives)

Mordecai Manuel Noah (1785–1861). Journalist, diplomat, and social planner; advocated a separate Jewish colony at Grand Island, New York. Portrait by John Wesley Jarvis (American Jewish Archives)

August Bondi. German-born abolitionist, fought with John Brown in the Missouri-Kansas border wars. (American Jewish Archives)

Ernestine Rose. A Polish rabbi's daughter, she was an abolitionist and early feminist leader. (Arthur & Elizabeth Schlesinger Library, Radcliffe College)

Julius Meyer, Indian trader, with some of his customers. Left to right: Meyer, Red Cloud, Sitting Bull, Swift Bear, Spotted Tail. (American Jewish Archives)

Julius Meyer's trading post, the "Indian Wigwam." Known as the "curly-haired white chief," Meyer also acted as an interpreter. (American Jewish Archives)

am Gimbel, a Bavarian immigrant who dled his wares along the banks of the ssissippi River. His success as a peddler to the founding of Gimbel's Department e. (American Jewish Archives)

Levi Strauss, the inventor of Levi's pants. His idea, to use tent canvas for work pants, made him one of the most successful of all the "merchant princes." (American Jewish Archives)

Menken brothers of Cincinnati in military uniform of the Federal Army during the Civil War. "Fraternal blood has been spilled by violent hands . . . the hand of the Southern Israelite has been found raised against his Northern brother." (American Jewish Archives)

Judah P. Benjamin, Confederate Secretary of State and key to its early successes by his skill in supplying ordnance. (American Jewish Archives)

Michael Goldwater, grandfather of Senat Barry Goldwater, came to Arizona in the late 1860s. As a freighter, army supplier, a merchant, he laid the foundation for the Goldwater influence. (American Jewish Archives)

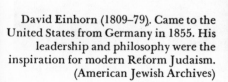

David Einhorn (1809–79). Came to the United States from Germany in 1855. His leadership and philosophy were the inspiration for modern Reform Judaism. (American Jewish Archives)

the 82nd Illinois Infantry was created to support a "vigorous prosecution of the war."

In the Confederate States there was an equal response to the call to arms. After the *Jewish Messenger*'s plea to "stand by the flag" was read by Rabbi Julius Lewis to the Hebrew congregation of Shreveport, Louisiana, the assembly passed a resolution to "scorn and repel" the advice of "a black republican paper . . . not worthy of Southern patronage. . . ." Pridefully, they asserted that as "Southern rebels," they would "stand by, protect, and honor the flag . . . and the Constitution of the Southern Confederacy with [their] lives, liberty, and all that is dear to [them]."

The intense devotion to the southern cause was more clearly expressed by Lewis Leon, who in the first days of the war enlisted in Company C of the 1st North Carolina Regiment. His zeal for Confederate independence and his worship of Robert E. Lee testify to his commitment as a rebel. After the crushing defeat at Gettysburg, he revealed his adoration for the Virginia-born general:

> We can never forget this campaign. We had hard marching, hard fighting, suffered hunger and privation, but our general officers were always with us, to help the weary soldier carry his gun, or let him ride. In a fight they were with us to encourage. Many a general have I seen walk, and a poor, sick private riding a horse, and our father, [Robert E.] Lee, was scarcely ever out of sight when there was danger. We would not feel gloomy when we saw his old, gray head uncovered as he would pass us on the march, or be with us in a fight. I care not how weary or hungry we were; when we saw him we gave that Rebel yell, and hunger and wounds [were] forgotten.

Others displayed equal devotion to their respective causes. In New York City, J. Barrett Cohen "promptly closed his [law] office and hastened to share the fate of his fellow Southerners," and in Baltimore, David Einhorn fled from a secessionist mob, vowing never to return until his "congregation was . . . prepared fearlessly to receive the [antislavery] doctrine from the lips of their teacher."

The decision of which side to support caused deep anguish. When General Pierre Beauregard's artillery began the siege of Fort Sumter, Major Alfred Mordecai was on special assignment at Fort Monroe, Virginia. Hearing of the assault, he returned to his command at the Watervliet Arsenal, at Fort Troy, New York, where he was confronted with the most serious decision of his forty-year military career: to remain in the Union Army or return home and join the Confederate ranks.

Born and raised in North Carolina, the West Point-educated ordnance expert, married to a Northerner, was sympathetic to the Confederate position yet loyal to the Union. Torn by pressure from both his southern and northern family, he resigned from the Army and took his family to Philadelphia, where he remained neutral for the duration.

Similar situations often tore even deeper into family relationships. Congressman Philip Phillips was a southern Unionist who "looked with profound amazement upon the efforts made by many Southern leaders to induce the South to believe the secession would be peacefully received in the North." He never waivered from his unionist stance. His wife and daughters, however, "were strongly on the Southern side" and openly expressed support for the rebellion. In direct conflict with the philosophy of her husband, the Charleston-born Eugenia Levy Phillips urged "Southern women [to give] free expression to [their] feelings [and] sustain their rights by encouraging . . . every resistance to tyranny exhibited by the Republicans."

The best description of the political division of America's two hundred thousand Jews appeared in a Rosh Hashana editorial in the New York *Jewish Record* (1862): "Fraternal blood has been spilled by violent hands, and, to our regret, we are compelled to add that the hand of the Southern Israelite has been found raised against his Northern brother."

Rabbis of both sides added their voices, and though they most often spoke for themselves, in many instances they gave expression to the thoughts of their congregations. Of those who immediately came to the defense of the Union—Liebman Adler and Bernhard Felsenthal of Chicago, David Einhorn of Baltimore and Philadelphia, S. M. Isaacs of New York, Max Lilienthal of Cincinnati, Sabato Morais of Philadelphia, Morais was the most vociferous. "We must have peace," he told his congregation, "but not at the cost of our national experience."

Not every free-state rabbi shared the views of the energetic Morais. Isaac Mayer Wise prayed for the end of hostilities rather than the achievement of a Union victory. "Force will not hold together the Union," he asserted, "[for] it was cemented by liberty and can stand only by the affections of the people." As a pro-Confederate neutral, he defended southern Jewry for their support of the rebellion: "If the largest proportion of the Jewish population of [the Confederate states] give aid and comfort to rebellion . . . they do exactly as others do in the same localities. . . . Why do you [pro-Union rabbis] expect the Jews there to stand in opposition to the masses of the people?"

In the Confederacy the clergy was just as outspoken. Once their choice was made, both Union and Confederate Jews committed themselves to the fratricidal blood bath of civil war. In the North the Jewish community participated in every aspect of the war effort: men joined the military, their organizations engaged in war relief, and their spokesmen gave unstinting support to the cause. Yet despite their total devotion to the Union, they were confronted with discriminatory policies of both the civilian and military authorities.

The issue of Jewish chaplains for the armed forces was the first sign of anti-Semitism condoned by American government officials. In December 1861, Rabbi Arnold Fischel submitted a statement to the United States Senate Committee on Military Affairs in which he charged that "Jewish ministers [were] being by law excluded from the office of chaplain in the Army." Acting as a spokesman for the Board of Delegates of American Israelites, he noted that the law that provided for "a regular minister of some Christian denomination" was a "violation of the principle of religious equality, guaranteed to all American citizens by the Constitution."

Immediately, pressure was brought to amend the discriminatory legislation. Congressman Clement L. Vallandingham, the "copperhead" Democrat supporting the Jewish position, charged that there was "a large body of [fighting] men . . . of the Hebrew faith . . . whose rabbis were excluded from giving spiritual comfort. Rabbi Wise also spoke out in defense of Jewish rights and called the exclusion an "unjust violation of [Jewish] constitutional rights." Demands for the establishment of Jewish chaplains faced bitter opposition in Congress and in the Christian press. The Cincinnati *Presbyter* wrote: "Our government has already gone a great length in this respect in appointing Roman Catholic and Universalist chaplains to the army; but here is a proposal immeasurably beyond anything it has yet done. These denominations at least call themselves Christians, and profess to honor the Lord Jesus, however much they may really dishonor Him. But Jews regard Jesus of Nazareth as an imposter, a deceiver, and one worthy of every term of reproach."

Lincoln was not as narrow-minded as the editors of the *Presbyter*, and after consideration of the Jewish protest promised Fischel that he would "try to have a new law broad enough to cover what is desired by [him] in behalf of the Israelites." After a year of Congressional in-fighting, Senator Henry Wilson of Massachusetts introduced a bill to satisfy Jewish demands. Finally, on July 1, 1862, Congress granted Jewish chaplains the right to administer religious guidance to Jewish members of the armed forces. For the remainder of the war, Jews who died in defense of the Union went into battle with the same spiritual comfort as their Christian comrades.

A short time later, anti-Semitism again was an issue. On this occasion, however, it was a military policy and a "class action" directed against the entire Jewish community. On July 17, 1862, General Ulysses S. Grant issued the infamous Order No. 11 from his headquarters at Holly Springs, Mississippi:

> The Jews as a class violating every regulation of trade established by the Treasury Department and also department orders, are hereby expelled from the department [northern Mississippi, Kentucky, and Tennessee] within twenty-four hours from receipt of this order.

The decision to expel the Jews was made after Grant heard of the active commercial trade being carried on across military lines. Though the stories were true, he refused to recognize that the business traffic and speculation, which did strengthen the Confederate economic position, were being conducted by members of *all* religious groups, including officers in his own command. Nevertheless, he singled out the Jewish merchants for punishment.‡

Almost immediately, the Jewish community protested the harsh policy—especially the "twenty-four hour" evacuation. One of those affected, Caesar Kaskel of Kentucky, went to see Lincoln and told him of the unfair treatment. Lincoln listened patiently and said to the outraged Jewish Unionist, "And so the Children of Israel were driven from the happy land of Canaan." "Yes," responded Kaskel, "and that is why we have come unto Father Abraham's bosom, asking protection." "And this protection they shall have at once," replied Lincoln. The President wired General Halleck, who in turn informed Grant that "the President has no objections to your expelling traitors and Jew peddlers, which, I suppose, was the object of your order, but as it is in terms [which] proscribe an entire religious class, some of whom are fighting in our ranks, the President deemed it necessary to revoke it." With a single firm directive, Lincoln put an end to the first anti-Semitic act of the

‡ No doubt, his decision was motivated by the heightened anti-Semitism during the conflict. Interestingly, commerce across the lines continued after the order was issued.

United States government. Jews would not be Grant's convenient scape-goat.

Though Lincoln quickly countermanded Order No. 11, anti-Semitic sentiments still prevailed on the battlefield. One soldier remarked that many Jewish fighting men did "not care to make their religion a matter of notoriety," because to be "known as [a] Hebrew, would expose them to [the] taunts and sneers of . . . their comrades." Others practiced their religious rituals in secret:

> It is quite common for Jewish soldiers indeed belonging to the same company, to meet together for worship on Sabbath, in some secluded spot, and I know a young soldier, who was on [Yom Kippur] morning, ordered to take part in a skirmish, near Harper's Ferry, which he had to go through, without having tasted food, and as soon as the enemy retreated he returned to the woods, where he remained until sunset, reading his prayers. The character of these devotions is not the less interesting from the fact, that they are always performed in solemn silence, and in some secluded spot, where the noise of the camp cannot penetrate.

But there were Jewish troops who did not hesitate to practice their religion openly. J. A. Joel of the 23rd Regiment of Ohio troops described a Passover Seder on a West Virginia battlefield:

> . . . being appraised of the approaching Feast of Passover, twenty of my comrades and co-religionists belonging to the Regiment, united in a request to our commanding officer for relief from our duty, in order that we might keep the holy days. . . .

Once permission was secured, the

> next business was to find some suitable person to proceed to Cincinnati, Ohio, to buy us matzos. Our sutler being a co-religionist, and going home to that city, readily undertook to send them. About the middle of the [next] morning, a supply train arrived in camp, and to our delight [it included] seven barrels of matzos. On opening them we were surprised and pleased to find that our thoughtful sutler had enclosed two Haggadot and prayer books. We were now able to keep the Seder nights, if we could obtain the other requisites for that occasion. We had consultation and decided to send parties to forage in the country while a party stayed to build a log hut for services.

Sometime after the Seder, Joel gave thought to the experience:

There, in the wild woods of West Virginia, away from home and friends, we consecrated and offered up to the ever-loving God of Israel our prayers and sacrifice. I doubt whether the spirits of our forefathers, had they been looking down on us, standing there with our arms by our side ready for an attack, faithful to our God and our cause, would have imagined themselves amongst mortals, enacting this commemoration of the scene that transpired in Egypt.

Since then a number of my comrades have fallen in battle in defending the flag they volunteered to protect with their lives. I have myself received a number of wounds all but mortal, but there is no occasion in my life that gives me more pleasure and satisfaction than when I remember the celebration of Passover of 1862.

Though Private Joel did not experience discrimination firsthand, there were others, especially those at home, who found themselves targets of anti-Semitism. The New York *Herald* made it a point to identify Jews who were arrested as rebel spies but never mentioned religion when reporting casualty lists or acts of heroism by Jewish soldiers. In the same manner, the Boston *Transcript* identified a Mr. Mordecai as "a wealthy Jew of Charleston, S.C. [who] presented to his belligerent state and city $10,000, to aid the purpose of secession"; the Harrisburg (Pennsylvania) *Telegraph* asked Lazarus Barnhart, who supported the Democratic Party, to "please inform his Christian fellow copperheads who murdered the Savior," and the Evansville (Indiana) *Journal* told its readers "that our fellow citizens of the Hebrew persuasion are, with few exceptions, all afflicted with Copperhead mania."

Far from the battlefields, in California, the press joined the anti-Semitic tide. Upset by a Republican defeat in a local election, the Los Angeles *News* vented its anger on the Jews:

The Union party has been utterly defeated in the country. Secession and disunion have carried the day and years of repentance cannot wash away the stain. . . . Nearly the whole of the Jewish population of this city voted the secessionist ticket . . . that a foreigner should come from a land of tyranny and oppression to a free and enlightened republic, from a land where he is no better than a serf, having no choice in the selection of his rulers; should come here and give his vote and influence against our government and in favor of the same state of affairs he left behind in the old world, seems passing strange.

But the press neglected to report Colonel Marcus M. Spiegel's appeal to the 120th Ohio Infantry, for it truly reflected the fierce loyalty of those Jews who took up arms for the Union. Several months before this soldier gave his life at Snaggy Point, in Louisiana, he urged those under his command "to defend the good old flag" and "the good cause, for which [they] were enlisted." If there was "one man in [his] Regiment who would refuse to shoot at a rebel" he asked that he "step three paces to the front on order that he can be *marked as a coward* and *receive the reward of a traitor.*"

Like Colonel Spiegel, Jews who fought for the Confederacy did so with equal vigor. Though some had strong reservations about rebellion, once their states withdrew from the Union they joined their fellow Southerners to repel "northern aggression." Without question, the devotion of Eleanor H. Cohen, a South Carolinian, to the dying Confederacy was shared by most southern Jews:

> . . . the Yankees shelled Columbia [South Carolina] without notice. On the seventeenth the city was evacuated by our soldiers and surrendered by the mayor. Oh, God, can I ever forget that day? Can time with lethean draughts ever efface from my memory the deep sorrow, the humiliation, the agony of knowing we were to be under Yankees, that our beloved flag was to be pulled down, and the U.S.A. flag wave over the city; that flag that carried loathing to every Southern heart; that flag whose sway is ever characterized by villainy, by outrage, and violence of every kind.

Though the Jews of each side remained loyal to their respective causes, they still retained emotional ties with those across the battle lines. Whenever possible they maintained relationships and followed the experiences of their brothers in the enemy army. When "Yankee Jews" entered Confederate territory, they sought out Jewish families and houses of worship; at times they were rebuffed, other times received warmly. In one instance, after the Federal occupation of Natchez, two Union soldiers, Henry Frank and Isaac Lowenburg, were welcomed into a southern Jewish family and in time "helped to make its history." According to Clara L. Moses, the men visited her father and identified themselves as Jews. The father, being the president of the Hebrew Kadusha Congregation, invited them to attend services during the Holy Days. Shortly after, the soldiers were invited to the Moses home, and being cordially received, became frequent visitors. "Many were the heated discussions between these Yankees and our rebel family," wrote Moses, "until Mother forbade political wrangling, but encouraged social affinity. . . ." Due to the mother's tact and good sense, "these Yankees became loved and loving [sons-in-law]."

For most, however, war on the home front was cruel. Emma Mordecai, of Richmond, described "the end of the old South" and the conditions of defeat:

> Several corps of Grant's Army had been passing up the turnpike all day, returning to Washington, there to be disbanded. I went on top of the house to see the living stream, in one compact mass, pouring up the road as far as the eye could reach in both directions. . . . they have finished their work of destruction and subjugation, and are going in triumph to uninjured, undisturbed homes . . . , only ruining a few more farms in their progress, the owners of which have just returned from our army destitute of everything and having some hope to making something to live on, as the surrender took place in time to plant.

Mordecai shared her neighbors' fear when the rumor spread that Sherman's army was also to pass her way. "If so, all farming operations on their line of march had as well be suspended," because this particular Yankee general was "perfectly ruthless."

In spite of their allegiance, the Jews of the Confederacy were still subjected to the ugliness of anti-Semitism. In the Confederate Congress, anti-Jewish outbursts were not unfamiliar. Congressman Henry Foote of Tennessee told his colleagues that if economic conditions were not to improve, "the end of the war would probably find nearly all the property of the Confederacy in the hands of Jewish Shylocks." Together with Foote, Chilton of Alabama and Hilton of Florida voiced their anti-Semitism. Hilton charged that the Jew "had swarmed here" and "ate up the substance of the country." Anxious to be part of the attack on Jews, John Beauchamps, an official in the Confederate War Department, echoed Hilton's denunciation: "The illicit trade with the United States has depleted the country of gold and placed us at the feet of the Jew extortioners. . . . they have injured the cause more than the armies of Lincoln [and] if we gain our independence, instead of being vassals of the Yankees, we shall find all our wealth in the hands of the Jew."

Even Secretary of State Judah P. Benjamin was not immune to the abuse of Confederate bigots. Though a principle figure in the struggle to defeat the Union, he was nevertheless characterized as "Judas Iscariot Benjamin," whose "Nero-like despotism" was responsible for "all the distresses of the [southern] people. . . ." According to Isidor Straus, a young Confederate businessman, "the blockading of all Southern ports, which cut off supplies that Southern merchants had theretofore procured from the Northern markets, made all the better dry goods, clothing, etc., very scarce. . . ." As a result, all merchants, Jews and Christians alike, entered Union territory to purchase the goods so desperately needed at home.

Since the law of supply and demand dictated the high cost of these goods, those who were engaged in this enterprise, wrote Straus in his diary, "were denounced as extortionists, speculating on the necessities of the people while many of their breadwinners were at the front." A scapegoat being needed, the Jewish merchants were "singled out as if they alone were the perpetrators of what was termed as iniquitous practices."

Once the wave of anti-Semitic denunciation started, added Straus, it was easy for suffering people, without examining the facts, to attribute their deplorable situation "to one and the same cause, and thus a prejudice against the Jewish merchants was inaugurated that found utterance in official and semiofficial quarters." Swept along by the tide, a Georgia grand jury denounced the "evil and unpatriotic" behavior of the Jewish mercantile houses who had engaged in this "nefarious business."

When Isidor Straus's father was told of the indictment, he was furious and let it be known that he would leave the community which he loved and which had cast such unpatriotic aspersions on him. He was the only Jew living in the town and it was obvious that the denunciation was directed at his mercantile exchange. "Father's [re]action caused such a sensation," wrote Isidor, "that every member of the grand jury, [and] all the ministers of the different denominations, assured him that nothing was further from [their] minds [and] that had anyone had the least suspicion that their action could be construed as they now saw clearly it might be construed, it never would have been permitted to be worded." Thus, Talbot County's anti-Semitic indictment would apply to all Jews but the senior Straus.

For every Jewish businessman who did "turn a dollar" at the expense of the war effort, there were countless other Jews who saw in the conflict a release from "northern tyranny and oppression." Eleanor H. Cohen, who recorded her thoughts on the Confederacy's crushed hope, wasted life, and fruitless exertion, was more representative of southern Jewry. After Lee surrendered at Appomattox, she noted in her diary:

> Slavery is done away with. Our noble Jeff Davis, as well as all of our great men, are prisoners; even the governors of the several states have been arrested. Confederate money is worthless, and greenbacks rule the day. Columbia and all the principle [cities] are garrisoned by Yankees. How it makes my Southern blood boil to

see them in our streets! Yes, we are again in the hated Union, and over us floats the banner that is now the sign of tyranny and oppression. . . . Sad, sad is the change since the days of Washington. My brothers are all home after fearful deprivations and hardships. Thank God, they are spared. Poor Joseph Moses, the flower of our circle, was killed. . . . He was a noble man, another martyr to our glorious cause.

Major Louis A. Gratz of the United States Army, confirmed her observations on the "end of the old South." After four years of war, he wrote his uncle Aaron Kurtzig, ". . . in the South the soil is unploughed and deserted; all men physically able to life even a finger are drafted into the army; their slaves are deserting them. Their elegant ladies who once had been too lazy even to dip a finger into water, and who indeed were unaccustomed to work, are now forced to enter our lines in order to beg literally for bread from a government which they had once treated with contempt. So deep has the proud South fallen."

The country as a whole was spared no tragedy. As Rabbi Elban Cohen of San Francisco's Temple Emanuel was about to deliver his Sabbath sermon, he was handed a message announcing Lincoln's assassination. "He was so overcome," reported *The Hebrew,* "that, bursting into tears, he sank almost motionless." Recovering from the shock, but his voice still trembling, he announced that the President "has fallen a bloody victim to treason and assassination, and is no more." The news fell upon the congregation's "ears like a thunderbolt—[everyone was] moved to tears."

Three thousand miles away, the same somber scene was repeated. At New York's Shearith Israel, the rabbi recited the prayer for the dead,* which, according to the *Jewish Messenger,* was the first time it had been chanted in a synagogue for a Christian. Once the memorial services were completed, the congregation filed out of the house of worship to join their Christian neighbors in a public procession. Seven thousand strong, New York's Jews marched and, under the banner of the Free Sons of Israel, paid final tribute to the slain leader:

> The Father of his country is dead.
> The Nation Mourns him.
> LINCOLN
> He is not dead but he still lives in
> the hearts of the nation.

* *Hashkavah.*

In San Francisco those who gathered to mourn Lincoln made up the largest public demonstration that had ever been witnessed in that city. *The Daily Alta California* (San Francisco), made special note of the fact that the marchers, led by the two hundred members of the Independent Order of the Sons of the Covenant, included almost the entire Jewish community. Los Angeles Jews were prominent in their city's memorial tribute. On April 17, the Stockton Street Synagogue resolved "that with feelings of deepest regret, [they deplored] the loss that [the] country has sustained" and pledged that their entire membership "in a body [would] join the procession."

While marching through the streets, California Jewry was undoubtedly aware of Lincoln's action in the two most serious incidents affecting Jews during his presidential tenure: the chaplain controversy and Grant's order No. 11. Yet, in the sobriety of the moment, they perhaps forgot that on several occasions, because of the language of his state papers, he had been criticized by Jewish leaders.

In his "General Order Respecting the Observations of the Sabbath Day in the Army and Navy," he announced:

> The importance for man and beast of the prescribed weekly rest, the sacred rights of Christian soldiers and sailors, a becoming deference to the best sentiments of a Christian people, and a due regard for the Divine will demand that Sunday labor in the army and navy be reduced to the measure of strict necessity.

In response to the order, B. Behrend of Narrowsburg, New York, whose son was serving with Union forces, asserted that "thousands in the army who celebrate another day as Sunday should be allowed to celebrate that day which they think is the right day according to their own consciences." Most of the Jewish press supported Behrend's assertion and urged that "Jews in the military be excused from unessential duty on their Sabbath." On another occasion, Jewish spokesmen censured the President for his first inaugural order, which declared that "Christianity, and a firm reliance on Him [Jesus Christ] who has never forsaken this favored land are still competent to adjust in the best way our present difficulty."

Though Lincoln erred in his choice of words, he by no means dismissed the wartime contributions of Jews. His quick action on Order No. 11 and his dealings with the problems of individual Jews attest to his concern for and fairness to the Jewish community. Lincoln's religious neutrality is perhaps best told by Rabbi Benjamin Szold, of

Baltimore. On a trip to Washington, the rabbi visited the White House to obtain a pardon for a Jewish deserter from the Army of the Potomac. While waiting for the President to complete a Cabinet meeting, Szold sent in to the chief executive a Bible marked with a passage from Deuteronomy and a personal plea to spare the condemned trooper. Though the meeting had not yet ended, Lincoln emerged from his office with Bible in hand and "tears rolling down his cheeks." A number of others in Meade's army—men of all religious denomination—awaited execution, and the President asked the clergyman if he was pleading for his coreligionist only, or all the condemned men. Szold took one look at the remorseful face and knew he had lost his appeal.

Simon Wolf, the unofficial Jewish representative to Republican Presidents, was more successful in his effort to acquire a pardon for a Jewish deserter. As he sat in his Washington office, a letter arrived stating that a Jewish soldier was to be executed at sunrise the next morning. Apparently, the young man had been refused a furlough to visit his dying mother, who "had begged for his return [only] to lay her dying hands lovingly on his head and give him a parting blessing." The trooper was so overcome with grief that he deserted his post and was subsequently "arrested, tried, and condemned to be shot." After reading the communication, Wolf "was dazed and uncertain as to the course to be pursued." As night fell he decided to call on the Honorable Thomas Corwin of Ohio, a close friend of the President, to seek assistance. Corwin, however, told the lawyer that it was impossible for anything to be done, because "the President has been maligned for being too generous and liberal in this respect."† Nevertheless, Wolf continued to plead and "begged so hard that . . . word [was sent] to the White House, inquiring whether an interview could be secured." An answer was soon received indicating that "later in the night" the President would see the two men.

The 2:00 A.M. meeting was described by Wolf:

> The President walked up and down with his hands by his side, his face wore that gravity of expression that has been so often described by his historians and biographers, and yet he greeted us as if we were his boon companions and were indulging in an interchange of anecdotes. . . . Corwin told him why we had come. He

† Apparently, the war was going poorly for the Union, and every man was needed. It has been said that Secretary of War Edwin M. Stanton threatened to resign unless Lincoln stopped pardoning deserters.

listened with deep attention, and when Corwin had exhausted the subject the President replied: "Impossible to do anything."

Corwin turned to Wolf and said: "I told you, my dear friend, that it was hopeless. . . ." In a final effort, the Jewish representative faced the President squarely and respectfully asked: "What would you have done under similar circumstances? If your dying mother had summoned you to her bedside to receive her last message before her soul would be summoned to its Maker, would you have been a deserter to her who gave you birth, rather than deserter in law but not in fact to the flag to which you had sworn allegiance?"

Lincoln stopped, touched the bell; his secretary, John Hay came in; he ordered a telegram to be sent to stop the execution. Some months later, the soldier Lincoln had saved was killed in action at the battle of Cold Harbor while "fighting . . . for the country of his birth." When Wolf informed Lincoln of the trooper's fate, the President became visibly moved and with great emotion said: "I thank God for having done what I did." It was "an impressive scene," wrote Wolf, "one full of pathos and sublime humanity, and is engraved [in my] memory as no other incident of my . . . life. . . ."

The interviews granted by Lincoln to Jewish citizens were not always for pardons; some were for promotions to higher rank in the armed forces. On one such occasion, a day on which the President issued a Fast Day Proclamation, Rabbi Morris J. Raphall, the dynamic defender of the "peculiar institution" in "The Bible View of Slavery," came to Washington seeking a first-lieutenancy for his son Alfred. After hearing the request, the President turned to the rabbi and indignantly asked, "As God's minister is it not your first duty to be at home today to pray with your people for the success of our armies as is being done in every loyal church throughout the North, East, and West?" Raphall, stunned by the question, could only answer that his "assistant is doing that duty." "Ah," said Lincoln, "that is different." The President returned to his desk and on a small card wrote the Secretary of War "to promote Second Lieutenant [Alfred] Raphall to a First Lieutenantcy." With the promotion granted, he turned to the rabbi and with a smile all his own said: "Now, Doctor, you can go home and do your own praying."

On April 14, 1865, during the Feast of Passover, Lincoln was assassinated. In the expressions of public anguish that followed, the American Jewish community was prominent. At New York's Union Square "the archbishop of the Roman Catholic Church . . . and a Protestant minister walked side by side in the procession, and a Jewish Rabbi performed a part of the funeral service." In Boston Jews marched to Temple Ohabei Shalom, where Rabbi David Meyers delivered an address. In St. Louis, A. S. Isaacs, President of the United Hebrew Congregation, arranged to have the synagogue draped in mourning, and at Philadelphia's Mickve Israel, the congregation passed a resolution describing Lincoln as "one of the best and purest presidents, who like the law-giver Moses brought a nation to the verge of the haven of peace, and like him was not allowed to participate in its consummation." Even Rabbi Isaac M. Wise, who had once characterized Lincoln as "a country squire who would look queer in the White House with his primitive manner," now claimed him "to be bone of our bone and flesh of our flesh. He supposed himself to be of Hebrew parentage," wrote Wise, "and indeed he possessed the common features of the Hebrew race both in countenance and features."

These expressions notwithstanding, perhaps the best summation of the reverence for Lincoln's memory appeared in the *Jewish Messenger*.

On Abraham Lincoln, Assassinated Nisan 18th, 5625
My heart overflows with a good speech.
I address my work unto a King.
Psalms, XLV. 2.

I.

Happy art thou, Lincoln. Who is like thee!
Among Kings and princes thou art exalted.
Much thou didst with an humble spirit.
Thou art like a unique person in the land.
Who among princes is like Lincoln?
Who shall be praised like him?

II.

Thou hast also a name among heroes!
Thy right hand has achieved prowess against them.
Thou hast girded on the sword of the slain.
Thou hast drawn the bow by night and by day.
One Father has created us, thou hast said;
Therefore thou hast proclaimed Freedom in thy land.
The black people thou hast redeemed into Freedom:
Forever they will praise and bless thy name.
Who among princes is like Lincoln, and who can be
    praised like him?

In the fifteen years after the assassination, the American Jewish community managed to put its communal house in order. Immigration from Germany was at its ebb, and most Jews had become American by birth or acculturation. Philanthropic agencies were beginning to unify, the Board of Delegates of American Israelites was becoming more influential as a civil defense organization, and the idea of religious union was abandoned in favor of separate internal development. The long respite and the stabilization that followed allowed American Jewry to prepare for the massive influx of their East European brothers. Indeed, the American Jewish community would meet its most serious challenge in the coming century.

CHAPTER III

East European Invasion

"To America, Brethren! To America!"

"One afternoon in the summer of 1881," wrote Abraham Cahan, "when the Jewish quarter of Kieff was filled with groans and its pavements were strewn with the debris of destroyed homes, a group of young men entered one of the synagogues of the ancient city." As they made their way down the aisle, the worshipers turned to gaze at the well-dressed newcomers who had joined them. When the marchers reached the holy ark, a silence fell upon the congregation, for these young Jews were students at the University of St. Vladimir and, although they were coreligionists, their presence at the synagogue was an unusual sight.

Struggling to hold back his sobs, a spokesman for the delegation addressed the gathering:

> Brethren, . . . we are a committee of the Jewish students of the University, sent to clasp hands with you and to mingle our tears with your tears. We are here to say to you, We are your brothers; Jews like yourselves, like our fathers! We have striven to adopt the language and manners of our Christian fellow countrymen; we have brought ourselves up to an ardent love of their culture, of their progress. We have tried to persuade ourselves that we are children of Mother Russia. Alas! we have been in error. The terrible events which have called forth . . . these tears have aroused us from our dream. The voice of the blood of our outraged brothers and sisters cries unto us that we are only strangers in the land

which we have been used to call our home; that we are only step-children here, waifs to be trampled upon and dishonored.

In the protective warmth of the synagogue the articulate student leader finally uttered what all of Russian Jewry had known for generations: "There is no hope for Israel in Russia." Let us go, he urged, to "a land beyond the seas which knows no distinction of race or faith, which is a mother to Jew and gentile alike. . . . To America, brethren! To America!"

The pogroms of the early 1880s, which caused these students to seek reunification with other orthodox coreligionists, were rooted in the emerging spirit of anti-Semitism a decade earlier. In the 1870s, Russian officialdom, as well as liberals and intellectuals, established the rationale used by rampaging *pogromnicks* who believed that Jewish life and property merited no protection. Among those responsible for rekindling this ideology were Jacob Brafman, a converted Jew, whose *Book of the Kahal* (1869) was adopted by government officials as an anti-Semitic manual, and Ippolit Lutostanski, whose writings reignited the myth of the Passover blood ritual. There can be little doubt that these events, coupled with the economic hard times of the early eighties, motivated the terrorsome Barefoot Brigades* as they pillaged the Jewish communities of Kiev, Odessa, and the Pale of Settlement, killing countless numbers of Jews.

Encouraged by a regime trying to divert attention from hunger and unemployment, the rioters visited 160 Jewish communities. When their work was done, twenty thousand Jews were homeless, $80 million in Jewish property was destroyed, and one hundred thousand Jews were reduced to abject poverty. Gleefully, the procurator-general of the Holy Synod looked at the government-sanctioned atrocities as the final solution to the Jewish problem: "One third," he said, "will die out, one third will emigrate, and one third will disappear without a trace."†

Contrary to past policy, czarist officials stamped out all hopes that the Jew could one day return to a "normal" existence. On May 3, 1882, Russian Jewry witnessed the enactment of the infamous Temporary Edicts—legislation designed to make Jewish life untenable.‡ Jews were forbidden to resettle outside their designated communities or conduct

---

* Gangs of peasants who murdered, raped, looted, and burned the various Jewish communities.
† To "disappear without a trace" referred to conversion.
‡ Also known as the May Laws. The legislation lasted until the February 1917 revolution.

business on Jewish or Christian holidays; they were refused admittance to their own homes after a few days' absence; they were expelled from their communities if they sought to change their residence in their own localities; and the already small number permitted to attend educational institutions was further reduced. To hasten the end of the Jewish community, the Russian Government, for the first time in its history, encouraged Jewish emigration across the borders. On January 16, 1882, Count Nicolai Ignatiev, the Minister of the Interior, declared "the western frontier is open for Jews." Though the ban on emigration was not officially rescinded, the new policy was clear: Jews would not be stopped if they sought refuge elsewhere.

Russian Jewry began their trek to Brody, in Austrian Galicia, where in the summer months of 1881 four thousand helpless immigrants arrived. In response to the refugee situation, the Alliance Israélite Universelle, a West European agency established to protect Jews, dispatched Charles Netter to co-ordinate relief activities. Once in the Austrian frontier town, Netter provided the immigrants with the basic necessities of life and arranged transportation to Hamburg, Germany, where those bound for America boarded ships for the transatlantic crossing. Ahad Ha'am witnessed the Brody erodus:

> The city was full of refugees from Russia. Charles Netter and his aides stayed there, directing group after group to America. One of the groups was in the train in which I travelled to Vienna, and I could see Netter, that worthy man, standing in the station and distributing money to the refugees. His face expressed the kindness and compassion he felt for them. The refugees were gay and in high spirits. One could read in their eyes how hopefully they looked into the future. As the train started to move, they called out: Long live Netter! Long live the Alliance!

The few who made the trip from Brody to Hamburg, as well as the many who remained in Russia, were on occasion warned by some of the European Jewish press to consider carefully any decision to go to America. In the United States, asserted *Hatzfirah* (Poland), there would be little financial aid for refugees. The newspaper cited the Russian settlement at the Agudat Achim Colony in North Dakota, where, after several months, recent arrivals had not received any financial support—"not even a penny."

A Louisville correspondent to *Ha-Melitz* (St. Petersburg) called for a halt to Jewish immigration:

General immigration to this country is not suited for the Russian Jews; the conditions of its life require other men. Any attempt at mass immigration will be in vain . . . it will not succeed. Only a few in number, a chosen few, who have decided to seek and attain success by means of their own strength . . . a chosen few like these, after their struggling with tremendous difficulties, will find a way to hold up the banner of this country on which is written the great principle: Help yourself!

Another correspondent added that to leave Eastern Europe was to abandon Judaism. "The abundant freedom which is practiced in America can sometimes be like an ever-swelling breach in the wall of religion, [which] destroys its foundation." A communication from Scranton, Pennsylvania, supported this assertion: "in America, they have no synagogue, they have no *shochet* [ritual slaughterer] and neither expect nor seek one; they do not teach their children *Torah,* and with neither *Torah* [religious training] nor *derech eretz* [proper manners] they are growing up wild." A New Jersey observer warned: Who is the man who wants to be free of the commandments of God?— let him go to America, a land which collects all those who forget God and abandon religion, a land which devours the faith of its inhabitants. . . ."

Some correspondents submitted dispatches that encouraged emigration. From Chicago, the *Ha-Melitz* reporter told his Polish readers about the paved streets, the splendid buildings, and the "spirit of commerce." This spirit, he wrote, pervaded the population and caused "every [religious] difference and division to be forgotten." Promoting the concept that the United States was the land of opportunity, a second correspondent declared that "if all the inhabitants of Russia were to come here, even then there would be sufficient work to support them. . . ."

Among those influenced by these favorable reports were the Antin family, in whose town, Plotzk (Russia-Poland), "America was in everybody's mouth." According to Mary Antin, businessmen discussed it in their shops; women who sold from pushcarts chattered about it from stall to stall; those who received letters from relatives abroad read their contents at public gatherings; and youngsters, caught up in the excitement of the moment, played at emigrating. Though "all talked of it," wrote Antin,

scarcely anybody knew one true fact about this magic land. For book-knowledge was not for them; and a few persons—they were the dressmaker's daughter and a merchant with his two sons—who had returned from America after a long visit, happened to be endowed with extraordinary imagination (a faculty closely related to their knowledge of their old countrymen's ignorance), and their descriptions of life across the ocean, given daily for some months, to eager audiences, surpassed anything in the Arabian Nights.

Encouraged by the stories of the good life across the ocean, Benjamin Antin thought seriously of resettlement. After holding several family meetings, he made up his mind to go. Unfortunately, economics made it impossible for the family to emigrate as a group, and as was characteristic of this migration, Mary's father went alone—anticipating a reunion with his family as soon as he established himself in the new country. Accompanying her father to the railway station, Mary watched her family and friends wave a tearful good-by. Benjamin Antin also watched the heartfelt demonstration of love. Suddenly the train started to jerk, and as it pulled away from the platform he shouted his final farewell, "Good-by, Plotzk, forever."

In the ensuing years, others followed the Antins across the ocean. Among this continuous flow of immigrants were the Wayfarers (*Fusgeyers*), who were driven from Romania after the outbreak of the May 1899 pogroms. Throughout the Romanian Jewish community, groups of Wayfarers banded together to journey on foot to the West European ports of embarkation. This particular band of travelers were not the untrained and poverty-stricken people of the Russian Pale, but skilled workers whose appearance spoke of youth, energy, and health. For months before their departure, the Wayfarers had made ready to leave their homeland—selling their personal possessions, pooling their money, and pledging to share their resources until *all* reached America. *Die Welt,* a Viennese Zionist journal, described one group as it walked across Western Europe: "They wear large home-made sandals and carry valises and flasks of water on their backs, and staffs in their hands. Each group also has with it several tents and lanterns."

The first of these groups (there were ninety-four in all) were the "Wayfarers of Barlad." Others followed their example, and soon the Students, Workers, and Clerks of Golatz, Bucharest Wayfarers, One Heart, The Wandering Jews, Romanian Exodus, and Painters and Dyers of Bucharest were marching toward Hamburg, Germany. Interestingly, there were several groups composed entirely of females. One such band, *Bat Ami,* began their trip with the distribution of a flier:

We were and are working girls. All our life from early childhood we have been working. Long winter nights we have spent, bent over our work, with needle in hand. With hard toil we have earned our bread. And now—a shiver runs through our body, when we have to appeal to you for pity and sympathy. . . .

Throughout the last two decades of the nineteenth century, East European Jewry converged on Hamburg. The poor, the uneducated, the skilled, and the young—boarding ships for the voyage to the New World. Tomorrow they would be in America, tomorrow they would begin a new life.

To protest the Russian atrocities, American Jewry called for demonstrations in Philadelphia, New Orleans, Pittsburgh, and New York. On February 2, 1882, a meeting presided over by Mayor William R. Grace was held at New York's Chickering Hall. The proclamation, inviting the attendance of the New York community, appealed not only to Jews but to all religious groups who had "heard with sadness and indignation of the sufferings inflicted upon the Jews of Russia." The gathering, supported by such notables as ex-President Grant, Carl Schurz, Whitelaw Reid, and Leland Stanford, also attracted a substantial number of Christian clergymen, both Protestant and Catholic, who, in a collective statement, endorsed the activities: "We sympathize with our fellow citizens of the Hebrew faith in their sorrow for their afflicted brethren in Russia, and in their energetic efforts for the welcome of the exiles."

Moved to action, the Jewish leadership began a campaign for refugee relief. Leading financier and philanthropist Jacob Schiff organized the Russian Refugee Relief and Colonization Fund, contributed ten thousand dollars to establish the "Schiff Refuge" on Ward's Island, and used his influence to attract other affluent Jews to the cause. Yet, the collective attitude of America's 250,000 Jews toward the Russian immigrant was tainted by indifference, apathy, and callousness.

In response to the anti-immigrant feeling, *American Israelite* characterized the reception of the newcomers as the "gloomiest chapter in the history of the American Jewish community." In an attempt to touch the conscience of his readers, Isaac Mayer Wise filled his newspaper with reminders "that the fullness of the misery of the Russian Jews has not been appreciated in America." According to Wise:

The American Jewish community, untrue to its best traditions, has not yet done its duty. It is urgently necessary to put forth our best endeavors to aid these exiles from their homes which have been cruelly devastated; it is our duty to give material aid to them, enabling them to become industrious citizens. Many are seeking shelther and home on our shores; they have the bones and sinew that are needed to build a peaceful, thrifty citizen; they have been trained to a life of labor, as well as a sphere of thoughts and morals; all that they need is the firsthand encouragement that shall set them on their feet in their new environment.

Though Wise's appeal did cause many American Jews to reverse their position, the community as a whole still refused to commit itself to a full-fledged support of immigration. Charles Netter of the Alliance Israélite Universelle was handed a telegram from Isidore Loeb urging him to "stop all transports to America." Shortly thereafter, another communication was sent to the Alliance: "We absolutely do not agree with you," wrote the American leadership, "that immigration to America is the only solution for the Russian Jews."

Protests were also heard from American Jewish philanthropic and fraternal societies. In 1882 Moritz Ellinger, of the Hebrew Emigrant Aid Society, declared:

America is not a poorhouse, [or] an asylum for the paupers of Europe. [European Jewry] may ask us what they are to do with the sick and aged and infirmed. [My] reply would be: "That is your business; we take care of our own sick, aged and infirm, and ask assistance of no one."

In an effort to put this philosophy into practice, HEAS officials informed the superintendent of immigration at Castle Garden that aid to future Jewish emigrants would cease. Again, in 1884, the president of New York's United Hebrew Charities asked the European relief agencies "to refrain from sending on a fruitless voyage any unfortunate coreligionists who cannot prove . . . their willingness and ability to lead a life of industry on these busy shores."

Others joined the assault: the New York *Commercial Advertiser* condemned the Europeans for encouraging the spread of disease by sending the infirm, and the New York *Sun* implied that increased immigration would lead to an upsurge of anti-Semitism. Even *The Menorah,* the journal of B'nai B'rith, added an unsympathetic voice: "There is no well-constituted nation that could possibly absorb such a large mass of immigrants as are thrust in exile by the Russian tyranny." In response to these charges, the Hebrew-language *Haivri* declared that "the advice of our own brethren is worse than that of our enemies."

The American Jewish reaction was unexpected by the Christian community. The commissioner of immigration felt that the Russian immigration was exaggerated. Though Jews were coming in steady numbers, he reported that the total was "not nearly as many as one could think." In an attempt to calm the "nervous" Jews, he denied that the Russians were "flocking here like a cloud of grasshoppers." He asserted that the number of Jews arriving was small when compared to the Italians and thus the fear of Russian inundation was hardly worth considering. "I can say," he declared, "that only a small number [of Jews] are detained by inspectors and that almost invariably we allow them to enter, because it is shown to our satisfaction that while they are very poor they will not become a burden." Even the New York *Sun,* in an apparent change of attitude, tried to alleviate the fear of Jewish pauperism by reporting that "the same influences which determine the great majority of the Christian emigrants to prefer the United States will act no less powerfully on the exiled Jews."

Though some of these efforts were successful in easing Jewish fears about the creation of a permanent pauper class, American Jewry still looked with disfavor on the Russians. After all, it was reasoned, they came from a different cultural milieu than earlier Jewish settlers. "Aren't they too pious?" said one observer. Another added that "they speak Yiddish!" And a third called them "uncouth!" On various occasions, the Russians were characterized as "lazy and shiftless" and as a "class [of people] that reflects no credit upon their brethren." "Until [their] old orthodox notions . . . have been modified or eliminated," added Martin Butzel, president of the Hebrew Relief Society of Detroit, "there is little to be expected from their children." Let them stay in Russia, declared another spokesman, "where they are as capable of rising to the full stature of manhood as are the negroes in the [American] south. . . ."

The best summation of why American Jewry refused to accept a greater responsibility for the resettlement of the Russians was stated by Rochester's United Hebrew Charities:

> They are a bane to the country and a curse to the Jews. The Jews have earned an enviable reputation in the United States, but this has been undermined by the influx of thousands who are not ripe for the enjoyment of liberty and equal rights, and all who mean well for the Jewish name should prevent them as much as possible from coming here.
>
> . . . it is no relief to the Jews of Russia, Poland, etc., and it jeopardizes the well-being of the American Jews.

Despite the negative reaction, efforts were made to ease the burden of the refugees. In St. Louis, Marcus Bernheimer established the Associated Hebrew Charities of the United States; in a communication to most major Jewish communities, he urged the creation of other, similar agencies. Meyer S. Isaacs organized the Russian Emigrants' Relief Committee, and in December 1881 the Hebrew Emigrant Aid Society (HEAS) was formed "for the purpose of aiding and advising Hebrew immigrants . . . in obtaining homes and employment, and otherwise providing means to prevent them from becoming burdens of the charity of the community."

With immediate aid as its objective, HEAS established a refuge for new arrivals on Ward's Island. The temporary shelter, which was funded by a grant from the United States Immigration Commission, provided housing, temporary employment for those willing to commute back and forth to the island, *kosher* food, and English classes. HEAS also founded an employment center in New York City, a labor bureau at Castle Garden, a *kosher* restaurant and boarding house in Greenwich Village, and a shelter in Greenpoint, Brooklyn. In some cases, HEAS placed newcomers with private citizens who "took in" one or more people until suitable accommodations could be found.

As the flow of immigrants rose, agency activity increased. In 1891, Baltimore's three major Jewish philanthropic institutions, The Hebrew Benevolent Society, The Hebrew Hospital and Asylum Association, and The Hebrew Orphan Asylum, jointly posted a two hundred thousand dollar bond with federal authorities in order to obtain the release of detainees who had been classified as paupers, and the Free Employment Bureau of Boston placed over two thousand refugees in jobs throughout the nation. In the first decade of the twentieth century, philanthropic activities were even more varied: the Hebrew Immigrant Aid Society (HIAS) maintained agents at Ellis Island to assist the united Hebrew Charities, the Clara de Hirsch Home for Immigrant Girls in New York City aided newcomers in the search for relatives, and the New York Council of Jewish Women boarded thousands of newly arrived single females.

In addition to providing aid, the Jewish community, in anticipation of limiting the swelling populations of New York, Boston, and Philadelphia, sought to disperse into the interior as many newcomers as possible. In 1882, New York's HEAS settled over two thousand immigrants in 166 cities across the nation. Sometime later, the Association of Jewish Immigrants of Philadelphia took similar measures to relocate 242 people in fifty separate areas. Having met with success, this same agency found homes for an additional 224 immigrants in sixty-four communities. Though successful, the plan for the dispersal of newcomers was never meant as an open invitation to those East Europeans who had not yet made the Atlantic crossing. In 1886, the Jewish Protective Society of New York warned:

> The object of the [dispersal plan was] *not to invite or encourage immigration,* but to protect and assist those that are landed here, so as to induce them from the start to "Americanize" themselves, dissuade them from overcrowding in the already overcrowded wards of their countrymen, and guard them from the cries of shrewd "sharpers" who take advantage of the inexperience of "greenhorns."

Concern with urban overcrowding in the northeastern cities led to the foundation, in 1890, of the Jewish Alliance of America. One year after it was organized, the alliance issued a "Plan of Action . . . with Regard to Russian Immigration":

> It may be stated as beyond question that the gravest evils attending the present great tide of immigration, both with regard to the immigrants and the community at large, may be directly traced to the massing of the newcomers in the great centers of population. . . . The immediate purpose to be kept in view is the settlement of small Jewish communities in the towns and villages of the interior throughout the country. It is manifest, that if two or three families could be settled anywhere in self-supporting conditions, they would soon become the nucleus of further growth through the accession of relatives and friends for whom the first comers would have made more or less adequate provision. . . .

Not all agencies agreed with the aims of the Jewish Alliance. Louis B. Schram, of Milwaukee, threatened, "If you send any more Russians, whether it be to this Society or *to whom it may concern,* they will be shipped back to you without permitting them to leave the depot." Cleveland Jewry told their East Coast coreligionists that they could accommodate no more immigrants, and the Jewish leadership of Providence, Rhode Island, warned "that for every new emigrant you send here we will return two." Letters were also received from Baltimore, Rochester, Boston, and Canada stating that "we have all the emigrants we can attend to." Many East Coast relief agencies informed their

European counterparts that no new immigrants would be received unless they were healthy and had some skill by which to earn a livelihood.

The resistance to the dispersal policy also motivated some Jewish agencies to encourage the return of unskilled immigrants. In 1887 the United Hebrew Charities of New York returned 1,082 Russians, and a year later, via the U.S. immigration authorities, managed to prohibit 3,500 additional refugees from entering the country. Those selected to be returned were "interviewed" before plans of the return trip were made, and in some cases, in order to make the returnees more agreeable, the frightened newcomers were informed that in America it might be extremely difficult to keep their religious way of life. Some of the more pious immigrants, disturbed by the thought that they might not be able to retain their orthodoxy, offered no resistance when told of their fate.*

As the decade of the 1890s began, the American Jewish community was by no means alone in its opposition to increased Russian immigration. President Benjamin Harrison informed Congress that although "the Hebrew is never a beggar [and] lives by toil [the] sudden transfer of such a multitude under such conditions . . . is neither good for them nor for us." More direct in his opposition was the New England intellectual James Russell Lowell, whose concern with Jews might be characterized as a paranoic anti-Semitism: he saw Jews everywhere. The fears expressed by Harrison and Lowell were also present in the more popular journals of the day. "Most men," reported the *Forum,* "if asked what class of immigrants they considered the least desirable, would answer, the Russian Jew."

Consequently, the U. S. Congress, on March 3, 1891, enacted legislation prohibiting "assisted immigrants"—paupers and those likely to become public charges—from entering the country. Eighty Jewish passengers on the S.S. *Marseilles* were detained at the Port of New York and denied entrance to the country. Immediately, Jewish immigrant aid societies protested the exclusion and, in a reversal of their position, declared that they would guarantee that no Jewish immigrant would ever become a public burden. Secretary of the Treasury Charles Foster re-

* Some American agencies, fully aware that the lack of orthodoxy in the United States would deter some immigrants from coming, requested that the European relief societies "explain to all men before they start their journey, . . . that a rigid adherence to the rites of Judaism will in many cases be entirely impossible."

fused to lift the restriction. Aid provided by relief societies, he maintained, "is a tax on the country even when paid by private funds." Shortly thereafter, another effort was made to reverse the restrictionist ruling, and with the aid of a sympathetic press and some "friends" in Washington, the *Marseilles* detainees were permitted to enter the country.

Several years later, Congress again took steps to bar "undesirable" immigrants. This time, the restriction was not directed against those in need of financial assistance but at those immigrants over sixteen years of age who lacked literacy in English or another "recognized language." Once more, Jewish leaders sprang into action as they launched a campaign to list Hebrew and Yiddish as approved languages. Initially, their efforts failed, but a presidential veto by Grover Cleveland defeated the proposed prohibition, permitting the entrance of Jews who were literate in the two "Jewish languages."

Congressional attempts to exclude "assisted" and Yiddish-speaking immigrants marked a turning point for American Jewry. The fear of a "Russian invasion" was put aside as Jewish philanthropic agencies finally recognized their obligation and responsibility to their less fortunate coreligionists. "To deny [the refugees] a resting place on God's footstool, because temporarily devoid of material wealth," declared the national Jewish leadership, "would be endorsement of cruelty and encouragement of its continuance."

The new attitude was in part due to the anti-Semitic undertone of the new legislation as well as to the creation of the Baron de Hirsch Fund, a European-based philanthropic agency established to ease the burden of immigrant resettlement. Founded in 1890 by the German industrialist Baron Maurice de Hirsch, the fund provided, via American Jewish agencies, agricultural and vocational training, employment opportunities, redistribution of newcomers to the interior, and programs for the rapid assimilation of immigrants into American society. By the turn of the twentieth century, American Jewry, no longer feeling that they were solely responsible for their Russian brethren, accepted the obligation for immigrant resettlement with a more enlightened attitude.

Soon after these attitudinal changes took effect, the New York *Times,* on April 24, 1903, informed its readers about a new "Massacre of Jews in Russia":

> Twenty-five Jews were killed and 275 were wounded, many of them mortally, in the anti-Semitic riots at Kishinev, capital of Bes-

sarabia, on April 20, when a number of workmen organized an attack on the Jewish inhabitants.†

The shock of the savagery at Kishinev suddenly made vivid the suffering and oppression of Russian Jews and brought swift reaction from many diverse groups in America, Jewish and gentile. The impact of the slaughter on public opinion was comparable to that of the massacre at My Lai seventy years later.

Immediately, the American Jewish community called for financial aid to alleviate the suffering of the victims. In response to the appeal, Samuel Dorf established the Kishinev Relief Committee, Professor Richard Gottheil of Columbia University sponsored a collection in New York City, and *The American Hebrew* urged its readers to contribute heavily because "not in the days of the inquisitor were such horrible deeds done as those inflicted upon the Jews in Kishinev." Among the first to answer the call was the New York theatrical community. The Windsor Theatre staged a benefit performance of *The Destruction of Kishinev,* at which Mayor Seth Low, after watching the special performance, asked the religiously mixed audience to contribute as much as they could for the Kishinev victims. Interestingly, New York's Chinese community backed three different productions with the Kishinev theme, at which postperformance appeals were made in English, Chinese, and Yiddish. Other non-Jews responded with equal vigor. The Hearst newspaper chain raised fifty thousand dollars, the Salvation Army suggested bringing "over to the United States 1,000 selected families" to settle in the rural South, and Louis Klopsch, editor of the *Christian World,* urged his readers to "be so generous as to convince the sufferers that the treatment they have received is regarded by the Christian people of our land . . . as alien to every principle of humanity. . . ."

At the same time, however, Arnold Kohn, treasurer of the Kishinev Relief Committee, declared that "we are not conducting an immigration movement. . . ." The Jewish survivors of Kishinev paid little attention to this disclaimer, for the Russian riots of 1903, even more than the crisis of the 1880s, sparked a new and even greater immigration to the United States. There were also American Jews who rejected Kohn's

† The true figure was 120 dead, 500 severely injured, and over 100,000 homeless. The *Yiddish Daily News* published a communication from its sources in Russia declaring "the anti-Jewish riots in Kishinev, Bessarabia, are worse than the censor will permit to publish," and *The American Hebrew* reported that it was "popular belief among the Russian peasants that the Czar decreed the slaughtering of the Jews."

statement; Daniel Guggenheim pledged support for those who sought refuge in America, and Chicago Jewry donated enough money to pay for the resettlement of six thousand survivors.

In addition, Jewish leaders sought the aid of the federal government. Ten days after the outbreak of the riots, Simon Wolf urged Secretary of State John Hay to instruct the American ambassador to Russia "to secure reliable information as to these outrages . . . and how far the Russian government will permit [relief agencies] to send supplies and aid financially those who are in distress." To Wolf's disappointment, the American ambassador at St. Petersburg "denied that there is any want or suffering among the Jews in southwestern Russia" and declared that "aid of any kind is unnecessary."

Not satisfied with the ambassador's response, Wolf and Leo N. Levi, president of the New York B'nai B'rith, led a group of national B'nai B'rith leaders to the White House to confer with President Theodore Roosevelt. Levi, acting as a spokesman for the committee, handed Roosevelt a petition the leaders wished sent, via diplomatic channels, to the Russian Government. After carefully examining the document, the President turned to the group and said:

> I need not dwell upon the fact so patent as the widespread indignation with which the American people heard of the dreadful outrages upon the Jews in Kishinev. I have never in my experience in the country known of a more immediate or a deeper expression of sympathy for the victims and of horror over the appalling calamity that has occurred.

The President went on to discuss some of the Jewish police officers who worked for him while he was police commissioner of New York City. "I had experience after experience of the excellent work done [by] what I might call the Maccabee type—by police officers of Jewish extraction. Let me give you one incident bearing upon this question of persecution for race and religious reasons." Roosevelt went on to describe an incident about an anti-Semitic clergyman who called public meetings to assail the Jews.

"Of course" asserted the President, "I had no power [as commissioner] to prevent those meetings. After a good deal of thought I detailed a Jewish sergeant and forty Jewish policemen to protect the agitator while he held his meetings; so he made his speeches denouncing the Jews protected exclusively by Jews, which I always thought was probably the very most effective answer that could possibly be made to him, and probably the best object lesson we could give of the spirit in which we Americans manage such matters."

At the conclusion of the story, Roosevelt congratulated the leaders on the work of their organization, consented to send an autographed picture to B'nai B'rith headquarters, and agreed to forward their petition "relating to the condition of the Jews" to the Russian Government. On July 16, Secretary of State John Hay informed the committee that ". . . the Imperial Government of Russia has declined to receive or consider your petition." Though disappointed at the news, the B'nai B'rith group decided not to press the federal government for further action. They realized that they lacked the political power to pressure their representatives to intercede in a Russian domestic matter.

The Kishinev pogroms of 1903 had far-reaching consequences for American Jewry. Again the Jewish leadership prepared for a second great wave of immigrants and, perhaps as important, realized that B'nai B'rith, a fraternal organization, was not designed to deal with matters of Jewish self-defense. As a result of their "Kishinev experience," a number of Jewish leaders called for the establishment of a national organization designed to protect Jewish rights at home and abroad, reasoning that such an agency might politically unify the Jewish community and create a voting bloc—a political phenomenon that always captured the attention of public officials.

In order to put this concept into operation, Cyrus Adler, Louis Marshall, Jacob H. Schiff, Simon Wolf, and thirty other prominent Jews met on February 3, 1906, in New York City to organize the American Jewish Committee.‡ True to its constitutional pledge "to prevent infringement of the civil and religious rights of Jews," the AJC in the ensuing years would maintain links with the federal government to protect its brethren abroad, oppose America's racially motivated restrictionist immigration policy, fight for separation of church and state, work for the abrogation of diplomatic agreements that restricted the rights of Jews abroad, battle against domestic anti-Semitism, and in an effort to "Americanize" the European newcomers, support the speedy assimilation of Jewish immigrants into American society.*

In the years since the Russian pogroms of 1881, the flood of immigrants so distended the Jewish population that by America's entrance

‡ The AJC was the first ethnic or religious self-defense agency in America to organize for the *sole function* of protecting the civil rights of its coreligionists at home and abroad.
* The work of the AJC as a self-defense agency is discussed in Chapter V.

into World War I the Jewish community numbered about 3.3 million, and by the closing years of the 1920s grew to approximately 4 million, of whom 80 per cent were of East European origin. It was the culture of these newcomers that shaped the American Jewish community of the twentieth century.

One who came with this torrent of East Europeans was Edward Steiner. "With tickets fastened to our caps and with our bills of lading in our trembling hands," he wrote, "we pass between rows of uniformed attendants, and under the huge portal of the vast hall where final judgment awaits us." From here the frightened newcomers pass before the inspectors. "Already," noticed Steiner, "a shifting process has taken place; and children who clung to their mother's skirts have disappeared, families have been divided, and those remaining intact, cling to each other in a really tragic fear that they may share the fate of those previously examined."

A Polish woman, wrote Steiner, suddenly becomes aware that one of her children is missing and begs for her return. A man shouts, *"Gdeye maya shena?"* ("Where is my wife?"), and a little girl, not quite five years of age, cries, *"Mitter, mitter, ich vil zu meiner mitter gehen!"* (Mother, mother, I want to go with my mother!") One by one they pass the inspector, answering questions, declaring money, and rehearsing silently the answers to anticipated questions.

Among the last to pass through the gates are a Russian Jew and his son. "Why did you come?" the inspector asks abruptly. "We had to" is the reply. "Are you willing to be separated; your father to go back and you to remain here?" The two look at each other with no visible emotion, for the question came too suddenly. "Then," wrote Steiner, "something in the background of their feelings moves, and the father, used to self-denial through[out] his life, says quietly, without pathos and yet tragically, *Of course.*" After casting his eyes to the floor, ashamed to look his father in the face, the son repeats, "Of course." Thus the healthy youngster is permitted to enter America, and the physically depleted father is detained, "for" said Steiner, "this was their judgment day."

Conditions of Life in the Urban Community

With the arrival of thousands of East Europeans in the 1880s, American Jewry feared the creation of a Jewish ghetto; within ten years of the first migration, these fears were fully realized. The Lower East Side of New York, the North End of Boston, the West Side of Chicago, and the downtown area of Philadelphia housed Jewish enclaves that ranked among the worst slums in the Western World.

The largest of these concentrations was on New York's Lower East Side, where, by 1890, the population was so dense that 330,000 people were crowded into an area of less than one square mile. According to contemporary observers, this quarter, which was bounded by Allen Street, Essex Street, Canal Street, and Broome Street, was the world's most densely populated community, more so than the poorest slums of London. "It is said," wrote Jacob Riis,

> that nowhere in the world are so many people crowded together on a square mile as here. The average five-story tenement adds an extra building on the rear lot, and yet the sign "To Let" is the rarest of all there. Here is one seven stories high. The sanitary policeman whose beat this is will tell you that it contains thirty-six families, but the term has a widely different meaning here and on the avenues. In this house, where a case of small-pox was reported, there were fifty-eight babies and thirty-eight children that were over five years of age. In Essex Street two small rooms in a six-story tenement were made to hold a "family" of father and mother, twelve children, and six boarders. . . . There are samples of the packing of population that has run up the record here to the rate of three hundred and thirty thousand per square mile. The densest crowding of Old London . . . never got beyond a hundred and seventy-five thousand.

William Dean Howells observed the living conditions within the Jewish quarter:

> . . . it was a most preposterous place for people to live. . . . To be sure, it was not very light and all the dirt may not have been visible. One of the smiling women who were there made their excuses, "Poor people; cannot keep very nice," and laughed as if she had said a good thing. There was nothing in the room but a table and a few chairs and a stove, without fire, but they were all contently there together in the dark, which hardly let them see one another's faces. My companion struck a match and held it to the cavernous mouth of an inner cellar half as large as the room we were in, where it winked and paled so soon that I had only a glimpse of the bed, with the rounded heap of bedding on it; but out of this hole, as if she had been a rat, scared from it by the light, a young girl

came, rubbing her eyes and vaguely smiling, and vanished upstairs somewhere.

Even these living quarters were sometimes too expensive for the average immigrant. Boarders were sometimes encouraged to share a family's tiny apartment. In 1889, a New York City police report described the "boarder" phenomenon:

A tailor lived with his wife, two children and two boarders in two rooms on the top floor. . . . But this tailor, with his immediate household, including the boarders, occupied the larger of the two rooms. The other, a bedroom eight feet square, he sublet to a second tailor and his wife; which couple, following his example . . . divided the bedroom in two by hanging a curtain in the middle, took one half for themselves and let the other to still another tailor with a wife and child.

Even the streets, which were by no means an adequate escape from the inhuman conditions within the tenements, spoke of filth, congestion, disease, and despair. Yekl, the central character of an Abraham Cahan novel, vividly described the outdoor scene: "[I] had to pick and nudge [my] way through dense swarms of bedraggled half-naked humanity; past garbage barrels rearing their overflowing contents in sickening piles, and lining the streets in malicious suggestion of rows of trees; underneath tiers and tiers of fire escapes, barricaded and festooned with mattresses, pillows, and feather-beds not yet gathered in for the night. The pent-in sultry atmosphere was laden with nausea," as "the teeming population of the cyclopic tenement houses were out in full force *for fresh air,* as even these people will say in mental quotation marks."

Other areas of primary settlement mirrored New York's Lower East Side. In Chicago there were three types of ghetto houses: the one- or two-story "pioneer" wooden shanty, erected before the streets were graded, and thus several feet below street level; the four-story brick tenement, with poor lighting, little drainage, and no indoor toilet facilities; and the deadly rear tenement, with little light and the frightful odor of the rear alley.

According to investigator Kate Levy, Chicago's "west-side settlement of Russian Jews [was] essentially a community of homes." The "bunk" system, cheap lodging houses, trashy restaurants, men's boarding houses, and the free-lunch saloon were conspicuously absent. In this community, single males and females without homes either rented furnished rooms or lived with families that seldom took in more than two roomers. The poorest individual, she reported, could pay a family one dollar a week for lodging and coffee or tea in the morning. A penny roll for breakfast and another for dinner often made up the morning and evening fare of some of these lodgers. Sometimes, a kind housewife would add "five cent's worth of meat to her pot for the lodger and furnish [his or her] cooking free."

Even these "better" conditions were at best unhygienic. Levy reported that few homes were fitted with screens, and flies carried disease from house to house. There were no laundry rooms. Chimneys were defective and rooms were cold and smoky in winter and oppressively hot during the summer. Frequently, dead rats rotted underneath the floorboards in these old shanties. "Pavements [were] broken and steps [were] rickety," and "ventilation without the admission of draughts [was] almost impossible."

Though all immigrant groups were subjected to similar living conditions, statistics reveal that the general health of the Jewish immigrant was substantially better than many non-Jewish ghetto inhabitants. The general mortality rate in New York's ghetto was 25.96 per thousand; among Jews it was only 16.23 per thousand. Yet the spread of tuberculosis and the fear of epidemic haunted the Jewish family. According to Riis, "typhus fever and small-pox [were] bred here," and health officers who labeled the New York Jewish quarter "the typhus ward" were almost always confronted by Jewish parents who hid their sick children because "they firmly believed" that the authorities would carry "them off to the hospital to be slaughtered." The fear emanating from the unco-operative and frightened families sometimes caused health inspectors to isolate entire streets to prevent the spread of communicable diseases.

Conditions were so unsanitary, reported Riis, that

> health officers are on constant and sharp lookout for hidden fever nests. Considering that half of the ready-made clothes that are sold in big stores, if not a good deal more than half, are made in these tenement rooms, this is not excessive caution. It has happened more than once that a child recovering from small-pox, and in the most contagious stage of the disease, has been found crawling among the heaps of half-finished clothing that the next day would be offered for sale on the counters of a Broadway store; or that a typhus fever patient has been discovered in a room whence perhaps a hundred coats had been sent home that week, each one with the

wearer's death warrant, unseen and unsuspected, basted in the lining.

The most descriptive account of these conditions was reported by Dr. George Price, who, in 1890, was appointed sanitary inspector for the Lower East Side. In the spring of 1885 Price investigated one thousand buildings inhabited by almost ten thousand families. Nine tenths of these dwellings were inhabited by Jews, mostly Russian immigrants. Even the cold pages of his official reports convey the frightful poverty, the tribulations, and the utter helplessness of these people. Price was not born with a silver spoon in his mouth, and during his first few years in this country went through considerable suffering and misery. From his very first moments as an inspector, the horrible sights that repeatedly met his eyes made him utterly depressed and almost ill.

"These buildings in which the Jews lived," he wrote,

> were crowded, damp, without elementary sanitary facilities, half in ruins. . . . The flats were dark, dank, emitting an unbearable stench, particularly those flats which also served as shops. The inhabitants were in a poor state of health. Children died like flies during the frequent epidemics. . . . Parents were forced to have their children help them in tobacco or tailoring work, or else send them—at the age of six or seven—to work in a shop, which meant physical, psychological and moral deterioration. . . . Not infrequently, we came across buildings housing one hundred families with eight persons [800 people].

Like the health statistics, the Jewish rate of alcoholism was also lower than other immigrant groups. In his investigation of the New York community, Riis recalled that he had never seen a Jewish drunkard, and Howells declared that he "saw none of the drunkenness or the truculence of [other immigrant groups]." Apparently, the low rate of alcoholism characterized other Jewish communities. In Philadelphia, Charles S. Bernheimer rarely saw a drunken Jew. "The temperateness of the Jewish population," he asserted, "is so patent a fact, even to the ordinary observer, that there is hardly any necessity for dwelling on the subject. . . . Russian tea may be said to be [their] national beverage."

Despite the reported sobriety of immigrant Jews, it still remained that they had their share of social dregs: swindlers and other criminals. Benjamin Antin writes of New York's "poolrooms, . . . gangsters, brothels and cadets . . . of peddlers, battling with the storms and typhoons of life, slaving and paying—to grafters and politicians and gangsters and buying tickets. Tickets for raffles. Tickets for balls. Raffles which never happened and balls where danced citizens of the underworld—all for the right to live and work and slave and sweat."

The dancing academies described by Antin were often hangouts for exploiters—Jews and Christians—who took advantage of the confusion and loneliness experienced by many unmarried immigrant girls. According to New York journalist George Kibbe Turner, these dance halls were "the largest and most profitable field for exploitation of the [Jewish] girls of the East Side . . . in procuring them for the white slave trade." His investigation of the "trade" revealed that on New York's Second Avenue, Jewish cadets—teen-agers who promoted the unsuspecting females into prostitution—actively carried on their business.† Bernheimer noted that prostitution, practically unknown to Jews, made its appearance in Philadelphia. He cautioned that the previous absence "of the Jews from [this social evil] rather overemphasizes [its] spread [in the Jewish community]."

The conditions of slum life in the areas of primary settlement led to other forms of antisocial behavior. "Thirty years ago [1875]," wrote Adam Wiener, "the conviction of a Jew for a felony was almost unheard of in the city of New York. Today [1905] there is not one penal institution within the area . . . which does not harbor some offenders of the Jewish people." According to Wiener, a number of Jews were found awaiting trial at the Tombs Prison, on Ludlow Street; 10 per cent of the inmates at Elmira Reform School were Jewish; at Auburn Prison there were at least a dozen Jewish convicts sentenced for "heinous crimes"; and at Sing Sing approximately 10 per cent of the inmates were Jewish.

The conditions of slum life, which encouraged the increase in crime, took an even greater toll of the children. Indeed, juvenile delinquency among newcomers aroused considerable discussion. The causes of this phenomenon were again largely economic: living conditions were intolerable; parents who worked fourteen hours a day found it impossible to pay adequate attention to the family; and living quarters were often so sparse that many children were driven into the streets to grow up wild. Some of these youngsters, due to the forces of assimilation, found them-

† Many of these cadets were members of the strong East Side political clubs and, according to Turner, were "determined thieves as well." The local politicians protected these youthful criminals when apprehended, as all had, largely through the owners of their special hangouts, direct access to the political machines.

selves in conflict with the Old World traditions of their parents. This widening cultural gap and the subsequent deterioration of parental authority led some into a life of teen-age crime.

Many of these children joined street gangs—a phenomenon endemic to all ghettos. Some of the gangs were self-defense units organized to deter anti-Semitic hoodlums who took pleasure in attacking Jews—especially the elderly and orthodox. According to composer Irving Berlin, on All Saints Day Jews who ventured onto Irish turf were often in danger of being thrown into the East River. Berlin himself almost lost his life as a result of such a "bath."

Other Jewish gangs were formed to engage in criminal activities. Eddie Cantor, described how as a teen-ager he hung out in poolrooms, joined a gang, and "became a gangsters' tool. Who could tell," he pondered in his later years, "by looking at a group of East Side youngsters, which would become a Gyp the Blood or Lefty Louie and which a Marcus Loew or Irving Berlin?"

As a teen-ager, Cantor "sizzled with purposeless energy." He pulled his cap down over his eyes, carried a huge club, and, "looking for all the world like the chief of a gas-house gang," hired himself out as a "guerrilla to guard strike-breakers." Being all for the life of a teen-age tough, he "spat sideways" and carried a gun for a local hoodlum. "If the gun had ever gone off," he wrote, "I'd have gone with it." Yet he was a gang member, and as such, he was often required to crawl between bars and through fanlights in order to gain illegal entrance to the stores of local merchants.

He described his role in a burglary:

> One of the gang's prize loots was a bicycle shop. I was lifted on a big chap's shoulders and slid through the transom over the door. After I unlocked the door, the whole gang mounted bicycles and rode them to 110th Street near Central Park, where the leader assembled the booty and made sure that none of his loyal crew had cheated him. The other youngsters and I were rewarded with a cup of coffee and two doughnuts apiece, and we got a nickel each for carfare home. The distracted storekeeper knew who had committed the theft, but dared not squeal, and the next day the leader came down to see him and sold him back his own stock of bicycles.

Though misdirected Jewish youth caused many a *tsore* (worry) for the hard-working parents, in the final analysis, as Lillian Wald, founder of the Henry Street Settlement, declared, the East Side still produced its share of "judges, teachers, actors, musicians, playwrights, and public leaders."

More indicative of this immigrant community were the bookworms who spent countless hours in the public libraries learning English and reading science, philosophy, economics, and classical literature. According to Carl W. Ackerman, a New York librarian, the Jewish immigrant was much more interested in self-education than in a life of moral turpitude. "His appetite for knowledge," he wrote, "is more insatiate than the seminary student in the university." On one occasion, a deep-eyed, dark-complexioned Russian came to the East Side's Seward Park Library seeking books on advanced chemistry. He had read everything available in the local library, and since he lacked funds to purchase more-advanced books, he requested the librarian's aid in obtaining the literature. His request was similar to those the librarian had frequently heard and because of lack of funding was so often compelled to refuse. She knew the young man, and in an attempt to help him sought the assistance of a chemist from one of the city's largest chemical firms.

In the spirit of adventure, the interested chemist climbed the stairs of a narrow Canal Street tenement and knocked at the attic door. When the Jewish youth admitted him, the chemist stood at the doorway dumfounded. He thought he was calling at the "bunk" of an immigrant. Instead he walked into a shabby but fully equipped laboratory hidden under the rafters of a five-story tenement. Here was a young student who had been banished from Russia because he was a Jew. He had sought political and religious freedom in the United States and did his first work in a sweatshop. From there he went on to a clothing store, and in the evening tutored himself with books from the public library. His meager earnings went for scientific instruments.

Several days later, the student was supplied with the most up-to-date books. He passed his Regents' examinations and was given employment as a professor of chemistry at a Brooklyn, New York, educational institution.

Many families thought of leaving their area of primary settlement and moving to an adjacent area of secondary settlement, across the river to Brooklyn, or the Bronx, or uptown to Harlem, or to the West End of Boston or the South Side of Chicago. With the money they put away and the improvement in inner-city transportation (trolley cars and subways), they could seek out fresh air and trees. They might even move to the comforts of a "spacious" apartment building or a relatively private three-family house, where they might share with others a plot of land called "the back yard."

While most families were still in the dream stages of their semisuburban relocation, the concentration and congestion of the primary settlements went on unabated. Several organizations, led by the United Hebrew Charities and B'nai B'rith, called for suggestions to alleviate the intolerable conditions of the urban communities. In 1901, the Industrial Removal Office (IRO) was established for the purpose of relieving the overcrowded cities of the eastern seaboard by relocating newcomers to the geographic heart of the nation. Agents were dispatched to find employment opportunities; sponsors were sought for the relocated families; and local aid committees were organized to administer the program in the prospective locations.

In Omaha, Nebraska, Esau Fleishman was appointed as the IRO's agent. With the aid of a local committee, he welcomed every trainload of newcomers and assisted them in the transition from their former lifestyles. He was so committed to the program that he often put up families at his own home until suitable accommodations could be found. Not all, however, who came via the relocation scheme remained in the interior. Some, as was expected, found life in these areas poorly suited to their orthodox orientation. Others, lonely for their friends, also expressed a wish to return to the crowded streets of the eastern cities—to their *landleit* (fellow countrymen).

Between 1901 and 1917, the IRO managed to resettle over one hundred thousand people in 1,670 interior locations. In Omaha alone, 2,135 people found new homes. Of course, no program to aid "assisted immigrants" was without its critics. Some rabid restrictionists considered the entire project "a bluff of the Jews and steamship companies to throw dust in the eyes of the ignorant [in order to] prevent proper [legislation against assisted immigrants]." Responding to the charge Cyrus L. Sulzberger, chairman of the IRO, testified before the House Committee on Immigration and Naturalization. In 1910 he asserted that relocated families

> have been distributed to all parts of the United States, towns and villages as well as cities, and according to the records of the [IRO], 85% of the breadwinners are engaged in gainful occupations at the places to which they were sent. These persons are distributed through the cooperation of friendly committees in the receiving places, excepting where the receiving places are small. Where we send a larger number, we have a reception committee to

whom we send these people, not in response to immediate requisition, but from a general knowledge of the conditions as to what kind of working men they can use, and we send such classes of workingmen. . . . These reception committees consist of public-spirited citizens of the Jewish community in the locality, who are interested in the work. They know perfectly well that they are able to place them; otherwise they would not ask us to send them.

Though the IRO's concept worked well, when one considers the total number of Jewish immigrants arriving daily, removal to the interior must be considered a failure. Though East Europeans found their way to such places as Nebraska, Missouri, Michigan, Montana, Wisconsin, North Dakota, and California, over 73.5 per cent who landed at the eastern ports remained. Many of the families that did relocate, either through the IRO or on their own, eventually drifted back toward the cities of the East.

Another attempt by the IRO to settle newcomers in the western states was the "Galveston Plan." This time, the immigrants were not to be landed at the eastern ports but were to be taken directly from Europe to the port of Galveston, Texas where it was anticipated, they could be easily distributed to the sparsely settled areas of the interior. According to Jacob Schiff, a principal promoter of the plan, the Galveston movement represented "an immediate outlet in the next two decades for 2,000,000 of our coreligionists."‡ While the American leadership pressured immigration authorities to establish stations on the Gulf Coast, the European-based Jewish Territorial organization and the Kiev Emigration Society publicized the plan, assumed responsibility for its European organization, and arranged with the North German Lloyd Steamship Company to carry passengers directly from Bremen, Germany, to Galveston, Texas.

The first boatload of immigrants arrived in the summer of 1807. As they departed from the ship, each newcomer received a welcome by Galveston's mayor. In response to the warm greeting, a spokesman for the group declared:

> In our country, Russia, this scene would not be possible. The mayor of our city would take absolutely no notice of us or of any people of our station. You have welcomed us, Mr. Mayor, and we

‡ Israel Zangwill, head of the Jewish Territorial Organization, was instrumental in bringing the concept to Schiff's attention. As a result, Schiff contributed $500,000 to implement the plan.

are grateful. There may be a time when the American people will need us, and then we will serve them with our blood.

Standing alongside the mayor was Morris D. Waldman, who had been dispatched to Galveston to facilitate the distribution of the new-comers. Galveston city officials, for what might be considered selfish reasons, displayed an unusual co-operativeness toward Waldman and his party. The establishment of a receiving station at the port had focused public attention on the little city as an important seaport—a fact that could not be ignored by the local business community. Wald-man and his organization did not care to question the motivations for the aid—Galveston seemed ideal to begin the process of relocation.

> Baltimore was rejected because it was too near New York and we feared a general drift of the immigrants to the metropolis, which in our judgement was already overcrowded, and it was further over-crowding that the Galveston movement sought to check. Charles-ton and Savannah were rejected because the meagre industrial de-velopment of the South afforded no prospects for satisfactory settlement below the Mason and Dixon line. San Francisco was hardly considered because of the great distance from points of ori-gin, combined with the limited industrial opportunities of the Pacific Coast. New Orleans received more consideration as the me-tropolis of the Gulf region and because it was the terminus of sev-eral of the largest railroad trunk lines of the west. It was more remote, however, from the prospective territories of settlement. Moreover, we feared that being a large city, many of the immi-grants might be tempted to remain there and so produce a sudden increase of Jewish population that would prove embarrassing to the city itself and its Jewish community, with resulting distress to the immigrants themselves.

While traveling west by train toward the Texas city, Waldman met a Jewish salesman who, after several minutes of conversation, asked: "Brother, what's your line?" Determined to have some innocent fun with his traveling companion, Waldman suddenly assumed a very mys-terious look. He rose from his seat and drew the curtains closed. After looking around to make sure he would not be overheard, he sat next to the salesman and in a low whisper replied: "I sell Jews." The salesman was startled by the answer and probably "wondered whether he had made the acquaintance of a white-slave trafficker." Waldman assured him that he should not be frightened—that he carried no samples. "If I had, I would surely experience some difficulty in disposing of my merchandise."

Upon arrival, Waldman was met by Rabbi Henry Cohen, who was very excited about the relocation plan. The rabbi "thanked God for this extraordinary privilege of service to his people." Securing the co-operation of the Jewish community was not difficult. As with most of the nation's Jews, the pogroms shocked Texas Jewry and "evoked an overwhelming pity not only for the victims but also for the millions of [coreligionists] who were living under unspeakable conditions then existing in Russia." Yet there was some resistance to the plan, as in the case of one midwestern Jew who had sponsored an immigrant several years prior to the Galveston movement.

This angry Kansas City businessman, who owned the largest shoe-repair shop in his community, had sponsored the resettlement of an immigrant cobbler from New York. He gave the newcomer a job, supplied him living quarters at a reasonable rate, and arranged to have his children sent to school. Ironically, within two years, the newcomer showed his appreciation by opening a shoe-repair shop within a stone's throw of his benefactor. In spite of this experience, the businessman still agreed to co-operate with Waldman in securing living quarters and employment for the relocated immigrants, agreeing only "on the condition that no cobblers would be sent to his town."

The Galveston movement was not as successful as its promoters had anticipated. The depression of 1907 and the subsequent rise in unemployment sparked angry protests by labor leaders and the Department of Labor and Commerce that these particular immigrants were violating the "contract labor law" and taking away employment needed by native Americans. Under pressure from restrictionists, government officials used the depressed economy to renew its campaign against the admission of "assisted immigrants."

In response, Schiff reported that the Galveston newcomers were not public charges but, on the contrary, were vocationally established throughout the West. In a sharp rebuttal of the restrictionists, he warned that

> The damage done by reason of the now hostile attitude . . . is already great, and if this attitude results in the entire breakdown of the Galveston movement, it will end all efforts to deflect immigration from New York and the North Atlantic seaport towns, which . . . is the sole purpose of the work which is being done in Galveston.

In the period between 1907 and 1912, the Galveston movement aided the immigration of five thousand people and at the cost of $150,000 managed to resettle these immigrants throughout the interior of the nation. By the outbreak of World War I, the number of these "assisted immigrants" reached ten thousand.

The opening of hostilities on the European battlefields in August 1914 brought to an end, as it did all immigration, the shipment of Jews to Galveston. The growing conflict between the forces of restrictionism and those who advocated "interior settlement" was temporarily abated. After the European peace was restored, in 1919, however, racist restrictionism appeared once more. Nativist sentiment, coupled with the fear of an alien tide from war-torn Europe, managed to capture the imagination of the United States Congress. In the early 1920s, Congress established immigration quotas that reduced to a mere trickle the number of Jews and others from Southern and Eastern Europe arriving in America.* For the most part, the days of Jewish immigration were over.

THE RURAL EXPERIENCE

As part of their program to relocate refugees in the interior, Jewish spokesmen suggested the establishment of agricultural co-operatives. This concept was not new. Throughout the nineteenth century, several such projects were initiated: Mordecai M. Noah had conceived of Ararat, William Renau founded a colony of Jews near Chicago, and Moses Cohen established the Shalom Colony in Ulster County, New York. In the 1840s, Julius Stern called for a Jewish "agricultural district" in the Mississippi Valley, and in the following decade, B'nai B'rith proposed the foundation of a Hebrew Agricultural Society.

When Jacob Schiff and Michael Heilprin recommended co-operative farms as an alternative to urban settlement, they were simply following a precedent of earlier American Jewry. Between 1881 and 1914, agricultural colonies appeared in such far-flung places as Louisiana, the Dakotas, Oregon, Colorado, New Jersey, Wisconsin, Utah, Arkansas, and Tennessee.

While Jewish leaders pondered the possibility of agricultural colonies, there were at the same time two East European organizations, *Bilu*

* The story of the fight against immigration restriction is discussed in Chapter V.

("House of Jacob, let us go!") and *Am Olam* ("The Eternal People"), that coupled their emigration from Europe to the founding of agricultural communities. The *Bilu* movement was motivated by Zionism and directed its activities toward Palestine, while *Am Olam,* headed by Moses Herder and Manya Bakal, aimed in the direction of America. *Am Olam* expounded self-reliance and urged its followers not to depend upon the aid of philanthropic organizations but to reach their goals by means of their own endeavors.

Though most American Jews appreciated the self-reliance displayed by *Am Olam,* the leaders of the various aid societies would not be denied the opportunity to render their assistance in the establishment of these agrarian projects. Ironically, in response to *Am Olam*'s determined effort at independence, Jewish agricultural societies were established in Philadelphia, Chicago, New York, and New Orleans. Together with these organizations came advice: the Hebrew Emigrant Aid Society willingly supported the projects but announced that "no colony should be organized in a communistic or cooperative plan" and Julius Ochs asserted that help should be given only to those who were familiar with "the American way of farming."

Joining those who advocated the "agricultural way" was Isaac M. Wise, who urged support for Jewish settlement upon government land. "They must be," he wrote, "supported to enable them to settle down on the land and protect their families . . . till they can help themselves. Send the funds," he exhorted,

> and you will be astonished how fast we will settle on government land every able-bodied Russian immigrant. We think that the long-deferred project of teaching our people agricultural pursuits can now be speedily realized, and the problems of what to do with the Russian can at once be solved.

A committee of New York rabbis issued a similar appeal:

> We say to you, never in the history of American Judaism has such an opportunity as this been afforded to promote the welfare of our brethren and the advancement of the best interests and the glory of our eminent faith. Here are the means to refute the oft-muttered calumny that our people are unfitted by habit, nature and sentiment for honest toil.
>
> . . . in colonizing them and settling them as agriculturalists, we feel, therefore, every moral assurance that they will become worthy

citizens repaying the protection and rights they receive, by becoming faithful and loyal denizens of the soil . . .

In the 1880s, members of *Am Olam* emigrated to America and established colonies at Sicily Island, Louisiana; Crémieux, South Dakota; and New Odessa, Oregon. HEAS helped settle refugees at Alliance, Carmel, and Rosenhaym in New Jersey and at Cotopaxi, Colorado. The Baron de Hirsch Fund also established the Woodbine colony in New Jersey and was the financial and organizational inspiration behind the Jewish Colonization Society, the Baron de Hirsch Agricultural School,† and the Jewish Agricultural and Industrial Society. The fund also provided scholarships for promising horticulturalists, subsidized the publication of *The Jewish Farmer,*‡ and contributed to the support of several agricultural settlements. Even the Yiddish press supported the movement toward the soil. In 1914, *The Morning Journal* (New York) declared that the American Jewish farmer was more "similar to the small nobleman of our old home rather than to the degraded and oppressed peasants."

The first colony to appear in this decade was founded by Herman Rosenthal and a group of *Am Olam* members on Sicily Island. With three thousand dollars of their own and an additional $4,600 contributed by European and American agencies, Rosenthal led 160 families from Kiev and Yelisanetgrad (Russia) to "twenty-eight hundred acres, situated . . . three hundred and fifty miles from New Orleans, and seventy-five miles from Natchez, Mississippi." According to the president of HEAS, Sicily Island, which could be reached only by way of the Mississippi and Ouachita rivers, was an ideal location: "This land is rich and is not subject to overflow [of the Mississippi River]. It is in the vicinity of several thriving towns, but New Orleans is its best market, which can be reached by boat within forty-eight hours." His optimistic description was encouraging: "[Sicily Island] is regarded healthy. The temperature rarely ever rises above 90° in summer and seldom falls below freezing in winter. The winters are generally mild enough to admit of good gardens. . . ."

Soon after the publication of this statement, the respective settlers arrived in New Orleans. After a brief stay, the men bade farewell to their families (women and children stayed behind until housing could be

---

† The first Jewish agricultural school in the United States.
‡ A Yiddish newspaper. In time, the journal was published in both Yiddish and English.

built) and departed for the island. Upon arrival, the newcomers were greeted by the "islanders" and, in a display of brotherhood, were assured of their co-operation. At a special meeting held by the natives of the island, the following resolutions were adopted:

> . . . [we] hereby extend a cordial invitation to these persecuted people to settle in our midst; and that we heartily favor the immigration of all honest, industrious, and peaceful citizens, irrespective of clime or creed, knowing that they will greatly assist us in developing the untold riches of the country.
>
> . . . Further, that we shall do all in our power to assist them in making a happy home with us, and that we will extend them every facility and protection in our power.

In anticipation of rejoining their loved ones, the colonists set about to dig wells, erect buildings, repair roads, and plant crops. They organized a government and wrote a constitution, much of which testified to the communal nature of the joint venture: "All lands, farming utensils, implements, stock and furniture," it stipulated, "shall remain the property of the . . . colony."

Initially things went well, and though most of the newcomers detested the climate, they expressed satisfaction with their progress. Some even sent word to Europe urging their friends and relatives to join them. One such communication appeared in the pages of *Russki Yevrei* (St. Petersburg):

> We have organized ourselves into a society and have written a constitution and by-laws. . . . Our wives and children will remain in New Orleans until we build houses on the land in which they will dwell. All of our necessities, agricultural implements, horses and mules and provisions which we need until the harvest season have been given to us on credit. There is no winter here. Trees blossom all year around.

Soon after this letter was written, the colony was plagued by a multitude of setbacks. As spring approached, the heat became unbearable, many expressed disappointment that their families still remained in New Orleans, all complained about the shortage of drinking water, and many were stricken with malaria. To make matters worse, the Mississippi River broke its levees and flooded almost everything that had been built or cultivated during the initial settlement. Expressing his discouragement, one colonist wrote:

We left for the colony with high hopes, but after having spent a few months here, we found conditions unbearable. The heat affected most of the colonists, and malaria has stricken the women and children.

Other communications appeared in the European Jewish press that reflected the general discontent of the refugees. In 1883, *Ha-Melitz* reported:

. . . it is impossible for a person to live in this territory; as even emancipated slaves steered clear of it since the land abounded in swamps and marshes and was three days journey from a city. Eight months out of the year the climate is so hot that the thermometer rises above blood heat, during which time there is the stench of the swamps and the bodies of animals and birds dead from the bites of snakes and scorpions that abound here.

In such a devastating place the first colony for Russian refugees was established. For eight months the colonists worked on the fields, plowing and harrowing the soil and chopping down the trees. Then the terrible weather came upon them. Many became ill with fever and too weak to work. One by one, they left the settlement, all their labor in vain and their hopes crushed. Some, however, refused to abandon their agricultural dream so easily and, under the leadership of Rosenthal, headed for the Dakotas to establish still another colony. The most poetic summation of the Sicily Island experience was written by A. Peissokovitch, secretary of the colony: "Work—mostly useless, hope, despair, love, song, poetry, happiness and misery—life as we lived it there in Louisiana."

In the pattern of Sicily Island, the refugees established several colonies in the Dakotas. Again, unfavorable conditions, poor choice of location, and lack of funds dictated their failure. At Painted Woods, one disaster after another prevented the colony from becoming successful. Hard winters, crop failure, and an emerging anti-Semitic atmosphere sealed its doom. Similar conditions plagued the Jewish farmer throughout the Dakotas. At the Iola settlement, one observer witnessed barefoot children trying to keep warm burning dried manure. "When [the settlers] threshed," reported David Rubin, "they slept in the straw piles, and drank slough water, and they decided almost anything would be better than farming, so they left." Again, at Bethlehem

Yehudah, poor harvests and an empty treasury caused the colony to liquidate in 1885.

At Crémieux*, where Herman Rosenthal and some of the Sicily Island people had resettled, the farmers were beset with difficulties from the start. Water had to be hauled over long distances, underground springs were too deep to afford easily dug wells, and prairie fires played havoc with the crops. During the first winter, the weather was so severe that some people used ropes, one end tied to a doorpost and the other end tied around their waists, "to prevent losing themselves in the blinding sheets of ice and snow." Once again, Jews failed to sustain their agricultural way of life.

Unlike the private ownership which characterized Crémieux, the colony at New Odessa, Oregon, was established on socialistic principles. Due to its communal orientation, the colony provoked a great deal of comment. One of the foremost critics was Dr. Judah Wechsler, the founder of Bethlehem Yehudah:

> While there is unity in their midst and may it be forever, nevertheless turth to tell, a communistic colony is not able to succeed. As long as they follow this policy there is no hope for permanent existence. So I told them openly and did not hide my words of despair.
>
> I asked them about their religious faith and whether they observe the Torah of Israel. Their replies made me sad. . . . They do not observe the Sabbath. They desecrate the Holidays and they told me directly that they are completely disinterested in Judaism.
>
> I continued to talk to them that it is their responsibility to remain true to their people Israel—but I doubt very much whether my words penetrated their hearts. . . . if it were not for their communistic and religious ideas, . . . these colonists would have a prosperous future in store, [but] I regret exceedingly that this otherwise intelligent community holds not steadfast to the principles which are generally accepted, and are led astray by many views which sooner or later will be an obstacle in their way to promote their welfare.

For several years, New Odessa worked to build a utopian society. In the end, however, it failed. Like the others, it was plagued by financial reverses, natural disaster, and most important, internal ideological

* The colony was named in honor of Adolphe Crémieux, president of the Alliance Israélite Universelle. Unlike the other Dakota projects, Crémieux was not a co-operative; farms were privately owned.

conflict. The colony was abandoned, and with empty buildings left as a remembrance, the project drifted into history.

The tiny village of Cotopaxi, Colorado, contained several stores, a small hotel, and a railroad station. At this site, one of the most disastrous attempts at colonization, Jewish or otherwise, took place. The moving force behind the Cotopaxi project was Emanuel H. Saltiel, owner of the Cotopaxi Silver Mine and president of the Cotopaxi Town Company. In an effort to bring Jewish settlers to the town, Saltiel contacted HEAS officials and convinced the society of the advantages of establishing a colony upon the fertile lands of the Wet Mountain Valley. "Here," he said, "a family could become self-supporting in no time at all." Impressed by his glowing report and encouraged by his enthusiastic presentation, HEAS gave him ten thousand dollars with which to found a colony.

Sixteen families, sixty-three people in all, arrived at Saltiel's "paradise." Their hopes, however, soon faded as they quickly realized that Saltiel not only exaggerated but lied about conditions in the region. Instead of possessing fertile land, the site was a barren desert. According to Idel Grimes, a seventeen-year-old settler, "it was the poorest place in the world for farming, poor land, lots of rocks and no water. . . ." Simply stated, Saltiel's proposal masked a swindle. There were no tools and no seed, and the houses that were to shelter the settlers were poorly built and without furniture. To make matters worse, the land was laden with stones, dry as desert sand, and separated from the fertile Wet Mountain Valley by a mountain range two thousand feet high. With only two plows for the entire community and no way of irrigating the soil, the colony was doomed from its inception. Saltiel and his partner, Julius Schwartz, had no intention of developing an agricultural settlement.

Yet the colonists remained, and in the initial months tried their best to cultivate the land. The most common question heard was "How do we feed our families?" One settler, Zedak, a carpenter from Kiev, managed to grow a few potatoes for his wife and four sons. Most of the others were unsuccessful with the land. A few of the men abandoned the soil and sought employment at Saltiel's silver mine. They walked four miles to and from work and earned $1.50 a day, all of which was shared by the starving families; the colony barely survived. According to the Denver *Jewish News,* Saltiel, for no apparent reason, fired these workers and forced them to find work in Salida and Monarch Pass cutting logs and digging ditches for the Denver and Rio Grande Railroad.

As winter set in, conditions at Cotopaxi became worse. Food and clothing were scarce, medical care was non-existent, and the hastily erected shacks provided little protection against the bitter winds and severe blizzards. The repeated appeals to Saltiel, a coreligionist, were answered with repeated indifference. Unable to endure the sight of his suffering family any longer, Bezald Pregant, a Polish refugee, met with Saltiel. With tears in his eyes, he pleaded for the freezing women and children. "Please," he begged, "give these people the provisions provided by [HEAS] for their needs." Saltiel listened patiently and, after several minutes, shrugged his shoulders and walked away.

The colonists dispatched David Korpitzky and Boruch Millstein to Denver to apprise the Jewish community of the situation at the colony. Upon hearing the news, an indignant Denver Jewry immediately collected five hundred dollars and a large amount of clothing for the refugees. They sent two agents, L. Witowsky and George Kohn, to investigate the conditions described by Korpitzky and Millstein, and after a short visit to Cotopaxi, the Denver investigators informed HEAS of the suffering:

> We are a loss to account for the sum of the $8,750 said to have been expended [by Saltiel and Schwartz] up to October 23, 1882. We can assure you that the New York Society, and therefore the refugees, have paid more than twice as much for what they received as an honest administration of the fund would warrant. In conclusion we could earnestly recommend that immediate relief in the shape of clothing and provisions be at once and without delay sent to the colony and that some means be immediately devised for the care and treatment of the sick and those about to be confined. And we recommend to the Hebrew Emigrant Aid Society of the United States the immediate removal of the colony to some other place.

As a follow-up, HEAS dispatched Morris Tusker, who, after conducting his own investigation, informed his superiors "that Mr. Saltiel used the money put in his hand for his own purpose." Almost immediately, HEAS provided each family with one hundred dollars, relocated them to other regions, and terminated the colony. Some of the refugees remained in Colorado, while others began again in the Dakotas and California. Samuel Shadsky was so disillusioned that he and his family returned to Russia.

Though Cotopaxi was a disaster, similar projects sprang up throughout the nation. Late in 1882, one hundred and fifty *Am Olam* members founded the Arkansas colony; still others established colonies at Beer Sheba, Montefiore, Lasker, Hebron, Gilead, Touro, and Lesser, in Kansas.

The best known of the Kansas settlements was Beer Sheba. Initiated by Cincinnati's Hebrew Union Agricultural Society, the colony was hailed as a new chapter in the history of the Jewish people. "If the colony succeeds," wrote Isaac M. Wise, "it will open the way for thousands of families to follow [its] example." With the aid of Cincinnati Jewry, on August 10, 1882, sixty colonists left for Kansas City and their new homesteads on the Great Plains. Unlike the experience at Cotopaxi, these particular settlers received everything that was promised. Food was provided, supplies and tools were made available, and housing was built to shelter the newcomers. Even a schoolhouse, which also served as a synagogue, was erected. A teacher was hired to instruct the adults at night and the children during the day. Beer Sheba was on its way to becoming a successful experiment.

One year after the colony was founded, M. H. Marks, in company with Max Isaacs, visited Beer Sheba and in a report to Moritz Loth, president of Cincinnati's Hebrew Union Agricultural Society, described the progress of the settlement. When the two men arrived in Kansas City, the first person they met was a Jewish merchant who, though he had no firsthand knowledge, claimed that the colony was a failure. "Nothing could be raised" where the colony was located, he said. The merchant reported that the settlers "were all running off and becoming a burden to Kansas City."

Not discouraged by this information, the two investigators called at the same merchant's store to meet with three families who had indeed abandoned the colony. The deserters were Messrs. Zukerwasser, Liebersohn, and Gidanzki. Surprisingly, all three asked Marks to help them return to their farms. They had no money and were stranded. "Mrs. Gidanzki begged us," wrote Marks, "with tears streaming down her cheeks, to take them along." Though moved by the appeal, Marks told the group that the society had a definite policy of not helping deserters and that they would have to find an alternative way of returning. As he left the store, Marks turned to his companion and said that he was confident that the three families would return on their own to "reclaim their land and become farmers without our assistance."

Upon arrival at Cimarron, Kansas, the two agents hired a team to drive them the twenty-six miles to the colony. Before boarding, they were introduced to "young Cohn," the son of one of the colonists, who worked on the Santa Fe Railroad. Though he earned only $1.30 a day, Cohn's ambition was to save enough money to buy five cows and start a cattle ranch of his own. The youngster's enthusiasm raised Marks's hopes that the "Kansas refugees" were taking to the land.

After a tedious four-hour drive over a dusty prairie, Marks and Isaacs arrived at their destination. After meeting Beer Sheba's superintendent, Mr. Baum, the two men "had the pleasure . . . to lodge in a [Jewish] settlers mansion—a dugout." In the morning, they began their investigation:

> The colony consists of eleven families, fifty-nine persons in all, of which thirty-six are children, and one a single or rather unmarried young man. Each family owns one hundred and sixty acres of land, upon which they have built a dwelling (a dugout). The majority are now building additions, such as kitchens, alcoves, etc. Each house has a well with good water. The houses are kept clean, and are all nicely whitened with whitewash, some even making attempts to decorate the interior with bric-a-brac and such fixings as only ladies know the names of. . . .

> The eleven families live on an area of land covering six miles, that is the first settler lives six miles from the last, the first being Mr. David Klein . . . with his happy family of six children. The last settler is Mr. Schwartzman, a Russian refugee with five children. One of Mr. Schwartzman's daughters was married to the son of Mr. Cohn (not the one previously mentioned). This was the first wedding in the colony.

Everyone was in good health. "Not a single case of sickness," reported Marks. At the time of the visit, the settlers were engaged in collecting fuel for the coming winter. Since there was little wood in the region, the fuel consisted of cow manure obtained from the nearby Texas cattle trail. Though coal was available, Marks declared that its cost was so high "as to make it an article of luxury out of the question for the new settlers. The refuse, however, furnished a good article of fuel, answering every purpose for cooking and heating, and . . . they are engaged in laying in their winter supply just as we do our coal."

While sitting in the dugout writing his report, Marks pondered the question "Can Jews become successful farmers?" His experience at Beer Sheba led him to believe that Jews "can become again that which, according to tradition, they have been before, an agricultural people." This, he asserted, "is established beyond reasonable doubt. There may have been failure of other colonies, but has it ever been properly investigated whether the failure was due more to the originators or to the farmers?"

Despite Marks's optimistic conclusions, Beer Sheba failed. By 1884, conditions had turned for the worse: internal strife ripped through the community, insufficient funds plagued the managers, and dry spells, cold winters, and hot summers ruined the crops. Like the other Kansas projects, the colony was abandoned. After deserting their land, some settlers borrowed on their farms to start again elsewhere, while others sought employment in the immediate vicinity. Most, however, simply drifted toward other sections of the nation.

To this decade also belong the agricultural projects established in New Jersey: Alliance was founded by the Alliance Israélite Universelle, Carmel by the Montefiore Agricultural Society; Rosenhaym by the Hebrew Emigrant Aid Society, Woodbine by the Baron de Hirsch Fund, and Mitzpah by the Mitzpah Agricultural and Industrial Company. Similarly, Montefiore, Riga, and Ziontown, all of a very short duration, were settled on the Jersey landscape.

In 1882, the Alliance Israélite Universelle, in co-operation with HEAS, sought to bring Jewish farmers to New Jersey. Hearing of the project, the Leach brothers offered HEAS an opportunity to purchase their property: an area situated several miles from Vineland and quite close to railroad transportation and the markets of New York and Philadelphia. According to *The American Hebrew,* the location was ideal: "The advantage for these new settlers consists in the fact that they [will be] able to produce in their second and third year, so that beyond the first labor of getting the trees and vines, no further skill or work is necessary than is required in keeping the soil fresh and free from weeds."

In 1882 the land was acquired, and one year later, under the direction of A. C. Steinberg, a Connecticut farmer, the colony had over fifty producing farms. In order to provide employment and supplement income, the colony also established shirt, cigar, and clothing factories. The initial success of the project was welcomed by all. *The American Hebrew* declared that "a glance at the colony would suffice to remove the slightest shadow of doubt into the bright prospect of the greatest Jewish colony in the world. . . . The success at the Alliance colony is a retort to those who say that the Russians are not fit for colonization." This optimistic outlook was followed by a very favorable report by the manager:

Nearly all the adult males are employed in agricultural pursuits, which are conducted so as to illustrate the methods employed in the United States in developing virgin soil. Some of the men who are expert handicraftsmen we have employed at their respective trades. . . . Most of the women having large families of young children to care for are engaged in domestic avocations. . . . I take pleasure in announcing the satisfactory hygienic condition of the colony. . . . We have not now, nor have we had, a single case of serious sickness. . . . In consequence of the greatest opinion so confidently expressed in many quarters that the Jew would never make an agriculturalist . . . it is with the highest pleasure here, that during my work as a practical farmer, I have rarely found beginners who have proved pupils more apt than the refugees.

A colonist added his voice:

I had the privilege of being one of the men to settle in the Alliance colony. . . . Our thought was to live in the open. . . . We desired to be dependent for our living on Mother Earth . . . we wanted to live a healthy life. . . . Our goal was to own a home and be faithful citizens of our adopted country. . . .

Our farms were cleared and we mastered the rudiments of farming by bitter and most trying experience. . . . our children had to walk a long distance to a school. Finally, we managed to build our own schoolhouse. We inaugurated a Sabbath school, we established a library. Now we have a dramatic club, and we arrange periodic library and social meetings which excel in interest and content. Our colony can be termed a real success.

Alliance, which lasted until 1908, was a success.† These farmers, as well as other New Jersey colonists, were still tilling the soil in the third decade of the twentieth century. During those years, however, the concept of co-operative agriculture was abandoned in favor of individual ownership and operation. One original settler observed the changes:

Today, in 1932, as we "old timers" return [we find] the landscape presents a vast change. The old farmsteads are no more . . . in their places have sprung up many small poultry farms . . . the houses are modern in every sense of the word, and a majority of the residents are perhaps as much urban-minded as are those of later generations who migrated to the cities.

Some of the descendants of the original New Jersey settlers are still producing agricultural products for the eastern metropolitan markets.

† In 1908 the colony was taken over by the Jewish Agricultural Society. The primary objective of the society was to encourage self-reliance and individual ownership.

Others, primarily those who established farms in the Catskill Mountains region of New York successfully converted their holdings into vacation resorts. Grossinger's Hotel was once a dilapidated farmstead. Purchased by Selig Grossinger for $450, the property, with the aid of Harry and Jenny Grossinger, was turned into one of the nation's leading vacation playgrounds. The conversion of some of these farms was an outgrowth of the "summer boarder" phenomenon. In many cases crops failed, livestock died, and poultry products found dwindling markets. Often, these particular farmers expended more money in producing a crop than it was worth in the market place, so some enterprising farmers provided space for vacationers. "If it had not been for the revenue derived from the summer boarders," declared the United States Immigration Commission in 1911, "it [would have been] scarcely probable that the Hebrew [farmers] could have retained their farms. . . ."

Except for the settlements in New Jersey,‡ all the Jewish agricultural colonies in America failed. On Sicily Island it was the ravage of flood, in Arkansas it was disease, at Bethlehem Yehudah and Crémieux it was an inhospitable climate and prairie fire, at Cotopaxi it was aridity and corruption, and at New Odessa it was ideological conflict and drought. Just as important, these projects had been hastily organized and poorly planned. All were in unfavorable geographic areas, all were underfunded, and many were settled by people who, in addition to having little farming experience, also harbored conflicting ideological beliefs. The Jewish colonist had no aversion to the soil; on the contrary he tended to idealize it. These settlements, however, came at a time when all American agriculture was in an economic decline. As a result of the nation's urban and industrial revolution, these several decades are characterized by rural abandonment in favor of the opportunities of urban life. In spite of the motivation of the settlers and of their philanthropic benefactors, these projects were destined to fail.*

‡ According to most sources, these colonies survived only because they were turned from collective into individual ownership. These farms were situated near large metropolitan areas and were thus able to sell their products more readily. Consequently, New Jersey managed to retain a few of its Jewish agriculturalists.

* To discuss each of the agricultural colonies is of course pointless; reasons for settlement were the same, conditions of life were similar, and most of their outcomes tell parallel stories. Mention should be made of the minor and thus lesser known communities established in the decades that encompassed the 1880s to the 1930s. They were Carp Lake, Michigan, 1882; Washington, D.C., 1883; Water View, Virginia, 1886; the Palestine Colony at Bad Axe, Michigan, 1891; Hebrew Colonial Society, Maryland, 1903;

"MAKING A LIVING"—PUSHCARTS AND PEDDLERS

Once the newcomers were settled, their initial concern centered on earning a living. Almost anything would do in order to provide food and shelter.† "With very few exceptions," wrote Dr. George Price, a New York City health inspector, "the immigrants did not find work which they wanted or for which they were suited." Skill, inclination, or desire was by neccessity put aside in favor of a weekly salary. "Everyone," he noted, "grabbed the type of job he could get, and changed it very often." One day the "greener" was a shoemaker, the next day a garment worker, and the following week a day laborer; later, a cigar maker, and so on ad infinitum. Price himself followed this familiar pattern:

> I worked in the following factories,—basket platting, chair factory, shirt factory, paper-collar and paper-fabrics,—and in a boiler factory. I also was a ditch digger, a farm hand, a conductor on a railroad, an owner of a grocery store, a bank clerk, a medical student, a health inspector, a superintendent of a house, a school teacher, an editor of a weekly newspaper and finally a contributor to a number of American newspapers.

"As you can see," he declared, "my occupations varied, but I know many who even had to change their occupations more often than I did."

Arpin, Wisconsin, 1904; Flora, Illinois, 1908; the Clarion Colony, Utah, 1910; Bay Minette, Alabama, 1912; The Ida Straus Colony, Georgia, 1915; and the Jingo Colony, Tennessee, 1916.

Other settlements not entirely devoted to agriculture but more concerned with a co-operative life-style were also established. Among them were The Fellowship, 1912, and Ferrer, 1914, at Shelton, New Jersey; the Chatham and Harmonia colonies, New Jersey, 1923; and the Mohegan Colony, near Peekskill, New York, 1925. Also, in the 1930s, the Jewish community witnessed the creation of the Sun Rise Cooperative Farm, near Saginaw, Michigan, which drew its settlers from the ranks of the urban radical community and was conceived as a collectivist community, and in that same year, a similar experiment known as the Jersey Homesteads, Inc.

† The average immigrant family of the 1880s landed with approximately $20 in their pockets. Some even arrived penniless. Those without funds were often the *luftmenschen* (people of the air), who, in their former homelands, possessed no skill or visible means of support. Accoring to one observer, the *luftmensch* lived "from hand to mouth [and as a] petty merchant, broker, [and] commission-man all rolled into one, [ran] from client to client, from shop to shop, like a wild animal hunting for a bite of food."

One such newcomer who was denied the opportunity to follow his desire was garment manufacturer Bernard Baum. As a fourteen-year-old immigrant, the youngster had expressed a wish to obtain an education; instead he entered the needle trades. "Before I could fill my lungs with free, American air," he remarked. "I found myself in a blouse factory." At the Yale Waist Company, young Baum put aside his quest for schooling and joined the ranks of the working class.

Three months later he became a "helper" at the notorious Triangle Shirt-Waist Company. There, with speed and diligence, he "sewed backs together" while trying "to find favor in the eyes of the foreman." Though he earned a meager salary, he still managed to periodically send a small sum to his father; and each time he mailed the bank-draft, he was reminded of his promise "to remain a pious Jew and to continue [his] studies. . . ."

His desire for formal education subsided, "for the new conditions," he wrote, "compelled me to turn in a different direction, to study the language of my new country and the harsh aphorism of *help yourself.*" His "mind, . . . dulled from being amidst the tumult, noise, and confusion, toil and sweat, of the sweatshop," he continued to work "for sixty and even seventy hours a week."

Another newcomer who "fell prey" to the exploitation of the American economy was Anzia Yezierska. She did not immediately enter the garment industry—she managed to acquire a position as a domestic with an assimilated Jewish family. These people were "so successful," she wrote, "that they were [even] ashamed to remember their mother tongue."

"What were to be my wages?" she timidly asked the well-dressed couple. Suddenly silence filled the room as the faces of her employers turned grim. "Was it so low for me to talk of wages?" she thought. "Maybe they're so high up in well-being they can't any more understand my low thoughts for money." Angered by the mention of money, the man stared at the servant-girl and exclaimed that she "must not be so grabbing for wages!" that she should instead be thankful "to associate with Americans." The wife assured Anzia that the position guaranteed a summer vacation in the country and that working in their household would be a wonderful opportunity "to become an American." Made to feel ashamed and ungrateful, the youngster dismissed her thoughts about money and began her "life in the sunshine."

When it was time to be paid, Yezierska "trembled breathlessly for the minute [she'd] get [her] wages. . . . Like a hungry cat rubbing up to its boss for meat, so I edged and simpered around them as I passed the food. Without my will, like a beggar, my hand reached out to them." Yet, still no wages were offered. *"Gottuniu!* [my God]," she thought, "maybe they forgot." *"Oi veh!* The money—my money—my wages!" she finally cried out.

With this scream, the husband turned toward the panicky girl and shouted:

> Wages? Money? . . . Haven't you a comfortable bed to sleep, and three good meals a day? You're only a month here. Just came to America. And you already think about money. Wait till you're worth any money. What use are you without knowing English? You should be glad we keep you. Other girls pay money yet to be in the country.

Shocked by his outburst, Anzia was lost for words. Even her tears, which she wanted to shed, remained dry. Not a dollar for her labor; she left and found employment in a sweatshop. "For a long, long time the thought of ever working in an American family made me tremble with fear. No—never again would I trust myself to an American family, no matter how fine their language and how sweet their smile."

Others were also exploited. Even their coreligionists took advantage of the newcomers' helplessness and ignorance. "Sometimes," wrote one observer, "so-called Jewish philanthropists" used the greenhorns in their own shops and factories: "they were exploited mercilessly," charged George Price, "[they] even forced them to work for a third or fourth of the standard wage and treated them like beggars and dogs." In one such instance Price described how one hundred families were sent to Brooklyn under the pretext that they would be taught a trade and employed in a chair factory. Though their work was satisfactory, they nevertheless received "dog kennels" to sleep in and "rotten food" to eat. The hunger strike that followed captured the attention of New York's Jewish community.

In spite of the exploitation, which appears to have greeted all immigrants, the East Europeans still managed to acquire gainful employment in a variety of occupations. At the turn of the century, three of five were employed in manufacturing, particularly the garment trades, a fifth were in retail trade (storekeepers) and approximately one tenth entered clerical and professional positions. Jews became cigar makers, butchers, and painters. A few remained as day laborers, and almost one out of a hundred made their living at some sort of peddling.

Many of them found a living in New York's *Khazermark* (pig market).‡ "Thursday night and Friday morning," wrote Jacob Riis, "[were] bargain days in the Pig-market." Concentrated on Hester Street, the market offered, at extremely reasonable prices, anything that could be sold from pushcarts: "Bandannas and tin cups at two cents, peaches at a cent a quart, damaged eggs for a song, hats for a quarter, and spectacles . . . at the optician's who has opened shop on a Hester Street door-step, for thirty-five cents; frowsey-looking chickens and half-plucked geese . . . are the great staple of the market. Half or a quarter of a chicken can be bought here by those who cannot afford a whole."

Among the rows of pushcarts one could see a woman churning horse-radish on a machine she has chained to a tree "lest someone steal it [and] beside her a butcher's stand with cuts at prices the avenues never dreamed of." Coats were hawked for fifty cents "as good as new" and pants "at any price offered." Also, there were the peddlers, the ever-present peddlers, calling to the potential buyers and grabbing the arms of possible customers:

> Yes, stop! . . . for this pair [of pants] thirty cents [calls the customer]; a dollar and forty was the price asked. The peddler shrugs his shoulders, and turns up his hands with a half pitying, wholly indignant air. What does [the buyer] take him for? Such pants—. The [customer] has turned to go. With a jump like a panther's, the man with the pants has him by the sleeve. Will he give eighty cents? Sixty? Fifty? So help him, they are dirt cheap at that. . . . the [buyer] takes them and goes, well knowing that at least twenty cents of the thirty, two hundred percent, were clear profit. . . .

As the day stretches on, the people jostle each other at the carts and sidewalk shops, "where a plank on two ash-barrels serves as a counter. Pushing, struggling, . . . and shouting in foreign tongues," the bargaining goes on. Suddenly, in the middle of the "organized chaos" there is a scattering of people, a hustling of goods from the street into cellars, into yards, a slamming and locking of doors hidden under the improvised shelves and counters. "The health officer is coming!" shouts one of the street vendors. Once the feared official and his crew have finished shoveling up "the eatables"—the musty bread, decayed fish, and stale vegetables—they leave. Indifferent to the curses shouted from the stoops and windows, they vanish as quickly as they appeared. Once more it is safe,

‡ The name given to the area was derisory, for pork was one item that was not sold in the market.

and the peddlers again emerge frm the doorways and cellars to continue the street trade.

Good jobs were difficult to find—especially for those who came with little or no skill. Boris Bogen arrived in the United States penniless. He tried to find steady work but with his halting English, lack of training, and "bewildered look that betrayed the greenhorn," he was unsuccessful. In the midst of his search he received a letter from Uncle Matvey offering him a position at a Baltimore furniture factory. This was his chance to escape ending up in a sweatshop. Bogen relocated in Baltimore.

"When you go for the job," cautioned Uncle Matvey, "don't, whatever you do, act like a greenhorn. Say you are experienced in this line. That is [a] bluff. In America one gets along like that." So Bogen assured the factory owner that he was an experienced furniture finisher and went to work that very same day.

As his first task he was sent to the basement, where they stored newly built sideboards: "Take it up to the second floor and varnish it," ordered the foreman. He seized the sideboard with a powerful grip and, "staggering, tugging, and pushing," got it to the first floor. Triumphant in his effort, he was nevertheless exhausted, but he dared not stop to rest, for looking at him was "someone with an air of authority." Once again he "took hold of the monster" and resumed the climb. At last he reached the top. While congratulating himself on the accomplishment, he unfortunately relaxed his grip and watched the sideboard go crashing down the stairs. "I ran after it," he exclaimed, "with some desperate notion of beating it to the bottom and breaking its fall." The race, however, ended in a tie; the sideboard was wrecked and Bogen was terrified.

After examining the shattered remains, the owner informed Bogen that as a finisher he was finished. Once more, the unskilled immigrant was walking the streets of an American city looking for work. While doing so, he made up his mind that he would postpone any future bluffing until he had become "more of an American and had improved [his] technique."

Jacob Cash's assault on the American economy met with greater success than his less fortunate, furniture-finishing coreligionist. Impressed by the commercial opportunities of New York, Cash left Philadelphia to take up residence on the Lower East Side. After several weeks of exploring the possible avenues of success, he became convinced that the phonograph would become the mainstay of the home-entertainment industry. He joined the Columbia Gramophone Company on a commission basis, rented a store to display his products, and waited for the greenhorns to knock down his doors.

Few people ventured into his establishment, and in order to attract business, he hired a youngster to "watch" the store while he made a house-to-house canvass of the neighborhood. Trying to convince his customers that they needed this form of entertainment, he borrowed the popular slogan "What is a home without a piano?" and changed it to "What is a home without a phonograph?" Still no business, for though Jews were willing to purchase the machine, they claimed that they had nothing to listen to—they wanted their own music.

Suddenly Cash realized how he could turn his failing business into a success. Whenever anyone told him he would buy a machine if there were Jewish records, he took him to the store, placed a blank cylinder in the reproducer, and sang a Yiddish song into the horn. "Then I let him listen to the song I recorded," he wrote, "and the delighted customer would buy the phonograph and order records."

Cash's reputation spread throughout the Jewish community. He no longer had to go out to seek customers; they now came to him. All he had to do was put on a recording of "Kol Nidre," keep the door open, and let the shoppers hear the chant. Almost always, a crowd gathered to listen. Then Cash would stop the record and deliver a sales talk: "Perhaps I would invite a mother to bring in her child and let the little one recite or sing into the reproducing machine, and then I'd play it back. You can readily imagine how quickly I sold that record . . . and, fortunately, also a machine to play it on."

Unlike Jacob Cash, the overwhelming majority of Jews arriving each day did not become entrepreneurs. Rather, they turned for employment to the rapidly growing needle trades. They did so not because of any innate aptitude of skill for the sewing machine but in response to that industry's demand for cheap labor. These workers did not bring these particular skills with them but learned to operate the "Katrinka" (sewing machine) only after setting foot in America. The clothing industry was, before the 1880s, practically the only one in which Jews were employers and it was natural that many newcomers were drawn to the craft. One report, issued in 1884, noted: "Nearly all the smaller tailor shops belong to Jews, and the ready-made clothing without exception are owned by [Jews]. [Consequently,] the [workers] are also nearly all Jews. . . ."

According to an investigator of New York's clothing industry, Jesse

E. Pope, the owners of these shops understood the peculiar characteristics of the Jews and were willing to adjust the industry to their needs.

> The industry itself was particularly fitted for the employment of the grade of labor which they could furnish. It suited their lack of capital and physical strength [a common belief at the time], yet it offered excellent opportunity for the exercise of the dexterity which has been mentioned as one of their prominent characteristics. [Most important], it did not interfere with their peculiar religious customs. It is not surprising, therefore, that the clothing industry absorbed the great majority of the newcomers.

In New York, Boston, Philadelphia, and Chicago, thousands of East Europeans utilized the shears, the iron, and the sewing machine to earn a living. In the decades that followed, Jews entered the industry in increasing numbers; there was always a *landsman* willing to teach another, as there was always a relative offering to bring a "greenhorn around to meet the boss."*

That so many Jews entered the needle trades should not obscure the fact that not a few were employed elsewhere, at times due to their unique talents brought from Europe—as often a result of knowing "someone in the business." Jewish newcomers also rolled cigars, worked in the building industry, and plied their skills as painters, glaziers, and carpenters. Others entered the printing, jewelry, and amusement industries, and still more were employed in every corner of the economy except in heavy industry, mining, and agriculture.

Another economic pursuit was peddling. Encouraged by the oft-repeated stories of the earlier Germans, numerous peddlers went from house to house offering such items as "suspenders, collar buttons, 'lastic, matches, and hankeches." Some, of course, after acquiring a little English, ventured out of the immediate neighborhood to offer their wares to non-Jews; at times, they were met with a hail of rotten vegetables or the mocking cries of anti-Semitic hoodlums. In order to cope with the cold and hunger, wrote Dr. George Price, some "greeners" spent their last ten dollars: "five for a peddlers box; three or four dollars for goods, consisting of thread, socks, kerchiefs and handkerchiefs, combs; . . . and one dollar for a basket in which [to put the

---

* The early introduction of Jews into the needle trades explains why so many, in future years, became both small- and large-scale manufacturers of garments.

EAST EUROPEAN INVASION 165

goods], then [placed] it on their backs and [went out to satisfy their customers]."

There were several types of peddlers: some carried a back pack and went from house to house selling a limited assortment of items: pins, shoelaces, combs, suspenders, and soap; others sold a greater variety of goods from a pushcart; and still more reached the highest and perhaps the most respectable level of the trade: customer peddler. The latter was a man who had acquired steady accounts, or what was commonly called "a route."

When Louis Feldstein, a Brooklyn peddler, arrived in the United States, he managed to acquire a job at an East Side sweatshop. Knowing no English and never having operated a "Katrinka," he was, to say the least, not the best of operators. His wife, Ida, recalls that the first sweater he produced "was large enough to fit an elephant!" Louis Feldstein was not long for the garment industry.

Within a year, Louis abandoned the needle trades and tried his hand at peddling. Like those before him, he acquired a stock of goods, placed a pack on his back, and began knocking on doors. Business was good, and encouraged by his initial success, he ordered new merchandise and expanded his territory. Eventually he graduated to the customer-peddler class. Most of his trade was not Jewish but Italian—immigrants like himself. He became fluent in English and Italian and began to push even more merchandise: "Curtains, slip covers, dry goods," he told the eager housewives, "whatever you need I can provide." And provide he did. Monday he shopped "downtown," along Grand Street, for goods; Tuesday he made his way through the streets of lower Manhattan; Wednesday it was the Italian section of Greenwich Village; and the remainder of the week he canvassed Brooklyn—selling his wares and noting the fifty-cent or dollar collection in the black account book.

Eighty per cent of those who made up his route were related or at least knew each other: cousins, aunts, uncles, daughters, and friends. "Mistreat one and you mistreat all," he told his son in later years, "but be fair with your people and they will provide you with a decent living." As time passed, his business improved. Now Louis carried an even greater variety of merchandise, if he had a contact, the item was yours. *Shlepping* (carrying) his bundles, which were always wrapped in a familiar brown paper and tied with a thorny twine, he made his way up the apartment-house stairs. "Louie the Jew is here," cried the youngster who responded to the knock on the door. "Where's the card?" "Where's the dollar?" "Tell him next week—it's holiday," came the reply. Many a customer peddler went home without his "collection" in the days before Christmas, Easter, or Thanksgiving—the money having been spent elsewhere. Even a niece's birthday or a nephew's confirmation served as an acceptable excuse to "skip"—to tell Louie and the thousands like him, "next week."

Though they "skipped" and bargained for the difference of a few pennies, Louis still developed a close personal relationship with many of those on his route. After all, he entered the same house for over thirty years. Considered a part of the family by some, he often danced at their weddings and cried at their funerals. "Have a Merry Christmas, Mrs. Durando," and "here are a dozen towels for the family." "I'll see you after New Year's." At other times he was not offering gifts but, rather, providing money, interest-free, for emergencies. One wonders if Mrs. DeMarco's children remember that Louie made their mother's operation possible. "Louie the Jew" was there when no one else was.

As the children of his customers grew to adulthood and moved to the areas of second settlement, he followed them. Once again he had new homes to furnish and new families to add to the route. He now owned an auto, and in its trunk, rather than on his back, were the bundles. What he could not fit into the trunk he had delivered: furniture, carpeting, and appliances. Even men's and ladies' garments were now part of his stock. "You need a suit for Johnny's graduation?" he asked. "No problem" was the reply to his own question; "just see Gerry at 66 East Broadway and tell him Louie Feldstein sent you."

"You're married to this business," he once told his wife, "but it's a good living." Yet he never wanted his children to peddle. "They must have something better than me," he constantly remarked in the presence of his brother Moe or to his relatives at the monthly family-circle meeting. Louie's children did not follow in their father's footsteps but, rather, went to college in order to enter a profession. The fact that few children joined their fathers in this business was a primary cause for the decline of this unique "Jewish economic institution." As important, in the ensuing decades, the stores began to give "credit" or encouraged their customers with "time payments." Armed with charge accounts and subjected to massive newspaper advertisements, the grandchildren of his original customers turned their shopping into an entertainment. "Buying on time" from a peddler, like so many of those early immigrant institutions, became a thing of the past.

Jews were also prominent in the junk, or waste, business. This industry consisted of the process whereby discarded products were collected, grouped, and processed. The material was then sold to a consumer who converted the discarded matter into new products. Almost anything was recycled—from old scrap iron to old rags and bottles.

In Detroit, Jews took a leading role in the collection of junk. Jewish involvement was not accidental but, rather, was the result of waste dealers' taking their friends and relatives into the business; by the first decade of the twentieth century, Detroit's Eastern European "junk aristocracy" ruled over a vast empire of discarded articles.

The low status assigned to the collection of junk mattered little to the pious Jew as long as he was able to devote time to the *shul* (synagogue). This assertion is supported by the findings of Maurice Fishberg. "It will be found," he wrote,

> that in a large majority of instances [Jewish] occupations [such as the waste business] are determined by their religious needs. . . . And, as a general rule, those trades are most favored by Jews which afford them opportunities for arranging their own time for work and leaving them free for their festivals and religious duties generally. Piece work rather than time work, domestic industries rather than factory work; in fact, occupations in which they can be, to a certain extent, masters would naturally be chosen by a people whose holidays differ from those of their neighbors.

Some Detroit Jews found their previous European vocations made them ready-made specialists for the waste industry. Tailors were familiar with rags, and merchants had experience in buying and selling discarded articles. Joseph Jacobs remarked:

> In [Europe] . . . it was customary for the Jews . . . to send out their sons every Monday morning to neighboring villages as hawkers, who would return in time for the Friday-night meal, meanwhile helping circulate goods and bring back secondhand products.
> . . . The same practice was at the root of Jewish commerce in Russia, where these itinerant agents were known as "Wocher."

Immigrant Jews also found employment in the thousands of small tobacco factories that dotted the cities. In the numerous New York shops, George Price reported, "about ten to sixteen per cent [of the Jewish immigrant population] worked as tobacco strippers, cigaret and cigar makers." In Chicago, thousands of Russian Jews were also engaged in the trade. "A fair proportion of the Chicago workers," noted Abraham

Bisno, state deputy inspector of factories for Illinois "were in business for themselves, as store keepers or manufacturers or both." His particular findings indicated that those who found work in this trade encompassed the cigar manufacturer worth twenty thousand dollars and "the man who keeps shop at night and works in a factory during the day. . . ."

Jacob Riis commented on the disproportionate number of Jews in the trade. In New York he saw "men, women and children work together seven days in the week in these cheerless tenements to make a living for the family, from the break of day till far into the night." On East Tenth Street he observed a "man and wife work at the bench from six in the morning till nine at night. They make a team stripping the tobacco leaves together; then he makes the filler, and she rolls the wrapper on and finishes the cigar. For a thousand they receive $3.75, and can turn out together three thousand cigars a week."

Many of these cigar makers were displaced by machinery or forced out of business by anti-tenement legislation.† Some ignored the law and continued manufacturing tobacco products in their homes, and many became deathly ill. The number of people who contracted tuberculosis was enormous. In one case, Riis observed a cigar maker who suffered from consumption, "which the doctor said was due to tobacco fumes." Though a shoemaker by trade this immigrant helped his wife roll cigars for thirteen years. After he fell ill and "was warned out of the industry," his wife was laden with the responsibility of supporting the family. Having no place to turn, she remained as a tobacco worker, earning eight dollars a week.

The children of those who toiled in the sweatshops, when the opportunities presented themselves, moved in other economic directions. For some it was not a new sweatshop they sought but, rather, the professions. Medicine proved the most attractive. According to one contemporary observer, "the awe of a doctor's title . . . contributed to the glamour of this vocation." Yet teaching probably drew more of these searching youngsters than any other field of professional endeavor. For obvious reasons, only those born on American soil or who arrived at a very early age moved in this direction. According to Isaac M. Rubinow of the United States Bureau of Statistics, "it [was] certainly . . . a revelation to many an American to learn how many Russian Jewish young men and girls are doing this work of Americanization, and not only of Jewish, but of Irish, German, and Italian children."

† The statute forbade such shops in tenement houses.

Jews entered law, dentistry, engineering, and pharmacy. "There are about one hundred druggists," noted Dr. George Price in 1893, "and their number [in New York] has been increasing. . . . The apprentices," he reported,

> receive from five to six dollars; the assistants, six to twelve; and the full-fledged druggists from fifteen to twenty-five dollars a week. The majority of the Russian druggists are employed by their own countrymen, owners of pharmacies, many of which have recently been opened. An experienced assistant or full-fledged druggist can always find a good position.

Jews also managed to find employment as clerks, electricians, mechanics, midwives, journalists, and translators. Insurance salesmen were everywhere. In response to the untapped market, the major insurance companies created "Russian departments" and employed thousands of part-time agents to staff them. "There is hardly a tenement house on the East Side of New York," wrote Burton J. Hendrich, in a contemporary study of life insurance, "in which the Big Three [insurance companies] have not each a representative. In every factory and every sweatshop have deferred dividends been sold. Bakers, grocers, butchers, and push-cart peddlers have done an insurance business on the quiet. Of the 5,000 employees of one of New York's largest clothing establishments, at least 1,500, it is said, have carried a rate book."

The pattern of Jewish economic growth was followed by those who settled in the interior. In Chicago, the transition from junk dealer to iron-yard owner, from dry-goods peddler to retail merchant, from cloak maker to cloak manufacturer, was relatively short. Abraham Bisno claimed that the immigrant Jews seemed "to develop business methods of their own, which, in many instances, successfully defy or modify well-established laws."

> They can do business [he said] with little money, or practically no money, right next door to a large house, ignoring the economic rule that the latter, through competition, drives the smaller house out of business. They continue to hold their own in the trades in which they engage, growing in strength as the years go on.

"A Jew would rather earn five dollars a week doing business for himself than ten dollars a week working for someone else," remarked one Chicago Irishman. This statement was confirmed by Bisno: "Quite a large proportion of the men who worked with me in the same trade ten or fifteen years ago are now in business for themselves or have entered professional life." Others, he reported, became salesmen, commission brokers, insurance agents, and the like. "I have met very few wage-workers among Russian Jewish people who regard it as their permanent lot in life to remain in the condition of a laborer for wage," he declared.

> Almost all are bending their energies to get into business or to acquire an education so that they may fit themselves for some other calling than that of the wage-worker of the ordinary kind. More of our boys and girls who have attended the public schools enter stores and offices than shops and factories. This is especially true of the more intelligent of the population.

In spite of Bisno's optimistic findings, there were scattered throughout Chicago's industries thousands of East European Jews engaged in a variety of wage-earning occupations: from common laborers to highly skilled merchanics. They were employed as iron molders, machinists, locomotive engineers, seamen, farm laborers, boilermakers, butchers at the stockyards, street sweepers, section hands on the railroad, and motormen and conductors on streetcars. A number were also found employed in the building trades as bricklayers, carpenters, steam fitters, and plumbers. In addition, Bisno's investigation placed them "in manufactories of electrical appliances, of iron beds and springs, of shoes, of wood work, and of upholstery; in tin, mattress and picture factories; and in bakeries."

Like their coreligionists in Chicago, the newcomers who settled in Milwaukee used the same petty trades as their steppingstones to retail and wholesale businesses. Few engaged in that city's major industries: beer, iron, steel, tanning, and machinery. Finding employment in these areas was difficult due to certain self-imposed religious restrictions—many refusing to work on their Sabbath or holidays.

They turned to the "street trades," and through the sale of such items as dry goods and the operation of fruit stands and the collection of junk, managed to feed their families. Their relative prosperity was noted when the *Jewish Daily Forward* (New York) called "Milwaukee a golden land for peddling, especially for rags and dry goods. . . ."

Like the East Europeans elsewhere, Milwaukee Jewry turned to junk. From early in the morning till late in the evening, these dealers would go from street to street calling for *"alte zachen"* (old things) and *"alte shmatehs"* (old clothing). Once their wagons or back packs were filled, they carted their merchandise to the paper mill or iron foundry to bargain for the day's best price. The industry grew to such proportions that the Progressive Rag Peddlers Union was formed and, with a membership of almost two hundred, managed to establish fixed prices for the wide assortment of items offered to the respective users.

In the midst of this upward economic climb, the most common expression heard in the immigrant community was "up from the gutter." The sons of cantors, influenced by the music that permeated their homes, became composers and singers. The children of rabbis took to acting, prize fighting, law, and journalism. The tailor's son entered teaching, the newspaper boy was awarded a university chair in philosophy, and the peddler's daughter headed a nursing school. Apparently, the advice offered by Jacob Riis in *The Children of the Poor* influenced many of these second-generation youngsters:

> Hold fast, this is most necessary in America. . . . Select a goal and pursue it with all your might. No matter what happens to you, hold on. You will experience a bad time but sooner or later, you will achieve your goal. If you are neglectful, beware for the wheel of fortune turns quickly. You will lose your grip and be lost. A bit of advice to you: Do not take a moment's rest. Run, do, work and keep your own good in mind. . . . Do not say, "I cannot; I do not know how."

Rebekah Kohut, a writer and teacher on the Lower East Side of New York, observed many ghetto youths following this advice as they rose to economic independence and professional recognition. "I had a visitor," she once wrote, "who thirty years ago attended my evening classes in English. . . ." She was flattered by the visit, which she called a "testimonial to [their] relationship." Her former student was reluctant to talk of the past; rather, "he spoke of yachts, important [law] cases, country houses, and of how one is always so busy." When he told his teacher of his new swimming pool and his country home, she reminded him of the "hot days on the old East Side, when, in company with other happy young rascals, he had jumped into the East Broadway fountain, the gift of Jacob H. Schiff, while the good-natured Irish policeman looked the other way." Though the story brought a smile to his face, it was evident that he was annoyed, "as if it recalled a world that was remote from him, a world which perhaps he preferred to forget."

Their continued conversation testified to the success of those who managed an early escape from the ghetto: "Most of the boys who went to the Educational Alliance in those days have made good, a higher average certainly, than any other group I can think of."

"There's [Lenny]," replied the visitor. "Whenever he is on the other side of a case I begin to worry."

"And there's [Arnie]," she suggested. "He's teaching philosophy classes out west, and critics seem to like his new book. [Robert] is a general manager of a bank, [Bernard] has just had his third play produced. [Irwin] is head of one of the largest woolen firms."

One of the young men she was talking about might very well have been Samuel Zemurray, the Jewish "banana king." According to several contemporary accounts, there were some New Orleans and Mobile residents who claimed they knew Zemurray as a pushcart peddler. Though he never did sell from a cart, he was in fact a fruit jobber who bought carloads of bananas in Mobile, Alabama, for distribution to retail dealers. After a time at this endeavor, he went to New Orleans to negotiate with the United Fruit Company for the purchase of "ripes," bananas that ripened on the ship before arrival at American ports, which he sold to small dealers. Successful at this venture, he therefore decided to pursue a career as a fruit importer. He entered into partnership with Ashbel Hubbard and, in anticipation of competing with United Fruit, purchased an old steamer to import bananas from Honduran plantations.

This enterprise led to even greater profits, and in 1910, he organized the Cuyamel Fruit Company. As president, he went everywhere and did everything. He learned Spanish like a native and could outcurse any man in the tropics in either blistering Spanish or waterfront English. Within the next five years Zemurray expanded his operation and began to challenge United's leadership; the masters of the Caribbean were more than annoyed with this trespasser in their own backyard.

Though United placed a variety of obstacles in his economic path, by 1929 he accumulated between twelve and fifteen million dollars, thirteen banana steamers, several sugar plantations, and an estate in San Pedro Sula. Here he presented the community with a school and a brewery. He was the pride of Omoa, where he and his partner also constructed a railroad, several small shops, "and a small, screened, sanitary town." Zemurray won the gratitude of Honduran officialdom.

By the end of the twenties, United's directors had had enough of the "tropical tramp" and decided to send their "legal bloodhound," Bradley W. Palmer, to find the Jewish "banana king" and to "come back with Cuyamel." Over his twelfth bottle of ale, Zemurray agreed to sell. Gladly, Palmer purchased the firm for three hundred thousand shares of United and a promise that Zemurray would never operate a competitive business. Palmer failed to include in the agreement that Zemurray would never operate United.

After acquiring the shares in United, Zemurray watched the Wall Street panic of 1929 shrink his holdings in the company from twenty million dollars to two million dollars. Worried by the loss (United stock had gone from 158 to an all-time low of 10¼), he gathered his personal resources, which amounted to twelve million dollars, and purchased as many shares of United as he could. One July morning, the former peddler of "ripes" walked into a board of directors' meeting of the United Fruit Company and flung a handful of stock certificates and proxies down on the long oval table and, selecting his words carefully, stated: "You've been ——ing up this business long enough. I'm going to straighten it out."‡

Zemurray left the meeting with a new title, unwieldy but brutally clear: "managing director in charge of operations." Immediately, things began to happen: he hired some of his old Cuyamel subordinates, eliminated scores of employees, and reduced the number of loans made to independent planters. "Within two weeks after he took charge," reported *Fortune,* "United Fruit stock had climbed to 26."

In the years after the 1880s, many of the virgin opportunities for economic growth were no longer there for the East European newcomers. Yet these Yiddish-speaking "greeners" managed to nudge their way into the American economic mainstream—or at least that part of the stream open to them. Some nurtured their pushcarts into large enterprises, others remained as workers, and not a few found their economic mobility linked to the classroom. No matter what path they chose, most found their place in the nation's growing economy.

‡ According to the editors of *Fortune,* "He said, in explaining the proxies he flung on the table, that he had New York friends who were large stockholders and were just as worried about United Fruit's future as he was. However much of their holdings were bought with his money they were quite willing to go along with Sam Zemurray, so much so that when he strode into the directors' meeting . . . he was able to offer the Boston gentlemen their choice of doing as he wished privately—or having the stockholders with abhorrent publicity do it for them."

CHAPTER IV

The Mushrooming of a Community

THE SWEATSHOP CULTURE

In the decades surrounding the turn of the century, Yiddish intellectual life found a home in the Jewish "coffee saloon." In a favorite café, restaurant, or wine shop, "the radical literati and journalists, the compositors on the Yiddish dailies, and students and insurance agents and others" discussed "politics and society, poetry and ethics, literature and life. The talk was good," wrote Hutchins Hapgood, "for there assembled [were] the chosen crowd of intellectuals." Even the café keepers were "thoughtful and often join in the discussion—a discussion never light but sometimes lighted up by the bitter wit and gloomy irony."

"The best that is Russian today is intensely serious," remarked Hapgood. "What is distinctly Jewish has always been serious. The man hunted from his country is apt to have a serious tone in thought and feeling."

Whether it was to play chess, or discuss Marx or Bakunin, or to analyze Tolstoy or Ibsen, or to debate the relative merits and demerits of the naturalistic or romantic drama—or the wonderful voice of the previous night's prima donna at the Metropolitan, or to denounce the critics of Jacob Adler, the actor, or to castigate the traducers of Jacob Gordin, the playwright—these subjects were handled best, thoughts came lucidly and words flowed eloquently, over a glass of steaming Russian tea, with a floating slice of lemon, and a cigarette.

If well acquainted with the "coffee and cake geography" of New York's Lower East Side one knew exactly where to find the intellectual diversion most to his liking. "It is each to his own," reported A. H. Fromenson, English editor of the *Jewish Daily News:* "The Socialist has his own chosen headquarters, the chess-crank his, the music-lover his, and so on right down the line." While the poets of *Di Yunge* were occupying the tables at Goodman and Levine's, on East Broadway, the theater crowd could be found late into the night discussing Gordin's latest tragedy at Schreiber's Cafe, on Canal Street. Descending on their favorite haunt, the actors and their admirers gathered to pose, sneer, joke, romance, fawn, and flatter until the gray light of dawn. Perhaps it was the "great star" or playwright, about whose table sat the worshipers, who gave the signal that it was time to depart. Everyone knew the meaning of his prodigious yawn: time to go home, time to put the discussion to bed. Tomorrow they would continue their talk when, once again, they would position themselves around the table to sip the strong Russian Tea.

Where the cigarette smoke was thickest and denunciation of government loudest, wrote Fromenson, "there you find women!"

> One wishes he could write these women down more gently. But to none would gentle words sound more strange than to the women of the radical coffee "parlor," who listen to strongest language, and loudest voices, nor fail to make themselves heard in the heat of the discussion. Yet it is hard to criticize them. The hall-bedroom is such a dingy, dreary place; the walls so close they seem to crush the unfortunate whose "home" is within its oppressive limits. The "coffee saloon" is light and cheerful, the noise is only the swelling chorus of spirits and with whom they are in harmonious accord. If they are not the objects of fine courtesies and considerateness, they do not miss them; perhaps they never knew them. The stern realities of life, the terrible disappointment of thwarted ambition, the bruising friction of tradition and "emancipation," the struggle for existence,—all these have conspired to rob them of the finer attributes of womanhood.

"These are the stalwarts of the radical movements," he said, "the Amazons, or, as they have been dubbed, *die kaempferinen,* whose zealotry rallies the flagging courage of their *genossen.*"

> Unromantic, perhaps, and yet we hear of them tailoring, slaving, denying themselves until some man has won a degree and an entry into one of the professions. But, as they sit there in an atmosphere

of tea-steam and cigarette smoke, one who does not know sees them only as unwomanly women; pallid, tired, thin-lipped, flat-chested and angular, wearing men's hats and shoes, without a hint of color or finery. And to them, as to the men, the time of night means nothing until way into the small hours. When one must sleep in a hall-bedroom there is no hurry about bedtime.

Seated nearby these women are perhaps a group of East Side literati: Morris Winchevsky, David Edelstadt, Menachem Dolitzki, Joseph Bovshover, and Morris Rosenfeld. These were the "sweatshop poets," whose pens helped give birth to America's Yiddish literary tradition. Morris Rosenfeld drew his inspiration from the "shops" and through his writings laid bare the struggle of immigrant "sweaters." "He is a class poet," said Hapgood, "a worker's poet." Rosenfeld's poetry bore out this analysis:

> I work, and I work, without rhyme, without reason—
> produce, and produce, and produce without end.
> For what? and for whom? I don't know, I don't wonder
> —since when can a whirling machine comprehend?
> Away rush the seconds, the minutes and hours;
> each day and each night like a wind-driven sail;
> I drive the machine, as though eager to catch them,
> I drive without reason—no hope, no avail. . . .

Soon the poets of *Yiddishkeit* came on the scene. These writers were steeped in Jewish tradition and, through their work, wanted to close the cultural gap separating the East Europeans in America from their coreligionists who remained in Europe. Among the most prominent of this school was Abraham Liessin, whom Hapgood described as "an imaginative critic, a violent Socialist, and an excitable lover of nature. He is a short, stocky man, with a suggestion of physical power."

> His eyes are brilliant, and there seems to be going on in him a sort of intellectual consumption. He is restlessly intense in manner, speaks in images, and is always passionately convinced of the truth of what he sees so closely but seldom expresses in cold logic. His fevered idealism meets you in his frank, quiet gaze and impulsive, rapid speech.

He disliked the United States, because it lacked "the ebullient activity of moral, imaginative life." Russia, he said, "was idealism and hope, and America is realization."

I thought it would not be as interesting as Russia, and when I got here I saw that I was right. America seemed all worked out to me, as if mighty things had already been done, but it seemed lifeless at the core. Russia, on the other hand, with no external form of natural prosperity, is all activity at heart, restless longing. Russia is nothing to see, but alive and bubbling at the core. The American wants a legal wife, something there and sure, but the Russian wants a wife behind a mountain through which he cannot penetrate, but can only dream and strive for her.

Hapgood described Liessin's poetry as a blend "of Socialism and nature" in which "one form [was] as turbulent as the other."

He writes, for instance, of the prisoner in Siberia, his verses are filled with passionate rebellion. Then he tells how he dreamed beside the gleaming river, and of the fancies that passed through his brain—not merely pretty fancies, but passionately moral images in which rebellion, longing, wonder, are by turns expressed; never peaceful enjoyment of nature, simply the humble eye that sees and questions not, but always the moral storm and stress.

After the *Yiddishkeit* poets appeared, there emerged, in 1907, another group of writers—*Di Yunge*—who produced a publication called *Yugend* (Youth). With no political ideology to promote, *Di Yunge* poets such as Mani Leib and Zisha Landau sought to "cleanse" Yiddish poetry of its commitment to the labor movement and social idealism. Due to their isolation from the literary emotions of the Yiddish-speaking ghetto, *Di Yunge* have been credited with being the first modern Yiddish-American poets.

In the midst of the growing Yiddish literary community there appeared numerous periodicals, journals, and newspapers. In New York City between 1885 and 1914 over one hundred and fifty different publications made their appearance. Seeking the free expression denied them in Europe, Jewish novelists, journalists, and poets submitted their work to a variety of dailies, weeklies, monthlies, and quarterlies. The Yiddish-speaking community was besieged with publications promoting anarchism, socialism, and Zionism; periodicals that were humorous and philosophical; and journals that were geared to "mature literary tastes."

In the 1880s, Abraham Cahan's radical weeklies, *Naye Tsayt* (1886) and *New Yorker Yiddishe Volks-Zeitung* (1886) told the immigrant Jews of the Haymarket riots, while at the same time, the Socialist *Naye Welt* (1888), the anarchist *Wahrheit* (1889), and the radical-oriented *Volksadvokat* (1888) pursued their respective ideologies. The labor journals made their presence felt: the United Hebrew Trades published the *Arbeiter Zeitung* (1890), Israel Barsky edited the *Schneider Verband* (1890), and the United Trade Unions established the *Union Zeitung* (1894). These labor journals were supplemented by the *Papier-Zigaretten Macher* (1907), the *Idisher Baker* (1910), the *Neckwear Macher* (1910), the *Painter* (1911), and the *Knitter's Haffnung* (1913).

For the business community there was Shaikewitz's *Vegveiser in der Amerikaner Bizness Velt* (1892) and *Shtadt Anzeiger* (1893); the dramatist Abraham Goldfaden published the *New Yorker Illustrierte Zeitung* (1897), and Morris Wechsler and David Apotheker established the *Weibershe Zeitung* (1888) for women. *The Schach Jurnal* (1906) appealed to chess players, the *Shadchan* to singles; *Di Yiddishe Puck* (1894) to those seeking humor, and *Hovev Zion* (1886), *Di Naye Shtunde, Di Yiddishe Zukunft,* and *Volksstimme* to the various shades of Zionism.

If on a particular evening one was not interested in reading any of these publications, one could always attend a lecture. For the Jewish intellectual, the lecture podium was perhaps the most stimulating activity of ghetto cultural life. At the *Arbeiter Ring* (Workmen's Circle) or the Educational Alliance, one would be enlightened by speakers who discussed anything from simple arithmetic to the philosophical foundations of Friedrich Nietzsche.

"There were scores of lectures every week," wrote Marcus E. Ravage:

> I found, and I went to, as many as I could. One night it was Darwin, and the next it might be the principles of air pressure. On a Saturday night there were sometimes two meetings so arranged that both could be attended by the same audience. I remember going once to a meeting at Cooper Union to protest against the use of militia in breaking a strike somewhere in the West, and then retiring . . . to the anarchist reading-room on Eldridge Street to hear an informal discussion on "Hamlet *versus* Don Quixote." It did not matter to us what the subject was. There was a peculiar, intoxicating joy in just sitting there and drinking in the words of the speakers, which to us were echoes from a higher world than ours. . . . It was something more valuable than information that we were after. Our poor, cramped souls were yearning to be inspired and uplifted. Never in all my experience since . . . have I seen such earnest, responsive audiences as were those collarless men and hatless girls of the sweatshops.

While some were listening to a lecture on Shakespeare, others might be attending a talk delivered by Planton Bronoff, the Russian immigrant whose American Indian opera *Ramona* was based on Helen Hunt Jackson's novel of the same name. The crowds might have been attracted to a discussion of George Luks's oil painting "Hester Street" or some remarks on the sketches of Jacob Epstein, which depicted sweatshop workers, street peddlers, and pushcart women. No matter what the topic, those who attended displayed a passion for information and understanding.

As the East European community grew, so too did its cultural and informational needs. In the four decades of mass immigration there appeared a variety of Yiddish newspapers. The most influential of all was the *Jewish Daily Forward*. Established by a group of Socialists in 1897, the *Forward* became a journalistic institution for Socialists and non-Socialists alike. True to its pledge to be non-profit, the paper used its excess revenues to establish editions in Philadelphia and Chicago, to support striking workers, and to aid a variety of labor organizations.

With Abraham Cahan as its editor, the *Forward* was not only a newspaper but a Socialist Party organ and an instrument for the building of labor unions. The Jewish working class flocked to its bosom for protection, sought its counsel on how to deal with employers, and solicited, through the "Bintel Brief" (Bundle of Letters), advice on how to handle their everyday personal problems:*

> *Dear Editor:*
>
> My son was against my marriage, but I have left my second husband and I am getting a divorce. My son reads the *Forward,* and I plead with him to forgive me. I am lonely as a stone.
>
> My husband reads the *Forward,* but where does he read it? In the barbershop where he goes all the time with those other card players. Let him see this letter.
>
> Is it a sin to use face powder? Shouldn't a girl look beautiful? My father does not want me to wear face powder. Is it a sin?
>
> My son is already twenty-six years old and he doesn't want to get married. He says he is a socialist and he is too busy. Socialism is socialism and getting married is important too.
>
> I am a socialist and my boss is a fine man. I know he's a capitalist but I cannot hate him. Am I doing the wrong thing?

Cahan's insistence that the paper reflect the everyday life of the Lower East Side was due to the training he received as a reporter for Lincoln

* The Bintel Brief was the letters-to-the-editor section of the paper.

Steffens as the New York *Commercial Advertiser*. Under the tutelage of the crusading Steffens, he learned how "to see actual tragedies and comedies and to report them."

> Here [said Steffens to Cahan] is a report that a man has murdered his wife, a rather bloody, hacked-up crime. We don't care about that. But there's a story in it. That man loved that woman well enough once to marry her, and now he has hated her enough to cut her all to pieces. If you can find out just what happened between that wedding and this murder, you will have a novel for yourself and a short story for me. Go on now, take your time, and get this tragedy, as a tragedy.

Due to his journalistic training under Steffens, Cahan turned out a realistic and sometimes sensational newspaper. At times he even urged his readers to "join" his staff: "Under the tenement roofs are stories of the real-life stuff, the very stuff of which great literature can be made. Send them to us. Write them any way you can. Come and tell them to us." If there was ever a community newspaper, the *Forward* was it!

The *Forward* was politically vibrant and at Cahan's insistence a vehicle for assimilation. Its editorials discussed the nature of the American political system; its coverage of news was in depth and explanatory and, after 1921, its columns included lessons in English. Cahan also held classes in manners. Responding to one lesson on etiquette, suggesting that *mama* supply her *kinder* (children) with handkerchiefs, some irate readers inquired as to how the advice was tied to Socialist ideology. "And since when has socialism been opposed to clean noses?" was Cahan's answer.

In trying to reach the everyday reader, Cahan also introduced colloquial Yiddish as it was spoken on the streets, in the shops, and in the home. If he had doubts about the use of a particular word, he would approach the elevator operator and ask him to read the article. If this "average worker" understood its contents, the item went to press; if not, it was rewritten. This practice did not compromise the intellectual integrity of the paper. In his attempt to lift the cultural level of his readers, Cahan encouraged the publication of art, theater, and book reviews, short stories, and poetry.†

Ironically, though the *Forward* was the organ of the Jewish Socialists,

---

† The Yiddish press was a mainstay for Yiddish literary talent. Having these vehicles in which to publish, writers such as Sholom Asch, Sholom Aleichem, Abraham Reisen, Peretz Hirschbein, and I. J. Singer turned the Lower East Side of New York into the center of Yiddish literary activity.

it was never fully committed to official Socialist doctrine nor was it hindered by the party's course of action. In its independence, it published news and not propaganda and adopted a "human," rather than doctrinaire, approach to this particular ideology. "The *Forward* is a party paper," declared Cahan, "but it is first of all a newspaper. I think that party affiliations of newspapers are compatible as long as newspapers remember their primary responsibility."

As the need grew, other journalistic organs appeared in the Yiddish-speaking community. In 1901, Jacob Saphirstein established the orthodox *Jewish Morning Journal;* four years later, the middle political ground was occupied by the *Independent Wahrheit,* and, in 1914, there emerged the *Day.* Once the Bolsheviks seized power in Russia, it was not too long before Jewish Communists founded the *Freiheit.*

New York stood alone in the number of Yiddish dailies published. Though Chicago boasted three between 1908 and 1920, most other cities—Milwaukee, Philadelphia, and Cleveland, for instance—were hard-pressed to support even one Yiddish daily for more than a short period of time. The lack of Yiddish editorial opinion in these cities caused some people to rely on the New York press—newspapers that perhaps reflected their own political philosophies. An Orthodox Philadelphian might get his news, though a few days old, from the New York *Morning Journal* rather than depend upon the local Socialist press for the most up-to-date information.‡

The Yiddish theater was also a direct result of the growing East European community in the United States. In New York the various Yiddish playhouses "with seating capacities equal to the largest patronized by the non-Jewish elements (one built for the specific purpose of housing a Yiddish stock company) were located within five minutes' walk of each other in the down-town Ghetto." According to Fromerson, theatergoing was so much a habit with New York's Russian Jews that an estimated five to seven thousand patrons a night were drawn to the performances. With presentations given on each of the seven nights in the week and with matinees on Saturday and Sunday, "the importance of the theater as a source of amusement . . . may be realized."

Outside of New York, similar developments took place. In Philadelphia, Yiddish-speaking audiences flocked to the Arch Street, the

‡ Rather than the daily, it was the weekly which survived outside New York. In Baltimore, Alexander Harkavy established *Der Yiddishe Progress,* and in Philadelphia *Das Licht* and *Die Yiddishe Press* meet some of the needs of the Yiddish-speaking community. Interestingly, the Los Angeles *Jewish News* and the St. Louis *Jewish Record* were published in both Yiddish and English.

Standard, and the National, and in Chicago, Glickman's was almost exclusively devoted to the presentation of Jewish historical and religious plays. "I saw [at Glickman's theater]," wrote I. K. Friedman, a Chicago journalist,

> a play which was a Yiddish adaptation of Hamlet. . . . Shakespeare was most neatly adapted out of the tragedy to make room for up-to-date melodramatic situations, for orthodox Jewish religious ceremonials, and for the dramatic triumph of the production —the singing of the Kaddish (prayer for the dead). A line or two copied from the programme may suffice to give even those who were not privileged to see "The Jewish Hamlet" an idea of the broad license that the adapter allowed himself. "Act IV, Scene 2— Great scene of the Jewish cemetery. Beautiful scenery painted specifically for this production. Sad wedding of *Vigder* (Hamlet) and his dead bride, *Esther* (Ophelia), according to the Jewish religion.

These performances, which catered to the Yiddish-speaking audience, also attracted non-Jews. Hutchins Hapgood was one who took in a night of New York City Yiddish play-acting:

> Joseph Latteiner is the most popular playwright in the Bowery, and Boris Thomashefsky perhaps the most popular acter. Latteiner has written over a hundred plays, no one of which has form or ideas. He calls them *Volksstucke* (plays of the people), and naïvely admits that he writes directly to the demand. They are mainly mixed melodrama, broad burlesque, and comic opera. His heroes are all intended for Boris Thomashefsky, a young man, fat, with curling black hair, languorous eyes, and a rather effeminate voice, who is thought very beautiful by the girls of the Ghetto. Thomashefsky has a face with no mimic capacity, and a temperament absolutely impervious to mood or feeling. But he picturesquely stands in the middle of the stage and declaims phlegmatically the hero, and satisfies the "romantic" demand of the audience.

Hapgood declared that the Yiddish stage was "deeply and painfully realistic." In the plays of Jacob Gordin, he said, "we have realism worked out consciously in art, the desire to express life as it is, and . . . the frequent expression of revolt against the reality of things. . . ."

Gordin adapted and wrote approximately seventy plays. He translated Ibsen, Tolstoy, and Gorky and modeled many of his own works on plots borrowed from Euripides, Shakespeare, and Victor Hugo. While Thomashefsky was entertaining his audience with Latteiner's operettas, Gordin was presenting *De Yiddisher Kenig Lear* (The Jewish King Lear)—adapting this Shakespearean tragedy to Jewish needs. More than one greenhorn who saw the production was reminded of the generational conflict he had with his own children. For some, Gordin mirrored the heartache of raising their *vilder* (wild) offspring in a strange American environment. Some frustrated parents "dragged" their rebellious youngsters to see his adaptation of *King Lear* in anticipation that they would learn how to behave toward their parents. More important, however, Gordin also brought maturity to the Yiddish stage, offering his audiences serious plays and not melodramatic operettas. He turned the Yiddish theater into an arena where emotions exploded and ideas clashed.

The problem play had its representation in the Yiddish community. According to Hapgood, these productions showed "the hideous conditions of life in the Ghetto—the poverty, the sordid constant reference to money, the immediate sensuality, the jocular callousness,—and underlying the mere statement of the facts an intellectual and passionate revolt."

And what of the audiences who came to see the Goldfaden melodramas or the Gordin tragedies? Who was sitting out front as Jacob Adler and Bertha Kalich performed? Who listened to the words written by "Professor Horowitz or Leon Kobrin or Solomon Libin? Who came to see the adaptations from Ibsen, the Yiddish version of *The Three Musketeers* or *The Jewish Hamlet?* Almost everyone!

> Into these . . . buildings crowd the Jews of all ghetto classes—the sweatshop woman with her baby, the day laborer, the small Hester Street shopkeeper, the Russian-Jewish anarchist and socialist, the ghetto rabbi and scholar, the poet, the journalist. The poor and ignorant are in the great majority, but the learned, the intellectual, and the progressive are also represented, and here, as elsewhere, exert a more than numerically proportionate influence on the character of the theatrical productions, which, nevertheless, remain essentially popular. The socialists and the literati create the demand that forces into the mass of vaudeville, light opera and historical and melodramatic plays a more serious art element, a simple transcript from life or the theatric presentation of a ghetto problem. But this more serious element is so saturated with the simple manners, humor, and pathos of the life of the poor Jew that it is seldom above the heartfelt understanding of the crowd.

From coffeehouse intellectuals to sweatshop workers, the Jews descended on the playhouses. Buying tickets ranging from twenty-five cents to one dollar, they packed the houses on weekends and ran benefits on weekdays. "It is on the *benefit* nights that the Yiddish theater is best worth visiting," wrote Fromenson, "providing that the play is not the thing."

> The audience is made up of family parties and neighboring groups; from the grandsire to the infant and the boarder the whole tenement house is there with its luncheons and its bedlam. Half of the audience has never been to the theater before, and would not have been there now, only they could not "insult" by not buying tickets, or because it is a "mitzvah" (good deed) to contribute to the good cause for which this "benefit" is given. And having earned the "mitzvah" why not partake of the earthly joy in its train? Here and there is the "veteran" theatre-goer, who may be a member of the society, or also could not "insult" by refusing to buy a ticket, or also wanted the "mitzvah" and all that goes with it.

The "veteran" was easily spotted, as he stood at the center of the group explaining the play, naming the actors, "criticizing them audibly if they are lesser lights, telling where the laugh will come in and repeating lines lost in the noise." The benefit was a joyous occasion. Presents were passed over the footlights to the stars, the officers of the society made "spitches" between the acts, those who sold the most tickets had medals pinned on their palpitating chests, and all would bathe "in a sea of ecstasy," with a feeling of good deeds well done, philanthropic purposes well served—if the benefit was successful.

After the death of Jacob Gordin, in 1909, Yiddish theatergoers witnessed the deterioration of the dramatic quality of the Yiddish play. There were several reasons for this downward trend. Stage productions had come to mean large investments, and the backers of these performances, in anticipation of attracting large crowds, opted for melodramatic spectacles rather than plays of serious social or political significance.

More important, the Yiddish-speaking community was becoming "American": many had learned English and were "wearing" their Americanization by speaking the language of their new homeland. "With very few exceptions," asserted I. K. Friedman, "the younger Russian Jews are neither proud of their Yiddish jargon nor of the ways of their ancestors and they are quick to accept anything that may have an Americanizing influence." The Chicago Yiddish theater, he said, was "not likely to outlast the life of the present generation [1905], and it is fairly open to question whether it will endure that long."

The assimilatory trend of the East Europeans, coupled with the drastic limitation of immigrants after the Immigration Act of 1924, hastened the decline of Yiddish audiences. Deprived of Yiddish theatergoers by death and acculturation, the Yiddish theater ceased to be an important cultural force in twentieth-century America.

UPTOWN VERSUS DOWNTOWN

For the Jews who arrived before the East European influx, Jewish indentification was an important aspect of settlement. Yet, many curtailed their religious "uniqueness" in the society into which they entered. They wished to be viewed by their Christian neighbors as merchants, not "Jewish merchants," as professionals, not "Jewish professionals." To be a Jew was significant; being *Jewish* was frequently quite undesirable.

With the arrival of *Jewish* Jews from the East European *shtetl*, resentment by the earlier arrivals arose, and antagonisms between the two groups grew. They who had introduced organs, choirs, and Sunday services to the Reform Movement, who were members of elite social groups, who were accepted by upper-crust Christian America, who had shed the *shtetl* mentality, were truly mortified by the ghetto life-styles of the most recent immigrants.

The American Jews "are ashamed of us," declared Morris Winchevsky, "not as one is ashamed of poor relations, but of a scoundrel in the family." The established Jewish community characterized their Russian coreligionists as "repulsive, ill-bred savages." B'nai B'rith refused to charter a group of Russian newcomers because they "[were] not yet civilized," and the Harmony Club, perhaps the nation's most influential Jewish social fraternity, barred East Europeans from membership; its byword for many years was "more polish and less Polish."

In a more extreme instance, the *Zeitgeist,* a midwestern German Jewish journal, declared:

> Russian Jews are half-barbarians, like the unfortunate Russian people to which they belong. . . . Moreover most of the Russian-Jewish immigrants stem from the poorer classes. The Jewish aristocracy, the rich and cultivated remain in Russia. . . . But even if the better Jewish classes should also be compelled to emigrate because of further persecutions, their bearing, their language, their manners, and their religion would soon demonstrate that we are

dealing not with persons of European education and culture, precisely because they are Russians. . . . Their ways are not our ways . . . even their language [Yiddish] is not our language. . . . if the ancestors of the Russian Jews had remained in Germany, they would be quite different by now.

Native American Jewry was not psychologically prepared for the masses that shuffled down the gangplanks at Castle Garden and Ellis Island. Upset and sometimes shocked by what they witnessed (women wearing *shaytlin* (wigs) and men in long beards and gabardine coats), they were hard-pressed to decide which was worse: the radical anarchist or the orthodox rabbi with side locks. "What can we do with these wild Asiatics!" exclaimed *The American Hebrew*. "Are we waiting for the natural process of assimilation between orientalism and Americanism? This will perhaps never take place. . . ." *The Hebrew Standard* repeated this foreboding: "The thoroughly acclimated American Jew . . . has no religious, social or intellectual sympathies with them. He is closer to the Christian sentiment around him than to the Judasim of these miserable darkened Hebrews."

Even David Philipson, the influential leader of the American reform rabbinate, expressed dismay at the activities of the orthodox community. Responding to the news that Cincinnati's newcomers were soliciting funds to build a mikveh [ritual bath], he exclaimed, "My God, is it possible that in this late day such a custom should be revived? In this age of bath-rooms public and private!! Oh! the shame of it. That even the most orthodox man, if he were but a little enlightened, should permit this. Much, much have I thought them capable of doing in their fanatic and ignorant zeal, but this never."

Nothing that was part of the East European settlement was accepted. Yiddish was imputed to be "piggish jargon," immigrant garb and ceremonials were called "disgraceful" and rabbinical divorces were denounced as "medieval."* The Yiddish theater was termed "savage," the Yiddish press was labeled "radical," and contempt was expressed for the proliferation of *kosher* restaurants, tailors who were arrested for working on Sunday, and the practice of "begging" at cemeteries. What irked native Jews more than anything were the radicals and trade unionists. Calling their activities "moral hydrophobia," the *Jewish Messenger* urged its readers not to associate with "Nihilists, socialists or anarchists." Underlying this condemnation of the customs and ac-

---

* Some members of the orthodox community did not bother to obtain a civil divorce.

tivities of the slum-dwellers and sweatshop workers was the ever-present fear that American Jewry would be *Russified*.†

One contemporary observer who vividly described the conflict between the "uptown" and "downtown" Jews was Isaac Max Rubinow. "The German Jew," he wrote, "accepted axiomatically the fact that the Russian Jew was incapable of transporting his cultural treasures with him to his new environment. He held this Russian savage in contempt. . . ." According to Rubinow, their contempt soon led to "open warfare" at New York's Educational Alliance.

This institution, which was established to promote the free exchange of ideas, became the arena in which the German community launched a campaign against the principles of unionism. "Jewish and non-Jewish professors alike, as well as religious leaders, Jewish and Christian," reported Rubinow, "preached from this platform about the detrimental influence of socialism. The esteemed leaders were somewhat embarrassed before their Christian neighbors when it became evident that the Jewish masses were becoming the vanguard in the struggle for these ideals. After all, we all feel ill-at-ease when our relative or even our name-sake places us in an awkward position."

In addition to the anti-union rhetoric of the German Jewish community, there were "sermons on the vanity of earthly goods," lectures on the "rewards in the life to come," and discussions on "tolerance" toward the "uptown" benefactors. The "downtowners" rejected the crudely stressed propaganda. According to Rubinow, the "educational" activities of the "uptowners" merely "aggravated the situation and caused dissatisfaction, suspicion and lack of confidence . . . toward the philanthropic motives and communal leadership of the uptown Jews."

In the cafés and on the streets the familiar topic of conversation "was on the way the millionaires [were] trying to raise the morals of the working class and the blunders which the German Jews had committed. . . ." As time passed, these conversations were replaced by action.

On one occasion the "downtown" community was invited to a demonstration with the following leaflet: "We do not need anyone's pity and benevolence. . . . This relationship is not that of benefactors and recipients of charity." The protestors decided to utilize a stage performance to attract a large crowd and turned to Jacob Gordin, the popular Yiddish playwright and ardent supporter of the Alliance "downtowners," for aid.

† The anti-Semitic term "kike" was first used by the German Jews to identify East Europeans whose names ended with "ki."

Entitled *The Benefactors of the East Side,* the Gordin drama was set in the home of a Jewish millionaire, where the cast of characters met to discuss the moral, intellectual, and economic level of the Lower East Side. Among those present at the gathering were several concerned "uptown" ladies; a Christian, to whom the Jewish philanthropists were catering, the Reverend Dr. Knobel [Yiddish for garlic]; and Goldberg, a "downtown" labor leader. In the opening scene, Knobel turns to Goldberg and explains his philosophy, which is the importance of a rapprochement with the "uptowners" and a minimizing of the Russian background.

One of the benefactors then recommends that model bathhouses be built where the immigrants would be taught how to take baths, and another suggests the introduction of athletics, because the people of the ghetto "devote too much time to reading and thinking." Rev. Knobel, of course, emphasizes the importance of religion. "All of these proposals," notes Rubinow, "were interspersed with expressions of contempt for the Jews of the East Side, whom the host designates as *schnorrers* and paupers." Finally, Goldberg rose to defend his community and made a fervid speech denouncing the patronizing attitude of the "uptown" benefactors. When the curtain fell, the audience applauded enthusiastically.

In Philadelphia, the East Europeans also clashed with their German brethren. Native Jewish Philadelphians remained aloof from any movement seeking to concentrate the Jewish vote or the formation of any political organization composed wholly of Jews. Such concentrations, however, because of the large Russian settlement in one district and a communal interest intensified by close religious and social union, mutual responsibility, and need, seemed much more palatable to the new immigrants.

Objections to such organization were soon heard from Philadelphia's German Jews. In a petition to the court in 1895 against the granting of a charter to the Fourth Ward Hebrew Republican Club, the petitioners asserted that "a racial or religious political club" was "against public policy in that it [tended] to the union of church and state" and that its object was "to introduce religion into politics and to excite racial and religious prejudices." Adolph Eichholz, an attorney acting for the petitioners, expressed the views generally held by the native community:

> . . . not only is it opposed to the spirit of American institutions that any set of men belonging to one race or one religious denomination should band themselves together for political pur-

poses, but it is also reasonably certain that the members of such organizations will be made the victims of unscrupulous schemes. One of the prime motives prompting the filing of these exceptions on the part of a co-religionist is a solicitude for the welfare of the misguided members and prospective members of this and all other so-called "Hebrew" and "Jewish" political clubs. The organizers of such clubs are, as a rule, men who, for their own selfish ends, use this means of impressing party leaders with the fact that they control a large number of "Hebrew" votes. Organizations formed upon such lines must necessarily interfere with elevation of the standard of true citizenship. Hebrew citizens take an interest in politics, and there is no reason why they should not do so after the manner of all other citizens, but their political activity has been and should be solely and purely that of good, loyal, and patriotic American citizens regardless of what may have been the country of their birth and independent of any religious belief or racial connection.‡

Detroit's German Jewish leaders, who were fearful that such organizations made Jews highly visible, were also opposed to separate Jewish political clubs. "There can be no political organization among Jews as Jews," stated Leo Frankel, a Detroit rabbi. "Those among us who attempt to unite the two are neither Jews nor Americans." The Russian Jews who organized "Jewish Democratic" and "Jewish Republican" clubs sent shock waves throughout Detroit's native Jewish community. Always conscious of their public image, the German leadership denied responsibility for the conduct of their orthodox brethren and made sure to tell their Christian neighbors that "the ways of these people are not our ways nor their thoughts our thoughts."

Detroit's native community was touchy about its image and was embarrassed and frightened by the East Europeans. "The conditions among the newcomers breed discontent, which opens the way for orthodoxy and anarchism," echoed the *Jewish American*. "These must be alleviated as quickly as possible lest the acts of these Jews bring discredit on all Jews." With little sympathy for the feelings of the Russians, Detroit leaders condemned them as backward and "oriental" and, almost always, characterized them as an inferior breed whose level of morality was beneath the Americanized native.

The Russians reacted to the charitable efforts of their Detroit coreligionists with attitudes that ranged from appreciation to resentment to

‡ Denial of a "Jewish vote" appears to have been a constant theme in the American Jewish experience. Indeed, there are those in present-day America who still reject the allegation.

bitterness. Though these poverty-stricken newcomers desperately needed the aid, it was at times accepted with feelings of humiliation. "The charities [are] organized for the purpose of bettering the conditions of the poor workingman," wrote one recipient, "but I do not like to beg." In 1914, the bitterness grew to such proportions that the Detroit Russian community, in protest, virtually boycotted the facilities of the German-dominated United Hebrew Charities.

In Chicago also, conflicts that embraced the religious, social, and economic life of the East Europeans were waged with the German community. In 1907 a movement began to install a kosher kitchen at Michael Reese Hospital, the only Jewish hospital in the city. At a meeting called to discuss the question, Dr. Emil G. Hirsch rose to address the gathering. He declared that "Michael Reese . . . is the finest institution of its kind throughout the land . . . but alas it gives no comfort to the Orthodox Jew for it lacks a *kosher* kitchen." Hirsch concluded that many of these people chose to suffer unrelieved pain rather than violate their religious principles. Despite his plea, a rebuttal submitted by Dr. Moses G. Greenbaum, one of Hirsch's opponents, that a *kosher* kitchen would be too expensive to build and maintain, proved more convincing. The project of a *kosher* kitchen for Michael Reese Hospital was defeated.

The fight over the kitchen facilities masked an even greater issue: Why weren't physicians of East European background permitted to serve on the hospital staff? According to a writer of the period, Philip Bregstone, the reason was obvious if one examined the attitude of the staff members toward their West Side colleagues:

> Since the beginning of the existence of the Michael Reese Hospital a group of physicians and surgeons whose fathers were contributors towards its maintenance formed a monopoly and permitted no Jewish doctor who was not of German descent to become a member of its staff, regardless of his ability or renown. Even the interns, although selected by competitive examination, were, oddly enough, all German Jews. This condition was not only an insult to the Jewish doctors on the West Side, but it even affected their economic position. When one of them had to send his patient to the . . . hospital, it meant the loss of a patient, for he was barred from attending and giving further medical treatment.

The quiet battle went on for several years, during which time the West Siders repeatedly expressed their desire for a hospital of their own. Their aims were obvious: to free themselves from their medical dependence on the Germans, to provide a *kosher* facility with a Jewish atmosphere, and to gain equal opportunity with those who discriminated against them.

The West Side medical men, led by Dr. Benjamin H. Breakstone, organized the Orthodox community in the fight for "medical emancipation." Translating words into action, Breakstone and others spearheaded a movement that had as its result Maimonides Hospital, Chicago's first *kosher* medical facility. Despite their initial triumph, "when the rooms [of Maimonides] were all furnished and the doors thrown open to receive patients, [a] war for extermination was waged against [the hospital] by the [German-dominated] Associated Jewish Charities. Maimonides Hospital could not long survive the terrific pressure it was subjected to—both from within and without," wrote Bregstone, and its doors closed shortly after they were opened. "Scientific charity," he exclaimed, "was once more the victor over sentiment and uncontrollable ambition."

The vacant hospital was purchased by the Associated Jewish Charities and renamed Mount Sinai. After improving its condition, the doors were opened and, writes Bregstone, "almost all of the evils that prevailed in the Michael Reese Hospital were eliminated." Chicago's orthodox community finally had its *kosher* kitchen.

Another midwestern example of the division within the Jewish community was described in the pages of the Kansas City *Star*. In September 1899, the infamous trial of France's Captain Alfred Dreyfus was on the lips of almost every American Jew. When news of his second conviction on grounds of espionage reached Kansas City, the Orthodox Hebrew Ladies' Relief Society passed a resolution recommending the boycott of the Paris Exposition. The *Star* published a letter written by a German Jew urging the public not to accept the "orthodox" position as being representative of the entire Jewish community. In a rather nasty manner, the author wrote that he doubted if any of the orthodox petitioners "earnestly contemplated a visit to the Paris Exposition" and asserted that "if they stay away not much harm will be done."

In the American South also, the established and newly settled Jews were engaged in similar combat. In Atlanta, Georgia, the Russians, finding themselves "different" from the earlier Jewish inhabitants, founded their own synagogues, established separate communal organizations, and went their own way socially and culturally. At the same time, the Germans discouraged intermarriage, prevented the Russians from joining B'nai B'rith, and thwarted all attempts at temple membership. On one occasion, relations were so strained that when a Russian infant died, members of the reform congregation *begrudgingly* acceded to a request for a plot to bury the child.

The conflicts between "old" and "new" immigrants lingered for decades. The labor-management splits between working-class "down-towners" and "uptown" employers further heightened the estrangement, and the separate cultural and institutional life of the ghetto diminished the communication between the groups. The division continued well into the twentieth century.

In the same manner that the Germans and Russians were waging their "war," the East Europeans themselves were afflicted with their own internal strife. Perhaps most important was the anti-religious sentiment that ran rampant through the ghetto settlements. The most noted manifestation of this clash was between the adherents of orthodoxy and the radical intellectuals. "We have none of the accepted beliefs regarded as religious," wrote Philip Krantz a prominent New York radical. "We do not believe in the God who negotiated with Moses our preacher." Even Abraham Cahan, through his fictional character Rabbi Nehemiah, echoed these sentiments: "I had ears but could not hear, because of my ear-locks; I had eyes and could not see because they were closed in prayer. . . . I am Rabbi Nehemiah no longer, they call me Nehemiah the atheist now."

David Edelstadt, the editor of the *Freie Arbeiter Shtimme,* attacked all religious institutions. In a dedication to the "Defenders of Darkness," his prose rang with liberation from religious tradition:

> Börne, Lassalle, Marx
> Will deliver us from the diaspora
> The world will recognize no
> distinctions
> All will be free, whether Turk,
> Christian or Jew
> Every age has its sacred message
> Ours is freedom and justice.

The most tragicomic manifestation of the clash between the radicals and the orthodox community was the Yom Kippur Ball. This form of anti-religious activity was initiated in 1888 by London radicals who placed the following advertisements in the *Arbayter Fraynd:*

> We hereby notify all our friends that we are preparing a dinner to be held in our club. This will take place in honor of the great festi-

val of the slaughter of fowl, Yom Kippur, when all asses and hypo-
crites beat their hearts, repent of the sins they have committed, and
fast. For one shilling you can receive a good dinner and spend a
most enjoyable day in fine company. The dinner will be followed
by singing and dancing. There will also be a number of brief lectures and recitations. On the occasion of this feast we have invited
as cantors and preachers the good lord himself and his entire suite:
Moses, Aaron, King David and his Harp, Jesus Christ, John the
Baptist. . . . We will post bills for those who, sitting in the synagogue and sneaking out now and then for a smoke and a bite to
eat, will not read this notice.

Jewish anarchists in America followed the example set by their London counterparts. An admission ticket to the American affair read:

Grand Yom Bom Kippur Ball with theater. Arranged with the consent of all new rabbis of liberty. Kol Nidre Night and Day in the
year 6851 (5651), after the invention of the Jewish idols, and
1890, after the birth of the false Messiah. . . . Music, dancing,
buffet, Marseillaise and other hymns against Satan.

Almost immediately, orthodox and reform leaders joined forces to
stop the event. *The American Hebrew* called it "malicious imbecility"
and urged everyone *"in every way* to abstain from association with [the
leaders]. Everyone has certainly the liberty, if he chooses," declared
the editors,

to alienate himself from religious associations, and go on his own
way. When, however, an organized body of Israelites propose to
publicly desecrate the most sacred sentiments of the Jews and the
most solemn traditions of Judaism, and ostentatiously invite others
to join them in their disreputable scandal, we cannot ignore them
and leave them to the contempt which they would receive from all
respectable people, whether Jews, Christians, or unbelievers. . . .
Absolute social ostracism should be the lot of such depraved crea-
tures who are so far lost to every sense of decency as to go out of
their way to outrage the religious feelings of those of their racial
kindred. . . . The Jews of this city [New York] owe it to themselves to disavow them, and in every way *in every way* to abstain
from association with them.

In response to this editorial and the activities of the religious leaders,
the anarchists distributed the following notice:

The orthodox and reform religious swindlers have set afloat a rotten, filthy lie, to the effect that the ball . . . has been called off.

One group tried to bribe the owner of the hall [where the ball was to be held]. Fortunately its shameful offer was rejected. We hereby notify the public that the rumor that the ball will not be held is wholly false. The concert and ball will definitely be held, and all will be in order, at the time and place, and with the program, which has been announced.

We therefore appeal to every right-thinking person to support this struggle against the swindle which religion is, and to come in large numbers.

On the evening of the event, there were, as promised, singing and dancing and a buffet. Speeches were made in German, Russian, and Yiddish, and street parade, which made "a terrible racket," topped off the festivities. Each of the anarchists, wrote one observer, "had a lit cigarette in his mouth and a piece of pork in his hand" as they walked along "growling the Marseillaise and other street songs. . . ." "From morning to night," reported the anarchist *Fraye Arbayter Shtimme,* "they danced, ate and sang, instead of deadening their spirits and bodies in a synagogue filled with bad air and even worse goings-on. . . . It is difficult to understand how all the good friends of our dear lord were able to sit by so quietly while a band of Yom Kippur celebrants gathered and deprived God of His holy halo this past Yom Kippur."

At other locations, similar events were held. In Providence, Rhode Island, Moshe Katz, an anarchist traveling among Jewish communities to stir up anti-religious sentiment, delivered a "Kol Nidray sermon" and the following morning he was in Boston, where, he said, "every gambling house is turned into a synagogue, every saloon into a temple of God, and every pool of muck into a mikve." "We really achieved something that day," commented a Boston participant. "We replaced stupidity by enlightenment, superstition by conviction, darkness by light."

Opposition to the anti-religious celebrations were more than verbal: sometimes there was violence. In 1893, on the day of Yom Kippur, New York's Anarchist Club, situated next to a synagogue, was broken into and destroyed. The *Fraye Arbayter Shtimme* declared "the pogromists" to be "none other than swinish saloonkeepers," "social-democratic hangers-on," and "Irish and American bums." The Hebrew-language *Haivri,* however, reported another account:

. . . this year, too, they held a party on Yom Kippur, and from their clubhouse on Pike Street much noise and merriment resounded, causing a great deal of pain to all Jewish passersby. Evidently, the anarchists had not been very diligent in praying "protect me from evil neighbors," for, according to the version of the anarchists, they were attacked by people from the neighboring synagogue.

In time, the anarchists abandoned their custom of the Yom Kippur Ball. In 1902, the *Fraye Arbayter Shtimme* called upon their readers to stop the practice of "making the Days of Awe in any way as being different from any other day of the year. Don't have any balls," it urged, "but don't suddenly become pious either. Ah, if only each freethinker would quietly go about his ordinary business . . . how much closer we would be to our goal."

The anti-religious outbursts of the radicals was a tactical error. Many East Europeans, even those who had abandoned orthodox observance, still had roots in Jewish religious tradition. The assault on their religious customs was seen as a frontal attack on their *raison d'être*. No matter how far they drifted from religious observance, this kind of insult could not be easily forgiven. The Yom Kippur Ball, which was used as a vehicle to gain support of the masses, only served to alienate and drive away the Jewish working class. "The war against God," admitted one anarchist, "played a great part in the decrease of anarchist influence in [American] Jewish life."

Less seething, but hardly less sensitive, was the linguistic division between the Hebraists and Yiddishists. While the masses spoke Yiddish, the intellectual wrote in Hebrew, Russian, and German. The vast majority of literary contributions of the period—via the press, poetry, prose, and theater—all indicated a "golden age of Yiddish culture." Hebrew attracted very few: only those steeped in Hebraic literature and concerned with retention of this ancient language.

In time, however, the Hebraists were drawn to the Jewish masses and in the process compromised their position: they learned Yiddish. Even Philip Krantz, the radical editor of the *Arbeiter Freind,* "tolerated" the language: ". . . everybody knows what a fine and rich language our *Mame Loshon* [mother tongue] is," moaned Krantz. "You must practically break your head to find the right word." Responding to the remark, the Yiddishists labeled Krantz as "a *goy* [gentile] who speaks Yiddish."

The armistice between the Yiddish-speaking masses and the Hebraist intellectuals had far-reaching consequences. It interfused, for a short time, the concern and outlook of the opposing groups. Despite the *rapprochement,* because the second and third generation turned to English, Yiddish also was relatively short-lived as a cultural movement.

In spite of the conflict raging within the East European community and the deepening cleavages between "uptowners" and "downtowners," the Jews of the Yiddish-speaking ghettos still managed to develop a complex, vibrant, and decidedly stronger American Jewish community than the earlier immigrants. Significantly, as the decades advanced, the hostility amid the "old" and "new" immigrants lost its intensity. The common fear of American anti-Semitism, the Hitlerian nightmare, and the concern for a Jewish homeland all served as vehicles for the unification. As important, the Eastern Europeans would shed their self-consciousness and the Germans their long-standing position of exclusiveness. In time, the two groups would meet and from necessity become one.

To Become Americans

On April 26, 1655, the board of directors of the Dutch West India Company instructed Governor Stuyvesant as follows: "After many consultations, we have decided . . . that [the Portuguese Jews] shall have permission . . . to live and remain there, provided the *poor among them shall not become a burden to the company, or to the community, but be supported by their own nation.*" What in Stuyvesant's day was obligatory and mandatory was, at the height of the Russian immigration, accepted as a voluntary responsibility. The axiom that "the Jew cares for his own" overshadowed the friction between newcomer and native and gave birth to a spirit of philanthropy aimed at establishing the East Europeans as self-sufficient members of the American community.

Emma Lazarus, who zealously undertook the work of assisting the newcomers, suggested that "every Jewish school . . . in the land, religious or secular, [offer] a system of instruction in some branch of productive activity. . . . We require this kind of instruction to be furnished to Jewish boys and girls who are not [only] orphans, who are [not] only wards of public institutions, but who, subjected to all the normal friction of life in the poorer, middle, and even higher classes, should be brought up to consider their education incomplete until it has supplied them with the art of using their hands and earning their livelihood in at least a single branch of productive activity."

Consequently, a number of technical schools were established: the Hebrew Technical Institute, modeled after the Odessa Trade School, gave instruction to 120 people as mechanics, tinsmiths, cabinetmakers and electricians; the Hebrew Free School Association founded a technical institute for females; New York's United Hebrew Charities operated a factory to teach "needle skills"; and Philadelphia's Hebrew Educational Society established programs to prepare men and women for the "garment, cigar and millinery" industries.

The American Baron de Hirsch Fund also established programs for industrial education. "The Jewish neighborhood was excited," reported George Price, "[as] rumors spread that Baron de Hirsch's agents were counting Jews; and paupers began to build castles in the air." No one knew what the census meant. Nevertheless, the New York ghetto was alive with talk that the baron was giving each person one hundred dollars. Some even estimated the gift at five hundred dollars. Whatever his reason, the wealthy European philanthropist was counting Jews and all Lower East Siders saw it as their obligation to prove their poverty and enlarge their family, for the census at least, by six. "Ah," muttered one would-be recipient, "what calamity would it be if the baron were to give an additional $100 per child; the baron would not become poorer."

The dream of acquiring the baron's money remained just that—a dream. Rather than distributing cash to the newcomers, the fund instead established a temporary trade school at the Hebrew Technical Institute. One hundred immigrants were enrolled and under the direction of six instructors were taught basic carpentry and cabinetmaking. For three months, "during which time the students were given a subsidy— three dollars per week, to those who were unmarried; and five, to those married," the school carried out its program.*

In addition to technical training, the philanthropists moved in other directions. Slum conditions provided constant pressure for proper medical care; tuberculosis was a major threat, and trachoma was extensive among the children. Malnutrition and heart disease, for which medical care was virtually non-existent, were also widespread among the newcomers. To exacerbate the problem, many of the recently arrived refugees chose to suffer from the effects of these illnesses rather than be treated at public medical facilities. For them, the city-owned hospitals were places crowded with abusive alcoholics, aggressive anti-Semites,

* Though similar schools opened in St. Louis, Chicago, Boston, and Detroit, most immigrant adults, rather than go through the "extensive" training period, sought immediate income and employment. This particular philanthropic endeavor directed its efforts at the young. In time, the public schools offered parallel programs and there was a noticeable drop in attendance.

and proselytizing Christian missionaries. "If I am going to die," said Sam Ratner, a New York tailor, "let it be among Jews."

In response to this situation, the charitable agencies rushed to open dispensaries and clinics. New York Jewry founded Montefiore Hospital, Chicago's Michael Reese Hospital established a dental clinic and maternity service, and the New Orleans Touro Infirmary gained a reputation for its excellent convalescent care. The National Council of Jewish Women helped to introduce milk stations, penny luncheons for school children, and educational campaigns among the Yiddish-speaking community; Lillian Wald, director of New York's Henry Street Settlement, spearheaded a drive to organize a visiting-nurse service; and B'nai B'rith founded the National Hospital for Rheumatism and Blood Diseases, in Hot Springs, Arkansas. Still others provided periodic medical examinations and summer camps for poorly nourished and handicapped children.

Jewish agencies also concerned themselves with the swelling number of fatherless homes. Though this was not specifically a "Jewish problem," almost all were alarmed by the increasing number of "desertions." According to one source, "in 1909, 7% of the charitable cases in St. Louis were deserted women, in Baltimore 16%, in Chicago 11%, and in New York City 10%."†

Concern over these statistics led to the creation of the National Desertion Bureau in 1912, which, among its many activities, published pictures and descriptions of "deserters" in the *Jewish Daily Forward* and, when necessary, participated in their criminal prosecution. As the immigration ebbed, those concerned with the problem discovered that desertion was not caused solely by good-for-nothing husbands but by the conditions of the new American environment. "Arranged marriages," asserted one investigator, "which may have worked satisfactorily in the Old Country, sometimes could not take the strains imposed by transplanted life in the United States. Long periods of absence before the breadwinner could bring his family to the United States also contributed to the estrangement of some. Punitive measures could not solve the problem of desertion."

Though the German Jewish community gave of their finances and time liberally, the newcomers were still skeptical about the natives, who held the philanthropic purse strings. "We are not *schnorrers!*

† The rate of desertions was higher among non-Jewish immigrants. Nevertheless, New York-based Jewish agencies campaigned to make desertion a felony.

[beggers]," exclaimed one Russian spokesman, "and we want to take care of our own." Thus, armed with a mixture of pride and distrust, the East Europeans set about to establish welfare organizations of their own.

The most outstanding manifestation of their efforts were the *Landsmanschaften* and *Vereins*—burial and mutual-aid societies made up of people from the same town or village in the old country. In New York, the Galicians established the Federation of Galician and Bukovinian Jews of America and founded Har Moriah Hospital, the Russian-Polish community organized the Federation of Russian-Polish Hebrews of America and established Beth Israel Hospital, the Romanians founded the Federation of Romanian Jews and operated a convalescent home, and the Bessarabians supported an orphan asylum.

"These societies," reported Hutchins Hapgood,

> curiously express at once the old Jewish customs and the conditions of the old world. They are mutual-insurance companies formed to support sick members. When a brother is ill, the president appoints a committee to visit him. Mutual-insurance societies and committees are American enough, and visiting the sick is prescribed by the Talmud. This is a striking instance of the adaptation of the old and the new.

Landsmanschaften appeared wherever the East Europeans concentrated. In Philadelphia, for example, Hachnosas Orchim (Hospitality to Wayfarers) founded a temporary shelter for immigrants waiting to find employment or lost relatives, the Independent Chevra Kadisho (Independent Burial Society) provided free burial in cases in which the families were too poor to bear the expense, and the women's society Gemilas Chasodim (Deed of Loving-kindness) made interest-free loans to "deserving persons in amounts of five to twenty-five dollars, repayable in installments. The Malbish Arumim (Clothing the Naked) provided needy children of the Talmud Torah schools with clothing, and the United Relief Association cared for those requiring immediate attention and furnished matzos to the poor and "wine and eggs to the sick." The value of these societies cannot be overestimated. According to Morris Raphael Cohen, the hundreds of *Landsmanschaften* dotting the ghettos helped the East Europeans "adjust themselves to the new land" and to keep their self-respect while making "a home for the new generation. . . ."

The most important benevolent-fraternal society to be established by the East Europeans was the *Arbeiter Ring* (Workmen's Circle). "The Workmen's Circle," wrote sweatshop poet Morris Rosenfeld, "was founded when Eighth Street [the location of several Jewish charities] was the Wailing Wall of the Jewish worker in New York. There the unemployed, hungry, sick worker would cry for bread, medical aid, clothing, coal and rent. There the worker's pale wife would groan, there his drawn and pallid children would sigh."

Established by two cloakmakers in 1892 and reorganized as a national organization in 1900, it stressed self-help and, unlike the German-dominated societies, *self-respect*. Those who provided funds for the needy on Monday knew very well, from experience, that they themselves might be requesting similar aid on Tuesday; equality and working-class solidarity were uppermost concepts at the influential "labor-fraternal order."

Assistance to members in time of need was not the only goal of the society, its fundamental philosophy being socialism. "We Fight Against Sickness, Premature Death, and Capitalism," read the masthead of a report to the 1905 convention. In the ensuing years, as the organization emerged as an important arm of the Jewish labor movement, it accepted only trade unionists for membership, urged those members to vote for Socialist candidates, and established, in order to stem the influence of "capitalist" public education, schools with a Socialist flavor.

At one Chicago school, where Jewish subject matter was "taught in the broad and free spirit of international socialism," a teacher described opening day:

> The celebration took place in the huge . . . auditorium. The hall was filled to capacity with 3,000 Jewish workers and decorated with red flags. . . . The newly registered children, over seven hundred of them, sat in the first rows, all dressed in red blouses. These youngsters, most of whom were actually snatched out of the teeth of the Talmud Torahs and *heders*,‡ who attend our school only for one week, filled the audience with enthusiasm and brought a thunderous applause with their singing of the "Internationale."

At the "Arbeiter Ring Socialist Children's Schools," where instructors were hired according to their devotion to socialism, the ideological aims were quite clear. "It is a regrettable fact," declared the sponsors,

> that in a capitalist society the public schools are controlled largely by capitalists, the enemies of the working class . . . the teachers

‡ The education offered by the Talmud Torah and the *heder* are discussed in the following section.

are forced to plant in the young innocent hearts the greatest reactionary chauvinism. Therefore every clear-minded worker who strives for a more beautiful and better world for humanity cannot permit himself to remain indifferent to the education of his children. . . .

The foundation of the new order must be carefully prepared. . . . Without the younger generation . . . the future of the ship of life and the workingman's fight will be lost. . . . It is a recognized fact that so long as nations with various tongues and cultures exist, the Jewish people will be no exception, for like all other nationalities, the Jewish people possess their own culture and the Yiddish language which is spoken by its largest majority. The American melting pot built a stone wall between the parents and the children, in that the children spoke a new tongue, thus making it impossible for parents and children to understand each other. This lack of understanding seriously disturbed the child's education. To eradicate this difference the Workmen's Circle decided to establish daily Jewish Socialist schools.

These schools, noted Menakhem Karson, a Chicago-based writer, satisfied the desires for an educational institution that embodied a synthesis of two ideologies: "that of secular Judaism and that of Socialism." This desideratum led to the creation of these "Yiddish, Socialist, and free-thinking schools.*

Acculturation had been relatively easy for the small and dispersed German community, but for the Russian newcomers, living in tightly knit urban centers, accommodating to American society was somewhat more difficult. Yet the assimilative pressures exerted by the new environment began to take effect. Hutchins Hapgood observed the initial stages:

The man who has been only three weeks in this country hates few things so much as to be called a greenhorn. Under this fear he learns the small vocabulary. . . . Of this modest vocabulary he is very proud, for it takes him out of the category of "greenhorn"—a term of contempt to which the satirical Jew is very sensitive. His dress received rather greater modification than his language. In the old country he never appeared in a short coat; that would be enough to stamp him as a free-thinker. But when he comes to New York and his coat is worn out, he is unable to find any garment long enough. The best he can do is to buy a cutaway, or Prince Albert, which he often calls a Prince Isaac. As soon as he imbibes the

* A broader discussion on the Yiddish-secular school movement will follow.

fear of being called a greenhorn he assumes the Prince Isaac with less regret. Many of the old women, without diminution of piety, discard their wigs, which are strictly required by the orthodox in Russia, and go even to the synagogue with nothing on their heads but their natural locks.

It was the children, however, who assimilated the fastest. Even before entering public school, the youngsters were in conflict with their Old World traditions. On the streets they learned some English, with a little slang, and often returned home to repeat the tales about the prize fighter named Bernstein. More important, at public school the child of orthodoxy ran up against an even greater set of influences that were at total variance with the orthodox tradition. As public school students they received no religious instruction but, rather, non-sectarian subject matter. English became the student's first language, and he achieved "a growing comprehension and sympathy with the independent, free, rather skeptical spirit of the American boy. He rapidly imbibes ideas about social equality and contempt for authority," writes Hapgood, "and tends to prefer Sherlock Holmes to Abraham as a hero."

While the public schools were making every effort to incorporate the newcomers into the American scene, other forces were also at work in anticipation of hastening the transformation. Native American Jewry did not sit idly by while their recently arrived coreligionists "shamefully" paraded their Old World ways before the Christian community. In every area of primary settlement, institutions armed with programs to help the newcomers become members of the American commonwealth appeared.

At the Educational Alliance, on the Lower East Side of New York, assimilation was a constant theme. Isidor Straus, president of the Alliance, described its policy: "We strive to help immigrants to understand American ideas—the dignity of American citizenship; to appreciate the American atmosphere of obedience to law and to recognize the rule of the majority." Echoing the same theme, Lee Kohns, the Alliance vice-president, declared: "Our aim is to Americanize without de-Judaizing the immigrant and his children."

To fullfill their aims, the Alliance conducted English and citizenship classes, held lectures (sometimes in Yiddish) on the nature of American government, maintained adult organizations, and offered "dramatic, musical, and social entertainments, often attended by more than five hundred persons at a time. . . ." Its method of teaching English was eventually adopted by the New York City Board of Education for its own "English for Foreigners" program.

Across the East River, in Brownsville, an area of secondary settlement, the Hebrew Educational Society (HES) maintained similar programs. Its Mothers' Club sought to acquaint foreign-born Jewish mothers with conditions affecting their children. According to Charles Bernheimer, clubs of this type played a vital role in aiding parents to meet the problems that arose "by reason of a difference of point of view between the parents who are influenced by old-world ideas, and their children who are affected by ideas of the new-world."

The cultural estrangement between the children and their parents tore at many family relationships. "Our children see salvation through different eyes," wrote one immigrant. "I have to listen to my son and keep silent, because to tell him the simple truth, to tell him the story of my entire fifty years of life, would simply mean that his father is still groping around in God's world and has prepared him for nothing definite."

Perhaps Hapgood, in his *Spirit of the Ghetto,* best describes the cultural estrangement that afflicted so many immigrant families:

> The growing sense of superiority on the part of the boy to the Hebraic part of his environment extends itself soon to the home. He learns to feel that his parents, too, are greenhorns. In the struggle between the two sets of influences that of the home becomes less and less effective. He runs away from the supper table to join his gang on the Bowery, where he is quick to pick up the latest slang, where his talent for caricature is developed often at the expense of his parents, his race, and all foreigners; for he is an American, he is "the people," and like his glorious countrymen in general, he is quick to ridicule the stranger. He laughs at the foreign Jew with as much heartiness as at the Italians, for he feels that he himself is almost as remote from the one as from the other.

Once on the street, he is safe. Surrounded by his friends, he talks of prize fighters, crime, and budding business opportunities. At thirteen he is *bar mitzvah,* and his first act as "a man" is to abandon the synagogue in favor of "uptown places of amusement . . . [the] latest American fashion . . . and . . . the right thing in neckties." Some even refuse to attend the Friday-evening meal. "Then, indeed," writes Hapgood, "the sway of the old people is broken."

"Amerikane Kinder, Amerikane Kinder!" wailed the old fathers as

they shook their hands in the air. Indeed, the trend was too strong for the men of the eternal Talmud and ceremony.

The estrangement that settled over some immigrant families—the process of Americanization—continued. At the settlement houses, acculturation made strong gains as American traditions were instilled in the minds of the young and old alike. At the Henry Street and University settlements, in New York, large numbers of Jews washed out the stains of Europe in preparation for a lifetime in America. They flocked to St. Louis's Educational and Charitable Association, Chicago's Educational Alliance, and San Francisco's Emanu-El Sisterhood to attend dances, athletic events, and cultural activities so they might absorb the traditions of their new homeland. In Atlanta, Georgia, also, they entered the Schoen Free Kindergarten, some learned typing and shorthand and were taught how to cook "American style."

Some of the immigrants' own cultural baggage was utilized in the assimilative process. In Cincinnati the Jewish settlement houses stressed the use of Yiddish in their lectures on American history and civics. More important was the Yiddish press as an Americanizing agency. By spending their precious pennies for these journals, the newcomers acquired editorial opinion, coverage of national and local news, interpretation of events, and special "features" on American history, geography, education, and government. The *Tag* published several articles on American history written by Woodrow Wilson.

The Yiddish newspaper increased its Americanizing effort by publishing special English sections. The *Tageblatt* (New York) introduced an English page in 1897 and, when the editors found certain words too difficult for their readers, they translated them into Yiddish and included Yiddish explanatory notes. The *Tag,* which merged with the *Wahrheit* in 1919, carried a weekly English supplement, a special English editorial on the front page, and an English section on Sundays.

The *Jewish Daily Forward* attempted to introduce the language to its readers on November 26, 1920, when it announced the publication of English lessons: "This Sunday we will begin to print in the *Forward* short English stories, translated and explained in Yiddish, so that the reader may learn the English language easily."

The purpose of these lessons is to acquaint the Jewish immigrant little by little with a thousand of the most important English words. For many, a smaller number of words is sufficient. Even if one knows but several hundred words well, one is able to increase his vocabulary by hearing the English language used at meetings, on the street, or at home, where children speak English. Before one notices it, one soon begins to read English newspapers, and the knowledge of the language increases rapidly. This is a very practical plan. The purpose of it is to avoid having the reader strain himself. We expect the reader to enjoy the content of the lessons, and while reading he will learn the language at the same time.

At the opposite end of the Americanizing spectrum were the assimilationist forces of the Christian community. The Daughters of the American Revolution, or *Techter fun de Amerikanishe Revolution,* as the name appeared on their Yiddish literature, offered a wide range of advice for the newcomers; they equated patriotism with religion and designated the nation's capital as "the *Kedisha Kedo-shum*—the Holy of Holies—fun de Amerikanishe nation." In their Yiddish guidebook they told the newcomers that

> The Jew like any other foreigner is appreciated when he joins the American social life. Until then he counts for nothing. Join American clubs, read American papers. Try to adapt yourself to the manners and customs and habits of the American people. Have your name placed on the roll of the league or union of your trade. . . . Become an American citizen as soon as you can. It is an excellent thing for a Jew to join a military company. . . . Membership gives social advantage, and the opportunity of healthful exercise in athletic games and drills is very important to a man who lives in a great city.

"MOTHERS!" they exclaimed:

> the home should be made a happy place to which the young people will bring their friends. Encourage your daughter to introduce to you all her men friends. Win her confidence by sympathy with her desire for proper amusement and pretty clothes. Do not prevent her attending dances held in respectable halls, but insist upon her returning home early. Be sure you know the conditions of your daughter's employment. Do not take your children to Court for commitment to an institution.

More concerned than the DAR with the rapid assimilation of the immigrants were native American Jews. "How can we Americanize them?" asked David Philipson, spiritual leader of the American reform rabbinate. Apparently, the answer to his question, for many, was quite simple: public education. "No levellers . . . like the public schools," wrote a contemporary of Philipson. "These children will become thoroughly American and forget the terrible ordeals through which in a barbarous land they were compelled to pass. They will become self-respecting and not look to the benevolent societies for assistance."

Mary Antin was proof of this assertion. "Education is free," she wrote. "No application made, no questions asked, no examinations, rulings, exclusions; no machinations, no fees. The doors stood open for every one of us." It appears that almost all took Antin's advice as thousands of Yiddish-speaking "greeners" passed through the doors of the nation's public schools. For most, this was the first encounter with public education, and to the surprise of some, they did very well. "As scholars," observed Jacob Riis, "the children of the most ignorant Polish Jew keep fairly abreast of their more favored playmates."

> In . . . class-rooms in the great building, which is devoted entirely to the cause of Americanizing the young Russian immigrants, hundreds of children get daily their first lessons in English and in patriotism in simultaneous doses. The two are inseparable in the beneficent plan of the instructors. Their effort is to lay hold of the children of the newcomers at once; tender years are no barrier. For toddlers there are kindergarten classes, with play the street has had no chance to soil. And while playing they learn to speak the strange new tongue and to love the pretty flag with the stars that is everywhere in sight. . . . the ease and rapidity with which they learn is equalled only by their good behavior and close attention while in school. There is no whispering and no rioting at these desks, no trial of strength with the teacher, . . . these children come to learn.

The Jewish immigrant, more than most, took full advantage of the free public schools. In Pittsburgh, the disproportionate number of Jewish children compared to their percentage in the school-age population was noted by the Council of Churches:

> The people here seem anxious to start their children to school. In Forbes School District only 4% of the children between 6 and 8 are not enrolled. Of those between 16 and 21 years, 25% in our district remain in school. Only 14% in whole city do this. *There is evidence that these facts are largely due to the presence of the Jewish population.*

Very quickly, the public school teacher became a strong influence in the lives of these children. "They learn to look upon [them] as models of good taste," reported J. K. Paulding, a New York journalist. "First, it is true, chiefly in external things, such as clothes and manner of speech—but afterwards, very often, as a pattern of deportment as well." The teachers characterized the educational ability and desire of these children as unique. "They rank among the highest," said one New York educator. "They are far more earnest and ambitious [than others] and many of them supplement their school work with outside reading." Most teachers agreed that the young Jews were exceedingly patriotic. One principal expressed the opinion that Jewish boys of the Lower East Side "are born politicians, and their chief interest in American history arises from the fact that the subject furnishes an area for political contests." A Philadelphia school-board member noted that they "manifest a lively interest in American history and institutions; that the encouragement of education by parents is *active* and that they are . . . as a rule brighter and more studious than other nationalities."

One cause of complaint, however, almost universally centered on the failure of immigrant parents to send their children to school on the days preceding holidays and the Sabbath. "Evidently," wrote a Philadelphia observer, "they are required at home to help *clean-up* previous to these special days, and both parents and children do not seem to realize the importance of conforming to the school routine when it comes into conflict with some of the set habits of the home."

Attendance at evening schools at times required a break with the Sabbath and at other times prevented the orthodox from enrolling in large numbers. In Pittsburgh, after the Sabbath candles were lighted, many missed the Friday-night class, which began at 7:30 P.M. Others chose to violate the Sabbath in order to attend the lesson. One who compromised his orthodox life-style described his experience at a Pittsburgh night school:

> As soon as I came here in 1910 I went to work for a stogy [cigar] maker. Everyone there spoke Yiddish. I didn't see how I would ever learn English. I worked from 7 A.M. to 6 P.M. and then I would rush home, get cleaned up, grab a bite, and run to school.
>
> At Franklin School, there were so many immigrants, 1,500 to 2,000, that our class had to use the kindergarten room and we had to sit on the small chairs. It was very hard to learn. The teacher taught us isolated words, not conversation. Later, one of my teachers was a college student who was himself an immigrant. He became a well-known judge.

The attraction of free public education and the external pressures to Americanize apparently caused a decline in the quality of Jewish education. The *heder,* the makeshift religious school generally held in an instructor's home or in a basement after school hours, was, to say the least, unappealing. Many youngsters expressed contempt for the Hebrew teacher, who dressed "in a long black coat, outlandish tall hat," and most often spoke no English. "In America," reported Hapgood,

> the *chaider* assumes a position entirely subordinate [to public education]. Compelled to go to the American public school, the boy can attend *chaider* only before the public school opens in the morning or after it closes in the afternoon. . . .
>
> Contempt for the *chaider*'s teaching comes the more easily because the boy rarely understands his Hebrew lessons at all. His real language is English, the teacher's is commonly Yiddish, and the language to be learned is Hebrew. The problem before him is consequently the strangely difficult one of learning Hebrew, a tongue unknown to him, through a translation into Yiddish, a language of growing unfamiliarity.

Jewish education via the *heder* did little to attract the younger generation. "The *rebbe* and the basement classroom," asserted one youngster, "are symbols of the greenhorn," and "this is what we detested most of all." The language of instruction, the poor teaching methodology, and the *rebbe*'s ever-present disciplinary strap—"that rap across the knuckles," as it was described by one youngster—added to the alienation. Despite the opposition, *hedarim* sprang up by the hundreds—over saloons, in back rooms of dance halls, in vacant stores, and in dingy basements. And to them went thousands of children. Carrying their neatly piled set of public school books—topped with the familiar, blue-covered Hebrew notebook—they rushed from classrooms where they were taught the rudiments of American government to the waiting *rebbe* to learn the mechanical reading of prayers and the chanting of the *haftarah* as preparation for *bar mitzvah*.

In order to counteract the poor quality of *heder* education, some of the newcomers organized Talmud Torahs—supplementary religious schools most often associated with a synagogue, where Hebrew, religious ritual, and Jewish history were taught. Others called for the establishment of all-day institutions, yeshivahs, in which the greater part of the curriculum was devoted to Jewish studies and only a few hours, enough to satisfy state educational requirements, to secular studies.

The Jewish labor movement also sought to expand the opportunities for a Jewish education. They directed their efforts at the establishment of modern Jewish secular schools. In the Bronx, the Sholem Aleichem

School was opened, and uptown, in Harlem, a Yiddish Socialist school was established by the Jewish Socialist Federation. The Workmen's Circle established schools that stressed "education and achievements relating to Jewish secular life and activity: Yiddish language and literature, Jewish folk creativity, [and] Jewish culture." This was done, they asserted, "to acquaint our children with the treasures of Jewish culture and literature, new and old, in order to assure the continuity of Jewish cultural life."

Also, in Chicago the National-Radical Yiddish School, with the motto "The Jewish Child for the Jewish People," was opened. *Der nayer dor* (the new generation) outlined its program:

> All subjects are taught in Yiddish. Hebrew is recognized as a language of substantial importance and it is studied as a separate subject in the higher grades.
>
> History is taught rationally and scientifically. Historical legends are taught separately and not in chronological order so that children will not assume that legends are history.
>
> The School celebrates all Jewish holidays, and the 1st of May.
>
> Conversations and discussions regarding social problems and movements are held in classrooms. The following personalities are studied and discussed: Robert Owen, Karl Marx, Ferdinand Lassalle, Moses Hess, Bakunin, Kropotkin, the Gaon of Vilna, Baal Shem Tov, Moses Mendelssohn and others. The aim of this course is to imbue the children with the desire to join the ranks of the fighters of freedom and give them the appreciation of the movements which contributed to the progress of humanity.

This institution was not founded by any one group but by several individuals who represented an assortment of ideologies—Poale Zionism, (Labor Zionism) socialism, and territorialism (seeking a Jewish homeland, but not necessarily Palestine). United in their effort to perpetuate Yiddish culture and seeking to utilize Yiddish to bind the Jewish people together, they "adhered," writes historian Mark Klug, "to a secular, though not necessarily anti-religious approach to Jewish history and Jewish group existence."

In 1914 the Poale Zionists abandoned this school and established their own Maccabee Folk School. Here the non-religious sponsors stressed the "nationalistic value of the Jewish religion as a crystallizing force. It is this living, striving and hoping Jewish nationalism," they declared, with which we saturate the mind and spirit of our children and we deeply imprint in their tender hearts that they are forever bound with the Jewish nation, being one with it and with all its kith and kin, in joy and sorrow, in pain and privation, in toil and persecution, in the mighty struggle of modern Jewry for its deliverance, in the glorious hope for salvation.

The Jewish Communists also established educational units. In Chicago, the "Non-Partisan Labor Children's Schools" emphasized the importance of the Soviet Union and the downfall of American capitalism. "While the Sholem Aleychem Folk Schools, supported as they are by well-to-do elements, find themselves in a pitiful condition, and the Arbeiter Ring schools which receive fat subsidies from Uncle Sam are in their last dying days. We," declared the Communists, "the class conscious workers of Chicago, have united. . . ."

The objectives of the "Non-Partisan Labor Children's Schools" were quite clear:

> The acceptance of the [Dalton] project method [an educational program borrowed from the Soviet school system] made it possible to bring the proletarian realities into our schools. It has assured the affirmation of the class struggle as a principle of education. The project method activated the children in all the branches of the movement. Thus for example the children worked on a project of a celebration of the October Revolution, collected money for the *Morgen Frayhayt,* took part in a Lenin memorial meeting, participated actively in the revolutionary appearances of the older comrades. . . . Our children did particularly well in their participation in the picket demonstration during the bread-strike as well as in the hunger-marches in Chicago.

Though the primary objectives of the Yiddish secular schools, except for the Communist-operated institutions, were the promotion of Socialist and Jewish ideals, the motivating force behind them was Jewish nationalism—a concept neglected by other Jewish educational institutions.† These schools emphasized the importance of teaching Yiddish, the first language of the immigrants, to offset the growing linguistic and ideological conflict between the children and their parents, and therefore to stop the separation of the family into two opposing camps without a common perspective or language.

† At the "Non-Partisan Labor Children's Schools," Zionism was equated with British imperialism, and stress was placed on allegiance to the Soviet Union.

Though religious and secular schools proliferated, most of the new-comers gravitated to public institutions for their education. Perhaps then, when the *Jewish Daily Forward* declared, "to the list of Jewish holidays should be added another important holiday, graduation day," they were expressing the thoughts of thousands of proud "greeners" who sat through their children's graduation exercises at the nation's public schools. Rightfully so, graduation day was a great holiday for Jewish parents—"a true Jewish holiday in tradition and spirit."

To the contemporary gentile observer, the religious conduct of the newcomers testified to their religiosity. "The sweatshops are full of religious fanatics," remarked one eyewitness, "who, in addition to their ceremonies at home, form Talmudic clubs and gather in tenement-house rooms, which they convert into synagogues." On the Sabbath and High Holidays the Jewish business districts were calm, in *shul* the orthodox *minhag* (ritual) prevailed, and on the streets the proliferation of *kosher* restaurants and shops was evidence enough to indicate that the East Europeans observed the rituals of *kashrut* (dietary laws).

The appearance of orthodoxy, however, was deceiving, for in reality there was an increasing indifference to religious life in the Jewish ghettos. Though the hundreds of synagogues dotting the community projected a pious image and were attended in large numbers on *Yom Kippur* and *Rosh Hashanah,* there was nevertheless an appreciable drop in attendance at Sabbath and daily services.

Religious laxity, though the elders still stubbornly maintained the Old World ways, was effected by the New World surroundings. "The pious scholars," reported Hapgood, were "submerged . . . in their own com-munities," as even some of the Sabbath observers, bending under the pressure of assimilation, "looked upon these rabbis as greenhorns." In Philadelphia, an investigation conducted by Rabbi Julius Greenstone revealed that the younger generation was not necessarily antagonistic to religion but indifferent to it. "They are unsympathetic with the existing synagogues," he reported, "because the synagogue offers them very lit-tle, it being managed by the older people, who do not and cannot un-derstand them. They are indifferent to Jewish practice, because it has never been presented to them in a light that would appeal to their more modern and cultivated tastes."

In anticipation of reversing this situation, New York's Association of Orthodox Hebrew Congregations called for the appointment of a "Chief Rabbi in America." Such an authority, they asserted, would "promote the observance of the Orthodox religion" and "improve and

elevate the moral and spiritual condition of the Jewish people. . . ."
Soon Rabbi Jacob Joseph, an outstanding European scholar, was on his
way to America. Immediately after his arrival, because of his attempt to
oversee the *kosher* meat industry, he became a controversial figure. Apparently, the "Chief Rabbi" opposed any financial charge to the consumer for the supervision of *kashrut* (dietary laws). Ordinarily, his
effort to eradicate this abuse would have been welcomed, but the association that hired him derived part of its operating income from the
"*kosher* surcharge" and refused to support his opposition to the practice. Though he continued to maintain that the charge be absorbed by
the association and not the consumer, in the end he gave in to the
wishes of his "superiors."

He did win part of his demands: that the tax for *kashrut* supervision
be placed on poultry and not on meat. "Poultry," he said, was the staple of the rich and if there was to be a tax, "let it be paid by those who
can afford it." Thus, in both Yiddish and English, the following circular
was distributed to the Lower East Side community:

> Herewith I make known to all our brethren, the children of Israel,
> who tremble at the word of the Lord, that inspectors have already
> been appointed in the poultry slaughter houses to test the knives
> and to have supervision of everything in their care. From this day
> forward every bird slaughtered in the abattoir under our supervi-
> sion will be stamped with a *plumbe* (lead seal).
>
> . . . and we make it known to you that if you find any butcher's
> chicken not so stamped, that it was not killed under our supervi-
> sion and we cannot guarantee it to be kosher.

The charge for the metal tag attached to the chicken's leg was one
penny: "The fowl bearing seals should not be sold for any higher price
than others, except one cent on each fowl for the seal," read the announcement.

As soon as the tags made their appearance, the Jewish community
rose in protest. Housewives objected to the payment of an additional
penny; butchers howled at the new controls; orthodox rabbis, who had
previously certified *kashrut,* feared the loss of income; and the radical
press, always looking for an excuse to attack religion, called it "price
gouging." Cries of *"Karobka!"*—the Czarist tax on *kosher* meat—were
heard everywhere. Indeed, all remembered that similar taxes were used
by Russian officialdom for anti-Semitic programs.

The "anti-tag" movement also had its poet. In a poem entitled
Karobka, Getzel Selikovitch wrote:

> Dance, orthodox chickens;
> Make merry, have no fear
> For the Rabbi an order has issued
> Shining medals you'll wear.
> You'll wear them after your slaughter
> That the Chief Rabbi may live;
> They flay the skin off the worker
> A fat salary the Great one to give.

Opposition was also heard from the Hebrew Poultry Butchers Association:

> The *Karobka plumbe* on chickens which evil men wish to import from the old country to the New World is an insult to Judaism and an affront to Mosaic law, because these men mean only to flay the skin off our backs through this despicable tax and put us to shame in our city, New York. Therefore . . . we declare as Terefah [non-kosher] all meats sold by the butchers who have made common cause with the charlatans who impose *karobka*.

The "anti-tag" assaults on Rabbi Joseph diminished his authority. Other groups challenged his appointment by naming "chief rabbis" of their own. The Galicians and Hungarians, known for their conflict with the Litvaks (Lithuanians), appointed Rabbi Joshua Segal, and a small group of Hassidim installed Rabbi Hayim Vidrowitz as their own "Chief Rabbi of America." Perhaps it can be said that a chicken with a metal tag led to the failure of the establishment of a rabbinical hierarchy in the orthodox community.

As though seeking forgiveness for the abuse they heaped upon him, the entire East Side community turned out for Rabbi Joseph's funeral procession. The anti-religious *Jewish Daily Forward* eulogized him as "a man who lived and died in America as a sacrificial offering to business-Judaism," and the orthodox *Jewish Gazette* declared: "In spite of all that was said against the Rabbi during his lifetime, we all loved him, because of his estimable qualities and the blameless life he led."

In death, as in life, the "Chief Rabbi" was in the center of conflict. As the funeral procession made its way through the streets, the Irish workers from R. Hoe and Company attacked the mourners with bottles, stones, and chunks of metal. Within seconds, bearded orthodox Jews were scrambling for the protective cover of East Broadway's hallways. In the midst of the fighting, the police, claiming they could not "tell the difference" between the "uniquely dressed" mourners and the Irish rioters, vomited up their anti-Semitic feelings and attacked the Jews with nightsticks and fists. The mayor's official investigation clearly showed that this was a "police riot," that New York's "finest" joined the workers to spill Jewish blood on the streets.

It was yet another encounter with the police, this time verbal, that led to the temporary unity of New York's Jewish community—the New York *Kehilla,* 1908–22.

In September 1908, New York's police commissioner, Theodore A. Bingham, in an article for the *North American Review,* asserted that 50 per cent of the city's criminals were Jewish. He wrote:

> It is not astonishing that with a million Hebrews, mostly Russian, in the city (one-quarter of the population) perhaps half of the criminals should be of that race when we consider that ignorance of the language, more particularly among men not physically fit for hard labor, is conducive to crime. . . . They are burglars, firebugs, pickpockets and highway robbers—when they have courage; but though all crime is their province, pocket-picking is the one to which they take naturally. . . . Among the most expert of all the street thieves are Hebrew boys under sixteen who are brought up to lives of crime. . . . The juvenile Hebrew emulates the adult in the matter of crime percentage, 40 percent of the boys at the House of Refuge and 37 percent of those arraigned in the children's court being of that race.

The Yiddish press labeled the commissioner an anti-Semite and denounced the story as untrue. The *Wahrheit* questioned Bingham's credibility, recalling a similar anti-Semitic article written for *Harper's,* and the *Tageblatt* warned that the future of American Jewry was at stake. As expected, there began a procession of Jewish spokesmen, all claiming to represent the Jewish community and each calling for conferences and demonstrations. Two weeks after the article appeared, no less than sixteen "leaders" offered explanations to the press—all with their own statistics or rational refutation of the charge. The Jewish community was unprepared for a unified reply. "What have we done" asked the *Wahrheit* "so that we will be reckoned with and respected . . . so that in such situations we can protect ourselves . . . ?" The *Tageblatt* editorialized: "We have a million Jews in New York. Where is their power? Where is their organization? Where are their representatives?" Turning to the "uptown" community, the same editorial scathingly declared:

When someone refused to allow a [Jewish] aristocrat into a Gentile hotel. . . . the Jewish four hundred did not rest until the guilty party had been dismissed; and now . . . they are quiet! Is it possible because the ones insulted are Russian Jews?

Responding to this charge, *The American Hebrew,* the journalistic voice of the natives, asserted that the "downtowners" overreacted. In an editorial entitled "Jewish Sensitiveness," they declared:

The cry goes up to heaven from all quarters that a serious insult has been put upon the Jews of New York, and some hot heads are even clamoring for the removal of the Commissioner. . . . The whole incident illustrates the excessive sensitiveness of Jews with regard to any statement derogatory to their highest claims. So many of them have passed their lives under the withering fact of repression, that in this land of liberty they tend to go to the other extreme and insist upon the right of freedom with undue emphasis. . . .

The *Tageblatt* condemned the apologetic editorial: "Is this the Torah of Americanism which you teach us!" they exclaimed. "Instead of teaching us to be proud citizens . . . of the land of freedom you preach [instead] the old Torah of fawning, to bend the back and be still. No doubt we cannot be dependent on our grand moguls."

In the midst of the verbal clash, the Jewish League, an *ad hoc* group made up of members of the Federation of American Zionists, in anticipation of putting up a united front, called for a conference to include "different shades of opinion of the Jews of Greater New York." They invited Louis Marshall, Isidor Straus, and Jacob Schiff to represent the "uptowners" and Congressman Henry Goldfogle and Assemblyman Moritz Graubard to speak for the "downtowners." Also asked to represent the Lower East Side were the heads of the various fraternal orders, spokesmen for the *landsmanschaften,* the Socialists, the Zionists, the publishers, and the influential Yiddish journalists.

Though the "uptowners" refused to attend, the democratically established conference still proved fruitful. The meeting demonstrated, though there were wide differences of opinion present, the ability of the East Siders to initiate a movement that had been previously characterized as "wishful thinking" and "inoperable" in the American environment. On September 6, the conference announced the appointment of two committees: one to collect information on the criminal activities on New York Jewry and a second to represent the Jewish community if similar charges were ever made again.

While the Lower East Siders were organizing, Louis Marshall, the influential leader of the American Jewish Committee, without fanfare or extensive press coverage, intervened on behalf of the "downtown" community. "I am very much opposed," he wrote to Dr. Adolph Radin, "to the holding of any meetings for the purpose of protesting against the remarks of Police Commissioner Bingham . . . because I consider it inadvisable to meet his statement by any sensational methods. A clear and pointed statement of facts would be much more effective and convincing than a tirade."

Several days after he wrote these comments, Marshall met with Arthur Woods, deputy police commissioner, to arrange peace between Bingham and the Lower East Siders. Marshall told Woods, if Bingham retracted his remarks, he would see to it that the "downtowners" would "make a statement to the effect that they accept the explanation . . . and that they regard the incident closed." In order to fulfill his part of the bargain, Marshall needed the co-operation of the Lower East Side leadership and the recently convened conference, now headed by Judah Magnes. It was the only unified organization in sight. Thus, when the terms of settlement were arranged, Marshall journeyed downtown to seek ratification. With Marshall representing the "uptowners" and Magnes the "downtowners," an organization representing a unified New York Jewish community was finally established.

Within a few days, Bingham retracted the challenged statement without reservation. "The figures used in the article," he said, "were not compiled by myself but were furnished . . . by . . . others. It now appears, however, that these figures were unreliable." The "downtown" committee, now called The Jewish Council, accepted the explanation and declared that "in view of this retraction [The Jewish Council] is willing to allow the incident between Commissioner Bingham and the Jews of New York to be regarded as closed."

After the Jewish Council accepted the Marshall proposal, it called on "representative Jews of the city" to meet for the "purpose of forming a permanent organization to foster the interests of the Jews in every proper way." "The one million Jews in New York," declared Magnes, "should draw the proper deductions from this incident. They need a permanent and representative organization that may speak on their behalf, that may defend their rights and liberties and that may also cope with the problems of criminality. . . ." On February 28, 1909, six months after the publication of Bingham's remarks, representatives of 222 Jewish groups ratified "the Constitution of the Jewish Community of New York," which Louis Marshall of the American Jewish Committee helped to write.‡

ORGANIZING THE UNIONS

One of the most notorious aspects of American industrial life was the sweating system. The term was applied to the process in which manufacturers distributed material to contractors who, in turn, subcontracted the work to people performing the tasks in their homes. At the turn of the century, nearly three quarters of the workers in Manhattan's sweatshops were Jews.* The well-known sweating district of New York, bounded by Eighth Street, the Bowery, Catherine Street, and the East River, had some 450,000 persons, including many children, who lived and worked in their homes. The denizens of the sweatshops toiled long hours for low wages and under terrible conditions, producing mainly garments. "The Jew," declared Abraham Cahan, "did not bring [the system] with him. He found it already developed here." The sweating system began in the early-nineteenth century among the native workers who then dominated the clothing trade. Later, when the Irish moved into the field, they inherited the "in-residence" method of production. With the massive influx of East Europeans, the Yiddish-speaking Jews became the chief source of sweatshop labor.

Throughout the Yiddish-speaking sections of New York, Boston, Chicago, and Philadelphia, sweatshops seemed to appear like magic, and in them it was not uncommon for men, women, and children to work from sixteen to nineteen hours a day.

"Lipman's," wrote Abraham Cahan,

‡ The New York *Kehilla,* which lasted until 1922, aided in the foundation of a school for communal work, operated the Bureau of Philanthropic Research, participated in the creation of the Bureau of Jewish Education, stimulated the formation of New York's Federation of Jewish Philanthropies, and published the Jewish Communal Register, which described every aspect of New York's organized Jewish life. After the *Kehilla* was abandoned, the New York community was never again to organize itself centrally.
* The figures vary for Philadelphia, Boston, and Chicago. However, in these cities, the East Europeans made up a very large part of the sweatshop labor force.

was a task shop, and, according to the signification which the term has in the political economy of the sweating world, his operator, baster, and finisher, while nominally engaged at so much a week, were in reality paid by the piece, the economical week being determined by a stipulated quantity of made-up coats rather than by a fixed number of the earth's revolutions around its axis; for the sweatshop day will not coincide with the solar day unless a given amount of work be accomplished in its course.

"Well, I get twelve dollars a week," said David, the fictional character of Cahan's *A Sweatshop Romance*. "Now a working week has six days, but—hem—that *but* gets stuck in my throat—but a day is neither a Sunday nor a Monday nor anything unless we make twelve coats. The calendars are a lot of liars."

"What do you mean?" asked Meyer.

"They say a day has twenty-four hours. That's a bluff. A day has twelve coats," answered David.

David worked for Leizer Lipman, one of the many contract tailors classified as a "cockroach." In the language of the sweating world this meant that he operated a very small shop and employed a single team, consisting of one sewing-machine operator, one baster, one finisher, and one presser.

> The shop was one of a suite of three rooms on the third floor of a rickety old tenement on Essex Street, and did the additional duty of the family's kitchen and dining room. It faced a dingy little court yard, and was connected by a windowless bedroom with the parlor, which commanded the very heart of the Jewish markets. Bundles of cloth, cut to be made into coats, littered the floor, lay in chaotic piles by one of the walls. . . .
>
> Dangling against the door or scattered among the bundles, were cooking utensils, dirty linen, Lipman's velvet skull-cap, hats, shoes, cotton-spools, and whatnot. A red-hot kitchen stove and a blazing grate full of glowing flatirons combined to keep up the overpowering temperature of the room, and helped to justify its nickname of sweatshop in the literal sense of the epithet.

Jacob Riis described "the sweaters of Jewtown" on Ludlow Street:

> Up two flights of dark stairs, three, four, with new smells of cabbage, of onions, of frying fish, on every landing, whirring sewing machines behind closed doors betraying what goes on within, to the door that opens to admit the bundle and the man. A sweater, this, in a small way. Five men and a woman, two young girls, not

fifteen, and a boy who says unasked that he is fifteen, and lies in saying it, are at the machines sewing knickerbockers, "knee-pants" in the Ludlow Street dialect. The floor is littered ankle-deep with half-sewn garments. In the alcove, on a couch of many dozens of "pants" ready for the finisher, a bare-legged baby with pinched face is asleep. A fence of piled-up clothing keeps him from rolling off on the floor. The faces, hands, and arms to the elbows of every-one in the room are black with the color of the cloth on which they are working. The boy and woman alone look up at our entrance. The girls shoot sidelong glances, but at a warning look from the man with the bundle they tread their machines more energetically than ever.

"Who are the youngsters?" asks Riis. "They are learners," replies the woman who turns out to be the boss's wife, "and have come over only a few weeks ago." "How much do they earn?" Riis quickly snaps back. The woman shrugs her shoulders with an expressive gesture. The workers themselves, asked in Yiddish, reply indifferently: "From two to five dollars." "They turn out one hundred and twenty-dozen 'knee-pants' a week," Riis finally learns, "for which the manufacturer pays seventy cents a dozen."

The "in-residence" method of production gave way to the more so-phisticated sweater: the factory. Though more organized in its method of production, the exploitation remained the same and in many cases was worse. In these firetraps, where disease was rife among the workers, the wages remained low and the heat was intense, the ventila-tion poor, and the hazards many.

Many of the Jewish workers were employed by their own coreli-gionists—marginal manufacturers who arrived shortly before the most recent "greeners" and who subscribed to the system's laissez-faire philos-ophy. The truth of this assertion is confirmed by testimony given before an Illinois state senatorial committee, in 1913, investigating the plight of Jewish women in Chicago's West Side "sweaters."†

> Senator Juul:
> Q.   What is your nationality—what country were you born in?
> INTERPRETER: She is a Russian Jewess.
> Q.   Who are you working for?
> INTERPRETER: She does not know . . . she is working in the shop.
> Q.   Ask her if she knows how much money she brings home Sat-urday night for the work she does.

† Almost all of the shops mentioned were owned by Jews.

A. Three dollars and forty cents a week.

Q. How many hours a day do you work?

A. From 7:30 till 6

Q. Do you ever get paid anything for overtime?

A. Twenty-one cents for three hours.

Q. Do they pay you supper money besides?

A. No, sir.

Q. She supports herself on this $4.00 a week?

A. She boards.

Q. How much does her board cost her?

A. She pays $6.00 for the room and then makes her meals herself.

Q. And she gets $16.00 and pays $6.00 for her room. That leaves $10.00. What does she eat—how much does the food cost her?

A. Well, she doesn't know exactly; she says when she has more money she eats better and if less she eats less.

Q. How much was short in the envelope that week?

A. About a dollar and sixty-nine cents. We don't keep any books, and we never knew anything about it; we don't know how much is coming to us; he used to write it on his books, and one Saturday I thought I ought to have five dollars and something. . . . I says, "I am short of money," and he says, "Can you prove it to me?" Of course you can't remember what you made all week, and I says, "No, I can't, but I am short."

Senator Woodward: Have you ever spoiled any goods under this foreman?

A. No, sir.

Q. Do you know anybody that has?

A. I know one girl that spoiled a waist and she had to pay for it.

Senator Tossey: Did this foreman ever swear at the girls?

A. Yes, he used to call them funny names.

Q. What do you mean by funny names?

A. I don't know as I can call it in English. He used to call us, we were all Jewish, he used to call us "lousy Jews." Every girl had a name back there.

Q. A nickname?

A. Yes.

Chairman O'Hara: What name did he give you?

A. He used to tell me, but it is just a funny name; I don't think it is nice for me to pronounce it.

Q. Do you mean vile names? Names that you would not call decent?

A. Yes, that is what I mean.

It was under such conditions that Anzia Yezierska found employment—in a close, ill-ventilated, and unsanitary shop on New York's Delancey Street. While the morning darkness still shrouded the streets, she entered the shop and she was met by the same darkness when, after tedious hours at her machine, she left to return home. Day after day and week after week, she fastened buttons on garments, the money earned hardly enough for bread and rent. "I didn't have a room to myself [or] even a bed," she wrote. "I slept on a mattress on the floor in a rathole of a room occupied by a dozen other immigrants. I was always hungry—oh, so hungry! The scant meals I could hardly afford only sharpened my appetite for real food."

When the busy season began, the piles of buttons grew and the long days stretched out even longer. With fingers turned numb from her work, she watched her employer turn "into a huge greedy maw for wanting more and more buttons." With a glass of steaming tea and with a piece of herring over the black bread, the employer would tempt the hungry workers to remain even longer—till there seemed no end to the exploitive day.

Young Yzierska rose in protest.

"I don't want the tea," she said boldly. "I don't want your herring. I only want the evening to myself."

"You fresh mouth, you!" replied her boss. "You learned already too much in America. I want no clock watcher in my shop. Out you go!"

"I was driven out to cold and hunger," she wrote. "I could no longer pay for my mattress on the floor. I no longer could buy the bite in the mouth. I walked the streets. I knew what it is to be alone in a strange city, among strangers. . . ."

The most tragic result of the conditions described by Yezierska and the Jewish women called to testify before the Illinois investigating committee took place on March 25, 1911, at the Triangle Shirt-Waist Company in New York City. On that day, the allegedly "fireproof" building in which the company was housed was engulfed by flames. When the fire was finally brought under control, 146 girls had been either burned to death or had died after frantically leaping from a ninth-floor window.‡

‡ Apparently *the doors were locked!*

"Thud-dead, thud-dead, thud-dead," wrote William Shepard, reporter who witnessed the girls jump from the windows and crash to the streets below. "I call them that," he said, "because the sound and the thought of death came to me each time at the same instant."

As Shepard watched in horror, he saw

a young man [help] a girl to the window sill. Then he held her out deliberately away from the building, and let her drop. . . . He held out a second girl in the same way and let her drop. Then he held out a third girl who did not resist. I noticed that. They were as unresisting as if he were helping them onto a streetcar instead of into eternity. Undoubtedly he saw that a terrible death awaited them in the flames, and his was only a terrible chivalry.

He brought another girl to the window. Those of us who were looking saw her put her arms around him and kiss him. Then he held her out into space and dropped her. But quick as a flash, he was on the window sill. . . . His coat fluttered upward—the air filled his trouser legs. I could see that he wore tan shoes and hose. His hat remained on his head.

"Together they went into eternity," wrote Shepard. "I saw his face before they covered it. You could see in it that he was a real man. He had done his best. We found out later that, in the room in which he stood, many girls were being burned to death by the flames and were screaming in an inferno of flame and heat. He chose the easiest way and was brave enough to even help the girl he loved to a quicker death." Girls stood in horror at other windows, watching their co-workers fall. "I . . . watched one girl falling. Waving her arms, trying to keep her body upright until the very instant she struck the sidewalk, she was trying to balance herself."

Others, too frightened to jump, jammed the windows, their clothing on fire:

. . . One by one, the [window] jambs broke. Down came the bodies in a shower, burning, smoking—flaming bodies, with disheveled hair trailing upward. These torches, suffering ones, fell inertly, only intent that death should come to them on the sidewalk instead of in the furnace behind them.

The floods of water from the firemen's hose that ran into the gutter were actually stained red with blood. I looked upon the heap of dead bodies and I remembered these girls were the shirt-waist makers. I remembered their great strike of last year in which these

A dream of Jewish Agriculture settlement failed at Cotopaxi, Colorado, in the 1880s. "It was the poorest place in the world for farming, poor land, lots of rocks and no water." (American Jewish Historical Society)

S. H. Drachman (to right of pole, with derby), a general merchant in the Arizona Territory, 1883. Men like Drachman began as traders supplying the Army. (American Jewish Archives)

Earning a living in Richmond, Virginia, 1887. "Coats were hawked for fifty cents as good as new and pants at any price offered." (American Jewish Archives)

The Touro Guards, 1898. A Rhode Island chartered command composed solely of Jewish youths. (American Jewish Archives)

Hester Street "Pig Market," 1895. "Thursday night and Friday morning were bargain days in the Pig-Market. Bandannas and tin cups at two cents, peaches at a cent a quart...." (Museum of the City of New York)

Peddler on New York's Lower East Side, 1895. "... the people jostle each other at
the carts and sidewalk shops where a plank on two ash-barrels serves as a counter.
Pushing, struggling ... and shouting in foreign tongues."
(Staten Island Historical Society)

Sweatshop on Ludlow Street, New York, 1889. "The flats were dark, dank, emitting
an unbearable stench, particularly those which served as shops." (The Jacob A. Riis
Collection, Museum of the City of New York)

Baron de Hirsch Agricultural School, Woodbine, New Jersey, 1905; established to train Jewish immigrants. "We wanted to live in the open and desired to be dependent on Mother Earth. . . ." (American Jewish Archives)

Jacob Schiff (1847–1920). Social activist, philanthropist, and founder of one of America's great investment banking houses. (American Jewish Archives)

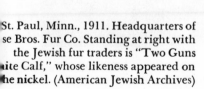

St. Paul, Minn., 1911. Headquarters of [Ro]se Bros. Fur Co. Standing at right with the Jewish fur traders is "Two Guns [Wh]ite Calf," whose likeness appeared on [th]e nickel. (American Jewish Archives)

Lazar Freed, Celia Adler, and Maurice Schwartz, in Sholom Aleichem's *Stempenyu* presented by the Yiddish Art Theatre in 1929. (Museum of the City of New York)

Jacob Adler as Shylock, in *The Merchant of Venice*, the first Yiddish production at the People's Theatre, on the Bowery, in 1901. Adler later played the role on Broadway, where the rest of the cast spoke English but he spoke Yiddish. (Museum of the City of New York)

Grand Theatre, New York's Yiddish showcase, 1908. "Into this building crowded the Jews of all ghetto classes . . . the Hester Street shopkeeper, the socialist, the poet, the journalist." The Byron Collection (Museum of the City of New York)

waist makers' strike by damning the bosses in Yiddish to workers gathered at Cooper Union. "A pint of trouble for the bosses." (ILGWU — Justice Photo)

Cloakmakers demonstrate in New York at the turn of the century. The sign reads: "Our leaders say the strike was settled, but this demonstration proves otherwise." (ILGWU — Justice Photo)

Samuel Gompers, president of the American Federation of Labor, addresses historic, November 22, 1909, Cooper Union meeting which voted for shirtwaist strike. (ILGWU — Justice Photo)

Shirtwaist makers march on New York's City Hall to petition the mayor for police protection, December 3, 1909. (ILGWU — Justice Photo)

Triangle fire, New York, 1911. "The floods of water from the firemen's hoses that ran into the gutter were actually stained red with blood. I looked upon the heap of dead bodies . . . these girls were the shirtwaist makers." (ILGWU — Justice Photo)

Amalgamated Clothing Workers' strike, New York, 1915. "Here there went arm in arm an old Jew with a young Italian. A little further on there marched an old Italian worker, gesticulating to the young Jewish worker who was his partner on the line. . . ." (American Jewish Archives)

same girls had demanded more sanitary conditions and more safety precautions in the shops. These dead bodies were the answer.

Before the smoldering cinders of the Triangle factory were fully extinguished, the East Side rose in protest. Morris Rosenfeld, the Sweatshop Poet, wrote:

> Over whom shall we weep first?
> Over the burned ones?
> Over those beyond recognition?
> Over those who have been crippled?
> Or driven senseless?
> Or smashed?
> I weep for them all.

Rose Schneiderman, of the Women's Trade Union League, added her thoughts. In a voice slightly above a whisper, she told a memorial audience:

> The old Inquisition had its rack and its thumbscrews and its instruments of torture with iron teeth. We know what these things are today: the iron teeth are our necessities, the thumbscrews are the high-powered and swift machinery close to which we must work, and the rack is here in the firetrap structures that will destroy us the minute they catch fire. . . .
>
> This is not the first time girls have been burned alive in this city. Every week, I must learn of the untimely death of one of my sister workers. Every year, thousands of us are maimed. The life of men and women is so cheap and property is so sacred! . . .
>
> I can't talk fellowship to you who are gathered here. Too much blood has been spilled. . . . It is up to the working people to save themselves. And the only way is through a strong working-class movement.

Almost from the very beginning of the East European settlement, Jews were involved in the workers' struggle to "save themselves." In the summer of 1882 a strike was called by five thousand Irish and Italian longshoremen who worked on the Erie Railroad docks at the New York waterfront. Company officials appeared at the Castle Garden reception center to hire "scabs"—greenhorns who knew no better. Among those recruited were approximately five hundred Jews. With the aid of interpreters provided by HEAS, the Jewish strikebreakers, though none knew the meaning of the term or the consequence of their action, went to work in place of the striking workers. To conceal the facts of their employment, the newcomers were swiftly spirited back and forth to work by ferry.

Unfortunately, the Jewish scabs learned about the strike from Irish fists. One of the Jews wandered away from the dock and walked right into an angry mob of pickets; he was beaten brutally. When news of the assault reached the main body of Jews, two of the newcomers who spoke some English arranged a meeting with the strikers at Battery Park. "Why," they wondered, "was this man beaten? After all, this is America and men have the right to work here." After having been told, however, that they were being used as scabs, the Jewish workers joined the strikers and, arm in arm, marched to the Bowery, where, in front of union headquarters, they held a rally.

In order to explain the meaning of their strikebreaking and also to establish a *propaganda farein* (propaganda society), several Jewish revolutionaries who had recently arrived from Russia called a meeting in the heart of the Lower East Side ghetto. One of those who attended was Abraham Cahan. When the speeches were concluded, the chairman asked if there was anyone in the audience who wished to say something. "I walked toward the platform," wrote Cahan, "with a thumping heart." After he spoke, however, there was a "storm of applause. The crowd gathered around us," he said. "Everybody wanted to know who I was, where I came from. I was the hero of the day."

Cahan felt that the leadership of the newly organized group was laboring under the misinformation that the Jewish masses spoke Russian. "If [the speeches delivered tonight are] for Jewish immigrants," he asked, "why are [they] in Russian and German."

"What language do you suggest?" they replied derisively. "What Jew doesn't know Russian?"

"My father," he replied.

When Cahan suggested the use of Yiddish, those surrounding him chuckled. Yiddish, they said, was suitable for the home, the *shul,* or in the street when buying from a peddler. However, the use of Yiddish for a serious political discussion appeared humorous to the crowd of Russian-speaking intellectuals.

"Well, why don't you deliver a speech in Yiddish?" they taunted him.

"Why not?" he replied daringly.

> During the week, I worked on my speech. I paid for the printing of a handbill in Yiddish, which Bernard Weinstein and I distributed in the Jewish neighborhood.
>
> The meeting . . . took place in a small hall in the rear of a German

> saloon. . . . The hall was crowded with some four hundred people. Mine was the first socialist speech in Yiddish delivered in America.
>
> I explained at some length Karl Marx's theory of surplus value, his theory of the class struggle and the inevitability of the coming of socialism. For two hours I spoke in the simplest Yiddish.

The creation of separate Jewish trade unions was motivated not by religion or nationalism but by linguistic identification. Yiddish was the *mame loshon* of the Jewish masses, and its utilization as a rallying point seemed quite natural. Furthermore, the concept of building a trade union around a language was not new to America; German- and Russian-speaking locals were already in existence, so those who advocated Yiddish-speaking unions were simply following an established precedent.

With Yiddish as its focal point, the East Europeans set about to organize a Jewish trade union movement. In 1885 they established *De Yiddishe Arbeiter Farein* (Jewish Workingmen's Union) and several years later, the Yiddish-speaking wing of the Socialist party founded the New York United Hebrew Trades—*Di Fareynikte Yiddishe Geverkshaften*—the first Jewish labor federation in America. "It is time," read the invitation to the delegates,

> that the Jewish proletarian should know the protection of a central union to which he can apply for help in his many wage struggles, as well as for advice as to how to attach himself to the ranks of organized labor. It is time that such a central body should be called into being and the Jewish workman should have the opportunity more quickly to free himself from the "Pig Market," to throw off the yoke of different kinds of contract systems . . . and the other living examples of the vile, capitalistic system of wage slavery.

At its inception the UHT had three locals: the Jewish choral singers, actors, and typesetters. Within four years, twenty-eight others affiliated with the federation. The concept was so favorably received that the Yiddish labor movement in Chicago, Philadelphia, and Baltimore followed the New York example.

At the same time, the AFL, infamous for its anti-immigrant posture, chose the UHT as its target in a new and highly vicious anti-alien campaign. "These Jewish newcomers are radicals," declared one spokesman, and "it is our duty to protect the federation from the spread of their socialism." In 1901, the Central Federated Union (CFU), New

York's AFL central labor body, refused to recognize a delegate from the UHT because of his "open hostility to American unionism," and several years later, an AFL organizer urged the CFU to forbid their locals from joining the Jewish federation. "The UHT," he declared, "[understands] little or nothing about the trade union movement. Its entire knowledge extends from East Broadway to Houston Street, and from the Bowery to Sheriff Street."*

In 1907, at the AFL national convention, the New York locals took the lead in censuring the UHT for organizing along "religious and racial" lines. The United Garment Workers of America (UGWA), for example, despite a large Jewish membership, was foremost in its opposition to the Jewish trade union movement.† "The United Hebrew Trades," declared their newspaper, "has no place in the labor movement of this country and we hope the Jewish workingmen will give it no recognition and treat its efforts as inimical to their interests." It is important to remember, however, that this very same union was also anti-alien: "While there is any amount of room for desirable immigrants in this country," asserted its journal, "the undesirable elements should be kept out in the interest of the American workingmen." "European workers," they advise, "should stay home . . . instead of fleeing to the imaginary land of promise, only to be thrown upon the labor market to bear down upon the workers of this country."

In spite of AFL opposition, in the last decade of the nineteenth century the UHT managed to organize the Jewish barbers, shoe workers, tinsmiths, theater employees, bookbinders, and bakery workers. In 1889 they helped establish the United Tailors' Brotherhood and, encouraged by their success, went on to call for a national convention in order to form a national garment workers' organization. The International Tailors' and Cutters' Union was established, but it lasted only one year. In 1891 the UHT made another attempt to establish a national organization, suggesting, at a meeting in New York, that a coalition of garment workers be created. This, too, was short-lived, and when its dissolution came, there emerged the Amalgamated Clothing Workers of America.

The most important national organization to appear at the turn of the

---

* In 1900, the AFL supported literacy tests as a means of restricting immigration.
† Interestingly, the non-Jewish leadership of the union looked upon its Jewish members as greenhorns. Some writers have implied that the leadership flirted with anti-Semitism.

century was the International Ladies' Garment Workers' Union (ILGWU). The convention from which this union sprang was attended by only eleven delegates representing 2,310 members from seven locals, in Brooklyn, Philadelphia, Baltimore, and Newark. The membership, however, was militant and extremely anxious to change their horrible working conditions. Within a short time after its foundation there were 189 strikes. "As a result," declared general secretary Bernard Braff, "wages had been generally increased 20 per cent; conditions of employment improved; the [local] organizations [were] recognized and, in some cases, a shorter work day obtained."

The militant activities of the women soon attracted others, and by its 1904 convention, four years after the original eleven delegates banded together, 5,400 workers from sixty-six locals in twenty-seven cities were paying dues. The growth of the union, however, was still slower than expected. The policies of its leaders, apparently under the pressure of the more conservative AFL, had much to do with this trend. "There was a definite desire to restrain the workers from striking often," asserted Louis Levine, the union's semiofficial historian. "Organization and preparation were the main slogans. High dues were advocated as a means of building up a strong treasury. A system of sick-and-death, strike, and out-of-work benefits was recommended to the local unions. Boycotts were advocated and used. But, above all, faith was pinned on the union label. . . ." "The best means of emancipation of the working class," declared John Dycke, secretary-general of the union, "from the oppression of capitalism [is the union label]." Shortly after these remarks were made, it was reported that only one manufacturer in the nation agreed to place the label in his garments; three years later, in 1917, the figure stood at three.

Some union officials were infatuated with the union label. At one New York shop, a union organizer confronted an operator sporting a new coat. Automatically he examined the garment for the telltale label. None could be found. Swelling with anger, the official walked over to the operator and screamed:

"Scab! get the hell out of here! You're a member of a union and you buy non-union-made goods!"

The startled worker jumped to his feet and tried to explain that the garment was not purchased in a store; that he had made it on his own machine using his own material. He even had witnesses who would testify to his innocence. The official, however, was so distraught over not finding the label that he continued to demand that the "scab" be ejected from the factory.

Most of the leaders of the Jewish unions were Socialists. In spite of Samuel Gompers' declaration "that socialism is partisan politics and has no place in the trade union movement," the ILGWU still passed a resolution at its 1904 convention calling for the study of socialism at future meetings.

Many of the Russian newcomers brought with them a knowledge of socialism, some by way of their membership in the illegal Jewish Bund‡ and others through their participation in the revolution and labor conflicts that rocked Russia in 1905. In the first decade of the twentieth century a number of Russian refugees established branches of the Bund and other Socialist labor and Zionist organizations on American soil. It is important to note, however, that Jewish radicals were functioning in America as early as the 1870s. In New York the Jewish Socialists were active in the 1886 mayoral campaign of Henry George, and the following year they requested that the Socialist Labor Party establish a separate Jewish chapter.

Though all Jewish Socialists were committed to Socialist ideology, they found themselves in the midst of an ideological struggle over the relationship of the party to the Jewish trade union movement. The New York Socialist community, which was heavily Jewish, wanted to work within the unions, and the national leadership, which also had Jews among them, stressed the importance of establishing their own radical labor organizations.

Though the New Yorkers eventually had their way, the conflict was far from over. In 1882, Daniel DeLeon, a Columbia University professor and West Indian Jew, gained control of the national organization and immediately called for an assault on the AFL. He ordered all Jewish Socialists to withdraw from Gompers' organization and affiliate their locals with the Socialist Labor Party. DeLeon's directive also forbade any member of the SLP to hold office in any labor organization not under the control of the Socialist Trade and Labor Alliance.

At first, DeLeon's strategy was successful: almost two hundred locals, representing twenty thousand workers, heeded his call. Soon, however, his dreams of success were shattered; by 1898 only fifty-four locals had remained with the SLP, while the AFL still boasted a

‡ A Jewish workingmen's organization officially called the General Jewish Labor Federation of Lithuania, Poland, and Russia. While active in Russia it fought against Czarist terror and "industrial oppression."

membership of three hundred thousand dues-paying members. The "voice of the Jewish Socialists," the *Jewish Daily Forward,* bolted from DeLeon's leadership and with other anti-DeLeon forces established the Socialist Party of America (SPA) and the Federated Hebrew Trades, which affiliated with the AFL. It was to these new organizations, and not to DeLeon's Socialist Labor Party, that the majority of Jewish Socialists turned. By 1905, the SPA had twenty-five thousand members; seven years later, that number had grown to 118,000.

In time, the Yiddish-speaking members of the SPA created the Yiddish Agitation Bureau to deal with the problems of the newcomers and, at the urging of the Russian Bundists, formed the influential Jewish Socialist Federation. Within three years the federation, as a semiautonomous branch of the party, published the *Yiddish Socialist*—a Yiddish journal read by five thousand members in twenty-one states and the District of Columbia. Not all Jewish Socialists, however, joined the federation. The *Jewish Daily Forward,* the leaders of the UHT, and other prominent Jewish figures were opposed to its sectarian objectives.

The growth of the Jewish labor movement did not of course come easy: the strikebreakers, thugs, and police who willingly assaulted the workers attest to this fact. In 1909 the working conditions of the shirtwaist makers were miserable, and "rebellion," said Pearl Straus, a garment worker from the Bronx, "seemed to fill the musty air of almost every New York sweatshop." Working fifty-six hours a week and paying for the electricity to operate their machines, Straus and her co-workers decided that they "had had enough—things had to change." On November 22 a meeting was called to discuss strategy.

"We came to Cooper Union by the thousands," declared Straus, "hoping to hear our leaders call for militant action. We must answer the insensitive employers with the full force of a solidified and determined effort." The thousands who came, however, were treated to words of indecision and caution. Meyer London and Joseph Panken, the representatives of the Socialists, and Mary Dreier, the spokeswoman for the Woman's Trade Union League, were ill-prepared to deal with the swelling discontent of their predominately female audience.

Suddenly, dashing down the aisle came a thin teen-ager named Clara Lemlich, who on reaching the platform, turned her back on the indecisive leaders and addressed her co-workers in impassioned Yiddish: "I am a working girl, one of those striking against intolerable conditions. I am tired of listening to speakers who talk in generalities. What we are here for is to decide whether or not to strike. I offer a resolution that a strike be declared—now!"

Her words were met with wild enthusiasm. Everyone rose from their seats cheering. They stamped their feet, they waved handkerchiefs and shouted for action, not next week or next month, but now. "At last," asserted Straus, "the tension was eased. My friend Clara had turned the meeting around."

"Do you mean it in good faith?" shouted the chairman, Benjamin Feigenbaum. "Will you take the old Jewish oath?" Thousands raised their hands: "If I turn traitor to the cause I now pledge," responded the audience "may this hand wither from the arm I raise."

The next morning, almost every New York shop was closed as picket lines jammed the streets. Meeting the frail girls were, of course, the thugs and policemen, who at times showed no mercy as they opened heads with bottles and nightsticks. "The scar I carried for the rest of my life," declared Bertha Kutner, a nineteen-year-old picket from Manhattan, "is testimony to the hostility of the police." In a month, 723 strikers were arrested and nineteen were placed in the work-house. "That won't deter us," said little Ida Schneiderman, a worker from Brooklyn. "We will remain firm." Indeed, the striking women became even more determined as word spread that their "sisters" at Wellesley College collected one thousand dollars for the strike fund. "Guess who's providing bail money!" exclaimed one youthful picket. "Who?" shot back the collective reply from the line. "Mrs. Oliver Belmont and J. P. Morgan's sister, that's who!" came the excited answer.

McAlister Coleman of the New York *Sun* watched the strike of twenty thousand:

> The girls, headed by teen-age Clara Lemlich, described by union organizers as a "pint of trouble for the bosses," began singing Italian and Russian working-class songs as they paced in twos before the factory doors. [All] of a sudden, around the corner came a dozen tough-looking customers, for whom the union label "gorillas" seemed well-chosen.

> "Stand fast, girls," called Clara, and then the thugs rushed the line, knocking Clara to her knees, striking at the pickets, opening the way for a group of frightened scabs to slip through the broken line. Fancy ladies from the Allen Street red-light district climbed out of cabs to cheer on the gorillas. There was a confused melee of scratching, screaming girls and fist-swinging men and then a patrol wagon arrived. The thugs ran off as the cops pushed Clara and two other badly beaten girls into the wagon.

I followed the rest of the retreating pickets to the union hall, a few blocks away. There a relief station had been set up, where one bottle of milk and a loaf of bread were given to strikers with small children in their families. There, for the first time in my comfortably sheltered, upper West Side life, I saw real hunger on the faces of my fellow Americans in the richest city in the world.

Several months after the "uprising of the twenty thousand," came the "Great Revolt" of New York's cloakmakers. This time, however, the men walked out, and the strikers numbered almost sixty thousand. Abraham Rosenberg, president of the ILGWU, described the cloak district the moment the strike began:

> About two o'clock some members of the strike committee went to the cloak district to see how the order of the strike committee would be received. . . .
>
> Among those who were eager to see whether the workers would respond were Abraham Cahan and Benjamin Schlessinger, editor and manager of the *Jewish Daily Forward*. Our people naturally were excited, their hearts beat fast, and every minute seemed an age to them. When at ten minutes past two there was no worker to be seen, Cahan ironically asked, "Well, where are your strikers . . . ?" Hardly had he spoken when we saw a sea of people surging out of the side streets toward Fifth Avenue. . . . By half past two, all the streets were jammed with thousands of workers. . . . Many of our most devoted members cried for joy at the idea that their lifelong labors had been crowned with success. In my mind I could only picture to myself such a scene taking place when the Jews were led out of Egypt.

Though the cloakmakers, who were joined by thousands of raincoat makers and female tailors, were well organized and determined, the employers nevertheless still refused to negotiate. Louis D. Brandeis, the attorney for the Boston Cloak and Suit Manufacturers' Association, who had helped settle a recent Boston strike, was brought to New York to break the deadlock. The determined strikers wanted a "union shop," and the employers were just as resolute in their rejection of this demand. In spite of Brandeis's mediation, the positions of both sides remained unchanged.

Soon after the breakdown of negotiations, another "outside attempt" was made to settle the dispute. This time, the move was made by Jacob Schiff and Louis Marshall—representatives of the "uptown" community —who wanted to "protect the good name" of the Jewish community.

Through their intervention talks resumed, and Brandeis's suggestion of a "preferential shop" and not a "union shop" was eventually agreed to by both sides.*

In the "Protocol of Peace," as this agreement was later called, the cloakmakers, after nine weeks of striking, won a fifty-hour week, limits on overtime, several legal holidays, free electricity for their machines, salaries to be paid weekly, a sanitary committee to investigate and clean up the shops, grievance machinery, and arbitration. For this last and most important feature, a three-member board of arbitration was established: "One nominee of the manufacturers, one nominee of the union, and one representative [the impartial chairman] of the public."†

Three weeks after the protocol was signed, wages of seventeen female employees at the Hart, Schaffner and Marx factory in Chicago were reduced. Immediately, thousands of workers "hit the streets." Soon the real issues emerged: the strikers wanted "union recognition and a closed shop." The strike began without the approval of the union leadership, and when the conservative head of the United Garment Workers of America, Thomas E. Rickert, appealed to the strikers to return to their machines, he managed to give still others the needed incentive to walk out. "We will settle for nothing less than union recognition," yelled one picket. Within two days after this personal declaration, the strikers swelled to forty thousand. In spite of the militancy, however, Rickert agreed with company demands not "to press" for union recognition or the closed shop. When he reported to the membership on the position he took at the negotiating table, an infuriated mob chased him out of a back door of the meeting hall. "We all knew," asserted Thelma Rahinsky, "that this *bastard* was selling us out!"

Though 374 strikers were jailed and seven murdered, the rank and file still refused to return to the machines. After five more weeks of mounting violence, bitter cold, and hunger, the strikers reluctantly

* In a "preferential shop" the employer would give preference to union members but have the right to hire non-union members as well. In all but name, the cloakmakers won the "union shop."
† In May 1951 the New York Cloak Manufacturers terminated the agreement. Shortly thereafter, a strike was called, and in its aftermath the New York union *lost* all the features included in the protocol except the "impartial chairman." The protocols agreed to in Philadelphia and Boston were also abandoned by the manufacturers. By 1920, the concepts agreed to in the original Protocol of Peace had all disappeared.

trusted their future to arbitration. "The strike was summarily ended by the leaders [mostly through the efforts of Rickert] of the United Garment Workers of America," wrote labor historian Selig Pearlman, "sending these workers back to work without any guarantees whatsoever." "Free to return to their old miserable conditions," lamented Sidney Hillman, "many . . . were victimized for months afterwards."

The most momentous strike of all took place when, in the winter of 1912–13, one hundred thousand workers in New York's men's clothing industry took to the streets. Initially, these workers were unorganized, but in the fall of 1912, as murmurs of a strike were heard in the shops around the city, the UHT decided to take the initiative and organize a small local. Word went out that only union members could cast a vote on the question of a walkout, and thousands rushed to join the new local. When the ballots were counted, it was more than evident that the men's clothing industry would come to an abrupt halt.

On December 30, 1912, Moe Feldstein, a pants presser from Brooklyn, said good-by to his family and joined seventy-five thousand others on the picket lines. By the end of the week, they were joined by twenty-five thousand others.‡ Marching side by side with the Jewish tailors were also Hungarians, Greeks, Germans, Lithuanians, and Italians. "The vitality of the Italian workers," declared the *Jewish Daily Forward*, "was wonderful, their energy is simply incredible, their devotion exceeds everything." Describing the nature of the interethnic picket line in front of one shop, the *Forward* wrote: "Here there went arm in arm an old Jew with a young Italian. A little further on there marched an old Italian worker, gesticulating to the young Jewish worker who was his partner in the line. . . ."

Some owners capitulated to the union's demands. News of these individual settlements raced through the garment center like a brush fire. "This victory could be sweet," thought Jack Siegel, a garment worker from Manhatten. "Imagine," he told his wife, Sarah, "a 20 per cent increase, only forty-eight hours of work, limited overtime, and they will even pay for the electricity we use." Siegel, however, was soon to be disappointed, for shortly after his enthusiastic outburst he was forced to face reality: "They're offering a fifty-six-hour week," he told his son Hershel, "and about one dollar more for our labor." Like his coworkers, Siegel rejected the offer and again was off to join the picket lines.

‡ Thirty-five thousand of the strikers were women.

In the midst of renewed talks, however, the despised Chicago labor leader Thomas E. Rickert came to New York to impose his own settlement. Once more, disregarding the aspirations of the local leadership— Max Pine of the UHT and Ben Schwertzer of the UGWA—Rickert negotiated an agreement that was described by one striker as "shameful and insulting . . . a sellout." The *Jewish Daily Forward,* which had been a strong supporter of the strike, like a "bolt from the blue" threw its support to Rickert and advised the strikers to accept the settlement. "Never!" declared Samuel Ratner, a pattern maker from the Bronx, as he marched to the *Forward* building, there "to break its windows and lay [his] hands on the traitors." On March 14, 1913, Ratner put aside his pledge of "never!" and with his fellow strikers, ratified an agreement that gave him a fifty-two-hour week, a small increase in salary and, most important, union recognition.

In the second decade of the twentieth century the Jewish labor movement, particularly through the Amalgamated Clothing Workers and the ILGWU, established itself as a militant and constructive force in the struggle against the abuses of American laissez-faire capitalism. It was also during this era, asserts Will Herberg, that due to America's participation in World War I, "the Jewish unions as well as other sections of the Jewish labor movement, . . . despite surface appearances, [went through] a fundamental *de-radicalization* and a preparation for the thoroughgoing integration into the [American] nation. . . ."

Immediately after Congress declared war, the Socialist Party, meeting in convention at St. Louis, condemned the action "as a crime against the people of the United States and against the nations of the world. . . ." The Jewish unions followed suit: "Yes, the capitalist class has forced us into a war with Germany expecting that the workers will make peace with them during the war," declared Jacob Panken to the Jewish Capmaker's Union. "But this day, the 1st of May, 1917, I cry to you, comrades, *No peace with capitalism.* On with the fight against war. On with the fight for peace; on with the fight against an expeditionary force to Europe; on with the fight against conscription; on with the fight for liberty, for solidarity, for humanity."

The ILGWU and the Amalgamated Clothing Workers, unlike the AFL, refused to pledge not to strike; the Workmen's Circle, in support of the St. Louis anti-war declaration, "shouted down" William Edlin as a "murder-patriot" when he attempted to deliver a prowar address to their convention; and the International Fur Workers' Union called on its members "to speak out against militarism, [and] against the domination of those who would conquer the world. . . ." The Russian Revolution, supported by large segments of the Jewish trade union movement, and the eventual withdrawal from the conflict of the new Bolshevik government also heightened the anti-war sentiment.

There were, nevertheless, elements within the Jewish labor movement supporting the American war effort. William Edlin, the Socialist editor of the *Tag*,* labeled as a "traitor anyone who will try to avoid doing his duty [conscription] because it is inconvenient or because of his previous sympathies," and the prowar Socialist M. Baranov wrote in the *Jewish Daily Forward* that Jews should "act as natives, not as foreigners. . . ." The prowar Socialists, who "stormed out" of the St. Louis convention, established in August 1917 the Jewish Socialist League of America; Jacob Milch, the ex-secretary of the New York UHT, branded German anti-Semitism "far more dangerous than Russian pogroms," and Louis E. Miller, a pioneer figure in the labor movement, warned that anti-war Jews were in fact supporting Germany and thus entertaining "momentary . . . interests and sacrificing the universal culture and civilization of humanity."

In time, anti-war exponents suddenly "wrapped themselves in the flag" and openly advocated an allied victory. Wilsonian idealism (the Fourteen Points) and the German military campaign against the revolutionary government of Russia motivated the greater part of the trade unionists, and to a lesser extent the Socialists, to take a prowar position: the ILGWU purchased one hundred thousand dollars in Liberty bonds, the Jewish Socialist Federation voted to repudiate the St. Louis resolution, the Amalgamated Clothing Workers and the Workmen's Circle pledged to support the war effort, and the UHT and the Furriers' Union raised twelve million dollars at a Lower East Side bond drive. "By the middle of 1918," asserts Herberg, "decisive sections of the Socialist Party were no longer opposed to the war, and the Socialist unions in the needle trades had begun quite openly, if not very enthusiastically, to favor it."

In the early decades of the twentieth century the Jewish labor movement, guided by the Jewish Socialists, managed to change Emma Lazarus' "huddled masses" and "wretched refuse" into a powerful political and economic force. Organized around the *Jewish Daily Forward,* the United Hebrew Trades, and the Workmen's Circle, the Jewish

* A liberal but not Socialist newspaper.

working class was molded into unions that, in the ensuing decades, fought not only for Jews but for all who joined their ranks.

THE ZIONIST IMPULSE

Almost a century before the publication of Theodore Herzl's *Der Judenstaat* (The Jewish State), American Jews were known to have advocated the restoration of a Jewish Palestine. In the 1780s, for example, Gershom Mendez Seixas, hazzan of New York's Shearith Israel, spoke of "a return to Zion," and several years after his death, in 1818, Mordecai Manuel Noah called for the recovery of the Jewish "dominions." "The Jews," he said, "never will relinquish the just hope of regaining possession of their ancient heritage."

Isaac Lesser, the most influential Jewish spokesman in mid-nineteenth-century America, also envisioned a Jewish state. "The Jews," he declared, should once again become "a nation, a unit, a people having a government and a home of their own . . . in no other country than the land of Palestine." To Lesser, the Land of Israel and the Jewish people were one and the same:

> . . . our religion is in its nature permanent, and requires at the same time a certain location for its perfect execution; it follows that a time will come when the people professing this religion shall be enabled to fulfill to the letter all the duties enjoined on them . . . it likewise follows that our redemption from our present state of bondage cannot be accomplished by a mere civil emancipation. . . . We do not ask merely to be free from tyrannical rule, but to see the supremacy of our code restored.

Lesser witnessed the anti-Semitic outbursts brought on by the high-pitched emotionalism of the Civil War. "The parties threatened," he declared, "were not Christians, not even Negroes, nothing but Jews." After reading Grant's Order No. 11, he was even more convinced that a Jewish homeland was the only hope for security. "There is no hope for Israel's tranquillity save in their own land" he said.

> No matter how just our cause may be, we shall always have to complain of slights and insults, of being overlooked by accident or design, of being scorned by the many and denounced by zealots . . . all for the sake of our faith. . . . Why should our religion always be the suffering one . . . ? Why should every religion have a

home where it is triumphant and Judaism have to receive the law from a dominant system? Without a home, ours by right, this must always be.

The same "Zionist impulse" was felt by Christians. Warder Cresson, a Philadelphia Quaker who was appointed the first U.S. diplomatic representative to Jerusalem, in 1844, also espoused the rebirth of a Jewish Israel. To fulfill this dream, Cresson remained in Palestine after his tour of duty, changed his name to Michael C. Boaz, and converted to Judaism. "I remained in Jerusalem," he wrote,

> in my former faith until the 28th day of March, 1848, when I became fully satisfied that I never could obtain *Strength* and *Rest* but by doing as *Ruth* did, and saying to her *Mother-in-law,* Naomi, (The Jewish Church) "Entreat me not to leave thee, or to return from following thee; for whither thou goest, thy people shall be my people, and thy God my God. . . ." Upon the 28th day of March, I was circumcised, entered the Holy Covenant, and became a Jew.

Boaz returned to the United States, and through his writings in *The Occident,* urged American Jewry to make the Holy Land "a great centre to which all who want may come and find rest to their persecuted souls."

Something like Boaz's project was being promoted by still other Christians. Clorinda S. Minor, also from Philadelphia, visited Palestine in 1849 and, after seeing the deplorable economic conditions, decided that the Jewish residents must be instructed in modern agricultural methods. On her return to America she appealed to a number of like-minded Christians and urged them to support the creation of a Palestinian agricultural colony. Soon Minor led a small group of "non-Jewish Zionists" to the land that now borders the city of Tel Aviv and established the colony of "Mount Hope." Here, assailed by financial reverses, poor soil, and hostile Arabs, the tiny community began the "restoration of Palestine." In 1857, however, Minor died, and with her loss the project came to an abrupt end.

The non-Jewish community retained its Zionist interests well into the nineteenth century. In Chicago, the Reverend William Blackstone assembled a group of Christians and Jews in anticipation of restoring the Jews to their ancient homeland. After describing the horrid conditions under which European Jewry lived, he urged his audience to draft a petition calling on the President of the United States "to secure the holding . . . of an international conference to consider the condition of the [Jews] and their claims to Palestine as their ancient home."

The petition, entitled "Why Should Palestine Not Be Restored to the Jews?" went unnoticed by President Benjamin Harrison and Secretary of State James G. Blaine. Having been endorsed by such notables as John D. Rockefeller, J. P. Morgan, and Speaker of the House Thomas B. Reed, it did cause extensive comment. While the spokesmen of Reform Judaism were aghast at Blackstone's action, the Zionist-minded Jews applauded his effort. "Let the Christians do whatever they can to help us in the resettlement in Palestine," wrote the Hebrew journal *Ha-Pisgah*. "As to the question of our faith, let that rest until Elijah returns and then we shall see whether or not their dream materializes."†

"The return to Zion" also attracted a diversity of Jews. Emma Lazarus, who had worn her assimilation with pride, had displayed little concern over the plight of her coreligionists. In the 1880s, however, she was awakened to the distress of the East Europeans and suddenly developed a keen sense of responsibility. Her passionate expressions of Jewish nationalism became more and more common. "While a few year ago," she wrote,

> the most enlightened Jews, yielding to the indolent apathy of comparative security, would have ignored or ridiculed the vision of a restoration, today it is no exaggeration to say that whenever two Israelites of ordinary intelligence come together, the possibility, nay the probability of again forming a united nation is seriously discussed. . . .
>
> There is something absolutely startling in the world's sudden awakening to the probable destiny of Israel. To judge from the current literature of the day, as represented by the foremost European periodicals, it has been reserved for Christians to proclaim the speedy advent of that Jewish triumph for which the Jew has hoped during his prolonged agony of twenty centuries. In all such questions as this, that which is agitated today is formulated and acted upon the morrow, or as Emerson put it, "the aspiration of this century is the code of the next."

While Lazarus was making a full turn toward Zionism, other Jews responded to the call for a Jewish homeland. In the 1880s, *The Lovers of Zion* (Chovevei Zion) established groups in Baltimore and New York; Rabbi Joseph Bluestone published *Chovevei Zion,* the first American

---

† This last comment was evoked by Blackstone's belief that the Jewish redemption would precede the second coming of Christ.

Zionist journal; Aaron Bernstein edited a Hebrew Zionist periodical called *Observer in the New Land;* and some newly arrived East Europeans established the Isaac Ber Levinsohn Association, where Henrietta Szold, the founder of Hadassah, was initiated into Zionist activities. By the 1890s the concept of Zionism had spread, and under the leadership of Henrietta's father, Rabbi Benjamin Szold, and Rabbi Aaron Wise (Stephen Wise's father), it commanded a reserved respectability in the minds of more and more American Jews.

The publication of Herzl's *Der Judenstaat* was the single most important event for American Zionism. "[It] created a sensation," wrote Bernard Horwich, president of Chicago's first Zionist organization, and "it became at once the topic of conversation and debate among Jews all over the world." However, he declared, "the idea of political Zionism, of a Jewish state,

> was attacked by the American Jews, of the Reformed as well as the Orthodox groups. It was approved by neither the rich nor the poor. The well-to-do Jews proclaimed that we were American citizens and this was our home; that we belonged to the American nation and therefore had no right to form a special Jewish nation; that if we did so, we would be disloyal and unpatriotic. They felt that if the movement succeeded, it would furnish anti-Semites here with an excuse to tell us to go to our own country, thus giving them an additional weapon.

"The Orthodox Jews," he reported "[also] opposed the project from a religious standpoint, claiming that Dr. Herzl was not interested in the Jewish religion or in Jewish affairs as such; that Palestine did not have for him a deep religious significance; that nobody had ever heard of him before, as he had taken no active part in Jewish life, and that he was not the proper person to be the leader in such a holy cause."

Despite the opposition, Bernard's brother Harris "became wild with enthusiasm" and insisted that Bernard "get busy at once and do something about it. I told him," wrote Bernard, "that since I knew very little about Herzl's plan, I did not feel qualified to call together a group of people [in order to] discuss a matter without learning more about the subject."

Harris, who was in favor of immediate action, called together several men to discuss the matter. "About fifty people attended," wrote Bernard, "and the discussion lasted from two in the afternoon until six. . . ."

Harris was the chief speaker in favor of forming an organization to further the movement, and submitted innumerable arguments. He employed his resources of wit and humor to cause the audience to burst into laughter. Then, changing his style, he described the tragedy of the Jews in Russia, Poland and other countries, stressing the Dreyfus case, and moved many to tears. His brilliant efforts, however, were of no avail. When the vote was taken, it was found that those present were against the plan about five to one.

Disregarding the negative reaction, Harris called another meeting, this time of several influential Jewish scholars, for more discussion. At the end of the evening, declared Bernard, "they urged me to call [still] another meeting and would not let me rest until I had promised to do so." Within two weeks, the gathering Bernard had promised was held. "Then and there," he wrote, "was formed the first Zionist group in America, of which I was made president. It was called The Chicago Zionist Organization No. 1." Several months later, a second group was established, in New York City. "In the meantime," said Bernard, "[we] increased our membership substantially and had become strongly imbued with the spirit of Zionism."

Horwich heard that Herzl was calling on Zionists throughout the world to send delegates to a Zionist congress, in Basel, Switzerland. "It goes without saying," he declared, "that we were very eager to send a delegate to such an epochal gathering." Without adequate funds, however, Horwich was forced to call upon the membership to pledge their own money. "In this way," he reported, "we raised $100."

We further formed a committee to go from store to store, and from house to house, to collect whatever they could get, from a dime up, so that we might be enabled to send our delegate in a proper manner. For a whole week, I spent half-days collecting, with different partners. It was a very hard and unpleasant task. For every quarter we received, we were treated to a dollar's worth of abuse. But finally enough money was raised to defray the necessary expense.

One of those who joined Horwich's delegation at the first Zionist congress was Richard Gottheil, professor of Semitic languages at Columbia University. Deeply moved by what he witnessed, he returned to the United States and, with the assistance of reform Rabbi Stephen S. Wise, called a Zionist conference of his own. One hundred delegates, claiming to represent five thousand Zionists, attended Gottheil's meeting. When the talk was over and all their views had been aired, Gottheil was elected president of the newly formed Federation of American

Zionists (FAZ). While the leadership of the new organization was made up of assimilated Jews from the eastern cities, the membership was largely composed of recently arrived, Yiddish-speaking East Europeans.‡

This explains why not all American Zionists wished to be affiliated with the eastern-dominated FAZ. Chovevei Zion, which found new life after Herzl's book was published, united with the religious Zionists to form the United Zionists of America (UZA), and the midwestern Zionists, also opposed to the FAZ, went off in a third direction to establish the Knights of Zion, an organization controlled by western Jews.*

Almost immediately, Milwaukee emerged as an influential midwestern center for the Knights of Zion, and the political power of the Milwaukee Zionists was quickly recognized by the city's aspiring politicians. "I do not hesitate to say that no good American citizen does wrong to his citizenship in enrolling himself in the cause you represent," declared David Rose, Milwaukee's mayor, to the fifth annual convention of the Knights of Zion. "Your banding together to alleviate the suffering of those who are bound to you by blood, tradition and history is noble. . . ."

Yet Milwaukee Zionists, like pioneer Zionists everywhere else, had to struggle to attract both contributions and membership. The dramatic appeal of their literature is unmistakable proof of this assertion:

> Are you in sympathy with the movement to bring Jewish life into the land of our ancestors and our hope? A hope which we have not given up for 2000 years? Do you want to help in the development and spread of Hebrew thought and the Hebrew language? Do you want to be considered as a participant in the great national labor of firmly establishing the Jewish people as one body?

"If you firmly believe in the Jewish home in Palestine," urged their literature, "you will join with your co-religionists everywhere and buy a Zionist *shekel*."† The number of *shekalim* purchased, declared another appeal, showed "the world the number of Jews who demand that the land of Israel shall belong to the People of Israel."

"Do not listen," cried the Milwaukee Zionists, "to the [Jewish] as-

‡ The meeting was conducted in English.
* Though divided at first, the midwestern societies united as the Federated Zionist Societies of the Middle West.
† A contribution. In some cases, a membership fee to help an organization pay for administrative costs.

similationists . . . who work with destructive force against the survival of the Jewish people. In which camp do you belong? Are you for a Jewish people? Then,

BUY A SHEKEL!

Milwaukee Zionists stressed their movement as a means of stemming the assimilationist tide:

> OUR PEOPLE ARE IN DANGER OF DECLINE IF WE REMAIN INDIFFERENT to the present conditions and changes in life, and *naygung* of our younger generation.

"The only answer is," they declared,

> to build up a Jewish people and Jewish life in Palestine. There we can have our own way of life; there our children can attend our schools, study in our own tongue, till our own soil, build our own cities and teach our own history. Such a kind of Jewish life in our Holy Land will have the right effect in keeping the Jewish people united in one strong body.

JUST THIS IS THE PURPOSE
OF THE ZIONIST MOVEMENT.

With a vitality that matched the zeal of the Zionists, the anti-Zionist Reform Movement declared their opposition to the establishment of a Jewish state. "Such attempts," asserted the Central Conference of American Rabbis,

> show a misunderstanding of Israel's mission. Such attempts do not benefit, but infinitely harm, our Jewish brethren where they are still persecuted, by confirming the assertion of their enemies that Jews are foreigners in the countries in which they are at home and of which they are everywhere the most loyal citizens.

The strongest proponent of this point of view was Rabbi Isaac M. Wise. "The idea of the Jews returning to Palestine is no part of our creed," he said. "We, rather, believe it is God's will that the habitable world become one holy land and the human family one chosen people." Judaism, declared Wise, was a world-wide religion:

> The Jew's nationality is not endemic; it is not conditioned by space, land, or water. The Jew's nationality . . . is not in his blood. . . . It is all intellectual and moral, without any reference to soil, climate, or any other circumstances. The Jewish nationality . . . has been made portable.

If Wise was the foremost "soldier" in the reform assault on Zionism, then Hebrew Union College, the training ground for reform rabbis, was its prominent fortress. "In this citadel of reform," asserted Boris Bogen, a Jewish social worker, "Zionism was an enemy held in no respect. The Reform Jews were sure that to be a Jew was to be a member of a religious communion and nothing else. To suggest that to be a Jew was any sort of national distinction was altogether un-American; this had always been taught at the . . . College."

Indeed, due to the school's anti-Zionist orientation, there were, on occasion, several pro-Zionist faculty members who were forced to resign. In 1907, for example, professors Henry Malter, Max L. Margolis, and Max Schloessinger, all Zionists, were ousted by President Kaufmann Kohler, the most outspoken anti-Zionist in the reform camp. According to Margolis, Kohler had declared "that as a Zionist I could not be trusted with teaching Biblical exegesis at the college." Several students, who were fearful that this represented an attack on *Lehrfreiheit* (academic freedom), threatened to organize a strike. In spite of the threat of disruption, the Board of Trustees continued to uphold the school's anti-Zionist policy and supported Kohler's position.

The anti-Zionist message of Hebrew Union College was carried far and wide by its graduates. Rabbi Isaac W. Bernheim, of Louisville, proclaimed in a letter to the Central Conference of American Rabbis and also in a speech before the Union of American Hebrew Congregations that Zionist "nationalism" could be interpreted by non-Jews as disloyalty to the United States. "Zionism," he declared, "political or otherwise, of the imported or domestic brand, is not a thing to our liking, nor can it ever receive our support. Here is our Palestine, and we know no other."

To assure that Christian America would recognize the difference between "loyal, anti-Zionist Jews" and those who advocated the dual allegiance inherent in Zionism, Bernheim suggested that the terms "Jew and Jewry" be replaced by "Israelite" and that Reform Judaism be renamed "The Reformed Church of American Israelites." Only in this way, he asserted, would it be possible for the Reform Movement to prove that "we are American by nationality, that our longings are not for an Oriental Palestinian homeland, that our hearts are here, our homes are here—here in America."

Detroit's reform community reacted in a similar fashion to the activities of the East-European Zionists. "They are trying to separate us from the Christian community," said one spokesman. "And this act will only serve the anti-Semitic forces who can't wait to level the charge of Jewish disloyalty to America."

Forever reminding Detroit Christendom that Zionism was the product of a small but vocal East European group, the anti-Zionists never missed an opportunity to display their loyalty to the United States: "It is eternally untrue that the Jew is a man without a country," declared the Detroit *Jewish American*. "He has found his Canaan in America. Let dreamers hail the renationalization of Israel as loud as they please —Zionism is a political impossibility, an historical inconsistency and a religious mistake. All talk of Zionism in a national sense by American Jews is nothing short of arch treason to the best government on earth and should be so dealt with."

Even among segments of the Yiddish-speaking community, though for different reasons, there was opposition to Zionism. To the extreme orthodox, Zionism was an attempt to "force the hand of God" and to those in the labor movement the credo remained "the world [and not Palestine] is our fatherland, and socialism [and not Zionism] is our religion." The Socialist labor leaders looked at the nationalistic aims of the Zionists as "reactionary, bourgeois, and obscurantist"—a "mirage of religious romanticism and chauvinism."‡

Conversely, there were segments of the orthodox, conservative, and labor community that rushed to the aid of the fledgling movement. The Union of Orthodox Jewish Congregations declared that "the restoration of Zion . . . in no way [conflicts] with our loyalty to the land in which we dwell," and Solomon Schechter, the leading spokesman for conservative Jewry, was instrumental in turning the Jewish Theological Seminary into a school not only for rabbinical students but for Zionists as well. The graduates of this institution, noted the veteran Zionist leader Louis Lipsky, "carried the message of Zionism into all parts of America." The Mizrachi, originally established in Lithuania in 1902, furnished an outlet for orthodox Zionists, and the National Radical

‡ As one of the voices of the Jewish labor movement, the *Jewish Daily Forward* was anti-Zionist. There were, however, some attempts, via the paper's editorial page, to link Jewish nationalism and socialism. On October 31, 1902, for instance, Dr. S. Peskin reminded the Zionists that they had allies in the Socialist camp:

We do not want to see all peoples cooked in one stew. We believe that, even as I have a right to wish that there be no poor and rich, so do I have a right to wish that Jews remain a nation with its own language, its own folkways, its own culture, etc. Every other nation may strive toward the same end. In this sense there is no conflict between socialism and nationalism. Everybody can fully be both a nationalist and socialist.

Verein Poale Zion did the same for labor Zionists. "Our platform," declared the Poale Zionists "[is] to create an organization in which both trends—the national and labor—can unite and meet on common ground."*

In the midst of the verbal clash caused by Zionism, World War I erupted in Europe. The American Jewish community, like the nation as a whole, wanted to stay out of the fighting. Despite Wilson's appeal to remain neutral "in thought," segments of American Jewry became belligerent in opinion and sympathy. While most Americans, due to strong ethnic and cultural ties, sided with England and France, the East Europeans, motivated by an intense hatred of czarism, welcomed a German victory. "What I fear," asserted a recently arrived Polish Jew, "is that the Russian thief wants to grab Galicia, and then we shall become Russians. They will make pogroms against us. . . ."†

Side-stepping the President's plea for neutrality "in thought," Polish synagogues prayed for a German victory, HIAS allowed a number of German reservists to use their facilities before returning to the Kaiser's army, and from Cincinnati came news of a group of Jews who wished to enlist in the Austrian Army. "We are ready to carry out our plans," they wrote to the *Wahrheit*, "but we want to know precisely whether it

---

* Almost from its inception, the Poale Zionist movement divided itself between the Socialist Territorialists (those who would accept any area as a Jewish homeland) and the Palestinian Zionists (those who would accept only Palestine as a Jewish homeland). In April 1905 the organization met in Philadelphia, where it became apparent that the territorialists had a clear majority. As a result, the minority members bolted the organization and established the Poale Zion Palestinian Society and endorsed the Basel Zionist Congress, which rejected territorialism and insisted on Palestine as the goal of Zionism. The split, however, did not last long. In 1909, representatives of both camps met in Chicago to settle their differences and unite the two factions.

In 1903, the Zionists had an opportunity to fulfill the aspirations of the territorialists. In response to the Kishinev pogrom, the British Government offered the Zionists the East African colony of Uganda. When Herzl presented the proposal to the Zionist congress, the delegates, who were passionately divided on the issue, rejected the offer. Chaim Weizmann made a vehement anti-Uganda speech, 175 delegates voted no, and the Russian delegation walked out in protest. "These people have a rope around their necks," cried Herzl, "and still they refuse." In the final analysis, however, the acceptance of Uganda as a Jewish homeland was not left for the Zionists to decide. On hearing of the offer, Uganda's British settlers declared their opposition, and shortly after the stormy Sixth Zionist Congress was held, the British Colonial Office withdrew its offer.

† This attitude paralleled that of the American-Irish, who, in being anti-British, were automatically branded pro-German.

is logical and correct that Jews should be willing to fight for a land which is no longer actually theirs?"

Most Jews, orthodox, reform, and non-religious, viewed the war as a struggle against the tyranny and barbarism of czarism. "The Jews support Germany," declared the *Tageblatt,* "because Russia bathes in Jewish blood . . . who will dare say that it is a crime for Jews to hate their torturers, their oppressors and murderers? . . . It is natural that Jewish sympathies should be on the side of learning and not on the side of ignorance."

Ironically, the assimilated American Jewish community found themselves in the same ideological camp as their East European coreligionists. Jacob Schiff blamed the conflict on czarist expansionism, and the Yiddish-language *Morgen Journal* declared that the Kaiser's "army had a right to go through Belgium when Berlin became convinced that the Belgians were in open sympathy with the French. The French Republic deserves to be punished for her unclean love for Russia, and if she takes this attachment so seriously as to go to war for her barbaric lover, she will in the end get what she deserves." Even Abraham Cahan, the Socialist editor of the *Jewish Daily Forward,* declared that he "was convinced that in the interests of general progress and for the Jews specifically a Russian defeat would be fortunate . . . that it would be fortunate for all of Europe and for the whole population if Germany would take all of Poland and also Lithuania from Russia."

In contrast to the pro-German sentiment, there were of course elements of the Jewish community that declared their support for the Allied cause. Max Barkin, of the Jewish Socialist Federation, urged Jewish support for the Allies in anticipation of better treatment for those Jews still under czarist control, and a Poale Zionist spokesman declared that France and England, "the helpers of Belgium," should not be punished for Russian crimes. "If you wish to punish the guilty," he said, "why should the innocent suffer . . . ?"‡

Despite the official neutrality of the Zionists and though many harbored pro-Allied sentiments, friendly overtures were made toward Germany's ally Turkey. Keenly aware that the Turks controlled Palestine, *Dos Yiddishe Folk* declared:

‡ The Socialists and trade unionists were anti-war and remained neutral. Other organizations that passed "peace resolutions" were the Union of American Hebrew Congregations, the New York Kehilla, the Independent Order Brith Abraham, the Federation of Galician and Bukovinian Jews, and the Central Conference of American Rabbis. These resolutions were at odds with the sentiments of some of their members.

We have felt, and have often expressed the feeling, that in a well-ordered Ottoman Empire the Jews had the best opportunity to develop their cultural and economic life in Palestine. We have based our policy upon the traditional friendship of Turks and Jews. We have assumed . . . that the kinship of the Jews and the Turks would allay any suspicions on [the Jews] with regard to [our] endeavors in Palestine, and from the Jewish point of view, this kinship gives assurance of a splendid future for the Jewish people in the Ottoman Empire.

More to the point were the remarks of Louis D. Brandeis, head of the Provisional Executive Committee for General Zionist Affairs: "Zionism," he told the Turkish government,

is not a movement to wrest from the Turks the sovereignty of Palestine. Zionism wants merely to establish in Palestine for such Jews as choose to go and remain there, and their descendants, a legally secure home, where they may live together . . . where they may expect ultimately to constitute a majority of the population, and march forward to what we should call home rule.

Brandeis's conversion to Zionism and subsequent commitment to its goals caused quite a stir in Zionist circles. "During most of my life," he told an audience in 1915, "my contact with Jews and Judaism was slight. I gave little thought to their problems, save in asking myself, from time to time, whether we were showing due appreciation to the opportunities which this hospitable country affords." Through experience and observation he became convinced that Jews were "by reason of their traditions and their character peculiarly fitted for the attainment of American ideals. Gradually, it became clear to me that to be good Americans, we must be better Jews, and to be better Jews, we must become Zionists."

According to Rabbi Stephen S. Wise, Brandeis's public leadership of American Zionism lasted only two years. "But what enriching years they were," he exclaimed, "and how inspiring [he was] to his colleagues."

He was our leader in the most critical years of American Jewish history. . . . I can affirm . . . that since the days of Herzl, Brandeis was indisputably and incomparably our greatest Jew. I think not of his gift as an economist, or even his genius as a statesman, least of all his boundless personal generosity. Rather do I think of the spirit he brought to our cause that I can best describe by using the Hebrew term *Kedusha*—holiness.

Though Zionism had divided American Jewry into factions, all recognized their obligation to provide immediate aid to those trapped in the war-torn areas of Europe.

"The war! My family. Not a word from them. Every week I heard from them. But now not a word for a month! This," wrote social worker Boris Bogen, "was the universal cry. The advancing months brought no news. . . ."

> Their remittances to Europe were not accepted. . . . The receipt of money sent shortly before the outbreak of the war had not been acknowledged. . . . The drumfire of the war echoed by day and by night. . . . The contending armies were grinding under their feet the towns and villages of their beloved Warsaw, Lodz, Cracow, Lemberg, Przemysl. . . .

"We must go to the aid of our brethren," urged the New York orthodox community, and, immediately, the Central Relief Committee for the Aid of Jewish War Suffers, under the direction of the Union of Orthodox Jewish Congregations, was organized. "These were the first to raise the banners of brotherhood," said Bogen. "They were well-meaning people but with no experience in the broader fields of philanthropy. They were still devoted to the conception of the quaint charity box [*pushke*] that was nailed to the doorpost of one's house and to the intinerant charity collector who went through neighborhoods hunting Jewish homes." Yet, by 1917, led by Leon Kamaiky, editor of the *Tageblatt,* the orthodox organization raised over $1 million.

The "uptowners," through the American Jewish Committee, established the American Jewish Relief Committee. "So that now," asserted Bogen, "there were two helping hands reaching with bread for the hungry in Europe—one Orthodox and the Reform. And across the path of both marched [the Workmen's Circle]—the People's Relief Committee for the Aid of Jewish War Sufferers. . . ."

Though it was possible for the three diverse groups—orthodox, reform, and Socialist—to work by each other's side, each among its own people, in collecting money for relief, "it was obvious," noted Bogen, "that if they attempted separately to transmit the money overseas and distribute it themselves, duplications, overlapping, overhead waste, and inevitable confusion must result." Thus the Joint Distribution Committee, which co-ordinated the distribution of funds, was established.

"One remembers," wrote Bogen,

the amazement of Jewry when in the first year of the war there was raised a million and a half dollars for relief. A million and a half! Our philanthropies had been measured by hundreds until then. Philanthropy had been small finance. It was something for which we could dig into the pocket easily—and fish out a ten-dollar bill.

Now we were learning to give, and "serving" was almost like a new word in our vocabularies, and the meaning of sacrifice was becoming clear. A million and a half! Certainly, we thought, the hunger of our brethren now would be appeased, the naked would be clothed, and the homeless sheltered. In our safe and distant habitations, we had not yet come to measure the extent of the disaster that had fallen upon mankind, and we were not to comprehend it fully until years later, when we would give twenty-five millions as willingly as we gave a million and a half that first year.

Throughout the nation, wherever the "pleaders of Jewry" spoke, "multitudes of Jews assembled and everywhere women took jewels from their fingers to enrich the fund. . . ." At one meeting held in New York, for example, Judah Magnes collected four hundred thousand in cash and almost a half million more in pledges. At the close of 1916, $4.75 million had been raised.

In the midst of the philanthropic effort, news of the Russian Revolution swept through the Jewish community. "There were sighs of relief," stated Morris Gartman, a Chicago store owner. Some celebrated with their best schnapps, others danced in the streets, and still more went to *shul* to thank God for bringing the czarist tyranny to an end. "My father cried," said Philip Bernstein, a Philadelphia teacher, "for, at last, the people he left behind could live in dignity and without fear." Amid the jubilation, the mass meetings, and the happy parades, the pro-German sentiment, which had pervaded the immigrant ghettos, all but disappeared. "Overnight," remembered Sol Schwartz, a cigar maker from New York, "the people in our tenement switched their allegiance to the Allies."

On April 6, 1917, when the United States entered the war, Jewish declarations of support, except for certain elements within the labor movement, were spontaneous. Every rabbinical society, each of the fraternal orders, and all the Zionist groups declared they were ready to serve "in the war to end all wars." "We Jews of America stand by our land and government," declared *Dos Yiddishe Folk,* "united and strong, and are happy that our victims shall serve the holy cause of justice all over the world."

The Poale Zionists held a mass meeting at New York's Cooper

Union, where they welcomed the war as a means of furthering "the principles of democracy and free nationality." All who attended expected that these "truths" would be applied to the creation of a Jewish state. Several days later, the Lower East Side community staged another rally. This time it was called by the League of Jewish Patriots to mobilize "the forces of the Jewish race with the view of placing them at the disposal of [the American military]." Approximately two hundred thousand Jews enlisted in the various services and, of them, thirty-five hundred were killed in action and twelve thousand received wounds.*

Just prior to America's involvement in the conflict, German officialdom, seeking to capitalize on Jewish sympathy, announced that the Jews in the captured Russian lands would be allowed to establish democratic councils to govern their own communities. In a countermove, the British Foreign Office nervous about the pro-German attitude of the Jews, suggested to its Russian ally that "it is clear that by utilizing the Zionist idea, important political results could be realized. One of the results would be the conversion of the Jewish element in the . . . United States of America, and other places, to the use of the allies; elements whose attitude is at present rather antagonistic to the allies." British concern with Jewish attitudes thrust the American Zionists into positions of importance and helped to focalize the Zionist movement in the United States.

The American Jewish Committee, long an opponent of Zionist aims, was not very happy with the new-found influence of the American Zionists. The "uptowners" were even more alarmed when news reached them that the 1914 Zionist Conference passed a resolution calling on the establishment of a "Jewish Congress Committee"—and organization intended to include not only Zionists but representatives of the entire Jewish community.† In response to the congress movement, one angry AJC spokesman asserted: "If this congress is successfully established, its Zionist majority will be able to pass resolutions which will be in conflict with our aims. Without question the term congress implies

---

* A total of 1,132 Jewish military men were decorated for bravery. Among the citations were 147 Distinguished Service Crosses and three Congressional Medals of Honor.

† The Jewish Congress Committee, which sought to incorporate the anti-Zionist "uptowners" and the various labor organizations, eventually became a permanent American Jewish Congress. One of the major fears of the American Jewish Committee was that this new group, representing a wide variety of Jewish organizations, would attempt to speak for all of American Jewry.

that [Jews] are an independent nation with separate [from the United States] national interests."‡

Driven by their opposition to a strong rival organization, AJC leaders sought to influence the structure and goals of the proposed congress. To start, the "uptowners" asked that the name "Conference" be substituted for "Congress"—a term that indicated that the organization was *ad hoc* and thus would be dismantled when its work was completed. After negotiations, however, the title "Congress" remained, but the AJC won the following concession: the Congress Organization Committee agreed to dissolve itself as soon as its work was completed.

In spite of this concession, the AJC, along with the National Workmen's Committee, was conspicuously absent when delegates from thirty-three organizations met at the first preliminary session of the congress, in Philadelphia. Welcoming the group reform Rabbi Stephen S. Wise declared that the congress represented a new beginning for American Jewry: "Let it be said that whatever may have been the necessities of the past, the time is come for a leadership by us to be chosen, a leadership that shall democratically and wisely lead rather than autocratically [like the AJC] command."*

After the Congress heard these encouraging words, American Jewry received the news of the Balfour Declaration:

> His Majesty's Government view with favor the establishment in Palestine of a National Home for the Jewish people, and will use their best endeavor to facilitate the achievement of this object, it being clearly understood that nothing shall be done which may prejudice the civil and religious rights of the existing non-Jewish communities in Palestine or the rights and political status enjoyed by Jews in any other country.

‡ Other groups were equally opposed to the creation of the congress committee. The National Workmen's Committee on Jewish Rights in the Countries at War, composed of the United Hebrew Trades, the Workmen's Circle, the Jewish Socialist Federation, the Socialist Territorialists, the Labor-Zionists, the Bundists, and the Jewish National Workers' Alliance, refused to co-operate with the Jewish "bourgeoisie" who proposed the congress.

* In 1920, the congress met to receive the report of those who attended the Paris Peace Conference. After the report was given, in accordance with its original agreement the congress was dissolved. The Zionists, however, who made up the bulk of the delegates, were unwilling to accept the dissolution of the congress and, within minutes, met to lay the foundation for a permanent organization. Two years later, the group assembled again in Philadelphia and established the American Jewish Congress.

In response to the declaration, *The America Hebrew* declared that "the daily prayers of Israel for the restoration of Zion have at last been answered," and *The Jewish Exponent* hailed the news as "the greatest occurrence in modern Jewish history." Even some anti-Zionist journals modified their views after it was learned that Woodrow Wilson, in a letter to Rabbi Stephen S. Wise, endorsed the British pronouncement. "President Wilson speaks for America," declared the Zionist *Maccabean,* "[and this] makes our American loyalty stronger because American idealism has been strengthened."

Though more subdued in their response, others were somewhat satisfied with the announcement. Louis Marshall, when writing to the staunch anti-Zionist Max Senior, asserted:

> I am confident that the Balfour Declaration and its acceptance by the other powers is an act of the highest diplomacy. . . . All the protests that non-Zionists may make would be futile to affect that policy.

He also wrote to New York *Times* publisher Adolph S. Ochs:

> You know very well that I am not a Zionist and that I am opposed to the establishment of a Jewish State, but that does not, however, mean that I cannot sympathize with the aspirations of those Jews who desire to establish a home in Palestine. . . .

There still remained those who were unmoved by the promise of the Jewish homeland. "We herewith affirm the fundamental principles of Reform Judaism," asserted the central Conference of American Rabbis, "that the essence of Israel, as a Priest People, consists in its religious consciousness . . . and not in any political or racial national consciousness." The extreme orthodox also remained uninfluenced by the declaration. "We reject any and all efforts to restore Palestine as a Jewish homeland," said one spokesman, "by any means other than divine intervention."

Most of the Yiddish-speaking community received the news with jubilation.† "The Jew HAS Taken His Place among the Nations of the World," read the headline in the *Tageblatt:* "The dry bones of Israel were quickened to life. Not all the machinations of the anti-Zionist could stem the tide of Jewishness sweeping over the Jewish world." *Dos Yiddishe Folk* reported that this "would be known as the greatest day

† The trade union movement was as divided in its response to the Balfour Declaration as it was to Zionism.

in the life of the Jewish people since their loss of statehood to the Romans."

In order to stem the Zionist tide, now made "respectable" by the British declaration, President Wilson was handed an anti-Zionist "Statement to the [Paris] Peace Conference" signed by 229 influential American Jews. The petition rejected Palestine as a Jewish homeland "for the present and the future. . . . The bonds uniting Jews," read the statement, "[were] not of national character."

To counter this move, Brandeis, now a trusted presidential adviser, urged Wilson to represent Zionist demands when he met with the heads of the allied governments. Brandeis's pro-Zionist advice and Wilson's concern for self-determination overshadowed the anti-Zionist request. "As for your representation touching on Palestine," he told a delegation from the American Jewish Congress, "I have before expressed my personal approval of the declaration of the British Government regarding the aspirations and historic claims of the Jewish people in regard to Palestine. I am, moreover, persuaded that the allied nations are agreed that in Palestine shall be laid the foundations of a Jewish commonwealth."

Wilson took to Paris the concerns and interests of the American Zionists. This assertion is confirmed by the fact that the "U. S. Intelligence Section," sent to Paris to aid the American peacemakers, recommended "that there be established a separate state of Palestine. This state," they advised, should

> be placed under Great Britain as mandatory of the League of Nations. . . . that the Jews be invited to return to Palestine and settle there, being assured by the [Peace] Conference of all proper assistance in so doing that may be consistent with the protection of the personal and property rights of the non-Jewish population and being further assured that it will be the policy of the League of Nations to recognize Palestine as a Jewish state as soon as it is a Jewish state in fact.
>
> It is right that Palestine should become a Jewish State. . . . It was the cradle and home of their vital race . . . and is the only land in which they can hope to find a home of their own.

CHAPTER V

Between Two Wars/
The 1920s

JEWISH RADICALISM

"IT was an era of lawless and disorderly defense of law and order, of unconstitutional defense of the Constitution, of suspicion and civil conflict, . . ." wrote Frederick Lewis Allen. "In a very literal sense [it was] a reign of terror." In the postwar decade, America's "superpatriots," caught up in the lingering wartime campaign for "100 per cent Americanism," repudiated the nation's libertarian heritage in favor of the "Red Scare" of 1919–20, restrictive immigration laws, and rampant racism.

As for all minorities, this era, which rang with Anglo-Saxon superiority, was not a pleasant one for Jews. For the first time in their American experience, home-grown anti-Semitism was threatening Jewish survival. No longer was it a matter of offensive resort advertisements equating Jews with consumptives and mosquitoes; now there were cries of "Jew Bolshevik," quotas at educational institutions, exclusion from the professions, the Ku Klux Klan, and the Jew-baiting articles of Henry Ford's Dearborn *Independent*.

After the Central Powers laid down their arms, the anti-foreign hostility of the "100 per cent Americans" was expressed in a campaign against the activities of the nation's "alien radicals." "That the threat to American stability should rest with the newcomer," asserted Prescott Grant, a nativist at a Boston rally, "is only natural. After all, weren't foreign-born workers in the forefront of the violent strikes of

1919? And was not the newly organized Communist Party, like many other radical groups, supported by recently arrived aliens—especially Jews?" To support the charge, Grant reviewed the wartime activities of Jacob Abrams and his companions:

On the morning of August 12, 1918, a group of men were standing at the corner of Houston and Crosby Streets, in New York City. While waiting for their factory to open its doors, they noticed someone throwing scraps of paper from a fourth-floor window. Seconds later, the street was cluttered with English and Yiddish leaflets protesting the presence of American troops on Soviet soil. "Workers—Wake Up," read the bold print of the Yiddish leaflet littering the hot pavement:

> You who have emigrated from Russia, who are friends of Russia, will you carry on your conscience in cold blood the same spot as a helper to choke the Workers Soviets? Will you give your consent to the inquisitionary expedition to Russia? Will you be calm spectators to the fleecing blood from the hearts of the best sons of Russia?
>
> America and her allies have betrayed [the workers]. The robberish aims are clear to all men. The destruction of the Russian Revolution, that is the politics of the march to Russia.
>
> Workers, our reply to the barbaric intervention has to be [a] general strike! An open challenge only will let the government know that not only the Russian worker fights for freedom, but also here in America lives the spirit of revolution.
>
> Do not let the government scare you with their wild punishment in prisons, hanging and shooting. We must not and will not betray the splendid fighters of Russia. Workers, up to fight!
>
> THE REBELS

Soon after the circulars hit the sidewalk, federal agents took into custody Hyman Rosansky, a Russian Jew, who admitted responsibility for tossing the leaflets from the hat-factory window. Six other Russian Jews, all belonging to the anarchist Jewish organization *Frayhayt* (liberty), were arrested: Jacob Abrams, Samuel Lipman, Hyman Lachowsky, Gabriel Prober, Jacob Schwartz, and Mollie Steimer.

Indicted for violating the Espionage Act of 1917, the group was brought to trial on October 15. The evening before, Jacob Schwartz died of influenza. Abrams claimed that "the death was caused by the police and [federal] agents." Schwartz, who had suffered from a heart ailment, had described the brutality of his jailers: "Our arrest," he had written his codefendants from New York's Tombs Prison, could be compared with the Spanish Inquisition and the blackest pages of man's brutality to man. This was a night of enraged devils in a lion's cage—the most horrible that man's mind could conceive, from tearing the hair to pulling the tongue; from black-jacks to the leg of a chair was used on us because we would not speak. For our declaration that we are Anarchists and one of us a Socialist, we had to endure the most horrible tortures which the Twentieth Century will not be able to erase. Yes, dear comrades, it would take too much paper, which is so precious to me now, to describe our sufferings during the first night of our arrest.

As the guards removed Schwartz's body from the cell one of them noticed a note, written in Yiddish, on the plain wooden table that adorned the room: "Farewell, Comrades. When you appear before the Court I will be with you no longer. But this is life itself." As the trial began, the six remaining defendants entered the courtroom displaying buttons bearing Schwartz's portrait.

As a result of the evidence, Prober was acquitted and Rosansky was given three years imprisonment. The others were punished more severely; Abrams, Lachowsky, and Lipman were sentenced to twenty years, and Mollie Steimer, the lone female, age twenty-one, was ordered confined for fifteen years. The punishments did not end there. Once Judge Henry De Lamar Clayton, who had been brought from Alabama to preside,* completed the reading of the sentences, he turned the court record over to immigration agents so that deportation proceedings might begin once the prison terms were served.

An appeal reached the Supreme Court of the United States, but the sentences were upheld. Only Oliver Wendell Holmes and Louis D. Brandeis declared their opposition to any law abridging freedom of speech. Holmes argued that "Congress cannot forbid all effort to change the mind of the country. . . . In this case, twenty years imprisonment have been imposed for the publishing of two leaflets that I believe the defendants have as much right to publish as the Government has to publish the Constitution of the United States now vainly invoked by them."

When he surrendered at the federal penitentiary in Atlanta, Georgia, Lachowsky expressed the sentiments of the condemned radicals: "If Dreyfus at Devil's Island was a shining disgrace before all the world, to France; if Robert Emmet's death on behalf of Irish freedom has been

---

* A federal judge was brought in from a district where there was absolutely no sympathy for radical activities. Some observers have claimed that if a judge from the New York, working-class area had been appointed, the results might have been different.

one of the blots on English history; so my imprisonment for the next twenty years will be a shining disgrace to America."

> As an alien and an Anarchist, I am willing to be deported to Soviet Russia, and have so stated at Immigration hearings, but if America wants to support me in jail for 20 years; if America wants that blot on her history, I am willing to be that sacrifice in the hope that by it, the true liberty-loving heart of America will awaken from its deadly sleep caused by the Espionage Law under which I was convicted.

Though the war was brought to a successful conclusion, the fear of radicalism still grew in intensity. In the next several years the Red Scare, highlighted by the raids of Attorney General A. Mitchell Palmer in 1919 and 1920, led to the arrest of almost ten thousand people and subsequent deportation to Russia of three hundred aliens.

The most noted Jewish radical on the passenger list of the U.S.S. *Buford,* nicknamed the "Soviet Ark," was Emma Goldman. "On the deck above us," she wrote,

> I felt dizzy, visioning a transport of politicals doomed to Siberia, the *étape* of former Russian days. Russia of the past rose before me and I saw the revolutionary martyrs being driven into exile. But no, it was New York, it was America, the land of liberty! Through the port-hole I could see the great city receding into the distance, its sky-line of buildings traceable by their rearing heads. It was my beloved city, the metropolis of the New World. It was America, indeed, America repeating the terrible scenes of czarist Russia! I glanced up—the Statue of Liberty!

"As the days rolled by," remembered Bernard Straus, a Philadelphia dentist, "federal agents continued to swoop down on the nests which were allegedly infested with foreign-speaking and foreign-looking revolutionaries. Almost anyone with a beard—a radical anarchist or an orthodox Jew—became suspect. I remember, on the second anniversary of the Bolshevik Revolution, how Palmer and his special assistant, J. Edgar Hoover, rounded up almost five hundred radical-looking types —even my friend Meyer, who had voted Republican for the past twelve years."

On New Year's Day, 1920, Straus witnessed Palmer's greatest raid, when almost three thousand people were arrested in thirty-three cities. "Some of us were so frightened," he recalled, "that many shaved their beards and spoke no Yiddish for weeks."

Many public leaders, Jewish and Christian, expressed shock at Palmer's activities. Secretary of Labor William B. Wilson declared that the raids were unlawful and could result in "injury to innocent parties," and Francis Fisher Kane, United States attorney for Philadelphia, resigned his position in protest. In a letter to Palmer, he asked if "it is necessary to protect our American workingmen . . . from the influence of a handful of Russians and Russian Jews . . . ?" He noted that the deportation of one "Russian Jew barber" from Philadelphia was "not only foolish but [also] an outrage to take him from his wife and children. I cannot regard him as a menace to society just because he was a member of the communist party."

The obsession with "wild-eyed and bearded Russian radicals" seeking to overthrow American society, however, overshadowed the protests. Congressman Victor Berger, leader of Milwaukee socialism, was refused his seat in the United States House of Representatives, and five Socialist New York State assemblymen, most of them Jewish, were excluded from that legislative body.†

"The [New York] Assembly was called to order," wrote Louis Waldman. Among the 150 members who found their seats were five Socialists: August Classens, Louis Waldman, Charles Solomon, Samuel Orr, and Samuel A. DeWitt—all legally elected from five, predominately Jewish, working-class districts. As the first-day, carnival atmosphere in the chamber disappeared, an uneasiness fell over the hall. Looking up from his seat, Waldman observed the sergeant at arms escorting his Socialist colleagues to the speaker's desk. A moment later, he joined the group.

"You," said Speaker Thaddeus S. Sweet, "whom I have summoned before the bar of this house, are seeking seats in this body; you have been elected on a platform that is absolutely inimical to the best interests of New York State and the United States. . . ." The Socialists eyed each other in silent disbelief.

Going back to 1917 and the St. Louis anti-war resolution, Sweet read a sentence from the document: "As against the false doctrine of national patriotism, we uphold the ideal of international working-class solidarity." Wetting his lips, he continued in his own words: "In order that

† Victor Berger, who had made anti-war remarks, was arrested and indicted for violating the Sedition Act. Though re-elected after his indictment, he was still tried, convicted, and sentenced to twenty years in prison. Free on bail while his appeal was pending, he was still denied his seat by a special session of the Congress. Again elected, in a special election, he was once more, in January 1920, amid cries of "Bolshevik," denied his seat.

we may understand what this solidarity means, I quote from the Communist International: 'Civil war is forced upon the laboring classes by their arch enemies. The working class must answer blow by blow if it will not renounce its own object and its future.'"

"I looked at Sweet," said Waldman, "and saw a marked resemblance to the ignorant New York policeman who had clubbed the anti-Socialist because he didn't care *what kind of Socialist* he was. All he needed was a blue uniform and a club."

The Assembly was silent. Then there was a scattering of timid applause. August Classens spoke: "Mr. Speaker, do I understand we have no rights until this body officially decides?"

"Yes," replied Sweet.

In an attempt to speak, Charles Solomon rose and faced the legislators.

The speaker reacted quickly. "The gentleman who rises has no privileges on the floor. The gentlemen involved will please retire to the back of the rail."

"We refused to budge," said Waldman.

> In the silence that followed, every eye in the chamber was fixed upon us. Sweet commanded the Sergeant-at-Arms to escort us out. We refused to move and stayed in our seats. At last, the Sergeant-at-Arms escorted us, one by one, from the Assembly. It was then that the House seemed to realize what was really taking place. As I passed up the aisle, my arm firmly held by the Sergeant-at-Arms, a few of the Democrats muttered to me: "Sorry, Waldman, we just couldn't help it."
>
> All the others, however, were silent. All eyes were averted and heads were downcast. And so the blackest day in the history of the New York Legislature came to an end. . . .

Protests were heard from both ends of the Jewish political spectrum. Unmoved by advice that a defense of the New York Socialists might inspire anti-Jewish activity, Louis Marshall declared that "the greatest peril to our democratic government is the tyranny of the majority. . . . We have fought," he said,

> against the right of a majority to sit in judgment not only of political parties, but of religious organizations. The same reasons which underlie the action of the New York Assembly in respect to the Socialist members whom it has expelled, would constitute a precedent for the exclusion of Catholics and Jews. . . . Let it be said

when I am gone, that I never feared to do what was right merely because it was momentarily unpopular among people who have become crazed by their hatreds and their prejudices and their stupidity.

More to the point were the remarks of labor leader Morris Hillquit: "Red baiting," he declared,

and heresy hunting became the fashion. Brutal force in dealing with everybody and everything suspected of radicalism met with general public favor. America had reverted to the practice of witch burning. Many a third-rate politician won fame and recognition in the disgraceful crusade, and many more envied them their laurels.

While the New York lawmakers were barring Socialists, a U. S. Senate Judiciary Committee was hearing testimony on the extent of Bolshevik propaganda in the nation. Chaired by Lee S. Overman of North Carolina, the special subcommittee heard witnesses link Jews to Bolshevism and thus spread the rapidly growing image of the Jew-Bolshevik. Rev. George S. Simmons, a Methodist minister who conducted church activities in Russia, told the committee that "the predominant element in this Bolshevik movement in America [are] the Yiddish of the East Side."

Immediately, Marshall dashed off a letter to Senator Overman: "The residents of the East Side," he wrote,

are, as a whole, as reputable, honorable and patriotic a body of people as are to be found in any part of the country. They are industrious, law-abiding and intellectual; they perform the duties of citizenship; they pay their taxes; they participate in elections; they have ideals; they educate their children; they understand the spirit of America, and are in every way entitled to fair treatment.

Marshall lamented that "it has become fashionable for newspaper men who desire copy, to treat the East Side as a bugaboo. By this time," he asserted,

the average citizen of other States imagines that the East Side is . . . the dwelling place wherein evils of every kind lurk. Consequently, . . . Bolshevism, with gnashing teeth and scraggy beard and dripping dagger, is pictured as stalking through noisome alleys in the imaginary East Side. The actual picture of the East Side . . . would lead [one] to wonder how it is possible in these days and generation, to permit prejudice and ignorance to malign an entire community which possesses qualities which will eventually be recognized as constituting one of the most valuable assets in American life. . . .

Though Marshall eloquently defended the Yiddish-speaking community against the smear tactics of those who equated Jews with radicalism, there were still others who promoted the Jew-Bolshevik apparition. The Better America Lecture Service, which provided materials for discussion on international events, added remarks to some of its slides declaring that "264 Hebrews from the Bowery district of New York" were leaders of the Soviet Government, and Dr. George Simmons appeared before a Senate Judiciary Committee on Bolshevik Propaganda and stated that "more than half the ruling minds in Russia are Jewish." Lothrop Stoddard, a leading advocate of "scientific racism," dubbed the Soviet Government "largely Jewish," and *Current Opinion,* a widely read journal, described Leon Trotsky as "distinctly Jewish."

Also gripped by this stereotype, the Committee of American Citizens of Polish Birth and Descent claimed that Jews were subverting Polish and American democracy; the American Red Cross called Bolshevism a Jewish plot to control the national economy; spokesmen for the Greater Iowa Association, a business society, went before Rotary Clubs and echoed the threat of the "Jewish Bolshevik," and in Brooklyn, New York, *The Anti-Bolshevik, A Magazine Devoted to the Defense of the American Institutions Against the Jewish Bolshevist Doctrines of Morris Hillquit and Leon Trotsky* declared that "most of the funds needed to carry on the propaganda of the revolution undoubtedly came from the Jews in the United States."

While America's "superpatriots" were promoting the Jew-Bolshevik image, there suddenly appeared in the United States a document purporting to describe a diabolical plot on the part of international Jewish leaders to dominate the world: *The Protocols of the Elders of Zion.* The *Protocols,* later proved fraudulent, were a concoction of the Russian Secret Police in the late-nineteenth century and were used to blame Jews for the 1905 uprising. Not until 1917 did they become a serious political weapon, employed by counterrevolutionary forces to fix the theme of "Jewish conspiracy" as the basis for the Bolshevik victory. They were brought to America by Boris Brasol, a czarist official who was then working for the overthrow of the Soviet Government. The document found its way to the director of the New York section of Army Intelligence, Dr. Harris A. Houghton. Houghton translated *The Protocols* into English, and gleefully distributed copies to his colleagues.

According to Houghton, there was now conclusive evidence that the Russian Revolution was part of an international Jewish conspiracy.

Soon congressmen, government officials, journalists, and business leaders were reading *The Cause of World Unrest*—the American version of the anti-Semitic document. Published by George Haven Putnam, the new, English-language edition revealed the workings of the "Jewish plot." In part, the conspiracy involved the following:

> We will represent ourselves as the saviors of the working class who have come to liberate them from this oppression by suggesting that they join our army of socialists, anarchists, communists, to whom we always extend our help under the guise of the fraternal principles of universal human solidarity.

> To wear everyone out by dissensions, animosities, feuds, famine, inoculation of diseases, want, until the Gentiles see no other way of escape except an appeal to our money and power.

> We will so wear out and exhaust the Gentiles by all this that they will be compelled to offer us an international authority, which by its position will enable us to absorb without disturbance all the governmental forces of the world and thus a super-government.

Among those receptive to the fraud set forth in *The Protocols* was the "man who put America on wheels": Henry Ford. Shortly after the publication of the tract, Ford launched the Dearborn *Independent,* a journalistic enterprise that warned America of the international Jewish conspiracy.

Ford, like other industrialists of the time, was born into a rural America, the Jeffersonian dream that was just beginning to decay. He was a major force in the creation of the modern, urban society he hated, and spent his life, in memory of his youth, re-creating villages, building museums of Americana, and despising the entrance of the exotic immigrant into Protestant American life. Though many ethnics powered his factories, the Jew became fair game to Ford, settling in the cities, a symbol of the crowding, disease, poverty, and herd mentality he detested. But in this he was little different from other Americans in the 1920s. "In America alone," asserted the *Independent,*

> most of the big business, the trusts and the banks, the natural resources and the chief agricultural products, especially tobacco, cotton and sugar, are in control of Jewish financiers or their agents. Jewish journalists are a large and powerful group here. . . . Jews are the largest and most numerous landlords of residence property

in the country. They are supreme in the theatrical world. They absolutely control the circulation of publications throughout the country.

. . It is becoming more and more the conviction of men all over the world that the labor question, the wage question, the land question cannot be settled until first of all this matter of an international super-capitalistic government is settled.

The *Independent* struck out in other areas as well; Bernard Baruch was described as the American dictator during the recent war, Presidents Taft and Wilson were portrayed as "Gentile fronts" of the Jewish conspirators, and the Federal Reserve System was labeled a "Jewish tool." Benedict Arnold was accused of being a Jewish agent, Jews were blamed for the outbreak of the Civil War and the murder of Lincoln, and Jewish gamblers were charged with masterminding baseball's Chicago "Black Sox" scandal. For the Jews of New York City, Ford's journal had special words:

The Jewish problem in the United States is essentially a city problem. . . . In no other city of the United States can the Jewish problem be studied with greater profit than in the city of New York. . . . As a population, the Jews exert more power in New York than they have ever exerted during the Christian Era in any place, with the exception of the present Russia. The Jewish Revolution in Russia was manned from New York. . . . Politically, while the rest of the country is entertained with the fiction that Tammany Hall rules the politics of New York, the fact is rarely published that the Jews rule Tammany.

After reading a copy of the *Independent,* Louis Marshall wrote directly to Ford. "[Such] statements," he told Ford, "are palpable fabrications and the insinuations with which they abound are the emanations of hatred and prejudice."

They constitute a libel upon an entire people who had hoped at least in America they might be spared the insult, the humiliation and the obloquy which these articles are scattering throughout the land and which are echoes from the dark ages. . . . On behalf of my brethren I ask you, from whom we had believed that justice might be expected, whether these offensive articles have your sanction, whether further publications of this nature are to be continued, and whether you shall remain silent when your failure to disavow them will be regarded by the general public as an endorsement of them. Three millions of deeply wounded Americans are awaiting your answer.

Marshall and the Jewish community received an answer—not from Ford, but from The Dearborn Publishing Co.:

> Your rhetoric is that of a Bolshevik orator. . . . Incidentally you cruelly overwork your most useful term which is "antizamitism." [sic] These articles shall continue and we hope you will continue to read them and when you have attained a more tolerable state of mind we shall be glad to discuss them with you.

As a consequence, Congressman Sol Bloom in 1926 called for an investigation of Ford's claim that Jews controlled the American economy. No action was taken by the Congress, and the fight was left to the Jewish community.

Due to the insulting answer to Marshall's inquiry, the American Jewish community sprang into action. Jewish agencies urged federal legislation making such publications illegal, attorneys for B'nai B'rith asked for stronger anti-libel laws, and the American Jewish Committee, perhaps the strongest of the defense agencies, called for a Congressional investigation of Ford's anti-Semitic campaign.

Individual Jews brought lawsuits against the automobile manufacturer. Morris Gest, a noted theatrical producer and son-in-law of David Belasco, sued Ford for 5 million dollars for damaging his reputation in the entertainment world. "I'll make that peace ship Henry pay dearly for what he has said and more, too, I'll make him eat his own words," said Gest. Ford's private secretary coolly replied: "Mr. Gest will be ignored." Ford stayed out of New York to avoid being served with a summons, and thus Gest's legal action never reached the courts.

Herman Bernstein, whose writings had helped to expose the *Protocols* as fraudulent, also attempted legal action against the auto tycoon. Because of an article that branded Bernstein an international Jewish spy, he filed suit for two hundred thousand dollars. Again Ford avoided New York's jurisdiction and managed to stay out of court. Bernstein, however, did receive some minor satisfaction. Through a court order, the author managed to tie up, for several months at least, $115,000 of Ford's money in a New York bank.

It was, however, the assault on Ford products that made the greatest impression. The Jewish press reminded its readers that the "next time you ride in a Ford car, think of what Ford said about you," and the American Jewish Committee urged Jewish newspapers not to publish advertisements of Ford merchandise. William Fox, the Hollywood film producer, in response to the *Independent*'s threat to smear the movie-maker's reputation, warned the auto magnate that he would initiate a newsreel campaign calling the public's attention to the fact that Ford automobiles were involved in more accidents than any other cars on the road.

The semiofficial boycott of Ford autos, which seems to have spread among Christians as well, finally commanded the attention of Ford officials. A southwestern car dealer reported that affluent Jews living in his territory had not purchased a Lincoln for several years, and Ford representatives in Missouri were told, after investigating a sudden decrease in sales, that Fords would not be driven by some people even if provided "free of charge by the company." Because of the refusal to purchase Ford products and the increasing competition from Chevrolet, the emerging workingmen's car, Ford sales by the middle of 1927 had fallen by a half million units.

Confronted by the growing hostility of the Jewish consumer and learning of the decline in sales, Ford decided to bring his anti-Semitic campaign to a halt. In 1927, representatives of the company approached Louis Marshall, the only man they felt could arrange a settlement, with the American Jewish community, and asked for peace. "They told me," wrote Marshall,

> that they thought that Ford would be willing to do whatever I thought was right for the purpose of putting an end to existing conditions, that he had found that Cameron, the editor of the Dearborn Independent, had been deceiving him, and that he had no idea of the publications which appeared in the Dearborn Independent. . . . I told them I was interested merely in protecting the good name of the Jews and in procuring from Ford a document which would be acceptable by the Jews and which would so far as it was possible make amends for the harm that he had tried to do them. . . .

"They left me," said Marshall, "saying they would confer with Ford and see me later." In the apology which followed, though Marshall and the Jewish community knew better, Ford was permitted to claim ignorance of the contents of the *Independent*. "For some time," read the Ford statement,

> I have given consideration to the series of articles concerning Jews which since 1920 have appeared in The Dearborn Independent.

Some of them have been reprinted in pamphlet form under the title "The International Jew." Although both publications are my property, it goes without saying that in the multitude of my activities it has been impossible for me to devote personal attention to their management or to keep informed as to their contents. It has therefore inevitably followed that the conduct and policies of these publications had to be delegated to men whom I placed in charge of them and upon whom I relied implicitly.

After pleading ignorance,‡ Ford continued:

Those who know me can bear witness that it is not in my nature to inflict insult upon and occasion pain to anybody, and that it has been my effort to free myself from prejudice. Because of that I frankly confess that I have been greatly shocked as a result of my study and examination of the files of the Dearborn Independent and of the pamphlets entitled "The International Jew." I deem it to be my duty as an honorable man to make amends for the wrong done to the Jews as fellowmen and brothers, by asking their forgiveness for the harm that I have unintentionally committed, by retracting as far as lies within my power the offensive charges laid at their door by these publications, and by giving them the unqualified assurance that henceforth they may look to me for friendship and good will.

On June 30, 1927, Ford officially brought to an end the most vicious anti-Semitic campaign to have visited America.

Though Ford had declared an end to his venture into anti-Semitism, the Ku Klux Klan, the most infamous hate group of the 1920s, certainly

---

‡ It is interesting to note that Ford lost approximately $5 million on his publishing venture. One therefore wonders if the plea of ignorance can be accepted even by the most naïve observer. Company officials were constantly after their salesmen to promote the distribution of the journal. Indeed, the following letter was sent to those dealers who did not actively distribute the publication:

Dear _____:
1. You have not sent in a single *Dearborn Independent* subscription this year.
2. You have disregarded our special requests to send in your estimated monthly subscriptions so we can remove your name from the non-producer list sent to the Home Office each month.
3. You signed a sales agreement to secure _____ subscriptions during 1925.
4. You are fully expected to live up to this agreement.

If the automobile division of Ford's company was aware of the *Independent* and so concerned with its distribution, I would imagine that Ford himself had "some" knowledge of its existence and contents.

did not follow suit. Revitalized in 1915 by William J. Simmons of Atlanta, Georgia, and especially strong in the Southwest, Midwest, and Far West, the secret society dedicated itself to "one hundred per cent Americanism." By virtue of this proposition, "Catholics, Foreigners, Niggers, and Kikes," were to be excluded from the "real America."

Though the major anti-Semitic thrust of the Klan highlighted Jewish cultural, political, and economic themes, it also reminded America of the Jew-Bolshevik. Not only did Jews cause the Russian Revolution, asserted one Klan journal, but were also "creating war between blacks and whites and working to overthrow all the gentile governments of the world." The *Fellowship Forum,* a "national masonic and patriotic weekly" and one of the unofficial voices of the Klan, declared that "Jews and Catholics Maintain [a] strong Invisible Government in the United States." "Senator Hensley of Oklahoma State Legislature," read the bold print of the headline, "Reveals Yiddish Have Powerful Clan and Jews of World Flock to New York not Palestine in Conspiracy to Internationalize America."*

In addition to the "International Jew" theme, the Klan claimed that Jews were unpatriotic city dwellers who exploited the American economy. "The Jew produces nothing," cried Imperial Wizard Hiram Evans, "anywhere on the face of the earth."

> He does not till the soil. He does not create or manufacture anything for common use. He adds nothing to the sum of human welfare. Everywhere he stands between the producer and the consumer and sweats the toil of the one and the necessity of the other for his gains.

"By deliberate election," declared Evans, the Jew

> is unassimilable. He rejects intermarriage. His religious and social rites and customs are inflexibly segregative. Law-abiding, healthy, moral, mentally alert, energetic, loyal and reverent in his home, the Jew is yet by primal instinct a Jew, indelibly marked by persecution, with no deep national attachment, a stranger to the emotion of patriotism as the Anglo-Saxon feels it.

On the heels of this verbal poison there were of course direct anti-Semitic activities. In numerous areas of Klan concentration, boycotts of Jewish stores were organized and the outcomes of elections were orchestrated. In Montgomery, Alabama, the following leaflet was distributed to voters as they walked to the polls:

* Reference was to the New York *Kehillah.*

Vote the Gunter ticket and help swell the ranks of the Catholics, the bootleggers, the immoral men and women, the Jews, the theater owners, gamblers and Un-Americans. Vote the Bob Jones ticket and help swell the ranks of loyal Americans, real citizens, moral men and women who are trying to raise children in a decent town. Judge a man by the company he keeps. Who are Bob Jones friends. They are the Pastors of our own Protestant Churches and their congregations. Who are Gunter's friends. They are the libertine Catholic priest and the whiskey-swilling, card-playing pro-German Jews.

As Klansmen gained a stranglehold on local governments, their statements and activities grew bolder. In Fort Worth, Texas, an attorney boasted that juries were generally composed of "brothers of the Klan" and warned that any "Kike Jew wouldn't stand much shot before such a jury." In Pocatello, Idaho, a leader of the Jewish community received the following threat: "You are being watched. If you appear on the streets of Pocatello in ten days from this date, God Help Your Soul. We are going to rid this beautiful city of all Catholics, Jews, Greeks, and Bootleggers."

Louis Marshall urged his coreligionists not to involve themselves in any public anti-Klan activities but to leave the fight to the Christian community.† "The only way to fight the Klan," he asserted, "is in the open, and that fighting should be done [not by Jews but] by the Protestant Church, at whose door lies this iniquity, because, besides masquerading in sheets and pillow cases, [the Klan] is seeking to make [itself] appear that it is the protagonist of Protestantism."

In spite of Marshall's suggestion, many Jewish leaders still called for a vigorous campaign against the night-riding terrorists. The American Jewish Committee passed a strong anti-Klan resolution, the Independent Order of B'rith Sholom urged Congress "to use . . . the armed forces . . . to exterminate this vicious and unhealthy organization," and the *Jewish Daily Forward,* which branded the Klan a capitalist tool, compared the night-riding terrorists to the czar's pillaging Cossacks.

There were others, both Jew and gentile, who refused to fight back with merely resolutions and editorials. In Chicago, Illinois, a bomb ripped through the office of a Klan newspaper; in Pittsburgh, Pennsylvania, an angry mob threw stones and bottles at a Klan parade, killing

† Marshall felt that the Klan was not a serious threat and that the "un-failing sense of fairness and decency of the American people as a whole" would, in time, win out.

one of the hooded marchers; in Steubenville, Ohio, three thousand outraged citizens invaded a gathering of one hundred Klansmen; and in
Perth Amboy, New Jersey, six thousand people, led by irate Jews and
Catholics, marched on a Klan meeting. There they "pushed aside" the
entire police and fire departments, which had been assigned to protect
the gathering, and attacked five hundred Klansmen, stoning, beating,
and kicking them as they fled for safety.‡

CLOSING THE GATES: IMMIGRATION RESTRICTION

The war years had all but ended the massive flow of immigrants, and
in the midst of the Red Scare, American xenophobes heightened their
campaign to terminate the policy of free and unlimited immigration.
Organized labor blamed the newcomers for depressing wages, sociologists and social workers decried the "insoluble" social problems, na-
tivists "reminded" the country of the diminution of its "Anglo-Saxon
stock," and the super-patriots, fearing an increase in radical activity,
"warned" America that it was "being turned into a dumping ground for
agitators and Reds."

A nation blinded by anti-foreignism, obsessive loyalty, and heightened racism abandoned its traditional policy of free immigration and
bowed to the demands of the restrictionists; in 1917, Congress overrode
President Wilson's veto and enacted a literacy test, and in 1921 established quotas for immigrant admission. The principle of classifying
immigrants by race and religion became the foundation of the nation's
immigration policy and the law of the land.

One of those touched by the new legislation was Samuel Ratner, a
Polish shoemaker who had spent the war years dreaming of the day
when he would be reunited with his brother in New York City.

"I remember," he declared, "how officials and health officers delayed
our crossing. I almost felt like a criminal the way they examined and re-
examined our papers. I really think they were disappointed that we
were approved for the crossing.

"Not even bribes," he asserted, "which were sometimes successful in
cutting through the massive paper work, were useful. It was then that I
realized that people like us were undesirable and unwanted."

In spite of invalid visas, Ratner reported, some European shipping

‡ In each of these incidents, Jews joined with other religious and racial
groups.

agents still encouraged emigrants to board vessels bound for America. "Some agents," he said, "even sold passage for the return trip—anticipating the newcomer's rejection at the port of entry." When he reached Ellis Island, his youthful friend Meyer, whose "papers were not in order," joined a group of detainees sitting behind a mesh cage.

A blue-uniformed official approached Meyer and explained that he had the right to appeal his deportation. "Appeal!" exclaimed Ratner; "in addition to being scared to death Meyer didn't even know the meaning of the word."

Ratner's brother, who had come to meet the newcomers, witnessed the incident.

"Don't worry about your friend," Jacob told young Samuel, "I know some people at the local political club who can provide us with an immigration expert—an East Side attorney who is known as *the fixer*."

The fixer, armed with injunctions and writs, descended on the Immigration and Naturalization Service. "Once these means were exhausted," asserted Ratner, "our *fixer* used every type of legal harassment—trying to delay the deportation decision until election time—when it was anticipated that some East Side politician would lend a helping hand."

"I soon discovered," remarked the newcomer, "that it was common for both parties, generally before an election, to influence deportation decisions. Most often, the politicians concentrated on the more heartrending cases which appeared in the Yiddish press."

Due to political influence, noted Ratner, "my friend and his family were saved." Still wearing their HIAS identification tags and surrounded by friends, relatives, and local political bosses, the grateful newcomers journeyed to Hester Street, where signs hanging from fireescapes and written in Yiddish, welcomed them to America.

Designed to encourage immigration from northern and western Europe, and to bar newcomers from the eastern and southern portions of the continent, the immigration law of 1921 limited the number of admissions to 3 per cent of the foreign-born elements in the nation in 1910. This drastically lowered the number of Jewish immigrants. In the pre-war years of 1904 to 1914 approximately one hundred thousand Jews a year entered the United States. In 1922, a year after the measure went into effect, that number stood at approximately fifty thousand.

The sharp drop effected by the first quota law still did not satisfy the nationalistic and religious bigotry of the exclusionists. In 1924 Congress responded with a new and even more restrictive statute that even the strongest proponents of restrictionism would accept. Known as the National Origins Act, the new quota limited the number of immigrants to 2 per cent of the foreign-born in 1890. This further reduced Jewish immigration by 75 per cent, so that, for all practical purposes, the East European immigration that began in the 1880s was finally halted.

The anti-Semitic theme, which sometimes surfaced during restrictionist debate, was one of the many forces that helped close the gates of America. In a letter to Louis Marshall this sentiment was expressed: the "spiritually inferior" Jew, wrote one woman, must be barred from American society. "We are populated enough now and do not want the low refuse that Europe is sending us. Of course, the nordic race is superior. He has settled this country, given us law, religion, decency, and is not on a soap box trying to overturn the Government after he is here six weeks."

More vehement in his opposition to Jewish immigration was A. E. Potter, a Methodist minister from Belleville, New York:

> For a real American to visit Ellis Island and there look upon the Jewish hordes, ignorant of all true patriotism, filthy, vermin infested, stealthy and furtive in manner, too lazy to enter real labor, too cowardly to face frontier life, too lazy to work as every American farmer has to work, too filthy to adopt ideals of cleanliness from the start, too bigoted to surrender any racial traditions or to absorb any true Americanism, for a real American to see those items of filthy, greedy, never patriotic stream flowing in to pollute all that has made America as good as she is—is to awaken in his thoughtful mind desires to check and lessen this source of pollution.

The most publicized anti-Semitic assault on Jewish immigration was made by Burton J. Hendrick. In a series of articles for *World's Work* in 1922 and 1923, he called for "bars against [Jewish] immigrants until the day comes when those already here are absorbed. Happily," he concluded,

> this conviction has at last become a fixed one in the popular mind. There is no more hopeful manifestation in American life to-day than the fact that the Nation, after fifty years of fumbling and discussing, has at last reached the point of wisdom in the restriction of immigration.

Though claiming to "have no animus against the Jew," Hendrick expressed his delight that "Congress has passed and the President has signed an immigration law chiefly intended . . . to restrict the entrance of Jews from Eastern Europe."

There were others, specifically government officials, who shared the concepts put forth in Hendrick's writings. Wilbur J. Carr, the director of the U. S. Consular Service, reported to a Senate committee that the Jews of Poland

> are filthy, un-American, and often dangerous in their habits. . . . The increase of immigration from Poland raises two important questions for the United States—first, public health, and second, public safety. Many bolshevik sympathizers are in Poland. It is difficult through visé control to keep out the undesirables.

Marshall again took a leading role in defending the Jewish community. This time he questioned the credibility of the source: "I have repeatedly heard from reliable sources," he told Secretary of State Charles Evans Hughes, "that Mr. Carr has practically forced out of the consular service of the United States the Jews who belonged to it. He has made it uncomfortable for them. He has made promotion impossible. He has given them assignments where there was no hope for advancement. He is known as a pronounced anti-Semite."

Marshall repeated a story told to him by Judge Elkus, a former U.S. minister to Turkey. After returning from that mideastern nation, Elkus called on Carr to request an appointment for a former staff member attached to the Ankara legation. Though Elkus spoke highly of the candidate, Carr, on hearing the gentleman's name, which "sounded" Jewish, replied "that there was no position available. . . ." Elkus, who knew of Carr's sentiments, quickly responded: "Of course, you know that the man is not a Jew, but a Pennsylvania Dutchman." Almost instantly, reported Elkus, Carr found "a position that this man could fill. . . ."

There were also leaders of the labor movement, though not necessarily anti-Semitic,* who shared many of the beliefs of the restrictionists. "The American Federation of Labor," declared Cyrus Adler, of the American Jewish Committee, "in spite of its fine phrases, is one of the most potent of these [restrictionist] influences." The AFL, apart from economics, declared that unrestricted immigration went beyond the nation's ability to Americanize. In support of the literacy test, Samuel Gompers, a foreign-born Jew, highlighted the need for American character and national unity. "America," he said, "has not yet become

---

* Though some were.

a nation. It is still a conglomerated mass of various and diverse ethnic groups . . . honeycombed with foreign groups living a foreign life." Again, in 1919, he repeated this sentiment. While addressing the Committee on Emigration of the International Labor Conference, he declared that "America has come to the conclusion that it is necessary at least for a time to stop the influx of immigration."

The world of science also contributed to the restrictionist verbiage. "Our scientific men," noted Adler, "especially the biologists and anthropologists, have taken up the subject of mixed race, which they declare is being produced here, and have issued all kinds of warnings against it as tending to degeneracy."

These views, he reported, "are being spread not only among the masses through a five-cent paper like the *Saturday Evening Post,* but in college and university circles by leading professors. . . . The people who are promulgating these ideas are sincere in their conviction that the American people, the American spirit, and the English language are seriously threatened."

Responding to the growing popularity of "scientific-racism," the American Jewish Committee utilized "science" to fight "science." It distributed a study of sixty-eight thousand patients in mental hospitals, published by the United States Public Health Service, which indicated that immigrants from northern and western Europe had "shown a higher percentage of mental illness."

The AJC also published a report by Dr. Raymond Pearl which, using the federal Census, found that "on June 1, 1923, in alms houses in America, 26.7% [of the cases] came from Ireland, 20.8% from Germany, 8% from England, and only 4.4% from Poland, 2.2% from Russia, 3.1% from Italy."

Other Jewish institutions sought to prevent the enactment of the restrictive immigration quotas. B'nai B'rith approached Catholic leaders but was unsuccessful in persuading them to join the battle.† Pressure from the B'nai B'rith was applied to the major political parties, attorneys for a number of organizations filed briefs, influential leaders

† The fight on the part of the Jews to halt or delay the restrictionist laws was, more often than not, made on behalf of the entire foreign-born community—including Catholics. Simon Wolf of the AJC had once declared: "I want [it] distinctly understood, that whatever we ask we ask as citizens and not as Jews. Immigration laws are made for all and not for a particular class, and we must put ourselves on a high plane of citizenship; and not as partisans of any particular cult."

flooded Congress with letters, and civic and religious leaders jumped at the opportunity to testify before Congressional committees.

Rabbi Stephen S. Wise used a Congressional hearing to express, in the most moving terms, the devotion and Americanism of the foreign-born.

"I tell you," he told a Committee on Immigration and Naturalization, "that postwar hysteria which still remains continues to work in America and [is] inflicting . . . a great wrong upon thousands . . . of citizens of America who live as Americans, who love it as I do, although I am foreign-born."

> You are creating among the Hungarians, the Czechoslovaks, the Serbians, the Jews of eastern Europe, none the less effectively, a sense of inferiority, that sense of inferiority . . . which is essentially and instinctively felt when a man is proscribed against, as if, later on, he will not be helpful and serviceable to America.

To crystallize the fact that most newcomers were intensely loyal, Wise related the following incident:

> I happened to tell [Theodore] Roosevelt . . . about my father, who was a student in the German University at Leipzig in 1865, . . . that I had learned from two friends of my father (all of them, of course, European; all of them Austrians, as my father was an Austro-Hungarian) that the three of them stood together on the day after the assassination of President Lincoln and my father turned to the other two men and said, "Someday I am going to live in the land of Lincoln. . . ."

Roosevelt, touched by the story, had turned to Wise and said, "When did your father come to America?"

"He came to America in 1874," answered the rabbi, "almost immediately after my birth in Budapest."

"And your father said he was going someday to live in the land of Lincoln, in 1865?" Roosevelt again asked.

"Yes," replied Wise.

"Then, I should say," declared Roosevelt, "that your father was an American nine years before he ever touched the soil of America with his feet, because the soul of America was his in the making and in the hoping, long before he dreamed physically of becoming a part of the United States."

"Forgive this digression," the rabbi told the members of the committee, "but I think it not without significance, because it bears just a little upon the discussion of a moment ago with respect to the vested right of any European.

"No European," he concluded,

> has any vested right in America, but . . . I point out to you that we may commit a wrong even against those who have rights vis-à-vis or respecting us. We may wrong one man if we deny him that which on any arbitrary and indefensible grounds we grant to another. And, Mr. Chairman, I dissent most heartily from the notion, most earnestly and solemnly from the notion that just because X, Y, Z in Czechoslovakia, Yugoslavia, Romania, have no vested rights in America, therefore the United States of America can do no wrong to them if we exercise, as against them, an attitude which is discriminatory. Discrimination, even though it cloak itself under the name "selection," is always fundamentally unjust.

Meyer London, the Socialist congressman from New York's East Side, also denounced restrictionism, before the House of Representatives, as an "exaggerated nationalism. . . ."

"At whom are you striking with this bill?" he asked rhetorically. "At the very people whom a short while ago you announced you were going to emancipate," he reminded the federal lawmakers.

Although most of London's Congressional colleagues were listening with "half an ear," his denunciation of their sentiments rang loud and clear: "We sent . . . men to make the world safe for democracy, to liberate these very people. Now you shut the doors on them. Yes, so far you have made the world safe for hypocrisy."

Turning his attention to the two principal arguments of the restrictionists, the need to bar European radicals and the protection of American industry, he continued his harangue. The first contention, he quickly dismissed as ridiculous:

> The supporters of the bill claim that the law will keep out radicals. The idea that by restricting immigration you will prevent the influx of radical thought is altogether untenable. You cannot confine an idea behind prison bars; you cannot exclude it by the most drastic legislation. The field of thought recognizes no barrier. The fact that there was almost no immigration during the war did not prevent us from importing every abominable idea from Europe. We brought over the idea of deportation of radicals from France—from the France of the Bourbons. We imported the idea of censorship of the

press and the passport system from Russia—from the Russia of Nicholas the Second. We imported the idea of universal military service from Germany—the Germany of the Kaiser. Ideas can neither be shut in nor shut out. There is only one way of contending with an idea and that is the old safe American rule of free and untrammeled discussion. Every attempt to prove any other method has always been disastrous.

In response to the second argument, the safeguarding of the nation's industrial growth, London offered information known to every thinking person: that the most developed areas of America were those with the greatest number of foreign-born. "Our most backward states industrially," he declared,

> and in the point of literacy are those which have had no immigration to speak of. The extraordinary and unprecedented growth of the United States is as much the effect as the cause of immigration. Defenders of this bill thoughtlessly repeat the exploded theory that there have been two periods of immigration, the "good" period . . . up to the year 1900 and the "bad" period since.

"The strange thing about this," he said, "is that at no time in history has any country made such rapid progress in industry, in science and in the sphere of social legislation as this country has shown since 1900. Besides that, identically the same arguments were used against the old immigration."‡

Though the protests were many, and in most cases eloquent and rational, the United States still made the quota system the law of the land.* The Statue of Liberty would remain in New York Harbor, but the immortal words at its base would from then on be but an accolade to a forgotten ideal.

‡ Like London, the *Jewish Daily Forward* also took a strong, Socialist-oriented, anti-restrictionist position. Drawing a parallel between the repressive legislation and the Red Scare, the editors asserted that the new quota policy was directed at radicals and Jews.
Describing the new restrictions as "inhuman," the *Forward* decried the fact that the number of newcomers would not be increased to reunite "broken families" but would be extended for the sake of the business community, since the Secretary of Labor was empowered to permit the entrance of laborers in excess of the respective quota.
* It is important to note that the quota system would have been legislated without the aid of the racist-nativist element, for the majority of Americans had themselves decided to terminate the historic principle of free and just-about-unlimited immigration.

BIGOTRY AMERICAN STYLE

One Saturday morning, an attorney and a professor were leaving the Synagogue together. After stopping for a few moments to wish their fellow congregants a "good *Shabos,*" the two men strolled up the avenue. Suddenly the lawyer turned to his companion and exclaimed: "Why is the rabbi getting so hysterical over this Goldfarb business!" referring to a recent case of anti-Jewish discrimination that had been the topic of the morning sermon.

"Why!" answered the professor, "because these incidents are happening all too often. That's why!"

"Look," the lawyer quickly shot back, "if not for these overly sensitive Jews, you would never even hear about anti-Semitism. I say we keep our mouths shut and let this Goldfarb affair die."

"But it's not only Goldfarb," declared the professor, "and you know it. Didn't you yourself protest to the school board when Sophie Rappoport was fired? And were you not furious when your opposition used Jew-baiting tactics in the last election?"

"That may be true," replied the attorney, "but, then, many people are confronted with similar treatment. What I am really opposed to are the people who kick up a fuss every time a Jew yells foul. Do you realize how much resentment we create? Listen, we only make things worse by broadcasting our *tsoriss.* I'm sure that if we kept still, the term anti-Semitism would vanish from the language."

"The term, yes," replied the professor, "but not the act. Most people won't admit they dislike Jews; but just the same they do; just open your eyes and you'll see discrimination all around you."

"Nonsense! I can't accept your analysis," said the attorney.

"O.K. then, let me prove it to you," responded the professor.

At that very moment the two men came upon the entrance to an exclusive social club. After motioning to his companion to follow, the professor entered the swinging doors and approached the doorman: "Where can we find Mr. Schwartz?" he said.

"I think you have the wrong address," snapped the attendant icily; "this is a restricted club."

In the decades following the turn of the century, anti-Semitism reached crisis proportions. Some of it was covert and subtle; much of it, however, was overt, direct, and crude.

The most vicious anti-Semitic incident to take place in prewar America was the lynching of Leo M. Frank, an Atlanta, Georgia, pencil manufacturer.

On April 26, 1913, the South's Confederate Memorial Day, Mary Phagan, a worker at the National Pencil Company, went to the factory to collect her wages. At three-thirty the next morning, the young employee was found murdered. Her clothing was torn to shreds, a deep gash crossed her head, and a rope, apparently the murder weapon, was tightly wrapped around her neck. By his own admission, Frank, a New York Jew, was the last one to see the girl alive.

After the body was discovered, the police found strands of the victim's hair and bloodstains in a workroom near Frank's office. When questioned about the evidence, so close to where he had been working the day of the murder, Frank seemed to be "nervous." His emotional response to the questions convinced the police that "they had their man." Leo Frank was arrested for the murder of the Phagan girl.

Within hours after the arrest, rumors of Frank's alleged sexual encounters, which did much to convince the townspeople that the "Jew pervert" was truly the killer, spread throughout the city. Without even the slightest shred of evidence, stories circulated over backyard fences about his "second" wife in New York, of pornographic pictures that decorated the walls of his office, and of the offensive manner in which he "bothered" the female workers at the factory. Even a policeman claimed to have seen "the damned sheeny," approximately a year earlier, fondling a woman while walking in a wooded area of the community.

The most damaging story of Frank's "sexual exploits" was told by the proprietor of an Atlanta whore house. Under oath, the madam testified that the accused had phoned her on the evening of the murder and asked for a room to which he could bring a female companion. Though Frank had witnesses who swore they were at his home playing cards with him on the night in question, the public and the authorities chose to believe the whore. Even after the madam retracted her statement and publicly declared that the police had intimidated her into lying, the angry crowds were still convinced that the "New York Jew" was with the murdered girl that evening.

Anti-Frank feeling, blinded by anti-Semitic sentiment, grew during the grueling legal fight to prove his innocence. "The crowds," reported one observer, "surrounded the court house as though it was a carnival tent." "Crack the Jew's neck," they shouted; "lynch him!" Inside, spectators followed suit; many cheered when the prosecution presented its evidence, and even more jeered when the defense rose to object. "Some officials," declared another spectator, "received threatening phone calls and notes demanding that they hang the Jew or we'll hang you." One member of the jury reported that he "wasn't sure of anything except that unless [we] convicted Frank [we] would never get home alive."

"The very atmosphere of the courtroom was charged with an electric current of indignation which flashed and scintillated before the very eyes of the jury," wrote the Atlanta *Journal*.

> The courtroom and streets were filled with an angry, determined crowd, ready to seize the defendant if the jury found him not guilty. Cheers for the prosecuting counsel were irrepressible in the courtroom throughout the trial, and on the streets unseemly demonstrations in condemnation of Frank were heard by the judge and jury. The judge was powerless to prevent these outbursts in the courtroom and the police were unable to control the crowd outside. . . .

During the final presentation by the State the Atlanta *Journal,* fearing that, "a verdict of acquittal would cause a riot such as would shock the country and cause Atlanta's streets to run with innocent blood," urged the judge to adjourn for at least a day.† "The mob," said one eyewitness, "was breathing vengeance in the very face of the judge and jury."

As expected, the foreman of the jury returned a verdict of guilty. Leo M. Frank was to be hanged by the neck until dead. "If Christ and his angels came down here," remarked presiding judge Leonard Roan, "and showed this jury that Frank was innocent, it would bring him in guilty." In the midst of Georgia's medieval justice, there were a few who recognized the miscarriage being committed. "Leo Frank has not had a fair trial," wrote the Atlanta *Journal*. "He has not been fairly convicted, and his death without a fair trial and legal conviction will amount to judicial murder." Nonetheless, the voice of intolerance was louder: Innocent or guilty, replied the local populace, we will get the damned Jew.

After the verdict was announced, Frank's lawyers filed for a new trial, but Judge Roan refused to grant the motion. The Georgia Supreme Court, voting five to four, followed suit. The United States Supreme Court, however, did hear the case, but they, too, upheld the

---

† In response to the threats, the Fifth Georgia Infantry was placed on alert the evening before the judge charged the jury.

decision of the Georgia judiciary. Only Oliver Wendell Holmes and Charles Evans Hughes, declaring that "mob law does not become due process of law by securing the assent of a terrorized jury," dissented.

Having lost in the courts, the defense turned to Georgia's governor, John M. Slaton, whose term of office was to expire one day before the scheduled execution. Convinced that justice was not served, Slaton, under a cloak of secrecy, transferred the condemned man from the Atlanta facility to the Milledgeville Penitentiary and announced a commutation of sentence. Leo Frank was to spend the rest of his natural life behind bars.

After hearing the news, angry crowds threatened to "take Frank by force and lynch [both] him and Slaton." *The Jeffersonian,* Tom Watson's anti-Semitic newspaper, added to the bitterness among the citizens:

> Our grand old Empire HAS BEEN RAPED! We have been violated, AND WE ARE ASHAMED! . . . The great Seal of State has gone, LIKE A THIEF IN THE NIGHT, to do for an unscrupulous law firm, a deed of darkness which dared not bask in the light of the sun. . . . We have been betrayed! the breath of some leprous monster has passed over us, and we feel like crying out, in horror and despair, "Unclean! UNCLEAN!"

In the summer of 1915 Watson's journal continued its assault on Frank and the decision of the now ex-governor Slaton. Charging that Slaton had been "bought" by wealthy Jews, *The Jeffersonian*'s headline called for Slaton's "INDICTMENT FOR TREASON." Going a step further, Watson urged the "good people of Georgia" to take Frank from his cell and lynch him: "The next Leo Frank Case in Georgia will never reach the courtoom," he said. "The next Jew who does what Frank did is going to get exactly the same thing that we give the Negro rapists."

The sentiments expressed in the pages of *The Jeffersonian* quickly spread throughout the state. In several towns the citizens burned Slaton in effigy. Attached to the burning figures were signs that read: "John M. Slaton, King of the Jews." A mob warned all Jews out of the town of Canton, and in the northern outskirts of Atlanta a vigilance committee tacked the following leaflet to the doors of Jewish-owned shops:

> You are hereby notified to close up this business . . . by Saturday night, June 29, 1915, or else stand the consequences. We mean to rid Marietta of all Jews by the above date. You can heed this warn-

ing or stand the punishment the committee may see fit to deal out to you.

Cards were distributed to those who approached Jewish establishments:

(CARRY ME IN YOUR PURSE)

STOP! and THINK!
Before you spend your money.
Shall It Go To A Fund to
PROTECT MURDERERS
To Buy Governors. Stop and
Think. Now is the time to
show your colors, to show your
true American Blood.—
IS IT STREAKED?
Can't you buy shoes from an
AMERICAN
Can't you buy the Necessities of
Life from an AMERICAN
AMERICAN GENTILES,
IT IS UP TO YOU
This little card is only a little ant
hill to start with. HELP it grow into
a MOUNTAIN.

On the evening of August 16, 1915, a group of vigilantes stormed into the Milledgeville Prison, cut all communications, overpowered the two guards, and kidnaped Frank. "We want you to come with us," said one. "Don't bother with your clothes," snapped another as the bewildered prisoner reached for his pants, "just come as you are."

The next morning, the armed auto convoy containing Frank and the vigilantes arrived at a location near the birthplace of Mary Phagan. Moments later, Leo Frank was lynched. "It was," said Reuben Arnold, Frank's defense attorney, "the most horrible persecution of a Jew since the death of Christ."

In 1921, American Jewry again witnessed an innocent member of their community indicted and tried for the "crime" of being Jewish. In October 1918, Captain Robert Rosenbluth, Major Alexander Cronkhite, and Sergeant Pothier, of the United States Army, were spending an afternoon on the pistol range. Cronkhite, who was Rosenbluth's commanding officer, accidentally shot and killed himself. Though cleared by an army investigation of any wrongdoing, three years after the incident occurred the Jewish captain was arrested for murder.‡

During the trial, Rosenbluth's attorney had proved that his client was nowhere near the shooting but had been drilling recruits in an open field some distance away. All the evidence pointed to the fact that the wound was self-inflicted. Taking the defense in yet another direction, the attorney branded the case "an American Dreyfus Affair," charging that Rosenbluth was being harassed simply because he was a Jew.

American Jewry saw in the assault on the Jewish army officer an overt endorsement of the growing anti-Semitic menace. "Uptowners," "downtowners," Zionists, and Socialists all agreed that an acquittal was essential to Jewish survival. "If we allow the injustice of the Leo Frank case to repeat itself," declared one observer, "we can expect this to happen with greater frequency. It must be stopped here and now!"

Due to the solidarity displayed by the various groups within the Jewish community, the anti-Semitic press had a field day. They repeated the charge of the Jewish conspiracy; this time, they said, the Jews were tearing at the very fabric of American justice by trying to save a guilty Rosenbluth.

Incensed by such editorials, Louis Marshall answered the accusation:

> Learning that Rosenbluth is a Jew, that damning fact was enough to serve the malign purposes of the ignorant fanatic [Henry Ford] to embark on one of his characteristic crusades to compass the destruction, nay the judicial murder if possible, of a fellow-being. For weeks and months his columns reeked with vile falsehoods, wicked and insane imaginings, cunningly contrived appeals to passion and prejudice. . . . It is interesting to speculate as to what this intellectual brother of the Ku Klux Klan, whose textbook is his "International Jew," will do now. . . .

After three years of agonizing litigation, the court finally agreed that not a shred of evidence had been submitted to justify the arrest and indictment. On October 16, 1924, Rosenbluth was acquitted when the New York State Court of Appeals dismissed the case. The editors of the Dearborn *Independent* were shocked. Charging that the verdict was the result of "shameful interference of [Jewish] social organizations," Ford's journal declared that the solid front put up by the Jewish community was "illustrative of the length to which an alien type of mind

‡ This action was taken at the insistence of the dead man's father, Major General Adelbert Cronkhite.

will go to neutralize the confidence of the people and our laws and courts."

By the beginning of the 1920s, anti-Jewish discrimination was well established. During this decade, employment agencies openly advertised that "no Jews need apply," quota systems were adopted by universities, membership in social and professional organizations was limited to "Christians only," and "gentlemen's agreements" were reached to keep the "sheenies" out of the "better residential communities."

The more affluent members of the Jewish community were the first to react to these discriminatory practices. Unlike their poorer coreligionists, who were still living in the areas of primary settlement and concentrated in working-class occupations, the wealthier and more educated Jews were quick to react and even quicker to develop countermeasures.*

Particularly resentful to the "uptowners" were the restrictive measures of the exclusive social clubs. "We are in no sense foreigners," wrote one perplexed Jew who was barred from such an organization. "My wife and I are both descended from generations of cultured people; I was educated at what is generally regarded as one of the most famous American universities . . . and have occupied positions of trust and responsibility. We do not even have very pronounced Jewish names."

Whether one had a "very pronounced Jewish name" or not, the fact remained that Jews were not welcome at most Christian-dominated social clubs. Even at the YMCA, though not an "exclusive" social organization, exclusionism became the order of the day. Two investigators related the following incident.

"A Jew and a non-Jew decided they needed more exercise and ought to take up handball," they wrote. The two friends went to New York's Twenty-third Street "Y" to apply for membership. They told the gentleman in charge that they wanted to play that afternoon and had brought along their gym shorts and shoes. The man at the desk handed them a form to fill out on which, since it was a religious institution, there were questions relating to religious affiliation. The Christian completed the form and was the first to return the card.

"All right, sir," said the clerk, "if you will just let me have the membership fee, you may go right up to the gymnasium now." Moments later, the Jew handed in his application. The clerk hesitated for a few

* In 1914, the B'nai B'rith established the Anti-Defamation League to combat the rising tide of anti-Semitism. In the 1920s, the American Jewish Congress followed suit.

seconds and then finally said: "I am sorry, but the rule is that men of your religion must first be interviewed by the membership secretary. I think it is because there is a percentage." Though disappointed, the two handball partners waited. The membership secretary never showed up.

Patterns of exclusion also reached the hotels. Tales involving the restrictive policies stretched from Lake Placid to Palm Beach and out to the West Coast. Typical is the story of Julius Weinstein, who, in preparing for a vacation, wired an "upper-class" hotel for a reservation for himself and his wife. His name, being a dead giveaway, immediately elicited the all too familiar response: SORRY, NOTHING AVAILABLE. ALL FILLED UP. Not deterred by the rejection, Weinstein asked a gentile friend to send the same request. Just as quickly as the previous communication was answered, the hotel wired back: RESERVATION MADE. THANK YOU. Weinstein and his friend were reminded of another Jewish couple, Joseph and Mary, who were informed "some years ago" by the keeper of an inn at Bethlehem that "no space was available."

Some hotels barred Jews unconditionally, others admitted them freely, and still others admitted them reluctantly. "The hotels do not cater to Jews" read one letter to a Baltimore rabbi from a vacationing congregant. It continues, "In other areas, we were given undesirable rooms during our stay and were not being shown the comforts and privileges given to the other guests." Miami Beach resort owners declared that their "finest hotels . . . do not accept Jews"; those in the Pennsylvania highlands advertised: "Altitude 2,500 feet, too high for Jews."

Hostility toward Jewish vacationers sometimes led to violence. In the fall of 1929 the Jewish owner of a group of cottages at Pewaukee Lake, on the outskirts of Milwaukee, received the following letter:

> Listen, Jew! We noticed that you are again trying to rent your cottages to the same _____ you had last summer. We'll murder you and all the rest like ducks, if you move in again. Remember, this is not a threat, we'll do it.

The author of the letter proved that he was serious: ten cottages were burned to the ground, and people from the surrounding area looted the remaining cottages of their furnishings.

The incident shocked a portion of the Christian community, eliciting the following editorial from the Milwaukee *Journal:*

> Listen, Gentile! Moved by the lowest form of race prejudice, you have practiced an outrageous persecution upon a citizen of this state. You have stepped from the levels of decency, fair play and

tolerance to the level of a coward, acting by stealth like a rat. Moreover you have broken the laws against arson.

. . . And if, by proper evidence, it can be established who helped to persecute and loot the Jew, . . . neighbor, resident of Pewaukee, or passerby—will be punished to the full extent of the law so that this shame upon the state may be wiped as clean as such a smudge ever can be wiped. This is the word of the decent people of Wisconsin who, as Americans, acknowledge no intolerance and practice no persecution against any creed or faith or sect.

Unlike those who harbored the noble sentiments that concluded this editorial, the people who sought "to protect their neighborhood" extended the practice of restrictionism to the selling of homes and renting of apartments. Those Jews, trapped for so long in the ghettos, who finally were able to make a move toward the "sunshine and fresh air," often ran up against the infamous "gentlemen's agreement" not to sell to "their kind." Even more direct was an advertisement on a New York City bus extolling the advantages of a Jackson Heights, Queens, apartment house. It read: "Restrictions, Convenience, Service."

In "The Coming of the Jews," Francis Russell vividly described the fear caused by the first Jewish family to "crack" his Boston neighborhood.

"Then came the catastrophe," he wrote. "Suddenly and in secret the Robinsons sold their two-family house to Jews."

Everyone . . . was appalled. At the tennis club they talked of nothing but the perfidy of the Robinsons, who, during their remaining months on the Hill, stayed in semiretirement with the shades drawn. Oscar Dobbs, their neighbor across the street, was all for a boycott of the new owner. Wellington Holbrook [the local real-estate agent] . . . selected a committee of ten to meet at his house. The only thing to do, he maintained, was to buy the Robinsons' place back again. If twenty people would give fifty dollars apiece, that would be enough to buy off this Isidore White.

They agreed. Fifty dollars apiece, even if they lost it, would be cheap enough for saving the Hill. They were protecting their homes. Yet even the committee members knew in their hearts that they were whistling down the wind.

For the Neighborhood "changed."

The most humorous incident of restrictionism, if that policy can in any way be funny, was the story of an affluent Jew who asked a Park Avenue rental agent the cost of an apartment.

"I'm sorry, sir," answered the agent, "but I can't quote the price, because nothing is available."

"What's the cost, anyway? When will one be available? Why won't you give me some information?" snapped the Jew in a series of questions.

"Well," said the agent, "I guess I will have to be honest with you. We do not take Jews."

"Oh!" exclaimed the Jew, "forgive me. I didn't understand what you were driving at. I am not interested in renting, but the fact is I'm keeping a blonde here, and I wanted to see if she was telling me the truth about the rent."

As the tide of Jews moved from the ghetto neighborhoods to the areas of second settlement, the residents of these semisuburban communities became more and more defensive. As history has recorded, sometimes their efforts were futile. In New York City, thousands of Jews crossed the rivers bordering Manhattan and flooded the apartment houses of Brooklyn and the Bronx. The gentile residents, often overwhelmed by the vast number of Jews "moving in," were either "forced" to accept their new neighbors or leave. In a reversal of roles, one woman's reply to a question about the number of Christians in Bensonhurst, an area of heavy Jewish concentration, was "not enough to be annoying."

Not every community in the path of the Jewish "trek" gave way as easily as Bensonhurst. In Sea Gate, an exclusive gentile enclave surrounded by Brooklyn's Coney Island, the residents employed one restrictive tactic after another before finally letting down the bars.

"What walls, what citadels shall withstand your march, all-conquering Jew?" asked William Schack, in "The Conquest of Sea Gate."

> What avails it for proud hostelries to bar the door—brave summer places, with edicts, signs and court injunctions to oppose your arms? The same sad fate awaits them all. From coast to coast you blow your trumpet blasts outside the battlements; the Gentiles flee, and their strongholds pass into your hands. . . .

As one walked west on the Coney Island boardwalk, there soon appeared an iron fence topped with barbed wire and maintained in perfect condition. If one followed the barricade, one soon reached the entrance to Sea Gate—guarded by private police and a small but meaningful sign:

SEA GATE
Private Residential Colony
Restricted Bathing Beach

From Williamsburg to Brownsville and East New York, to Bensonhurst, Sheepshead Bay, and Coney Island, the Jews marched across Brooklyn. Having arrived at Coney Island, the last stop on the elevated electric train, these refugees from the tenements of the Lower East Side proliferated throughout the popular summer resort. With their "beachhead" secured, some of the newcomers, generally the more affluent, spearheaded a drive to penetrate the "forbidden zone" surrounded by the ominous wire fence: Sea Gate.

"The entering wedge was made," wrote Schack,

> during the war, when some of the Sea Gate people, pressed for funds, sold out at a good price—as it happened, to Jews. This in turn made others sell out who were not pressed for funds, but who turned up their noses at the new neighbors. A few years later, when the Jewish invasion was on in earnest, a great many new houses went up to meet the demand. The newcomers were willing to pay good prices.

Boardinghouses sprang up, and Jews crammed their newly acquired homes with people from cellar to ceiling. "After all," noted Schack,

> the newcomers were accustomed, in the Catskills and at the seashore, to live a little crowded, scores of families in one building, and all cooking in a tiny common kitchen. The smell of good Jewish cooking penetrated into the streets; private cottages became noisy tenements.

"And worse!" he declared with tongue in check:

> The Jews are a hospitable people, not selfish and exclusive like the Gentiles. Having such a fine place near such a wonderful beach, how could the golden-hearted Jewish women who lived there understand that they should keep this blessing entirely to themselves? So they invited cousins and aunts and uncles, and brothers and sisters, and friends from Brownsville, to come over for the weekend, and go bathing with them. The restricted beach began to take on almost as crowded an appearance as the one on the other side [of the fence]. The older residents began to grumble also that, at the new boardinghouses, not only the regular guests but even tran-

sient diners were being given the privilege of bathing. These visitors, held up at the gates for want of a pass, would raise a commotion, and argue. The lot of the policemen at the gates was not a happy one.

Disturbed by the number of new arrivals and further alarmed by the many guests the newcomers invited to the enclave, the gentile-dominated Sea Gate Association established new rules to govern their Jewish neighbors. "Except in the case of established and recognized boardinghouses and inns," read the principal regulation, "the Guard will not permit entrance to more than ten guests on any one day to any one destination, except as a special privilege for such special occasions as weddings, funerals, receptions, or entertainments, for which the . . . Association, through its office, shall have been notified in advance, and for which it shall have issued a permit."

The new regulation found at least one Jewish opponent who was willing to do legal combat with the association: Wolf Drabinsky. In a court contest, the Jewish residents of the community emerged victorious. Drabinsky and his coreligionists (including non-Jewish residents of course) could have as many guests as they pleased.

Not deterred by the court ruling and still seeking to limit the number of visitors, the association erected new restrictions. After the decision was handed down, new fences were built along the private beach, and guards were stationed at every entrance. It was now "necessary to have one card for entering the grounds, and still another for entering the beach." The association ruled that there were to be no more than two boarders in a bedroom, and only two beach passes were issued to each room. "You may bring your friends," the association said, "but they must do their bathing elsewhere."†

By the 1920s, the restrictive codes that governed the selling of homes and the renting of apartments were also applied to higher education. Numerous colleges and universities, through formal and informal methods, limited the admission of Jewish students.

At New York University, in addition to signs (erected by students) decorating some of its dormitories (at its Bronx campus) declaring that "scurvy Jews" and "strictly *koshers*" were not welcome, a prominent dean exclaimed that "this is a Christian university.‡ The best service you can perform," the told a group of Jewish leaders, "is to tell Jewish students not to come in such numbers to the . . . university."

† The beach pass could be used only twice a day, once in the morning and once in the afternoon. According to Schack, "This rule [was] sternly enforced."
‡ NYU has always been a private, non-religious institution.

NYU did not enforce its quota system at all of its campus locations. The Washington Square Campus, situated in the heart of Greenwich Village, was non-restricted and housed the nation's largest body of Jewish undergraduates.* Conversely, the University Heights Campus, nestled in a wooded Bronx community, made a serious effort to preserve "a conventional college atmosphere and spirit" by installing "selective admissions." Substantially smaller than its "downtown sister" and still the darling of the trustees, "The Heights," as it was affectionately called by Jew and gentile alike, remained the pride and joy of the old guard.

"Selective admission," or more accurately, the quota system, was instituted at the school in 1919. In defense of the policy, Dean Archibald L. Bouton declared:

> We were at that time threatened . . . with nothing less than the immediate disintegration of our college body as it was then constituted at University Heights. . . . It is still true as it was in 1919, and in this metropolitan environment it will long be true, that our chief problems center in students of Russian, Polish and Central European parentage.

The dean went on to say:

> . . . We do not exclude students of any race or national origin because they are foreign, but whenever the student body is found to contain elements from any source in such proportions as to threaten our capacity for assimilating them to the standards of national life, which, as an educational institution, we hold, then in the interest of our functions as a college, as we interpret it, we seek by selection to restore the balance.

In response to the dean's assertion that the university was not discriminating against Jews, a former student sent the following letter to a national publication:

> My brother, a Jewish student of irreproachable reputation . . . was elected president of the junior class (the first time in NYU history that a Jew received that honor in the college of Arts and Sciences). With him other Jews were elected to a majority of class offices. Whether this was good judgment or not, they were of the class and were elected by and for the class.

"When the elections were announced," continued the letter,

> the faculty—mind you, the faculty—called off the elections, using the pretext that, first, the officers elected were Bolshevists; sec-

* For a private university or college.

ondly, that there had been ballot-stuffing; and thirdly, fourthly and fifthly, that the elections were null and void. To add insult to injury, the [Jewish] officers were threatened with expulsion for the offense of being elected.

In the spirit of co-operation, the former student was granted an interview with Bouton. "We had a long and startlingly frank talk . . ." said the student. "The worthy Dean (and he really is that, in spite of his dilemma) finally agreed that Bolshevism and ballot-stuffing were not the issue—that it was simply a Jewish question—that . . . the percentage [of Jewish students] now threatened to be over fifty and would be if not restrained."

By no means was NYU the only institution of higher learning to introduce these practices. *Almost every private university* that faced the possibility of a large Jewish enrollment set limits on Jewish admissions.†

At Columbia University, Jewish enrollment was "controlled" by means of "psychological" and "character" tests. The following college song might have served as one reason for the restrictive policy of the trustees.

> Oh, Harvard's run by millionaires,
> And Yale is run by booze,
> Cornell is run by farmers' sons,
> Columbia's run by Jews.
> So give a cheer for Baxter Street
> Another one for Pell,
> And when the little sheenies die,
> Their souls will go to hell.

Annoyed by the publicity of this popular collegiate tune, Columbia's officials set about to limit the number of Jewish students. Morton Levy, an honor student from a Bronx high school, wanted to attend the Ivy League enclave on Manhattan's upper West Side. He sent for an application and anxiously waited for the school to respond. Soon the application was on the kitchen table of his family's two-bedroom apartment

---

† According to contemporary observers, "In the tax-supported state and city colleges the theory of equal opportunity [applied] strictly so far as admission [was] concerned. In many cases, however, it [did] not go much farther." At the University of Wisconsin, for example, a football player declared at a public meeting that "we are getting so many damned Jews here that something must be done." At the same university, "A Jewish girl brought suit against . . . a dormitory on the ground that after her application and fee were accepted for admission as a resident, she had been thrown out because she was a Jewess."

in the Bronx. After filling in his vital statistics—name, address, and date of birth—he came to a section that included the following questions: "Have you been a student at any other college?" "Place of birth?" "Religious affiliation?" "Have you been known by another name or used any variation of your name?" "Father's name, occupation, place of birth?" "Mother's maiden name in full, place of birth?"

The next step in the admissions procedure was the "psychological" test. This was followed by a "character" examination and a personal interview. "We favor students from outside New York," the interviewer told the candidate from the Bronx. "But since yours is an early application we can place you on a waiting list." It was common knowledge, said Levy, that "with a waiting list, college officials could do almost anything."

Having gone through the ritual of Columbia's admissions procedure, Levy relaxed and waited for the results. "With my grades," he said, "how could they not want me?" Every day he could be seen sitting on the stoop of his apartment house waiting for the postman. Finally it came. He took the letter, ran up the five flights of stairs, and opened the envelope.

"We regret to inform you . . ." read the first sentence. "Why?" he asked his family; "with my grades—" Quickly his father interrupted. "Why? Because they can't forgive you for being born Jewish."

Four years later, Levy, who was perhaps the best stickball player to come out of his neighborhood, graduated with honors from the City College of New York.

At Barnard College, Columbia's "sister school," the policy of "selected admissions" was repeated. In a letter to *The Nation,* Rebecca Grecht related the ordeal of her rejection:

> In June, 1918 . . . I applied for admission into Barnard College. I offered a record of uniformly high scholarship—I was fourteenth on the list of winners of State scholarships, with an average of 92 per-cent—excellent references from my high school, and a certificate of perfect health.

> In July I received a letter notifying me that I had been rejected. When I went up to the College for a personal interview, I was assured that my rejection had not been due either to scholarship, character, or health. What then could have been the cause but my race, my religion? The references I had given had not even been referred to.

As a result, Grecht took the matter up with her high school counselor:

> The head of the [high school] scholarship department held a conference with the [Barnard] Dean, but learned nothing more definite. Various excuses were given, among them, that Barnard preferred students who took college entrance examinations, though I had neither seen such a statement in the bulletin of information, nor had been informed when I made my application; that, furthermore, the standard of that high school was not high enough, though non-Jewish applicants had been admitted from the school with records appreciably lower, as was well known; that finally, the capacity of the college had been filled before my application was considered, though students had been admitted even as late as a week after the opening of the semester.

The disappointed student continued:

> I made two more attempts to enter Barnard, once after my freshman year at Hunter College, and again in my sophomore year at New York University. Nothing availed, however. After all, what intrinsic worth had I to offer Barnard? I was an intelligent student of high attainments, true enough, but I was only a Jew. I lived on the East Side, and I had no high social connections.

"I might add," she wrote, "that I graduated from Washington Square College, New York University, in February, 1922, receiving the degree of Bachelor of Arts, *cum laude*."

In response to the letter, Barnard's Dean Virginia C. Gildersleeve wrote: ". . . the only reason we had for rejecting this applicant was that, in the judgment of our Committee on Admissions, she did not seem as promising a student as others whom we admitted. No doubt, being human, we sometimes make mistakes."

Even greater than the obstacles erected to block Jewish college admissions were the barriers surrounding the medical schools,‡ forcing many promising would-be physicians to leave the country to study abroad; others entered dentistry or pharmacy, two professions where Jews were more readily accepted.

Some medical colleges were quite open about their "Jewish policy." An admissions officer at Loyola University of Chicago bluntly told one

‡ Significantly, few law schools practiced discrimination against Jews, for they were profit-making institutions and simply expanded to meet the rush of Jewish law students.

applicant that "your application for admission to the school of medicine cannot be acted on favorably because the quota for Jewish students has been filled," and Creighton University School of Medicine, Omaha, Nebraska, declared that "our policy is to admit [only] ten percent of Jewish students."

The most noted case of the medical profession's anti-Jewish discrimination occurred at Brooklyn's Kings County Hospital. In June of 1927, three Jewish interns complained that they were pulled from their beds and thrown into a tub of ice-cold water. Several days before the "dunking" occurred, the three doctors were warned by their colleagues to resign from the staff. "This a Christian institution," said one of the irate physicians, "and we will tolerate no Jews here."* The three Jewish interns claimed that nurses refused to carry out their medical orders, they were refused admittance to the hospital's tennis court even though they were willing to contribute to its upkeep, they witnessed the mistreatment and neglect of Jewish patients, and were deliberately isolated in the dining room and forced to sit at what was dubbed the *"Kosher Table."*

An investigation of the "dunking" incident revealed that

> Jewish interns were not summoned promptly to the bedside of patients in urgent need of treatment—when a telephone call came for a Jewish doctor, the operator was told that he was not there, or the receiver was slammed back in place. Some such procedure was followed in a case when a gravely ill woman was admitted to the hospital, with the result that she was not attended for two hours and . . . died an hour after she was finally attended.

Also, Jewish females seeking to enter the nursing profession were subjected to discrimination. In one such case, a young girl went from hospital to hospital gathering information about the programs each offered. When she finally found a school she wished to attend, the head nurse immediately set the girl straight: "Oh," she said, "I see your name is Goldstein. Why don't you apply to a Jewish hospital?"

Jewish lawyers were accepted at "strictly Jewish" law firms, Jewish doctors found it difficult to join the staffs of non-Jewish hospitals, and Jewish engineers were not surprised to read the following job offering in the January 1930 issue of *Industrial and Engineering Chemistry:*

PATENT EXPERT, CHEMICAL—Progressive, rapidly-growing chemical corporation requires full services of patent expert capable

* Kings County Hospital was and still is a tax-supported institution.

of assuming executive responsibilities. Legal training not essential but highly desirable. *Christians Preferred.*

College professors and lower-grade teachers faced the same difficulties.

"How can I get a professorship in an American university?" exclaimed one job-hunting scholar who had just completed a Ph.D. in history.

"That's easy," replied a fellow student, "simply have one of our millionaires endow a chair for you."

There were also Jewish applicants for teaching positions in the grade schools who insisted, after failing the interview portion of their teaching examination, that they were rejected because they were Jewish. In New York City, the Board of Education required each candidate, in addition to passing a written test, to pass an oral examination. If the examiner did not like your appearance, the color of your tie, or the sound of your last name, he could easily discover that you did not pronounce "she sells sea shells at the seashore" correctly. "What they really meant," asserted one applicant who failed, "was my Yiddish inflection."

"What about Tim O'Hara?" said the young man's father. "He has an Irish brogue."

"Papa," replied the son, "the examiner's name was O'Malley."

Jews seeking employment in non-professional positions were also blocked by the barriers erected by business enterprises and employment agencies. Western Union refused to hire Jewish students on summer vacation, the New York Telephone Company declared that it could not "take on Jewish women as switchboard operators because their arms are too short," and banks and Wall Street firms, except those controlled by Jews, simply refused to offer any reason why Jews would not be employed in even the most subordinate position.

Job discrimination, though it was present at the turn of the century, slackened somewhat during the war years of 1914–18. In the 1920s, however, the employers reintroduced their "no Jews need apply" policy. The following representative ads, for example, were commonplace throughout the nation:

STENOGRAPHERS—Many attractive positions for well-groomed Christian American young women, immediate placement in almost all lines of business. . . .

Boy, 17 or over (Christian), some high school education preferred; excellent opportunity for boy with large insurance company. . . .

It was common knowledge that employment agencies, either at the direction of their clients or on their own initiative, refused to place many Jewish job seekers. In a study of twenty-three commercial agencies, the Bureau of Jewish Research found that

> One flatly refused to register any Jews; another stated that he could place no Jews; eight more were very discouraging and emphasized the futility of registering since Jewish girls stood no chance of being placed.
>
> Seven were willing to register the girls but explained that there would be difficulty in placing them since so many employers did not want Jews; six of the agencies were encouraging and asked the girls to register. . . . In brief, in ten out of twenty-three agencies the Jewish girls had very little chance and at only six they had as good a chance as if they were not Jewish.

"Presumably," wrote Bruno Lasker, the employers and the agencies had *"some* reason—even if a poor one—for reducing [their] possible choice of personnel." Anxious to know this reason, he sent a response to several newspaper ads that stipulated or implied that the positions posted were for Christians only. The letter, signed with a Christian name and stating that the survey was being made to "secure facts about the reasons which determine many employers, in advertising vacancies in their personnel, to express a preference for Protestants or gentiles or to exclude others altogether," elicited some interesting responses. Here are a few:

A druggist declared:

> Seventy-five per cent of the graduates in pharmacy in the Metropolitan district colleges are foreign-born Russian Jews. My experience with them, in the laboratory, the prescription department or at the general sales counter, qualifies me to state that they are as a class undesirable. Their work is unclean, clumsy and careless. I am not a bigot, nor am I filled with intolerance against the Hebrews, but being associated with the nice ethics of pharmacy, and with a profound comprehension of the responsibilities entailed thereby, and finding these virtues absent in the Jews, I'll take the Christian, if he is to be had, any time.

A factory owner said:

> We try to have only white American Christians in our factory regardless of religion. This rule was based on past experience. Some time ago we had the Bolshevik class of Jews in our place who caused a strike, although we paid the same rates as other factories in our line. We also found that they stole from us and from other employees. We found the Christians are more to be trusted.

Lastly, an irate advertiser wrote:

> One only needs to emply the other kind to find out. If you do not believe it, try it. Anyone sending out such a letter as this is not worthy of receiving a Christian's confidence.

In order to avoid the almost certain rejection that followed an application bearing a Jewish-sounding name, some decided to change their names. The most noteworthy comment about this trend was stated in the preface to the 1926 Who's Who in American Jewry:

> Doubtless many names have been omitted which should have been included. . . . Unfortunately, some persons preferred to be omitted rather than associate their names with those of their racial colleagues. A few even rejected with indignation the proposal of being included in a volume where their Jewish identity would become a matter of public knowledge.

During the great immigration of 1890–1910, many Jews had their names changed at Ellis Island upon arrival, when immigration officers misheard, misread, or simply picked the nearest approximation to the European name. The father of composer Aaron Copland, born Kaplan, had the name changed when he pronounced Kaplan in a heavy accent. The harried officer, besieged by clamoring thousands, heard it as Copland and pushed him through. Siegelovich became Siegel. A man named Mendelowitch was told by a kindly Irish officer that the name was too unwieldy for America and bestowed Mandell upon him.

Few German Jews changed their names, which were more palatable, more like those of other Germans who emigrated to America in the 1840s. Long assimilated into American life, generally respected as bankers and merchants and scholars, they wore their names as badges of honor rather than the distorted and comic labels associated with East European Jews. One of the rare cases on record was August Belmont ("beautiful mountain" in French), whose original name was Schoenberg ("beautiful mountain" in German).

The first generation of Jews who came from Russia-Poland, generally tradesmen and artisans, rarely changed their names. Their lives were so insular and ghettoized, there was no function to a name change. Indeed, it was better to be Rabinowitz on Ludlow Street dealing with a Dubrowsky on Madison Street. Not until the 1920s, when Jews entered the mainstream of American business and social life, was there an impulse, as in other immigrant groups, to change the name, shorten it, make it more representative of the person who had left his greenhorn days behind.

In many instances, Jews turned to the courts in their effort to "sound American." Levy wanted to be called LeMay, Wishnofsky wished his name changed to Winters, Schwartz opted for Shore, and Louis Goldstein asked for the name Golding. Interestingly, Louis Goldstein's case was heard by Judge Louis Goldstein. "The reasons advanced in the petition," asserted Judge Goldstein, "are that the name 'Goldstein' is not euphonious and un-American. . . . The court believes that the request of this petitioner is a subterfuge for the purpose of covering his religion and racial identity. Therefore I am opposed to granting a change of name on such flimsy reasons as advanced in this petition."

Justice Aaron Levy, who was assigned the case of Everett Levy, said:

> Character and courage are essential in fighting off these vicious and bigoted influences, but, as he prefers to run, let him. Doubtless he is wholly ignorant of the fact that the Bible tells us that the tribe of Levi never worshiped the Golden Calf. Let his application be granted, so that his people may well be rid of him.

The most famous American court case involving the change of a Jewish name was that of the Philadelphia Kabotchnicks. In spite of legal action by the blue-blooded Cabot family of Massachusetts to prevent the change, the court allowed the Kabotchnicks to become the Cabots. As a result, the following parody was repeated in both upper- and lower-crust circles:

> Then here's to the city of Boston,
> The town of the cries and the groans,
> Where the Cabots can't see the Kabotchnicks
> and the Lowells won't speak to the Cohens.

The changing of one's name to escape "Jewishness" was not very humorous to writer and teacher, Rebekah Kohut. "My criticism," she wrote "of the pastime of changing names is the plain, practical one that it does not work. Lopping off extra syllables, [the Jew] lops off some of his own vitality. He loses some of his essential Jewishness; the best part of him. Losing it, he becomes lost, because it is something that he needs with which to find his way through the world we live in."

Torn by the conflict described by Kohut, one name changer declared, "I went through hell. There were always awkward moments coming up, and I got so thin-skinned that I would shudder at the word Jew. If anyone had called me a Jew, I might have killed him. I hated the people as well as the word. I found myself saying, 'I can't stand Jews.' And it was literally true. I couldn't. I was never on good terms with myself, because I couldn't be honest with myself. And honesty is, after all, the first consideration in life."

Those who felt guilty about hiding their Jewish identity were even more disturbed after viewing the 1927 version of Cecil B. DeMille's *King of Kings*. After the motion picture was released, Jewish organizations, namely B'nai B'rith and the American Jewish Committee, were flooded with protests that labeled the film anti-Semitic.

In an effort to determine the validity of the charge, William Fox, the well-known Hollywood filmmaker, invited several Jewish leaders to a private showing. Among them were banker Felix Warburg, Rabbi David de Sola Pool, and Cyrus L. Sulzberger of the New York *Times*. When the group left the studio, they were convinced that the "DeMille classic," which showed Jews as barbaric murderers of Christ, would heighten anti-Semitism among the nation's theatergoers. Rabbi Stephen Wise called it "vicious, defiling, and wanton."

The New York Board of Jewish Ministers urged all Jewish organizations to do whatever was in their power to prevent its showing. Louis Marshall, however, speaking for the American Jewish Committee and B'nai B'rith, warned his coreligionists not to take public action. Fearful that Jewish pressure would only publicize the movie, he suggested that Jews simply avoid theaters where the film was playing. After being informed by Will Hays, president of the Motion Picture Producers and Distributors Association, that Christian ministers were demanding the movie be shown "without cuts," Marshall was even more convinced of his position.

After *King of Kings* had completed its tour of the movie houses, Marshall did admit that its portrayal of Jews as "Christ killers" further inflamed the nation's anti-Semites. "But," he told Alfred M. Cohen, president of B'nai B'rith, "not much more than is occasioned by the reading of the New Testament or the teaching in Sunday schools or the traditions that are passed on from generation to generation."

More disturbing than *King of Kings* was the tremor of excitement caused by the disappearance of a Christian child in Massena, New York, on the eve of Yom Kippur, 1928.

Immediately, the blood libel rent the air: "Barbara has been killed," shouted one of the local residents, "killed by the Jews who needed her blood for their holiday ritual." Other rumors spread like wildfire as long-standing Jewish members of the community came under suspicion.

"Perhaps the Jew tailor did it—he's always carrying those long shears," shouted one frantic woman.

"Yes," cried another, "the Jew doctor could have used ether to keep the child quiet."

"Hey," exclaimed a third, "I saw something that looked like a coffin being delivered to the Jew who owns the Emporium—maybe she's in it."

Fearful that the crowd, which had gathered in the center of town, would march on the synagogue, where the Jewish community was holding services, Mayor Hawes went to the police station to confer with Corporal McCann of the State Police.

"We can't arrest every Jew in town," said the police officer, "we don't have the room to keep them all."

After conferring for a few more minutes, the two officials decided to question the rabbi. Though every Jew in the community had already been questioned about the whereabouts of the little girl and had denied the practice of human sacrifice, the local authorities still wanted to hear it from the rabbi. McCann went to the synagogue and, in the middle of services, asked the Jewish spiritual leader to accompany him to police headquarters. Moments later, the rabbi, guarded by the state trooper, met with the town's mayor.

"This is outrageous," exclaimed the rabbi, "to interrupt our services on this most holy of all our holy days! Vile slander," he shouted, "of ignorant country bigotry and fanaticism!"

Unmoved by the outburst, McCann again asked: "Is tomorrow a big holiday, a fast day?"

"Yes," replied the rabbi.

"Can you give any information as to whether your people in the old country offer human sacrifices?" said McCann.

The rabbi expressed his amazement that any public official would ask such a question. The officer continued with this line of questioning.

"Was there ever a time when the Jews used human blood?" he again asked.

"No," replied the rabbi, "not only is the use of human blood forbidden by the Jewish faith but also the use of animal blood."

McCann assured the rabbi that he himself did not believe that Jews used human blood, but "that a foreigner had impressed me with it."

Later that day, the little girl was found unharmed. She had been looking for her brother and had lost her way in the woods. Exhausted from her search, she'd fallen asleep. Luckily for her, and for the Jews of Massena, two women discovered the weary child, totally unaware of the excitement her disappearance had caused.

When the news of the discovery reached town an embarrassed mayor promptly apologized for the reaction of the townspeople. The members of the Jewish community just as quickly refused to accept the apology.

"I never had the slightest suspicion," the mayor told Rabbi Brennglass; "some of my best friends are Jews."

ZIONISM IN THE TWENTIES

In the decade following World War I, American Jewry took a front seat in the struggle for a Jewish Palestine. Its representatives negotiated with the world's leaders on the creation of a Jewish homeland, almost two hundred thousand American Jews showed their support for Zionist aims by purchasing *shekalim,* and the non-Zionist "uptowners," in a dramatic reversal of position, contributed substantial sums for Palestinian economic development. Even the Central Conference of American Rabbis, though still opposed to the establishment of a Jewish state, declared their support of unrestricted Jewish immigration to the ancient land. "The Jewish people are," asserted the reform rabbinical organization, "and of right ought to be, at home in all lands."

The conflicts within the Zionist Organization of America (ZOA), however, which had been submerged by the turmoil of war, resurfaced. An intraorganizational conflict between the Brandeis faction and the supporters of Chaim Weizmann, the undisputed leader of the World Zionist Organization (WZO), was laid bare for everyone to see. At the International Zionist Conference held in London in 1920, a schism that rocked the Zionist world was dramatically played out. The chasm between the philosophies of the two leaders was so deep and so uncompromising that Weizmann told the American delegation: "I do not agree with the philosophy of your Zionism. . . . We are different, absolutely different. There is no bridge between Washington and Pinsk."

Brandeis, who led the American delegation to London, rejected Weizmann's appeal for continued political Zionism. "The work of the great Herzl was completed at San Remo," he declared, and therefore the need for a politically oriented WZO was no longer present. The Jews, said Brandeis, had their homeland.†

Weizmann rejected the notion that political action was made unneccessary by the statesmen at San Remo. Political Zionism, he asserted, "is far from finished. . . . the Balfour Declaration and the San Remo decision are the beginning of a new era in the Palestine struggle, and the Zionist Organization is our instrument of political action." When the vote was taken, the conference supported the Weizmann position.

After losing the battle over the philosophical direction of the WZO, Brandeis again found himself at odds with his European counterpart. This time the conflict was over money. Learning that Weizmann called for approximately 25 million pounds sterling a year for economic development—most to come from American Jewry—Brandeis became outraged.

"Astronomical" he said. At best, he told Weizmann, the Americans can raise five hundred thousand dollars.

"If this is all you can find in America," replied Weizmann, "I will have to come over and try for myself."

When the smoke of the charges and countercharges cleared, Brandeis emerged a defeated man. Weizmann was named president of the organization, his American rival was diplomatically given the title of honorary president, and a contingent of pro-Weizmann Americans, headed by Louis Lipsky, planned to strip Brandeis of his power in the ZOA. The anti-Brandeis revolt was set to take place in Cleveland at the ZOA's twenty-fourth annual convention, in June 1921.‡

In the months before the American Zionists were to gather, Weizmann made good his promise to come to America in search of money. On April 2, 1921, the international Zionist leader was peering through a porthole at New York's skyline.* He recalled that eventful afternoon:

† At the San Remo Conference, held on April 18, 1920, the League of Nations gave the British the Palestine mandate. Though the terms of the mandate were still to be worked out, it was understood that Palestine was to become a Jewish homeland.

‡ Also to be ousted was Julian Mack, president of the ZOA and Brandeis's strongest supporter.

* Officially, Weizmann came to announce the start of the *Keren ha-Yesod*—the fund-raising arm of the WZO.

We intended . . . to proceed straight to our hotel, settle down, and begin planning our work. We had reckoned—literally—without our host, which was, or seemed to be, the whole of New York Jewry. Long before the afternoon ended, delegations began to assemble on the docks. Pious Jews in the thousands came on foot [it was Saturday] all the way from Brooklyn and the Bronx to welcome us. Then the cars arrived, all of them beflagged. Every car had its horn and every horn was out in action.

"By the time we reached the gangway," wrote Weizmann, "the area . . . was a pandemonium of people, cars, and mounted police."

The car which we had thought would transport us quickly and quietly to our hotel fell in at the end of an enormous procession which wound its way through the entire Jewish section of New York. We reached the Commodore at about eleven-thirty, tired, hungry, thirsty and completely dazed. The spacious hall of the hotel was packed with another enthusiastic throng; we had to listen to several speeches of welcome. . . . It was long after midnight when we found our rooms.

In the space of time between Weizmann's arrival and the opening of the Cleveland convention, the Zionists acquired conclusive proof that the need for political action, contrary to Brandeis, was far from over. In the early days of May, the Arabs rioted in Jaffa and British High Commissioner Samuel announced a limit on Jewish immigration to Palestine. When the ZOA convened, in June 1921, the majority of delegates were solidly behind the Weizmann program. Bernard A. Rosenblatt, who aligned himself with the pro-Weizmann faction, recalled the Cleveland meeting:

It was indeed a battle of giants. On the platform sat Dr. Weizmann, Shemarya Levin and Menachem Ussishkin—silent, because they were not delegates, but nevertheless, serving as a reminder that in their persons, they represented the unity and welfare of the World Zionist Organization. Presiding at the opening of the convention was Judge Julian W. Mack, whom everyone respected for his selfless devotion to the cause which he embraced so warmly late in life. As champions of the absent Judge Brandeis—whose spiritual presence was nevertheless felt—there were Professor Felix Frankfurter, . . . the mighty voice of Rabbi Stephen S. Wise, backed by Rabbi Hillel Silver and Jacob de Hass. Against the formidable phalanx, the initial attack on the policy of the administration was left to the "Young Turks," led by Abe Goldberg, Louis Lipsky, Emanuel Neumann, Morris Rothenberg, and myself.

"I was perhaps at fault," wrote Rosenblatt, "when I interrupted Dr. Wise as he sought to nominate Judge Mack [the pro-Brandeis president of the ZOA] as permanent Chairman of the Convention." Quickly, however, Wise turned to Rosenblatt and asked: "Do you think this is a Tammany courtroom?"

A hush fell over the meeting. Rosenblatt then delivered his retort: "No, Dr. Wise; neither is this a Free Synagogue." Indeed, the air was filled with tension.

After each side presented its case, the delegates voted 153–71 to reject the Brandeis leadership. Julian Mack resigned the presidency, and Brandeis, through a letter read by Mack, also withdrew his active participation. The split between Weizmann and Brandeis was fully realized.

Once the Cleveland meeting adjourned, Weizmann began his fundraising activities on behalf of the newly created Palestine Foundation Fund (*Keren ha-Yesod*). Wherever he went he met poor Jews whose contributions amounted to a few dollars, rich Jews who gave in the hundreds, and "big donors," whose pledges reached as much as five thousand dollars. The meetings were long and grueling, he said, "and the arrangement always was that the guest of honor should speak last, lest the public should be tempted to leave, thus depriving some of the other speakers of their audience." From each, he had to endure the repeated criticisms of the pro-Brandeis people or the nasty taunts of assimilated anti-Zionists. As often, he heard crank schemes for the immediate creation of a Jewish homeland and paternal advice from successful Jewish businessmen. To all, however, he listened attentively and courteously.†

Excited by the presence of the Zionist leader, Brownsville‡ Zionists urged Weizmann to visit the community.

"I have heard and read so much about Brownsville, which you call the Jerusalem of America," Weizmann said to noted Yiddish orator Shemarya Levin. "Tell me, where is Brownsville?"

"Brownsville is Brownsville," replied Levin, "and the city of New York is built around her."

---

† Almost everyone asked him about the part he had played in the invention of T.N.T. To the surprise of many, he explained that he had had nothing to do with the explosive.
‡ In Brooklyn, New York.

Fascinated by Levin's reply, Weizmann accepted the invitation. Immediately, local Zionists initiated plans for a proper reception. A parade was organized, a mass rally at the Liberty Theater was announced, posters were placed in every store window and news releases were distributed to the press.

"Weizmann is coming!" shouted the children as they ran home from *heder*. "In this community," said Izzy Goldberg, "he will find the real American Jew. The real lover of Zion."

When the eventful day finally got underway, the entire Brownsville-East New York community turned out to see the Zionist leader. After the activities culminated at the "jam-packed" theater, the Palestine Foundation Fund was $125,000 richer—truly a fantastic sum for the working-class people of this community to raise. "In Brownsville," said Levin, "was laid the foundation for the *Keren ha-Yesod*. God came to our help."

Though Weizmann returned to Europe with almost $2 million, he was still convinced that the primary battle was political and not economic. Knowing that the British were in the process of drafting the final text of the mandate and fearful that "Jewish rights" might be compromised, he urged all Zionists to maintain a constant political vigil. Weizmann was correct. When the terms of the mandate were announced, the promise of a Jewish homeland was as vague as it had been in the Balfour Declaration. Though the British approved "Jewish immigration under suitable conditions" and encouraged "local autonomy," the mandate implied rather than stipulated the creation of a permanent, self-governing Jewish state.

Though the Jews were promised nothing by the terms of the mandate, an angry Arab community protested vigorously to London. As a result, the British issued the White Paper of 1922. A masterpiece of confusion, the statement managed to placate both Arab and Jew. In part, it read:

> When it is asked what is meant by the development of the Jewish National Homeland in Palestine, it may be answered that it is not the imposition of a Jewish nationality upon the inhabitants of Palestine as a whole, but the further development of the existing Jewish community with the assistance of Jews in other parts of the world, in order that it may become a centre in which the Jewish people as a whole may take, on grounds of religion and race, an interest and a pride. But in order that this community should have

the best prospect of free development and provide a full opportunity for the Jewish people to display its capacities, it is essential that it should know that it is in Palestine as of right and not on sufferance.

At the same time the British were seeking to deny the promise contained in the Balfour Declaration, the United States Congress passed the pro-Zionist Lodge-Fish Resolution. Much to the chagrin of American oilmen, who were then negotiating for concessions in the Middle East, the joint resolution, which was a reaffirmation of the Balfour Declaration, called for the establishment of a Jewish homeland in Palestine.

"Whereas . . . the Jewish people believed in and yearned for the rebuilding of the ancient homeland," read the resolution, "the Jewish people are to be enabled to re-create and reorganize a national home in the land of their fathers which will give to the House of Israel its long-denied opportunity to re-establish a fruitful Jewish life and culture in the ancient Jewish land. . . ." The political pressure of the organized Jewish community to shape U.S. foreign policy vis-à-vis Palestine was becoming more evident.*

After the passage of the Lodge-Fish Resolution by the Congress, Weizmann attended the World Zionist Congress at Carlsbad. Here, the militant Vladimir Jabotinsky attacked Weizmann for accepting a mandate that did not contain the promise of an independent Jewish state, and the delegates set about to create an "appropriate Jewish agency" to advise the British on matters of Palestinian Jewish concern. The WZO established the Jewish Agency.

The Jewish Agency was the WZO. Weizmann, however, wanted the new organization to attract wealthy non-Zionists. He hoped that American philanthropists, who were well known for their financial support of

---

* According to the anti-Zionists, Senator Lodge, who was not popular with "the Irish and Catholics," introduced the Senate version of the resolution to court Jewish voters. Though there may be some truth to this assertion, it was well known that Lodge was an early supporter of Zionist aspirations. In 1917 he supported the Balfour Declaration and, several years later, in 1919, declared that "the efforts of the Jewish people to establish a national home in Palestine is not only natural but in all ways desired."

Hamilton Fish, who was an "America Firster" during the 1930s and was accused of being pro-Nazi and anti-Semitic, two charges he denied, claimed that he introduced the resolution on his own initiative. Apparently, his friendship with the Holtzmann family of Brooklyn, his concern with the tyrannical treatment of East European Jews, and his evangelical belief in the return to Zion had something to do with his action.

Jewish and non-Jewish causes, would align themselves (and their money) with Palestinian development. Weizmann knew that the Jewish Agency as an arm of the WZO would make this impossible.

Several months after the Congress was held, he urged the Zionist leaders to pass a resolution making the Jewish Agency "responsible to a body representative of the Jewish people"—not only Zionists but non-Zionists as well. Though the opposition to this proposal was formidable, the Zionist leadership bowed to his wishes. Having accomplished this ticklish maneuver, he returned to America in search of more funds.

On this second trip, Weizmann made impressive headway with America's non-Zionist community. Felix Warburg, who at a meeting with Weizmann denounced the behavior of the Jewish colonists in Palestine, eventually "saw the light" and contributed a half million dollars for the construction of the Hebrew University in Jerusalem.† Louis Marshall, won over by Weizmann's persuasive arguments concerning the cultural and spiritual importance of a Jewish homeland, also lent support to the fund-raising activities of the Palestine Foundation Fund.

The most unusual find Weizmann made in America was Samuel Zemurray, the New Orleans "Banana King." After hearing of Zemurray's background and financial success, Weizmann journeyed to New Orleans to meet the "Jewish fruit merchant." Zemurray was just as impressed with the world Zionist leader. He canceled his own plans to leave the city just so he could make the meeting. "I found [Sam Zemurray] not only interesting," wrote Weizmann, "but also profitable." Accordingly, Zemurray was the highlight of Weizmann's "swing through Jewish America."

Not every encounter was as rewarding as the one with Zemurray. In New York and Philadelphia, areas of heavy Zionist concentration, the response was good. In Chicago, however, the anti-Zionism of Julius Rosenwald, the man behind Sears, Roebuck & Co., was reflected in the meager sums donated. Even more difficult was Cincinnati—the headquarters of militant anti-Zionism. There, claimed Weizmann, the comparatively small East European community was confronted by the powerful opposition of the anti-Zionists. The appeal to Zionism faltered even more as he moved father west. "California," he said, "was a different world, remote from the Jewish interests of the eastern states, and practically virgin soil from the Zionist point of view."

† Apparently, a trip to Palestine, at Weizmann's insistence, turned Warburg into a "dollar Zionist."

Though his second tour can be termed a financial success, Weizmann was still convinced that more had to be done to incorporate the wealthy non-Zionists into the movement to rebuild Palestine. In January 1927, he sent an appeal to Marshall. "I have" wrote Weizmann,

> travelled throughout America over a period of years and have met various types of Jews. I can, therefore, vouch for the abiding interest in the welfare of Jewry the world over on the part of those who have been engaged in the work of the United Jewish Campaign. To be sure there are differences of opinion among us. We do not always agree. There are many who have been unwilling to subscribe to the possibilities and hopes which we have for Palestine. Yet I have always respected their viewpoint and have hoped that the time might come when all the Jews of this great land [America]— whether they be Zionist or non-Zionist—could be helpful and participate in Palestinian development.

Weizmann continued:

> Although we Zionists have consecrated ourselves to the task of rebuilding and remaking Palestine, I am urging upon all Zionists the importance of realizing that every Jew has the right to his own opinion as to what is needful for the good of Jewry. We must endeavor to co-operate amicably with our non-Zionist brethren who do not concede the priority of the claims of Palestine over those of our brethren who live in other countries whether the help given to them be of a palliative or of a constructive nature, or whether it involves the settlement upon the land of those who desire that opportunity.

In response to this appeal for peace and unity, Marshall advised the Zionist statesman that he "accurately diagnosed the situation. . . . Speaking for my associates and myself," he wrote:

> I convey to you with profound satisfaction, our acceptance of the proffered olive-branch. In your act we perceive convincing proof that strife has ceased in the ranks of American Jewry. Let us once more cultivate and practice the virtues of that peace upon which, as remarked by our sages, the world is built, and it may be added, upon which the preservation of Jews and Judaism depends. With restored fellowship we may be enabled to demonstrate to friend and foe alike that with unity as the very essence in our lives and thoughts, we shall continue to make significant contributions to civilization and culture and to the welfare of mankind.

On March 22, 1927, Weizmann and Marshall celebrated the new "alliance" at New York's Biltmore Hotel.‡ First Weizmann spoke. Then Marshall addressed the gathering:

> I am not a Zionist and have never been one. I have always felt that I am something better than a Zionist or non-Zionist: I am a Jew. I can stand on that platform. You can stand on that platform. Our ancestors all stood on that platform. They died upon that platform and they lived upon that platform. The time has come when we should forget everything but the fact that this problem of Palestine is a Jewish problem. There have been differences in the past. There may be differences in the future. It would be a most uninteresting world if we all agreed on all points at all times. There should be differences of opinion, because out of differences of opinion can eventually come truth. We forget the differences of the past. They are unimportant. . . .*

As a result of the *rapprochement,* Weizmann went before the Sixteenth World Zionist Congress to ask for an expanded and non-partisan Jewish Agency. Now 224 delegates would hold membership—half appointed by the Zionists and half by non-Zionists. The American Jewish Committee was given forty-four seats—the largest number of any non-Zionist group.

Brought together by "the Pact of Glory," Zionists and non-Zionists finally sat together in an effort to direct the reconstruction of a Jewish Palestine. Marshall, however, the key man in the making of the alliance, would never know if the co-operative venture would last. One day after the historic meeting at Zurich took place, he fell ill and died. Weizmann lost his strongest non-Zionist supporter.

The elation following the "Pact of Glory" did not last long. Within days after the historic meeting, Palestinian Arabs rioted in the streets of Hebron, Safed, and Jerusalem. Attacking Jews who were in the midst of Sabbath prayer, the mufti's followers painted the streets of these ancient cities with Jewish blood. Some were murdered while praying at synagogues, others lost their lives on the streets, and still more were killed in their homes.

‡ The meeting, which took the form of a dinner party, was hailed by *The American Hebrew* as "a prelude to the appointing of a non-partisan commission" for Jewish Palestinian affairs.
* A formal agreement of co-operation was signed on August 14, 1929.

Pierre van Paassen, a Christian observer, gave an eyewitness account of the Hebron massacre:

> After killing the Jews in the synagogue, the Arab mob . . . went down the road . . . where stood a *yeshivah* . . . and massacred both students and professors. . . . After this the mob . . . attacked the home of the local rabbi, called Slonim, where a number of men and women had taken refuge. . . . But the Arabs came in through the windows . . . and made short shrift of the thirty-eight persons in the room. Their throats were slit and both men and women were horribly mutilated.
>
> . . . I found that the dead in Slonim's house had had their genital organs cut off, in the case of the women, their breasts. This was really nothing very extraordinary; it was the usual practice of Arab mobsters in those days and still is.†

Almost as shocking as the riots was the news of the Passfield White Paper of November 1930. This British statement, which was an outgrowth of the Shaw Commission's investigation of Palestinian conditions, recommended severe limitations on future Jewish immigration; it was tantamount to a retraction of the Balfour Declaration.

In the protest against this latest British move, Weizmann resigned the presidency of the Jewish Agency; Felix Warburg, the non-Zionist representative, gave up his chairmanship of the Agency's Administrative Committee, and the American Jewish Committee vigorously expressed "its profound disappointment with the policy of the British Government." Even members of the British Parliament, specifically Lloyd George, declared their dissatisfaction at what they felt was a betrayal of Lord Balfour's promise.

As a result of the outcry, Prime Minister Ramsay MacDonald announced that, for the present, the restrictions outlined in the Passfield White Paper would not apply. The second serious attack on the Balfour Declaration was repelled. In the ensuing years, thousands of Jews would still manage to use Palestine as a refuge from the oppressive forces of European anti-Semitism.‡

† In both the 1967 and 1973 Arab-Israeli wars, captured Israeli soldiers received similar treatment.
‡ Between 1931 and 1935, approximately 150,000 Jews resettled in Palestine.

CHAPTER VI

The Depression Decade

CRISIS AND REACTION

"WITH the depression," wrote novelist Arthur Granit, American Jewry "was assailed on all sides. The men began to lose their jobs and appeared wheeling baby carriages. Soon they began to shop for their wives and argue with the peddlers. And as times grew worse, the long, fascinating noses of our Jews got closer to the ground and began to sniff through the very walls to see what was transpiring on the other side."

As the decade of the thirties wore on, the occupational transformation of the Jewish community, which had begun in the twenties, was obscured by the widespread unemployment and prevailing poverty. The movement into white-collar positions and government service was cut short; teachers, pharmacists, accountants, and lawyers drove taxicabs; doctors, dentists, and architects, who had already been contending with the hardships of the quota system, worked as waiters; graduate students completing higher degrees were hopeful of entering civil service; garment-center workers who had "turned manufacturer" went bankrupt; real estate holdings vanished overnight; and medium-size retail outlets, unable to compete with the large chain stores, were driven out of business.

The major philanthropic organizations, which were often headed by affluent "uptowners," were also faced with the multifarious problems created by the total collapse of the American economy. "Economic conditions in the United States during the past year," noted the American Jewish Committee in June 1932, "were such as to compel the Jew-

ish community to apply by far the greater part of its energies to the so-
lutions of its own domestic problems and, in some cases, preventing the
dissolution of institutions and agencies which had been created by the
community in previous years. American Jewry was prevented therefore
from taking as active an interest in its sister communities overseas as in
former years. . . ."

Jewish agencies were set upon by thousands of coreligionists in desperate need of financial aid.* Baltimore's agencies reported a 77 per
cent increase in requests for assistance, Minneapolis a 100 per cent increase, Chicago 62 per cent, Milwaukee 47 per cent, and in Los Angeles the available funds managed to reach only a handful of families
living from day to day. Harry Weiman, his wife, and his three children
were on the verge of starvation until news of their plight was brought to
the Los Angeles Jewish Social Service. "Mr. Weiman," reported agency
officials, "is working as a [pants] presser irregularly, averaging $3.50
per week. Family is unable to manage and requests supplemental assistance." A single subsidy, of twenty-seven dollars for the year, was
granted.

The same agency went to the aid of a divorced woman with two children: a son of twenty and a daughter of seventeen. The Los Angeles
Board of Welfare refused to entertain their appeal because the son
earned thirty-six dollars a month. "Since this is an unemployment
case," noted a Jewish caseworker, "and thirty-six dollars equals the
BCW budget, they will give no relief." The Jewish agency had no
choice but to supplement the applicant's meager income.

Coupled with direct cash payments were other measures to relieve the
crushing effects of depression life. Living up to the oft-repeated motto
that "Jews take care of their own," the Anglo-Jewish and Yiddish press
provided free space for "Job Offerings," Jewish employment bureaus
were established to help the flood of unemployed, and direct appeals to
Jewish businessmen were made "to stretch their overhead in order to
find work for a less fortunate brother." In Los Angeles, the plight of
unemployed Jewish carpenters reached the ears of Jewish community
leaders. "Two hundred Jewish carpenters cannot find work," noted an
appeal to local businessmen, "and this group have been out of employment . . . for many, many months. They are neither radicals nor com-

---

* In the early years of depression, relatively few Jews sought aid from
government agencies. Indeed, many vacillated and fought with their new
humiliation even before turning to their own agencies.

munists" but upstanding citizens and Jews in need. As was expected, the business community was asked to absorb the group.

Some relief agencies provided rent money to forestall eviction until the son or daughter completed college; and still others, notably the "Self-Support Funds," helped professional men establish "a practice or furnish an office." These same agencies provided "feed" for a peddler's horse or distributed milk to children, both Jewish and gentile, threatened with malnutrition.

Also doing an outstanding job of relief were the *landsmanschaften*. After being told about a coreligionist who was only steps away from becoming destitute, their working-class members were quick to answer an appeal. "If they didn't answer the appeal," said Meyer Rabinowitz, a butcher on Pitkin Avenue in Brooklyn, "their seat at the weekly gin game would suddenly disappear."

The *landsmanschaften* were slow to contribute directly to the major Jewish philanthropic agencies. "Perhaps," said Morris Schwartz, a Philadelphia postal clerk, "we might give to some relief worker who was directly involved in helping a needy family. But we almost always refused to entertain the requests of the fund raisers, who we knew never came in direct contact with the people they solicited for. The only way to give," he exclaimed, "was *directly!* After all, how many of those uptown *big shots* would walk six flights to deliver a grocery order for *Pesach* [Passover]?"

Discouraging the well-dressed fund raisers from attending or crashing their meetings was by no means an easy trick. "They smelled us out wherever we met," recalled motion-picture projectionist Abe Cohen. "Once, we had to find a basement in the Bronx to get away from them. Even there, one of those college-educated fast talkers found us."

Often, they met in secret and almost always their bolted doors were guarded by a rather large member, whose specific instructions were "No strangers!" "Sometimes," recalled Schwartz, "the fund raisers, in their persistence, would relentlessy bang on our doors in order to gain admission—in order to make a special plea for this or that charity." "Sorry," was the oft-heard response of the burly sergeant at arms barring the entrance. "Come back in the future."

The Jewish community, like the rest of the nation, was divided over whom to blame for the economic crisis. *The American Hebrew,* a journal generally associated with the older and more affluent Jewish community, was optimistic in outlook: "We believe," declared the editors in 1931, "that the so-called depression will be short-lived and that the country with its excellent recuperative powers will be in excellent shape within a few months. By the Summer the crash of last October and its effects will be pretty much out of the picture." In 1932, the same newspaper expressed the same confidence: "Whatever the cause of the setback that has hit so many so hard, America will not long indulge in lamentation. Though, alas, too many are jobless, the world is still on the job and the universe spinning in its groove."

There were other Jews who refused to view the economic crisis through the *Hebrew's* rose-colored glasses. This group, composed mainly of East Europeans and their offspring,† did not have the years of assimilation (and thus the confidence) or the same economic entrenchment as did their German coreligionists; nor was their meager wealth invested in the same fashion. The suffering was more direct and more severe. "We were not really worried about losing our investment in AT&T," remarked Morris Goldberg, a Chicago tailor. "What we were concerned about was putting bread on the table, paying the rent, keeping the children in school, and preventing the collapse of the family." It was from Goldberg's segment of American Jewry that the cry to revamp the nation's economy was heard.

Speaking for the working class, *Justice,* the organ of the ILGWU, and *The Advance,* the voice of the Amalgamated Clothing Workers, institutionalized these sentiments. "No humanitarian point of view can possibly justify a system that breeds poverty because that system also creates millionaires who cast some of their surplus upon the waters," declared the editors of *Justice.* "The existing order with its chaotic distribution of wealth by the interplay of chance, chicanery, oppression and submissiveness, is an absurdity and is indefensible from the viewpoint of economic sense and ordered progress."

As American Jews were divided in their response to the causes of the depression, they also had a very definite and separate reaction to FDR's plan to restore the nation to economic sanity: the New Deal. While some affluent Jews attacked Roosevelt's program and worked for the election of Alf Landon in 1936, others, along with the majority of Americans, supported the program. "Roosevelt," noted the *Jewish Spectator,* "was a friend of the oppressed" and "the voice of reason, humanity." Louis Kirstein, of Filene's Department Store, urged Jews to support the New Deal: "I think that it is particularly fitting for Jews to help in this program," he said, "because certainly [it] has done a great deal for the industry in which so many Jews are interested and engaged

† This group also included those of German background.

in, . . . the needle industry, and the distributive trades, to say nothing of the great good that has been accomplished in the elimination of the sweatshop."

Some Jewish social workers were quick to recognize that the New Deal was far from successful. In 1935, a group from the National Conference of Jewish Social Service, who were painfully aware of the vast number of jobless and were equally disturbed over the unfulfilled relief needs of the nation, issued a paper that voiced skepticism of New Deal accomplishments. "After two years," declared the paper, "we can see that this attempt to benefit the forgotten man and business has resulted only in bringing benefits to industrial owners. . . ."

> Profits and dividends of the large industrial concerns were not only safeguarded, but increased as much as 600 percent in 1933 over 1932. In contrast to this we find that during the period the [real] wages of the industrial worker declined. . . . Speed-up and mechanization have further intensified the problem of unemployment and have helped considerably in swelling the number of unemployed. In agriculture under the New Deal we find the lowering of income, reduction of standards of living, increase in tenancy, forced sales, mortgage indebtedness, and heavy taxes. Unemployment stood at 17,157,000 men, women, and young workers in November, 1934. This is 800,000 more than the estimate for November, 1933.

More critical of Roosevelt's program were the forces of the Jewish left.‡ The Workmen's Circle, the Socialist-fraternal arm of the Jewish labor movement, through its journal *Workmen's Circle Call,* sharply criticized Roosevelt's program.* Its stance is perhaps best illustrated by a satirical feature called the "Diary of a President's Cook":

> The President is in a very bad mood today. He threw my wonderful dessert, lemon meringue with whipped cream, out the window. He

‡ Since the New Deal was designed to save capitalism, the Socialists, in the initial stages of the program, were divided in their opposition. Abraham Cahan was one Socialist who was delighted with the reforms. At a Madison Square Garden meeting, he gleefully announced that FDR should be carrying a Socialist membership card.

* The Workmen's Circle, unlike other Jewish Socialist organizations, did not join the "New Deal coalition" until the outbreak of World War II. In 1933, while Sidney Hillman was working to formulate the NRA codes, the labor movement hailed the New Deal as "an entirely new departure from American legislative practice," and in 1937, the labor Zionists called for support of the President's program. At the same time, they warned their followers not to be fooled by the "amorphous sea of Rooseveltism." By the end of the decade, the Jewish Socialists had reversed their position and gave their unqualified support to the New Deal.

said it tasted like cotton in his mouth. Can it be there is a textile strike imminent?

The islands [Hawaii] are in an uproar. A Suspicious man was found wandering through the city. He claimed he was an American, but as he could not prove he was working for the Sugar Interests, he has been arrested and is to be deported.

Most often, however, the Workmen's Circle journal was not satirical but came straight to the point: "In its appraisal of the New Deal youth must comprehend that the NRA does not go to the roots, does not meet the difficulties involved in Capitalism: the profit motive and the failure to plan enterprises to meet the needs of the nation."

In a play entitled *Five Out of Nine Have It,* the *Workmen's Circle Call* also charged that the Supreme Court, though made up of both liberals and conservatives, was engaged in a conspiracy to oppose what was best for the nation's working class:

JUSTICE HUGHES: I am Big Chief Justice
                            Charley Evans Hughes.
                            I'm quite a reactionary
                            With very liberal views;
                            The dear old Constitution
                            At last has reappeared.
                            It really wasn't lost at all;
                            It was hiding behind my beard.

JUSTICE BRANDEIS: And I am Louis Brandeis.
                            A Liberal I'm supposed to be.
                            It never does you any good,
                            Because I'm in the minority.
                            It makes a perfect set-up
                            For Morgan and his minions.
                            The Masses are demanding bread,
                            And they get dissenting opinions!!

Though the American Jewish community expressed varying opinions on the New Deal, the fact remains that *almost all Jews* firmly supported Roosevelt during his long tenure as president.† "The Jews," said Judge

† As the economic crisis deepened, Jewish social workers, lawyers, professors, and jurists descended on Washington to join the numerous alphabet agencies created by the New Deal; others flocked to Detroit to join the troops of the CIO commanded by Walter Reuther and Philip Murray. Many, of course, came from the German Jewish community and were educated at Ivy League schools. Others, however, were graduates of CCNY and the University of Chicago, where, though working by day and attending classes at night, they still managed to achieve the highest academic honors. These, of course, were the sons and daughters of the East Europeans.

Jonah J. Goldstein, "have three *velten* [worlds]: *di velt* [this world], *yene velt* [the next world] and Roosevelt." Indeed, the truth of Judge Goldstein's pun is clearly proved by each and every survey of Jewish voting habits since Roosevelt's second bid for office. "In 1936," asserts Lawrence Fuchs,

> the Twenty-fourth Ward in Chicago was probably the most Jewish ward in the nation. There Roosevelt received 96 percent of the vote. Elsewhere Jews were not as solidly Democratic. Four years later, Jewish wards in Boston and assembly districts in New York showed appreciable increase in Democratic strength. Over 90 percent of the Jews in New York County's Seventeenth Assembly District cast ballots for FDR. In 1944 Jewish Democratic strength increased further. In Boston's Jewish Fourteenth Ward, more than 95 percent of the Jewish votes cast went to Roosevelt.

"The results of national surveys," added Fuchs, also showed "that more than 90 out of every 100 Jews voted Democratic in 1940 and 1944. . . . According to . . . Public Opinion surveys in 1944 the Jews were the only high economic status group to look with favor on governmental guarantees against economic insecurity. The results show that 53.8 percent of the Jewish business and professional men were for such governmental guarantees, as compared to an average of about 20 percent for non-Jews in these same professions. Other survey evidence showed that, even though there were proportionately fewer Jewish manual laborers than in any other religious denomination, a higher proportion of Jews than any other group wanted to give more power and influence to working people."

Jewish allegiance to reform and liberalism was not only grounded in self-interest but also expressed their moral concerns. "Politics," wrote political scientist Daniel J. Elazar "even to the Jews who came to America from an unpolitical environment, was considered to be a matter of morality, a device for achieving justice and establishing the good commonwealth."‡

IDEALISTS AND RADICALS

"The depression was a nightmare for us," said Meyer Goldberg. "My graduation from CCNY seemed doomed and my mother's dream of get-

---

‡ "*Tsedakah* [charity]," wrote political scientists Lucy Dawidowicz and Leon J. Goldstein, "love of learning and rejection of asceticism are thought to have molded the political outlook of Jews, as has their constant sense of identification with persecuted minorities."

ting out of the East Side shattered. First we worried about Papa's job. When that was gone, we worried about the rent. Soon we were at each other's throat. It wasn't that we couldn't get along, it was the tension; that *goddamned* tension. What do you say to a man, my father, who after raising five kids on a stinking cutter's salary, has to go to his younger brother for a handout? It took us more than a week to convince him that Uncle Louie was the last resort, that the job was gone forever."

"Go get some money from your brother," Meyer's mother begged. "It's snowing outside! Do you want I should freeze? Do you want relief?"

"Relief!" exclaimed Meyer's father. "Never! Let that bastard Hoover go on relief. I'll bet the White House is heated. Maybe he'll take us in for a few weeks. Maybe I can get rid of this rotten cold."

Suddenly there was a knock on the door. "Who's there?" snapped Meyer's sister in the direction of the knock.

"It's me," came the reply. "Who the hell is me?" young Rose Goldberg shouted back at the voice. "Louie, your Uncle Louie. What's the matter, you don't recognize my voice any more!"

"Quick," said Mama, "let him in. Now's the time to ask."

"Molly," said the elder Goldberg in a meek tone, "he has two kids in college."

"What's family for?" questioned Meyer's mother. "Go ask him now."

Uncle Louie entered the apartment, glanced at his brother's family, and walked over to the kitchen table. On it he placed an envelope and, without saying a word, disappeared through the door. "A few seconds later," said Meyer, "we heard his familiar farewell."

"See ya later," shouted Louie.

"What do ya mean see ya later!" exclaimed Jake Goldberg. "I can't pay ya back." Then he started to cry.

"I'll never forget that scene as long as I live," Meyer told his classmate as they entered the campus of New York's City College.

"Louie, Uncle Louie," Meyer muttered. "Who'd ever think he'd use a system he hated so to make so much god-damned money. My uncle was a Communist in the twenties, a real radical," he told his companion. "I'll never forget the day Louie needed my father to bail him out of jail after being arrested in Passaic, New Jersey. What do you think the guy does after getting out?"

"What?" asked the classmate.

"Goes right back to the demonstration!" exclaims Meyer. " 'Can't desert my comrades,' he says. That 'can't desert my comrades' cost him broken nose and six stitches."

Like Louie Goldberg, some Jews who marched on Washington in the demonstrations of the thirties or who delivered revolutionary speeches to the crowds standing on the wind-swept street at New York's Union Square just might have received their radical "baptism of fire" at the 1926, Communist-led, Passaic, New Jersey, textile strike.

"The strikers," noted Joseph Freeman, a left-wing writer of the 1930s "were unarmed, peaceful . . . the women smiled, some of them carrying children in their arms." Suddenly, like a bolt of lightning, the "hard-jawed men in blue uniforms plowed the line." Heads were cracked, noses broken, perhaps Uncle Louie's, and those who fell under the rap of police clubs were kicked into unconsciousness. The pickets singing "Solidarity Forever," continued to march, and the police, still unable to break their spirit, called for reinforcements. "The firemen," remembered one participant, "hooked up the hoses and blasted us with stinging streams of water. Men, women, and children hit by the powerful bolts of water, were driven from the line. Some of them, frantically seeking shelter, ran down the street, their bodies drenched, their hair and clothing flat against their bodies as though held by glue."

Across the street, the press recorded the action with cameras. The "next morning," commented Freeman, America would read its news papers "over ham and eggs" and would know "that workers, their wives, their children have been clubbed, drenched [and] gassed for demanding bread, milk, shoes, coal for winter, the merest necessities of life."

The pickets, not deterred by gas, water, or clubs, return the next morning. There to greet them are the police. Suddenly, the men in blue leave the pickets and head for the reporters. This time, the press will feel the sting of water and sharp rap of the billy club. "They beat up the newspapermen," said another observer, "smashed their cameras," and "chased them down the street." The strikers watched in horror: the fleeing journalists, the rushing cops.

"Long live a free press," shouts a picket.

"Now," declares another, "they know what we are up against."

After their victory over the unarmed reporters, the police return; now it's the pickets' turn. Enraged by the taunts of the pickets, the police rush the line with clubs, and Louie Goldberg, the radical who turned capitalist, lies in the gutter, his face covered with blood, his nose twisted into the shape of the Italian Peninsula. "Thank you," he says to a fe male picket who helps him to his feet. "You better run; if the bastards don't kill you, they might rape you. Female comrades are lower than whores to them. On second thought you might be safer than me. Word has it that most of them are *queers* hiding behind a badge and a gun." She pays no attention to his ramblings and walks him to the safety of a doorway. "There," said Louie, "a woman who was looking out of a second-floor window shouted: "beat it, you Red Jew-bastard, good people don't want you bleeding all over the hallway. Besides, I just mopped up the place!"

"The next day," wrote Freeman, "the war veterans among the strikers got out their wartime gas masks and helmets." Six thousand strong, "the men in the front lines wearing masks and helmets as in battle" and the women in the rear, the strikers marched again. "At the head of the parade was little Barbara Miscolocsy, wheeled in a baby carriage by her grandmother. Everyone was singing and shouting and waving, full of cheer and courage and the will to win."

The children of these workers, and thousands like them, reached college age during the thirties. The pain and uncertainty of depression life, coupled with the radical atmosphere of their homes, sent many of them in search of radical outlets. Some found their opportunity at New York's City College. "Arguing excitedly about politics, about the depression, about anti-Negro prejudice, about anti-Semitism and how to fight against German and Italian fascism," wrote Paul Jacobs, a student radical at the City College of New York, "took up a lot of time at City College . . . where informal student life centered in an area known as The Alcoves. . . ."

> There, in huge recesses set around the perimeter of the building, I watched the other students eating their sandwiches from paper bags, studying and playing chess, and, among the politicals, always arguing. Each political group had its own alcove, and an informal understanding existed that no other group would attempt to dispossess it. Very often, though, the "members" of one alcove drifted over to another, either for a discussion if there was any common political bond between them or for a violent argument when the groups were as widely separated as, say, the Stalinists and the Trotskyists.

"As far as I was concerned," said Jacobs, "those alcove discussions were the most important part of life at City College. I knew there were classes, for I had to attend them, and I knew there were other student activities, for the posters advertising the clubs and lectures were everywhere. . . . But, for me," he added, "there was only one world into which I wanted to be taken and accepted: the radical atmosphere which dominated City College in those years."

> We were a pretty damn serious lot, with the whole weight of the world on our grim shoulders; a weight we carried humorlessly, except for the bitter satire that was one of our favorite weapons against the Stalinists. In Max Schachtman we had a really virtuoso performer of this art, and listening to him rip apart with savage satire some Stalinist hack capable only of parroting the party line made up in small way for the usual abuse we took from the Communists. Some humor emerged, too, in the semisocial postmeeting gatherings we held over cups of cafeteria coffee.

The cafeterias, said Jacobs, "were our clubs. . . ."

> We would meander over to the cafeteria and pull a small oblong ticket with two rows of numbers on it from the gaping mouth of a machine that stood just inside the entrance. Each pull was announced by a bell. . . . Then we bought our cups of coffee and perhaps . . . a cheese danish. In the early days of cafeteria sitting, you didn't have to buy anything but could simply sit with a glass of water and then leave, returning the unpunched check to the cashier, who would take it back with a very sour face. And since most of the young comrades were either students or unemployed, and so dependent for money on what they could scrounge from their families, they had very little to spend. Eventually, though, the cafeteria owners got tired of providing free sitting space to indigent young revolutionaries, and signs began to appear on the walls announcing a minimum charge of five cents (the price of a cup of coffee) for every ticket. Later the minimum went up to a dime.

"We Trotskyists," said Jacobs, "were partial for a long time to a cafeteria just off Fourth Avenue on Fourteenth Street itself, and when it closed we decided to rendezvous at another one, near Fifth Avenue."

> I can still recall the horror in the face of the proprietor the first night we descended on his premises and took over six or seven tables. He looked at us as if to say, "What have I done to deserve this fate?" and we looked back at him, arrogantly, with Benny the Ape saying loudly, "Fuck you, buddy. We like it here and we're going to stay."

"It is easy," wrote Jacobs, "to recollect the radical movement of the thirties through a sentimental haze of warm and happy moments, as if it had been a political idyl in which, charged to a high emotional pitch, we sang revolutionary songs, marched in glorious parades, sat for hours talking about politics, went on week-end hikes, and made love to each other on narrow beds underneath Diego Rivera prints of Mexican workers. . . . Although it is true that we did sing and march and hike and talk and study and try awkwardly to make love, all those experiences were, for me at least, also accompanied by moods of pain and deep depression."

In the wake of the Bolshevik Revolution, America's East European community breathed a sigh of relief. Almost the entire Jewish population of the East Side was on hand when, in July 1917, the recently arrived Russian ambassador addressed his ex-countrymen. "I salute you in the name of my sisters," he told the crowd of thousands, "who were tortured in Russia; of brothers who were tortured in Siberia; and of my dead father, whose eyes were burned out in a pogrom."

For some, the response to the czar's overthrow went beyond cheering the remarks of the distinguished speaker. In May, approximately one hundred Russian Jews, known as the "Former Prisoners," returned to their childhood homeland. M. Litwin, a *Jewish Daily Forward* reporter, evaluated the exodus:

> When New York Jews found out about the Russian Revolution they were exuberant. . . . We would all leave America and fly to Russia, and Jewish New York would be emptied out; East Broadway and Harlem and the Bronx would be covered with grass, as they were fifty years ago when the first Litvaks set foot in America. But we are sobering up and realizing that Jews in America are here to stay. I talked with lots of people; only a few thousand can and will leave immediately. Most of these are greenhorns who can't assimilate. *Luftmenschen* drifting between the United States and Russia and always ready to move. The majority of the two million Russian Jews in America have struck roots and will remain. They have hundreds of cemeteries here, where their relatives are buried. Those with children born here will remain. And economic ties are strong.

Among the millions who chose to remain in America were five members of the Jewish Socialist Federation: Frank Geliebter, Harry Hiltzik, Lazar Kling, William Abrams, and Benjamin Solomon. Significant, it was this tiny group which in 1919 gathered in a basement restaurant humorously known as the "Jewish Smolony Institute" (a girls' school used by the Bolsheviks as their central headquarters in Petrograd during the Revolution), to establish the "left wing" of the Jewish Socialist Federation.

The new faction, in the tradition of all Jewish radicals, published a newspaper. "We are not seeking a split in the [Socialist] party," declared an early issue of *Der Kampf*. "We publish this paper with peaceful intention. . . ."

> Our official leaders avoid entirely the discussion of the problems—left in the wake of the war—and do not permit others to discuss them either. Or they take an ambiguous stand to satisfy everyone.
> . . . And in our Jewish labor, things are quiet as usual. . . . The advanced workers feel as though they were in a house with closed windows and doors. . . . To "open the door" . . . , to unite our scattered people, to create a tribune for opinions that do not carry the O.K. of the official leaders . . . these are the tasks of our review.

In time, the "open door" promised by the editors of *Der Kampf* was shut. The left wing of the federation drifted nearer to the general American left, and *Der Kampf,* echoing the feelings of the Yiddish-speaking Communists, urged the Socialists "to organize the Bolshevik sentiments among the masses. . . ."

The Socialist camp, rife with splits and fusions, was divided into two hostile groups. "There are no more branch meetings," wrote the editors of the *Jewish Daily Forward,*

> because each meeting consists of hostile elements which refuse to listen or to understand each other. The only question is who can muster enough "hands" in electing a chairman or in any other vote. . . . Discussing party problems is impossible, and still less possible is it to carry on constructive activity. The question then arises: "Perhaps a divided existence will be more practical than a forced existence? . . .

The "divided existence" discussed by the *Jewish Daily Forward* in 1919 finally came to pass at the federation's 1921 convention. Here, the Yiddish-speaking Communists captured control of the organization. And were vilified by a defeated right wing. "If the Jewish revolutionary would steadfastly remember his responsibility for the sufferings of his people," said Abraham Liessin, "he would be more tactful and take better account of the conditions surrounding him: he would then not clamor for the impossible, as our Jewish revolutionaries now do." Philip

Krantz accused the left of being "a guileful [transmutation] of DeLeonism. . . . They have affiliated themselves . . . with a government of a faraway land . . . that, as everyone knows by now, does not always stick to the ideas it preaches and the slogans it formulates, that will do everything to serve its own interests and to further its own power."*

Stripped of their power within the federation, the Socialist leadership, which indeed had a majority of the members behind them, left the organization and formed the Jewish Socialist Farband. The Farband retained control of the most important federation institutions and maintained close ties with the *Jewish Daily Forward*—the single most effective force in preventing the Communist bid for power in the Jewish labor unions. "From the start," said one observer, "the left wing saw the *Forward* clique as their principal opponents."

Quick to respond with a journal of their own, the Yiddish-speaking Communists soon announced the publication of the *Freiheit*. Under the editorship of Moisaye Olgin, the *Freiheit* began as more than just a political mouthpiece. It published novels, short stories, poetry, feature articles, and literary criticism. With a host of prominent contributors that included such notables as Abraham Reisen and Mani Leib, the *Freiheit*'s pool of literary talent could be matched by few Yiddish papers.

These writers were not attracted to the *Freiheit*'s political position but to the seeming resurgence of Yiddish culture in the Soviet Union. "Their contributions to the paper," wrote Jacob Rabinowitz, a trade unionist, "were regarded by them as simply a vehicle to reach their isolated Soviet brethren. Perhaps as important was the *Freiheit*'s readership." Though fewer than the other Yiddish journals, *Freiheit* readers were "younger, livelier, and more responsive. Often," said Rabinowitz, "we met with the writers at Communist-run social clubs, dramatic societies, summer camps, and educational institutions. At these places all of us had an opportunity to discuss, face to face, their writing. Plainly this was one activity very dear to both the writers and their readers."

In 1929, most of these prominent Yiddish writers broke with the

* In 1921, the Communist leadership of the JSF established the Workers Party of America. The new organization, noted Will Herberg, acted as the "overground" of the Communist Party. By 1925, the non-Communist pretense of the Workers Party was abandoned. Its name changed to the Workers Party of America, the organization became the American section of the Communist International. "The Communist triumph," said one contemporary observer, "was an unqualified success."

paper. In that year Arab terrorists murdered several Jewish colonists in Palestine. At first, the *Freiheit,* in line with its readership, condemned the bloodshed. Later, pressured by the Jewish Bureau of the Communist Party, the editors reversed their position and presented the Arabs as "fighters for national liberation." The Yiddish literati turned away in dismay.

Joining the intellectuals in their rejection of the paper's editorial policy were thousands of others. Led by the *Jewish Daily Forward* and the "downtown" Zionists, a call went out to boycott the paper. "I agree with [Abraham] Cahan," said Izzy Goldstein, the owner of a newsstand on East Broadway. "I won't carry this rag any more. If they are so anxious to buy it, let them go elsewhere. I want to make a living, but not at the expense of Jewish blood."

The unofficial boycott of the *Freiheit* soon took on greater proportions. For years its circulation staff had sought, through its readers and sympathetic businessmen, to attract a larger share of national advertising. To most large American companies the *Freiheit* was simply another Yiddish-language paper and, not aware of its political posture, they placed ads in anticipation of reaching the Yiddish-speaking market.

"We organized," said Jacob Schwartz, a Manhattan dry-goods dealer, "a campaign to deprive the *Freiheit* of the revenue produced by these big companies. I myself went uptown to the advertising agencies and told them, in no uncertain terms, that the Jewish community was betrayed by the paper's editorial policy on Palestine. You keep supporting this paper with your ads," he told one executive, "and the downtown community will make sure no store in the area stocks your product. We don't care how good your products are, if it appears in the pages of the *Freiheit,* we will make *your* soap, *your* hats, *your* anything, look anti-Semitic!"

Stunned by the tone of Schwartz's threat, the bewildered representative asked that the request "be put in writing so he could show it to the boss." "Never mind putting it in writing," replied Schwartz. "Just tell the man in charge that if it appears in the *Freiheit,* it's the same as throwing money out the window!"

Apparently, the threats were successful. National advertisers began to desert. The smaller, local ads followed. Even the Yiddish playhouses, though conscious that offending a paper could lead to poor reviews of their shows, joined the boycott and canceled their weekly ads. "So they will read about us in the *Forward,*" said one theater manager. "Offending this community means an empty house—and who the *hell* can afford that!"

The Communists sought to expand their activities to a broader front, and in the Jewish labor movement they anticipated their most successful venture. The instrument for their infiltration was the Trade Union Educational League (TUEL), an organization established in 1920 by William Z. Foster. Initially designed as a propaganda organ, TUEL soon adopted the policy of "boring from within" and rapidly achieved, for an organization of limited size and strength, remarkable success.

Sidney Hillman, president of the Amalgamated Clothing Workers, feared TUEL's master plan. But at the same time he attacked the Communists, he also resisted the Tailors' Council, a Socialist organization established to counteract the Communists.

"For the Reds," said one contemporary of Hillman, "Sidney's even-handed approach was not acceptable. They figured sooner or later Sidney would turn on them." Hillman was not anxious for the Amalgamated to be split by internal strife. He appealed to all groups, right and left, for harmony. "The difficulty of negotiating with the employers is nothing," said Hillman; "the most deadly enemy of the whole labor movement is internal dissension!"

TUEL, however, which by now controlled a large local of coat makers, saw Hillman's approach as weakness. "Rather than make the sacrifices Sidney called for," commented a member of the rank and file, "the left wing decided to intensify its struggle for power." In the months that followed, Hillman was under strong pressure to expel a TUEL-controlled local. Nevertheless, he repeatedly told his associates that he "never wanted to come to the point where he would have to revoke a charter."

"But how long can we put up with this business?" asked one associate. "As powerful as we are, such tactics will eventually pull us apart."

Momentarily Hillman seemed without an answer. Suddenly, he turned to his colleague and said: "This union has to be tolerant of different opinions and has to encourage free discussion among its members." The Communist effort to "bore from within" was effectively countered by Hillman's tolerant and enlightened point of view. "Less than a score of members were suspended," wrote Hillman's biographer, Matthew Josephson, "and the right of reinstatement was always held open to them; only one local was disciplined. . . ."

Unlike the Amalgamated, the struggle for Communist control of the ILGWU reached civil war proportions. Apparently, the demoralized state of the ILGWU's membership during the postwar years and the long-standing dispute between the international and the New York City locals, made the union a prime target. "The Communists," remarked one Seventh Avenue cutter, "flocked to us like sharks to the smell of blood."

The conflict within the ILGWU was rapidly reaching its climax when its president, Benjamin Schlesinger, who had held that position since 1914, threatened to resign, as he had numerous times. Everyone at the General Executive Board meeting remained silent. Again he repeated the threat. Suddenly Joseph Breslaw, leader of the New York Cloak Pressers' Union, leaned forward and, to the surprise of everyone, said, "Well, brother Schlesinger, if you want to resign, here is a sheet of paper. Put it in writing."

Stunned by the challenge and too proud to back off, he grabbed the paper and quickly wrote out his resignation. Breslaw swept the document from the table and held it up for the board members to see. The ILGWU found its new leader in Morris Sigman, who immediately attacked the Communists in the union by ordering the suspension of three Communist-led locals. The left wing, however, did not remain silent. In response to Sigman's actions, over forty thousand workers, not Communists but angered by Sigman's high-handedness, gathered at Yankee Stadium to protest; there were large demonstrations elsewhere. "Thousands of us," said Morris Benson, a non-Communist trade unionist, "crowded into the East Side meeting halls to condemn Sigman's disregard for union democracy."

Unmoved by the Left's massive response, Sigman continued with plans to rid the union of all Communist taint. But other voices counseled compromise. Sigman finally realized that compromise, rather than total warfare, should prevail.

The peace was short-lived. At a special convention in Philadelphia called to mend fences, the two factions continued the fight. The Communists, outnumbered 60–40, were handed a resounding defeat. But the war was not over. The New York Cloakmakers' strike of 1926 was led by Communists, whose leaders wanted a short walkout, a quick victory for the union, and thus a victory for the TUEL. "They made some headway in this direction," wrote Max Danish, a writer, "and then decided to put the question of terminating the strike before the Communist Party's trade union commissars."

> Characteristically, although it involved the well-being of some 50,000 workers and their families, the tentative settlement ran

headlong into a snarl of party factions and quickly foundered on the rock of "right-wing deviationism." [Charles] Zimmerman and [Louis] Hyman [the leaders] were instructed to continue the fight and try to get "a little more."

Five months after the Communist-initiated walkout, the non-Communist leaders of the union summoned the strikers to New York's Cooper Union. After listening to reports of strike developments and hearing Sigman and David Dubinsky highlight the helpless status of the conflict, the rank and file voted to turn the strike leadership over to the ILGWU's General Executive Board. In January 1927, a settlement was reached. "After twenty-six weeks," said union delegate Mike Rabinowitz, "the strike was over. We got *gornisht* [nothing]. We followed the Communists, listened to their promises and in the end we won less than we were offered before it all began. I can only speak for myself but I know a lot of people were thinking the same as me. It was time to get rid of these people. We lost a whole season's wages. And for what? So the damn Reds could sink their teeth into us, that's what!"

It was the worst defeat in the union's history—and marked the end of TUEL's infiltration. Though the Communists met with failure in their attempt to control the ILGWU, they by no means gave up their program to penetrate the Jewish needle unions. Indeed, their persistence eventually paid handsome dividends as the policy of boring from within gave them their most successful victory: control of the Furriers Union. The labor struggle was long and fierce. During the Communist-led strike in 1926, the employers hired New York hoodlums to break heads.

Ben Gold, the Communist leader of the union, was the man the mobsters were after. One afternoon, a hood burst into Gold's office. "Send the men back to the shops," he warned Gold, "or you'll end up in the ground!"

"Get the hell out of here," Gold quickly replied, "or you're the one who'll end up in a box."

"I'll be back," the hood warned, "and I won't be alone."

"I'll be here," replied Gold. "Now, get the *hell* out!"

The mobster, surprised by Gold's courage, rushed down the stairs. Gold, in a rage, shouted: "Come back again and we'll break your head!"

That evening, Gold had dinner with S. J. Zuckerman, the labor editor of *The Day,* at a Broadway restaurant, and when they left they saw a crowd across the street. Suddenly Gold realized that the "crowds" were mobsters: leading them was the hood he had thrown out of his office that afternoon.

Gripped by fear, the two men edged close together, their backs to the restaurant door, and prepared to defend themselves. Suddenly, as if in a Hollywood B film, hundreds of fur workers came running up from each end of the block. The mobsters were surrounded. Outnumbered, frightened, they fled.

The fur district was a place of terror and brutality. Police guarded each building, arresting or at times assaulting anyone who told a scab not to cross the line; thugs from the infamous Lepke-Gurrah gang patrolled the streets ready to attack strikers with iron pipes wrapped in the *Jewish Daily Forward*. "The paper muffled the noise," said one gangster. "Besides, it would give the *schmuck* something to read in the hospital."

The Workmen's Circle also experienced a split within its ranks. Hoping for unity, its Board of Directors at first tried to remain neutral. The left wing was interested in power and control, not neutrality. In 1926 they seized several of the Workmen's Circle's schools, its Harlem center, and Kinderland, the children's camp. They then abandoned the circle entirely in favor of their own fraternal society: the International Workers' Order (IWO).

The IWO was quick to follow the anti-religious, anti-Zionist, pro-Soviet ideology of the Yiddish-speaking Communists. Kinderland's bunks were renamed "the thirty-six Soviet Republics," and at their schools the aim was not to teach *Jewishness* but to politically indoctrinate the children of the workers. There was not a trace of Jewish subject matter in students' books, which were dedicated to "our comrades . . . the Soviet textbook writers." The books highlighted such personalities as Lenin and Stalin and gave descriptions of the Paris Commune, May Day demonstrations, hunger marches, and anti-black racism. Also included were such class projects as the painting of the hammer and sickle on classroom walls and the creation of a Soviet Union corner in the classroom.

In addition to the IWO's activities, there were other cultural and social events designed to attract the Jewish Left. Throughout the cities were numerous left-wing social clubs, noted Melech Epstein, a prominent radical, "excellent recruiting places for the revolutionary unions and the Communist Party."

Epstein described a "workers' club":

A club occupied a floor in an office or apartment building. The inner walls were taken out, and a stage built on one side. The walls were painted and decorated with posters and placards, and the ceiling was festooned with colorful crepe paper. Facing the stage was a buffet for sandwiches and hot and cold drinks, served by the girls. Larger clubs had dramatic groups, dance groups, mandolin bands, sport sections, libraries, and the inevitable "wall newspaper," an institution brought over from Russia.

Friday night was lecture night. Saturday was given over to dancing. Sunday, to the literary evening, with invited writers or poets. During the week there were rehearsals and classes. The clubs existed on dues and on the income from the various affairs.

The clubs were an outlet for native talent, and, last but not least, boys met girls there. There were *shotkhonim* (matchmakers) for many a couple.

"During the summer months," added Epstein, "the social life of the clubs was transferred to the Communist-controlled camps." One of the most prominent Nitgedeiget ("No Worries"), at first opened only on weekends. Equipped with sleeping tents and a shanty for dining, the retreat attracted those Yiddish-speaking radicals who had little money, providing swimming, lectures, fellowship, and fresh air. Chores, except for the cooking, which was done by professionals, were rotated. Campers waited on tables, washed dishes, and cleaned the grounds. "It was an inexpensive and intellectually stimulating vacation," said radical school teachers from Brooklyn, George and Dora Stein. "All that we could afford and all that we desired."

Over the years, thousands came to Nitgedeiget. "It was so successful," recalled one camper, "that the tents were soon replaced by wooden bungalows and the stream by plumbing and showers. After a while we didn't recognize the place. They added a dining room and a social hall, where we enjoyed concerts, plays, and discussions."

The favorable response to Nitgedeiget motivated the party to open Camp Unity for the younger, English-speaking crowd. But some people were disappointed by their stay at the Communist camps. "I went there," said Mel Lasky, a teacher from New Jersey, "because I heard everyone believed in free love. This, I must say, proved to be untrue."

The Communists also established the Freiheit Singing Society and the Mandolin Orchestra. "The basic theme of our concerts," said Nat Zelman, a non-Communist music lover from the Bronx, "was the glorification of the Soviet Union. But for many of us it was the music—the opportunity to sing or play—rather than the ideology that attracted our participation. Each day after work," he said, "Harriet Frank and I would leave the shop and go uptown to rehearsal to prepare for the big night at the Brooklyn Academy of Music. It was the cultural highlight of my younger years."

For many, however, their days with the Freiheit Singing Society were over when news of the Hitler-Stalin Non-Aggression Pact reached the Jewish community. "The pact," declared Melech Epstein, "hit the [Jewish] Communists like a bolt from the sky."

> The anguish of the Jewish Communists and left-wingers was acute; the non-Jews were less touched. The Jews suddenly found themselves angrily repudiated by their shop mates and neighbors. . . . In the first couple of weeks it looked as though the Jewish segment of the party had suffered a blow from which it could hardly recover.

Most Communists who happened to be Jewish by birth were shocked when they read the news. Those who presented themselves as *Jewish* Communists, operating within a *Jewish* framework, suffered the most humiliation and the greatest agony. "All of us," said one Yiddish-speaking Communist, "who put our trust in Stalin were exposed in front of the world as a pack of idiots."

Even *The Day,* which often took a soft stand on the Soviet Union, now spoke in icy terms: "A horrible treason. The worst has come . . . an infamous document for a country which in the last few years has pressed the democratic countries to its bosom, . . . which moved heaven and earth for collective security . . . a country which claims to be Socialist . . . is bringing on a world catastrophe with open eyes. . . . Millions of Jews . . . are now in the hands of Hitler."

The *Freiheit* portrayed the pact quite differently: "Soviet Russia," they said, "was saving the Jews from the Nazis." "The saving," declared Melech Epstein,

> referred to the march of the Red Army into Poland and the Baltic States; occupying a large area inhabited by Jews. This adroit campaign provided the dispirited Communists with a talking point, and their agony was turned, at least in their own mind, into self-righteousness. Each town's occupation by the Red Army was made the occasion for a celebration and mutual *mazel-tovs* by the Communist-left *landsleit* here.

In response to the *Freiheit*'s justification of the pact, the Yiddish *Morning Journal* urged the destruction of the Yiddish-speaking Communists: "The Jewish enemy of the Jewish people," declared the editors, "raises its head, and it is our duty to hit him with an iron bar on the head, as one would a snake." The labor-Zionist journal, *Yiddisher Kemfer,* took the same stance: "We reject with loathing the saving of a million Jews when it is bought at such a price. Explanations [among the Communists] change daily. . . . It is difficult not to form the impression that the [party] faithful do not themselves believe in their own arguments."

Also buzzing with talk about the pact were the lunch-hour crowds created by the Seventh Avenue garment workers. Prudently, the Communists avoided mixing with the street-corner gatherings.

"Who could have believed it?" said one pattern maker. "If someone had told me this a month ago, I would have opened his head. . . ."

Another exclaimed: "If I could force my way into the *Freiheit* office, I'd make a little pogrom there. . . ."

A third remarked: "The *Freiheit* is now telling me that condemning Moscow means siding with Chamberlain. But Chamberlain is not going to help Hitler. . . ."

Soon the desertions began. Leading Yiddish-speaking Communists, shocked by the news photo of Ribbentrop and Molotov shaking hands, resigned. One of them expressed the heartache of the group:

> Thanks be to Stalin. He has cut open the abscess and the "pus" will run off and the blood will stop, and the patient will open his eyes and be cured. . . . How much pain and strain were required in the last ten years to maintain at least a shred of faith that everything going on in Moscow meant redemption! Iron dictatorship, concentration camps, the slaughter of comrades and builders of the Revolution, espionage, informers, servility, dehumanization. . . . All the shedding of innocent blood was forgotten. . . . Workers, liberals, intellectuals, Socialists labored to find vindication for all this, stifling their own conscience, explaining away through rationalization and casuistry, and with tooth and nail clinging to the consolation. . . . Still, Socialism is being built there. . . .

Ravaged by the internal battles of the 1920s and further crippled by the economic decline of 1929, the garment unions were at their lowest ebb; sweatshops returned; strikes were ineffectual; gangsters roamed freely.

Soon, however, under the umbrella of Roosevelt's New Deal, the

Jewish unions began to regroup. The most phenomenal progress was made by the ILGWU, whose membership increased from forty thousand in the early part of 1933 to over two hundred thousand by the middle of the next year. As a result of several whirlwind strikes during the "honeymoon" period of the National Industrial Recovery Act, the "needle unions" were once again a potent force in virtually every segment of the women's garment industry. By the time Schechter's "sick chicken"† destroyed the NRA's blue eagle, in 1935, the power of the garment workers soared to new heights.

With swelling membership, powerful financial resources, and a new-found influence in Washington, Hillman's Amalgamated and Dubinsky's International were forces to be respected.

"Clear it with Sidney" was the oft-heard answer FDR gave when asked about his administration's labor policy. Hillman's counsel and cooperation were the umbilical cords connecting the policy makers in Washington with the cutters and operators of New York's garment district.

Not everyone in Washington however had the same respect for the president of the Amalgamated as did the President. In March 1935, the Senate Finance Committee, during an investigation of FDR's labor policies, summoned Hillman to a hearing. Utah's Senator King, an outspoken opponent of labor and a leading member of the committee, was convinced that the President, along with Hillman, was turning the nation over to the Bolsheviks.

After the proceedings began, the tone of the questions reminded one of the "back room of a police station. The grilling," said one observer, "was reminiscent of a third degree."

Senator King, the most obnoxious of the committee members, immediately took the offensive: "You organized the Amalgamated Clothing Workers?" he asked Hillman. Not waiting for an answer, the Utah representative quickly added, "I have here a copy of your preamble and by-laws. . . ." King read a section concerning the eventual working-class takeover of the system of production.

"That is part of your creed?" he shouted at Hillman.

"That preamble has been out of our constitution for over fifteen years and—" Hillman was cut short: "You put that into your constitution? You put that into your program after you came from Russia?" asked King.

† In 1935 the Supreme Court held the National Industrial Recovery Act unconstitutional in *Schechter Poultry Corp.* v. *U.S.* ("Sick Chicken Case").

"Of course, I come from Russia—" replied Hillman.

King again interrupted. "No, that was put into your organization here after you had come from Russia? Please answer that—"

"Of course it was. I was born in Russia—" Hillman again replied.

Suddenly King was interrupted by Senator Costigan: "This is not a court-martial!"

A murmur of approval swept the room. For a moment, King backed off. Suddenly, however, King again stabbed at Hillman with his biting questions. But Hillman had had enough.

"Senator King," said Hillman, "instead of permitting me to give what I believe is my honest opinion of the policies of the New Deal, the question seems to be: Was I born in Russia?"

Banging his fist on the table, Hillman began his counterattack: "As if I had anything to do with where I was born. At least I can say, Senator, that this country is with me not merely a matter of accident [of birth], but it is the country of my choice!"

For a moment, Hillman digressed. He was going to tell the committee that the people of America were in pain, that they suffered terribly: "Talk about freedom for industry," he said to the senators. "What freedom has a girl compelled to work for a dollar a week? What freedom has the worker out of work and hopeless of finding a job? We are finding fault, indulging in philosophical interpretation of what is the solution two hundred years from now. You can afford to wait two hundred years, but the men and women out of work cannot afford to."

Before Hillman could complete his statement, the Utah senator again interrupted and again asked the same question: "Where were you born, Mr. Hillman?"

Exhausted of patience and absolutely livid, Hillman looked squarely at King and said: "I was summoned here to speak about the labor policies of the administration. Yet I am questioned about the Amalgamated and I am asked about whether I was born in Russia. Senator King, I'll be glad to give my record of where I was born . . . and about everything I have done since then. It will stand up with that of any man in this country."

"With those words," commented a spectator, "King dropped his questions concerning Hillman's place of birth and the committee ended its heckling." "Finally," said another observer, "Hillman and these elected clowns got down to the business at hand: the nation's recovery."

David Dubinsky also acquired enormous power and influence during the Roosevelt years. Born David Dobnievski, the son of a Russian baker, the sensitive youth spent his early life surrounded by czarist oppression. His schooling as a revolutionary came at an early age. "When most American youngsters were still in elementary school," wrote J. C. Rich, Dubinsky "had already been a professional baker; when they were busy with their high school education, he received his secondary education as a political prisoner in Russian jails. For a graduation journey, [he] had taken a long trek, first by railroad and then on foot, into exile under police surveillance in a Godforsaken Siberian hamlet."

His exile, however, was short-lived. With the aid of a peasant, the youthful radical escaped and returned to his home in Lodz.

"You must be a fugitive?" the peasant asked Dubinsky.

"Why do you say that?" the frightened youth replied with pretended indignation.

"The straw," said the peasant. "It's all over your body. You were hiding in the hay, weren't you? If you weren't hiding, why would you be sleeping in the straw?"

Dubinsky looked at his body and saw bits of straw clinging to his clothing.

"Yes," he said. "But will you help me?"

"Have you ever ridden a horse?" the peasant asked.

"No; why do you ask?"

"Never mind," the peasant replied. "Get on my horse. I'll help. Jews and revolutionaries aren't the only ones who hate the Czar."

"I knew," remarked Dubinsky in later years, "that I was in friendly hands."

> He brought me to his village and introduced me to another peasant, a friend of his. He told him immediately that I was a fugitive, a political prisoner. I shall never forget the expression on the face of this Russian peasant when he heard I was a political prisoner. He knelt . . . and prayed for me.

Once back in Lodz, Dubinsky took a pseudonym and changed his "sleeping place every night." Working as a baker, he waited for a chance to escape Russia. Soon that opportunity came: "My brother," he said, "who lived in New York, sent me a ticket to America. I had earned enough money by that time to take my other brother with me. We were smuggled across the border. Once outside Russia, we didn't need any passports. . . ."

On Sunday, January 1, 1911 standing on the deck of a ship, Dubinsky saw Manhattan's high buildings through a veil of light fog.

> Only a narrow strip of water separated me from America, but inwardly I was still in Europe, on the streets of Lodz with their crooked sidewalks paved with gray, brown, and sometimes, almost red flagstones, in the prison at Tcheliabinsk, and in the Paviak jail in Warsaw. I thought of my friends there. I was still with them, and America and my presence in New York Harbor seemed like a dream.

Soon after he landed, the "pink-cheeked youth with alert eyes" went to work as a knee-pants operator. In possession of a letter of introduction from Benjamin Schlesinger, he became a member of Local 10, the powerful cutters' union of the ILGWU. Thus started the long career of one of Jewish labor's most productive leaders.

Dubinsky rose rapidly through the ranks of Local 10. In 1919 he became a member of its executive board and one year later was its vice-president. In 1921, he occupied its presidency.

The erstwhile Russian revolutionary became a leading figure in the battle against the Communists. When he went to the assistance of Morris Sigman, president of the ILGWU, "The lefts," wrote McAlester Coleman, "promptly trained their heaviest fire on [him] . . . recognizing in him their most formidable foe."

Dubinsky used every weapon at his disposal against the Communists. "Those suspected of leftist sympathies," reported Coleman,

> were hurled incontinently out of the locals. There were many weird distortions of parliamentary procedure; red-baiting consumed more of the officials' time than routine union business.
>
> Soon Dubinsky developed an in-fighting technique that brought him to the top of many a scrambled heap. When the Communists would fire off a barrage of broadsides picturing him as the leader of "sluggers and gangsters," the head of a "fat-bellied clique of job holders," and announcing, "on behalf of the rank and file," that "we are through with Dubinsky," the little man would promptly hand in his resignation. As a result, vehement protests would pour in from hitherto neutral rank and filers, Dubinsky would withdraw his resignation—and be re-elected by a large majority.

As important to him as his anti-communism was the sanctity of his word. The fact that he never backed away from a pledge, no matter how strong the pressure to do so, was recognized by both the rank and file and the employers.

After the ILGWU's battle with the Communists, Dubinsky was convinced that a strike, to bring order to the industry and unity to the union, was needed. "Not one for wages or working conditions," he said, "but one which would unify the membership." The maneuver, however, needed the co-operation of the "responsible" manufacturers—those employers who recognized that a strong union, free of gangsters and internal dissent, would necessarily lead to a healthy industry.

To insure secrecy, Dubinsky got into a cab with I. Grossman, president of the Employers Association, and Samuel Klein, its executive director. In the eight-hour drive around the city, the meter rang up forty dollars.

"The industry," Dubinsky told the two men, "has to eliminate the hoods and the scabs. If not, both of us have nothing. Only an empty shell. You and I will be working for someone else. We're weak and you're in trouble. You need a union as much as we do. We're going to call a walkout to unify our organization, and we won't ask for more money. We just want you to co-operate by closing your shops and not bringing in *shtarkes* [hoodlums] or strikebreakers. Fair enough!"

Grossman and Klein agreed with Dubinsky but wanted certain assurances: "How do we know you won't turn around and hold us up for more money?" asked Grossman. "Look," said Dubinsky, "I can't go to a notary public; you just have to take my word."

Klein, who knew Dubinsky quite well, turned to Grossman and said: "His word is better than a notary. You can trust him."

The strike was a short one. The employers, as promised, co-operated. Dubinsky, true to his pledge, made no wage demands. As expected, word spread that Dubinsky "sold out the membership." In the face of this he set about getting the support of the rank and file—a task that would not be very easy.

"How can we return to the shops without more money?" said one Dubinsky associate. "Why didn't we ask for more money?"

"We won something more important," replied Dubinsky. "Unity—support, a union."

"But what about wages?" declared another associate.

Dramatically, Dubinsky walked over to a window and opened it. "You'll be able to ask for more money, but only after I jump out." With that gesture, the discussion was dropped. Dubinsky won the first round.

Now Dubinsky had to convince the membership. Though apprehensive, he went before a ratification meeting and simply told the group, "All I bring you is a union."

For a few seconds there was dead silence. Dubinsky waited. Then there were whispers, and suddenly, as if they were able to read Dubinsky's thoughts, the crowd knew why he had called the strike. The members rose to their feet and let out a thunderous ovation. Rather than rebellion, the workers lifted Dubinsky on their shoulders and paraded him around the hall. When news of the meeting reached Klein's office, he turned to Grossman and said: "I told you!"

Dubinsky, who sometimes was called "Papa," had another side to him. Often known to lose his temper, he could be ruthless, sometimes autocratic. "His rages," noted A. H. Raskin, "were fearsome."

"But," declared Raskin, "no matter how consuming his anger, he never allowed it to block the full utilization within the union of men whose talents he considered valuable." An incident with Louis Stolberg is a case in point.

In 1928, when Stolberg was working as a cutter and Dubinsky was managing Local 10, the two men backed different candidates for the presidency of the international. Apparently, Stolberg, who had been a union representative in Ohio, still wielded influence among a number of delegates from Cleveland and Toledo. When the two men met, Dubinsky was furious.

"Who the hell do you think you are!" Dubinsky roared at the Seventh Avenue cutter. . . . "If you don't fall into line, I'll see to it that you are washed up in this union! . . . Until hair grows on the palm of my hand," he warned Stolberg, "you don't get a job with this local!"

Sometime later, after the election was over, Dubinsky was searching for someone to become the local's new business agent. Unmindful of his previous threats, he asked Stolberg if he wanted the job.

"Turn your hands over and let me see your palms," Stolberg said. "I want to see if you need a haircut."

Dubinsky seemed puzzled. He did not remember his anger or his threat.

When Dubinsky was chosen to lead the international, the Socialists were engaged in a great debate over whether to support or oppose the "New Deal." At a rally held at New York's Madison Square Garden, Abraham Cahan, the outspoken Socialist editor of the *Jewish Daily Forward,* angered some and thrilled others when he suggested that FDR become a card-carrying member of the party. Among those who were delighted with Cahan's remarks were the leaders of the Jewish labor movement. Sensing that Roosevelt was something special to them, in a break with past tradition the leadership of the Jewish unions called on their rank and file to support the "capitalist" President. The membership, which also recognized the possibilities promised by the New Deal, responded with enthusiasm. In a single stroke, Jewish socialism was "brushed aside" in favor of the reforms advanced by the Roosevelt administration. The Americanization of Jewish labor had begun.

POPULAR CULTURE AND BEYOND

Soon after the stock market crash of '29, the lights of New York's theater district dimmed. "Now only the hits will make it" was the oft-repeated remark of the unemployed actors, stagehands, and directors. The ticket scalpers disappeared; producers scrambled for the rights to revivals; and low-priced productions became commonplace. "Veterans," wrote Howard Taubman author of *The Making of the American Theatre* (1965), "observed the deflation in salaries, royalties and profits and predicted bravely . . . that an era had ended." For many, "Brother Can You Spare a Dime?" was more than a popular song.

In the midst of it all, the theater was going through a renaissance. "In the grim, straitened years of the early thirties," noted Taubman,

> the soil was ripe for protest and experiment. Routine opportunities in the theatre were drying up. Impatience with the mindless entertainment that made up the bulk of New York's theatre offerings was endemic. Out of this discontent there emerged eager, young theatrical organizations dedicated to the proposition that the theatre should be something more than a place to kill an hour or two.

Most prominent among this discontented element were Jews, and through the Group Theatre, the Theatre Union, and the workers' theater organizations, they made a tremendous impact on the American stage. The graduates of these organizations, declared Taubman, "influenced the theatre into the next three or four decades."

As children and grandchildren of East European "greeners," the Jews associated with these innovative theatrical groups (and there were many) were imbued with the emotion of the Yiddish stage and deeply committed to the concept that the play was a proper vehicle for social commentary. Not everyone, however, agreed: *The Literary Digest* brooded over the fact that Broadway was "taking a back seat" to Second Avenue (the home of the Yiddish stage); and *Time* magazine portrayed the Group as nothing more than an outlet for left-wing ideology. New York *Times* critic John Corbin voiced his objection to the "downtown playwrights." While admitting that Broadway could learn from Second Avenue (". . . the Yids write plays first hand out of their daily experience . . . and their public flock to them enthralled and illumined") he still feared that the Jewish influence on Broadway would be ". . . corrosive, vitriolic, [and] anointed by the spirit of a separate minority. . . ."

The Group Theatre's trademark, said one contemporary observer, "was stage realism and plays of social significance. Without question, the Jews in the Group brought with them the very best of the Yiddish stage." Expressly, it was within this atmosphere that Lee Strasberg, a prominent Group director, introduced The Method.‡ Harold Clurman, a co-founder and director, described Strasberg's system:

> One was improvisation. This required the actors to do extemporaneous scenes based on situations emotionally analogous to those in the play, but not actually part of the play's text. A further step . . . was the acting of the play's scenes in the actor's own ad lib. speech. The purpose . . . was to make the actor face each of the play's situations spontaneously—that is, without the support of the play's actual lines, which often serve merely to disguise from himself his own lack of relation to the basic matter of the play.

"The second, and most striking, feature . . ." said Clurman,

> is effective memory. . . . In this "exercise" the actor was asked to recall the details of an event from his own past. The recollection of these details would stir the actors with some of the feeling involved in the original experience, thus producing "mood." These "exercises" were used to set the mechanism of the actor's emotions rolling. . . . When . . . in the grip of this mood . . . the actor was better prepared to do the scene calling for the particular mood that the exercise had evoked.

"Here," concluded Clurman, "was something new to most of the actors, something basic, something almost holy. It was revelation in the theater; and Strasberg was its prophet."

‡ Derivitive of the actor-training techniques of Stanislawsky, a cofounder and the director of the Moscow Art Theatre.

The list of Jews writing for the American stage during the thirties was prestigious: Most Hart, Lillian Hellman, George S. Kaufman, Elmer Rice, John Howard Lawson, Morris Ryskind, Irwin Shaw, and S. N. Behrman, to name a few. Yet, only a handful had the literary impact of the Group's exceptional find, Clifford Odets.

"By a considerable margin," wrote Robert Warshaw in an article entitled "Poet of the Middle Class," "the most important achievement in the literature of American Jews [during the thirties] is that of Odets." "He is of particular significance to students of Jewish cultural history in America," added Judd Teller, for while "most other Jewish playwrights dipped, from time to time, into Jewish [themes] . . . Odets produced a minor 'human comedy' [of] Jewish middle-class [life]." Indeed, Odets was the poet of this life.

In *Awake and Sing,* a depression play about a Jewish family, Odets proved Teller's assertion: His characters consider the insignificance of their lives; they are no longer communicating; all are confronted with their own unhappiness, using words as weapons. Though they speak, nobody listens:

BESSIE: I'm so nervous I can't hold a knife in my hand.

MYRON: Is that a way to talk, Ralphie? Don't Momma work hard enough all day?

BESSIE: On my feet twenty-four hours.

MYRON: On her feet—

RALPH: What do I do—go to night clubs with Greta Garbo? Then when I come home can't even have my own room? Sleep on a day-bed in the front room!

BESSIE: He's starting up that stuff again. When Hennie here marries you'll have her room—I should only live to see the day.

HENNIE: Me too.

Living in close quarters, in a loveless familiarity that is the reverse of the usual Jewish family solidarity, their unhappiness is manifested by constant and deep-seated antagonism; Ralph, for example, wants to marry:

BESSIE: A girl like that he wants to marry. A skinny consumptive . . . six months already she's not working—taking charity from her aunt. You should see her. In a year she's dead in your hands. . . . Miss Nobody should step in the picture and I'll stand with my mouth shut.

RALPH: Miss Nobody! Who am I? Al Jolson?

BESSIE: Fix your tie!

RALPH: I'll take care of my own life.

BESSIE: You'll take care? Excuse my expression, you can't even wipe your nose yet! He'll take care!

While the offspring of the East Europeans were invading the legitimate stage, others from the "downtown" community were captivating audiences with their song, humor, music, and dance. The list seems almost endless: Fanny Brice, Eddie Cantor, Al Jolson, the Gershwins, the Ritz Brothers, George Jessel, George Burns, Irving Berlin, the Marx Brothers, Sophie Tucker, Jack Benny, and many, many more. The influence of these performers, and the hundreds of others too numerous to mention, was great. Critic Gilbert Seldes measured their impact:

> In addition to being more or less a Christian country, America is a Protestant community and a business organization—and none of these units is peculiarly prolific in the creation of [these] individuals. [They] gave something to America which America lacks and loves—[they] are out of the dominant class. Possibly this accounts for their fine carelessness about our superstitions of politeness and gentility . . . [and their] contempt for artificial notions of propriety.

The fact that Jews gained control of a substantial segment of the nation's entertainment business led many of these personalities to enter American society through the stage door. The rise of Marc Klaw and Abe Erlanger's "booking syndicate" and the influence and power of such theatrical pioneers as the Schubert brothers, Marcus Loew, and Adolph Zukor did not go without notice in the Jewish community.

"During the time I had been [manager] at the Harlem Opera House," said George Blumenthal, a familiar Broadway figure, "a trust had been forming for the booking of combinations and shows with regular runs." The trust, also known as the "syndicate," was the brainchild of Marc Klaw and Abe Erlanger. "It was," declared Blumenthal, "showing all indications of becoming the most powerful theatrical booking concern we had ever known."

> The plan was to tie up theatres all over the country with contracts to be booked only by the Syndicate, then to tie up as many attractions as possible. That would force both ends; without Syndicate booking a theatre could get no attractions to fill the time, and attractions could not get a theatre unless they signed with the Syndicate.

Abe Erlanger was the "czar" of the Syndicate. He frightened almost every theater manager in the country with his power and his threats, and more often than not, "forced them to accede to his wishes at all times. I remember," said Blumenthal, "when I had a week open at the Harlem Opera House and less than a month's time to fill it. I went down to Erlanger's office to see what he had."

> In the outer office I met Ben Stern, manager of Fanny Davenport. When I told him of my dilemma, he called me aside and whispered that that was the very time he had open, that he would like to have Fanny . . . go into [my house] that week; it would be her first appearance in Harlem.
>
> In another breath he said to me, "If you go in to see Erlanger, for heaven's sake don't mention what I told you."
>
> And that is how afraid managers were to try anything independent of Erlanger.

The Schubert Brothers—Samuel, Jacob, and Lee—who came to New York in 1900 with fifteen thousand dollars in borrowed cash, took control of the American theater. "If America bought tickets to see a play," said Jerry Stagg, "two thirds of them were from Schubert."

> They created their own mythology about themselves and became legends in their own time. One part of the myth was the disguise they wore as great Trustbusters. They fought with the Theatrical Trust—and they compromised with it, and fought it again, and joined it, and fought it again and broke it. Then the Schuberts were the Trust—and more powerful and more ruthless than their predecessor. They fought the Trust and everyone else. Their competitors, their stars, their employees, their partners, their government;
> . . . they took on the press, the Tax Department, Equity, ASCAP, the Dramatists' Guild, local politicians, each other. Sometimes they lost. More often they won.

The Schuberts, declared Stagg, were "Horatio Algers with a Jewish accent; the immigrant dream; the carving of an empire; the power play in the world of high finance, of make-believe, talent, temperament, and the most beautiful women in the world!"

For Sol Hurok, it was a small distance from his home in Brownsville to the streets of Manhattan's theater district. Yet it was this journey which consumed most of his life. "Someday," he once told a friend, "I'm going to manage artists. . . . And I'll have my office," he said, looking across Broadway, "in that building." His companion neither laughed nor argued but merely shrugged his shoulders and reached into his pocket to see if he had the carfare back to Brownsville.

"Brownsville," said Hurok,

> was a steaming microcosm of culture in the heart of Brooklyn, alive with intellectual striving and artistic hungers. It was no garden spot to the eye, with its push-cart cluttered market streets and frame houses. . . . But it was a lush garden for the mind. In South America, Cuba, Mexico, in the capitals of Europe I have met musicians, artists and writers who first budded in Brownsville.

As a youth, Hurok watched as the people of Brownsville flocked to the neighborhood's cultural events. "I," said the young impresario, "was kept busy supplying the artists and organizing the events."

> Elsewhere in New York in those days music was not big business. Concerts offering artists of world renown, two or three of them in joint appearance, failed to sell out the thousand seats in the old Steinway Hall on Fourteenth Street.
>
> But music thrived in Brownsville. So, having tried my managerial wings on our local talent . . . I began to have bigger ideas.

The "bigger ideas" swirling around in Hurok's head caused many sleepless nights, "What I hatched," he said, "laying awake" on one of those nights, "was the biggest idea of all. I could get Efrem Zimbalist!"

Zimbalist, the famous Russian violinist, was the sensation of the 1911 season. "You did not merely *say* Zimbalist," noted Hurok, "you either whispered it in awe or shouted it in wild acclaim." Hurok, however, was quite apprehensive about approaching the world-famous artist. His performances in Europe had been followed by "rhapsodic reports," and his Boston debut "had set the music world to quivering with ecstasy." Asking him to play Brownsville, said Hurok, "was pure brass . . . *chutzpah!*"

Hurok, determined to bring Zimbalist to "the neighborhood," went to Carnegie Hall to see the artist's manager. He "listened politely to my proposition, which was of itself a surprise," said Hurok. "For I not only wanted Zimbalist to play at Brownsville's New Palm Garden for the benefit of the Socialist Party; I wanted him to play at a bargain rate, besides!"

Rather than throw the impresario out of the office, the manager sent him to see Zimbalist. It was a momentous occasion for the anxious Hurok: for the first time in his life he was face to face, "as manager to artist, with a Big Name." Hurok, however, carried the day. After a lengthy conversation, he walked away with a contract in his pocket. Zimbalist, though he refused to cut his fee, pledged $250 to the Socialist Party.

While watching the crowd file into the Brownsville meeting hall, Hurok thought: "If Zimbalist would play for me in the New Palm Gardens, why not Carnegie?" "With all my brashness," he said, "I could not yet imagine, in type on . . . cards . . . the words S. HUROK PRESENTS."

While Hurok was providing audiences with such outstanding talent as Zimbalist, America was laughing at the antics of Eddie Cantor and George Burns or tapping their feet to the songs of Sophie Tucker. The fact that so many of the people on the "booking or production end" of show business were Jewish certainly made it easier for a Jewish performer to break in. "This was not medical school," said one observer. "Here we all spoke the same language. And even if we didn't, a gentile audience didn't care if you were circumcised or not, just as long as you could put your act over."

Jewish entertainers, in an effort "to come up with new and unusual acts," sometimes buried their Jewishness. "Not because of anti-Semitism or shame," said one producer, "but strictly to put one over on the booking agent or audience." One such incident was related by A. J. Balaban, a popular New York booking agent.

> One afternoon we were interviewing the leader of a Hawaiian band we wanted to book. I ardently wished to present this foreign novelty but the price was too high. The leader, in a very hesitant, broken English tried to impress us with the enormous investment he had in the men of this orchestra brought so far from their homeland. . . . I took a long chance and threw a question at him. "Kennst redin Yiddish?" [Can you speak Jewish?] "Geviss" [Of course], he answered just as quickly and in a natural New Yorker's tone, without a trace of an Hawaiian accent. We quickly came to terms, complimenting him on his ability to impersonate.

For others, it was *Yiddishkeit* that counted. "[George] Jessel and I," wrote Eddie Cantor, played "the Paradise Theatre on the Grand Concourse in the Bronx." The Paradise, noted Cantor, was "like playing a big kitchen, a strictly homey place where the audience doesn't merely applaud, they virtually clasp your hand. There were people in that audience who hadn't been inside a theatre for years. They came because of loyalty and nostalgia for a couple of local boys who'd made good. Some of the women brought us homemade soup!"

On one particular afternoon, the manager of the Paradise, hoping to "squeeze" in an additional performance, asked Cantor and Jessel to cut some time off their act. Jessel said he would eliminate his popular "Chazan ov Shabbas" ("The Cantor on the Sabbath") song.

Just as the act was ending, however, someone shouted from the audience:

"Just a minute. Just a minute. What's the matter with Jessel's 'Chazan ov Shabbas'?"

"How did you know about that?"

"I heard it at the last show."

"So you heard it."

"I want to hear it again. There's a law against it, I shouldn't hear 'Chazan ov Shabbas' again?"

> There was no law. Jessel had to sing it before this customer would let us finish the act.
>
> I don't know how many shows he stayed for; a good part of the audience stayed indefinitely. A woman would come backstage and say, "Mr. Cantor, do me a favor. My two children have been in the theatre since twelve noon. They haven't eaten for six hours. Will you give 'em these sandwiches?" So I'd call their names and they'd come up on stage and get their dinner.

"Sometimes," said Cantor, as he went off stage he would see a familiar face and say, "Weren't you here for the last two shows?"

"Yes," came the reply.

"Well, aren't you hungry? What kind of a sandwich would *you* like?"

> The customer'd specify corned beef or chicken, and while Jessel was on I'd have a stagehand run next door and get the sandwich. I'd come back on carrying the paper sack. "Oh yes, and a pickle," and I'd pull a big dill out of my back pocket. Sometimes a fresh guy'd say, "What, no Coke?"

For fifteen to twenty dollars a week, Sophie Tucker put on blackface and toured the small-time circuit. Though the money was poor, she didn't care. "This, at last," she said, "is show business."

"Let me leave off the black," she pleaded with her booker, Joe Woods. "Try me out the way I am and see if I don't go over." Woods, however, refused to listen.

Tucker, who eventually rose to stardom singing "Some of These Days," was billed as a "World Re-nowned Coon Shouter." When she finally hit New York, it was "Sophie Tucker, Manipulator of Coon Melodies."

> When I started out . . . I wore the white satin dress, . . . and used burnt cork for make-up. But the difficulty of keeping the dress clean was too great. I soon changed to a high-yellow make-up and rented a black velvet dress which gave a contrast. I kept to the gloves, however. It made a good stunt at the end of my act to peel off a glove and wave to the crowd to show I was a white girl.

Tucker also played the ten-cent music hall owned by Marcus Loew, Adolph Zukor, and Nicholas Schenck. "All they showed was a one-reel slapstick comedy," she said, "and me in blackface for the ten afternoon shows and whiteface for the ten night shows."

> Twenty shows a day for a salary of twenty dollars a week. I would get to the theatre for the first show at noon and sit there until the lights went out a little before midnight. Marcus Lowe would bring me my food in between shows. He was very fond of me, even aside from the fact that he knew I brought in the dimes when I was singing there. He changed his singers weekly, but I played more return dates than any of the others.

Marcus Loew and Sophie Tucker maintained their friendship for many years. "It was a tribute," she noted, "to those days when he called on me [as a star] to help him open the first Loew's Picture Theatre. . . ."

> He used to say I was his good-luck charm. I never remember Marcus . . . coming into any city on business that he didn't ask, "Is Sophie Tucker playing in town?" And if I was, then there would be a note asking me to meet him for supper. . . . His interest was always keen. Was I happy? Was I saving my money? Was I still looking after the family? His theatres were always open to me to play at any time, from the days when I was a small-salaried performer up to the days after I had climbed into the big money. . . .

Everyone who watched Fanny Brice perform knew she was destined for stardom.

"I watched you work," said Flo Ziegfeld to the speechless, trembling young girl sitting in front of his desk. "You are very talented. . . . Would you like to work for me?"

Moments later, Ziegfeld showed her a contract. "It was on slick, shiny paper," she said, but she "would not exchange it for the Magna

Carta." She thanked him and walked out of the office. On her way to the street, she also thanked the secretary in the outer office, the cleaning man in the hall, and the doorman who let her out of the building. Once in the fresh air, she ran in the direction of Forty-seventh Street and Broadway—the burlesque crossroads of the world.

"Hey," she shouted, "Ziegfeld signed me!" I'd stand there every day and in five or six days the contract was torn to pieces. . . . it cracked and nobody could make it out. If they couldn't make it out, they couldn't read it. They wouldn't believe me. So I went to Ziegfeld's office.

"My mother threw the contract out," she told him. "You have to give me another one." He did. "I wore *that* one out in a week." She came for another contract. He gave her a fresh one. Brice, in showing her Ziegfeld contract to friends, wore out eight copies before the Follies ever went into rehearsal.

Like thousands of others, Groucho Marx broke into show business by traveling around the country with a small vaudeville act. And like thousands of others, he got stranded—broke in Cripple Creek, Colorado.

We played . . . Cripple Creek without getting killed. . . . I don't know where dire straits is, but I certainly was now in the neighborhood. No money, no job, a minimum of talent and far, far from home.

Alone and broke in the tiny Colorado town, Marx searched for work. "I saw a sign," he said: "Experienced boy wanted to drive grocery wagon. . . . Must know how to handle horses."

Having been born and raised on Manhattan Island, the only horses I had ever had any contact with were those on the merry-go-round at Coney Island. With this doubtful background, only the thought of my dwindling bankroll gave me the courage to go in and apply. . . .

"You come for the job?" asked the proprietor.

"Yes."

"Know anything about horses?"

"Oh, yes," he lied. "I've been around horses all my life. I was brought up on a ranch in Montana." A few seconds later, he added, "I won first prize in a Junior Rodeo in Cheyenne!"

The owner was convinced. "Go out back. You'll find two horses.

Hitch 'em to the wagon and take these potatoes to Victory [a town a few miles away]. I'll pay you five dollars a week—and if I catch you stealing any food out of the store, I'll beat the hell outaya. . . ."

Marx's knowledge of horses was quickly tested. "In addition to being afraid of horses," he said, "I hadn't the faintest idea of how to harness one." After trying for some time, the owner finally helped the youth hitch the team.

"Get going!" he shouted. The horses began to move. Seconds later Marx got the shock of his life:

> The horses charged forward and away I went. . . . I tried to slow my steeds down, but it was hopeless. We then hit a narrow mountain road, with the horses galloping wildly around the curves. I kept looking straight ahead. I had already taken a quick, nervous look over the side with the idea of jumping, but all I could see was a sheer drop of four thousand feet.

Marx reached his destination. "One of the horses," he said, "neighed loudly, staggered for a moment—either from fatigue or overexertion—and conveniently dropped dead." He got off the wagon, looked at the dead animal, and walked back to Cripple Creek. "I finally arrived at the boardinghouse," he said, "and hid until my mother sent . . . money. I didn't know where she got the money, but I have a hunch she hocked one of my brothers."

While America was laughing at the antics of the Jewish vaudevillians, they were also, since the twenties, being thrilled by the great quadrumvirate of American popular music: Irving Berlin, the Gershwin brothers, and Jerome Kern. All children of families who had emigrated to America shortly before or after their birth, each of them, by the time the depression rolled around, had launched a successful career.

Israel Baline, whom everyone called "Izzy," found a job as a singing waiter at Pelham's Café, more commonly known as "Nigger Mike's," at 12 Pell Street, in New York's Chinatown. One evening, a visiting European prince wandered into the place. The owner, who earned his nickname because he was a dark-complexioned Russian Jew, was honored by the presence of royalty and announced that the drinks were free. When the night was over, the prince offered his waiter a generous tip. The youngster refused. "No, thanks," he told the customer, "this one is on me." The next morning, a journalist who witnessed the incident, and who was "shocked" that a New York waiter had refused a tip, reported the story to his editor. This was the first time Irving Berlin made the press.

During his off-hours, Izzy and a companion sat around Mike's battered piano picking out tunes with one finger. Soon, they came up with "Marie from Sunny Italy," and the hunt for a publisher began. The two knocked on the doors of Tin Pan Alley for weeks. When it was accepted, the song writers were sixty-six cents richer—the total amount they made on their first tune. The money, however, was unimportant: Izzy was a song writer!

With the publication of his first song, Izzy Baline ceased to exist. Since his name was to be on a sheet of music, young Izzy decided to spell his name the way it was pronounced; it became Berlin. His first name also had to be changed. Israel was too solemn and Izzy sounded silly. "He always like the name Irving," said a contemporary, "but that, too, was also no good. The people at Mike's would simply laugh." Thus, Izzy's first piece of sheet music carried the credit "Words by I. Berlin."

Sometime later, Mike fired the musically gifted waiter. "Izzy had been placed in charge of the club for an evening," said a steady customer, "and during the wee hours of the morning, he fell asleep while sitting at the bar. When Mike saw this, he became furious!"

"Where's the money in the till!" exclaimed Mike. Izzy had no answer. "You're fired—get out!" shouted the Russian. Sometime later, Berlin was told that Mike had taken the money. "It was Mike's way," said an observer, "to teach the youngster a lesson."

Being fired by Mike was the best thing that could have happened. Now Izzy could truly become Irving Berlin. By the time he reached his twenty-third birthday, his songs were heard up and down Broadway. "The boy who had run away from home at thirteen," wrote author Katherine Bakeless, "wretched and miserable at heart, the boy who used to tramp the Bowery with empty pockets, peddling a tune to a publisher only to be laughed at, was now—ten years later" the most sought-after "song writer of Tin Pan Alley. . . ."

The composer John Alden Carpenter once said: "I am strongly inclined to believe that the musical historian of the year 2000 will find the birthday of American music and that of Irving Berlin to have been the same." Jerome Kern, however, disagreed: "Irving Berlin," he said, "has no place in American music, he *is* American music."

Like Irving Berlin, the Gershwin brothers had a tremendous impact on America's musical tastes. In his early years, even those not associated with the "Tin Pan Alley School of Music" recognized George Gershwin's unique ability. "He is a great composer," declared pianist Beryl Rubinstein during a newspaper interview. The interviewer was amused by the use of the term "great" and quickly asked Rubinstein for an explanation of the remark. "I am absolutely in earnest," replied the pianist. "This young fellow . . . has the spark of musical genius. . . ."

Surprised by the statement, the reporter continued to press Rubinstein. "With Gershwin's style and seriousness," continued the pianist, "he is not definitely of the popular-music school, but is one of the really outstanding figures in this country's serious musical efforts. . . . This young man has great charm and a most magnetic personality, and I really believe that America will at no distant date honor him for his talent. . . . That when we speak of American composers George Gershwin's name will be prominent on our list." Indeed, that day arrived when Gershwin gave the world *Rhapsody in Blue*.

At the first rehearsal of the *Rhapsody,* Paul Whiteman, the noted jazz conductor, became so excited that he often forgot he was conducting an orchestra. By the middle of the composition he dropped the "pretense" of directing and simply listened. "I expected George to write an interesting piece," he said, "but this was sheer genius." As the music continued, the conductor was so filled with excitement that his baton dropped to the floor. As soon as the music stopped, Whiteman rushed to the telephone: "I've got hold of something that you might sharpen your teeth on," he told critic Leonard Liebling. "And I don't mean breakfast."

America's response to the *Rhapsody* was nothing less than sensational—it was electric! Music critics, who had never heard the likes of it before, sensed that something very special was taking place. "This composition," declared Olin Downes, "shows extraordinary talent." "Mr. Gershwin," said Gilbert Gabriel, "has an irrepressible pack of talents, and there is an element of inevitability about the piece." William J. Henderson asserted: ". . . Gershwin will be heard from later, and one music lover who became an admirer of his art . . . earnestly hopes he will keep to the field in which he is a free and independent creator." And Deems Taylor declared that the *Rhapsody* "reveals a genuine melodic gift . . . it is genuine jazz music, not only in its scoring, but in its idiom."

Other critics went even further: Henry O. Osgood, of the *Musical Courier,* said the *Rhapsody* "is a more important contribution to music than Stravinsky's *Rite of Spring,*" and Henry T. Finck, the dean of the

New York music world, claimed that Gershwin was "far superior to Schönberg, Milhaud, and the rest of the futurist fellows."

This initial response to Gershwin's *Rhapsody* was only a flurry when compared to the storm that followed. The *Rhapsody* was hailed as the finest of all American symphonic pieces. The sale of its phonograph recordings and sheet music skyrocketed; it was arranged for piano, for two pianos, for eight pianos; for harmonica, for mandolin orchestra— and for the movies. At New York's Roxy Theatre, for example, the showplace of the cinema world, the management paid ten thousand dollars in order to play it for a week, and, at thousands of dance companies, producers rushed to adapt it for ballet and tap. "What was perhaps the final accolade," asserted renowned musicologist David Ewen, "was bestowed . . . when, on the afternoon of November 1, 1942, Arturo Toscanini conducted it over the radio for a nationwide audience."

Gershwin's musical triumph led others to the realization that jazz was an important musical idiom. "Directly or indirectly," noted Ewen, "it inspired John Alden Carpenter to write his ballet *Skyscrapers,* Aaron Copland to write a jazz piano concerto, George Antheil to write a jazz opera, *Trans-Atlantic.*"

In Europe, the *Rhapsody* made an indelible impression, as it fired Maurice Ravel to write the blues, Kurt Weill and Bert Brecht to write their opera *Rise and Fall of the City of Mahagonny,* and William Walton and Constant Lambert to produce jazz music for symphony orchestras. "The magic of the *Rhapsody in Blue* was irresistible," wrote Ewen. "It was the greatest artistic expression of a mad and turbulent era in American life."

Gershwin was more than the composer of the *Rhapsody.* "He was," said composer Kurt List, "a part of America's social history transposed into music."

> A symbol of the immigrant in the new world and of the newcomer to our national culture, George Gershwin was the first and so far the only composer to capture the essence of American life and art. . . . Surveying the host of composers who today try so strenuously to create a supposedly American music, one cannot resort but to a paraphase of André Gide's *bon mot* on Victor Hugo: "Gershwin, alas, is America's greatest composer."

To complete the trio of musical greats was of course Jerome Kern, the father of American operetta. Born in 1885 among the comforts and culture of an affluent German Jewish family, Kern, who leaned toward a cultured mother interested in music and art, spurned his father's wish to take up a business career.

Unlike Berlin and Gershwin, he was spared the usual struggle of the aspiring artist. "The gentility and well-being of his family," noted List, "gave [him] a security that was to remain one of the chief factors of his personality:

> From his mother, he gained a confidence and unrestrained feeling for the middle levels of culture. From his father, he gained a certain business sense that helped him greatly in his later dealings with publishers and producers—a business sense that never deviated, however, from the tradition of honest dealing of the well-established nineteenth-century merchant: Kern had no need of the pushing shrewdness that the sharper competition of later days and the resistance toward East European Jews forced on those Broadwayites who emerged from the East Side only by arduous efforts.

When Kern first picked up Edna Ferber's novel *Show Boat,* unlike most others he had some difficulty reading it. "I kept turning the pages," he told the author, "and I kept thinking that the book would make a wonderful light opera. Reading it was difficult because after every few pages I rushed over to the piano to put the words to music." Ferber was impressed, and shortly thereafter, Kern and the lyricist Oscar Hammerstein II were busily at work on a musical version.

The social implications of the music, borrowed from Negro spirituals, demonstrated that Kern was keenly aware of the black man's plight. Though "Kern might have been surprised," noted List, "to have been told that his 'Ol' Man River' was an attack on the American status quo, or that he felt akin to the Negro because he was himself a member of a minority group . . . the fact remains that these songs . . . betray the slight social discomfort that even the most integrated Jew . . . felt. . . ."

"Kern's audiences," said List,

> took the themes more seriously, perhaps, than he may have meant them in his own consciousness. It was not long before "Ol' Man River" became the song of Negro emancipation in the minds of white liberal audiences. *Show Boat* took on the aspects of a genuine American folk opera—in no small part because of its social implications. . . . In the ghetto tales it is always "Kol Nidre"; in *Show Boat* it is "Ol' Man River."

It was a Jew who wrote *Show Boat,* two Jews who put it to music, and a Jew who produced it on the Broadway stage. Thus it should come as no surprise that Jews, on two separate occasions, turned the Kern-Hammerstein musical into motion pictures.

"In 1909," wrote Benjamin B. Hampton, a historian of American cinema, "motion-picture investment was scorned; in 1919 it was a doubtful speculation; in 1929 it had become a favorite of conservative bankers. . . ." It was during the "motion-picture investment was scorned" period that Jews deserted their pushcarts, gave up peddling, and left factories to get into "moving pictures." Rushing into this risky business was a Chicago fur worker named Adolph Zukor; a garment maker called William Fox; a glove salesman, Samuel Goldwyn; a clothier, Carl Laemmle. Others joined the trek to Hollywood: Louis B. Mayer left his father's junk business, and Jack Warner walked away from his bicycle store.

As Samuel Goldwyn entered the Broadway theater, he had no idea of ever going into the movie business. "When I went out," he said, "I was glowing with the sudden realization of my way to fortune. I could hardly wait," he said, "until I told my idea to my brother-in-law, Jesse Lasky."

"Lasky, do you want to make a fortune?"

"Why not!" he replied.

"Very well, then, put up some money."

"In what?"

"Motion pictures."

"Motion pictures!" exclaimed Lasky, "you and I would be a fine pair in that business—me, a vaudeville man, and you a glove salesman! What do we know about the game . . . ?"

Though they knew nothing about "the game," these "pushcart Jews," as they were known to the established Hollywood filmmakers, made the trip to "the Coast." With nothing but energy, showmanship, persistence, and sheer *chutzpah,* they soon found themselves in control of the cinema world. They gambled the few dollars they made in their nickelodeons, penny arcades, and small-town theaters, and won. "Hollywood, we are here," they said. "And we're going to stay!"

The Jewish film moguls stamped an indelible impression on the movie world; Zukor, Lasky, Fox, Mayer, Loew, and Laemmle emerged as giants. Samuel Goldwyn, known for his often atrocious use of the vernacular—"Include me out," "In two words im possible," "A verbal contract isn't worth the paper it's written on," "Any man who goes to a psychiatrist should have his head examined"—nurtured M.G.M.;

Jack Warner and his brothers made their studio a movie household word; William Fox guided 20th Century-Fox; Adolph Zukor directed Paramount; and Carl Laemmle built Universal.

According to Michael Blankfort, a seasoned screenwriter who worked for most of these men, they "were accidental Jews, terribly frightened Jews, who rejected their immigrant background to become super-Americans.* They were," he said, "interested in power and profit. They would hardly ever touch a story with a Jewish character, and if they did they cast a gentile for the part." A case in point was Harry Cohn, also known as "White Fang," of Columbia Pictures. One day, a director asked Cohn to hire a particular actor.

"Nah," said Cohn, "he looks too Jewish."

"But he's a good actor," said the director.

"Around this studio," replied Cohn, "the only Jews we put into pictures play Indians." That closed the conversation.

As the industry proved more and more lucrative, competition among these pioneer filmmakers grew in intensity. Adolph Zukor, of Paramount, remembered that "they did everything but murder."

> I didn't raid anybody [for talent] because I started the whole business. But I had something others could take. They had nothing, and the only way they could have something was to take it from me.

"Then," said Zukor, "the business grew bigger, and there was room for us all.

> It was only a question of who made the best pictures, and I tried to stay in business on the quality of what we produced. If you don't make pictures that you anticipate the public will patronize, you don't exist. But if you use your head to pick the story and pick the cast and pick the director, that is a God-given gift. You can't learn it in college. If you have it, you succeed. Those people who have that quality are still in business. They still do well. Only illness, retirement, or death can stop them. Louis Mayer had it. Harry Warner had it. William Fox had it.

Though Zukor pioneered Paramount into a commanding position, he

---

* Rabbi Edgar Magnin, of Hollywood's Wilshire Boulevard Temple, characterized these men as "neither better nor worse [than] other American Jews. I don't believe they were ashamed of their Judaism, and they gave very generously to local Jewish causes."

also found out that the best planning sometimes backfired. Arthur
Mayer, a publicity man for Zukor, related the following incident:

> On one occasion it was decreed that all Ace Publix Theatres, re-
> gardless of local tradition or expense, must be rechristened to bear
> the Paramount name. I was assigned to the conversion of the well-
> established Riviera of Omaha, Nebraska. . . . I plastered Omaha's
> billboards, buses and business windows for weeks with slogans cel-
> ebrating the public's overwhelming demand for a new name for its
> favorite Publix Theatre.
>
> Came the day of the big christening and there arrived a quartet of
> Paramount's most illustrious brass, headed by Adolph Zukor him-
> self. I hurried to a waiting taxi.

"To the Paramount," Mayer proudly instructed the cabbie.

"Where?" asked the driver.

"To the Paramount," Mayer repeated.

"Never heard of it!"

Then Mayer weakly explained: "To your right and up the hill."

"Oh," the taxi driver responded, "you must be meaning the Riviera."

Zukor looked squarely at Mayer: "Did you say this campaign cost
twenty-thousand dollars?"

Though Harry Cohn refused to cast certain actors because they
looked "too Jewish," there is no denying that Jews were *very* prominent
among the "talent stables" of the Jewish movie moguls. Though few of
these performers were cast in an identifiable Jewish role, except perhaps
for Al Jolson in *The Jazz Singer* (1927), almost every week Jewish
actors thrilled audiences with the magic of their craft.

"I will never forget those wonderful afternoons I spent in the darkened houses," said Ida Feldstein, a Brooklyn housewife, "watching
John Garfield [Julius Garfinkle], Edward G. Robinson [Emanuel Gold-
berg], Melvyn Douglas [Melvyn Hesselberg], Theda Bara [Theodosia
Goodman], and Paul Muni [Muni Weisenfreund], make my fantasies
come true. Muni was my favorite. He could play anybody—just anybody."

Paul Muni, who, like many others, came to films via the Yiddish
stage, was one of the greatest actors of all time. "There was no way for
this man to be bad," said noted director Mervyn LeRoy. "He was a
perfectionist. . . ." Whether the infamous gangster in *Scarface,* or the
warmhearted physician in *The Last Angry Man,* or the hunted convict
in *I Am a Fugitive from a Chain Gang,* his performance was always remarkable. "If you're really *listening,*" added LeRoy, "you can take the

scene right away from the guy or woman who's talking. Muni did that —not intentionally—instinctively."

In *I Am a Fugitive from a Chain Gang,* Muni demonstrated this unique talent. "The ending of the picture," said LeRoy,

> a scene which lasts less than a minute, is mentioned constantly in film histories. . . . Muni as James Allen, weary, hunted, appears out of the night, for one last meeting in a garage alley with his girl. When she asks, "How do you live?" he answers, "I steal," as the black maw of night seems to swallow him up.

"It was an accident," noted LeRoy. "I was shooting way downtown in Los Angeles. As we were doing a take, there was a sudden power failure. Muni was haggard and bleary with fatigue. As he backed away, the light drained out of his face as if the life were ebbing out of him. . . . It was a great ending."

Muni's performance in *Fugitive* set the Hollywood colony on its ear. Everyone, but everyone, recognized the unusual ability of this gifted actor. "Part of that gift," said a veteran observer, "he got from the Yiddish theatre."

"In Russia," noted LeRoy, "they thought we were all Communists. Because the film showed the brutality of the [chain-gang] system. But we did a lot to help eradicate the chain gangs in the South. For years Jack Warner and I were barred from Georgia."

While Muni electrified movie audiences, still other Jews established beachheads in American literature. Their numbers were considerable: Daniel Fuchs, Michael Gold, Henry Roth, Nathanael West, Ludwig Lewisohn, Edward Dahlberg, Nathan Asch, Isidore Schneider, Benjamin Appel, Samuel Ornitz, Albert Halper, Meyer Levin, Jerome Weidman, and Budd Schulberg are only a few on the list.

Like other depression writers, the Jews were haunted by the economic crisis and thus questioned the system—capitalism—which permitted hunger and want amid potential plenty, and their "proletarian" novels, a term taken from Soviet literary critics, were imbued with themes at odds with American society. "Unlike their Socialist predecessors," noted Walter Rideout, they dealt "graphically and at length with violence and cruelty . . . and the disruption of their own lives. . . ." They wrote "of the decay of the middle class or of the sordid, terrifying lives of those at the bottom of the social pit—the 'bottom dogs,' as they were called from the title Edward Dahlberg's striking first novel."

The most significant piece of proletarian literature was Michael Gold's autobiographical novel *Jews Without Money* (1930). In his opening chapter, "Fifty Cents a Night," he described the East Side not in terms of nostalgic *Yiddishkeit* but, rather, as a sordid community replete with pimps, "peanut politicians," and prostitutes—women who sold their bodies because it was better than starving.

> The Jews had fled from the European pogroms; with prayer, thanksgiving and solemn faith from new Egypt into a new Promised Land.
>
> They found awaiting them the sweatshops, the bawdy houses and Tammany Hall.
>
> There were hundreds of prostitutes on my street. They occupied vacant stores, they crowded into flats and apartments in all the tenements. The pious Jews hated the traffic. But they were pauper strangers here; they could do nothing. They shrugged their shoulders, and murmured: "This is America." They tried to live.

Gold related how the women hurled garbage onto the street until "the East Side heavens rained with potato peelings, coffee grounds, herring heads and . . . soup bones." In the bitter cold of winter, these same people, while cursing Columbus, froze in their cold-water flats waiting for the Messiah. "At times," wrote Gold, "I seriously thought of cutting my throat. At other times I dreamed of running away. . . . I developed a crazy religious streak. I prayed on the tenement roof in moonlight to the Jewish Messiah who would redeem the world."

For Gold, the Messiah was "a man on an East Side soap-box" who, "one night, proclaimed that out of the despair, melancholy and helpless rage of millions, a world movement had been born to abolish poverty. I listened to him."

> O Workers' Revolution, you brought hope to me, a lonely, suicidal boy. You are the true Messiah. You will destroy the East Side when you come, and build there a garden for the human spirit.
>
> O Revolution, that forced me to think, to struggle and to live.
>
> O great beginning!

Among the younger writers of the decade was Albert Halper. He, like Gold, had little sympathy for capitalism. "I witnessed," he said in 1944, "fascism come to flower, reactionary big business hit its stride and the manufacture and dissemination of anti-Semitism, linked with fascism and big business, assume astounding proportions in our civic life."

-. . . here in America I, and other writers, are witnessing every day a different kind of pogrom—the pogrom of human decency. And it is not limited to Jews. It is also directed against Negroes, against labor and against little people. . . . Unaccompanied by the rattle of machine guns, it is played, instead, against the muted legal obbligatos of "free enterprise."

I am in deadly earnest. The enemy is in deadly earnest here. Being a Jew has helped me to see the terrifying deadliness of the whole business. We Jews are like undertakers; we have been to so many funerals, including our own, that we can smell a corpse quicker than any gentile can.

Halper characterized the Jewish writer as the vanguard of Jewish resistance. "Jews," he declared, "will be the first to write about the present in a way which the time calls for."

They will be the first because of their undertakers' noses. Do not forget that it was Kafka, a European Jew, who detected the smell of fascism as far back as 1919, and wrote about it.

So, we Jewish writers, because of our equipment (or heritage, if you want to call it that), or ought to get going. We ought to get going not because of the cries rising up to us outside our windows, but because our time is shorter than that of our Christian colleagues, and because of the possibility of the human race being forced to dig its own grave if it is not awakened. . . .

The best proletarian novel, if not the greatest *Jewish* novel of all, was Henry Roth's *Call It Sleep* (1934). Like *Jews Without Money,* Roth's book also describes the life of the Lower East Side, primarily through the eyes of young David Schearl. The son of a loving mother and a neurotic father, the sensitive youngster experiences the terror of the tenement cellar, the emotional insecurity of his top-floor apartment, and the "psychic release of the rooftop. What makes the novel so extraordinary," said one critic, "is its seemless web of concrete and abstract, of reality and symbol, of earth and spirit. Many of the events are grossly physical and are described in revolting detail. . . ."

Note, for example, David's encounter with a girl who wants to "play bed."

"Yuh know w'ea babies come from?"

"N-no."

"From de knish."

"Knish?"

"Between de legs. Who puts id in is de poppa. De poppa's god de petzel. Yaw de poppa."

"Perhaps," said Allen Guttmann, "it was not ignorance that let *Call It Sleep* drop into oblivion from its publication in 1934 to its reissue in 1960."

> Perhaps David Schearl's pain and terror and triumph came *too* close to the experience of the young men and women of the second generation as they moved from childhood to adulthood and from one culture to another. Perhaps Henry Roth had to wait for another generation to recognize that he wrote for every generation.

Many of the writers in the decades between the two world wars—the children of immigrants—expressed a kind of Jewish self-denial. "There's a great deal of beauty . . . in our tradition," declared one of Aben Kandel's characters in *Rabbi Burns* (1931). "But I haven't seen any of it in America. For that matter, I've met very few Jews here that I like. Something happens to them here."

Muriel Rukeyser, who distinguished herself as a poet, echoed these sentiments:

> I grew up among a group of Jews who wished, more than anything else . . . to be invisible. They were playing possum. They shrank away from the occasional anger of the rabbi, and said that such a man ought not to be in that pulpit; they were the people who read Sokolsky's column at breakfast, and agreed with him every time he said that Jews should be quiet and polite, and should never protest; if he would only leave the Jews alone. . . .

"They supported big charities," said Rukeyser, and

> they gave generously of their money. Some of the women even gave their time. But they wanted a religion of reassurance; . . . and refused to be involved in suffering that demanded resistance, and refused to acknowledge evil. If they had a mission as a responsible people, they did not want it. It was enough to be Jewish.

Howard Fast was even more critical in his self-denial. "I escaped," he said, "most of the Jewish mores and most of the fears. . . . I could not, nor did I desire to, go groping back into a Jewish past and rear the dangerous and always vulnerable walls of 'an Island Within.' For me, that past did not exist—and as I found it, through reading and hearsay, it held nothing attractive, nothing that I wanted."

A Jew is nothing special; I see him as no better, no worse than other human beings—no wiser, no more foolish. If he is distinguished by anything, it is by the fact that through his religion and situation he offered a fine target for political reaction. Then I say—let him fight that reaction. . . . Let him join with all others who fight reaction, who fight for decency and democracy.

Jewish writers in Germany, and latterly Jewish writers in America, discovered how slick and easy it was to lampoon the Jew, to treat him as an animal, to wallow in the mystical appraisal of his divine or deadly place in the world. They fed the fires of anti-Semitism, contemplated their navels, and repeated blithely, "I'm special."

This self-denigration—the rejection of "I'm special"—seems to be a recurrent theme of the Jewish literati. Ideology, either communism, Americanization, or the like, were, without question, the outstanding concerns of the second generation of American Jewish writers.

While some Jews took to pen and paper, others chose brush and canvas to express their innermost feelings. "Beginning in the 1920s," explained Harold Rosenberg, "an extraordinary development in art took place on the Lower East Side. . . ."

Under the influence of the American Ash Can School, this art (which might be called East Side realism) dedicated itself to studying the artist's environment—the prevailing idea was for the artist to paint what he saw and what he was deeply familiar with—and the environment happened to contain a multitude of Jews. Quantities of paintings and sculptures were done by Jews of old men with beards, grandmothers sitting in front of tenements on Essex Street, people going to synagogue, street ceremonies of dedicating a Torah —subjects that tended to branch out and include other Jewish themes. . . .

"I recall," said Rosenberg, "a very sensitive picture . . . by one of the Soyers in the '30s of the artist's parents

seated at the table after a Friday night supper. The candles are burning to melt, and the middle aged couple are also melting into half sleep. They look as if they had eaten a good deal—a golden glow as of chicken soup permeates the picture. With the droopy, worn quality of the parents in the midst of the Sabbath haze, the scene is thoroughly authentic, and it is beautifully painted.

Many of the artists of the "East Side School of Realism" received part of their training at the Educational Alliance Art School. Founded in the early part of the twentieth century, the school opened its doors to the sons and daughters of Yiddish-speaking cap makers and shirt cutters and used as its models "the people of the street": pushcart men, fish peddlers, talmudic scholars. "One of the most remarkable things about the school," said Moses Soyer, "was perhaps it models."

> They were the people who made up the teeming, multi-varied, East Side. After painting for years the eternal nude, male or female, against the eternally gray school wall, it was a relief and almost a rediscovery to face a bearded, Rembrandtesque Hebrew patriarch, a jolly Italian woman, a pregnant gypsy, or a wistful Negro child.

Soon after its inception, the school was brought to the attention of the world. "Out of the teeming squalor of New York City's East Side," wrote one newspaper, "will soon arise a great genius, . . . a great artist, and Abbo Ostrovsky [the director of the school] . . . is doing what he can to keep alive and fan the fire latent there that may make the artist."

Maxwell Anderson, at the time a cub reporter, wrote:

> An art school that grew up among the immigrants on the East Side would be interesting even if the work were only conventional. But when we find the East Side Art School doing work in painting, etching, drawing and modeling that equals or excels the best work produced in old-established and reputable schools we may be pardoned for enthusiasm and surprise. The immigrant evidently knows more about art than we have given him credit for.

Moses Soyer recalled his experience: "As luck would have it, I read one Sunday in a newspaper about a small school on the Lower East Side. . . . I decided to go there."

> The director of the School was a young Russian artist, Abbo Ostrowsky. He was . . . a true idealist but, like many idealists, academic and somewhat limited. He was imbued with a consuming desire to create an art center for immigrants and children of immigrants. It was this dedication, this singleness of purpose which gave the School its quality and flavor and set it apart from better equipped schools such as that of . . . the Art Students League. The students were allowed to come and go as they wished, for most of them were poor and had to work. Ostrowsky accorded them absolute freedom of expression, even though he may have differed (he often did) with their ideas, goals and motivations. He was young and didactic, and the students were young and rebellious.

"Consequently," said Soyer, "there were clashes, mostly ideological, and to the good, I think, because, to paraphase freely an old Hebrew saying, 'Clashes and jealousy in art and knowledge stimulate the latter.'"

> A communal spirit pervaded the School. In summertime we would go *en masse* to Woodstock to do watercolors. One summer Abbo took a group of us to spend several months as guests of the wonderful, shy Maxwell Anderson in Grand View on the Hudson. Another summer we lived and worked in a deserted estate on Long Island.

All of the Soyer brothers—Raphael, Moses, Isaac—were encouraged by their parents to develop their talent. "Everyone in the family," noted Raphael, "aspired to be something."

> Our father [who was a distinguished Hebrew scholar] wrote his stories every morning; our mother constantly and bitterly complained about her lack of education, the lack of time for reading, for improving herself. Even in those days Moses, Isaac and I were obsessed by childish dreams of becoming Rembrandts and Raphaels. . . . The atmosphere of our home was charged with overtones of ambition, frustration, rivalry and jealousy of one another's little triumphs. Once I secretly cried when my much younger brother, Isaac, made a drawing better than mine.

This driving ambition, at least for Moses and Isaac, found an outlet at the East Side Art School. "The life class to which I was admitted," said Moses, "consisted of unusual, dedicated boys and girls. . . ."

> I remember Saul Berman, hard working, mule-like. He could recite Shakespeare from memory by the hour, and would sing old English ballads; Leo Jackinson—a young genius who sculpted, painted, played the violin, wrote poetry, all equally well. . . . Later came Peter Blume, precocious, handsome, nicknamed "Dawn" by the girls. Then came Isaac Soyer, fresh from school; Jack Friedland, a punster who kept everybody gay; and finally, Chaim Gross, my old friend. . . . There were many others: Louis Schanker, Adolph Gottlieb, Mark Rothko, sleepy-eyed Barnett Newman—I list them together because some of them are today [1963] leaders of the New York school of non-objective expressionism, the school which is against my school. The evening classes were attended by Philip Evergood and Ben Shahn, today so universally famous; Louis Lozowick, a "walking encyclopedia," and others.

"Those were good days" noted Soyer. "We painted life-size canvases and carved heroic sculptures. We made alliances which lasted through life. We argued and fought endlessly about life and art, and the relative importance of Piero della Francesca and Cézanne. We differed in all things. Only one thing united us—the consuming desire to become artists."

Like Soyer, Jo Davidson had his start at the Educational Alliance Art School. "There were lapses between jobs and when they came I would . . . go to the afternoon drawing class of the Educational Alliance on East Broadway." Unlike Soyer, Davidson's family did not want their son to become an artist. "We were exceedingly poor," he said, "and often did not have enough to eat." To his family, an artist was simply "a loafer, a perpetual pauper, an absolutely useless person."

The ambitious youth, who spent his childhood surrounded by the "crowded tenements, strange smells, [and] drab unpainted walls" of the East Side ghetto, managed to overcome his family's objections and he went on to gain an international reputation for his busts of the world's cultural and political leaders. One of his subjects was a coreligionist— Albert Einstein:

"Tell me," said Einstein, "do you understand people as well as you see them?"

"I replied," said Davidson, "that I was rather like a dog—I sensed them."

"Oh," said the scientist, "I am like that; . . . only, I am so often wrong."

Then Davidson asked if he had ever sat before.

"Yes," Einstein answered, "when I was a student in Munich. I was really an artist's model and, between sittings, I was a physicist."

When it came time for lunch, Davidson offered Einstein a ride home. It was snowing outside and the artist noticed that the scientist was not wearing socks. Einstein, however, refused the offer, saying that he preferred to walk.

"He was wearing a light sweater," said Davidson. "He put on an overcoat and his hat and walked out into the snow. I was afraid he would catch cold."

When Einstein returned, that afternoon, Davidson noticed that "his face was red and nipped with cold. . . . When he sat down and crossed his legs," recalled the artist, "I saw that he had still not put on socks."

Jacob Epstein also grew up on the East Side and attended the Educational Alliance Art School. His parents, however, did not discourage him from becoming an artist but "could not understand how [he] could make a living out of art. Their idea of an artist," said Epstein, "was that of a person who was condemned to starvation."

Hutchins Hapgood, whose book *The Spirit of the Ghetto* was illustrated by Epstein, was one of the first to recognize the talent that the youth possessed. "There is character in every one [of his drawings]," he said. "He tells the truth about the ghetto. . . ."

While attaining international prominence, Epstein, who turned almost exclusively to sculpture, lost his infatuation with his boyhood community and severed his ties with Jewish life. "I have never joined in all-Jewish exhibitions of art. Artists are of all races and climes, and to band together in racial groups is ridiculous." Rather than becoming the Rembrandt of the Lower East Side, he left for Europe, where, as England's first modern sculptor, he achieved fame and knighthood.

A host of others—Ben Shahn, William Zorach, William Gropper, Max Weber, Maurice Sterne, Peter Blume, Mark Rothko, Louise Nevelson, Arnold Friedman, Ben Zion, Louis Schanker—were honored by the art world.

Maurice Sterne, who became a celebrated sculptor and painter, recalled that in his Latvian *shtetl* "religious Jews took very seriously the biblical injunction against 'graven' images . . . I was punished badly by the rabbi of the school for drawing his picture in the ground with a stick."

Sterne's sister was somewhat more enlightened and took her younger brother to the Tretiakoff Art Gallery:

> On our way out . . . I saw something that interested me far more than had any of the exhibits. A man stood before a painting . . . he was copying it! Rosa could not tear me away. Eventually the . . . artist asked . . . if I wanted to become a painter when I grew up. I . . . answered, "I don't know." He asked me whether I like to draw, but I could not be bothered with conversation, so engrossed was I in comparing the original with the canvas. . . . It was like a miracle to me to watch the colors on the palette being transformed into a painting.

"How do you like my copy?" the artist asked.

"I think it's better than the original, but—" came the self-interrupted reply.

He urged me to continue and I told him that I didn't know what was wrong but that something about the left eye disturbed me. The painter patted me on the cheek, and when I asked if I could hold the palette, [he] indulgently told me that I might put a few dabs of paint in the background. . . .

"If you don't mind," said Sterne, "I'd rather fix that eye. Now I see just what's wrong with it. The one on the wall has a much dreamier expression than yours."

"At that," declared Sterne, "my embarrassed sister whisked me away but I went home . . . determined to become an artist."

Sterne's determination, like the determination of many other Jews in the arts, found expression in America.

THE JEWISH CRIMINAL

"They all had killers' eyes," said Burton Turkus, the assistant district attorney who prosecuted the "troopers" of Murder, Inc. He saw it in Abe "Kid Twist" Reles, Allie "Tic-Toc" Tennenbaum, Mendy "I love to kill" Weiss, Martin "Bugsy" Goldstein, "Pittsburgh Phil" Strauss.

Killers' eyes. It wasn't scientific, but Turkus knew it was something he could dramatize to a jury. "You point it out and pretty soon the jurors see it." As each Murder, Inc., defendant entered the courtroom, he said, "I got the feeling the theory was perfect. . . ."

The gangster was a new phenomenon in Jewish life. A unique product of America—he was born and raised here—his sudden rise testified to the adaptability of the Jewish newcomer. Driven by the same criminal tendencies as his gentile counterpart, the Jewish gangster was often more daring, more violent than his Christian colleague. Often he was more merciless and more bitter—his criminal passion had no limit.

The East European immigrants were law-abiding people—a quiet and reticent type of humanity. "Some," said an observer, "were even afraid of their own shadows and would dodge anyone suspected of being aggressive. . . . They would actually pay money to be left alone." Where does the Jewish gangster come from? became an oft-repeated question in almost every Jewish household.

Many who asked this question were convinced that the Jewish criminal had his origins in the ghetto street gangs. "These gangs," reported an observer, "were made up of children of respectable and hard-working parents." "Some of them," added New York City policeman Ruby

Goldstein, "had good educations, but banded together in order to protect themselves and their parents from anti-Semitic attacks."

The truth of Goldstein's assertion was related by a young Jewish gang
leader:

> My father was a cantor [and] I went to the Henry Street School
> [on the Lower East Side]. At that time Didra O'Rourke [an Irish
> gang leader] would compel all Jewish peddlers to pay him a weekly
> tribute for protection from him and his gang. He who refused to
> pay discovered one day that his push cart was destroyed and his
> goods removed. My friends and I were very grieved that we could
> do nothing. One day we were attacked by the members of Didra's
> gang and were told that unless we paid them a quarter weekly we
> would be beaten up. A few of my friends succeeded in joining
> Didra's gang to escape the penalty.

"Finally," said the youngster,

> I too was admitted to the gang. I tried to persuade Didra to stop
> taxing the poor Jewish peddlers and storekeepers, but he ordered
> me to keep my mouth shut. . . . For the time being I was silent,
> although I was consumed with anger. However, I could not be si-
> lent, and took the matter up with my friends who belonged to the
> same gang. I told them that we had no right to be silent. The worst
> of it was that Didra used to attack the elderly Jews when they were
> on their way to [shul]. . . . The members of Didra's gang threw
> stones at them.

"One of the missiles," he said, "hit my father . . . and he fell to the
ground unconscious."

> When I told Didra that it was my father, he laughed. . . . This
> caused me to organize my Jewish friends into a gang and to declare
> war upon Didra. One attack followed the other and in the course
> of one of the attacks [Didra] was shot.

Some members of this defensive gang, which entered the world of
crime by a chain of noble, yet peculiar circumstances, became professional criminals and leaders of New York's underworld. "It is a fact,"
asserted an observer, "that even Kid Twist† [not to be confused with
Abe Reles of Murder, Inc.] started his stormy and colorful career" in
this manner. His hatred of the Irish gangster was manic. "No Irish or
Italian gang is going to invade our neighborhood," said the "Kid." "No
Wop and no Mick must rule on the Lower East Side" was his slogan.

† A Lower East Side Jewish hoodlum.

New York Jews parade in protest against British negligence in Palestine riots, August 1929. (American Jewish Archives)

Abraham Cahan (1860–1951), editor of the *Jewish Daily Forward*. "Under tenement roofs are stories of real-life stuff, the very stuff of which great literature can be made. Come tell them to us." (American Jewish Archives)

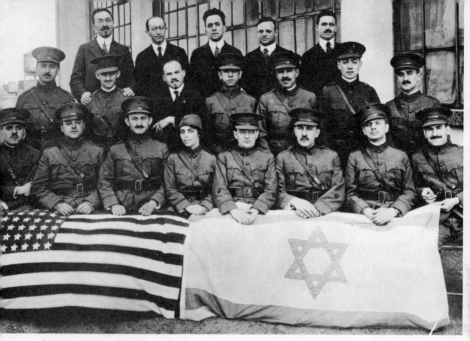

American Zionist Medical Unit sent to France during the First World War.
(Zionist Archives and Library)

American Jewish soldiers pray together in France during the First World War.
(U. S. Army Signal Corps)

American Jews lie next to their gentile comrades in a makeshift cemetery during the First World War. (U. S. Army Signal Corps)

Louis Marshall (1856–1929), defender of Jewish rights. He was identified with the affluent and assimilated Jew but acted in behalf of all Jews, especially vis-à-vis the Christian community. (American Jewish Committee)

On December 21, 1919, Emma Goldman, nicknamed the "Red Queen," was expelled from America because of her anarchist activities. "I do not consider it punishment," she said, "but an honor to be the first political agitator deported from the United States." (National Park Service)

Louis D. Brandeis (1856–1941). Supreme Court justice and president of the Zionist Organization of America. "Since the days of Herzl," said Stephen S. Wise, "he was our greatest Jew." (American Jewish Archives)

Henrietta Szold (1860–1945), the Zionist leader and founder of Hadassah. "She epitomized Brandeis' hope of bringing America to Zion, of investing American ideals and practices in the Jewish homeland." (American Jewish Archives)

David Dubinsky, visionary leader of the ILGWU, came to the United States in 1911. When most American youngsters were in high school, he was receiving his secondary education as a political prisoner in Russian jails. (ILGWU — Justice Photo)

In time, the motivation of these gangs changed and in the predawn of prohibition repeal, Jews witnessed some of their coreligionists gain prominence in the underworld. About this time, the nation's leading racketeers (Jewish and gentile) agreed to establish new rules for the conduct of murder under a loosely knit national crime network known as The Syndicate. Murder, however, was not The Syndicate's business. It did not murder for outsiders and did not kill for a fee. Instead, its rules sharply restricted the use of homicide to business needs. "The new handbook," noted Meyer Berger, a crime reporter, in 1940, "sternly forbids murder for personal or romantic reasons, or even revenge." Much as a Wall Street firm might discuss a maneuver in the stock market, the board of directors of The Syndicate dispassionately debated each murder before causing it to happen.

Once the decision was made, however, it fell to the specialists of Murder, Inc.—made up predominently of Jews from Brownsville, East New York, and Ocean Hill—to carry out the contract. They became the "Extermination Squad," the "Enforcement Arm," for The Syndicate.

As part of its "modernization," The Syndicate established a "judicial system." All "defendants" were entitled to counsel; not a lawyer, but some member of the underworld to present their case. Abe "Kid Twist" Reles, for instance, the infamous Murder, Inc., "trooper," fancied himself as a "master mouthpiece." After listening to his own attorney—he had been in court at least forty-three times—he was well acquainted with the language of the courtroom. He enjoyed uttering clichés such as, "If it please the court" and "I respec'fully except."

Appearing before "the court," Reles pleaded the case of Abe "Pretty" Levine, the son of a Brownsville shop owner, who, after working as a "trooper" for Murder, Inc., decided to leave the homicide business. Levine wanted to try a more prosaic way of making his living. At the "hearing," Reles used his full repertoire of legalisms. He defended Levine's right to leave the "business" and went as far as guaranteeing his silence. "Pretty will keep our secrets," he told the stone-faced judges.

Reles was proud of his performance, but he was indiscreet in his defense of Levine and he was marked by the leaders for the ice pick. With this knowledge, he quickly sought out District Attorney William O'Dwyer for protection. The meeting between the two was historic, for it was there that all the gruesome details of Murder, Inc., were brought to the public's attention.

"The killings," he told O'Dwyer, "were simply by-products of a business organization that involved millions." The Syndicate, he said, "is operated like the Lehman banks. It is practically one organization and spreads all over the country." He compared it to a "tree with all its branches branched out. . . ." It controlled gambling, prostitution, narcotics, the policy racket, bootlegging, and loan-sharking. Through terror, a Murder, Inc., specialty, it dominated certain unions and had an interest in nightclubs and cabarets. It operated some legitimate businesses and "muscled in" on others. It even had its own banking and credit system designed to lend gangsters money—at extremely high interest rates—to start businesses. It protected its members against rivals and murdered "its own" when they violated the rules of the organization.

When Reles' name made the headlines, Patrolman Frederick Murray thought back to the evening of March 14, 1921, when he walked a beat along Brownsville's Van Sinderen Avenue. "Four-family and two-family houses were going up all around for the Jewish families who were moving from the East Side now that the New Lots IRT had been extended through Brownsville into East New York," he said.

"This night . . . I heard somebody shout: 'Beat it, the cops.' Everybody ran," said Murray, "except one kid. He started to gather up the pennies that were on the steps. I got there before he was finished and grabbed him.

"I knew him. His name was Reles, a tough kid fifteen years old."

> Usually when I caught a kid gambling, I slapped him across the pants with my stick and told him to go home. Then I'd talk to his father or mother. I knew somebody in the neighborhood and during the five years I was there I learned to speak a little Yiddish.
>
> This kid was different, though. He used to slap the younger boys around, take their nickels from them, break up their little homemade carts. He was mean and tough. . . . I took him in overnight.

"He's not a bad boy," cried Mrs. Reles. When the judge discovered who she was, he asked her to approach the bench. He told her that Abe had a bad reputation; that he had been arrested before and that he wasn't afraid of the police. He wanted to send Abe to the Children's Village in Dobbs Ferry.

Mrs. Reles begged for her son's freedom. "We'll watch him carefully," she said in Yiddish. "He's not a bad boy, he's just been keeping bad company." The judge was taken by the plea of the concerned mother and, after giving Abe a tongue-lashing, sent the family home.

"That," said Murray, "was the beginning of Abe Reles's criminal record. . . . His dossier now [1940] contains forty-one accusations, and the latest is a murder indictment. . . ."

In the midst of prohibition, Reles's rise to power was rapid. Working in a print shop convinced him that he would "never get any place" that way. He saw that the most affluent, most powerful people in the neighborhood were in the rackets—people with expensive cars, endless amounts of money and political influence.

"You start stealing," he told O'Dwyer, "and you see how it reaches around, and you try to advance yourself. You see the next man in the rackets go higher and higher, and you want to go higher too. Everybody wants to get ahead in the world. Well, we also want to advance ourselves higher and higher." If you want to move up, thought Reles, you have to fight all the way. "There's nobody to help you go ahead," he explained. "Nobody approaches you and says, 'Come along with me.' No, you've got to be smart enough to dope the situation out for yourself. You have got to advance yourself, and how you make your bed, that's how you lay in it."

After Reles quit school, he and his two companions, Martin "Bugsy" Goldstein and "Pittsburgh Phil" Strauss, lived on the streets, in candy stores, in pool halls. They played cards, shot craps, stole from pushcarts, and extorted money from frightened youngsters.

"He ran around with his gang, and I saw him most often at baseball games," recalled an acquaintance who later became a Brooklyn high school teacher. "He was mean and tough. However, in those days most games ended in fights and we didn't mind having him on our side. He was a handy guy with a baseball bat and, knowing he was on our side, umpires frequently gave us most of the close decisions. Since we were playing for money, we didn't mind that."

As they matured, Reles, Strauss, and Goldstein graduated from minor crimes to confirmed hoodlumism. "The money," they said, "was in bootlegging, drug peddling, prostitution, gambling, and strikebreaking." These local enterprises, however, were controlled by the Amberg Brothers (Hymie, Oscar, Joe, and Louis) and the Shapiros (Irving, Meyer, and Willie), who had forced their way into several of Brownsville's breweries as "silent partners." Their "enforcers," who acted as "salesmen," used pipes and blackjacks to convince the customers that Amberg-Shapiro beer was "the best on the market."

Though the cabaret owners were "frightened to death," they still needed watching. Thus, the local mobs hired Reles (and his partners,

"Happy" and Louis Maione) for the job. As "troopers," they also guarded the stills, watched the beer trucks, and pasted labels on bootleg gin. Though underpaid, Reles recognized this as his opportunity to make the "big time." Where the Ambergs and Shapiros had control, Reles and his gang had power. Soon, as an integral part of the Amberg mob, he and his partners established their own rackets.

A series of underworld executions led to a redistribution of Brownsville's criminal power. The Shapiros, it was rumored, had invaded the garment industry, where the "Lepke-Gurrah" mob reigned. "The Shapiros," said Louis "Lepke" Buchalter, "had to be eliminated." The job fell to Reles and Maione. One by one, the Shapiros were murdered. The New York *Post* reported:

> . . . the Ambergs, acting for Lepke, arranged their demise, with . . . Reles as the principal executioner. Willie Shapiro, who was only seventeen when his brothers were killed, was hit on the head and buried alive in a Canarsie marsh . . . supposedly because he had announced that he was going to get his brothers' murderers.

The elimination of Irving and Meyer Shapiro left the Ambergs in control of Brownsville, and promoted Reles one degree. But the Ambergs themselves controlled Brownsville only because they were useful to bigger gangsters. As soon as they became too ambitious, they went the way of the Shapiros.

In 1935, Lepke called on Reles to fulfill a contract. "The Amberg brothers," said an observer, "were bucking Lepke." Their bullet-ridden bodies were found in burning autos. Reles and his gang were arrested, but there was a lack of evidence. "There were a good many other murders in Brooklyn at the time that Reles and Maione were winning and consolidating their new positions," reported the New York *Post*. Each of them were so horrible that Reles and his bunch gained the reputation of vicious and sadistic killers. Willie Shapiro was buried alive in a swamp; a small-time money lender named Irving "Puggy" Feinstein was drenched with kerosene and burned alive; George Rudnick was stabbed fifty-four times with an ice pick.

The path to success was clear. The Reles-Maione gang "seized" East New York and Brownsville and, learning from the experience of the Ambergs and Shapiros, did not try to "move in" on Lepke's territory. Other gangsters also took the cue. A stop was put to the bloody feuds.

From their start as petty thieves, Reles and his gang of killers, via Murder, Inc., became the local enforcement agents of The Syndicate.

Now Reles and his gang were making "big money," eating the best food and driving flashy cars. According to one observer, "Kid Twist did his work in a $6,000 Cadillac with a chauffeur to open the door for the loot," and "Pittsburgh Phil dressed like a regular Beau Brummell."

When Strauss was being questioned about a murder, New York's Police Commissioner Valentine came to see him in the line-up. Strauss, wearing a tailored Chesterfield, a pearl-gray fedora, flashy black shoes, and a tie to match his pin-striped suit, simply smiled at the police official. "Look at him!" exclaimed Valentine. "He's the best-dressed man in the room and he's never worked a day in his life! When you meet men like him, don't be afraid to muss them up. Men like him should be mussed up. Blood should be smeared all over his velvet collar. Instead, he looks just as if he had come from a barber shop." Strauss continued to smile.

Abe "Pretty" Levine also grew up in Brownsville. "This boy," said a reporter of Levine, "who has murdered many people with the frigid skill of the professional, appears to have atrophied emotions. Only when you mention his parents does he wince—'Please leave them out of this.'"

When Levine was thirteen years old, his father's grocery store was robbed. The next day, the thieves boasted to "Pretty" about the job but warned him to say nothing. A few days later, they again told him of another robbery. He joined the action.

"We are going to grab some slot machines," they said, "and you're going to help. . . . We'll give you half." He did, and very soon he discovered that "life on the street [was] more exciting than life in the school room." He graduated to the status of an independent hood and deemed it an honor when the local bigshots "patted him on the back and said [he was] a good kid."

Levine was sponsored by Reles for membership in Murder, Inc. "He has a gift for handling cars," said the "Kid," "and good drivers are needed for a clean getaway." Thus Levine, who was placed in charge of stealing autos for projected murders, took part in the killings and shared in the profits. As a Murder, Inc., trooper, he learned that he was no longer permitted to operate as an "independent." "The rule," said Reles, "was simple. If you get caught on business other than ours, your services are lost—and we don't want to lose the services of the man."

"Pretty" Levine was a loyal gang member and as such was given control of some pinball machines. When times were good, he earned as much as fifty dollars a week. During the slack season he was sometimes forced to borrow from the "shies" of Murder, Inc. He always made sure to pay back. "When needed," said a trooper, "we collected with a fist, blackjack or rubber hose." Once, Levine borrowed five dollars from the organization, paid fifty-two dollars in interest, and still owed the original five dollars. "Pretty" never forgot this.

On March 1, 1940, the police arrested Levine and charged him with stealing the car used in the ice-pick murder of George Rudnick. They told him that they "could put Reles, Goldstein . . . away for a long time." They also said that he, too, might go to the electric chair.

> "You're a kid," Captain McGown told him. You've got a pretty wife and baby. How will you feel when you go to the chair, knowing you'll never see them again? Why should you go to the chair for a bunch of rats who'd turn you in in a minute if it would do them any good? If you talk, it might help you, and we've already got you on this Rudnick killing.

They reminded him that he was always on the "dirty and dangerous jobs for the gang and had never made anything but a meager living. . . ." The others, they said, "were going around with money in their pockets." Nor did they forget to remind "Pretty" that when Reles was arrested, he pulled out "a roll amounting to $1,637 . . . and placed the one thousand dollars for bail." Levine, who thought of the five dollars he had borrowed, recalled that when he was arrested, he had only some small change in his pockets. Indeed, not every killer made "big money."

From youngsters like Levine, with backgrounds of dismal poverty, Murder, Inc., drew its troopers. But only a *tiny* faction of Brownsville's youth wanted to join the underworld organization, and even for them, it was not as easy as one might think. "To be recruited," said Reles, "you've got to have criminal tendencies. You begin as an independent and the big shots in The Syndicate keep an eye on you."

> They are just the same as employers in the shop. They see a man is very good and they give him a good job. Gang leaders may never talk to a prospective recruit until the moment of induction, but a man don't have to be on top of you to watch you. It's all up to the punk himself. You can't get into Murder, Inc., just by asking for it, or because you are related to some racketeer. You've got to have the caliber. . . . Then some gang chief, watching your good work, may say, "I think he's all right," and the kid is in.

When Reles was arrested by O'Dwyer, Brownsville's hard-faced youth, brandishing sticks and rakes, swarmed out of their poolrooms to poke through piles in vacant lots and rummage through the musty, cobwebbed cellars of abandoned buildings.

"You see," noted the New York *Sun,* "they are after big stakes—$75,000 in hard cash, the nest-egg Reles always boasted he had hidden away."

Everyone listened when Reles boasted about his hidden money. "Listen, mug," he often said, "I'm playing it smart. I got seventy-five thousand in cash and nobody but me knows where it is."

"Look, Kid," they responded, "why don't you stick it in a bank? Get one of them safe-deposit boxes."

Reles would laugh: "Yeah? Nuttin' doin'. That dough stays where it is. Why, with my reputation . . . the government would tie that up if anything happened to me."

"Look at Al Capone," he exclaimed. "Look where he ended up. After all he did, the G-men got him for taxes. Not me. I ain't takin' those chances. That dough'll stay where it is."

Reles's money became a favorite topic of conversation in Brownsville's gangland hangouts. Even some teen-agers hung around "de Kid hoping that he would someday slip and tell its location." Honor among thieves had its limit, and seventy-five thousand dollars in cash was considerably beyond that limit.

Reles's reputation always made him welcome at the popular bars. When "Kid Twist" was around, the drinks were free. He began, however, to notice that the liquor was coming faster and faster.

"Have one on me, Kid. Come on, have just another," was to be heard in more and more of the places he frequented.

He began to suspect and, according to local talk, he was correct. Everyone knew that liquor loosened his tongue, that he enjoyed talking about money. But Reles was too smart. Never a heavy drinker, he drank even less.

"Not me," he'd say, "and I ain't tellin' where it is." Indeed, the secret, if there was one, died with him.

On a sweltering summer evening in 1946, Louis and Ida Feldstein took their children, Thelma and Stanley, for a walk on the Coney Island Boardwalk. When the family reached the front of the Half-Moon Hotel, the elder Feldstein looked up to the fifth floor. "That's where it ended," he said.

"What are you talking about?" said the son.

"That's where they threw Abe Reles out of a window before he could testify."

"But I thought the police were guarding his room. How did they get in?" asked the daughter.

"*Shush* . . . , it's none of our business," said the father. "Here's twenty-five cents for the penny arcade. Mama and I will be sitting at the rail."

But Reles and the other Murder, Inc., assassins were only the enforcers. It was Louis "Lepke" Buchalter who conceived the idea and organized the squad of killers for The Syndicate. A rapacious thief who virtually owned New York City's small industries and trade unions in the 1930s, Lepke was one of the prime movers in the formation of warring mobs into nationwide cartel and was one of the half dozen most powerful figures in American crime.

When Burton Turkus looked into Louis "Lepke" Buchalter's eyes, he was "jarred." Unlike the other hoods', "they never hardened. . . ." This destroyed his theory that everyone in Murder, Inc., "had killers' eyes." As the undisputed head of the homicide ring, Lepke ordered the execution of over one hundred men.

J. Edgar Hoover called Lepke "the most dangerous criminal in America." Mark Sufrin was closer to the truth: "Make no mistake, Lepke was a criminal genius." He controlled more industries and had a firmer grip on more labor organizations than any other modern racketeer. He manipulated, all told, some 250 criminal ventures simultaneously, kept an eye on at least three hundred straw bosses, a corps of accountants and bookkeepers, and a staff of nutty triggers, strongarms, and industrial saboteurs, and other homicidal excesses—yet ordered the disposal of talkative witnesses ("No witnesses, no indictments. Simple," he used to say) or disobedient henchmen with all the blandness of a businessman getting rid of worn office fixtures.

The execution of Joseph Rosen, a garment-center trucker whom Lepke had put out of business, was proof of Sufrin's assertion. Rosen had spread the word that he was going to talk to Special Rackets Prosecutor Thomas Dewey unless he was "paid off." Lepke offered two hundred dollars; this, however, was not enough.

"I stood enough of this crap," he yelled. "That son of a bitch Rosen —he's around again talking about seeing Dewey. Not him or anybody is going to do any more talking."

Max Rubin, one of Lepke's garment-center straw bosses, never saw such rage. "Don't be foolish and do something that will get us into trouble, Louis," said Rubin. "Rosen just wants some cash."

"I'll give him dog crap. Nobody threatens me!"

Several days later, Rosen was killed. Mendy Weiss, one of the killers, told Lepke that "Pittsburgh Phil" Strauss, who did the actual killing, "acted like a crazy man. He just kept pulling the trigger until his gun was empty." "What's the difference," said Lepke, "as long as everyone is clean and got away all right?"

In anticipation of Dewey's investigation, Lepke sent Rubin, who knew all about his criminal operation, on a trip. First to Salt Lake City, then to the Catskill Mountains, and finally to New Orleans. In the midst of the traveling, however, Rubin "ducked" back to New York to see his family. Lepke became furious with each clandestine return to the city.

"Things are hot," he told Rubin. "You can't hang around."

Rubin agreed and left the city once more. "I won't sneak back again until you say its o.k.," he told his boss.

Several weeks later, Lepke was told that Rubin was back in town. "This guy," he said, "will get us killed. He's no longer an asset. Get rid of him."

"I saw Lepke standing under a dripping awning," remarked Rubin. "I went over to him, aware that something might happen."

"Why did you come back?" snapped Lepke.

"To see my family."

"How old are you, Max?" asked Lepke.

"I'm forty-eight."

"That's a ripe age."

Murder, Inc., shot Rubin in the head. One bullet was not enough to do the job, and Rubin's testimony would put Lepke in the electric chair.

Born in 1897 on the Lower East Side, "Lepkeleh," as his mother liked to call him (it means little Louis), was a rather shy youngster. After the death of his father and the break-up of his family—which moved west‡—he joined a group of neighborhood hoods who rolled drunks, picked pockets, and stole from pushcarts. It was in his "pushcart days" that he met Jacob "Gurrah" Shapiro ("Gurrah" was a contraction of the peddlers' yell, "Get out of here, Jake," when they caught him stealing fruit or other merchandise). The partnership in crime lasted more than thirty years.

‡ Lepke, who took a furnished room on the East Side, remained alone in New York.

In Lepke's rise to power, said one investigator, "he dreamed of the enslavement of meek garment workers, leatherworkers, painters, bakers, and the like—all easy prey." "With the rest of us," said Charles "Lucky" Luciano, "it was booze, gambling, whores, like that. But Lepke took the bread out of the worker's mouth." Buchalter saw more in his dealings with the labor unions and employers than just hiring out his troopers as *shtarkes*. "What can stop us from taking over an entire industry?" he once asked Shapiro. "The trick was a captive union and a captive trade association. That way you got both the boss and the worker in your pocket."

On one occasion, a labor organizer asked Lepke to "break some heads" of a few discontented union members. He did, and after the "rebellion" was over, he stayed on. He placed his own men in office and backed them up with the "gunsels" of Murder, Inc. That particular organizer was in no position to seek the aid of the police. Once inside, Lepke raised the dues, most of which he pocketed, rigged elections, and kept "rebels" in line with clubs and pipes.

"In the unions," reported Mark Sufrin, "this system never failed."

> The few who tried to get to the law with their stories got the acid treatment—in the face. It was difficult for even the guttiest men to stand up to the terror. They either quit the union or submitted. Lepke's system worked and became a legend. Within a few years, it gave him control over, among others—clothing workers, leatherworkers, bakery and pastry drivers, motion picture projectionists, flour and clothing truckers, taxis, the handbag and shoe industries, millinery, poultry . . . the income was prodigious. No official ever figured it out. $100 million is as far as law-enforcement accountants could come—a conservative estimate, they say.

In the same fashion that Lepke moved into the unions—through terror—he wedged his way into legitimate business. The employers who hired him and his troopers soon discovered that they had a partner. The courageous ones who tried to fight had their goods ruined by acid-throwers. "Send a 60-watter to So-and-So," he'd order (it was a vial of acid, a tear-gas bomb, or a stink bomb about the size of a light bulb). When a manufacturer surrendered, Lepke would place his men in the factory as managers or foremen, generally with an additional man "to help keep the books." Soon, he was telling the manufacturer where he could send his outside work on contract (he got a kick-back from selected contractors).

Even on Brooklyn's Pitkin Avenue, a major New York City clothing center, the mention of Lepke's name struck terror.

> . . . my shop was unionized. There was a strike before it happened and I went to Joey Amberg. . . . He sent down some boys to watch out for me. I paid Joey $50 a week.
>
> Anyway, when the strike is going on about a week, he comes to me and says he's sorry, but the union offered him $100 a week so he shouldn't keep his boys in my place. I tell him for a hundred it's cheaper to have the union, so I sign a contract.

"But Joey don't go away," said the owner. "Instead, he tells me I got to keep on paying him the fifty every week. I tell him I can't afford it, but he says I got to pay, and I pay him for almost six months. Then, one day he comes to me and he says I don't have to pay no more, but I better be careful."

> He says the gorilla boys have come to Brownsville and they told him and his brothers to lay off. For a while I don't pay any money. Then a fellow comes in and says he knows I been paying Joey. He wants to get money.

"I telephone Joey and I tell him. Joey tells me I better pay. These fellows, Joey says, are real tough guys, they work for Lepke. So I pay."

At the pinnacle of his power, Lepke was the feudal lord of New York's underworld. Even Albert Anastasia, high in The Syndicate hierarchy and boss of Murder, Inc., once quipped: "I don't ask Louis any questions. I just go along. It would be healthier that way."

By the time 1934 rolled around, Lepke helped organize The Syndicate. Sitting around an oval table, Lepke, Meyer Lansky, Johnny Torrio, Moe Dalitz, Nig Rosen, "Lucky" Luciano, Frank Costello, Phil Kastel, "Longie" Zwillman, and others decided that each boss would have his own territory, and there would be a loose working confederation with regional chiefs sitting together on the board of directors. It was Lepke who campaigned for a special enforcement group to keep the peace. He organized the gunsels of Murder, Inc., with Albert Anastasia as top sergeant to ride herd on the killers and assign contracts.

When Arthur "Dutch Schultz" Flegenheimer, who boasted that he "would do things his way," was killed, it was Charlie "the Bug" Workman and Mendy Weiss, two Murder, Inc., killers on orders from Lepke, who pulled the trigger. As soon as "The Dutchman" hit the ground, the mob started to grab: Luciano seized Schultz's numbers games and Lepke grabbed his restaurant protection racket. Schultz, who had threatened to kill Special Rackets Prosecutor Thomas Dewey, made Lepke nervous. "He'll have the whole world around our ears," he'd told Gurrah. "And that's no good."

At dusk, thousands of Harlem's citizens grabbed the evening papers. They read about the Schultz shooting and then turned to the sports pages to see what lucky number had won at Narragansett Park, in Rhode Island. They blinked with surprise. The winning number was 000. It hadn't turned up in four years.

"Triple zero!" a man standing on the corner of 7th Avenue and 117th street shouted. "That's Dutch's number. That means good-by Dutch. It's all over with that boy."

At 8:00 P.M., Dutch suddenly opened his eyes and shouted, "This is journey's end. It's death for me." His head dropped back onto the pillow. One of the doctors present pronounced him dead at 8:35 P.M. The next morning, every numbers regular read the time of death. They scrambled to get their money on what they thought was a sure winner: 835.

In November 1941, Lepke (sometimes called "The Judge" or "Judge Louis," but never to his face) had his criminal career ended—he was indicted for the murder of Joseph Rosen.

It was the testimony of Max Rubin, the one-time Lepke straw boss, that convinced the jury that "Judge Louis" ordered Pittsburgh Phil to carry out the execution.

Louis "Lepke" Buchalter was executed on March 4, 1944. To kill the three men convicted of Rosen's murder took approximately nine minutes.* The first to die, Lepke, one reporter noted, was quiet and unmoved as he was strapped into the electric chair. "Everything that followed," he wrote, "was anticlimactic after those first three minutes."

Benjamin "Bugsy" Siegel, unlike his colleague Lepke, was the archetype of the movie mobster. He was, according to author Mark Sufrin,

> handsome, hot-headed, the too ambitious kid out of the ghetto and on the rise, the petty thief and muscle man who became a sleek, powerful crime lord. A complex, charming murderer (who went into a rage when anyone called him "Bugsy"), he opened up Las Vegas for the mob, the man who partied with and bedded with movie stars. Bugsy was the hood who wanted "class." He loved a woman with crazy obsession, tried to cross the syndicate, and in the end was the first member of [The Syndicate's] board to be executed by his own. His words were prophetic.

* Also convicted were Mendy Weiss and Louis Capone. Phil Strauss, who actually pulled the trigger, was executed for another murder.

Once he told Del Webb, the contractor who built the Flamingo in Vegas for him, that he had probably killed as many as twenty men. When he saw Webb's startled look he laughed. "There's no chance you'll get killed, Del; we only kill our own.

One veteran New York City detective who dealt with them all— Dutch Schultz, Mendy Weiss, Abe Reles—said, "Bugsy was the worst. . . ."

> For ten bucks that Bugs-Meyer [Lansky] mob would break the arm of a man they'd never seen. They'd kill for less than fifty. Bugsy seemed to like to do the job himself. He just didn't give the orders or collect the payoff, that was more like Lansky's way. Bugsy enjoyed doing the blasting himself. It gave him a sense of power. He got his kicks out of seeing his victims suffering, groaning, and dying.

After Siegel left elementary school, he committed his first minor crimes. He snatched handbags from women, beat up drunks, stole from newspaper stands. As a sixteen-year-old, he gave his mother her share of *tsores* (worries). "I never sent Maurice to talk sense to Benjamin," said his mother, "because I was afraid for my younger son, my baby. Benjamin's temper, I knew. He would probably have beaten him up, or maybe worse, God forbid. So I sent the girls after him. But it didn't do any good. He wouldn't listen. He told the girls that he was a man and he wanted to lead his own life. A boy, he was. . . ."

By 1928, the Siegel-Lansky gang, known on the streets as the "Bugs-Meyer mob," sold protection to nightclubs, acted as troopers for Joe Adonis, Lucky Luciano, and Frank Costello, muscled-in on the labor unions, and dabbled in armed robbery, burglary, narcotics, and murder. When the national crime syndicate was formed, in 1934, Siegel, though only twenty-eight years old, became a "board member."

Known for his dependability as a "trouble shooter," he was soon chosen by The Syndicate to run their West Coast Operation. "Keep an eye on Nevada," Lansky told him. "They got legal gambling there."

For Siegel the West was an escape. "He hated the city that bred him," noted Sufrin, "was repelled by the gorillas he commanded. He killed, he once said, because he had to kill, but he knew that in the constant power struggle of the underworld, he'd be a target sooner or later. He hungered for respectability, the other side of the fence. California would change everything for him."

After several years of the fast Hollywood life, though he never forgot his mission for The Syndicate—to establish gambling, organize the narcotics traffic, exploit the rackets in the movie colony—he decided to move to Las Vegas.

"I've got a bitch of an idea," he told Meyer Lansky, "and the more I think about it, the hotter I get." He told Lansky that Las Vegas was a perfect spot for a fabulous gambling casino. "He envisioned himself," said a contemporary, "as *the* impresario of American gambling, with a casino surrounded by a plush hotel with all the elegant trimmings: nightclub, restaurant, bars, swimming pool, fine service, and exotic landscaping."

"Where'll your suckers come from?" asked Lansky.

"From L.A. at first. Then from all over. Hell, this joint'll have class. It'll be world-famous."

"Sounds like a lot of dough."

"Maybe a million or two. So what? Gambling's legal there and it'll stay that way. It's an investment. I swear I'll make it pay."

After the conversation, Lansky received The Syndicate's approval. He told Siegel to start the project. "You know," said Bugsy, "it'll be called Ben Siegel's Fabulous Flamingo."

"Call it any damned thing," replied Lansky, "but get it built."

The fact that the Flamingo was not an initial success did not bother The Syndicate chiefs. Siegel's threat to make Las Vegas his exclusive territory did. *"Fallo Furi!* Kill him," was Albert Anastasia's answer.

Lansky suggested another approach. "We owe Ben something," he told the board. "He's been with us through some rough days and he always did fine work . . . the Flamingo'll work. And there'll be a whole string of places. Let me go out and talk to him. If it doesn't work, I'll personally make the arrangements." Everyone agreed.

The Lansky-Siegel Las Vegas meeting was marked by bitter quarreling. Siegel would not listen to the advice of his associate. Rather, he told Lansky that the Flamingo was making it, that Las Vegas was his.

"I found it, made it, and I intend to keep it. It's all mine!" he shouted. "Screw The Syndicate. Screw you!"

"I had," said Lansky, some time later, "no choice."

On a warm June evening, a Murder, Inc., killer pointed a .30-caliber carbine at Siegel's face. The first round knocked out his right eye, smashing it against a wall. The other bullets weren't needed but were added for "good measure." Twenty minutes later, two Syndicate representatives, Moe Sedway and Gus Greenbaum, walked into the hotel and took over its operation.

In November 1972, a safe, buried in six inches of concrete, was discovered under a trap door in the Flamingo's executive suite. It took four hours to open. What secret, what treasure had Siegel hidden? Precisely nothing. It was empty. "It was," said Sufrin, "Bugsy's last prank."

CHAPTER VII

Struggle and Survival

THE NAZI FURY

AFTER Adolf Hitler came to power, American Jewry, safely guarded by the United States Constitution, had its first glimpse at Nazi tyranny. The terror began in March 1933, in Essen, Germany, when Jewish-owned shops were forced to display the swastika over their doors. This completed, brownshirted storm troopers stationed themselves at the entrance and "suggested" to shoppers that they "buy in German shops." The incident was repeated the next day in Kassel, Magdeburg, and Berlin.

Jacob Lestchinsky, the Berlin correspondent of the *Jewish Daily Forward,* was an eyewitness:

> One can find no words to describe the fear and despair, the tragedy that enveloped the German Jews. They are being beaten, terrorized, murdered, and to cap the climax, they are compelled to keep quiet. The Hitler regime flames up with anger because it has been compelled through fear of public foreign opinion to forego a mass slaughter of Jews. It threatens, however, to execute big pogroms if Jews in other countries make too much fuss about the pogroms it has hitherto indulged in.

In response to such reports, Julius Streicher, the Jew-baiting editor of *Der Stuermer,* called for sterner anti-Jewish measures.

> The Jew lies: "In Germany members of the Jewish people are being killed through cruel tortures."

The Jew lies: "In Germany even Jewish women are being killed in a horrible way and Jewish girls are being assaulted in the presence of their parents."

"The Jews spread these lies," he said, "in the same way and for the same purpose as they did during the [First World] War."

They want to excite the world against Germany. Moreover, they agitate for a boycott of German goods. The Jew thus wants to increase the misery of unemployment in Germany and ruin the German export trade.

German men and women! The instigators of this mad crime, this base atrocity and boycott are the Jews of Germany. They have called those of their race abroad to fight against the German people. They have reported lies abroad.

The leaders of the German movement of liberty have therefore decided to decree, in defense against this criminal agitation, a boycott of all Jewish stores [and] offices . . . to begin Saturday April 1st, at 10:00 A.M. We appeal to you, German women and men, to join this boycott. Do not buy from Jewish stores or department stores! Do not consult Jewish attorneys! Avoid Jewish physicians!

"The boycott is organized," wrote Goebbels in his dairy; "we need only press a button to set it going."

Tomorrow not a German man nor German woman shall enter a Jewish store. Jewish trade through Germany must remain paralyzed tomorrow. We shall then call a three-day pause in order to give the world a chance to recant its anti-German agitation. If it has not been abandoned at the end of that respite, the boycott will be resumed . . . until German Jewry has been annihilated.

As the most powerful Jewish community in the world, American Jewry were expected to come to the defense of their German brethren. Alfred Cohen, president of B'nai B'rith, called a meeting in New York City. There the "Big Three"—B'nai B'rith, the American Jewish Committee, the American Jewish Congress—and several other Jewish defense groups established a Joint Conference Committee to monitor the actions of the Nazi state. It was agree, for the time being, that public protest would be ruled out. "Direct action," said a participant, "would only increase the severity of the Nazi program."

After three weeks of co-operation, the major organizations split over the lack of public protest. "At one of the sessions," reported a B'nai B'rith spokesman, the representative of the American Jewish Congress insisted that public agitation should be sponsored. The . . . American Jewish Committee and B'nai B'rith believed such course unwise and . . . urged that such meetings sponsored by Jews would not help the situation. The representatives of the . . . Congress said that the Board of the Congress in charge of that branch of its activities insisted on such agitation meetings being held, and when the representatives of the B'nai B'rith and the American Jewish Committee in the Conference would not agree . . . the American Jewish Congress left the Conference. . . .

Congress leaders, joined by the militant Jewish War Veterans (JWV), announced a mass rally at New York's Madison Square Garden. "The time for caution and prudence is past," asserted Stephen Wise. "We must speak up like men."

How can we ask our Christian friends to lift their voices in protest against the wrongs suffered by Jews if we keep silent? . . . What is happening in Germany today may happen tomorrow in other lands on earth unless it is challenged and rebuked. It is not the German Jews who are being attacked. It is the Jews. We must speak out.

When Germany's Jewish spokesmen heard of the protest meetings sweeping America, they urged Wise to call them off. The charges against the German Government, they said, "are pure inventions and inexcusable distortions."* Wise replied that the request was "pitifully unconvincing. The denials," he asserted,

admit that there have been "acts of political revenge, also reprisals against Jews"; and it admits further that "the anti-Semitic aims in the various domains of life and business which are manufacturing themselves fill us, indeed, with grave concern. The [German-Jewish] Central Union goes on to say, however, that that is a "German domestic affair." This we in turn deny most vehemently.

Wise refused to cancel the Madison Square Garden meeting; neither would he stop the demonstrations scheduled in eighty other cities. "We have no quarrel with our Jewish brothers in Germany," he said, "but their policy of . . . super-cautious silence has borne evil fruit. They who have been virtually silent through the years of anti-Jewish propaganda cannot be followed by us as the wisest of counselors."

* There is no question that the Nazi regime had "something" to do with the request.

"That evening," recalled Marvin Goldstein, a student at New York University, "myself and fifty-five thousand other people, Jews and non-Jews, packed the Garden. I heard William Green of the AFL condemn Germany for trampling on the laws of humanity."

"It was quite a sight," he said, "when the Christians in the gathering joined us in cheering the words of Senator [Robert F.] Wagner, a German-American, and an Irishman named Alfred E. Smith.

"Too bad some of our own people weren't as militant as those two non-Jews," remarked Goldstein. "I have to admit, that I was lost for an answer when a woman sitting next to me, wearing a crucifix as big as my fist, asked: "Where's the B'nai B'rith and the American Jewish Committee? What are they doing?"

On March 20, those two organizations, in a joint statement, answered the woman's questions. "The American Jewish Committee and the B'nai B'rith," read a statement signed by Cyrus Adler and Alfred Cohen,

> . . . have requested the American Government to make proper representations to the government of Germany, and we pledge ourselves to continued and unremitting efforts in behalf of the Jews of Germany. We confidently hope that the enlightened opinion of the German people can be made aware of the gross injustice of these anti-Jewish actions and that they will demand the restoration of civilized standards in their own great nation.

The next morning, Patrick Sullivan, a California schoolteacher, read this statement in the *Los Angeles Times*. He placed his coffee cup down and looked over the top of his newspapers. "Are they kidding?" he asked his wife.

Mass rallies were one way to protest the rising tide of Nazi anti-Semitism. "They did not, however, have the impact we expected," said a participant in the Garden rally. "We needed something that would hurt—something dramatic—possibly a boycott of German-made goods."

America's anti-Nazi boycott movement was initiated after the March 1933 German elections and ended shortly after the Japanese attacked Pearl Harbor, in 1941. Though the smallest of the Jewish defense organizations, the Jewish War Veterans led the way. On April 10, 1933, a handful of ex-servicemen opened the doors of the first boycott office. "For Humanity's Sake," read its leaflet, "Don't Buy German Goods."

"If you believe in the doctrine of Life, Liberty and the Pursuit of

Happiness," stated its open letter to the public, "you will help our cause."

> The Jewish War Veterans of the United States, comprising men who fought in all the wars of our Republic, are conducting a national campaign of protest and enlightenment.
>
> The distribution of the enclosed seals is a part of our campaign. Please use them. If you believe our effort should be continued, a contribution from you will be appreciated.
>
> This is your battle as well as ours!

The JWVs were also the first to picket stores selling German-made products. "This tactic was," said former Army Sergeant Meyer Schwartz, "the most effective measure to keep a customer out of a store. Though other groups joined the boycott movement, our style—and make no mistake, we intended to break heads—set us apart from the others."

The "specialists" in "breaking heads" were quickly dubbed the "Anti-Nazi Minute-Men," and their publications, which at times were directed at "Jewish traitors," minced no words. "Parasites must be treated as such," read one of their leaflets, and "stern action will be taken with those fellow Jews who, for monetary gains . . . place profit above principle. . . ." "Jews who entered establishments selling German goods," said Schwartz, "would be rejected by their neighbors and business associates."

The militancy of the JWV helped create the image of the fighting Jew—something that had always been lacking in America. Realistically, the JWV, when compared to the Non-Sectarian Anti-Nazi League to Champion Human Rights† (NSAL or ANL) or the major Jewish boycott organizations, lacked the numbers to make a lasting impression, and, it fell to other groups—specifically the ANL—to lead the boycott fight.

From its establishment, in 1933, the anti-Nazi boycott movement welcomed non-Jewish support. The two outstanding non-Jewish boycott groups were the American Federation of Labor and the Volunteer Christian Committee to Boycott Nazi Germany (VCC).

William Green, the powerful AFL president, had promised his Madison Square Garden audience that the labor movement "will not remain passive . . . when the relatives, families and brethren of [our]

† Originally called the American League for the Defense of Jewish Rights (ALDJR).

Jewish members . . . are being persecuted and oppressed." Though the giant labor federation maintained an independent posture and declined invitations to co-ordinate their efforts with the NAL or the American Jewish Congress, Green kept his promise. In October 1933, the federation's Executive Council passed the following resolution:

> . . . because the Hitler Government refused to heed or respect the protests of the people in all nations . . . the AFL join[s] with other public-spirited organizations in our country in officially adopting a boycott against German-made goods and German services. . . .

As the decade wore on, American Christian scholars, who had remained on the side lines of the boycott movement, began to agitate for an organization of their own. Shocked by the news of Nazi atrocities, they, too, felt it was high time to stand up and be counted. Organized by Christopher T. Emmet, Jr., a free-lance writer, and Dr. William J. Schieffelin, chairman of New York's Citizens Union, sixty influential Christians established, on January 9, 1939, the Volunteer Christian Committee (VCC).

Schieffelin, chairman of the VCC, declared that his organization was formed to restrain Hitler and act "as the symbol of our own unity against prejudice and intolerance here. The movement," he said,

> is in the oldest American tradition. Long before the word boycott was used, our forefathers made great sacrifices in enforcing a general embargo against trade with Great Britain. The purpose of a widespread voluntary boycott is to bring the Nazis to their senses or else to justify our government in declaring an embargo.

Soon, representatives of the VCC approached the AFL and suggested that the two groups join forces to strengthen and consolidate their efforts. Green, however, anxious to maintain his organization's independence, declined the offer. Still wishing to build a formidable movement, the Christian leaders joined with two other groups: the American Boycott Against Aggression and the Joint Boycott Council. The new organization, known as the Coordinated Boycott Committee, remained active until the United States entered the war.

While Jewish, Christian, and non-religious boycott groups were mushrooming, the American Jewish Committee and B'nai B'rith, though expressing their anguish at Germany's "Jewish policy," still opposed public action. They did, however, continue to pressure President Roosevelt. Even B'nai B'rith felt it was time, in light of the government's inaction, to re-examine its anti-Nazi activities. In 1937, they witnessed their lodges in Germany seized and their order abolished; in 1938, they read of the terror of the *Kristallnacht;* and in 1939, they finally saw in the boycott a way to strike back at fascism.

The American Jewish Committee still refused to join the boycott movement and remained the only Jewish defense organization opposed to public action. "The Jews," asserted a confidential statement circulated among sustaining members, "must be concerned for the likely effects of the boycott in the future." As they were to discover, that future carried the code name of "the Final Solution."

In the midst of the boycott controversy, which began in 1932, the American Jewish community received news of the Nazi onslaught that surpassed anything that Germany had previously done. On the evening of July 15, 1935, approximately two hundred storm troopers, dressed in civilian clothes, descended upon Berlin's stylish Kurfürstendamm and savagely attacked anyone who "looked Jewish." Shouting "out with the Jews," the rioters were free to kick and beat anyone and everyone. "It was," said a newspaper correspondent, "the worst anti-Semitic attack since Hitler came to power."

Varian Fry, editor of *The Living Age,* was an eyewitness:

> I was informed at about eight o'clock last night that there was an anti-Jewish demonstration on the streets. I hurried out and presently heard shouting toward the east end of the Kurfürstendamm.
>
> When I got there I found a large crowd lined up on both sides of the street, forcing each car which came by to run the gauntlet, stopping all cars in which Jewish-looking men or women were riding, and dragging out the Jews and beating them up. . . .
>
> Nowhere did the police seem to make any effort whatever to save the victims from this brutality. Occasionally, they attempted to clear areas for motor traffic to get through or to prevent the crowds from collecting in front of certain . . . cafes. That was all. All along the Kurfürstendamm, the crowd raised the shout "Jude!" whenever anyone sighted or thought he had sighted a Jew. The cry sent the crowd converging on the poor victim, who was asked for his identification papers. If he could not prove himself a good "Aryan" he was insulted, spat upon, roughly handled, and sometimes knocked down, kicked and beaten.
>
> The cry "Jude!" would be raised at another point and the crowd would hurry off to a new victim.

"Everywhere," reported Fry,

the people were in a holiday mood; in fact, one German youth said to me, "This is a holiday for us." Old men and young men, boys, Storm Troopers, police, young girls of the domestic servant type, well-bred women, some even in the forties and over, all seemed to be having a good time.

This morning as I walked along the Kurfürstendamm to inspect the broken glass, I passed in half an hour eight or ten persons, . . . obviously Jews, with bandaged heads, and fresh slings of plaster over their noses.

This was a sight I never had seen in Berlin before. It pretty obviously was connected with last night's circus.

The Berlin riot of 1935, which sparked the racist Nuremberg Laws, shocked America's Jewish defense organizations. The American Jewish Congress and the Jewish Labor Committee were the first to act. In a joint communication, they urged "all Jewish organizations, societies, groups and all opponents of the Hitler Regime of whatever creed or class to meet in Emergency Conference. . . ."

The meeting, which was attended by representatives of almost one thousand groups, called for an intensified boycott of "the products and services of Nazi Germany"; sanctions to be imposed by the League of Nations; a rejection by America's Amateur Athletic Union (AAU) and Olympic Committee of Germany's invitation to the 1936 Berlin games; and a refusal by American universities to "exchange . . . professors and students. . . ."

The meeting did not produce a unified front. "A small but disciplined group made up of Communists," said an observer, "began to yell." They shouted at the speakers, especially Abe Cahan, and started to throw punches. "I think we went after the Communists first," said another participant. "No matter, I got a broken nose and the meeting ended in chaos."

When the American Jewish Congress met later that month, the incident was discussed. The Congress wanted to know why, in the midst of the Nazi tyranny, Jews were still fighting Jews:

Discussing the admission of [the] Communists to the meeting . . . Mr. Lipsky stated that the call to the conference was issued to all Jewish organizations, without any direct invitations being sent. "If we are calling a conference of Jews, of Jewish organizations and their representatives, has anyone the right to say, 'We exclude the Communists' without telling them in advance?" The question raised was whether we should exclude them at the door or admit them and hope that order would be maintained. By majority vote it was decided to admit them and try to keep them in order.

"The disorder created," said Lipsky, "was not related to the meeting itself but to an argument between Abe Cahan and the Communists which had nothing to do with the meeting. It was unfortunate that it should have had its outlet at this meeting."

In the aftermath of the meeting, the major organizations, in a rare display of unity,‡ sought the assistance of the State Department and the President. "Franklin Roosevelt," said an observer, "unlike past American presidents, was slow to bring diplomatic pressure. For months we searched the newspapers for a statement—nothing! When it finally came it was, to say the least, feeble."

"We have sought by every legitimate means," Roosevelt told the Congress of the United States on May 3, 1936, "to exert our moral influence against repression, against intolerance, and against autocracy, and in favor of freedom of expression equally before the law. . . ." After hearing these remarks on the radio, Sylvia Meyer, who proudly displayed "my President's picture on the living room wall," was puzzled. "Oh, well," she said, "at least Mayor La Guardia is doing something."

After the Berlin riot, New York's gentile mayor, Fiorello H. La Guardia, refused to issue a masseur's license to a German citizen. The denial was protested by the German Consul General, who maintained that the mayor's action was a breach of the 1935 German-American treaty. "Germany and America" said the diplomat, "guaranteed certain reciprocal privileges and in this case a German national was being denied his rights." La Guardia couldn't have agreed more but claimed that American Jews were being denied the very same privileges in Germany. "The Consul General certainly can't complain to City Hall," quipped the mayor, "because I am City Hall." Despite some pressure from the State Department, the "Little Flower" remained firm—he flatly refused to issue the license. "La Guardia" said one New Yorker, "belongs in the White House."

While La Guardia was registering his protest against Nazi tyranny, the nations of the world were preparing to send their finest athletes to the 1936 Berlin Olympics. Samuel Untermeyer, president of the Anti-Nazi League, appealed to America's athletes, especially Jewish ones,

‡ The American Jewish Congress, the American Jewish Committee, B'nai B'rith and the Jewish Labor Committee, in order to bring pressure on the American Government, created the Conjoint Consultative Council.

not to participate. He also charged the American representatives to the International Olympic Committee (IOC), in their eagerness to accept Germany's invitation, with glossing "over the race discrimination issue."

"My advice to the athletes and others of world Jewry," he said,

> is not only [not] to compete, but to keep away as far as possible from any form of participation in the Olympic Games. . . .
>
> Out of decent consideration for their race, it is unthinkable that any self-respecting Jew would accept the hospitality of a country that persists in so insulting, degrading and persecuting our people. Any with a Jewish ancestor, with a drop of Jewish blood in his veins, who crosses Germany's border, or accepts its hospitality, is deserving only of the contempt of his fellow-men, be they Jews or Christians.

Brooklyn Congressman Emanuel Celler also rebuked Avery Brundage, president of the American Olympic Committee (AOC), for failing to consider Nazi persecution of Jewish athletes. "In your article in . . . *Olympic News*," he told Brundage, "you urge the youth of the United States with athletic talent to bend their energies to the task of winning a place on the American team, and with a fanfare . . . made much of the fact the German Committee is making every effort to provide the finest facilities. . . . You, apparently, have prejudiced the issue."

Brundage dismissed Celler's protest. "I feel," he told the delegates to the AAU convention, "that since we have received unqualified assurances of non-discrimination from German athletic leaders, we should waive further argument and go ahead with Olympic plans. Both sides have had every opportunity to uphold all principles upon which the Olympic Games are based. I do not feel anything is to be gained by further agitation."

Brundage could not dismiss the issue with this glib comment. As the athletic contest drew nearer, the question of American participation became a national controversy. People and institutions from every area of American life—scholars, athletes, political spokesmen, labor leaders, church officials—soon were drawn into the argument, demanding that the United States withdraw from the games.

The Catholic War Veterans urged the AOC to reverse its position, and the *Christian Century* demanded that the Olympic site be transferred to another country. *Commonweal,* a Catholic publication, went a step further: it called for a boycott. "Participation in the approaching games," it told its readers, "means endorsement of wilful and violent persecution." The Catholic clergy, it said, should "warn the faithful concerning the issue involved so that no Catholic young man or his friends unwittingly gives to enemies of our faith [the] opportunity to question the sacred solidarity of the Christian belief." Even Father Coughlin, the Jew-baiting Chicago priest, urged his followers to stay away from the games. "Religionists of every type," he told his parish, "hardly feel free to go to Germany as long as the Germans prefer to patronize paganism. We suppose that the American athlete will not be too anxious to participate in the Olympic Games next year if the Hitler Government remains unfair in its treatment of every religion except his own."

As opening day drew near, the list of anti-Olympic spokesmen mushroomed. In the United States Senate, the representatives from Rhode Island and Massachusetts urged withdrawal; Celler pleaded with his House colleagues to prohibit the use of public and semipublic funds by the AOC; and the Friends of Democracy, a group of German-Americans, held a meeting in New York City's Yorkville, a German-American community rife with Nazi ideology, where they went on record against a "Nazi-sponsored Olympics."

Also joining the protest was the Committee on Fair Play in Sports, an *ad hoc* group that attempted to discourage American athletes from going to Germany. Its leaders, who included such notables as Henry Leiper, secretary of the Federal Council of Churches of Christ; Oswald Garrison Villard, former publisher of *The Nation;* Mary Woolley, president of Mt. Holyoke College; and James Curley, governor of Massachusetts, were convinced that the games would be "violated by open or concealed discrimination. . . . Germany is deliberately planning to use the Olympic Games to promote its political prestige. . . ."

Charles H. Sherill, America's leading IOC representative, dismissed the protests—Jewish and non-Jewish alike. He did, however, have special words for his Jewish "friends."

> As to obstacles placed in the way of Jewish athletes or any others in trying to reach Olympic ability, I would have no more business discussing that in Germany than if the Germans attempted to discuss the Negro situation in the American South or the treatment of the Japanese in California.
>
> I am surprised at the extent to which the movement to keep America out of the Olympic Games has gone in this country. I am

sorry that what I have done has not pleased all of my Jewish friends. . . . But I shall go right on being pro-Jewish, and for that reason, I have a warning for American Jewry.

"There is grave danger in this Olympic agitation," he warned the Jewish community.

Consider the effect on several hundred thousand youngsters training for this contest throughout the United States, if the boycott movement gets so far that they suddenly are confronted with the fact that somebody is trying to defeat their ambitions to get to Berlin. . . . We are almost certain to have a wave of anti-Semitism among those who never gave it a thought, and who may consider that about 5,000,000 Jews in this country are using the athletes representing 120,000,000 Americans to work out something to help the German Jews.

In answering Sherill, the Committee on Fair Play accused him of making the games a purely Jewish issue. "This issue," they said, "is not Jewry against Germany, but fair play." They reminded him that it was not only Jews who were being denied participation in the Games "but also Catholic and Protestant sport clubs which [did] not accept Nazi doctrines. . . ."

In response to the attacks, the AOC published a sixteen-page pamphlet. Its contents reflect the pitch the controversy reached. In an opening statement of *Fair Play for American Athletes,* Brundage wrote:

. . . the future of amateur sport in the United States is now being threatened as a result of the efforts of certain individuals and groups to involve sport in foreign political affairs, and keep American athletes out of the Olympic Games. It becomes the duty of those charged with the administration of amateur sport to fight off this invasion. *Shall the American athlete be made a martyr to a cause not his own?*

Despite all the agitation, a number of American Jewish athletes turned up in Berlin. Among them were sprinters Marty Glickman and Sam Stoller, members of the championship relay team; David Mayer, a weight lifter; Sam Balter, a basketball player; bobsledder Max Bly; and Hyman Goldberg, a baseball player who was in the line-up for an exhibition game. Only New York's 92nd Street "Y," in a last-minute decision, withdrew its athletes. "The Nazis will not be given the opportunity to insult these Jewish athletes," said a spokesman.

American Jewish participation in the games was not without its anti-Semitic incident. "When the American track coach replaced Glick-man and Stoller on the 400-meter relay," said one observer, "we all felt that certain pain that every Jew feels when a *member of the tribe* is kicked. Some say it was a tactical move, not motivated by politics but because the two sprinters weren't ready that day. Most of us knew that was *bullshit!* It was a last-minute decision and we knew it had to be be-cause a victory by Jews would be an embarrassment to *certain* people." When Glickman was asked about the sudden switch, he replied: "Sure, Jesse Owens and Ralph Metcalfe were faster than Sam and I, but we would have won the championship anyway."

Once the Committee on Fair Play was convinced that their fight was lost, as a protest they sent a group of athletes to Spain to participate in the Peoples Olympics. The Jewish Labor Committee carried the sym-bolic protest even further. Under the direction of Charles Ornstein, a Jewish Olympiad was staged on New York's Randall's Island. "Here we didn't allow any Nazis to compete," quipped a spectator. "I guess that made us even."

Within two years after the Olympics controversy, American Jewry witnessed the most brutal anti-Jewish terror of the decade. In Novem-ber 1938, Herschel Grynszpan, a young Polish Jew whose parents had been sent to a Nazi labor camp, walked into the German Embassy in Paris and killed the Third Secretary, Ernst vom Rath. Several days later, German Jewry was subjected to the most vicious pogrom in the Third Reich's history: the *Kristallnacht* ("The Night of the Broken Glass").

"It was a well-planned assault," remarked a newspaper reporter who witnessed the terror. "And there was little doubt that the Paris incident was simply an excuse to unleash the animals." Synagogues were burned, Jewish shops were looted, and gangs of Nazi criminals roamed the streets attacking foreign and native-born Jews. "This madness," recalled Max Greenberg, an American Jew who was visiting his family, "signaled the end of German Jewry."

The horror of the *Kristallnacht* evoked a chorus of protests in America. Few American leaders could remain silent. Al Smith, former governor of New York and past presidential aspirant, addressed the American people over NBC radio. "The German people," he said, "are incapable of living under a democratic government. The French might have been right in 1919—perhaps we do not know the Germans." Thomas E. Dewey, the crime-busting New York district attorney, voiced similar sentiments: "The civilized world," he told his audience, "stands revolted by the bloody pogrom against a defenseless people . . . by a nation run by madmen."

The anti-Nazi boycott, which had been rather sporadic in the years since 1933, suddenly gained renewed life. The importation of German-manufactured toys was brought to a halt by a group of New York importers, as were other products that bore the stamp MADE IN GERMANY. Quickly, people began to respect "the moral embargo." In every large city, pledges were signed by some exporters not to sell American materials and merchandise to the Nazis, announcements were made by prominent political and religious organizations to lend their support to the boycott, and signatures were collected, the goal being five million, of those who refused to "buy German."

Thousands of letters and telegrams flooded the White House demanding an end to German imports. Some of these communications reminded the President that another Roosevelt—Theodore—had acted quickly and forcefully in 1904, when the czarist murderers sanctioned similar anti-Semitic pogroms. Roosevelt, however, remained cautious in those first days following the *Kristallnacht* madness. "All we could get out of him," commented one reporter from the Yiddish press, "was a statement that he was 'deeply shocked' by the riots. But I must admit he did recall our ambassador from Berlin, and this move left little doubt in Berlin where his sympathies were."

German radio, of course, responded to the President's action with its usual anti-Semitic rhetoric. "America is a country burdened with unemployment," it told its listeners,

> . . . [and] its public affairs agitated and disturbed by corruption and scandals and its foreign policy guided by persons who go from one failure to another; a President who gives free rein to international troublemakers [Jews] and is backed by a Jewish influence seeking profit from a colossal rearmament.

Though the German propagandists portrayed Roosevelt as a "Jewish agent," the fact remains that the President, aside from recalling Ambassador Wilson from Berlin, took no effective action. After the *Kristallnacht,* Roosevelt became preoccupied with other things: rearmament and the European war. "The Jewish question," said an observer, "sank low on his list of priorities. Unfortunately, too many people, so comfortable in the safety of America, also pushed the memory of the *Kris-*

tallnacht to the back of their minds." Most also forgot historian Konrad Heiden's prophecy: "Sooner or later the consequences will come."

HOME-GROWN FASCISM

In 1933, the year FDR first occupied the White House, there were no fewer than 103 fascist organizations in America. Imitating the Nazi Brownshirts and the black-shirted Italians, these organizations dubbed themselves the Silver Shirts, the Blue Shirts, the Khaki Shirts, the White Shirts, and similar prosaic names. While many of these "shirt societies" were American in origin—the result of conditions in a depression-ridden land—a number of them were directly tied to Hitlerian Nazism.

"When Fritz Kuhn's German-American Bund marched in [New York City's] Yorkville," recalled Morris Rabb, a plumber from Manhattan, "East Eighty-sixth Street wasn't the most hospitable place. . . . There weren't any actual JUDEN VERBOTEN posters on the walls, but to many of us they seemed to be there just the same. Nazi songs shouted in the *Honaratiorenstuben* filled the air."

Yorkville, which runs from East Seventy-ninth up to East Ninety-sixth streets, was a hot-bed of Brownshirt activity. "It wasn't a pretty sight," said Rabb. "American-style storm troopers of the Amerika-Deutsche Bund paraded down the streets, arms raised in the Nazi salute, and swastikas were displayed everywhere. Sometimes, emissaries from Berlin drew huge crowds on Eighty-sixth Street . . . addressing rallies of *Auslandsdeutche* [Germans living abroad] on the evils of American Jewry. You could hear the cheering for blocks."

When the German-American *Vereins* and *Stammtische* expelled their Jewish members and "Gruppenführer" Fritz Kuhn assailed the Jews for the anti-Nazi boycott, he was cheered wildly. "The Jews in Germany," Kuhn once told a Yorkville gathering, "will be treated accordingly." Even those in his audience not wearing the Nazi arm band applauded the statement. Yorkville, for New York Jewry, was indeed an everyday reminder of the terror their German coreligionists faced. "That community" remarked Rabb, "had simply gone mad."

The most shocking Nazi demonstration came on February 20, 1939, when some twenty thousand people crowded into Madison Square Garden to hear Kuhn extoll the virtues of National Socialism. He spoke, ostensibly in celebration of George Washington's birthday, against a backdrop of the first President's picture, anti-Semitic signs, swastikas, and American flags. Hitler was "heiled," Roosevelt was booed, and mention of Father Coughlin's name brought thunderous applause. "Some fifty uniformed storm troopers," noted one newspaperman, "tried to eject Dorothy Thompson [a noted journalist] when she laughed loudly as one of the speakers declared that white Gentiles lived by the Golden Rule as a result of inborn racial virtues."

Prior to the rally, Garden officials were brought under strong pressure to refuse the Bund the use of the auditorium to desecrate Washington's memory. "Other groups and individuals," noted an observer, "including the American Jewish Committee, felt nevertheless that the Bund was entitled to free speech and assembly." Mayor La Guardia agreed, and ordered fifteen hundred policemen to protect the Bund's right to peaceful assembly.

Most of the nation's press supported La Guardia's decision. The Cincinnati *Times-Star* declared: "We believe [the mayor] showed a proper appreciation of free speech when he permitted the New York meeting to be held." And the Baltimore *Sun* paid tribute to "New York's finest":

> Thanks to the presence of many hundred of policemen, the rally Monday evening in New York's Madison Garden was a relatively decorous affair. Such order as was in evidence was due to the patience and competence of the professional policemen and not to the fake troopers inside nor to the milling mobs on the outside. . . . The German-American Bund has as much right as any group, orthodox or dissident, to hold a meeting and expound its doctrines.

Though they deplored the meeting, the editors of the Atlanta *Constitution* added:

> The meeting was called in honor of George Washington, for which all Americans offer their sincere apologies. It couldn't be helped. There is still the Bill of Rights that guarantees these strangers to the American ideal the protection of the very things they would destroy.

A minority of press opinion, however, felt the rally should have been banned. "Mayor La Guardia," stated an editorial in the Indianapolis *Star,* "must shoulder the blame for the un-American gathering . . . under the perverted notion of free speech. Far milder remarks made in Germany against Nazis would result in prompt imprisonment of the offender." "Why Must We Endure It?" asked the Detroit *Free Press,* expressing amazement that the American people stood for such "an impertinent insult to the memory of the first president."

The New York *Post* took a simpler but more straightforward position: "Had the meeting been banned, it would be the livest issue in New York today and for many weeks to come. Now the farce is over." Out of the city's seven million people, reported the *Post,* only thirty thousand, twenty inside and ten thousand hecklers outside, were involved. "The remaining ninety-nine and five eighths percent of the people," they said, "stayed home, listened to the radio, had friends in for dinner, went to the movies, or sat up with a nice new mystery novel. By doing that they said, 'Pooh, Pooh!' to the Bundists louder than if they had come to the Garden in person."

Dorothy Thompson and Ernest L. Meyer, however, two well-known columnists who attended similar rallies in Berlin, saw the spectacle as an ill omen. Thompson declared that the meeting should have been stopped, and Meyer, an ardent advocate of civil liberties, had misgivings. Both were worried that American liberalism might pave the way for the growth of Nazism. "I saw an exact duplicate of it in the Berlin Sport Palace in 1931," said Thompson:

> That meeting was also "protected" by the police of the German Republic. Three years later the people who were in charge of that meeting were in charge of the government of Germany, and the German citizens against whom, in 1931, exactly the same statements had been made as were tonight . . . were beaten, expropiated and murdered.

Meyer also recalled attending a Nazi rally in Berlin. At that time, he told his American colleagues that Hitler would never win out. "The Germans," he said, "are intelligent; they will let him go his way, for the Weimar Republic upholds freedom of speech, and good Germans know that Hitler will go nowhere."

After the Garden rally, however, he was not so quick to make the same prophecy. "All that I know is that witnessing this shocking demonstration I feel fearful for the future, less confident than I did in Berlin years ago."

At the peak of the anti-Semitic rhetoric, Isidore Greenbaum, a young New York Jew who managed to gain entrance to the rally, was gripped by anger. As he listened to Kuhn speak in front of the giant picture of Washington, his eyes caught a glimpse of the American flag, flying side by side with the swastika. Suddenly, unable to restrain himself any longer, he bolted up the aisle; the microphone was his target. He was going to tell the crowd that Kuhn was lying, that Nazism was evil. He was going to speak for his Jewish brethren. As he reached the foot of the platform, two brownshirted storm troopers grabbed him. Several others joined the melee and kicked him to the floor. The beating continued until the police reached the scene. Greenbaum went home that evening with a firsthand taste of Nazi brutality.

"I lost my head at the meeting," he said later.

> When I heard the abuse of President Roosevelt and the attack on the Jews made beneath the portrait of George Washington, who above all things stood for freedom of religion, I felt that the insults to our flag and to democracy were such as no red-blooded American could stand and so I came suddenly to the conclusion that I would rush on the stage and get to the microphone and cry that the speakers were lying. Before I knew what had happened I was attacked by storm troopers, was pummeled and buffeted and had my hair pulled, and if it had not been for the police, who deserve great credit, I do not think I should be here today.

The next morning, New York's official Bund newspaper, the *Deutscher Weckruf und Beobachter,* carried an eight-column streamer headline: JEWISH GUNMAN ATTACKS FRITZ KUHN, with the following subheads:

> Isidore Greenbaum flourishing gun
> knocked down by O.D. men
>
> Madison Square Garden Rally a smashing
> Bund hit
>
> Garden filled to top
>
> Thousands turned back
>
> Unprecedented enthusiasm for Christian
> Patriotic Americanism
>
> Stormy Applause Greets Father Coughlin's
> Name
>
> Notorious Dorothy Thompson Put Out

The Bundists distorted Greenbaum's courageous action, calling it "an attack upon the life of Fritz Kuhn. . . . Only the prompt action of the O.D. men, assisted by policemen, fortunately frustrated the event," declared their newspaper. "Eyewitnesses reported seeing the Jew aiming a gun at Kuhn, the gun being knocked out of the hand of the would-be assassin by the hard-hitting fist of a brave O.D. man."

"Not one reporter covering the event," said a non-Nazi journalist, "reported an assassination attempt, [and] no gun was found on Greenbaum or on the stage. The only charge the police made was disorderly conduct." When Abe Messner, a Bronx candy-store owner, heard of the incident, he remarked: "Too bad the kid didn't have a gun."

After the rally, La Guardia took steps to prevent the use of storm troopers at future Nazi meetings. He directed the various municipal agencies—fire, police, health, and housing—to warn building owners of their responsibility for the public's safety. "Under no circumstances," he said, "are organizations to be permitted to use their own guards or other persons for the ostensible purpose of preserving order. Owners will be required to use their own ushers when needed. . . ." In another move, undoubtedly to annoy the Bund, he ordered Jewish and black policemen to guard Nazi speakers and parade routes. "In the future," quipped a reporter, with tongue in cheek, "those who attended Yorkville's Nazi meetings would have to *endure* the protection of *racially inferior* policemen."

La Guardia's directives were not the only result of the Garden spectacle. A week after the rally, New Yorkers answered the Nazi "supermen" with a demonstration of their own—at Carnegie Hall. Among the notables who sat on stage, without the benefit of police protection, were La Guardia, Lieutenant Governor Charles Poletti, Congressman Bruce Barton, Dorothy Thompson, and Justice Jeremiah T. Mahoney. "No more effective answer to Fritz Kuhn's American Hitlerites can be imagined," wrote the New York *Herald Tribune,* "than the meeting at Carnegie Hall."

There were others, however, who wanted to answer the Bundists not with words but with lead pipes. Judd Teller, a reporter for the Yiddish press, received a telephone call from a Murder, Inc., trooper asking for the names of the Nazi "bastards that should be rubbed out." He forwarded the message to some New York Jewish leaders, who, in turn, told him that if this were done, they would call the police. When the reporter relayed the reply, the trooper simply said: "Tell them to keep their shirts on. OK, we won't ice the bodies; only marinate them."

"Marination," wrote Teller in *Strangers and Natives* (1968),

> began within a week. It was a miniature re-enactment of the night when God struck all the first-born in Egypt. All Nazi meetings in New York's Yorkville and Ridgewood sections, in Staten Island, in

Hoboken and Bergen County, New Jersey, were invaded suddenly one evening. Men inside, and strategically deployed outside, glanced at their synchronized watches and went into action everywhere at the same minute. Leaping from their seats, they lunged at the speakers at the precise time that their confederates outside rushed the unsuspecting sentries at the doors and burst inside. A third segment of the invading force had climbed the fire escapes and was entering through the windows. They worked expertly and with dispatch on a ten-minute schedule, causing no fatalities, no permanent injuries, only several dislocated limbs, many bloodied heads and noses, and a great deal of damage requiring dental attention. Like commandos, they were gone before the police could arrive. It was sufficient "marination" to have drastically reduced, for a while, attendance at these meetings and to have discouraged Christian Fronters and Bundists from appearing in uniform singly in the streets.

While New York Jewry was watching the activities of Kuhn's Yorkville Bundists, their coreligionists elsewhere were faced with similar crusades. In St. Louis, The Friends of Hitler, referred to by locals as "the Hitler Club," organized a boycott of Jewish stores. "Boycott the Jews," read the leaflet of the St. Louis Bundists. "Help Patriotic America Recapture the USA."

> Who is responsible for the Depression?
> The Jewish Banker.
> Who lets Gentile workers starve?
> The Jewish Industrialists.
> Who pays starvation wages?
> The Jewish SweatShop Owner.
> Don't expect relief. Too many Jews
> are in Government. Drive them out. . . .

By 1937, the St. Louis paramilitary organization German-American *Volksbund* stepped up their activities. In the summer of that year they established a camp, consisting of a single building on an acre of land, and trained young recruits "for the fight against Jewry and communism." At its opening ceremony, Bund members, wearing black pants, white shirts, and Nazi arm bands, listened to Dr. Gustav Mosen, a St. Louis dentist, shout "Heil Hitler—death to the Jews."

Marching under a swastika, which flew alongside the Stars and Stripes, more than one hundred Brownshirts vented their anti-Jewish hatred. When asked about their purpose by the local press, they proudly answered: "We are organized along purely American lines. We lay stress on German culture and uphold the constitution of this country. We believe in our government and that it can't be beat by any in the world. We are opposed to communism and to the Jewish boycott against German-made goods."

"Membership in the organization," added Anton Kessler, a group leader, "is for those with German blood; no Jews—no Negroes." When a reporter pressed him for the names of the officers, Kessler hesitated: "For economic reasons," he said, "I am not at liberty to tell you."

Since many of them were aliens, Kessler feared that membership in the organization might deny them the right to American citizenship. When the St. Louis *Star-Times* asked William Wolf, the divisional director of the Immigration Bureau, about this, he replied that "being a Nazi or a member of a pro-Nazi group is not enough to bar someone from American citizenship." When discussing Kessler and his activities as a storm trooper, Wolf again declared: "There is no reason why this bureau should become interested in his activities in pro-Nazi organizations. Even if he came in here and said he was a Nazi organizer, there is nothing we could do about it."

While St. Louis Jewry were witnessing the growth of their local Bund, they saw another threat to their safety in the form of Gerald L. K. Smith. Long active in the Midwest, Smith's America First Party launched an organizing campaign, holding rallies from St. Louis to Baltimore. At every one of his meetings, he warned Jews to stop their anti-Nazi agitation. Writing in his personal journal, the *Cross and Flag* of a recent anti-Semitic outbreak in Boston, he said, "What has taken place [there] is just a pimple on the skin of our great body politic. Similar outbreaks can be expected in every great center." More important, he threatened to establish a political party that would nominate a true "nationalist" if neither the Democrats nor the Republicans chose an America Firster for President, and advocated Charles A. Lindbergh, the heroic aviator, for the position.

Lindbergh, who became the darling of the isolationists, shocked many Americans—especially Jews—when, in his notorious Des Moines, Iowa, speech, he charged the Jews, along with the British and Roosevelt, as being one of the "most important groups . . . pressing this country toward war. . . ." Of the three, said Lindbergh, the Jews were "the most dangerous," because of "their large ownership plus influence on motion pictures, on press, on radio, and on government." The Des Moines *Register,* which commented on the speech the next day, noted that Lindbergh's audience reacted with mingled boos and cheers, adding that the reference to Jewish influence "brought out particularly heavy booing and applause."

Even the legitimate isolationist press, those newspapers against American involvement in the European conflict, agreed that Lindbergh's remarks were "inexpedient." "Mr. Lindbergh is no longer a dangerous enemy to American security," declared the Cincinnati *Enquirer,* "because he has discredited himself forever in the eyes of the American people."

After several weeks of silence, the America First Committee finally issued a statement declaring that neither Lindbergh nor the committee was anti-Semitic. Editorial opinion regarded this disclaimer as an endorsement of the aviator's remarks and political suicide for the committee. "The isolationist spell," said Michigan's Saginaw *News,* "was now broken. By apologizing for his speech it will raise honest doubts whether its objectives fit with its name."

Such a conclusion to the incident was totally unexpected. It transferred to the America Firsters the condemnation that had attended Lindbergh's address. "It was," said an observer, "the most impolitic thing the committee could have done." The editorial posture of the Des Moines *Tribune* proved this assertion: "Frankly, we are stunned. Positively stunned."

> It had not occurred to us, and we assume it had not occurred to the vast majority of Americans, that the America First Committee was so bankrupt of responsible leadership that its national executive committee would actually ENDORSE the introduction of this tragic element [anti-Semitism] into the debate [to enter the war].
>
> The America First Committee, by this step, has divested itself of the right to respect for its purpose. It has stigmatized . . . every person who clings to its fringe.

After Lindbergh's speech, Smith continued his anti-Semitic activities. In 1944, long after the United States had entered the war, he held a rally at St. Louis's Kiel Auditorium. Over six hundred people heard him defend isolationism and attack Walter Winchell, calling the journalist "Walter Lipschitz." "If there are any Jewish statesmen in the audience," he said, "and you want to stem the rising tide of anti-Semitism in this country, you had better choke off this rat." Some of his listeners turned to each other and, in German, discussed the remark. "One woman," noted a reporter for the St. Louis *Post-Dispatch,* "smiled and said: Just like the Führer."

William Dudley Pelley, the founder of the Silver Shirts, competed with Smith for a share of the anti-Semitic market. Pelley, who had been a newspaperman, a YMCA secretary, a Hollywood screenwriter, and a spiritualist—he claimed to have died but before returning to earth to have spoken with God—was described as an undersized man who "sports a goatee and wears an oversized military hat." "He looks ridiculous in the uniform of the Silver Shirts," reported another observer, "but make no mistake about the man, he is vicious."

In his battle with American Jewry, Pelley and his paramilitary organization made every effort to "expose" Franklin Roosevelt's "Jewish identity." "The architect of the Jew Deal," said a Silver Shirt spokesman, "was originally a Rosenfeld and he is permitting another Jew, Bernard Baruch, to rule this country." To support the charge, the spokesman quoted from a tract entitled *New Dealers in Office, with Their Red Front Personnel:*

> . . . the first Roosevelts to come to the United States were Claes Martenszen Van Rosenvelt and his wife, whose maiden name had been Janntje *Samuels.*
>
> Take note that the spelling of the name at that time was Rosenvelt, not Roose-velt.
>
> Claes' wife must have been a Jewess, for Samuels is by no means a Dutch name. . . .
>
> Seeking safety in Germany, Holland and other countries, members of the family . . . changed their names to Rosenberg, Rosenbaum, Rosenblum, Rosenvelt, Rosenthal, and Rosenfeld.
>
> The Rosenfelds in North Holland finally became Roosevelt, some becoming apostates with the first generation, and others following suit until, in the fourth generation, a little storekeeper by the name of Jacobus Rosenvelt was the only one who remained true to his Jewish faith.

Pelley also made much about Benjamin Franklin's alleged anti-Semitism. "This, too," said an observer, "was proven to be false."

On February 3, 1934, the Silver Shirts leader published a passage purporting to be a quote from the "Private Diary" of Charles Pinckney of South Carolina, in which Franklin was quoted as denouncing Jews equal to the savagery of Hitler's Propaganda Minister, Goebbels.

According to Pelley, Pinckney, one of the framers of the Constitution, took notes on "Chit-chat around the Table during Intermission." "Though the diary had been destroyed during the Civil War," said a spokesman, "a copy still remained in Georgia and that is where the quote was found." Where the diary was, or who had it, Pelley did not say. The alleged diary was never found.

"Although I was pretty well convinced . . . that the Franklin [quote] was a pure fabrication," wrote noted historian Charles Beard, "I had been taught by bitter experience the danger of drawing a negative conclusion. It is not easy in historical writing to prove a negative in the absence of authentic evidence." In his search for the document, Beard contacted an outstanding American scholar who was very familiar with the writings of Franklin and Pinckney.

> Should I mention his name, his authority would be immediately recognized, but I must not bring him into this affair. To my inquiry this scholar replied that there are indications which make it almost certain that Pinckney did not keep a diary of convention proceedings. He added that there is nowhere any evidence that Franklin ever made such a speech and that it is inconceivable that he should ever have done so. In addition, my friend declared flatly: "The alleged Franklin document is merely a forgery and a crude one at that."

While Pelley was providing false leads for historians to follow, others stepped up the assault on the Jewish community. "On the streets of America's largest cities," recalled Morris Steinberg, a Chicago cab driver, "hoodlums attacked Jews with words and clubs. These groups, who called themselves Christian Mobilizers or the Christian Front, instituted anti-Jewish boycotts, applauded Hitler and assaulted Jews. What seemed to anger many of them was Jewish support of loyalist Spain. To these animals, Franco was going to make the world safe from Communism."

The hero of the Christian Fronters was a Catholic priest, the radio voice from Royal Oak, Michigan, Father Charles E. Coughlin. With the onset of the depression, Coughlin's Sunday radio sermons struck out at greed, low wages, and those of the "old order" who caused the misery. In the late 1930s, he moved in another direction and warned America of the Communist penetration of American life, lashing out at Roosevelt's New Deal and blaming the "Jewish financial oligarchy" for the nation's economic ills. "Anti-Semitism," said a listener, "soon became uppermost in his Sunday tirades."

"Like his radio program," recalled Jack Ginsberg, a Brooklyn college student, "Coughlin's privately printed journal, *Social Justice,* could stand out with the worst of them—Pelley's *Galilean,* Elizabeth Dilling's *Round Table Letter,* Lawrence Dennis's *Weekly Foreign Letter*—it was a real vicious rag. It was through this organ that the Christian Front was established in my [Bay Ridge, Brooklyn] neighborhood. I couldn't believe it. People I had known for years avoided my father's store; others broke his windows, called my mother names and beat up my kid brother. That madman they called a priest—I could have killed him. How the hell could people have listened to him?"

Though *Social Justice* was read by approximately two hundred thousand Coughlinites, primarily Catholics living in Detroit, Cleveland, Cincinnati, Boston, and New York, several Catholic journals made it a point to tell the nation that it was *not* a Catholic periodical. The Pittsburgh *Catholic,* a diocesan organ, flatly declared that Coughlin's journal was an attempt to "promote disunity and provoke intolerance." The fact that his policies so frequently paralleled those of the Nazis, said the editors, "was sufficient reason why it would have to be rejected as a guide for Catholics."

Equally emphatic was the *Florida Catholic,* which issued a blistering denunciation of the "disloyal activities of that unAmerican paper misnamed *Social Justice.*" It condemned the magazine for its "obstruction, confusion and sabotage. . . ." More important was the disclaimer issued by Msgr. Edward J. Hickey, chancellor of the Detroit archdiocese. Writing in the *Michigan Catholic,* he repudiated any connection with the journal and declared that "no priest of this diocese has been authorized to associate himself in any capacity with its publication or circulation. . . ."

Other Catholic disclaimers included a story by Edward A. Lahey in the New York *Post* entitled "A Catholic Answers Father Coughlin," which stated: "Father Coughlin . . . appeals only to a small lunatic fringe who read *Social Justice.* . . . a recent issue of [the journal], which virtually justified the Nazi treatment of Jews, leads me to believe it is about time for Catholics in this country to declare themselves on Father Coughlin in no uncertain terms."

The outstanding exception in the anti-Coughlin campaign proved to be Patrick Scanlan's *Brooklyn Tablet,* the official journal of the Brooklyn archdiocese, which emerged as the radio priest's most ardent supporter. In an editorial entitled "It Has Happened Here," the *Tablet* charged that a man "can no longer speak his mind freely without being shouted down as a fascist, a Nazi, a red-baiter, a Jew-baiter or an anti-Semite." In view of this, the *Tablet* maintained, "Americans can no longer remain smug in their conviction that what is happening in Europe is impossible over here."

The Christian Front, which Coughlin promoted through *Social Justice,* first appeared in Brooklyn. Chapters were established throughout the nation. "Forces of destruction in the U.S.," proclaimed the journal in June 1938, "are seriously grinding away the heritage of American liberty. Human minds, clever and scheming, are engineering the mechanism of a juggernaut of hatred, slavery and death . . . the saving of America must be a Christian Front."

"It was no surprise," recalled Chicago truckdriver Julie Meyerson, "that it excluded Jews. Only Catholics and Protestants were admitted to membership. Where we lived, it was predominantly Irish Catholic—and they flocked to the organization in droves. One of my neighbors, an Irishman, went to one of their meetings out of curiosity. He came home very upset. Julie, he said to me, these bastards spent the night drinking beer and when they got good and tanked up, they called your people *kikes* and Communists. The President was referred to as Rosenfelt. I couldn't believe it." Meyerson recalls that no Jew was safe on the streets.

The Anti-Defamation League of the B'nai B'rith seemed powerless to deal with the situation. "The ADL," said Elliot Shapiro to Sheldon Marcus, Coughlin's biographer,

> received many complaints from Jewish people in Brooklyn who were being beaten by gangs of individuals who screamed that they were "Father Coughlin's brownshirts." . . . We arranged for meetings with Church officials of the Brooklyn archdiocese, but they were, on the whole, quite unsatisfactory in their outcome. They merely shrugged and said that they could not control the everyday acts of Brooklyn parishioners. Of course, they also denied any knowledge that it was Catholics who were beating up the Jews.

On the streets of the nation's largest cities, it was not uncommon for Coughlin's storm troopers to assault Jews—young children, old men, defenseless women. "I want to see Jewish blood flow all over America," shouted a Coughlinite after being arrested for beating up a Jewish woman of eighty, "every Jew in the United States hanged!"

Coughlin, who came under increasing attack from a variety of Jewish and Christian organizations for leading what was termed "the Catholic Klan," simply answered that he was "not running out on the fine body of . . . Christians who make up the membership of the Christian Front."

One of the strongest supporters of America's "home-grown fascist ideology was Abdul Hamid, a Harlem black man who paraded around in Nazi-style jackboots, a Turkish fez, and a Sam Brown belt. Though he had only a handful of faithful followers, his Bundist-style Harlem street rallies, which often attracted several hundred people, were frightening sights.

"I was assigned to one of those rallies," recalled Harold Rappaport, a New York City policeman. "He could scare the hell out of you! I remember him saying that the Jews were scared to death of him; the newspapers called him the Black Hitler.

"He told the crowd," said Rappaport, "that the Nazis hated only the polluted Jewish race, that the princely African was exempt from Hitler's racism.

"I laughed at the *schmuck!*" said Rappaport, "but I must admit I was upset when he quoted the mufti of Jerusalem and called Jews in Palestine Zionist imperialists. Most of the time, he directed his bullshit to us —the American Jew. If you would believe this madman, we owned Harlem and we ruled Washington."

During the thirties, Harlem blacks were harder hit than other New Yorkers by the economic decline. Jobs were scarce, living conditions abominable, and relief meager. "Unfortunately," remarked a black observer, "the Jews of Harlem—the storekeepers, the landlords, the salesmen—were the most visible whites, and some blacks vented their frustrations on them. I'm not saying it was fair, but they were the most available targets. They're white and we're colored—it was as simple as that."

When Harlem was ripped by riot in 1935, the Jewish "Mama and Papa" stores were perhaps the hardest hit. "Located on the side streets," said Patrolman Rappaport, "they were the least protected. Those on 125th Street, where the cops were assigned in large numbers, seemed to be OK. Riots happen; I can understand and accept that striking fact of depression life. But, for the life of me, why did they have to shout the anti-Semitic slogans? Why did they blame it all on the Jews? I wonder if they knew that, after the Jews, they were next on Hitler's list?"

In the aftermath of the Harlem turmoil, black community leaders and Jewish businessmen sat together in order to find a solution to the interracial conflict. "We need jobs," said a black minister, "and you can give us those jobs in your stores." "That sounds reasonable," replied Jacob Goldberg, the operator of a marginal tailor shop. "We'll try."

As part of the truce, Jewish personnel in the larger stores were replaced by blacks, and "Mama and Papa" enterprises, which in most cases could not afford or did not need an additional employee, took on local help. Some Harlemites, however, were still not satisfied with this arrangement and demanded still more—clearly, "payoffs."

To get their way, they "zeroed in" on selected establishments and set up picket lines. DON'T BUY HERE, read the signs, UNFAIR TO NEGROES.

"We realized," said a black spokesman, "many of these storeowners couldn't afford to hire help and the only reason they were being singled out by these self-appointed leaders was for a payoff. It was extortion, pure and simple. We finally put a stop to this. Apparently, they learned the technique from the Bundists downtown."

American fascism, which plagued the nation's Jews for the better part of a decade, achieved little success in the United States. Democracy, despite the ravages of depression and the activities of Kuhn, Pelley, and Coughlin, did not break down. As the hysteria created by America's self-styled Hitlers waned—due to the New Deal recovery programs and the nation's entrance into the war—fascism lost its charm. The nation's pro-Nazi sentiment, whether domestic or imported, deteriorated into insignificance, never having enjoyed widespread popularity.

WHILE SIX MILLION DIED

As the word *refugee* became more commonplace, many Americans, including some prominent labor leaders and liberals, went on record as opposing any relaxation of existing immigration laws. Some went even further. Robert R. Reynolds, the "restrictionist" North Carolina senator, urged his colleagues to stop "feeding, clothing, and housing . . . millions of people here from foreign shores, uninvited," and the Kansas City American Legion, alarmed at the arrival of 154 Jewish refugees, wrote down the names of the newcomers and kept close watch on them. In a similar gesture, the National Refugee Service characterized the aliens as the vanguard of a mass invasion of foreigners. "Many of them," said the NRS,

> sink to the lowest patterns of conduct; many of them bring their persecution complexes to our communities; many of them, if given a finger, take and seize the whole hand; many of them who are hypocritically grateful at the beginning soon seek to dictate to American residents how they should run their business, conduct their family affairs, deport themselves in their professions.

To compound the situation, the major Jewish organizations, except perhaps for the Jewish Labor Committee, maintained a deadly silence. "Their inaction," noted Nat Jacobson, a Los Angeles lawyer, "especially in the aftermath of [Congressmen] Celler and Dickstein's defeat to temporarily revise the immigration quotas upward was, to say the least, disturbing. They were *sha-sha* [quiet] because they didn't want to make trouble. The American Jewish Committee didn't even mention the bills in their *Review of the Year*."

The *sha-sha* approach of the defense organizations did not of course make the refugees disappear. "I will never forget that March [1938] morning," said Jacobson, "when I read about the German annexation of Austria. I knew then that there would be more helpless refugees and that nothing, absolutely nothing, was going to be done."

Ten days later, Jacobson heard about Roosevelt's proposed Évian conference; he breathed a sigh of relief. "Perhaps I underestimated the President," he said. "Perhaps I was wrong."

In an effort to find a home for the swelling numbers of refugees, Roosevelt invited thirty-three governments to meet at Évian, France. The invitation stipulated that no nation "would be expected or asked to receive a greater number of emigrants than is permitted by its existing legislation." Despite the qualification, the proposal was greeted with enthusiasm. "I think it is a splendid act on the part of our government," declared Cyrus Adler, president of the American Jewish Committee. "It indicates what I have never doubted—that there is a continuing feeling on the part of America, that when people are deprived of their rights for political or religious reasons, that asylum should be offered to them by civilized nations." The Jewish Labor Committee, the American Jewish Congress, and the Joint Distribution Committee also welcomed the plan. Harry H. Schaffer, commander-in-chief of the Jewish War Veterans, sent Roosevelt a communication: "The JWV of the United States warmly congratulate you and offer their assistance and cooperation to further your humane endeavor."

At Évian, however, Myron C. Taylor, the chief American spokesman, made it clear that his nation had no intention of modifying its existing immigration policy: "The quotas," he said, "will remain unchanged." "Taylor's announcement," said Eli Berkowitz, a Philadelphia dry-goods dealer, "was shocking. We placed our faith in Roosevelt and we felt cheated. I went home that evening and took his picture off the living room wall. My kids asked me why. I was at a loss for an answer."

After the American disclaimer, the other nations began to back off: Paraguay said it restricted its immigration to agriculturalists; Australia asserted that "as we have no real racial problem, we are not desirous of importing one"; Nicaragua, Costa Rica, and Panama jointly declared that they did not want "traders or intellectuals"; and New Zealand flatly refused to change its steadfast restrictionist policy. "It was simple," said Berkowitz; "no one wanted the Jews. All they got from the meeting were words and profound regrets."

As the world rejected the homeless Jews, the twenty-one Jewish organizations attending the proceedings could not agree on a unified policy. "The arguing was absolutely pitiable," said an American Jewish Congress spokesman. A. Leon Kubowitzki, who was also present at the meeting, described the scene:

> The [World Jewish] Congress sought to have a single common delegation of all major Jewish organizations . . . ; it also advocated that a single, joint memorandum be submitted in the name of all the associations concerned. In both of these endeavors it was defeated by Jewish disunity, rarely more in evidence than on this occasion. It was a sorry spectacle to see each of the Jewish organizations insist on appearing separately before the special sub-committee . . . and stating its own views on how to solve the refugee problem in the space of the three minutes allotted to each. . . .

In the aftermath of Évian, however, the hopes of American Jewry were again raised as they witnessed two legislators, Senator Robert F. Wagner of New York and Congresswoman Edith Nourse Rogers of Massachusetts, sponsor legislation—the Child Refugee Bill—designed to save the lives of twenty thousand homeless children. Eddie Cantor, the popular entertainer, as well as thousands of others of all faiths, welcomed the proposal.

"My dear Marvin," wrote Cantor to Marvin McIntyre, a presidential secretary:

> . . . for generations to come, if these boys and girls were permitted entry into this country, they would look upon our leader as a saint —they would bless the name of Franklin D. Roosevelt. . . . If [the plan] met with the approval of the President and Congress, I would furnish you with the names and references of the families willing to adopt these unfortunate children.

Cantor, instrumental in establishing and promoting FDR's favorite charity, the "March of Dimes," quickly discovered that not even the plight of defenseless children could pry open the restrictionist gate. "There is a general feeling," McIntyre answered Cantor, that "even among those who are most sympathetic towards the situation in which so many thousands of persons find themselves abroad, that it would be unadvisable to raise the question of increasing quotas. . . ." Roosevelt, too, was "hesitant" about supporting the legislation: "First things come first," he told his wife, an ardent supporter of the bill, "and I can't alienate certain votes I need for measures that are more important at the moment. . . ."

Wagner, disregarding hints from the White House not to push the bill, conducted a fervent fight. He told his Senate colleagues that the measure was supported by the clergy of all faiths and that only half of the children were to be Jewish. Pleading with a special subcommittee to show compassion, he told the story of a youngster who walked into a Prague travel agency to purchase a ticket.

"Where to?" asked the agent.

"Well, what kind of tickets have you got?" asked the child. The agent placed a globe on his desk.

The youngster studied every inch of the map, then asked, "Haven't you got anything better?"

He concluded his presentation with the New Testament injunction: "Suffer little children to come unto me and forbid them not; for such is the Kingdom of Heaven."

News of the Wagner-Rogers bill spread like wildfire among the restrictionists. Francis H. Kinnicutt, president of the Allied Patriotic Societies, an umbrella organization for thirty restrictionist organizations including the Daughters of the American Revolution, the United Daughters of the Confederacy, the Veterans of Foreign Wars, the New York County branch of the American Legion, and the Society of Mayflower Descendants, matched Wagner's zeal. "Strictly speaking," he told the very same subcommittee, "it is not a refugee bill at all, for by the nature of the case most of those to be admitted would be of the Jewish race. The bill, if passed, will be a precedent . . . in response to the pressure of foreign nationalistic or racial groups, rather than in accordance with the needs and desires of the American people."

The anti-children "patriots" continued to parade before the committee. "I am the daughter of generations of patriots," proclaimed Agnes Waters, who claimed to speak for the widows of World War I veterans:

This nation will be helpless to guarantee our children their rights, under the Constitution, to life, liberty, and the pursuit of happiness if this country is to become the dumping ground for the persecuted minorities of Europe. The refugees have a heritage of hate. They could never become loyal Americans. . . . [They are] potential leaders of a revolt against our American form of government. . . .

Rabbi Stephen Wise also testified. "His statement," said Michael Greenberg, a Baltimore librarian, "was quite disappointing. We certainly expected much more of him."

"I want to make it plain," said Wise, "that, as far as I am concerned, there is no intention whatsoever to depart from the immigration laws which at present obtain. I have heard no sane person propose any departure or deviation from the existing law now in force. . . . Speaking for myself as a citizen, I should say, of course, that our country comes first."

Asked if he approved of expanding the area from which the children might come, he replied:

Hard as it may be to answer your question, Mr. Congressman, I feel that the country and that Congress should not be asked to do more than take care of a limited number of children. The bill provides for 10,000 each year for a period of two years. After all, we cannot take care of all of them. Germany has a population of five or six hundred thousand Jews.

On June 1, 1939, the hearings ended. The next day, Roosevelt was handed a memo. Representative Caroline O'Day wanted the White House to comment on the impending legislation. After looking at the memo for a few moments, Roosevelt picked up his pen and wrote in bold letters: "File no action FDR."

Wagner, a German-born Catholic, knew his proposal was defeated. He withdrew the bill the next day. "The American patriots," sarcastically snapped a Wagner aide, "have won. It is a shameful victory for all Americans."

Almost as soon as the debate on the Wagner-Rogers bill ended, the nation was again caught up in the dramatic plight of the German Jewish refugee. This time, the drama was not played out in Congressional committee rooms but at sea—on board the Hamburg-American liner *St. Louis*.

"As the ship steamed into Havana Harbor," said Max Wishnofsky, a Chicago high school teacher, "I was teaching my students Edward Everett Hale's *The Man Without a Country,* in which the traitor Philip

Nolan was punished by having his wish granted never to see the United States again."

> Transferred from one ship to another, he travelled the oceans until he died, kept always beyond the sight of his native land. He was not permitted to hear or read any reference to home, and the agonies of homesickness he suffered distilled in him a feeling of fervent patriotism.

"The Jewish refugees on the *St. Louis*," Wishnofsky told his class, "were also men and women without a country, but they were not traitors. Their only crime against their homeland was in the accident of birth."

For the 930 passengers who had a "J" stamped on their passports, Cuba was someplace, so they thought, that Nazi tyranny could not reach. As they soon found out, this was untrue. While the ship lay at anchor outside the Cuban capital, anti-Semitic forces were busily at work in trying to prevent their landing. In the midst of Cuba's feverish attempt to stop their disembarkation, only the Havana *Post* pleaded for compassion: "Witness the care-worn faces of old and young, their bright eyes grown dull with suffering, and your heart will go out to them. Witness the stark terror in their expression, and you will realize they cannot be sent back to Germany."

The voices of humanity were few, however, and on June 2 the *St. Louis,* observed by one hundred thousand people and escorted by Cuban police boats—to pick up those who jumped overboard— steamed out of Havana Harbor. *"Auf Widersehen,"* cried some of the spectators standing on the pier as they watched the ship make for the open water.

As the *St. Louis* sailed toward the United States, like a helpless wanderer begging for refuge, the American people kept a close watch. "There should be some place" wrote the Washington *Post,* "where these victims of twentieth-century persecution can find at least a temporary haven."

The Philadelphia *Record* noted:

> Granted that the refugee problem is complex and difficult, there must still be a better solution for civilized peoples than sending out police boats to pick up those who jump into the sea.

And the St. Louis *Post-Dispatch* asked:

. . . why, in the name of humanitarian professions of this advanced day, cannot the nations—including the United States—
which still possess broad expanses of unoccupied or sparsely settled territory come together and agree on quotas which would solve
the refugee problem once and for all?

Steaming aimlessly off the coast of Florida—under the watchful eye
of the U. S. Coast Guard—the passengers wired an impassioned plea to
the White House: "Help us, Mr. President, the 900 passengers, of
whom more than 400 are women and children." The communication
was ignored.

On Tuesday, June 6, the *St. Louis* finally ended its aimless drifting
and set a course for Europe. "It is hard to imagine," wrote the New
York *Times,*

> the bitterness of exile when it takes place over a faraway frontier.
> Helpless families driven from their homes to a barren island . . . ,
> thrust over the Polish frontier, escaping in terror of their lives to
> Switzerland or France, are hard for us in a free country to visual-
> ize. But these exiles floated by our own shores. Some of them are
> on the American quota list and can later be admitted here. What is
> to happen to them in the interval has remained uncertain from
> hour to hour. . . . The cruise of the *St. Louis* cries to high heaven
> of man's inhumanity to man.

As the liner headed for Europe, an *ad hoc* passenger committee, in a
desperate effort to find refuge elsewhere, wired the Joint Distribution
Committee (JDC): "We ask in great despair your assistance for disembarkation at Southhampton [England] or asylum in benevolent noble
France."

Morris Trooper, head of the JDC's European operation, was assigned
the task of finding a friendly nation. The telegrams he received from the
New York office were anything but encouraging: "INTERVENTION
COLUMBIA WITHOUT PROSPECTS STOP IMMIGRATION
CLOSED"; "CHILE: NOTHING DOING ST. LOUIS ACCOUNT
POLITICAL SITUATION"; "PARAGUAY YET UNDECIDED";
"ARGENTINE UNDERTAKING STEPS DOUBTFUL RESULTS."

The next communication was the most menacing of all: "REGARD
THESE PASSENGERS AS DOOMED ONCE THEY REACH GER-
MAN SOIL. . . . WE WOULD WANT TO BE ASSURED NO SIN-
GLE POSSIBILITY OF ESCAPE SHOULD FAIL TO BE GIVEN
UTMOST CONSIDERATION. . . . TIME IS OF ESSENCE BOAT
HAS COMPLETED MORE THAN HALF OF TRIP."

Trooper's efforts proved successful. On June 13, he wired the passenger committee: "FINAL ARRANGEMENTS FOR DISEMBARKATION ALL PASSENGERS COMPLETED HAPPY TO INFORM YOU GOVERNMENTS OF BELGIUM, HOLLAND, FRANCE, AND ENGLAND COOPERATED MAGNIFICENTLY WITH AMERICAN JOINT DISTRIBUTION COMMITTEE."

The passenger committee quickly responded:

> THE . . . PASSENGERS OF ST. LOUIS DANGLING FOR LAST THIRTEEN DAYS BETWEEN HOPE AND DESPAIR RECEIVED TODAY YOUR LIBERATING MESSAGE. . . . OUR GRATITUDE IS AS IMMENSE AS THE OCEAN ON WHICH WE ARE NOW FLOATING SINCE MAY 13 FIRST FULL OF HOPE FOR A GOOD FUTURE AND AFTERWARDS IN THE DEEPEST DESPAIR. . . . ACCEPT THE DEEPEST AND ETERNAL THANKS OF MEN AND WOMEN AND CHILDREN UNITED BY THE SAME FATE ON BOARD THE ST. LOUIS.*

After five tension-filled weeks, the *St. Louis* entered the harbor at Antwerp, Belgium. One refugee exclaimed: "Eighty per cent of us would have jumped overboard had the ship put back to Germany." The relatively happy ending, however, was spoiled when the passengers saw standing on the dock members of Belgium's Nazi National Youth Organization distributing anti-Semitic leaflets. "We, too, want to help the Jews," they read. "If they call at our offices, each will receive gratis a piece of rope and a strong nail."

From Hitler's accession to power, in 1933, to America's entrance into the global conflict, in 1941, almost one hundred thousand Jews found safety in the United States. The Germans among them, unlike the earlier, East Europeans, were, for the most part, an educated and cultured group. Many had graduated from a *Gymnasium* or a university, and a goodly number of them had held positions as university professors, physicians, attorneys, or scientists, some with international reputations. A host of others were artists, bankers, merchants, inventors, chemists, and businessmen. Of course, many were also everyday working people.

"About half of them," recalled Jacob Kaminsky, a Manhattan bagel

---

* Unknown to the officials of the Hamburg-American Line, Captain Schroeder planned to run the ship aground on the English coast if the JDC failed to find refuge for his passengers.

baker, "settled on Manhattan's upper West Side. It soon was nicknamed the 'Fourth Reich.' "

"Walking along Broadway," noted Kaminsky, "it was not uncommon to run into some of the most prominent German or Austrian personalities. Writers like Franz Werfel or the psychoanalyst Theodor Reik. On a number of occasions I spoke with Kurt Weill, who would frequent the popular Broadway cafés catering to the new German community. The West Side had perhaps the most intellectual atmosphere in New York, if not in the entire country."

"At the same time," said Kaminsky, "many of us didn't like the Germans. They always had this air of superiority; they made nasty remarks about those of us who still spoke Yiddish. And they never missed an opportunity to flaunt their education or the fact that they held important positions in their native country. It's amazing how some of them still spoke of Germany, not the Nazis of course, with affection. They simply couldn't reconcile themselves to the fact that we wouldn't accept them at German values."

Joseph Rubin, a Brooklyn bus driver, agreed with Kaminsky's observations. He characterized the German refugees as self-centered and clannish. "Sometimes," he said, "we just had to laugh at them. To crystallize his point of view, he related a popular story about a German dachshund that refused to talk to a Boston terrier: "Don't tink I alvays vas chust a dachshund; back home in Germany I vus a Saint Bernard!"

A third observer, Gertrude Gainor, a nurse at Mount Sinai Hospital, had a more favorable impression of the German refugee. "Many of them were by no means contemptuous or haughty, but rather frightened." To drive her point home, she related the story of the newly arrived refugee couple that went into a grocery store and asked for oranges.

"For juice?" asked the clerk.

"Did you hear what he said?" the woman said to her husband in German, motioning him to leave the store. "For Jews? You see, it's beginning here, too. . . ."

Gainor, who spent most of her time helping the refugees get settled, noted that some of the newcomers, German and otherwise, contributed beyond measure to this country's cultural sophistication. "Think of it!" she exclaimed, "from France alone we got André Maurois, the novelist; André Spier, the poet; Henry Bernstein, the playwright; and artists Jacques Lipchitz, Manne Katz, and Marc Chagall. . . . As for the few nasty Germans, they made up a very small minority of this immigration."

In the summer of 1942, as reports filtered across the Atlantic that the Nazis were in the initial stages of the "Final Solution," American Jewry responded with demonstrations, moral protests, prayer, and fasting. As more shocking information arrived, the enormity of the slaughter began to be fully understood; by January 1943, two million Jews had been destroyed.

"I regret," wrote Under Secretary of State Sumner Welles to Rabbi Wise, "that [communications from Europe] confirm and justify your deepest fears."

Wise, who referred to Roosevelt as "the Boss," was sure his White House friend would come to the aid of the stricken Jews. "Dear Boss," he wrote, "I do not wish to add an atom to the awful burden which you are bearing with magic and as I believe, heaven-inspired strength at this time. But you do know that the most overwhelming disaster of Jewish history has befallen Jews in the form of the Hitler mass-massacres . . . and it is indisputable that as many as two million Jews have been slain."

After the message was received, Wise and a delegation of Jewish leaders handed the President a twenty-page report, *Blue Print for Extermination,* which gave a detailed account, country by country, of the annihilation. A somber Roosevelt thanked the group for past political support and pledged to save "those who may yet be saved. The mills of the gods grind slowly," he told the delegation, "but they grind exceedingly small. We are doing everything possible to ascertain who are personally guilty."

As the months passed, American Jewry waited for Roosevelt to act— to save "those who may yet be saved." Yet, rather than action, they saw apathy hover over the White House. "Roosevelt and those anti-Semitic bastards in the State Department," said one Yiddish newspaper reporter, "did nothing. Absolutely nothing. We couldn't believe it. Our people loved that man and yet he did nothing. Why?"

Hyman Rothstein, a New Jersey college professor, tried to answer his friend's question. "What do you expect from Cordell Hull!" he exclaimed. "Didn't he try to stop a boatload of refugees from entering this country a few years ago? Why should he be any different now?"

In 1940, a ship laden with Jews had sailed from France. Its destination was Mexico. "Their visas had been obtained illegally," explained Rothstein, "and the Mexican Government ordered the ship out of its waters. They knew it meant certain death."

Instead of returning directly to Europe, the ship and its doomed passengers stopped first at Norfolk, Virginia, to take on fuel. While in the American port, the plight of the passengers reached the desk of Mrs. Roosevelt. She arranged a meeting between several notable Jewish leaders and Hull. Dr. Nahum Goldmann, an ardent Zionist, pleaded with the Secretary of State to admit the refugees.

"Dr. Goldmann," said Hull as he turned toward an American flag hanging in his office. "I took an oath to protect that flag and obey the laws of my country and you are asking me to break those laws."

Goldmann, not one to be easily intimidated, reminded Hull of an incident that had taken place several weeks earlier in New York Harbor. As a German ship steamed out of the Hudson River, a number of anti-Nazi sailors leaped into the water. The United States, which was still at peace with Germany, ordered the Coast Guard to pluck the seamen from the water and land them at Ellis Island. There they were given political asylum.

After completing the story, the rabbi smiled at Hull and asked him to wire the refugees in Norfolk and suggest that they imitate the actions of the German sailors. "The Coast Guard will pick them up," said Goldmann, "and they will be safe for the rest of the war."

"Dr. Goldmann," replied Hull, "you are the most cynical man I have ever met."

"I ask you, Mr. Secretary," snapped Goldmann, "who is the cynical one—I who wish to save these innocent people or you who are prepared to send them back to their death?"†

"Even more of an obstructionist," remarked Reuben Feinstein, a Chicago dentist, "was that son of a bitch Breckinridge Long, the assistant secretary of state. He must have been delighted to have been so instrumental in the passage of rules and regulations which made it virtually impossible for Jews to get into this country."

In June 1941, one of those regulations noted by Feinstein denied refugees with relatives in German-occupied countries the right to come to the United States. One gets the sense that Catch-22 was a paragon of logic compared to the following regulation:

† Through the intervention of Mrs. Roosevelt, Hull allowed the refugees to land.

> . . . the fact that a relative of the first degree . . . [father, mother, sister, brother, wife, children], with whom the applicant had maintained close family ties, remains abroad in any country or territory under the control of a country whose form of government is opposed to the form of government of the United States may be considered with other evidence that the ties between such relative and the applicant would make the entry of the applicant prejudicial to the public safety . . . of the United States.‡

To make matters worse, the State Department issued still more obstructionist regulations. Hermann Kravitz, a refugee who managed to enter the United States, described the ordeal of cutting through the State Department's "paper wall." "Form BC," he said,

> had to be filled out six times and sent to the US Visa Department. They in turn sent copies to the FBI, Immigration and Naturalization Service, Naval Intelligence, Military Intelligence, and the State Department. Then we would wait—sometimes for several weeks. I have known people who waited as much as two months—all the time fearing that the Nazis would get to them first. If we were lucky we were permitted to contact our sponsor in America. Often this was difficult because of the war and the ocean which separated us.
>
> If you were a "Friendly Alien," those not fleeing from Germany, you had a chance. Those who were "Enemy Aliens," running from Germany or its conquered territories, you almost never made it.

"One of my friends," said Kravitz,

> was rejected and had to wait six months to reapply. He couldn't understand why he was not permitted to go to America. They wouldn't tell him why he was disqualified. He was an "enemy alien"—what a grisly joke, the Nazis wanted to kill him and they called him an enemy. His case went before a Primary Committee and then to something called the Interdepartmental Visa Committee. In a few weeks, his case was heard by the Board of Appeals. They rejected him. We said good-by one evening and both of us knew we were saying good-by for the last time. He was gassed in a concentration camp.

Albert Einstein, who came to the United States in 1933 to accept a post at Princeton's Institute for Advanced Study, enlisted Eleanor

‡ If a refugee's wife were in a Nazi concentration camp, he would be, according to this regulation, unable to enter the country.

Roosevelt's aid to stop the State Department's obstructionism. "I have noted," he wrote the First Lady,

> with great satisfaction that you always stand for the right and humaneness even when it is hard. Therefore in my deep concern I know of no one else to whom to turn for help. A policy is now being pursued in the State Department which makes it impossible to give refuge in America to any persons who are the victims of Fascist cruelty in Europe. Of course, this is not openly avowed by those responsible for it. The method which is being used, however, is to make immigration impossible by erecting a wall of bureaucratic measures. . . . I know that you will find it possible to bring the matter to the attention of your heavily burdened husband in order that it be remedied.

After reading Einstein's letter, a shocked Mrs. Roosevelt promised the scientist that the matter would be brought to her husband's attention "at once." If FDR saw the letter, and there is no reason to doubt that he did, he did nothing.

"Absolutely!" exclaimed a Jewish source close to the White House, "the President not only knew of the obstructionist tactics but himself engaged in them. Look at the way he dismissed the 'Free Port' concept. His inaction was a disgusting display of non-concern."

In April 1944, Samuel Grafton, of the New York *Post*, suggested the creation of "Free Ports for refugees" on the coast of the United States. "The need is for reservations of a few acres, here and there," he said,

> where a man who has been running for ten years can sit down and catch his breath, and where somebody can tell a story to a frightened child, a few reservations where it would be possible for those who cannot satisfy the requirements of law to rest a bit, without violating the law. We do it, in commercial free ports, for cases of beans, so that we can make some storage and processing profit; it should not be impossible to do it for people.

Grafton's concept was greeted by the public enthusiastically, and almost immediately Roosevelt received thousands of letters, petitions, and telegrams favoring the plan. "The Free Port idea has nothing to do with unrestricted and uncontrolled immigration," assured the New York *Times*. "It is simply a proposal to save lives of innocent people." The plea of the Emergency Committee to Save the Jewish People in Europe was more dramatic: "TWENTY-FIVE SQUARE MILES OR

2,000,000 DEAD," read its Washington *Post* advertisement, "WHICH SHALL IT BE?"

"Unfortunately," said a reporter, "FDR did not share the enthusiasm. He told those of us who gathered for a press conference that there were other places that the refugees could find safety. That it was not necessary for the country to initiate this plan, because many other countries were still open to the victims of fascism."

Several days later, due to the persistence of Roosevelt's own War Refugee Board, the President announced a "modified" version of the free-port concept. "With a lot of *hoopla* from the White House," commented an observer, "FDR declared that an abandoned military post at Oswego, New York, would be turned into an emergency shelter. Less than one thousand refugees were admitted." Henry L. Feingold, author of *The Politics of Rescue* (1970), described conditions at the refuge:

> . . . Harold Ickes welcomed 987 carefully selected refugees to the eighty-acre former army post. Almost immediately the project ran into trouble. The refugees, most of whom had come from camps situated in the mild climates of North Africa and Italy, found it difficult to adjust to the cold isolated northern location. Moreover, the conditions under which they had gained admittance proved to be so confining that the refugees were little more than prisoners. For people who did not feel that they had committed a crime, such treatment seemed irrational. A number of physical and mental breakdowns occurred. The unwholesome conditions, due mainly to a rigid interpretation of the regulations as administered by the army, were fully revealed by a Congressional investigation in 1945.

The turning point for American Jewry *vis-à-vis* the refugees came on August 29, 1943, when the American Jewish Conference convened at New York's Waldorf Astoria Hotel. In a historic show of unity, customary jealousies and political differences were put aside as every important organization—representing all strata of American Jewry—met to create a unified refugee policy.

"We cannot truly rescue the Jews of Europe," declared Rabbi Abba Hillel Silver to the delegates, "unless we have free immigration to Palestine. We cannot have free immigration into Palestine unless our political rights are recognized there. Our political rights cannot be recognized there unless our historic connection with the country is acknowledged and our right to rebuild our national home is reaffirmed. These are inseparable links in the chain. The whole chain breaks if one of the links is missing."

"Silver," said a delegate, "was magnificent. He voiced what all of us believed in our hearts—even the non-Zionists. Some of us wept; others cheered. Then the delegates rose to sing 'Hatikvah.'"

Once the debate was over, Joseph Proskauer, representing the American Jewish Committee, met with Silver and Nahum Goldmann. "He wanted to block the resolution calling for the re-creation of a Jewish commonwealth," said an observer. Silver, however, refused to listen to Proskauer's argument, and Goldmann, who did not want the Zionist momentum to be lost, declared that "in view of the tremendous pro-Zionist emotions generated throughout the country we would be torn limb from limb if we were now to defer action on the Palestine resolution."

The following day, the resolution was placed before the assembly; Henry Monsky, of B'nai B'rith, seconded it, and Wise called for a vote. Only four of the 501 delegates, three of them from the American Jewish Committee, were opposed. "After the vote was recorded," said a delegate, "all hell broke loose." When calm was restored, Proskauer stood and almost reluctantly told the assembly, "We regretfully dissent from concurrence with these resolutions," expressing hope that cooperation was still possible between his organization and the Zionists.

Zionism had finally triumphed. In the September issue of *New Palestine,* the jubilant editors wrote: "The Zionist position is now the position of American Jewry. The Conference has served to crystallize Jewish opinion in our own country. This marks the end of long discussion and debate. . . . The time has come for action."

The historic Waldorf Astoria meeting "solved" the refugee problem for American Jewry; it provided a refuge for the survivors of Hitler's death camps. "American immigration policy was no longer our concern!" exclaimed a Jewish Labor Committee delegate. "All of our energy was shifted to the creation of a permanent Jewish homeland."

You're in the Army Now

"Jews," noted former army Lieutenant Stephen Wolf, "went through enormous changes during the war." The transformation, he said,

> was due to the scattering of Jewish servicemen throughout the country. . . . Jewish kids in uniform from the sidewalks of New York, Chicago, and Philadelphia finally came into contact with the

isolated small-town Jew of the South, Middle and Far West. They also met Christians, not New York Italians or Philadelphia Irish, but "real Americans," those who had never seen a Jew before. People who discovered that their conception of Jews, as a result of their service-connected associations, changed. For that generation of urban northeastern Jews it was the first time they met America. It was also the first time America met them.

Jewish servicemen, who for the most part came from the urban centers of the Northeast, were frequently raised in orthodox homes. Yet, many of them were indifferent Jews. Most had a limited Jewish education and even fewer had an intimate knowledge of Jewish history. Jewish life to them was limited to the atmosphere of a social group; it meant dating Jewish girls, eating blintzes or pastrami, and going to *shul* on the High Holidays.

"Such Jewish boys," noted army Chaplain Lee L. Levinger, "may come suddenly to a training camp adjoining a small western or southern town."

> They look for a [*kosher*] delicatessen—of course, there is none; they inquire about Jewish girls—only to find out that the one marriageable girl in the community has just given her heart and hand to a sergeant from the preceding division. They ask about a synagogue and are shocked to find out that the fifteen Jewish families in town do not have a house of worship. Their first reaction is either incredulity or disgust.

Many of them, however, adjusted to the new surroundings and compromised with the traditions that had been with them since birth. They worked on their Sabbath, dated gentile girls and, unable to obtain *kosher* food, settled for unfamiliar and sometimes "offensive" dishes. Others quickly adjusted to ham and eggs and similar non-*kosher* delicacies. "The guilt associated with eating bacon," recalled one ex-serviceman, "soon vanished. In fact, when we were served *matzos,* some of us passed 'em up. It was the first time some of us ever ate bread on Passover. I somehow felt a sense of freedom when I took that first mouthful."

Many indifferent Jews, those who had been eating bacon long before their army service, suddenly clung to their Judaism. "Once we were deprived of it," said Jakie Schneiderman, "we wanted it more than anything else." A young soldier from Brooklyn declared:

For the first time in life I was alone both physically and spiritually. I was in a strange land among people who hardly spoke my own language. On this foreign soil one could not find lox and bagels or pumpernickel. Here Southern fried [chicken] and grits were the popular delicacies. Because I felt strange I immediately began to seek my fellow Jews, with whom I could speak freely about subjects we both understood. I found myself, rather than becoming assimilated with the local population, asserting my Judaism more than ever. . . .

Another soldier, from Chicago, reported:

I went to the various theaters and nightclubs in the city but I always seemed to turn up at this center [the Jewish Welfare Board] when I had the desire to be closer to home. . . .

Still another, from Philadelphia, said:

Religion has had little influence upon me. . . . Yet how can I explain the flow of tears, involuntarily streaming, when attending services at a synagogue . . . for the first time in twenty years? Was I moved by the spectacle of hundreds of men in uniform from all the states of the Union? . . . Can I attribute it to the loneliness I often feel here . . . the loneliness which comes not from separation alone [from my family], but that which invariably is sensed when a stranger comes among those who shun him?

Whether one was an indifferent, an estranged, or a practicing Jew, his military travels were directly responsible for his development of new ideas about Jewish life. He was startled to discover that some Jews opened their stores on *Yom Kippur,* amused that Jews preferred fishing to pinochle, and astonished that Jews had been mayors of southern and western towns. "Every departure from the ways of the big city," noted Levinger, "adds a further surprise."

Every departure from orthodoxy gives him pause—he was often skeptical himself, but with these people such neglect is part of their environment and of their personalities, too. He sees this at close hand, for the village Jews have proved themselves most hospitable to the visitors from the city. They have invited him to their homes, prepared just the feast he likes for Passover; they bring refreshments to the [army] camp for a party after services on Friday evening. Their breezy western ways, their separation from Judaism [as he knew it], has not separated them from the Jewish soldier from the East.

"And so," added Levinger, "his mind begins to include many types of Jews and Judaism it had never known before,"

> or had deliberately rejected as beneath consideration. He sees that other modes of Jewish worship, unfamiliar to him as they may be, have value, too. At least, they no longer represent apostasy to him, since he now knows these people who practice them. He may be sorry for these village Jews in their isolation, but he must recognize them as his fellows.

By the time the Jewish serviceman from the large eastern metropolitan area had completed his basic training in Texas, California, Georgia, Louisiana, or Florida, he was transformed; his insularity was broken down. When some returned to their homes, they were no longer content. "After seeing the Jewish life-style in California," noted Pfc. Henry Bernstein, "I wanted to go back. It seemed like the kind of life I wanted to live." The experience outside of the insulated New York Jewish environment had a similar effect on others. If anything, through their associations with Christians and small-town Jews, they returned home with a broadened view of Judaism and a greater understanding of their Christian countrymen.

This interaction had perhaps an even greater impact on the small-town Jew—it returned him to his people. As the ambassadors from New York and Philadelphia arrived, assimilated Jewish women, via the USOs, became hostesses; Jewish homes opened their doors to lonely servicemen from Boston and Chicago; village synagogues set up folding chairs to accommodate the crowds; eligible females dated those "nice Jewish boys from the Bronx"; and dying Jewish organizations, while serving the needs of their visitors, found new life. "The village Jew came into contact with the intense [and not so intense] Judaism of the cities," asserted Levinger, "the devoutly orthodox soldiers whose chief lament was the absence of *kosher* food; the larger mass who were less pious but whose Jewish backgrounds were just as intense."

The village Jew discovered that in spite of his long separation from Judaism he was still a Jew. His isolation was shattered, perhaps forever. "The process," noted Levinger, "was something like this:"

> a local committee was assembled to provide sandwiches or homemade cookies after the regularly constituted services for servicemen; soon the community became used to attending, and praying with the soldiers. Then came a *seder,* which involved arduous labor for the women of the community, who wished to serve the stranger

within the gates, but it also attracted Jewish families who had discontinued to practice for years. Many a small-town Jew, moreover, attended his first *seder* when one was prepared for the military visitors. The wholehearted appreciation of the soldiers, the presence of the Christian post chaplain and the commanding officer, combined to develop a new attitude toward Judaism among those who had long been negligent, or who, perhaps, had never known Judaism at all.

Their loyalty solidified, each among them learning that they all belonged to the same House of Israel. "We were very proud of those kids from the Northeast," said Arnold Ratner, a Texas feed-store operator. "At first we thought they would embarrass us—but we were wrong. Most of us had been ashamed of the Jews in the big cities—they were different. Now we were able to see and meet them on our terms. I'm happy we did. . . . My family and I discovered that we are all cut from the same side of beef."

Though some of the anxieties of Jewish servicemen were alleviated once they were welcomed so warmly by their village coreligionists, many were still fearful of the possible negative treatment they might receive at their military posts. Pfc. Mike Goldberg said, "we always had anti-Semitism on our minds. When I left home, the stories were circulating about the negative treatment of Jews. One of the most popular of all the stories was that the "crackers" from the South and the West would ask to see our tails and horns. It might have been anti-Semitism. Then, again, it might have been plain ignorance. . . ."

The military was cognizant of this sensitivity and did take steps to build the Jewish serviceman's morale. Major General Milton A. Reckord, commander of the Third Service Command, cited the "enthusiastic response of Jewish men to the call to military service. . . ." Similar pronouncements, however, did little to change attitudes about Jews—attitudes that were deeply imbedded in the thinking of so many Americans. Frank Weil, president of the National Jewish Welfare Board, commented on the problem: "There have been some complaints of anti-Semitism against this officer or that man. Some . . . have arisen out of oversensitivity, a few others have been substantiated, usually against some officer or man but recently come from civilian life. That there are anti-Semites among us is no news; that some of these will find their way into the army can be expected. . . ."

Pfc. Harold Ribalow was somewhat more optimistic. "A year in the U. S. Army," he wrote, "has taught me . . . this: there is no anti-Semitism in this army."

I have met soldiers from every state in the Union and from more cities and towns than I ever knew existed. I have met devout Catholics, pious Protestants of every denomination. On the other hand, they have seen all types of Jews: Orthodox, Conservative, Reform, "assimilationists," and what have you, and they learned that the Jewish soldier is just another "G.I." who has to go through the same military mill that they do. It is a good thing and a liberal education for most of us to be subjected to the army method of complete equality for all.

In an article entitled "You're in the Army Now," Ribalow, a keen observer of Jewish life, had a reassuring message for those who anticipated questions about their "horns and tails."

"Plump Dan Middleton . . . ," wrote Ribalow, "was talking in a loud voice, and there was bewilderment in his tone."

"Gee," he said, "when I came into the Army I thought that all Jews were home makin' the dough." Then he uncomfortably eyed the twenty men in his barracks, eight of whom were Jews.

"But wherever I go I find Jewish soldiers. Hell, there are more Jews in the Army than there are in Jerusalem."

Several weeks later, Middleton thought differently. He was not an anti-Semite, but he did harbor many of the misconceptions of the average civilian: that Jews were draft-dodgers, that they were too clever to be in service. "Some of the Jewish boys," said Ribalow, "had heard him, but rather than start a religious riot . . . they preferred to shut up."

Middleton was soon convinced, according to Ribalow, "that there was no difference between a Jewish and a non-Jewish soldier. He had been taught by the facts. There is no longer any need to talk to him. He sees for himself. There is no need to hand him carefully prepared literature that proves that Jews don't control industry, the movies, the press, etc."

Middleton's misconceptions about Jews, which were shared by many, were well known to the sensitive Jewish soldiers. "The image of the draft-dodger or the goof-off," said Army Air Corps Captain William Pinsky, "created among us [Jews] a feeling of collective responsibility. We watched our own conduct and the behavior of others to see that no one stepped out of line. I was particularly hard on the Jewish men in my own unit—much harder on them than on the gentiles. I didn't want anyone to think we were a bad lot."

In another incident, a radio commentator was telling his listeners the rags-to-riches story of Irving Berlin. When he told his audience that the songwriter was Jewish, a young soldier from Oklahoma suddenly said: "These Jewish guys sure did a lot for this country. He spoke," said Ribalow,

> in a deliberate voice. Surely Bartlesville [Oklahoma] does not have a large Jewish population, and Billy certainly did not meet many Jews before joining the Army, but his sincerity was spontaneous and his admiration clear. He had been listening to a success story and delivered his opinion. No prejudice colored him and no propaganda poisoned him.

That evening, while Ribalow was writing a letter, he noticed Billy looking over his shoulder.

> "What's that?" he said.
> "Hebrew," Ribalow answered.
> "Are you Jewish?"
> "Yes."
> "No kidding." Silence. Then, "Say, do you want to go to the show today?"
> "There was no change of attitude at all," recalled Ribalow. "Why should there be? There should not be. There isn't in the Army. But I've seen it differently at home."

On another occasion, a soldier from Ohio lying on the cot next to Ribalow asked what he was writing.
"I'm writing an article on anti-Semitism in the Army."
The young soldier smiled. "Come again?" he said. "Now tell me in plain language what you are doing."
"I'm writing about anti-Semitism," replied Ribalow.
"What the hell is that?"
"Are you fooling?" Ribalow asked.
"No," he answered.
"I explained to him what I was writing about," said Ribalow. "He is still a bit bewildered. Now, this is something that is true. Would you believe it? Neither would I, but it just happened, and I know it can happen only in the Army."
Ribalow wrote his essay to assure the Jewish community that although anti-Semitism did exist, the military was not rife with it. "I had met," he said,

> a few Jewish civilians who, when entertaining Jewish soldiers, asked, sooner or later, how we were treated. They were eager to

know and half expected us to tell them some horrible tales. But all of us said, with perfect simplicity, that we hoped there was as little anti-Semitism in civilian life as we found in the Army. They did not know whether to believe us or not. I still suspect that they don't, for the shadow of anti-Semitism has been built up so that it is now a solid pillar of darkness.

Ribalow of course, as did many other Jewish servicemen, encountered anti-Semites. "His name was Bob Burnham," he wrote, a curly-haired New Englander who said one day that "Jewish boys ask too many questions."

"That's a hell of a thing to say," snapped another soldier. "You ask as many questions as I do."

That started it. Within five minutes Burnham had delivered a diatribe against all Jews. He invoked all the old issues of how Jews controlled everything in America. . . . I entered the argument and gave him some of the answers to his complaints, or were they charges? I told him that the Jews don't control the newspapers of the nation, that they don't control the banks, and that they don't control the motion picture industry. The audience listening in on our talk was unconsciously taking sides.

"Well," he responded in a half snarl, "don't shout these damn facts at me. Say all you want. I don't care if what you say is true. I just feel it, here," as he put his finger on his heart.

"The significance of the . . . incident," said Ribalow,

is that he was the only soldier I have met who was anti-Jewish and declared himself so. I have lived in close contact for the past six weeks with more than forty men from seventeen states and thirty cities, and at no time have I heard anything, consciously or unconsciously, said against Jews in any way. True, there is much ignorance. The American from Macedonia, Ohio, does not know many Jews and, consequently, does not care or worry about the "Jewish problem." I am certain that the American Jew does not know much about the whys and wherefores of the Roman Catholicism of Heywood Broun or the Anglo-Catholicism of T. S. Eliot. Nor does he know the difference between Protestant denominations.

A second representative incident of individual and *not official* military anti-Semitism was reported by Howard Sachs, a soldier who worked in an army laboratory. Also working in the laboratory was a German-American who made constant anti-Jewish remarks. The Jewish soldier, however, said nothing; nor did any of the other G.I.s—all

Christians—who couldn't help but hear the shouts of the German from Pennsylvania. "I felt terrible," reported Sachs, "because I was under the impression that their silence meant approval of the remarks.

"One day," said Sachs, "the German came into the lab and announced in a very loud voice that the [U.S.] government should hand over all Jews to Hitler. 'Into the ovens!' he shouted.

"With that," asserted Sachs, "I had enough. I hit him square in the teeth and the blood began to pour from his mouth. Then I picked up a club and rapped him across his back. For a moment I wanted to kill the bastard!

"Suddenly, I realized that everyone in the room was walking towards me. I thought I was going to have to take on the entire bunch. I turned towards them, club in one hand, and showed my fist."

Much to Sachs's surprise, the others congratulated him. "It's about time you stopped that son of a bitch," said one.

"Why didn't you speak up before?" asked a surprised Sachs. "Why didn't you support me before it came to this?"

"Because it *had* to happen," responded one of the soldiers. "Only *you*, a *Jew*, was going to put a stop to it."

"Now that you taught him a lesson," said a third man, "let's get back to work."

What may be considered an official anti-Semitic act, the denial of a Jewish chaplain's right to speak at an interdenominational service, took place on the Pacific island of Iwo Jima.

"Here before us lie the bodies of comrades and friends," said Rabbi Roland Gittelsohn as he looked upon the graves of fallen marines.

> Men who until yesterday or last week laughed with us, joked with us, trained with us. Men who were on the same ships with us, and went over the side with us as we prepared to hit the beaches of this island. Men who fought with us and feared with us. Somewhere in this plot of ground there may lie the man who could have discovered the cure for cancer. Under one of these Christian crosses, or beneath a Jewish Star of David, there may rest now a man who was destined to be a great prophet. . . . Now they lie here silently in this sacred soil, and we gather to consecrate this earth in their memory.

It was assumed throughout the nation that Gittelsohn's sermon dedicating the Fifth Marine Cemetery was preached at an interdenominational service. The assumption was false.

The division chaplain, Warren F. Cuthriell, initially planned a common service. To open the ceremony, the commanding officer was to deliver a secular dedication. This was to be followed by a joint religious memorial service, after which each group would be at liberty to conduct its own religious exercise. In the spirit of brotherhood, Cuthriell invited Rabbi Gittelsohn, who represented the smallest religious group in the division, to deliver the sermon. "I learned later," said the rabbi,

> . . . immediately after the announcement of his plans, [that] two of our Protestant chaplains visited Cuthriell to express their vigorous objection to the Jewish chaplain preaching over graves which were predominantly those of Christians. His answer was that the right of the Jewish chaplain to preach such a sermon was precisely one of the things for which we were fighting the war. When that approach failed, the six Catholic padres with us on Iwo [Jima] sent their senior representative to the Division Chaplain to speak for all of them. They were opposed in particular to a sermon preached by the Jewish Chaplain! Furthermore, if he insisted on carrying out his original intention they would refuse to participate or attend!

After Gittelsohn had been invited to deliver the sermon, Cuthriell summoned him to explain the situation. "The objection of two Protestants [Cuthriell] could withstand," said the rabbi.

> The objections of an entire church, which would surely have made a *cause célèbre* out of the incident, was another matter. I had no right to expose my senior to that kind of embarrassment. I withdrew. After a brief secular dedication, each faith went to its own specified corner to hold its own Service of Memorial. The sermon I had written for the combined service was actually delivered at our own little Jewish service. Perhaps it should be added here that not one word of the original manuscript was changed as a result of the incident.

The home front also had its share of anti-Semitic incidents. From the start of the war, rumors circulated in many cities accusing Jews of not being 100 per cent behind the war effort. "It was part and parcel of the same campaign," said one observer, "that brought forth such whisper campaigns as *England is willing to fight to the last American. . . .* Jewish sensitivity was such that sometimes these rumors were unwittingly spread and exaggerated by Jews themselves."

"I was living in Pittsburgh at the time," recalled Marvin Goldstein, a radio technician, "and the rumor mill had it that several draft boards located in Jewish neighborhoods were classifying an unusually high percentage of Jews 4-F. The stories that were told included details and names that smacked of irrefutable fact.

"We heard," said Goldstein, "that some doctors were injecting draftees with drugs causing an irregular heartbeat; that others were suggesting to prospective inductees that they inject glucose into their veins to fake diabetes; that the government had looked into the charges and arrested an entire draft board; and that official records were falsified by Jewish draft-board officials."

The Pittsburgh rumor, which was repeated in New York, Philadelphia, Boston, and Chicago, led to a full-scale investigation by the FBI, the local press, Selective Service officials, city police, and the Allegheny County Medical Association. "Their collective findings," noted Goldstein, who was in uniform when the rumors began to circulate, "dispelled the anti-Semitic rumor. . . . We all breathed a lot easier after the investigation was over."

Into this climate of anxiety and rumor came reports of the patriotic and sometimes heroic conduct of Jewish servicemen. The behavior of these men was the unqualified answer to the anti-Semites. "Without question," remarked a ranking commander serving in Europe, "the account of Jews serving in my command exposed the lie of the Hitlers both here and at home."

WARTIME ZIONISM

In early 1942, American Zionists meeting at the "Extraordinary Zionist Conference" at New York's Biltmore Hotel showed increasing signs of militancy. In a marked change from previous, apologetic declarations, the broadly based group called for "a Jewish military force fighting under" the Star of David and, for the first time ever, demanded "that Palestine be established as a Jewish Commonwealth. . . ."

"The Biltmore Platform," noted one participant, "signaled the new voice of American Jewry. The hat-in-hand approach of the past had finally been replaced by a vigorous Jewish nationalism. Like falling dominoes, the organizations in attendance—Hadassah, Poale Zion, Mizrachi and ZOA—approved the platform. The day of appeasement," he exclaimed, "was over!"

The news of the Biltmore Platform shocked the anti-Zionists. "The day had to come when we must cry halt," declared a manifesto of non-Zionist rabbis meeting in Atlantic City:

> The conditioning of American Jewry by a Jewish flag and a Jewish army and a state in Palestine and a dual citizenship in America is more than we can accept. . . . We refuse any longer to be religious acrobats. We cannot pact with the untenable position in society which nationalism as a creed imposes on us.

The fear of foreign loyalty soon crystallized into the anti-Zionist American Council for Judaism. "This selfish organization," noted Aaron Geist, a St. Paul auto mechanic, "headed by Lessing Rosenwald, the heir to the Sears, Roebuck millions" and supported by such notables as Arthur Hays Sulzberger, publisher of the New York *Times,* "quickly mounted a propaganda offensive to neutralize the Biltmore Platform."

In response to the plethora of anti-Zionist rhetoric, the ZOA established the Committee on Unity for Palestine. Headed by Rabbi Arthur J. Lelyveld, the committee deployed speakers throughout the Jewish community and flooded the nation with literature bearing such dramatic titles as "A Stab in the Back," "They Sharpened the Dagger," and "'Anti-Zionism, a Fear Psychosis." They also enlisted the talents of Kurt Lewin, the noted psychologist, as their principal ideologue. His theory of "Jewish Self-Hatred" was soon leading the Zionist counter-attack. "Having achieved a relatively satisfactory status among non-Jews," he wrote,

> these individuals [anti-Zionists] are chiefly concerned with maintaining the status quo and so try to soft-pedal any action which might arouse the attention of the non-Jew. . . . They are so accustomed to viewing Jewish events with the eyes of the anti-Semite that they are afraid of the accusation of double-loyalty in the case of any outspoken Jewish action. If there is "danger" of a Jew's being appointed to the Supreme Court, they will not hesitate to warn the President against such an action. . . .

Not as sophisticated but as significant were the words of Chaplain Edward T. Sandrow, a Cederhurst, New York, rabbi serving with the armed forces in Alaska:

> . . . some of us would like to utter a word about the unfortunate and premeditated attempt to scuttle the Zionist movement in America. We in the Army—and I speak for hundreds and hundreds of men who have already gone to seek out the enemy, as well as those who are being prepared for huge and perilous tasks—were grievously pained . . . first, because we sensed an attempt to cast aspersions on our American loyalty. Here we are, wearing the uni-

form of our beloved country, training night and day for service overseas, risking life and limb for the land of which we are citizens, and whose every nook and corner we would die to protect . . . being challenged by those who, while good Americans, cannot claim to be doing a vital task for America, as we are. As Zionists, we thought that America was as precious to us as it purports to be to the members of the Council.

When we fight for the liberation of the Dutch, the Greeks, the Yugoslavs, the French, the Filipinos, the enslaved Catholics and Protestants, we also battle for the freedom of the Jews everywhere and for a Jewish homeland in Palestine.

Amid the debate raging between anti- and pro-Zionists, Ben Hecht, a newspaperman turned playwright and Hollywood screenwriter, suddenly found himself thrust into the fight for a Jewish homeland.

Born on the Lower East Side of Manhattan but raised in Wisconsin, Hecht was an "indifferent Jew." His identification with Judaism or Jewish causes was, to say the least, remote. In 1939, however, he "became a Jew and looked on the world with Jewish eyes. The German mass murder of Jews," he wrote in *A Child of the Century,* "had brought my Jewishness to the surface."

As Hecht watched the world through Jewish eyes, he assailed that segment of American Jewry that were "reluctant to speak out as Jews" but "preferred to conduct themselves as neutral Americans." The Hollywood film moguls, many of whom were his coreligionists, were among his prime targets. Quick to voice their objections to his biting commentary, some, rather apologetically, told the now militant journalist that they were pressured into remaining silent, that Joseph P. Kennedy, the United States Ambassador to England, whose financial empire reached the movie colony, warned them not to "make this a Jewish war."

Outraged by Kennedy's advice, Hecht responded with an article entitled, "My Tribe Is Called Israel." "My way of defending myself," he wrote, "is to answer as a Jew. . . . My angry [Jewish] critics all write that they are proud of being Americans and of wearing carnations, and that they are sick to death of such efforts as mine to Judaize them and increase generally the Jew-consciousness of the world."

Several days after this sharp criticism appeared, Peter Bergson, the Palestinian leader of the Revisionists (whose hostility to the American Zionists, though for different reasons, matched the American Council for Judaism) introduced himself to the screenwriter at New York's 21 Club. Hecht, who had had little interest in Palestine, joined Bergson's

Committee for a Jewish Army of Stateless and Palestinian Jews. Several persuasive lectures in Revisionist theory and a quick Revisionist course in Zionist history were enough. Hecht was now a committed Revisionist. Somewhat surprised by his new commitment, the journalist was soon asking his Hollywood friends for contributions for the *Irgun Zvai Leumi* (National Military Organization), one of the three Palestinian underground groups.*

"Approaching people one by one, however, wasn't the best way to raise large sums of money," noted one Hollywood writer,

> and Ben soon drew up plans for a mass rally. I received one of those invitations, as did a thousand others. Most of the Jewish executives—I guess it was expected—were frightened by the whole affair and refused to attend. The thought of supporting terrorism didn't sit well with them. But Ben's name, and it was a respected name, did get several hundred people to attend—Jews and gentiles. I know Hedda Hopper, David O. Selznick, and Burgess Meredith were there. Many, however, when they realized what the meeting was all about—the Irgun—were shocked. Some were frightened; others stormed out in disgust. I joined those who left.

Though the rally was not a smashing success, the ten thousand dollars collected (though $130,000 was pledged) was enough to send Bergson to Washington, D.C. Leon I. Feuer, who headed up a Jewish lobby in 1943, recalled Bergson's activities:

> He and his friends would tell congressmen and others not to pay any attention to the [American] Zionists, who did not really represent the Jews of Palestine. They, the Irgunists, claimed to be the real spokesmen for the Jewish independence movement in Palestine. *They* were the genuine freedom fighters. . . . The Bergson boys finally overshot their mark by staging, in the spring of 1944, a cheaply melodramatic "happening," the opening of a "Hebrew embassy." To mark the event, they called a press conference, covered for me by our young and brilliant public relations director, Harold Manson. The report he brought me that afternoon would have been unbelievably funny had it not been so tragically absurd. After a round of refreshments for the reporters, there was a flourish of trumpets, doors were thrown open, Bergson and his companions marched to the platform in the center of the room dressed—believe it or not—in black shirts and boots and proceeded to proclaim the Hebrew State. That was virtually the last we heard of the Hebrew Liberation Movement.

* *Haganah* (Defense) maintained by funds from the WZO was the largest.

Hecht continued to be heard from. In late 1943, as thousands of letters reached the White House demanding an end to immigration quotas, several show-business personalities—Kurt Weill, Billy Rose, and Moss Hart—helped Hecht organize a show called *We Will Never Die*. Promoted as a "Memorial to the Two Million Jewish Dead of Europe," the pageant was sponsored by the Emergency Committee to Save the Jewish People of Europe—an Irgun front group. Hecht, however, wanted broader support and thus invited over two dozen New York-based agencies to hear a reading of the script. "When the presentation was over," noted a participant, "Hecht asked for our support."

To everyone's surprise, Hecht did not ask for money—only an endorsement: permission to use their organizations' names on advertisements and press releases. Hecht recalled their reaction:

> . . . the representative of the American Jewish Congress stood up, and pointed a finger and cried out, "As an organization, we refuse to work with Morris Goldfarb! Never will the American Jewish Congress join up with anything in which the *Arbeiterring* [Labor-Socialists] is involved!" A man, possibly Morris Goldfarb, was on his feet yelling back, "And we will never work with the American Jewish Congress in a thousand years." Other voices arose. English and Yiddish outcries filled the room. Within five minutes a free-for-all, bitter as a Kentucky feud, was in full swing. The thirty-two Jewish organizations were denouncing each other as Socialists, as Fascists, as Christians, as undesirables of every stripe. The door opened and the thirty-third representative—he who had taken the wrong subway—entered. He understood what was going on and began yelling without taking his hat off.

The show, without major organizational support, was still produced. "By the thousands," recalled one observer, "volunteers came to help us —actors, singers, cantors, public-relations people, and stagehands." "They were like strange soldiers come from the moon to help the Jews," wrote Hecht.

"While we were rehearsing," said another observer, "Hecht received a telephone call from Stephen Wise. The rabbi wanted Ben to call the show off, but he refused. In fact, shortly before the performance, Billy Rose asked Governor Dewey to declare the day on which the pageant was to be performed a day of official mourning—sort of a memorial to the two million dead." The governor agreed, however perplexed he was by the internal madness of the Zionists.

As soon as Wise received word that Dewey was entertaining the request, he left for Albany. He was going to warn the governor that the Jewish vote might go to the Democrats if he insisted on helping those "dangerous and irresponsible racketeers. . . ."

Wise feared Hecht's association with the Irgun, right-wing militants who opposed the methods of the Jewish Agency headed by David Ben-Gurion, which sought a Jewish homeland through negotiation with the British and was willing to settle for a Jewish state coexisting with an Arab one in Palestine. The Irgun demanded *all* of Palestine and Transjordan. Its motto was "Judea collapsed in fire and blood. Judea will rise in fire and blood." Wise, like many moderate Jews, feared that the Irgun's campaign of terror and their obsessiveness would bring chaos and failure to the dream of a Jewish state.

In the midst of Hecht's Revisionist activities, the American Zionists found themselves confronted by still another sharp split—this time over belief in Roosevelt's assurances on Palestine. "Most of us," noted Ralph Pollock, a Rhode Island businessman, "followed Wise's trust in the President to live up to his campaign pledge." A minority, however, led by Abba Hillel Silver, charged that FDR was working against Zionist aims. "Though he [Roosevelt] was always quick to offer an encouraging pledge," noted Leonard Leibowitz, a New York attorney, "he managed to hide the fact that hundreds of thousands of Jews lost their lives while the British, along with his complicity, were keeping refugees out of Palestine."

Leibowitz's suspicions were well founded. On March 3, 1944, New York Senator Robert Wagner—at the time campaigning for re-election in the state with the largest Jewish vote in the nation—reminded the President of the size of the American Zionist Emergency Councils (AZEC) letter-writing campaign to the White House, noting "how the Jews of America feel about the situation."

"You know, Bob, where I stand on Palestine; my heart is still in the right place," said the President.

"Why don't you call leaders of American Zionism and tell them that?" Wagner quickly asked.

A week later, Roosevelt invited Wise and Silver to the White House to ask for their advice. "You have to make a reassuring statement on Palestine," Wise told the President. "American Jewry knows we are here, and we can't return to them empty-handed."

"What shall I say?" asked the President.

Almost before he finished the sentence, Wise placed a prepared press release on FDR's desk. Roosevelt read it, suggested some changes so as not to embarrass the British, and authorized its release. Few who read their newspapers the next morning knew that the statement was merely the wishful thinking of the two Zionist rabbis.

> The President has authorized us to say that the American Government has never given its approval to the White Paper of 1939. The President expressed his conviction that when future decisions are reached, full justice will be done to those who seek a Jewish National Home, for which our Government and the American people have always had the deepest sympathy, today more than ever in view of the tragic plight of hundreds of thousands of homeless Jewish refugees.

Zionists acclaimed the announcement a victory. "It was the first time," said an observer, "that FDR publicly supported the creation of a Jewish Palestine." Minutes after Wise and Silver left the White House, Roosevelt's duplicity was again evident as he congratulated Speaker Sam Rayburn for blocking a House resolution supporting a Jewish commonwealth.

Undaunted by such setbacks, the Zionists continued their agitation. "In the summer of 1944," recalled Hyman Goldman, a retired Kansas businessman active in Zionist affairs, "both parties were holding national conventions and our aim was to capture their attention—to get a Palestine plank in their platforms." The pressure, felt by both Democrats and Republicans, paid off handsomely. The Republican plank called for "the opening of Palestine . . . to unrestricted immigration [and] a free and democratic [Jewish] Commonwealth" and, less than a week later, the Democrats followed suit. American Jewry, for the moment, was jubilant.

On the heels of the two national conventions, the ZOA opened its own convention, in Atlantic City in mid-October. Aware that the meeting would be attended by key Zionists from every corner of the nation, Dewey went shopping for votes. "I hereby endorse the Palestine plank of the Republican platform," read a press release. "As President I would use my best offices to have our Government working together with Great Britain to achieve this great objective. . . ."

Several days later, Roosevelt put in his bid for the Jewish vote by asking Senator Wagner, an outstanding advocate of Zionist causes, to represent his views at the Atlantic City meeting:

October 15, 1944

Dear Bob:

Knowing that you are to attend . . . the convention of the ZOA, I ask you to convey to the delegates assembled my cordial greeting. . . .

Efforts will be made to find appropriate ways and means of effecting this policy [the Democratic plank favoring a Jewish Commonwealth] as soon as practicable. I know how long and ardently the the Jewish people have worked and prayed for the establishment of Palestine as a free and democratic Jewish commonwealth. I am convinced that the American people give their support to this aim and if reelected I shall help to bring about its realization.

"When we heard Wagner relate the President's pledge," declared a delegate from Philadelphia, "we were not only hopeful but jubilant. First Dewey and then Roosevelt. Most of us were convinced that the establishment of a Jewish commonwealth was now a bi-partisan policy." The Philadelphia delegate was of course wrong. "On the very morrow of this commitment," wrote historian Selig Adler,

the State Department, with White House approval, dispatched new guarantees to the Arabs. Two months later, another pro-Zionist resolution was killed in Congress as a result of presidential orders. Moreover, on three separate occasions Roosevelt approved a projected joint Anglo-American freezing, for the duration, the status quo in the Holy Land. The purported objective of this declaration [October 15 letter to the ZOA convention] was to silence Zionist agitation. . . .

With the exception of Abba Hillel Silver, most Zionist leaders blamed a pro-Arab State Department, and not the President, for undercutting Zionist aims. Several weeks before Roosevelt's death, however, the press reported a series of explosive events that finally exposed his double-dealing policy. "These electric events," wrote Adler, "involved the meeting between FDR and the King of Saudi Arabia on the President's return from the historic Yalta conference."

On a sunny February day in 1945, the USS *Quincy* lay at anchor in the blue waters of Egypt's Suez Canal. "What took place on board," said an aide of Rabbi Silver, "convinced most of us, even the die-hard Roosevelt lovers, that the President was, in no uncertain terms, an enemy of Zionism."

According to William A. Eddy, Roosevelt's interpreter, the President raised the question of the Jewish refugees and asked the Arabian ruler for suggestions. Ibn Saud quickly replied, "Give them . . . the choicest lands and homes of the Germans who have oppressed them. . . . It is the 'Christian' Germans who stole their homes and lives. Let the Germans pay. The Arabs would choose to die rather than yield their lands to the Jews." Impressed with the monarch's answer, FDR reassured the oil-rich king that he would make no move hostile to Arab interests.

Standing before a joint session of Congress, FDR reported on his Yalta meeting. Death seemed imminent as he addressed the assembled representatives. "He looked exhausted," noted one congressman. "He was hesitant and fumbled. At times, he rambled and was incomprehensible." Suddenly, the President injected an unexpected remark about his meeting with Ibn Saud: "Of the problems of Arabia: I learned more about that whole problem, the Moslem problem, the Jewish problem, by talking with Ibn Saud for five minutes than I could have learned in an exchange of two or three dozen letters."

"The remark praising Ibn Saud's knowledge of the Jewish question," said a member of the press, "hit like a bolt of lightning. Some people were angry, others astonished; the Jews, and not only the Zionists among them, were mortified. You could *feel* their humiliation."

"With all due respect to the President and King Ibn Saud," commented Colorado's Senator Edward Johnson, a staunch Zionist supporter, "I must say that the choice of the desert king as expert on the Jewish question is nothing short of amazing. . . . I imagine that even Fala [FDR's dog] would be more of an expert." "Almost bordering on the ridiculous," added Judge Samuel Rosenman, a close adviser and friend of the President, "a thought that must have popped into his head at just that moment."

To quell the Zionist outcry that followed, Roosevelt publicly assured Wise that he had not forgotten his campaign pledge favoring a Jewish homeland, and harassed by an anti-Zionist communication from Ibn Saud, FDR responded that his promise to the king "with regard to the question of Palestine . . . is unchanged. . . ." On April 12, 1945, FDR's duplicity once more surfaced as he authorized another communication—this time to Prince Abd-ul-Ilah, the regent of Iraq:

> I have received the letter which you sent me under date of March 10 and in which you outline the attitude of the Arabs toward the question of Palestine.
>
> I take this opportunity to express to you my appreciation for this statement of the Arab position. . . . I desire in this connection, to renew to you assurances which have been previously com-

municated to the Iraqi Government to the effect that in view of the Government of the United States no decision affecting the basic situation in Palestine should be reached without full consultation with both Arabs and Jews.

I am looking forward to meeting Your Highness on the occasion of your forthcoming visit to the United States. . . .

The meeting between the President and the Iraqi leader never took place. While FDR's staff was preparing to send the letter, the President suffered a massive cerebral hemorrhage at his Warm Springs, Georgia, home. That evening, Harry S Truman became president. "What," asked one Zionist leader on that fateful day, "will be his Palestine policy?"

CHAPTER VIII

No Longer Strangers

A NATION REBORN

"MA!" exclaimed nine-year-old Philip Zukerman as he ran through the lobby of his Bronx apartment house, "the President's dead!" Philip's mother shouted at her son to "behave. That's no joke," she told the youngster. "Go do your homework. Supper will be ready soon."

"But Ma!" continued, "they interrupted the Lone Range—" "Oh, my God!" exclaimed Mrs. Zukerman as she placed her hands to her mouth." "The boy isn't lying." For the first time in her life, Eva Zukerman fainted.

As though they had lost a father, American Jewry wept when they heard the news of FDR's death. "We lost a friend that day," said a Philadelphia housewife. "A member of the family. Someone who understood us. Who loved us. He loved the helpless—the oppressed and the downtrodden."

"Who can we turn to?" she asked. "Truman? Who's he? How can this man from the Midwest understand our anguish? How can he replace *the President?*"

In the emotionally charged atmosphere following FDR's death, even those who bitterly denounced the Ibn Saud remark acted as though an irreplaceable ally had been slain. A few, like the outspoken Ben Hecht, saw things differently. For him, Roosevelt offered only empty promises: "No humanitarian hero was lying dead for me," wrote Hecht. "A bold and fretful man, an arrogant and lusty man, but a stranger to love and goodness, had died for me. A man with the gift of making himself unreasonably loved, a man who had discovered the poor, like some happy political explorer come upon a hidden continent of voters, was being wept over, and all his great deeds acclaimed. In my mind his chief monument remained—the dead Jews of Europe."

When Harry S Truman took the presidential oath, he, too, was certainly no Zionist. "I have no desire to send five hundred thousand American soldiers to make peace in Palestine," he told a press conference on August 10, 1945. Several days later, however, while reading a report that spoke of "Jewish displaced persons," his humanitarian nerve was touched. "[They are] living under guard behind barbed-wire fences in camps," read the communication from Earl Harrison, Truman's emissary to Europe, "amid crowded, frequently unsanitary and generally grim conditions, in complete idleness, . . . waiting, hoping for some encouragement and action on their behalf. . . . The desire to leave Germany is an urgent one. . . . They want to be evacuated to Palestine now. . . . The civilized world," pleaded Harrison, "owes it to this handful of survivors to provide them with a home where . . . they can begin to live as human beings. . . . And for the vast majority of them, that home is Palestine."

Truman's response was instantaneous and humane. He ordered General Eisenhower to take immediate action to alleviate conditions at the DP camps and provide, for as many Jews as possible, outside housing. He also forwarded the report to British Prime Minister Attlee, accompanied by a letter stating his "belief that no other single matter is so important for those who have known the horrors of the concentration camps . . . as is the future immigration possibilities into Palestine. . . ."

Truman's efforts to persuade the British to open Palestine to Jewish refugees, which over the next two and a half years occupied an inordinate amount of his time, indirectly led to the creation of the State of Israel.

While Truman's tactful diplomacy tried to open the gates of Palestine, some American Jews, tired of empty promises, threw their support behind the clandestine military operations of Palestine's Jewish underground. Aware of this new militancy, David Ben–Gurion went "shopping." "Arms meant money," he declared, "and we had none."

> I did not expect to get arms from the United States but I did expect to get money to finance purchases which might be effected elsewhere. And for this I turned to a good friend, Henry Montor, who had directed with such success the United Jewish Appeal. . . . I

asked him for a list of twenty wealthy Jews whose devotion to the security of Palestinian Jewry was wholehearted, and I asked another friend, Rudolph Sonneborn, to offer his house for a meeting on a subject of great importance. The result of the meeting was several million dollars with which we could begin to "shop" for machinery and equipment to set up a proper arms industry.

Hecht, in a separate quest for funds, was busily dramatizing the exploits of the Irgun. Reacting to stories that boasted of commando raids on British installations, some American Jews began to ask: "Where do I join up?" "I want a gun," they said. "I want to fight."

"I watched with awe," Hecht wrote,

> as they rose out of the stores and workshops and came to our side. Jewish clerks and sales ladies, garage workers, plasterers, elevator boys, Yeshiva students, policemen, garment workers, prize fighters; Jewish soldiers and sailors still in American uniforms, Jews from nightclubs, tenements, farm lands, synagogues and even penthouses came boldly to the Irgun banner. . . . They poured their dollar bills and five-dollar bills into the Irgun coffers and the coffers swelled with millions. They crowded our rallies and theaters. They cheered with joy and there was no more fear in them than in any other group of humans whooping for victory. They were all Americans with no desire to settle anywhere else, but they stormed the [Irgun] offices demanding to be ferried to Palestine into the ranks of the Irgun.

The movie moguls refused to contribute to Hecht's cause. David O. Selznick said, "I am an American, not a Jew, and I am not interested in Jewish political problems." To win Selznick over, Hecht offered to phone three of the producer's closest friends and pose this question: "Is David O. Selznick an American or a Jew?" If only one replied, "an American," Hecht would give up. Selznick, to his consternation, lost the bet, but to his credit he threw himself into the struggle with furious energy and became the head of the motion-picture division of the UJA.

Even the Jewish "underworld" rushed to the support of Hecht's freedom fighters. Mickey Cohen, the czar of California's illegal gambling, held a fund-raising dinner of, wrote Hecht, "a thousand bookies, exprize fighters, gamblers, jockeys, touts and all sorts of lawless and semilawless characters; and their womenfolk." After Hecht addressed the group, "Madam Frankie Spitz took over the hat passing. There was no welching. Each of the bookies, toughies, and fancy dudes stood up and called out firmly his contribution."

"I stood against the back wall with Mickey," wrote Hecht. "He struck me a stinging blow on the arm and said, 'Make another speech and hit 'em again.'"

Hecht, exhausted, declined. The gambler turned to his bodyguard: "You tell 'em," he ordered. "Tell 'em they're a lot o' cheap crumbs and they gotta give double." The bodyguard, wrote Hecht, "roared inarticulately over the microphone for a spell. When he had done, Mickey came to the edge of the stage and stood in the floodlights. He said nothing. Man by man, the 'underworld' stood up and doubled the ante for the Irgun."

That evening, noted Cohen, two hundred thousand dollars was raised for "Jews ready to knock hell out of all the bums in the world who don't like them."

Following the "underworld Zionist meeting," Hecht, via a paid advertisement in the New York *Herald Tribune,* published a "Letter to the Terrorists of Palestine." The letter, picked up as a news item by other newspapers was read from coast to coast:

> My Brave Friends,
>
> You may not believe what I write to you, for there is a lot of fertilizer in the air at the moment.
>
> But, on my word as an old reporter, what I write is true.
>
> The Jews of America are for you. You are their champions. You are the grin they wear. You are the feather in their hats.
>
> In the past fifteen hundred years every nation of Europe has taken a crack at the Jews. This time the British are at bat.
>
> You are the first answer that makes sense—to the New World.
>
> Every time you blow up a British arsenal, or wreck a British jail, or send a British railroad train sky high, or rob a British bank, or let go with your guns and bombs at the British betrayers and invaders of your homeland, the Jews of America make a little holiday in their hearts.

Some Jews, added Hecht, were against the terrorists. "Unfortunately, this small percentage includes practically all the rich Jews of America, all the Jewish organizations whom the American newspapers call 'The Jewish Leaders.' They're all against.

> Every time you throw a punch at the British betrayers of your homeland, nearly all these Jews have a collective conniption fit.
>
> They rush in waving white handkerchiefs and alibis. They didn't do it—not they!
>
> Respectable people don't fight. They grabble.

Naturally, advertisements of this nature outraged the British. Americans, however, especially Jews, closed their ears to British protests. "We considered England a hostile nation," noted Albert Siegel, a recent high school graduate on his way to join Haganah. "England's Palestine policy is shameful." After hearing of the fate of the *Exodus,* a Haganah ship smuggling immigrants to Palestine, American Jewry agreed even more with the young volunteer. *Kol Yisrael* (the Voice of Israel), Haganah's secret radio, was the first to announce the tragedy:

> This is the refugee ship *Exodus 1947.* Before dawn today we were attacked by five British destroyers and one cruiser. . . . The assailants immediately opened fire, threw gas bombs, and rammed our ship from three directions. On deck there are one dead, five dying, and one hundred twenty wounded. The resistance continued for more than three hours. Owing to the severe losses and the condition of the ship, which is in danger of sinking, we were compelled to sail in the direction of Haifa in order to save the 4,500 refugees on board from drowning.

"The ship looked like a matchbox that had been splintered by a nutcracker," recalled an eyewitness. "In the torn, square hole, as big as an open blitzed barn, we could see a muddle of bedding, possessions, plumbing, broken pipes, overflowing toilets, half-naked men, women looking for children. Cabins were bashed in; railings were ripped off; the lifesaving rafts were dangling at crazy angles."

Amid the blare of loudspeakers directing people off the boat, the smashing of glass bottles which the refugees took along to hold drinking water, and the explosion of British depth charges to ward off swimmers who might attach mines to damage the ship, the slow, weary march of the refugees began to the prison boats. "The pier," said a British soldier, "began to take on the noise and smell and animal tragedy of a Chicago slaughter house. The cattle moved slowly down the tracks."

When news of this latest British action reached America the Jewish community swung into action. Full-page ads appeared in the nation's press pleading with sympathizers to boycott British goods, and rallies, attended by Jews and non-Jews alike, called on "all freedom-loving Americans to demand a stop to the British atrocities in Palestine." "Boycott British goods," pleaded the speakers. "No one use British goods or services. . . . No shipping, no insurance, no airlines, no tourist travel." Posters with similar themes soon appeared on subway platforms, at bus terminals, in store windows, and on automobile bumpers: DON'T BE A PARTY TO MURDER. DON'T BUY BRITISH GOODS.

With Palestine gripped by anarchy, the British Government began to consider walking away from its League of Nations mandate. Irgun terrorism was on the rise, the boycott was beginning to make itself felt, and most important of all, Truman was still trying to open the gates of Palestine to one hundred thousand refugees. "I am bound to say," declared Lord Altrincham, one of the few members of the House of Lords opposed to his government's Palestine policy, "that if the United States continues to claim to dictate a policy for immigration into Palestine regardless of the facts while we bear the brunt, then the only course for us is to return the mandate to the United Nations and to ask them to take action upon it."

Winston Churchill echoed these sentiments: "We should definitely give notice that unless the United States comes in with us shoulder to shoulder on a fifty-fifty basis, to take a half-and-half share of the bloodshed, odium, trouble, expense, and worry, we will lay our mandate at the feet of the United Nations." Significantly, the British would eventually do just that: lay the problem at the feet of the world assembly.

The day the United Nations voted to partition Palestine, almost ten thousand spectators sought admission to the Lake Success, New York, meeting hall. Rather than return home to join the millions glued to their radios, those denied entrance waited to hear the results. "The wait was worth it," noted an observer. "The news was as sweet as honey." "The Mandate for Palestine," read the U.N. measure,

> shall terminate as soon as possible, but in any case not later than August 1, 1948. . . . Independent Arab and Jewish States and the specific international regime for the City of Jerusalem . . . shall come into existence in Palestine two months after the [British] evacuation. . . .

"We've got it! We've got it! We've won!" cried a woman in the visitors' gallery. In the lobby there were kisses and tears and excited laughter. In the delegates' lounge a rabbi cried, "This is the day the Lord hath made! Let us rejoice in it and be glad." In the assembly, pandemonium broke loose. "Applause," said Dov Joseph, of the Jewish Agency, "rolled around the walls."

> Men embraced each other, sobbing with joy; women were almost hysterical with gladness. The face of the British delegate was grim and set, and the Arab representatives sat white with a fury which was to express itself, in a few short hours, in a wave of disorder, murder, and sabotage throughout Palestine. But, for the brief spell,

it was our moment. The President knocked good-humoredly for order with his gavel, but the hubbub continued to mount. The meeting was adjourned; the delegates streamed into the lobby; the galleries emptied, and the Jewish observers who were present were left to savor the sweet fulfillment of that moment of destiny.

"A JEWISH STATE—MAZAL TOV!" proclaimed a banner headine in the *Jewish Morning Journal.* "The whole Jewish world will say *mazal tov!"*

Mazal tov! American Jews were ecstatic. Parading through the streets, they wished the traditional *mazal tov* to friends and strangers. "I ran out of the house and embraced and kissed everyone in sight," said Morty Blum, a Chicago tailor. "There was joy in the streets. Wherever I went that day, there was spontaneous joy. . . . All meetings, all gatherings which were held [that] night," wrote Morris Duchovny, a reporter for the *Jewish Morning Journal,* "all weddings, all family celebrations were turned into national demonstrations. There was joy! There was *mazal tov!* There was the blessing of the new life for the nation Israel."

While American Jewry celebrated the UN's historic decision, Arab gunmen went into action. Snipers fired on civilians, synagogues were set ablaze, and Jewish shops were looted. "Near Lod Airfield," said an eyewitness, "a bus was ambushed." Another reported that an ambulance was attacked near Jersualem. "Arab mobs," he reported, "dragged out the occupants and brutally beat them." "Violence engulfed the Palestinian Jews," noted a third witness. "Seventy-four people were killed in that week of fighting. And to make matters worse, the British-trained Arab Legion occupied the West Bank."

To meet the emergency, the Jewish Agency mobilized Haganah. "But we needed guns," said a volunteer from Chicago, "and Truman's arms embargo to the Middle East made things worse: the Arabs were well equipped by the British."

American Jewry followed the events in Palestine with intense interest. And they, too, knew that their coreligionists needed weapons. "We came too far to allow our accomplishments to be destroyed by a lack of arms," said a California Zionist. "So we organized a national letter-writing campaign to tell the President just how we felt. We flooded the White House with thousands of postcards, letters, and telegrams. It would have taken Truman a thousand years to read them all."

Most of the mail Truman received in the wake of the Mid-East eruption was the result of a well-organized campaign. "In the middle of our *bar mitzvah* lesson," noted Samuel Schulman, a twelve-year-old student in Philadelphia, "the rabbi came into class and asked for our attention. 'Put aside whatever you're doing,' he said, 'and write this letter, in your own words, to the President.' The rabbi then placed a form letter on the blackboard:

> Dear President Truman:
> I am a student in _____ Hebrew School in _____ (place). I am ____ years of age. Please help the Jewish boys and girls in Palestine so they can win their battle for freedom. The Arabs are attacking them and they cannot defend themselves. We are told that their brothers and fathers do not have enough guns to defend themselves because they have no place to buy them. Why can't the United States furnish them with guns just like we did England and France? The United States promised to help the new Jewish State. As an American child, I feel sure our country will make good its promise.

"When we finished," said Schulman, "he asked us to take home a second letter—this one for our parents."

> Dear President Truman,
> We are proud of the U.S.A. and of your administration for having done so much to make possible the U.N. decision regarding a Jewish State in Palestine. But we are in great anxiety because evil men are trying to annul that glorious promise. . . . What happens to the setting up of the new Jewish State will be a barometer of faith or lack of faith in the efforts made to create a more united and better world.
> We respectfully beg of you, Mr. President, to use your powerful influence that—
> The United States should take the lead in the Security Council to send an international force to Palestine; and to give an immediate allotment of arms to equip the Jewish militia.

Besieged by countless letters and sought after by hundreds of supporters of the Jewish cause, a weary Truman refused to entertain a Jewish Agency request to meet with Chaim Weizmann.

"Individuals and groups," noted the President some years later, "usually asked me, in rather quarrelsome and emotional ways, to stop the Arabs, to keep the British from supporting the Arabs, to furnish American soldiers, to do this, that, and the other. I think I can say that I kept my faith in the rightness of my policy in spite of some of the Jews. When I say 'the Jews,' I mean, of course, the extreme Zionists. I know that most Americans of Jewish faith, while they hoped for the restoration of Jewish homeland, are and always have been Americans first and foremost."

"As the pressure mounted," noted Truman, "I found it necessary to give instructions that I did not want to be approached by any more spokesmen for the Zionist cause."

Political pressure and letter writing were not the only means by which American Jews responded to the crisis. "I went with my father to *shul* one night," said Marvin Schecter, a fifteen-year-old student from Brooklyn, "and in a crowded back room there were about two dozen men—some of them were holding packages."

"We'll take anything you have," said a stranger in broken English.

"Suddenly the men moved forward. They unwrapped their packages. They were guns! German and Japanese weapons they had brought home. Pistols, rifles. Maxie Schultz carefully placed three German pistols on the table and then unwrapped a rifle. I think it was an American-made M-1."

"The rifle," said Schultz, a CCNY student studying under the G.I. Bill, "is a gift from General Patton. I walked through Europe with it."

"Before the meeting broke up," said Schecter, "the stranger," who turned out to be a Haganah officer, "asked the men to spread the word. 'We will take anything, in any condition. Just get it here by the end of the week. You know where I can be found.'

"On our way home we stopped by a candy store and picked up several more rifles. . . . When my father came out he was beaming. Georgie Cohen had promised him a machine gun."

Also engaged in the illegal gun traffic were Joseph Untermeyer, the nineteen-year-old son of writer Louis Untermeyer, and Isaiah Warshaw. In April 1948, unlike Schecter and his father, these two members of the Zionist Youth Movement were arrested for possession of hand grenades, rifles, revolvers, and ammunition. The weapons, hidden in packages of clothing and food were destined for Palestine. Paul O'Dwyer, an early Irgun supporter who had helped to smuggle DP's into Palestine, acted as counsel.*

Standing before the judge, O'Dwyer declared that New York's gun-control law, the Sullivan Act, had been passed "to prevent gangsterism" while "these guns were to be sent to Palestine to protect people in their homes." The defendants, he insisted, had not known that the weapons were among the packages, but he said, even if they had had

* Mr. O'Dwyer is the former president of the New York City Council.

knowledge of the contents of the crates, "it would have been a worth-while act." "Case dismissed," declared the judge.

Other New York youths were arrested for possession of several boxes of weapons. O'Dwyer again represented the defendants and again he called for a dismissal. "If there is any conspiracy at all," he told the court, "that conspiracy exists with the State Department, and—" The judge interrupted: "Case dismissed."

On another occasion, six men were taken into custody in New Jersey for possession of sixty thousand pounds of T.N.T. bound for Palestine. Judge Sylvester Ryan heard the case. "You were endeavoring to provide means of defense to an otherwise helpless people," he told the defendants. "I do not regard you men as criminals and therefore will not impose any jail sentence. I likewise feel that it will serve no useful purpose to impose a fine."

A more dramatic case of arms smuggling was that of two California Jews, Leo Gardner and Sam Lewis. The two, who had served in the Army Air Corps, convinced the Jewish Agency to buy several surplus aircraft. The Jewish Agency gave the project its blessing and soon, with the aid of several others—Al Schwimmer, Ray Selk, William Sosnov, and Irvin "Swifty" Shindler—the group was overhauling what was to be the beginning of a Jewish air force.

Everyone believed that they would be ferrying refugees to Palestine. Early in 1948 they learned the real reasons for the project: to smuggle weapons for Haganah. A shipment of arms, they were told, was waiting for them in Hawaii; they were ordered to pick the weapons up.

After the order was given, the group contacted Hank Greenspun, a Las Vegas radio-station owner. They needed his help. After they told him of their plans, he immediately volunteered for the mission. He flew to Hawaii and picked up four hundred aerial machine guns and forty-five aircraft engines. The matériel, packed in crates marked AIRCRAFT ENGINE, was quietly brought to Los Angeles, entering the country uninspected by customs officials.

Quickly the weapons were uncrated and dispersed among Zionist sympathizers. The engines, which were legitimate enough equipment for an airline to have, remained at Schwimmer's Burbank headquarters. When the FBI raided Schwimmer's office, all they found were spare parts and engines. They left empty-handed.

Americans were not the only ones who volunteered to fly for Haganah. There were South Africans, Swedes, Frenchmen, and even a few British—men who opposed their nation's Palestine policy. "But for sheer picturesqueness," noted Benjamin Kagan, a Haganah air force officer,

> no group could compare with the Americans. Among them were dedicated volunteers, mercenaries, and adventurers out for anything. No two were alike. Almost all of them had to their credit a past history that would make the most imaginative novelist pale with envy. The majority were American Jews, some professed the convictions of ardent Zionists; others were indifferent to our problems, but that did not prevent them from fighting passionately for our cause. They felt that they were Americans first of all, and they remained that way throughout everything. However, each time that the existence of the Jewish people was threatened, we could count on them; we would find them ready to fight, and in the front lines.

One who fought in the front lines was West Point graduate Colonel David "Mickey" Marcus. Discharged from the U. S. Army in 1947, the Brooklyn-born combat veteran joined Haganah during the crucial days of the 1948 war for independence.

Marcus, who fought under the pseudonym "Brigadier General Stone," was killed during the siege of Jerusalem. "The day of his death," wrote Eve Kushner, a Tel Aviv housewife at whose home Marcus had stayed, "will remain for us a day of mourning for as long as we live, and our children and grandchildren will be taught to love and admire the American soldier who came to help us in this desperate, difficult fight." Ted Berkman, author of Marcus's biography, described the day the Haganah hero came home:

> His body had been flown to the United States . . . on June 30, fulfilling to the letter his pledge to be "home by the end of June." In the few days since his death, the tears and tributes had flowed from every corner of the world. A farewell toast was offered in a Normandy café; and there was a moment of sadness in the villa of a Soviet marshal outside Moscow. The Palestine struggle, editorialized the New York *Herald Tribune,* would henceforth be seen in a new light "because a good American came to it by a route that thousands of his countrymen followed a part of the way, over the beaches in Normandy . . . to the shame and shock of Dachau." At West Point the color guard came to a halt, and the bird choir fell quiet. Across the grave, the ten honorary pall-bearers from Mickey's Class of 1924 faced the family. Alongside Big Mike were two of Israel's doughtiest fighters, Moshe Dayan . . . and Yoself Hamburger, Haganah commander aboard the original SS *Exodus.*

Of the thousands of men who are buried at West Point, Colonel Marcus has the distinction of being the only one killed while fighting under a foreign flag.

Aware that its citizens were fighting for Haganah and Irgun, the State Department announced that passports would not be granted for "the purpose of proceeding abroad to enter foreign military service. . . . That while engaged in such service Americans will not be regarded as entitled to recognition as citizens."

The decree was aimed at the George Washington Legion, a military group organized by Hecht, and the Irgun's American League for a Free Palestine. Barney Ross, the Jewish prize-fighting great and ex-Marine Corps hero, took exception to the rule. Addressing an Irgun recruiting rally, he said that he would not like to lose his citizenship but "certainly [wanted] the right to fight for a cause that is just. All I've got left," said the champ, "is my heart and two good hands to talk for me." Two months later, the George Washington Legion claimed that five thousand of its supporters were willing to go to Palestine.

While Arab and Jew were spilling each other's blood, word reached American Zionists that the White House might temporarily withdraw its support of partition. "The only man who could convince Truman of the error of this," noted a Zionist official, "was Chaim Weizmann. The problem, however, was how to get the two men together. Eddie Jacobson, an old Kansas City friend of the President, was the answer."

When Harry Truman and Eddie Jacobson returned home in 1919 from the battlefields of Europe, they decided to open a men's clothing store in Kansas City. "The idea of a haberdashery was Eddie's," wrote Truman, "and it was agreed that he would be the buyer and that I would act as a salesman."

In their first two years, the two men sold over seventy thousand dollars' worth of merchandise. In 1922, three years after the store opened, the business was failing. "Our creditors and the banks we owed began to press us," wrote Truman, "and when we closed out, later in 1922, we were hopelessly in debt."

> Neither Jacobson nor I wished to go into bankruptcy, as so many were doing during that period. We both wanted to pay all the indebtedness in full. Still, we did not find that easy. . . . It was a struggle for both of us during the next several years, and in February 1925 Jacobson finally found himself unable to withstand the pressure.

Though Jacobson was never a Zionist, several Kansas City Jews knew of his long-standing friendship with the President. Thus, Mrs. Ernest E. Peiser, an influential leader of Missouri's Hadassah, set out to convert the wartime friend and former business partner of the President. Through her husband's business associate Herman Rosenberg, who also served with the two men in France, she met Jacobson. Immediately, the conversion began. She gave him Zionist literature, introduced him to several influential Zionists, and finally persuaded him to meet with Arthur Lelyveld, head of the Committee on Unity for Palestine. After several visits from the persuasive Lelyveld, the Kansas City merchant was a Zionist. The conversion complete, Jacobson agreed to arrange a meeting between Truman and Weizmann. "Mr. President," wrote Jacobson,

> I know that you have very excellent reasons for not wanting to see Dr. Weizmann. No one realizes more than I the amount of pressure that is being thrown on you during these critical days, but as you once told me, this gentleman is the greatest statesman and the finest leader that my people have. He is very old and heartbroken that he could not get to see you. Mr. President, I have asked you for very little in the way of favors during all our years of friendship, but am begging of you to see Dr. Weizmann as soon as possible. I can assure you that I would not plead to you for any other of our leaders.

"I waited impatiently for a reply," wrote Jacobson; "my anxiety increased during these intervening days, because I briefed myself in preparing to see the President."

On Friday, March 12, 1948, Jacobson left for the Capital. As usual, he did not make an appointment, but took his chances. He arrived at the White House on Saturday and was greeted by presidential assistant Matt Connelly, who advised and urged him not to discuss Palestine. He quickly told Connelly that that was why he was in Washington.

As Jacobson entered the Oval Office, he noticed that the President was looking well, that his trip to Florida had done him a world of good. For a few moments they talked about their families, Jacobson's business, and other personal matters.

Jacobson started to cry. "Great tears were running down his cheeks," wrote Truman.

"Eddie, you son of a bitch, you promised me you wouldn't say a word about what's going on over there."

"I haven't said a word but every time I think of the homeless Jews, . . . I think about Dr. Weizmann, I start crying. I can't help it."

"Eddie, that's enough. That's the last word."

"Harry, all of your life you have had a hero. You are probably the best-read man in America on the life of Andrew Jackson. I remember when we had our store together and you were always reading books and papers and pamphlets on this great American.

> Well, Harry, I too have a hero, a man I never met, but who is, I think, the greatest Jew who ever lived. . . . I am talking about Chaim Weizmann; he is a very sick man, almost broken in health, but he travelled thousands and thousands of miles just to see you and plead the cause of my people. Now you refuse to see him because you were insulted by some of our American Jewish leaders, even though you know that Weizmann had absolutely nothing to do with these insults and would be the last man to be a party to them.

As Jacobson spoke, Truman began to tap on his desk. Suddenly, the President swirled around and looked out the window. Then he glanced over to a picture of his family. Jacobson knew the sign. Truman was considering the request. "I don't know how many seconds passed in silence," wrote Jacobson, "but it seemed like centuries."

Truman turned and looked his friend straight in the eye "and," reported Jacobson, "said the most endearing words I had ever heard from his lips. . . ."

"Eddie, you son of a bitch, I ought to have you thrown right out of here for breaking your promise; you knew damn good and well I couldn't stand seeing you cry.

"I will see him. Tell Matt to arrange this meeting. . . ."

As soon as Jacobson left, Truman called the State Department and told them of his decision.

"What flag should we fly, Mr. President?"

"Look here," snapped Truman, "he's staying at the Waldorf Astoria in New York. Find out what they are flying and do the same."

The aging Weizmann was "hustled" into the White House through a side gate—the public was not to know of the meeting. "I told him," wrote Truman, "as plainly as I could, why I had at first put off seeing him. He understood. I explained to him what the basis of my interest in the Jewish problem was and that my primary concern was to see justice done without bloodshed. And when he left my office I felt he had reached a full understanding of my policy and that I knew what it was he wanted."

"You can bank on us, I am for partition," he reassured the Zionist leader.

On Friday, May 14, 1948, the British left Palestine. Meeting late that same afternoon in the Tel Aviv Museum, several hundred people listened as Ben–Gurion spoke under a portrait of Theodor Herzl: "We, the members of the National Council, representing the Jewish people in Palestine, and the World Zionist Movement, are met together in solemn assembly today, the day of termination of the British mandate . . . and by virtue of the natural and historic right of the Jewish people and of the resolution of the General Assembly of the United Nations, we hereby proclaim the establishment of the Jewish State in Palestine, to be called Medinat Yisrael [the State of Israel]."

Hours later, Truman was handed his first diplomatic communication from the new nation. "I have the honor to notify you that the State of Israel has been proclaimed an independent republic . . . ," read the letter from Eliahu Epstein, an official Zionist representative in Washington, D.C. "I have been authorized by the provisional government of the new State to tender this message and to express the hope that your government will recognize and will welcome Israel into the community of nations."

The President's reply was swift: "The United States recognizes the provisional government as the *de facto* authority of the new State of Israel."

May 15, 1948, was an eventful, yet fateful day for American Zionists. "Many of us," noted a veteran of the movement, "felt the anguish a mother must feel who gives up her only child in marriage. What more," he asked, "is there for us to do? What will be our *raison d'être?*"

These same thoughts were shared by Zionists from New York to California and from the Great Lakes to Florida. Their fund-raising activities had been submerged by the streamlined methods of the United Jewish Appeal, and political decisions, as they agreed they should be, were now determined in Jerusalem and not New York.

Some leaders harbored a secret desire that the new Israeli Government would, at least, consult with them. "After all," commented an official of the ZOA, "two heads are better than one. Didn't we demonstrate our effectiveness in bringing about the State?"

Israel's answer to the Zionists quickly and publicly shattered this hope. Seeking to take advantage of the support now being offered by a large segment of American Jewry not affiliated with *organized* Zionism, Ben–Gurion extended an invitation to Jacob Blaustein, president of the American Jewish Committee, to come to Jerusalem for a chat. "For years," remarked journalist Judd Teller,

> it had been the position of American Zionist leadership that the Zionists alone spoke for the overwhelming majority of American Jews. Now Ben–Gurion, by his invitation to Mr. Blaustein, gave reason to think that this was not, if it had ever been, his view. Indeed, when in the autumn of 1950 he invited a group of American Jewish leaders to Jerusalem to map out a four-point program of American aid, Ben–Gurion chose . . . representatives of the various fund-raising agencies who were largely non-Zionist. He completely ignored the indigenous American Zionist organizations, and it was only after some pressure that they were called in.

Zionist anger at Ben–Gurion's courting of the non-Zionists mushroomed. "We began to feel useless," noted an observer, "as though we were being discarded." Even more demonstrative of the Israeli attitude was the behavior of Israeli officialdom. When the American Zionists were preparing to apply pressure on their government to support Israel on the Jerusalem issue before the UN, Abba Eban coldly told them that his country would handle its own diplomatic affairs. In those first years of Israeli independence, Zionist morale, as well as prestige, deteriorated. "A Zionism without some certified declaration of Israeli approval," noted Teller, "seemed more and more of an oddity. Both affiliated and peripheral Zionists had begun to ask privately, and in some instances publicly: 'Is a Zionist organization necessary?' "

The decline of Zionism was deceptive. "The movement," noted an observer in the late 1950s, "merely underwent a change. It became more diffuse, less organized. All Jews are Zionists today. They may not belong to an organization, but they are Zionists just the same. To some degree, everyone works for Israel. They pressure their government to provide financial aid, clamor for military support and, when Israel is under attack, publish full-page ads or raise their voices over loudspeakers at well-attended rallies. Believe me, when they go to the polls on election day, the overriding question in their minds almost always is, 'Is he good for the Jews?' 'Is he good for Israel?' "

While *organized* Zionism steadily declined, except for Hadassah, *social* Zionism continued to occupy the hours of hundreds of thousands of Jews—men and women. "Simply," said Freda Klaus, a life-long member of Hadassah, "it was almost a pastime for many of us, an activity which had become so much a part of our lives that few of us would know what to do if it was gone."

Samuel Koenig, a sociologist, offered this observation:

> Most of the gatherings inspired by the movement are largely devoted to fund raising, and consist of tea, bridge, and theater parties, luncheons, dinners, concerts, etc. This is particularly true of the women's organizations, which are strongest numerically and the most active. Reports and informative and inspirational talks by local and out-of-town speakers, whereby the interest in the Zionist cause is sought to be aroused, are, as a rule, part of these gatherings, but their general character is mainly social. Individuals belong to those organizations chiefly because it is the thing to do, because they offer social opportunities, and because they serve a "good cause."

The slaughter of six million Jews in Nazi death camps also had much to do with making everyone, to some degree, a Zionist. "In a very real sense, each Jew," wrote George Steiner in *Life* magazine, "wherever he may live, carries with him a piece of that yellow star which European Jews were forced to wear under the rule of the Gestapo. 'There but for the grace of God go I and my family,' is what many an American Jew said to himself. And out of the horror grew a new sense of community, an awareness that being a Jew is something strangely different from merely belonging to a particular religious denomination. One did not need to know Hebrew to qualify for Buchenwald."

A veteran fund-raiser, however, offered a different explanation as to why Jews worked so hard for Israel, why they gave so much financial and political support: "They have intense pride in the country," he said. "For the first time in their lives they saw Jews fighting back rather than turning the other cheek. They gave their money because they got *nachas* [pleasure] when they read about, or indeed saw, how a people turned a desert into a garden. In a sense, Israeli accomplishments meant self-respect for the American Jew. Whether one gave five dollars or a thousand dollars, the donor felt a part of that nation's success."

"Others," he added, "give because it's a form of boasting. Open pledges at synagogues and contributions announced at fund-raising dinners was a way of telling your competitor or your neighbor how well off you were—kind of like a charitable conspicuous consumption."

"Competitive giving," noted a second fund-raiser, "was the key. You can't believe the amounts people give just to impress the guy sitting next to them in *shul*. If Schwartz gives one thousand five hundred dollars, it's a cinch that Horowitz would quickly jump to his feet and announce that he is raising his gift, that he is doubling his gift. But don't misunderstand what I'm saying. These people still give because they are Jews, because they want that nation to survive."

"The universal objective," reported a third fund-raiser, "is to make it impossible for a man not to give. You appeal to whatever you think is best: fear, vanity, sympathy. You want results. Vanity is usually the best of all."

Playing to people's vanity, many synagogues and organizations published a *Book of Life,* a handsome pamphlet containing photographs of Israeli accomplishments—schools, hospitals—and a thank-you letter from a noted Israeli personality—such as Golda Meir. The donor's name would appear in bold type. Sometimes the contribution would be right alongside the name. The larger the gift, the bolder the type. "A *Book of Life,*" said a veteran fund-raiser, "is one of the most effective ways to nail the stiffs. Not only that, it makes everybody give a little more. Look, you're in business. You're doing good, or you want everybody to think so. What are you gonna give, five dollars? Like hell."

"Of course," he added, "the most effective way to raise *large* sums is still the dinner," often held in honor of a big contributor; "everyone from his industry—say housecoats or motion pictures—would be there. No one, but no one, would dare walk away without honoring the guest of honor with a substantial contribution." Rabbi Morris N. Kertzer offered the following comments on one such UJA affair held by the New York ladies' underwear industry:

> The luncheon was held at a leading New York hotel and the mood was far from solemn despite the fact that we were brought together by the needs of the starving and the tempest-tossed. These men who were locked in bitter competition in their offices on Seventh Avenue were transformed into a pleasant social group very much like a Lions Club luncheon meeting. . . . But they remained in competition—and no one dared *not* give, with the eyes of the whole industry upon them. Any suggestion of a decrease from last year's generous level would be regarded as a sign that their particular business was on the decline! Might as well tell Wall Street as inform the UJA that things were not going too well at Adorable Undergarments!

Michael Katz, a Long Island lawyer, recalled a similar event held at his suburban synagogue. "We gathered a host of local notables for the dais, and for a guest speaker an aspiring politician. There were some speeches, a film on the 1967 war, and several representatives from the UJA. On one occasion, the guest of honor was an American volunteer on the *Exodus*.

"The master of ceremonies," said Katz, "told a few jokes and, when everyone was nice and comfortable, we began the appeal.

"'We all can sit around and laugh, eat well and know that when you leave you return home to a safe community. That your kids are safe, that your wife is safe,' said the M.C. "The tone is set," said Katz. "Now we get down to business.

"'It's not that way in Israel. Children are being killed by Arab terrorists, bombs explode in the streets. They still need us. This year more than ever.'

"The dinner guests listen while puffing on cigars and sipping coffee or tea. Many have their checkbooks lying next to their half-empty coffee cups. No one jokes. This is serious business.

"'If you care, you'll give! They're giving their blood. We're only giving money!'

"The roll call begins. First, of course, come the largest pledges. You can't start with one hundred dollars," said Katz, "when you know there are thousand-dollar givers sitting out there.

"'Last year, Max Abramowitz gave ten thousand. This year the Abramowitz family, which incidentally just had a beautiful affair [*bar mitzvah*] for their son in our temple, is raising that amount to twelve thousand dollars.

"'Things must be good on Forty-seventh Street,' quips the speaker in an apparent reference to Abramowitz's Manhattan jewelry business. Everyone laughs. Then the crowd quiets down and the roll call continues.

"After each pledge," said Katz, "the guests begin to recalculate their contribution. They are anticipating the next round. They know that a dinner of this size is at least a two-appeal affair.

"'OK,' says the M.C. 'We have fifty thousand dollars. That's better than last year, but it's only a beginning.'

"For a moment, there is silence. Then someone stands and asks for recognition. He is raising his donation to two thousand five hundred dollars. A second man gets up and pledges an additional two thousand dollars, 'only if the people at my table match it.' There is some quick figuring at another table. 'The Forsheit family, which incidentally purchased this entire table, would like to add. . . .'

"That starts the ball rolling again," notes Katz. "Soon everyone is raising their hand asking for recognition. They want to give. They feel good giving.

" 'Fifteen hundred dollars in memory of my father,' announces a retired high school principal.

" 'The family of Robert Feldstein would like to add five hundred dollars to its gift,' says an accountant.

" 'The firm of Schwartz and Solomon, in honor of its new partner, . . . ,' And on it goes.

"Noting that almost everyone has responded to the second appeal, the fund-raisers gather for a conference. 'How long should we keep it up?' asks one. 'A little longer' is the collective answer. 'There are still a few live ones out there.' A note is quickly slipped to the M.C.: One more round.

" 'Ladies and Gentlemen,' he announces, 'As always, you have been wonderful. But we can't stop now. What do you say? If everyone adds two hundred and fifty dollars to their pledge, we can provide one hundred hospital beds. We can give another ambulance. Maybe settle another one thousand refugees. Dig a little deeper. Cut the vacation a few days short this year. They need it more than you. *Come on!* ' "

As American Jewry poured millions of its dollars into the coffers of the fund-raisers, on three separate occasions the tension between Arab and Jew erupted into war. Each time, the conflict ended in a swift, yet unexpected, victory for Israel. And each time, the behavior of American Jewry revealed the emotional bond linking them with their coreligionists in the Middle East.

On the morning of June 5, 1967, Stanley Feldman, a Brooklyn high school teacher, automatically flipped on his car radio. Generally, he paid little attention to the news at this early hour. "Today was different," he said; "the news hit like a ton of bricks: 'War has erupted in the Middle East. . . . Aircraft from Jordan, Egypt, Syria, and Iraq have bombed Israel. Cairo Radio reports that Haifa is in flames. Egyptian troops poised for assault. . . . Tel Aviv bombed.'

"My God!" exclaimed Feldman. "They'll kill every one of them." Thoughts of another Nazi terror; of concentration camps, of murder, of rape, flashed through his mind. "It will happen again," he muttered to himself.

Suddenly Feldman's 1965 Buick headed for Manhattan. He was going to enlist. He was going to fight for Israel. "I was too young in

'48," he thought, "but I am going to do it now. For the first time in my life I realize what Israel means to me."

Like Feldman, thousands of others throughout the country—Jews and non-Jews—descended on the Israeli consulates with offers to help, to replace civilians who were mobilized—to fight if necessary. When they arrived, however, Israeli officials gave them a polite but firm "No. Only Israeli citizens are permitted to serve in the armed forces," they were told.

Rejected for service in Israel's military, Feldman quickly headed for the headquarters of the American Youth Zionist Foundation. He wanted to join a program that freed Israeli reservists for combat. He would carry mail, collect garbage, operate a switchboard. He had to get in on this war. He had to do his share. "It was almost as though I was being directed by a higher power," he said.

"From what we can judge now," noted Moshe Divorkin, the organization's national director, "many, many Jews and non-Jews are going to volunteer if we can get the flights in. . . . And we discourage the kind who want to go to fight. There are many romantic stories about 1948. If you could stand up they could use you then. But, today, Israel doesn't need it.

"Many of the kids coming around to volunteer," added Divorkin, "are associated with the dove position [on Vietnam]. But they really see it as two different situations. Vietnam is a civil war. This is the defense of a democratic state in an area where totalitarianism reigns."

"I can see," said a twenty-year-old Jewish dove from the University of Massachusetts, "how others might view me as hypocritical.

"My first night back home, I stayed up all night writing down my thoughts, trying to see if I were schizophrenic or not. I came to the conclusion that you have to judge any war on the basis of its own moral standpoint.

"For Israel, it was a question of defending itself, of preserving its very existence."

By Wednesday, fear had turned to pride, for it was evident that Israel had not only repelled the invasion but had thoroughly defeated the Arabs on all fronts.

"Who's winning?" shouted a garment-center salesman, almost as though he were asking the score of a World Series game.

"We are," came a crisp reply from a stranger with a transistor radio to his ear.

"Atta boy!" exclaimed the salesman, his face beaming with pride as he entered the showroom.

Wherever Jews gathered, they spoke of the war. "I really do feel prouder today," announced a twenty-six-year-old college student from Chicago.

"Though I'm reluctant to express pride," he added. "It has to do with humility, with not being boastful, with the Jewish feeling of walking humbly with God, with the Jew's reluctance to assert himself in America."

At another corner of the city someone shouted, "Moshe Dayan is another Moses." The comment was made by a man who had spent part of his childhood in a concentration camp. "I was always proud to be a Jew," he said. "But after the Israeli victory I'm a great deal prouder. . . ."

At a bar, a woman was "absolutely overwhelmed" by the "courage, skill, and spirit" of the Israelis.

Admitting that she was neither religious nor a Zionist, the thirty-year-old youth worker declared: "I felt a pride in being Jewish that I've never felt. I felt admiration for the manhood of Dayan, for his ruggedness, his vigor, his virility. It was a real change from seeing Jews as the long-suffering victims."

Elsewhere, the merits of the Israeli military were on everyone's lips. "Dayan's a mastermind." "No, it's Rabin who should get the credit." "They ought to stay in Sinai." "They should really give it to the Arabs." "The Syrians didn't get enough." "They should never pull back." "My God! Tanks and planes with the Star of David. I can't believe it!"

Suddenly the street-corner debate was halted. Laughter broke out as one of the group, a stocky many in his forties, said: "All I know is, this country is safe—as long as Israel is behind it."

At UJA headquarters the switchboards were flooded. "Everyone wants to help," said a spokesman. "People call up, they want to give money, blood, and packages. Some say they want to fight. . . . Most are being turned into 'instant dollar Zionists. . . .'"

"You've got it all now," read a note attached to a check for twenty-five thousand dollars from a professor at the Jewish Theological Seminary. The owner of two gas stations showed up with the deeds to his property. "Here," he told a fund-raiser, "it's all I've got."

Others crowded the UJA building armed with the cash surrender value of insurance policies, and still more sold securities and real estate in order to give to the multimillion-dollar fund drive. In Dayton, Ohio, seven men gave five hundred thousand dollars. At James Madison High School, in Brooklyn, the staff of 125 collected twelve thousand dollars. Someone called up the UJA and pledged $1 million. Four other callers offered a million each. In California, a Hadassah group raised $250,000 from five hundred members. In Okmulgee, Oklahoma, the twenty Jewish families sold the building that housed their synagogue and sent the proceeds directly to Israel. And at a New York City luncheon on the day the war erupted, about a hundred community leaders, in the space of fifteen minutes, pledged $15 million. "At that," jested a UJA official, "I resigned as an expert. None of us ever saw anything like it before."

"Industrial and business leaders," reported the New York *Times,*

> converged on New York from all over the country. They moved into a board-like room and took seats around an oval table. Each was supplied with a telephone, which he used almost constantly, calling friends and requesting contributions.

> Fund raising in other cities had gone this way: Chicago, $3.5 million; Milwaukee, $920,000; Norwalk, Conn., $115,000; Binghamton, N.Y., $300,000; Madison, Wis., $104,000; Des Moines, Iowa, $800,000; Cincinnati, $700,000; Providence, R.I., $1,540,000; Atlanta, $1,132,000; Pottsville, Pa., $100,000; Boston, $2.5 million; Newark, $1,250,000; Harrisburg, Pa., $462,000; Cleveland's Jewish Federation, $1 million.

"Money was everywhere," remarked a veteran fund-raiser. At UJA headquarters, for instance, a gray-haired gentleman walked in and timidly, almost apologetically, told an official he was pledging "another hundred thousand." On his way out, he turned and said, "I am now going to give my friends a talk. If the Israelis can give their blood, we can give what we have." When he was gone, the official remarked: "That man gave us one hundred thousand dollars yesterday, and had already pledged $100,000."

While vast sums were being pledged by the affluent, on the streets teen-agers with coin boxes and shopping bags solicited contributions at subway stations, bus stops, and shopping centers. In New York, four orthodox Yeshiva students stood on a corner of Broadway and Forty-second Street, a bed sheet spread between them. "There's no food being produced in Israel," shouted the bearded, black-hatted youngsters. "All able-bodied men are at the front. Give for medical supplies, for food and shelter, and for the children."

As people passed, they dropped quarters and frequently dollars into the make-shift collection "box."

Hundreds of thousands of non-Jews were also caught up in the wave of "dollar Zionism." They threw quarters and dimes into bed sheets, wrote checks for hundreds, and in a few cases matched the astronomical sums given by some Jews. "The gifts by non-Jews," reported the New York *Times,*

> included one of $250,000 from Robert T. Stevens, president and chairman of the executive committee of J. P. Stevens and Company, the textile firm. . . .

> Still other gifts from non-Jews included one of $300,000 from Roger Milliken, Inc., also a textile concern. The United Jewish Appeal of Greater New York also disclosed a gift of $5,000 from Rev. Leo P. McLaughlin, president of Fordham University, who wrote:

> "Our good and mutual friend Leon Lowenstein has alerted us to the acute situation in the Middle East, and as president of Fordham University, where students are accepted regardless of race, color, or creed, I am hoping to contribute $5,000 to this worthy cause.

Some fifteen hours after the first reports of the war had been broadcast by the American media, the London BBC read a dispatch from its Jerusalem correspondent: "Less than fifteen hours after fighting began, Israel had already won the war. Egypt is no more a fighting factor. . . . It's the most instant victory the modern world has seen." The report quickly raced around the globe.

"I couldn't believe it!" exclaimed Leo Capese, an Italian-American who had sought out a Jewish neighbor to ask where to send the check. "We won!"

Following the swift Israeli victory, Jews walked the streets of their respective cities with a new-found pride. "On *Shabbos,*" recalled Ida Feldstein, "I saw something I'd never witnessed before: The men were walking to *shul* wearing their *talaysim* [prayer shawls] and *yarmulkas.* They'd never done this, not even on the High Holy Days." What the Brooklyn housewife saw were Jews basking in Israeli valor.

In 1973, Jewish pride was suddenly mixed with fear. "MID EAST ERUPTS," read the banner headline in the New York *Post:*

EGYPT CROSSES THE CANAL
SYRIANS MARCH ON GOLAN
AIR WAR OVER GULF OF SUEZ
ISRAEL IS MOBILIZING

At New York's Kehilath Jeshurun synagogue, while the adults were in the midst of their Yom Kippur prayers, a group of children listened to a transistor radio in a side room. "We're at war again!" exclaimed one. Several of the youngsters edged their way through the crowd to whisper the news to their parents. Quickly, heads began to turn as the synagogue came alive with whispers. "It's started again." "The Arabs have—" "Shush!" whispered someone deep in prayer. "Maybe it's just a rumor," said another worshiper.

When the services ended, the rabbi confirmed the news. His voice quivering with emotion, he could not complete the sentence: "Israel has been attacked. . . ." Quietly, the crowd filed out.

"We prayed for a quick victory," remarked one observer, "but we knew that it wasn't going to be a repeat of the Six Day War." Indeed, confidence in Israel's military ability dwindled as TV anchor men reminded viewers of the number of Israeli aircraft destroyed; of the swift, almost perfect execution of the Egyptian crossing of the canal.

"This certainly wasn't '67," noted a volunteer headed for Israel. "When I saw films showing tanks bearing the Star of David destroyed and Israeli POWs guarded by Egyptian soldiers, I was frightened. The most frightening of all was the story told to me by a UJA volunteer: that the textile firms were donating thousands of terry-cloth dish towels because they absorbed blood easily."

Then came the atrocity stories: The Syrians were mutilating captured flyers. The Egyptians were executing POWs. "God! what will they do when they reach Tel Aviv?" asked a frightened Chicago merchant. "Is it the end?" "How did the Arabs learn to use those Russian weapons? The bastards didn't even know what toilet paper was in '67. How did they learn to use that fancy hardware the Russians gave 'em?"

The Jewish state of mind, the fear that pervaded the Jewish community, was described by Mark Sufrin, a free-lance writer whose identification with Judaism was, to say the least, minimal. "I felt at that moment that Jews, including myself, were threatened. It became symbolic. If they lost the war, I envisioned every anti-Semite in the world would find an excuse to come out in the open."

At the UN's Dag Hammarskjold Plaza, Jews were somewhat more confident. They showered thousands of single dollars into corrugated boxes, as a man hawked as though selling ice cream at a picnic. "Dollars for Israel, more dollars for Israel." The crowd shouted back: *"Am Yisroel Chai*—the Jewish people live!" and hoisted posters reading, "Cairo or Bust" and " '48, '56, '67, Arabs, you'll never learn."

In the aftermath of the Six Day War, Milton Himmelfarb had remarked on American Jewry's reaction to Israel's sweeping victory. "Some of us surprised ourselves and each other by our concern," he wrote.

> . . . The surprise is that some Jews still had to find a reassurance about themselves in the military valor of the Israelis. One would have thought that that had been taken care of in 1948, with the Israeli war of independence. Israel, it then became clear, provided for the Jews of the United States and countries like it a kind of contemporary pioneer or cowboy ancestry, reassuring us by showing us that we wanted and needed to have shown—that while Jews can be pretty good with a fountain pen and briefcase, they can also if necessary be pretty good with a rifle or tank.

In 1973, with Israel momentarily in jeopardy, that emotion was intensified.

How Secure These Rights?

In August 1946, an organization calling itself Columbians, Inc., was chartered by the state of Georgia. Its purpose was to "encourage . . . people to think in terms of race, nation and faith and to work for a moral reawakening in order to build a progressive white community that is bound together by a deep spiritual consciousness of a common past and a determination to share a common future." So began the nation's first fascist revolt—the Atlanta *Putsch* of American fascism.

As early as 1940, Homer L. Loomis, Jr., the Columbians' self-styled Führer, told a New York neighbor that "Hitler has the right idea. He's not going to let the German race get mixed up with a lot of inferior races." Six years later, after serving with the United States Army, the lover of facism left the city of his birth "to discover America, to get closer to the people. To get," he told a friend, "just one congressman into Washington, then one from every state. . . . Then I'm going to have a mighty army and we're going to march on New York. If I go to jail for a while, it'll give me a chance to think and to write a book, *Thunder in the South*. I'm going to be the Hitler of America."

Arthur Weiss, commander of Atlanta's Jewish War Veterans Post No. 112, was well aware of Loomis's activities, and thus was not surprised when word reached him that the Columbians had invited the public to an anti-Semitic meeting that evening. Quickly, the ex-Marine captain, who had fought at Guadalcanal, assembled 125 other Jewish veterans and descended on the Nazi rally.

"Lies!" shouted Weiss when Loomis announced that "the Jews . . . have never become part of the American way of life."

"The Jew is the original Nazi," Loomis screamed back, now aware that his audience had been infiltrated by hostile elements. "The Jew will die for what he believes in, but I've never seen one die for the American world."

As Loomis continued to rant, the JWVers stepped up their taunts. "If you're such a superman," yelled one, "why don't you step off that platform and come down here and prove it!" The brown-shirted guards at the foot of the stage suddenly looked frightened. "An even fight," noted a JWVer, "wasn't their style." Suddenly, Loomis, too, was stricken with fear. "There might be trouble," he told an associate. "Better call the police." When he returned to the platform, he was trembling. He could hardly get the words out. "This meeting," he announced "is closed to the public." Then, as several unidentified men walked toward the front of the hall, he bolted for the safety of a side room. Once inside, he pushed a desk against the door. Their mission accomplished, the JWVers left.

Several days later, Loomis made another public appearance—this time on an Atlanta street corner. One of his henchmen, ostensibly to demonstrate the group's peaceful intentions, cradled his sixteen-month-old daughter in his arms. Ironically, that same child had just come from the free children's health clinic maintained by Atlanta's B'nai B'rith.

"Everybody in America is free to hate," screamed Loomis. "Hate is natural. It's not un-American to hate. Why does the Jew think that he alone is above criticism and being hated?"

As his denunciations filled the air, a representative of the Georgia Attorney General's Office eyed the crowd of storm troopers. "Who the hell are these men?" he asked out loud. "What in the world makes them tick?"

"If you're really interested in an answer," said a bystander, "I'll tell you."

"I'm listening."

"That one over there, the tall one," pointing to a middle-aged man. "He's a real-estate broker who buys up white homes and sells to Negroes. At the same time, he joined the Columbians to fight the nigger invasion. . . . The short guy is a salesman who signed a contract with

Loomis to sell memberships at three dollars each, pocketing two dollars on every card. . . . And the blond was a mental patient. Word has it he's a fugitive from an asylum in South Carolina."

He raised his arm and pointed to another: "He's twenty-one years old. Spent his childhood in an orphanage and then joined the Marines. When he was asked why he became a Columbian, he said, 'To tell the truth, I had no place to go. I wanted to be with other fellows and get into something. Besides, I don't like niggers. . . .'" The knowledgeable observer gave a biographical sketch of still another: "He's seventeen years old. Ran away from home at thirteen and bummed around Chicago for a while, worked as a bellhop . . . and when he came back to Atlanta got a job in a hamburger joint. Then he joined the Columbians. He likes girls under ten."

In 1947, Loomis, who had boasted earlier that his organization was going to invade the "cities like storm troopers, parading, smashing windows of Jewish stores, and scaring people," was convicted of inciting a riot. He was sentenced to three years. "My fair-skinned brothers," shouted his father at the trial, "my son is being crucified like Christ by the Jews." So much for Atlanta's "Beer Hall *Putsch.*"

In the immediate postwar period, few people were attracted to lunatics such as Loomis. "World War II," noted Oscar and Mary Handlin, "made the decisive difference."

> The global struggle that began in 1941 called for the union of all Americans; at the same time, it totally discredited all those who had accepted the assistance of the Nazis and who preached doctrines similar to those that led Germany to destruction. The barbarities that culminated in the extermination camps horrified every sector of public opinion in the United States. Few wished any longer to be associated even indirectly with their country's foes; and anti-Semitism was now inescapably linked to the tragic events in Europe. The movements of the 1930s withered away and died.

"The war," added the Handlins, "had the decisive effect it did because the racism on which the hostility to the Jews had rested no longer misled substantial numbers of Americans. A new generation of social scientists and biologists had demonstrated the falsity of the old assumptions, and a public constantly being educated had become freshly aware of its own heritage of diversity. By mid-twentieth century, it was hard to find any serious defenders of the old ideas."

Unlike the established blatant racism, the established pattern of social discrimination still remained. "Habits are tough to break," noted a Jewish resident of San Francisco, "and even here, a city almost void of any anti-Semitic tradition, the practice of excluding Jews didn't disappear overnight."

For many, San Francisco was America's "white spot" of anti-Jewish prejudice. "In near top-level social and country clubs," wrote Earl Rabb in *Commentary Magazine* in 1950, "there is Jewish membership and even charter membership. Gentleman's agreements are quite uncommon in its quality residential sections, old and new. In filling public and quasi-public posts, there seems to be no trace of a policy of exclusionism or 'quota' or even discriminatory hesitation. At times Jewish citizens have concurrently held the presidencies of the Chamber of Commerce, the Community Chest, the Board of Education, Art, Fire, and Harbor commissions, and many other appointive and elective posts; it is a situation that cannot be duplicated in any other city with a 6 per cent Jewish concentration."

Rabb did note that some social discrimination lingered, that some employment agencies continued to mark applications with "No J's" or "Blonds only," that some private housing developments still refused to include Jews, that during sidewalk confrontations someone often turned "out to be not only a 'damned ———' but a 'damned Jewish ———.'"

Though the ugliness of discrimination remained, professional anti-Semitism—the type practiced by the city's defunct Nazi Bund—was never a paying proposition. "Efforts in that direction," said Rabb, "have always been short-lived. The tip-off is the latrine-wall type of anti-Semitic literature that has turned up . . . has been date-lined Chicago and Los Angeles, and mailed in.

"So far as the city and its institutions are concerned, the Jew is a first-class citizen. It may well be that he can live in San Francisco with a greater degree of personal dignity than in any other large city in the country."

Even more of a haven for Jews were the small towns of the South. "They were relatively free of discrimination," noted an observer from Greenville, South Carolina. "Here we were probably more integrated, more accepted, than any of our *landsleit* to the north or west, or for that matter, those who lived in the large urban centers of the South."

Harry Golden, a keen observer of southern small-town Jewry, agreed with this assertion. "He is 'our' Jew to the small-town Southerners," wrote Golden, "and they often take care of him with a zeal and devotion otherwise bestowed only on the Confederate monument in the square. There have been cases where the schools have closed an hour earlier for his funeral, in some towns they have flown the flag at half-mast on the Court House building, and high-school trophies have been presented in his memory."

The acceptance was so complete, noted another observer from rural North Carolina, that "the editor of the local newspaper made it a point to print an annual Passover or Purim story and always devoted space to a Jewish feature on the High Holidays. I never saw the announcement of a *bar mitzvah* in any New York or Chicago paper."

With his almost total assimilation, the small-town southern Jew, unlike his northeastern coreligionist, had a tremendous sense of security. Harry Golden commented on this solid tradition of philo-Semitism:

> It is a standing joke at the weekly civic and club luncheons in the small towns of the South to put a ham platter in front of the Jewish member just as he is taking his place. Everybody watches during the singing of "Onward Christian Soldiers," and then they all laugh as one of the serving ladies, in all likelihood a member of the True Blue Bible Class, comes running down the aisle with the "kosher" dish; fried chicken, black-eyed peas, and mashed potatoes. These Southerners are deeply concerned over the possibility of an "over-sight" occurring at their annual banquets. If pork is on the menu, they automatically serve you chicken, without comment or inquiry.

While small-town southern Jews were enjoying their black-eyed peas and memberships in country clubs, their coreligionists elsewhere recognized that only a strenuous effort could eradicate the silent conspiracy —the web of social discrimination—still blocking their way to full equality. "The rationalization that social discrimination does not exist in communities where we have become assimilated is false," commented a New Mexico observer. "Even in areas of the country like my own Southwest, where anti-Jewish discrimination was always insignificant, we find that it is still a barrier to our total equality."

In the aftermath of the war to stamp out a racist ideology, Jews still read about, or experienced personally, the sharp bite of prejudice:

"We trust you are not Jewish, as we cater only to a Christian clientele."

"You can bank here, but please don't ask for a job."

"Of course we'll install a telephone, but please don't file an employment application."

"Doctor, can you do something for my arthritis? but please don't join my club."

And on it went. "It was still with us," lamented Hy Saltz, an ex-G.I. blinded by a Japanese artillery shell. "That god-damn restriction. I thought the war would change all that, but it didn't. Nothing will ever change."

The ex-paratrooper, of course, was wrong. Things did begin to change. They began, rather slowly, to get better. "And most of us knew it," noted Simon Levine, an electrician at the Brooklyn Navy Yard. "We kept the jobs we got during the war, our children were finding it easier to get into a college, and we started to move out of the inner city. It didn't happen overnight, but it happened."

Unlike its defensive posture of the previous decades, the Jewish community, specifically organizations such as the American Jewish Committee and the Anti-Defamation League, moved swiftly to destroy the remaining citadels of anti-Jewish prejudice. "The times were right," noted an ADL spokesman. "The expanding economy almost eliminated unemployment, and the postwar boom opened up all kinds of economic vistas. With economic security people were receptive to new ideas. They could get away from the binding force of their old prejudices. They seemed to be willing to listen, to learn."

The Jewish fight for equality employed the concepts of the social scientists, the vivid power of the media, and most importantly, federal and state legislation. "The winds of change," noted an observer, "were perhaps best powered by the plethora of anti-discrimination legislation. If I can choose any one year as a real start, I think I'd pick 1948." In that year, he noted, over one million copies of the *Report of the President's Commission on Civil Rights* and the *Commission on Higher Education Report* were distributed; Truman issued two sweeping executive orders making discrimination in public employment and segregation in the Armed Forces illegal; the Supreme Court ruled that "restrictive covenants to limit the sale or occupancy of houses on the grounds of race and color are unenforceable by state or federal courts, . . ." making it illegal for the courts to "participate in facilitating discriminatory practices"; the New York legislature passed the first fair-educational-practices act prohibiting racial or religious discrimination in higher education, and the Philadelphia City Council, not waiting for state action, passed a Fair Employment Practices Ordinance.

Similar social measures were enacted in other parts of the country. In Evansville, Indiana, a Mayor's Commission on Human Relations was established. In Massachusetts, the legislature amended its public housing law, making it unlawful to discriminate by reason of race or creed against prospective tenants. Phoenix, Arizona, adopted an FEPC ordinance that applied to public employment and contractors doing business with the city. The 1948 Democratic and Republican national conventions included strong civil rights statements in their platforms. The G.I. Bill gave Jews freedom to attend universities where they had formerly been excluded, or in areas of the country where they had never been seen. "That alone," said an observer, "earned the Jews greater acceptance."

The media also helped make great inroads against prejudice, as films such as *Crossfire* and *Gentleman's Agreement* showed millions of moviegoers the ugliness of religious bigotry. The fight to bring anti-Semitism to the screen, however, was not an easy one.

At the end of World War II, RKO studios purchased Richard Brooks's novel *The Brick Foxhole*. Immediately, the screenplay was renamed *Crossfire* and the murdered soldier was changed from "gay" to Jewish, possibly in deference to screen censorship. Few studio executives threw their wholehearted support behind the project, and production was held up for over a year. Not until Dore Schary became production chief, almost two years later, did the screenplay finally "come off the shelf."

While RKO was debating the box-office results of a film dealing with anti-Semitism, at Twentieth Century-Fox, Darryl F. Zanuck was preparing to bring Laura Z. Hobson's novel *Gentleman's Agreement* to the screen. When news of the project was announced, influential Hollywood Jews became nervous. "A film on anti-Semitism," said one, "will only stir it up more. We don't need it. There is no point in bringing our problem to the public's attention."

In an effort to discourage the film's production, spokesmen for Hollywood Jewry met with Zanuck at the Warner Brothers studio. "We're doing fine," they told the filmmaker. "Why bring the whole country into this?" Zanuck, however, was determined to make the film. He gave them a flat "No" to their request. One writer has suggested that this incident, which does not appear in Hobson's novel, was deliberately included in the film version of the book as a "belated response to the people at the Warner Brothers meeting": Gregory Peck, playing writer Phil Green, says to magazine executives that he is anxious to do a series of articles on anti-Semitism. Irving Weissman, played by character actor Robert Warwick, seems upset at this announcement and tries to discourage Green. Any exposé of anti-Semitism, he fears, could only breed more trouble for the Jews. "You'll stir it up more!" he exclaims. "Let it alone; we'll handle it. The less talk the better."

In making *Crossfire,* Schary met similar opposition. The American Jewish Committee, frightened by the possibility of an anti-Semitic reaction to the movie, threatened to ruin the film by using its influence with the press if the project continued. "At least," said an AJC representative, "make the Jew a Negro. The same point will be made." Schary, like Zanuck, refused. Even a Warner Brothers threat, warning him that they would not exhibit *Crossfire* in their theaters, could not dissuade him.

Though *Crossfire* opened to mixed reviews, the Jewish establishment continued to assault the film. Elliot Cohen, editor of *Commentary,* called the movie, among other things, "potentially harmful. . . . many would have been happier if the producers of *Crossfire* could have found some more normal, more vigorously human character for its Jew than the stereotype of the eternal helpless victim of brute force. . . . Many of us would like to see the day when art presents Jews in America not as A Problem, but as a people."

In defense of the characterization of the Jew, Schary responded with an open "Letter from a Movie-Maker."

> . . . there is no characterization that overcomes the fear you express, because the Jew is labeled as something reprehensible by the anti-Semite, no matter what he happens to be.
>
> If the Jew fights (Barney Ross, Benny Leonard, and a host of others have fought well and expertly), he is a dirty fighter, yellow in the clinch, and very tricky in an Oriental way.
>
> If the Jew is poor, they all are Communists. If the Jew is rich, they are all dirty bankers. If the Jew is happily married, they're clannish, selfish, and anyway, they have Gentile mistresses. If the Jew is single or divorced, they all are libertines or homosexuals. If the Jew was in the Army, he was goldbricking—if he wasn't, he's a slacker. If he was an officer, be bought his commission—if a private, he avoided doing his job. If the Jew is communicative, he's a buttinsky. If he's uncommunicative, he's stuck up and thinks he's smarter than anybody else. If he works for a boss, he's a cheat and plotting to take away the business. If he is a boss, he's a miser and a crook.

"These opinions," wrote Schary, "are like everything else about anti-Semitism: absurd. It is equally absurd and surprising that you give them credence in your [Elliot Cohen's] open letter. No matter what the Jew had been in *Crossfire,* the anti-Semite would have read something evil into his character."

Crossfire, a morbid, violent film, had only moderate success at the box office. *Gentleman's Agreement,* a glossy, big-star, almost sedate treatment of anti-Semitism—this time, a Christian investigative reporter posing as a Jew—was a tremendous hit. Even Cohen, editor of the most respected Jewish publication in America, hailed *Gentleman's Agreement* as "moving" and "thought-provoking." "If there is any justice," he wrote, "it should win at least half as many Oscars [as *The Best Years of Our Lives*]."

In addition to films, national publications were a potent force in the fight against bigotry, publishing numerous incisive articles on civil rights.

In some instances, these articles were inspired directly by the *Report of the President's Commission on Civil Rights.* While others did not speak of the *Report* specifically, it was apparent that the publicity given the committee's findings made the subject important news. The most direct influence of the *Report* was apparent in an article written for the three million readers of *Collier's,* by Charles Luckman, president of Lever Brothers.

He appealed to the "good dollar sense" of the American businessman. In "Civil Rights Means Good Business," Luckman pointed out that where civil rights were most denied, the standards of living were lowest, property yielded the smallest taxes, and businessmen often ended up in the bankruptcy courts. He concluded that business would find it to their own advantage to "emerge as a fighting leader in the most liberal of democratic causes—the preservation of our Bill of Rights."

Other journals, many of which catered to a female audience, were publishing articles in an effort to bring about a greater understanding of different racial, religious, and ethnic groups.

Helen Huntington Smith, writing for *Woman's Home Companion,* showed what could be done by housewives who were quietly determined "to rub out the pattern of hate in America"; *Parents' Magazine* supported the case against discrimination by suggesting to its readership that they "take a refresher course in the ideals, principles, and goals of this democracy of ours"; and the 1,003,597 readers of *Seventeen,* in an article entitled "Memo to Teen-Agers," were urged to read the Civil Rights Commission's *Report* and to "get a group together and talk over

the day-to-day things you teen-age Americans can do to fight prejudice. . . ."

Reader's Digest demonstrated an increased interest in articles dealing
with discrimination. Their May 1948 issue, for instance, contained a
condensation of "Philadelphia Fellowship." Written by Margaret
Hickey, the article, which had originally appeared in *Ladies' Home
Journal,* described the achievements of Fellowship House, one of Philadelphia's main centers for combating intergroup tension.

In addition to the media's positive effect, there was a more intense
co-operation between Jewish and Christian organizations than earlier.
Illustrative of the joint effort were the interfaith and interracial camps
held in the summer of 1948 and sponsored by the ADL and the United
Christian Youth Movement. Jews and Christians, whites and blacks,
met in New York, Grand Rapids, Atlanta, and Minnesota in an adventure in mutual understanding. One of the campers who attended the
session at Lake Minnetonka, Minnesota, told about her experience:

> It isn't as though we sat down in a lecture hall and had all the facts
> organized for us and presented to us. It was living together, being
> able to watch each other studying and at play, being able to ask
> one another about ourselves and friends whenever we wanted, that
> created an atmosphere of ease, so that there were no hard feelings,
> nothing too delicate to talk about. We became good friends person-
> ally and got to know each other as *individuals,* so there was no
> problem created of having to accept one another as members of a
> group.

As the years advanced, Jews welcomed the slow but steady deterioration of social discrimination. At the same time, however, they
witnessed, as all Americans did, an anti-Communist hysteria sweep
across the land. "It was like those years after World War I," noted a
veteran of the Jewish labor movement, "only worse!

"Everywhere, people went on indiscriminate witch-hunts; some of us
were mute with fear. To many—government officials and business
leaders—everyone was suspect. Guilt by association, smear tactics, and
loyalty oaths were the order of the day."

The hysteria that gripped the nation in the early fifties posed a particular threat to the Jewish community. The American Jewish Committee
explained why: "For a number of years," noted a memorandum,

> anti-Semitic activists have assiduously promoted the smear that
> Jews are Communists. They have found this to be the most effec-

tive line with which they were left since the decline of organizational activity. The acceleration of the anti-Communist campaign has come as a windfall to them, and our reports indicate a steady procession of anti-Semitic operators from their regular sphere of activity onto the bandwagon of the general anti-Communist movement.

By the opening of the 1950s, the Red Scare mushroomed; China had fallen to Mao's forces, newspapers vividly described the details of espionage trials, the Soviet Union demonstrated atomic capacity, Korea exploded into a shooting war. Then came the anti-subversive laws, the rise of Senator Joseph McCarthy, and the loyalty investigations. "When Jewish names turned up in these investigations," said Howard Roth, a New Jersey dentist, "and anti-Semitic agitators joined the Peekskill rioters, I became frightened."

In August 1949, the quiet summer-resort town of Peekskill, New York, was the scene of two violent anti-Communist demonstrations. The disorders, touched off by an open-air concert of pro-Soviet singer Paul Robeson, quickly took on anti-Semitic overtones.

"When my husband and I arrived," reported Judith Stern, "we knew immediately that there was going to be trouble." The forty-year-old New Jersey nurse was correct. Blocking the entrance to the grounds were hundreds of townspeople. "They were led by a parade of anti-Communist veterans," said Stern.

"Go back to Russia, you god-damned Reds!" screamed a woman in a print dress. "If you're so fuckin' unhappy with this country, get out!"

Stern, a veteran of several left-wing campaigns during the thirties, remained calm. "The statements," she said, "I had heard before." Several hours later, she was gripped by fear. "As the pickets disbanded, fights broke out all over the place. The demonstrators began to hurl stones and bottles and began to turn over cars. I thought someone was going to get killed."

"Where's the police?" shouted a frightened concertgoer.

"They're part of the riot," answered someone while fleeing for safety.

"My husband, where's my husband?" screamed the nurse.

"He's over there by the tree!" answered a friend.

"My God!" she exclaimed as she looked at her husband. The ex-soldier was covered with blood. "An anti-Communist bottle hit me in the face," he said. "Thank goodness the bastard drank what was in it."

Apprised of the disorders, Robeson did not appear. The organizers of the concert, declaring that they would not be denied their right to assemble, rescheduled the event for Labor Day. "When that day arrived," said Edith Meyers, a Brooklyn music teacher, "fifteen thousand of us, this time protected by twenty-five hundred guards recruited from left-wing labor unions, descended on the abandoned golf course by car and chartered bus. As expected the same pickets were there—the very people who stoned us the previous week. What I didn't expect were the Jew-haters. When I saw the anti-Semitic stickers affixed to their cars and the vicious Jew-baiting leaflets, I wanted to scream. They not only hated our politics, but also Jews. Incidentally," she added, "I'm Catholic."

"When the entertainment was over," noted another eyewitness, "violence once again ensued." Cars were overturned, people were beaten, and shouts of "Red Jew bastards" filled the air. "Everyone knew the audience contained a hell of a lot of non-Jews," he noted, "but that didn't mean a *goddam* thing to the fascists."

As frightening as the stone-throwing antics of the Peekskill demonstrators was the tendency, on the part of some, to be more tolerant of patently anti-Semitic individuals and themes because they were anti-Communist. In 1954, veteran reporter James Rorty, described the anti-Semites' new look. "Today, he wrote,

> if you wish to move in the best anti-Semitic circles and at the same time have hopes of back-door entree and financial support from respectable corporation executives and businessmen who are not openly anti-Semitic, you will speak sympathetically of the good, upstanding Jews of B'nai B'rith and the American Jewish Committee, and in the same breath denounce Communists, Zionists, "Khazars," and the Anti-Defamation League, in approximately that order. As a patriotic publicist, you will denounce the menace, not of the Jews and "international Jewry" as such, but of the international Communist conspiracy and its agents and sympathizers in high places, most of whom you discover to be Jews, whose original names, where they have been changed, you restore parenthetically for the instruction of the unwary. It is *de rigueur* to support Joe McCarthy, and you will be the first to attack as Communists or Communist sympathizers all who criticize the Senator.

"That's the new anti-Semitic look," wrote Rorty, "—the fact that it is worn by some of the same faces that during the '30s bore a remarkable resemblance to Bundists . . . is purely coincidental. . . . The fact that these are some of the same people that screamed 'kike' at Joe McWilliams street-corner rallies in Yorkville fifteen years ago is something well-heeled ultranationalists . . . wave aside with a pained expression."

Joseph Kamp, a former editor of the pro-Nazi journal *The Awakener,* was one of the many who draped the American flag over his shoulders as he embarked on his anti-Semitic witch-hunt for radicals. Witness *his* description of how Senator Joseph McCarthy came to terms with the Jewish civil rights agencies.

"They had threatened," he wrote in an open letter to J. Edgar Hoover, "to label him with that damning little Communist smear word 'anti-Semitic.' They had forced him to repudiate a helpful friend, the nationally known radio commentator Upton Close. . . .

"Joe McCarthy had a bitter choice," wrote Kamp. "He could stand idly by and see his fight against Communism effectively sabotaged, or he could swallow his pride, betray his principles, and sacrifice his self-respect.

"It took guts to do what Joe McCarthy was compelled to do in order to continue his fight."

American Jewry was highly sensitive over the identification of Jews with communism. The trial of Julius and Ethel Rosenberg intensified that sensitivity.

"All this makes a bad impression," wrote Hillel Rogoff, editor of the *Jewish Daily Forward,* bemoaning the fact that the defendants, as well as other "accused, arrested and tried Communist traitors and spies," were Jewish. "We have no doubt that it is being used silently, if not openly, as propaganda." Every time "a Julius Rosenberg is arrested," he said, "the impression [that Jews leaned toward Communism] is strengthened."

On July 17, 1950, Julius Rosenberg had been arrested in his New York City apartment. One month later, his wife, Ethel, was taken into custody. Charged with providing atomic secrets to agents of the Soviet Union, the couple was tried, convicted, and subsequently executed at Sing Sing Prison, in the spring of 1953.

On the day the death sentence was announced, Louis Schafer, *Jewish Daily Forward* reporter, interviewed presiding judge Irving Kaufman. During their brief talk, the journalist asserted that while the Jewish community was ashamed of the Rosenbergs, they were at the same time pleased with the judge and the prosecutor, Irving Saypol, "for showing the world that there are Jews of whom we can be proud."

The next morning, an editorial in Schafer's own paper called Kaufman's sentence "too horrible." Two days later, another Yiddish journal took Kaufman to task—this time for the inflammatory remarks made during his sentencing speech. Though *The Day* editorial admitted that the crime was very serious, it nevertheless condemned Kaufman for tying the defendants to America's Korean War casualties. Such an accusation, it noted, would "lead to an intensification of the present hysteria in certain [anti-Semitic] circles." How would the Jew-hater use these remarks if Soviet bombs fell on the nation's cities? asked M. Danzis, editor of *The Day* (New York). "Are these the calm, thoughtful words of a jurist?"

As uncalled for, noted Danzis, was a New York *Daily Mirror* editorial calling attention to the two Jews—Kaufman and Saypol—"who did such a magnificent job for America. . . ." Danzis, who interpreted the remark to mean that the Jewish judge and prosecutor "should atone not only for the sins of the Rosenbergs, but of all other Jews," answered with an article entitled "Judge Kaufman and the Rosenbergs." In it he charged that the death penalty was imposed because the judge himself was a Jew; that Kaufman leaned over backwards in an effort to prove that Jews were loyal Americans. "[His] entire interpretation of the trial . . . left many people and especially Jews with a feeling of bitterness."

As criticism of Kaufman mounted, the Jewish community began to take sides. Rabbi George Fox, writing for the Chicago *Sentinel,* called the death penalty "unjust," noting that it was imposed as a result of the "hysteria which has overtaken our country. . . ." As to the possibility of an anti-Semitic retort that Jews were "soft on communism," he argued that "One does not have to bend his back backwards to avoid things that may bring on insecurity and perhaps danger. Anti-Semites will be anti-Semites whether the Rosenbergs are sentenced to thirty years or death." The death penalty, he repeated some time later, "was unjust, if not illegal," and urged his readers to save the Rosenbergs from the electric chair by wiring Truman and asking for clemency.

William Reuben, a writer, also joined the protest, asking in an article for *Jewish Life,* "What Was the Rosenbergs' 'Crime'?" Arguing that the couple was really convicted for harboring unpopular political beliefs, he warned that "if the courts uphold this conviction and sanction the execution . . . this will help to establish an invalid and fantastic connection in law between committing espionage and being a radical." One month later, Louis Harap, managing editor of *Jewish Life,* looked into the anti-Semitic aspects of the trial. The trial, he asserted, took place in New York City where a third of the population was Jewish. Yet not one juror was a Jew.

Even the anti-Communist editor of the California *Jewish Voice,* Samuel Gach, called the death sentence "shameful" and "legal murder" because of "national hysteria." Kaufman, he wrote, was a "berobed and politically anointed punk [who] was a scared and synthetic American and weaker than a no-good Jew."

Like Gach, Rabbi Franklin Cohn of Los Angeles also declared that the defendants were "framed," that the judge and prosecutor had murdered the Rosenbergs to show the nation that they were "super Jews. . . ."

As the criticism heightened, the "anti-Rosenberg" forces swung into action. In Chicago, the director of the ADL convinced officials of Temple Judea to close their doors to a Progressive Party demonstration protesting the death penalty. Appalled by the action, Nathan Dworkin, the temple's president, resigned, thus bringing about a division within the congregation's membership. Unable to resolve the dispute, the trustees decided to close the synagogue entirely. Similarly, in Cleveland, the Jewish Community Center withdrew permission for a gathering of the Sholem Aleichem Club after being told that William Reuben was the guest speaker, and in New York City, the Brooklyn Academy of Music, under pressure from the Brooklyn Community Council, refused to rent their facilities to a pro-Rosenberg group.

Meanwhile, the American Jewish Committee and the ADL vigorously campaigned to discredit the newly formed Rosenberg Committee, calling the group the "CP's fakery." Likewise, the National Community Relations Advisory Council, an umbrella organization speaking for the ADL, American Jewish Committee, American Jewish Congress, Jewish War Veterans, Jewish Labor Committee, and Union of American Hebrew Congregations, issued a press release denouncing the Rosenberg committee as a "Communist-inspired group [trying] to inject the false issue of anti-Semitism into the . . . case." The fact that the defendants were Jewish, noted the statement, was being used in a "fraudulent effort to confuse and manipulate public opinion for ulterior political purposes."

Of all the establishment organizations, the American Jewish Committee led the attack. In a memorandum to their community-relations councils, they provided "full details about the Communist machinations on the issue [and] made available to rabbis, educators, writers, opinion molders, and to community leaders" material explaining "the attempted exploitation of the case by the Communists for their own evil purposes." Irving M. Engel, chairman of the AJC's executive committee, explained the agency's intent: ". . . as Jews, we desired to repudiate the false claim of anti-Semitism raised by the Communists to deceive American Jews; and as Americans, we desired to protect our country's reputation from the circulation of Communist-inspired slander."

The AJC also kept close watch on the activities of the various Rosenberg committees. Frederick Schreiber, an AJC area director, described a meeting of the Los Angeles Rosenberg Committee. The defendants, he reported, were tried *in absentia* and found not guilty. For almost an hour, he reported, William Reuben presented the details of the trial to a crowd of several hundred. When he ended his presentation, Kaufman and Saypol were convicted of murder. "After that evening," said an eyewitness, "I was convinced that the Rosenbergs were tried for being Communists and not for espionage."

The campaign to save the Rosenbergs ended abruptly at 8:00 P.M. on Friday, June 19, 1953. Despite fresh evidence that indicated possibly perjury on the part of a key witness, and numerous appeals to President Eisenhower, the execution was carried out as ordered. "They were strapped into the electric chair several hours earlier than scheduled," noted a reporter, "so as not to desecrate the Jewish *Sabbath.*"

Amid the Rosenberg controversy, American Jewry witnessed still other incidents tinged with anti-Semitism, communism, and treason. At Fort Monmouth, New Jersey, a large percentage of Jews working at the radar labs were suddenly told that they were "security risks." The attorneys for the ousted workers turned to the AJC and the ADL for assistance, claiming that anti-Semitism and not "security" was the issue. Though evidence seemed to support their contention, both agencies refused to help, declaring that there was no proof to support the charge. "My client," lamented an attorney for one of the Jewish technicians, "was sacrificed on the altar of anti-Semitism" by the very agencies entrusted with his protection.

A more serious incident of anti-Semitism disguised as anti-Communism stemmed from an effort, in 1950, to stop the appointment of Mrs. Anna Rosenberg as assistant secretary of defense. Immediately after the Armed Services Committee approved her nomination, an outcry was heard from the ultranationalist right wing: "Anna Rosenberg is a Communist fellow traveler," cried the infamous Gerald L. K. Smith. "She is one of the most ominous and enigmatic figures in the secret . . . Jew machine."

Unlike their inaction during the Fort Monmouth affair, the AJC and the ADL rushed to defend Rosenberg against her accusers. They furnished the senators with material on her background and, as a result of their energetic efforts, the anti-Semitic assault on her collapsed. "The quick response to the crisis," noted an observer, "helped avert a potential Dreyfus affair."

By the late 1950s the Red Scare had run its course, and in the closing years of the decade relatively few acts of *overt* anti-Semitism were recorded. "Today," reported a survey taken in 1958, "anti-Semitism flows a quiet course, hidden, subtle and pervasive, just as harmful—and even harder to fight." Open anti-Jewish manifestations, noted the study, had gone underground because of the success of educational programs and civil rights legislation.

Shortly after this analysis was published, the nation was swept by a "swastika epidemic." Bricks were hurled through synagogue windows, anti-Semitic slogans were scrawled on store fronts and school-room walls, swastikas were painted on temples, Jewish centers, and Jewish-owned homes. There were also bomb threats, several of which were carried out. "Between Christmas 1959 and the end of February 1960," noted a report of the AJC's Institute on Human Relations, approximately 650 such cases were reported, with California and New York being the hardest hit. "The perpetrators—at least those who were caught—invariably were boys below the age of 21."

"I can't believe it . . . I can't believe it," exclaimed a father upon hearing that his teen-age son had smeared a swastika on the driveway of a Long Island family. A surprised neighbor added, "He's a model boy. . . ."

"He loved art and hated violence . . . he couldn't have done a thing like that," insisted the parents of another teen-ager, who was arrested for painting a swastika on an Atlanta synagogue.

"Most of the 12 youths who tormented a Jewish couple over a period of 15 months are from . . . 'better families,' " reported a San Francisco newspaper. "Some were in college or plan to enroll. . . . Some go to church regularly. . . . They looked and acted like Explorer Scouts, clean-cut, alert, 'normal.' "

"On the surface," said an AJC investigator, the youths seemed to be "*typical* American teen-agers. Seeing one on the street, one would scarcely suspect that he could engage in violence or in the ugly anti-Semitic episodes which shocked the nation." "The incidents," remarked another observer, "reminded me of Nazi Germany."

On a house in Absecon, New Jersey, were smeared the words "We want no Jews. If you don't move—liquidation." At a public golf course in New York, a fifteen-foot swastika and some obscenities were carved into the greens. On the walls of an apartment house anti-Jewish slogans were scrawled, and swastikas were spray-painted on fifty automobiles in the parking lot of another.

More disturbing were the firebombings of synagogues. In Kansas City, Missouri, a bomb ripped through Temple Kehillath Israel. In Springfield, Massachusetts, a crudely constructed explosive device shattered the stained-glass windows of Temple Beth El's sanctuary. And in Gadsden, Alabama, a seventeen-year-old high school dropout who was known for his infatuation with Nazism hurled a firebomb at that city's only Jewish house of worship. When two congregants rushed out of the building to investigate the blast, the youth opened fire on them with a shotgun. Interestingly, while the maladjusted Alabama teen-ager was free on bail, he drove an automobile into a tree, "dying almost instantly in the presence of a high school band rehearsing on a near-by field." Before committing this final act, he discharged a shotgun to attract everyone's attention.

After an intensive investigation, it was discovered that most of the youngsters involved in these incidents were members of Nazi youth groups. "In Kansas City," noted the *American Jewish Yearbook,*

> the detonation came shortly after police rounded up for questioning members of a so-called Nazi Club, operating in the high schools, . . . the Reich Nordic Youth Club and the National Socialist Workers party. Two of the youths admitted having previously defaced the temple with swastikas. . . . In the Springfield instance, three boys, 15 to 16 years old, were apprehended. At first they said they were part of a Nazi group. . . .

"Two 15-year-olds," continued the *Yearbook*'s report on "Anti-Jewish Agitation,"

> apprehended for having defaced a high school, a Catholic church, and a Baptist cemetery near Levittown, N.Y., were found to be members of a group bearing the hybrid name "Naz-Comms." Among other groups uncovered . . . were the National Socialist German Sympathizers, consisting of boys 12 to 14 years old, involved in swastika daubings in Detroit, . . . and the S.S. Elite Club of Yonkers, N.Y. . . . nine of its members ages 13 to 14. . . .

Imitating the antics of George Lincoln Rockwell's American Nazi Party and other such representatives of the "adult" lunatic fringe, these adolescents served to remind American Jewry of the level of anti-Jewish prejudice in American culture. In 1967, in the obscure town of Wayne, New Jersey, that prejudice became evident and significant in a school-board election.

Few suburbanites vote in such local elections, which are sometimes concerned with religious issues: Christmas observance, released time, prayer and bible reading, Sabbath classes, and similar concerns. In Wayne, however, a community situated twenty miles from New York City, not only did they go to the polls in droves, but the election commanded national attention.

Five candidates, two of whom were Jewish, were running for three school-board vacancies. A week before the polls opened, the Jewish office seekers were denounced. "Most Jewish people are liberals," said Newton Miller, school board vice-president, during an interview, "especially when it comes to spending for education. If Kraus and Mandell are elected . . . and Fred Lafer [who was not up for re-election] is in for two more years, that's a three-to-six vote. It would only take two more votes for a majority, and Wayne would be in real financial trouble.

"Two more votes," added Miller, "and we lose what is left of Christ in our Christmas celebrations in our schools. Think about it."

The next day, the local press printed the remarks under the headline "Miller Warns: Don't Put Mandell, Kraus on Board."

The story touched off an immediate response, as Wayne's civic and religious leaders collectively condemned the statement: "Mr. Miller," said George Schroeder, president of the school board, "has gone off the deep end this time . . . [his remarks] are so far off base that they are impossible to give credence to. They are ridiculous and shameless." David Caliri, another board member, called the statement "despicable."

"I deplore this kind of statement," added Richard Davis, a candidate for the school board. "There is no place for an appeal to prejudice."

Councilman Leonard Pine exclaimed, "These comments are uncalled for!" And Andrew Militello, president of Wayne's P.T.A., asserted: "I cannot put into words my reaction to this statement. . . . I am sick over this. I cannot understand bringing religion into this."

Overnight, the national media picked up the story, and, the next day, every home in the country received the details of the incident from their favorite TV anchor man. From near and far, political leaders, civic groups, and religious spokesmen hurled their denunciations at the New Jersey bigot. Wayne's residents were unhappy about the publicity. "My

Henrietta Szold (hand on hip) greets American Youth Aliyah arrivals, Palestine, 1934. (Zionist Archives and Library)

Menasha Skulnick and his wife, Sarah. Skulnick, active from the 1930s to the 1950s, was a popular comedian and musical-comedy actor in the Yiddish theatre who became a Broadway star in the later part of his career.
(Photo courtesy of Joseph Kutner)

Marty Glickman of Brooklyn (left) and Sam Stoller of Cincinnati en route to the 1936 Berlin Olympics. Pressure from American Nazi sympathizers, afraid of offending Hitler, kept these two superb sprinters from racing. (Courtesy of Marty Glickman)

Marty Glickman passing the baton to Jesse Owens in a post-Olympics relay race held at White City Stadium, London, August 1936. (Courtesy of Marty Glickman)

Away from home during World War II. "I went to the theaters in the city, but I always seemed to turn up at the Jewish center when I had the desire to be closer to home. . . ." (U. S. Army Signal Corps)

A study in irony: Jewish Mayor Henry Plitt (left) with his prisoner Julius Streicher (center) the most notorious anti-Semite among the Nazis.
(American Jewish Archives)

Jewish War Veterans march on Washington D.C., demanding that Palestine be opened for displaced persons, July 1946. (Zionist Archives and Library)

Haganah Ship *Exodus*, 1947. "The ship looked like a matchbox that had been splintered by a nutcracker. We could see women looking for children . . . lifesaving rafts dangling at crazy angles." (Zionist Archives and Library)

President Harry S Truman and Eddie Jacobson. "Well, Harry, I too have a hero . . .
I am talking about Chaim Weizmann, the greatest Jew who ever lived. . . ."
(American Jewish Archives)

Israel Goldstein kisses Abba Hillel Silver as news of the UN vote to partition Palestine is announced. (Zionist Archives and Library)

Colonel David "Mickey" Marcus. After combat against the Nazis, the West Point graduate fought for Haganah. He was killed during the siege of Jerusalem. Of the thousands of men buried at the U.S. Military Academy, he is the only one killed while fighting under a foreign flag. (Zionist Archives and Library)

In 1949, Chaim Weizmann presents President Truman with Torah.
(Zionist Archives and Library)

God," complained a resident, "they are making a wonderful town sound like Germany; it'll never get its good name back."

On the evening of the emergency meeting, nearly five hundred people, amid a crowd of TV and newspaper reporters, witnessed the school board, in an 8–1 vote, "censure Mr. Miller's appeal to bigotry" and call for his resignation. Miller, who cast the single opposing vote, refused to resign, explaining that he wanted to stay on in order to "serve out [his] term and do the job [he] was elected to do for the people of Wayne."

No doubt shaken by the no-confidence vote, Miller offered the best apology he could muster. "[I am] truly sorry for the incident," he said, but he nevertheless refused to retract his remarks. He insisted that he was not anti-Semitic, and to prove his assertion told the crowd that Jack Mandell, one of the Jews he attacked, was a friend. That some of his best friends were Jews. With that, Mandell finally spoke.

"Newt, you're right. We have been friends. But it grieves me to tell you that you are an anti-Semite and a bigot."

The audience greeted the remark with applause, while another board member, Mrs. Carl Yoder, quietly sobbed.

Due to Miller's rather feeble "apology," many of Wayne's residents rushed to the support of the school-board vice-president. "My God," noted one long-time resident, "Newt tried and tried to apologize and they [the Jews] wouldn't accept it. Now I tell you, what do you make of that?"

"We've discussed this in class . . . ," said a high school student. "We were upset. We thought the Jewish people should have pardoned Mr. Miller. It's much too blown up." Another student added, "People have said worse things in a campaign. It wasn't the right thing to say, but he apologized; what more can he do?"

Similar support was recorded in the local press's "Letters to the Editor." All were addressed to Miller:

One wrote:

> Apparently there are several persons who still want to degrade you, including some of your friends, and political leaders. If this is what is meant by the golden rule then I have nothing but compassion, sorrow and my prayers for them. You have made a mistake, you could have committed murder and been let off easier. . . .

Another:

> All of you who were "shocked," refusing his apology, including Mr. Mandell, are nothing more than you accuse him of being . . . Hypocrites. The news media love you all dearly!!

Finally:

To err is human—to forgive divine.

On the day of the election, many townspeople, because of the "religious issue," as they called it, were confident that Mandell and Kraus would be easily elected. "I was certain [they] would be a shoo-in," noted a resident. "Newt committed political suicide. I was sure that you just can't get away with open anti-Semitism in America any more." This observer was wrong. When the vote was counted, the confidence he had in his "enlightened" neighbors was shattered. Kraus and Mandell were buried in a pro-Miller landslide.

"If Jack Mandell had been understanding," declared a self-righteous Miller, "and extended his hand in the spirit of brotherhood, the Christians of this town would have backed him all the way."

Though the Wayne episode had little to do with religious emphasis in public education throughout the 1940s and 1960s, concern with Bible and prayer reading and with religious-holiday observance continued to be a source of tension between gentiles and Jews. "The tensions seemed to be mounting," noted the *American Jewish Yearbook* for 1959, "as more and more people were becoming active in educational matters and were expressing their views on school questions, particularly when they felt that religious or moral issues were at stake." The controversy over Christmas observance may be taken as a typical issue.

In 1956, in Ossining, New York, Jewish and Protestant citizens joined together in protest over a school-board proposal to erect a crèche on the lawn of the town's public high school. Though tensions ran high, school-board officials continued to support the project. The following year, in Valley Stream, Long Island, outraged residents stormed a local school-board meeting after hearing that James Devers, the district superintendent of schools, canceled a Christmas play based on the life of Christ. Several Jewish parents had inquired about the nature of the performance, but none had requested that the play be canceled or its contents changed. Though Devers insisted that he had not withdrawn the activity because of outside pressure, anti-Jewish feelings ran high.

Infuriated by Devers' decision, nearly a thousand parents descended on a meeting of the school board. "The decision, however, stood," noted a participant; "the performance would not go on." Almost overnight, a Citizens Guardian League was organized to help elect a future board "with a membership pledged to an acceptance of spiritual observance of the holiday in the public schools." The new organization published a full-page advertisement in the local newspaper apologizing to the children for the cancellation of the play.

In Ross, California, the annual Nativity play was not canceled. In January 1958, Ann Diamond, a housewife, complained to officials that a school Christmas play did not reflect the religion of her children. "It confused them," she said, "and they brought their confusion into our home. It was an experience outside their faith." The county attorney, however, dismissed her complaint as "insubstantial." The play in question, he said, did not discriminate and showed no "preference for one religion over another." It was simply a drama based on historical events and was related "to the talents of the students in the fields of speech and drama. . . ." In a letter to the superintendent of schools, he added that "the most that could be said of such a program" is that it possibly "[constituted] an incidental encroachment upon the constitutional principle of separation of church and state."

In 1962, representatives of Washington, D.C.'s Jewish Community Center repeated Mrs. Diamond's objections. They urged the local school boards to put an end to religious celebrations. School superintendent Carl F. Hansen, however, refused to ban the various Nativity pageants, asserting that to yield to the Jewish community would "create an artificial separation between events within and outside the school . . . difficult to reconcile with the purposes of education." The episode, noted an observer, "was followed with some narrow-minded talk tinged with anti-Semitism. Most of the opposition, however, was limited to abusive letters to the press."

In Florida, the Jewish community was also confronted with a school-related church-state issue. In an effort to ban religious celebrations in their public schools, several Miami Beach Jews, supported by a number of Unitarians and agnostics, filed a suit in the State Supreme Court. The court, however, ruled against the plaintiffs as "just another case in which the tender sensibilities of certain minorities are sought to be protected against the allegedly harsh laws and customs enacted and established by the more rugged pioneers of this nation. . . ." Several years later, the United States Supreme Court overruled this decision.

Throughout the 1960s, the trend toward secularization of the public schools alarmed certain American traditionalists. North Carolina Senator Sam Ervin asserted that the court had "made God unconstitutional." Alabama congressman George Andrews added, "They put the Negroes in the schools, and now they've kicked God out."

CHAPTER IX

Into the Present

Bittersweet Encounter

ON November 11, 1957, six sticks of dynamite were placed next to a synagogue in Charlotte, North Carolina. The bomb was discovered before it exploded. In the next two years the country was rent with a series of similar incidents. In the early-morning hours of February 9, 1958, worshipers found a suitcase filled with thirty sticks of explosives at the entrance to Temple Emanuel in Gastonia, North Carolina. In Birmingham, Alabama, fifty pieces of high-powered dynamite, contained in a valise, were uncovered on the window sill of Temple Beth-El. "It had rained the night before and the damp explosives failed to detonate," said a policeman. "If it had gone off it would have leveled the entire street." The school section of Atlanta's leading reform temple was rocked by an explosion on October 12, 1958. Several minutes after the blast, a journalist's phone rang: "This is General Gordon of the Confederate Underground," announced the caller. "This is the last empty building I'll blow up."

Before the Atlanta incident, an explosion had ripped through a Miami Beach temple, and later that same evening, Nashville's Jewish Community Center was also rocked by a blast. At 8:27 P.M., Rabbi William Silverman's telephone rang. His wife answered: "We have just dynamited the Jewish center," said the caller. "Next will be the temple and any other nigger-loving place or nigger-loving person in Nashville." The woman became so frightened that she slammed the receiver down as hard as she could.

In the early-morning hours of April 28, 1958, another bomb exploded, this time the target was the Jewish Community Center of Jacksonville, Florida. After the blast, a black public school was also destroyed. Within minutes of the two explosions, someone called the editor of a local newspaper and warned that "Jews must be driven out of Florida except for Miami Beach. . . . The bombings will continue until segregation is restored everywhere in the South."

The thunder-like blast that ripped through the school section of the Miami synagogue broke the stillness of early morning. Fortunately, the building was empty and no one was injured. The damage was extensive. "The explosion," reported Nathan Pearlmutter, "tore a gaping hole in the concrete rear wall of the school. It hurled a section of iron railing, cemented to the rear steps of the building, one hundred and fifteen yards onto the roof of a private home. The school's roof and walls were lifted from their foundation." Everyone who heard the blast thought "that an airplane had crashed."

Quickly, the excited, pajama-clad people were flushed from their homes. Dressed in housecoats and bathrobes, they watched as emergency vehicles raced to the blast area. "Fearful of panic if word of a 'synagogue bombing' raced through the alarmed neighborhood," wrote Pearlmutter, "police told the gathering crowd that it had been a gas explosion." The real cause, however, had already been discovered. It was dynamite, "wrapped, ironically enough, in paper *yarmulkas,* stolen from an outside storage bin."

When Nathan Pearlmutter, director of Florida's ADL, heard the news, a Ku Klux Klan meeting he had recently witnessed "some sixty miles north of Tampa, in the middle of 'cracker' country," quickly flashed before his eyes. "The rally," he said, "was a segregationist one. The loudest exclamations, however, the auto-honking that filled the night air, were in response not to anti-Negro but to anti-Semitic diatribes:

" 'If Ike wants to involve us in the Middle East, instead of sending Americans out there let him send American Yids to fight for Israel. . . .

" 'We don't hate the good nigger. A good nigger is black on the outside, but a Jew is white on the outside and black inside. We've got to segregate the Jew to the same second-class citizenship that the nigger thinks he has but don't really have.'

"Whereas mention of 'niggers' seemed to call forth no more than strong disapproval in the mob," noted Pearlmutter, "the term 'Jew,' 'kike,' and 'Zionist' caused them to stir angrily."

The desegregation crisis rocked southern Jewry more severely than any domestic event since the Civil War. "For three hundred years," asserted one southern Jew, "we accepted, with reservations of course, our region's customs and institutions: slavery, Jim Crow, the Democratic Party. We felt secure down here and most of us wanted to keep things the way they were." Sociologist Alfred Hero, Jr., supported this assertion: "Probably nowhere [else] in America," he wrote, "is the old principle of Jewish history *Wie es Christel sich, so Judel sich* [as the Christians do, so do the Jews]' so apparent."

Tradition-bound southern Jews became extremely uneasy by the ubiquitous presence of northern Jews in the Civil Rights Movement. When a young Jewish lawyer was told by a non-Jewish friend that "the president of the NAACP is Jewish," wrote Murray Friedman in *Commentary* magazine, he reacted with disbelief. "Within twenty-four hours, almost everyone in the Jewish community had heard the story, and the next day, a Jewish defense agency was phoned for information." They wanted to know if the story was true. "When the Virginians learned that Arthur B. Spingarn of New York, the NAACP's president, was indeed Jewish, there was grim silence at their end of the line. The knowledge that a northern Jew was head of the leading organization for Negro rights had shaken the security of this Virginia Jewish community."

In 1956 this security was again disturbed when Rabbi Seymour Atlas took part in a "Brotherhood Week" program and *Life* magazine published a picture of a black man standing next to him. Not five minutes after this issue was on the stands, the officers of his Alabama temple urged the rabbi to "demand" that *Life* inform its readers that "Brotherhood Week" was not associated with the 1954 school-desegregation decision or, for that matter, any integrationist activities. "The congregation," noted an observer, "was convinced that to remain silent on the issue of Negro rights meant continued harmonious relations with their non-Jewish neighbors."

The fear of anti-Semitic reprisals continued to grip southern Jewry as news filtered South of the integration efforts of their northern coreligionists. "When Jews from outside of the South marched in demonstrations down here," noted an Alabama observer, "we always reminded them of our touchy situation." One Birmingham resident told a visiting rabbi who was on a civil rights mission, "We are glad that you are doing what we would like to do but do not have the courage to do. Please do not endanger us; do not get our synagogue bombed."

Other Jews made firmer protests. "When a rabbi from New Haven, Connecticut, takes part in such demonstrations," said a Georgia Jew, "you have no idea the position Jewry in our state is placed in. . . . A rabbi from out of our area is detrimental to Jews in the South." "For the probable success in organizing an effective Klan in Albany, Georgia," wrote another furious Jewish resident to a rabbi who marched for civil rights, "you and your colleagues can take full credit." From Memphis came these angry words: "If only you Yankee Jews would keep your long noses out of our business. . . ." And a Jewish leader in Alabama said: "You're like Hitler; you stir up anti-Semitism against us."

Most southern rabbis also followed the cautious approach to desegregation. "I don't see how we can do much," said a rabbi from New Orleans, "until the Protestant ministry avows a more positive stand. They could change the situation overnight." A South Carolinian wrote: "While I have spoken against segregation and in favor of integration from my pulpit from time to time—to the discomfiture of my members —I have put nothing in writing [owing to] a dangerous powder keg in Florence which might explode at any time." A Tennessee rabbi declared, "As a southern congregation, we need not initiate or take an overly conspicuous role in advocating integration." A colleague from the western part of the state added, "We must move slowly and gradually. . . ."

Perhaps a dozen or so southern rabbis, not gripped with the caution or fear of their colleagues, plunged into the civil rights fight. Among the most notable were Perry Nussbaum of Jackson, Mississippi, Jacob Rothschild of Atlanta, Georgia, Emmet Frank of Alexandria, Virginia, and Charles Martinband, who was thought of by his Mississippi congregation as "crazy" or "ahead of his times."

Though told by his congregants to remain silent on the civil rights issue, Martinband nevertheless continued his activities. To further upset his board of trustees, he at times invited blacks to his home. On one occasion a neighbor saw several blacks entering the rabbi's home. Unnerved by the sight, he asked, "Who are those people?" "Some of my Christian friends," Martinband answered as he slammed the door shut.

The most outstanding southern rabbi to throw himself into the civil rights struggle was Emmet Frank. Unmoved by threats of reprisal, the

Virginia rabbi declared that "the Jew cannot remain silent to injustice."
He lashed out at the politically powerful segregationist Senator Harry F.
Byrd and at others who supported "massive resistance" to Virginia's
public-school integration. On Yom Kippur Eve, 1958, he delivered the
most noted of his sermons:

> I speak as a rabbi on this issue to a Jewish congregation on our
> holiest evening. The significance of my remarks is heightened this
> evening in that I have chosen one of our holiest days to devote to
> root out the evil in our midst in the form of bigots and hate ped-
> dlers who, for a headline, a misplaced vote, would attack minority
> after minority. When those who are not afraid to speak . . . sound
> like a voice crying in the wilderness—it is our moral obligation
> as Jews not to desist from being a light unto the nation. . . . I am
> afraid of silence . . . I will not be silenced! . . . The Jew cannot
> remain silent to injustice. . . . Let the segregationists froth and
> foam at their mouth. There is only one word to describe their
> madness—Godlessness, or to coin a new synonym—Byrdliness.
> Byrdliness has done more harm to the stability of our country than
> McCarthyism. . . .

The sermon quickly made Rabbi Frank a nationally recognized
figure, as letters and telegrams poured in from all over the country.
Most of the correspondence, including those from his Virginia congregants, supported his position. A few, however, did not. "As the years go
on," noted one opponent to his stance, "you will reflect on the damage
you have done to those to whom you were supposed to be a religious
leader."

In the desperate effort to block desegregation, the segregationist
swung a hard club, sometimes not looking at where it fell. As he fought
to maintain his "peculiar" way of life, he grabbed whatever he could
and too often at hand was a weapon tinged with anti-Semitism. Southern Jews knew this, and it was this knowledge that dictated their
prudence. More than mere social disapproval, the Jew feared social
ostracism or physical antagonism at the hands of the more extreme
segregationists.

Alfred Hero, Jr., a sociologist, commented on the situation:

> It was one thing for Judge X, descendant of several esteemed
> families of the region, leader in the Episcopal Church, and relative
> of the socially prominent in the Deep South, to write critical letters
> to the archconservative papers in the state, chair the discussion
> groups in the library on public issues, and inform all and sundry of

his views. . . . people merely said he was getting old and was just another genteel eccentric. A Jew who did likewise needed considerably more courage or less sensitivity to probable public reactions. The whole Jewish community might become a target for antagonism—other Jews would fear that one was risking the status of the entire ethnic group, and many local Jews felt that no one had any right to upset the delicate balance whereby Jews had been treated well and accepted generally as fellow Southerners.

Desegregation raked up many latent antagonisms in the South, and knowing this, Jews, though many believed that blacks should have equality, were simply too timid to openly express their opinion.

While most southern Jews were conspicuously absent from the civil rights struggle, their northern coreligionists helped to spearhead the movement. "We are no Johnny-come-latelies," wrote Rabbi Richard Hertz in 1964. "We had a head start in the civil rights race. After World War II, the Jewish civic protective agencies—the American Jewish Committee, the Anti-Defamation League, Jewish community councils and all the others—were in the forefront of the battle."

Jewish agencies openly co-operated with the NAACP, the American Civil Liberties Union, and other, like-minded groups in litigations and in support of civil rights legislation. As early as 1950, four years before the Supreme Court's historic school-desegregation decision, the Jewish agencies filed briefs contending that the doctrine of "separate but equal" resulted in economic, educational, and social inequality. Four years later, when *Brown* v. *Board of Education* (1954) was heard by the high court, these same agencies, acting as "friends of the court," filed additional briefs opposing the "separate but equal" principle.

Will Maslow, executive director of the American Jewish Congress, commented on the early alliance between blacks and Jews: "The truth," he told Lenora Berson, author of *The Negroes and the Jews,* "is that you can't fight discrimination against one minority without fighting it against others. It was logical for Jews and Negroes to co-operate. Besides, it was in our interest to help them. We had the staff, the money, and the political muscle to do it. Many [civil rights] laws were actually written in the offices of Jewish agencies, by Jewish staff people, introduced by Jewish legislators, and pressured into being by Jewish voters. In addition, literally hundreds of court actions were taken by Jewish attorneys on behalf of Negro plaintiffs."

According to Maslow, the controversy surrounding Manhattan's Stuyvesant Town housing project best illustrates the early black-Jewish alliance. Soon after World War II, the Metropolitan Life Insurance Company financed the construction of a middle-income housing complex. The land on which it was built, due to state action, was exempt from New York City taxes. In spite of the semipublic character of the financing, several black ex-servicemen were refused apartments. Immediately, the Commission on Law and Social Action, a unit of the American Jewish Congress headed by Maslow, joined the NAACP in support of the veterans. Negotiations with management, however, failed to produce positive results, and so the case was taken to court. The litigation, supported by attorneys and money from the Jewish agency, forced management to reconsider and allow the blacks to rent.

In the years following the Stuyvesant Town affair, the overwhelming participation of Jews in the civil rights movement was unmistakable. Their agencies played an important role in the introduction and passage of every piece of civil rights legislation, Jewish individuals marched on "Freedom Now" picket lines, and still others were manhandled and beaten during the "freedom rides" to integrate interstate travel. Allen Sherman, a Jewish songwriter and entertainer from Brooklyn, commented on these activities in a musical parody of "Frère Jacques": *And how's your sister Ida?* he sang. *She's a Freedom Rida,* was the comical answer.

The rabbis who answered Dr. Martin Luther King's call to help desegregate a St. Augustine, Florida, swimming pool did not take their arrest as lightly or as comically as some took Sherman's whimsical song, nor did the rabbis who participated in the Mississippi Freedom Summer Project or those who were beaten and jailed in Selma, Alabama, or Jackson, Mississippi. Cleveland Rabbi Arthur J. Lelyveld, who was clubbed by red-necks in Hattiesburg, Mississippi, must have found little humor in Sherman's tune.

The thousands of Jewish students who marched under the banner of King's Southern Christian Leadership Conference, or who participated in the various southern voter registration drives, shared Lelyveld's sentiments. "We found no humor in being beaten, jailed, whipped, or insulted," noted twenty-one-year-old Richard Shapiro. "I was frightened all the time I was in Mississippi. I thought I'd never get out alive. I thought I'd end up like Schwerner and Goodman."

On the evening of June 21, 1964, Michael Schwerner and Andrew Goodman, along with James Chaney, a Mississippi black, were murdered in the backwoods of Neshoba County, Mississippi. The two New York Jews were there, said a friend of Schwerner's, "to find fulfillment by helping Negroes improve their place in that portion of our society which still feels compelled to boast of white supremacy."

In 1964, Schwerner and Goodman went to Meridian, Mississippi, to "help crack that state's racial barriers." Told of the presence of the two civil rights workers, a Meridian Jew went to see the twenty-four-year-old Schwerner to urge him to return home. "You are already known as that god-damned bearded atheist Communist Jew from New York," he said. "All you will do is make trouble for us down here. Progress will come with time and from within; it will not come by outside agitation."

Schwerner and Goodman refused to take the advice. The two men were determined to stay and help organize the Mississippi Summer Project: a massive voter-registration drive. It was this project that indirectly led to the lynching of the three men.

Aaron Henry, president of the Clarksdale, Mississippi, NAACP and organizer of the Mississippi Freedom Democrats, commented on the tragedy. "In the fight for human dignity," he said, "we have never underestimated our opposition, but we have overestimated our support. We thought that naturally we would have the Jews on our side, because the enemies of the Jews were usually found in the same group that oppose us. But we don't have Jews supporting us." To Aaron Henry, wrote Lenora Berson, author of *The Negroes and the Jews* (1971), ". . . Michael Schwerner [as well as Andrew Goodman] wasn't a Jew. He was, as Schwerner said of himself, only a man."

With talk of the murders still fresh on everyone's lips, Jews began to witness, with mounting alarm, the rise of black anti-Semitism. In 1963, Judd Teller noted that "anti-Semitism among Negroes is a stark reality that cannot be ignored." Soon after, a reliable study reported that black college students exhibited "markedly prejudiced and authoritarian attitudes directed particularly against Jews, Orientals, . . . and non-Negro foreigners." The survey forewarned that "Freedom Now" and "We Shall Overcome" were being replaced with shouts of "Black power."

Anti-Jewish hostility on the part of blacks did not begin in the 1960s, but, rather, was present decades before. Past encounters between the two groups "in the northern urban centers," noted Robert Weisbord and Arthur Stein, "were scarcely the kind that promoted goodwill. . . . Instead, they were unequal-status, friction-generating contacts, between merchants and consumers, between landlords and tenants, between housewives and domestics."

In 1946, Kenneth B. Clark examined several sources of the friction:

Three Negro women appeared before a mediating panel of clergymen with complaints that a Jewish butcher was "refusing to sell meat to many Negro residents of the neighborhood, but selling to white Irish Catholics who live outside the area but formerly lived within it."

. . . A Negro actor states in bitter terms that he is being flagrantly underpaid by a Jewish producer. A Negro entertainer is antagonistic to his Jewish agent, who (he is convinced) is exploiting him. He vents his feelings to his friends, but admits that "If the Jews didn't get us bookings or parts we wouldn't work—but they make a gold mine out of us."

Antagonism toward the "Jewish landlord" is so common as to have become almost an integral aspect of the folk culture of the northern urban Negro. To him, almost all landlords are automatically Jewish and all his obvious housing ills are attributed to the greed and avarice of the "Jewish landlord."

High on the list of complaints were those of the domestics—cooks, maids and cleaning women—who worked for some Jewish families. The "Bronx Slave Market"—where domestics were hired in a fashion reminiscent of the ante-bellum slave mart—was an outstanding "sore spot" of black-Jewish relations. In 1942, Lawrence D. Reddick, a noted black historian, commented on the situation:

The majority of the inhabitants of the Bronx . . . are Jewish. In certain spots in this area the Negro domestic workers gather each morning to be hired for daily work at rates which are sometimes as low as fifteen cents per hour. These girls, bunched about the corners in all kinds of weather, are a very sorry sight. With the inevitable bundle under arm, they wait their turn to "sell" themselves to the housewives, who often haggle and bid for the cheapest price. The analogy to the old chattel slave market is not inapt.

In the East Bronx, the Simpson Avenue "slave market" illustrated the system at its worst. Ella Baker and Marvel Cooke, two black journalists, described the scene:

Rain or shine, cold or hot, you will find them there—Negro women, old and young—sometimes bedraggled, sometimes neatly dressed—but with the invariable paper bundle, waiting expectantly for Bronx housewives to buy their strength and energy for an hour, two hours, or even for a day at the magnificent rate of fifteen, twenty, twenty-five, or, if luck be with them, thirty cents an hour.

In Chicago, anti-Jewish hostility also stemmed from "slave market" conditions during the Great Depression. Two sociologists, St. Clair Drake and Horace R. Cayton, reported the following complaint:

> The Jewish woman that I work for tries to get a colored woman to do all of her work for as little as $2.00 a day and pay her own carfare.
>
> She is expected to do all the washing, including the linen and towels as well as the clothes for the five members of the family. She is supposed to finish the work, that is iron the entire wash—and then clean the house thoroughly—all for $2.00. Because there are some women who will do all the work for that amount, this Jewish woman feels that a colored woman who demands more is silly to think that she can get it. She says that she doesn't understand why, if some colored people can get along on that amount, all can't do the same.

Throughout the 1930s and 1940s, *some* blacks blamed their difficulties on Jews and peppered American Jewry with a barrage of anti-Semitic assaults. As journalist Chandler Owen noted in a 1941 article for the Chicago *Defender,* it was not uncommon for blacks to say, "Well, Hitler did one good thing: he put these Jews in their place."

Richard Wright, in his autobiographical *Black Boy,* examined a different source of black anti-Semitism. He recalled a childhood meeting with a Jewish grocer.

> I had never seen a Jew before and the proprietor of the corner grocery was a strange thing in my life. . . . All of us black people who lived in the neighborhood hated Jews, not because they exploited us, but because we had been taught that Jews were "Christ-killers." With the Jews thus singled out for us, we made them fair game for ridicule.
>
> We black children, seven, eight, and nine years of age—used to run to the Jew's store and shout:
>
> > Jew, Jew, Jew
> > What do you chew?
>
> Or we would form a long line and weave back and forth in front of the door, singing:
>
> > Jew, Jew
> > Two for five
> > That's what keeps
> > Jew alive

Or we would chant:

> Bloody Christ killers
> Never Trust a Jew
> Bloody Christ killers
> What won't a Jew do?

At the same time, there were a host of responsible voices being heard in the black community. In the worst days of the depression Adam Clayton Powell spoke out against the rising tide of anti-Semitism, calling the vicious diatribes "a deadly virus of the American bloodstream. . . . Let us stop blaming the Jew for the wrongs perpetrated and blame those who are really at fault," noted his column "Soap Box" in the *Amsterdam News:*

> Wherever the blame falls, let us not follow it up with hate. The fact is the Jew doesn't wrong us any more and probably much less than any other group. Maybe the corner grocer will short you a couple of ounces, but so will Joe the vegetable man and Sam the ice man. Cheating is not confined to any one race. Whereas one group might cut the change a little bit or pad the bill, it is the so-called white Christian that is giving us the most hell right now.

A. Philip Randolph, president of the Brotherhood of Sleeping Car Porters, echoed similar sentiments: "No Negro is secure from intolerance and race prejudice," he told a Madison Square Garden audience in 1942, "so long as one Jew is a victim of anti-Semitism. . . ." Ralph Bunche, then chairman of the Department of Political Science at Howard University, added his voice:

> Negroes are an oppressed people, such a people hits always upon the simplest and most convenient explanation of its troubles. It pounces upon a scapegoat as a means of psychological escape. The Jew is handy. In Negro communities he has daily contact with Negroes in the conduct of his business. And it is safe to scorn the Jew. His powers of retaliation are less great than those of the gentile whites, for the Jew himself is a victim of race.

Hardly twenty years after Bunche offered this observation, *some* blacks once again made Jews the victims of race. Perhaps the most outspoken among them were the Black Muslims. In February 1962, the *Führer* of the American Nazi Party, George Lincoln Rockwell, addressed five thousand Muslims at their Chicago convention. He hailed Elijah Muhammad, the Muslim leader, "as the Adolf Hitler of the black man" and added that Muhammad was "trying to do what I am trying to do."

Jeremiah X, Minister of the Muslims' Philadelphia Mosque, expressed Muslim policy toward Jews:

> As a Muslim, the Jews are the Negro's worst enemies among whites. Unlike other whites, Jews make it a practice to study Negroes; thus they are able to get next to him better than other whites. He uses the knowledge thus obtained to get close to the Negro, thereby being in a position to stab him with a knife.
>
> We regard him as the real Devil of the Bible where it is said, "those who say they are Jews are not, but are of the synagogue of Satan." Through their control of the press and of other mass media they are able to make the public feel sorry for Jews. It is so bad today that anybody who speaks out against Jews is immediately clobbered as "anti-semitic."

"They infiltrate the Negro neighborhood," he added, "with stores, and they exploit the Negro more than any other white group—housing, food, clothing—controlling the three basic things Negroes need. They claim to be friendly with Negroes but, when pushed to the wall, they are more injurious, more ruthless, than other whites."

A second representative incident occurred in 1965 in New York's Greenwich Village. There, playwright LeRoi Jones and jazz musician Archie Shepp attacked the "martyrdom" of Schwerner and Goodman. Shepp called the slain civil rights workers "artifacts" who went to Mississippi to "assuage their conscience." He then went on to tell his audience that he was "sick of you cats talking about six million Jews." Jones, who is known for poetry which speaks of "the slimy bellies of the owner-Jews" and "cracking steel knuckles in a jewlady's mouth," added that most of "our enemies are you in the audience." One member of the predominantly Jewish gathering stood up and told Jones and Shepp, "Go *fuck yourselves!*"

Anti-Jewish sentiments were again expressed in February 1966 by Clifford A. Brown of the Congress of Racial Equality (CORE), when he told an audience attending a Mount Vernon, New York, board of education meeting that "Hitler made a mistake when he didn't kill enough of you." Immediately, CORE officials denounced the remark as "intolerable" and began an investigation in an effort to determine the "context" in which the remark was made. Will Maslow, however, a member of CORE's national board and executive director of the American Jewish Congress, was disappointed with CORE's "tepid and ambiguous" response. He resigned from the civil rights organization, and in his letter of resignation asked James Farmer, CORE's national director, why Brown had not been ousted from the organization. "Can you conceive of any context that would make Mr. Brown's outrageous statement permissible?" he asked. "Can you conceive of any situation that would justify the kind of tirade that calls for more acts of genocide?"

Though Farmer responded to Maslow's letter with a strong denunciation of Brown's remark, asserting that "there is no room in CORE for racism or bigotry," another member of the organization reacted quite differently. "We are sick and tired," he said, "of white politicians telling us who our leaders should be." The alliance between Jews and blacks was coming to an end.

THE SUBURBAN DILEMMA

When New York City high school student Ruth Glazer was sixteen years old, her father decided to join the ranks of the self-employed. Like thousands of others, he joined the trek to suburbia to open what he felt suburban Jews missed most: "a real Jewish delicatessen."

At first he considered a traditional delicatessen. One with a "steaming grill warming knishes and frankfurters to be eaten on the spot," where a glass display case was decorated with ten or fifteen salamis, rolled beef, several cold pastramis, and two trays of franks—specials and regulars—flanked by pans of cole slaw and potato salad. On top of the counter would be the invariable plate piled with small chunks of salami. "A Nickel a Shtickel—Have a Nosh" read the sign. In the war years a new slogan found its way to the countertop: "Send a Salami to Your Boy in the Army."

The traditional delicatessen did not appeal to the new entrepreneur, because he sensed that the "emancipated" and "modern" Jewish suburbanites, who drove to *shul* for Friday-night and Saturday-morning services, "didn't care about such things." Confronted by this anachronism, the Glazers set out to satisfy Jewish taste for traditional food without offending their customers' "newly acquired dignity and propriety." The metamorphosis of their delicatessen "was a reflection of some of the painful minutiae of [Jewish suburbia's] social adjustment."

As soon as Glazer opened his door, the word went out: *There's a new Jewish Deli.* "The important word to the community," wrote Ruth

Glazer, "was not 'delicatessen,' but 'Jewish.' Uncertain of the articles of their faith, the Jews of the neighborhood could make one affirmation unhesitatingly. Jewish food was good."

> Requests for lox, sturgeon, whitefish, for sour cream, bagels, cream cheese, for gefilte fish and potato *latkes* besieged us. . . . The store, recognizedly a symbol of traditional Jewish living, became a center for the dispensation of knowledge on Jewish cookery, too. On Passover, women would come in and ask how to make *matzoh brei*. "My husband had some here, and he insists I learn how to make it." We closed on [most] Jewish holidays, served *matzoh* with meals on Passover, and gefilte fish on Friday.

Though Glazer also served clam chowder, hung a holly wreath on the door during Christmas, and occasionally filled an order for bologna and cheese, there was "a mysteriously fixed point he could not pass. His sympathies, principles and prejudices," noted his daughter, "shaped the atmosphere of the store and left no room for *treyf* meat. Unkosher cuts of meat—roast beef, leg of lamb, yes. Meat from a pig, no. A lamentable rigidity of adjustment, perhaps. But he had gone as far as he could. The next generation could begin serving the hams."

Like the Glazers, in the decades following World War II countless numbers of other Jews deserted America's central cities to establish themselves in suburbia. *And why not?* There lived the happy family of TV commercials, of magazines, of Doris Day movies. Few city dwellers could help but be attracted to newspaper ads beckoning them to resettle in communities where oak-shaded streets and wooded hills waited for their children to play. "A Superb Location," "There's Nothing Like Grandway View," "Gracious Suburban Living Starts Here," "If You're Moving Up in the World," and on they went, promoting the land of blue jeans and shopping centers, of bright new schools, of barbecues, garden clubs, PTA, do-it-yourself, and green lawns. "When I was growing up in Brooklyn, noted Martin Siegel, a Long Island rabbi, "I thought of the Five Towns," an affluent complex of bedroom communities on Long Island, "more than Israel, as the Promised Land."

To the new settler it was *Philadelphia Story*'s Mainline, *Andy Hardy*'s Carvel, and *Tom Sawyer*'s Hannibal, rolled into one. In reality, it was a land of station wagons and car pools, get-togethers over coffee and Danish, Chinese restaurants, pizza, and youngsters named Scott and Lisa proudly wearing scarlet jackets with *Hewlett High* emblazoned across the back. It was the home of lavish *bar mitzvahs* and weddings that resembled Hollywood premieres. Mothers chauffeured their children to band practice, baton-twirling try-outs, and ballet lessons; and fathers who had spent their childhood playing stickball on the concrete surface of Mrs. Goldstein's alley now occupied themselves with spreading fertilizer, praying for rain, and thumbing through the pages of *Consumer Reports* in search of the most potent weed killer.

"We came to the land with a full-blown insecurity that shows itself in constant comparison and seeking for advice," wrote Harry Gersh. "The neighbor's lawn always looks greener than yours."

> This is particularly true on my side. My lawn comes down from the fieldstone fence in a gentle slope, then down a steep bank, on to a level stretch, finally down to the street in a sharp slope of pachysandra. Passers-by can see the lawn only at an oblique angle. From that angle almost everyone's lawn looks like a green carpet. The brown spots, the crab grass . . . show only when you walk over the lawn and look directly down. This looking for trouble is done only on your own land.

In spite of the "brown spots," Gersh said, "it is pleasant to walk on your own earth and feel your own green grass and plan your own mysteries of birth and bloom and death."

> Only in our wildest dreams, the ones we didn't tell each other, did we include the ownership of broad acres, half-acres, quarter-acres. It is pleasant—but also worrisome. The clichés take on meaning. The cultural tags become things rather than words. When I spoke grandly of *my* house, *my* fourteen trees, *my* three varieties of lilac, *my* prize roses, my friends were envious. But they also were apprehensive. "Can you take care of things like that?" Even my wife, with all the required high school and college courses in botany, looked at the fertile earth and wondered would these growing things flourish under a new name on the deed of ownership?

Many of the Jews who followed Gersh to the rolling hills of suburbia —New York's Long Island, Chicago's Forest Park, Cleveland's Euclid, Boston's Newton, Los Angeles' San Gabriel Valley, Minneapolis' St. Louis Park—desperately wanted to escape the "old neighborhood." Away from the smelly *shuls* guarded by bearded old men who always seemed to be mumbling, candy stores where the second booth from the left was reserved for the bookmaker, nosy *yentas* and amateur marriage brokers who constantly investigated one's private life. They wanted no more of it. They wanted respectability, dignity. They hazily imagined the life of "country squires"—even if that life meant traveling over an hour to work or the Sunday-afternoon trip back to Mama for dinner.

Away from the invading *schwartzes* [blacks]. They also wanted out of the "Jewishness" which permeated their childhood.

Torn from familiar social moorings, however, many suddenly rediscovered their Jewishness and were overcome with the desire for their children to receive a Jewish education. "The very men who dropped out of Judaism after their *bar mitzvah,*" said Morris Bernstein, a retired merchant living in a New Jersey suburb, "now wanted their sons and daughters to know that they were Jewish. These were alien surroundings in the suburbs and there was no Jewish flavor here." "Out here," added his wife, Bluma, "God forbid it's too easy to marry a *shiksa!*" "The old neighborhood took care of this problem," noted a third observer. "You lived under heavy social pressures in a community of Jews. The signs were all around you. The *shul,* the kosher butcher, empty schools on Jewish holidays. Out here it was different. We didn't need an old *shul,* what we needed was a *temple,* something grand, something that reflected our aspirations."

In every suburban Jewish community the temple became the center of Jewish life. Unlike the traditional *shul* of the central city, these modern synagogues provided for more than mere religious needs; they also became centers for leisure-time activities. They became social clubs, amusement halls, civic centers, and lecture forums. They offered basketball courts, saunas, garden clubs, bridge clubs, men's clubs, women's clubs, sewing circles, book-review luncheons, and facilities for the *bar mitzvah* that "would be talked about for years." And, noted Rabbi Martin Siegel, the rabbi became their "property," paid to lead the congregation "in acting out their abstract sense of religion."

"This is the room that often sells our facilities for a wedding," proudly declared David Siegel, the director of a Jewish Center, to a visiting journalist investigating the Jewish condition in suburban Queens, New York City.

"We were in a small room with thick, flower-embossed carpeting," noted the journalist, "pink-and-silver papered walls, a pink brocade sofa, and a combined vanity and sink covered with pink formica and topped by a big, professional dressing-room mirror."

"There's a new [Jewish] center," said Siegel, "in which corners have been cut in everything but the bride's room. Theirs is probably the most elaborate bride's room in the city. It'll pay off, too."

The two men entered the auditorium. "This is the most active room in the building. . . . In addition to accommodating the overflow from services, we also do our catering here. Sometimes there may be four or five affairs on a weekend, *bas mitzvahs* Friday night, *bar mitzvahs* Saturday morning, a dinner, a wedding, a dance, a club meeting. We come close to resembling Madison Square Garden in making fast changes."

Martin Siegel, a Long Island, New York, rabbi, bemoaned the commercialization of Judaism. "Our Five Towns rival, Temple Israel," he wrote, "is symbolized to me by its new ballroom."

> I've heard that the ballroom, along with some other additions to the building, cost something around $1 million. God knows it has every conceivable luxury—special wood paneling, incredible crystal chandeliers, the most garish adornments. It can seat 700 people comfortably, and a *bar mitzvah* there, from matzoh-ball soup to nuts, can cost between $5,000 and $15,000. I find it an abomination.

"But it is hardly unique," he added. "All over the United States, Jews are building monuments to themselves at roughly the same speed and with the same taste as Colonel Sanders putting up his fried-chicken stands."

> I don't really want to be in the Judaism franchise business. I suspect that if we don't get our new building, some of our members, those who are looking mostly for a service station where they can fill up with religion and dinner parties, will defect to Temple Israel. The membership fees are about the same in the two synagogues, and I've actually heard prospective members say, "Why buy a Ford when I can get a Cadillac for the same price?"

As telling was an incident that occurred after Siegel conducted a funeral service. A member of the "rival" temple approached him and asked, "Rabbi, what do you think of the new ballroom at *our* temple?"

"I think," he replied, "that it is morally and aesthetically grotesque."

The woman gave him an icy look: "When your salary is as large as Rabbi Zion's, then you'll be able to talk."

Ironically, with all the pomp and splendor of the new temples, few people, except on the High Holidays, when overflow crowds were jammed into ballrooms and basketball courts, attended weekday or weekend services. The suburban synagogues' religious function ran a poor second to its social activities. "Our temple membership is high," noted Los Angeles businessman Sam Solomon, "and religious-school attendance is regular, but Judaism is absent in the personal lives of our members." "Judaism," added his wife, Sarah, "whether reform, conservative, or orthodox, is not mere synagogue membership or attendance at a lox-and-bagel get-together."

Despite the lack of religiosity, most suburban Jews still wanted their children provided with opportunities to "feel Jewish." *Happy* Jewish holidays, especially Hanukkah, were transformed into children's festivals, and Sunday schools proliferated. Many parents, however, still refused to practice traditional Judaism, thus making the task of the school more difficult. "Don't make him too religious," said one parent; "after all, I don't want my son to become a rabbi."

In a Chicago suburb, the drama of what should and should not be taught at Sunday school was played out between a rabbi and an audience of apprehensive parents. "You have a responsibility of preventing any inconsistencies which might arise from not practicing at home the content of the school curriculum." Immediately, the parents rejected the suggestion. "They insisted," noted an observer, "that the school teach *about* Jewish traditions and at the same time not put the parents themselves under pressure to *observe* these traditions at home."

After weeks of discussion a compromise was finally reached: "The children will not be taught that parents should follow the rituals," said a school official. "They will only be informed of the background of the ritual. . . . We're not teaching the child that he must do these things. We just teach him the custom. . . ."

"No wonder," wrote a critic of suburban Jewish education, "the children . . . suffer from a mild kind of schizophrenia."

> *Here* are the rabbi, director, cantor and teachers; *there* are the parents. . . . *Here* is supernaturalism, prayer, the Ten Commandments, Jewish customs and ceremonies. *There* is science, atomic facts, sex, Mickey Spillane, American ways and values. . . . So it comes about that the attempt to make children more secure as members of the Jewish community has in many cases the opposite result. Uncertainty and insecurity are increased and the children's suspicion of adult hypocrisy is strengthened, because the traditions, customs and beliefs of the religious school are at complete variance with home life.

"Interest in Jewish tradition has withered," noted Dr. L. H. Grunebaum, writer and chairman of a local committee on Jewish education; "ceremonials are not adhered to; the basic skills of prayer have been lost; their relationship to God bothers few people. . . . Hebrew is unknown. . . . We may regard the Christmas tree found in many homes

. . . as a perfect symbol of the well-nigh complete acculturation to suburban 'normality.'"

More and more Jews, not necessarily suburban dwellers, were caught up in the Christmas festivities because their own joyous holiday Hanukkah, which had similar external symbols, often fell within the same week. "The aspects of Hanukkah observance currently emphasized," asserted two sociologists in 1967, "—the exchange of gifts and the lighting and display of the *menorah* in the windows of homes—offer ready parallels to the general mode of Christmas observance as well as provide a Jewish 'alternative' to the holiday. Instead of alienating the Jew from the general culture, Hanukkah helps to situate him as a participant in that culture. Hanukkah, in short, becomes for some the Jewish Christmas."

For the most part, this assertion is correct. In one southern community, "Uncle Max, the Hanukkah Man" was invented. As a Jewish Santa, the patriarchal "Uncle Max" wears "traditional clothes and a nice yarmulke coming from Eretz Israel on a good-will mission." Other innovations are the "Hanukkah bush" decorated with Stars of David, "Hanukkah stockings," "Hanukkah gelt," and "Hanukkah dinners." Commercially, there are all sorts of Hanukkah gift wrappings, Hanukkah chocolate boxes, and Hanukkah greeting cards.

Some acculturated Jews, unsure of themselves in a Christian society, went a step further and decorated Christmas trees. An orthodox lawyer noted: "We get hundreds of cards at Christmas. I would say that about 80 per cent of them come from Jews. The explanation for such behavior, noted a national magazine, "lies in the changing nature of the holiday itself. With the increasing Americanization of Christmas, and emphasis on its secular rather than religious aspect, the holiday has become more and more acceptable to many Jews." A university professor put it this way: "The essence of Christmas—peace on earth, goodwill toward men, the carols, the presents—how can you resist that?"

Other Jews offered different explanations: "You're sending your kid to Hotchkiss, and he comes home for Christmas, and what are you going to do—celebrate Hanukkah?" A Los Angeles doctor said, "It's a lovely time of the year, especially for children. The actual literal definition of Christmas is of no consequence to me." Some, of course, were guilt-ridden over the tree in their living room. In Chicago, a young man recalled that he hid the tree when his rabbi unexpectedly dropped by to wish the family a happy new year.

By the mid-1960s, reported *Look* magazine, the new generation of

Jews, "sure of themselves as their parents never were," began "to reject Christmas celebrations in Jewish homes as unseemly." Though they continued to exchange greeting cards and gifts with gentile friends and associates, the day of the tree was over. "Twenty years ago, there was hardly a Jewish home that didn't have a tree," noted a Beverly Hills religious-school director in 1965. "Today, there are few that do."

The trend was obvious. A New York Jewish leader said, "the 'Hanukkah bush' used to be a big joke. Now it has a kind of derogatory sound." An Illinois man declared, "Putting a tree in my house would be like changing my name from Jack Goldfarb to Jordan Gray." The remarks of a San Francisco man who was attending a Christmas party for influential members of the city's Jewish community are perhaps the most telling. His wife was late for the festivities and so he stepped outside to wait. "There I was in my well-pressed tuxedo, and out came this gentile from next door in *his* well-pressed tuxedo. I almost fainted. I asked myself, 'What am I doing here?' "

"After you get somewhere," explained Rabbi Arnold Wolf of Illinois, "the tree gets smaller. It's no longer decorous to *goy* it up. Changing names and noses and having trees were inadequate ways of handling the problem."

Though suburban Jews, like their coreligionists in the city, continued to be a mainstay of the nation's cultural audience—they bought the books, supported the symphony orchestras, attended the ballets, and purchased subscriptions to public television—their *nouveau riche* "uneasiness" gave rise to what Irving Howe has called "a distinct alloy of vulgarity": driveways guarded by thousands of dollars' worth of shrubs, slate patios, *bar mitzvahs* complete with nightclub entertainment, sweet sixteens held at discothèques, weddings where champagne poured from the mouths of bronze cupids, weekend junkets to Las Vegas, and "finished basements" that housed mirrored bars stocked with every kind of bacchanalian paraphernalia.

In Philip Roth's *Goodbye Columbus,* we become voyeurs into the most secret heart of the Patimkins. In their basement there is "a freezer big enough to house a family of Eskimos."

> Beside the freezer, incongruously, was a tall old refrigerator; its ancient presence was a reminder to me of the Patimkin roots in Newark. This same refrigerator had once stood in the kitchen in an apartment in some four-family house. . . . After Pearl Harbor the refrigerator had made the move up to Short Hills; Patimkin Kitchen and Bathroom Sinks had gone to war; no new barracks

was complete until it had a squad of Patimkin sinks lined up in its latrine.

I opened the door of the old refrigerator; it was not empty. No longer did it hold butter, eggs, herring in cream sauce, ginger-ale, tuna fish salad, an occasional corsage—rather it was heaped with fruit, shelves swelled with it, every color, every texture, and hidden within, every kind of pit. There were greengage plums, black plums, red plums, apricots, nectarines, peaches, long horns of grapes, black, yellow, red, and cherries flowing out of boxes. . . . And there were melons—cantaloupes and honeydews—and on the top shelf, half of a huge watermelon, a thin sheet of wax paper clinging to its bare red face like a thin wet lip. Oh Patimkin! Fruit grew in their refrigerator and sporting goods dropped from their trees!

The Patimkin refrigerator, of course, could never match, though it came close, the ostentation of the "super *bar mitzvah*." The Werters, formerly of Brooklyn and now residents of Miami Beach, had such an "affair." "The Bar Mitzvah was everything we expected," they wrote to friends "back home" who could not attend the event; "the Go-Go girls were magnificent."

"The Bar Mitzvah boy," wrote Roger Kahn, "feels better than he did in the morning. The worst of it, the Hebrew, is behind him." The good part, the "affair," is about to begin.

"Be-e-e-e seated," announces a proud uncle.

Under the watchful eye of the caterer the meal is served. Everything goes smoothly. The Rock Cornish hen, served of course with *kiska,* a traditional dish to keep the party *hamish,* is outstanding. The best compliment that one can pay is to declare to your table-mates that "you can cut it with a fork."

The ballroom grows quiet as people turn their attention to the food. Once the chicken has been reduced to bones, the caterer, dressed as though he were the M.C. at a Miss America pageant, steps up to the microphone. "He gets a confirming nod from Barbara Farberman," the Bar Mitzvah boy's mother, "and proclaims, 'Ladies and gentlemen': dessert!"

The ballroom lights dim. In formation, the eight waitresses wearing red and white parade from the Temple Beth-El kitchen bearing aloft and ablaze Tarte aux Cérises, Flambée—flaming cherry tarts —the spécialité de la maison for Harry Aarons Kosher Katerers, Inc. A ripple of applause, proper now, begins. Flames from the cognac surrounding the tarts lick high in the half-dark room. With the girls marching in perfect formation, it is spectacular. The applause grows.

Bezalel Kantor, a journalist, attended several such events and invariably was asked, "How did you like the affair?" Always the gentleman, he would reply, "I have never seen one like it before." Pleased that her guest enjoyed himself, the hostess explains that she "wanted to show how a Bar Mitzvah should be celebrated."

As Kantor walked into the cold evening air he thought of the "thirteen well-fed, well-dressed couples marching arm in arm to the accompaniment of a jazz band and lighted candles." The ceremony "signified nothing," he mumbled to himself, "except the bare fact that a religiously ill-educated boy reached the age of thirteen."

Not everyone considered "Jewish ostentation" purely a suburban phenomenon. Some noted that it actually originated with the older immigrant communities and was transported, like the Patimkins' old refrigerator, to the grasslands beyond the subways and candy stores. "If you look at the current phenomenon historically," a rabbi told Morris Freedman, former associate editor of *Commentary,* "you can find a lot to explain it."

These new [Jewish] centers, by and large, are sponsored by persons whose main experience with Jewish tradition and observance, if they had any at all, was very likely to have been in the store *cheders* in the Bronx and Brooklyn. . . . Sometimes I think that the square boxes they put up now commemorate their origins, so to speak. Having become wealthy, they enlarge and shine up the tiny, grubby cube in which they used to prepare for Bar Mitzvah. However that is, you've got to admit that these centers are an improvement. They represent a striving to arrive, in Rockefeller Center terms, all marble and bronze, that is really touching. The catering is certainly more dignified, less commercial, than the kind of thing that went on in the lofts of Tremont and Pitkin avenues, or in the basements of the manors off Eastern Parkway. After all, you can't expect them to build on the model of the Touro Synagogue, which itself had its own tradition.

Let's be a bit realistic—how can one be a purist in these matters? If you're going to have Jewishness of any sort in this country you've got to start somewhere, preferably with familiar, easy-to-swallow things, even the near-pagan spectacles of Bar and Bas Mitzvah and operetta-like weddings. . . .

The rabbi concluded on an optimistic note: "I don't say that what goes on in many [Jewish] centers—the country-club atmosphere and so on—is better than no Jewishness at all. Nothing of the sort; it may be worse. But it is the beginnings toward revitalizing Jewishness, and maybe someday, when the offspring of the present members grow up, Jewishness everywhere in America will return to something of its seriousness. . . ."

There were many members of the country-club-type temples who were disturbed by the commercialization of Judaism: teen-agers, for instance, who because of religious-school affiliation sometimes chose to follow the rituals their parents ignored.

"I picked up *kashrut* at the United Synagogue Youth Convention," noted one youngster. When he came home he refused to eat his mother's non-*kosher* food, attended morning services while his father slept, and stayed out of school on even the most minor holidays. When his parents asked him, "Why the sudden passion for Judaism?" he argued, "Isn't this what you wanted? Isn't this what you sent me to Hebrew school for?"

"To [his] parents," wrote journalist Evelyn Rossman, "such acceptance seems as aggressive as their own rejection had been years before. [They] don't know whether to be pleased or unhappy at the sudden interest in ritual." Rather than try to understand the youngster's religious needs, they simply passed off the incident as "another passing phase of adolescence."

For whatever its lack of spirituality or cultural achievement, the suburban Jewish community still was decent and strongly knit and laid heavy emphasis on humanity and morality. If they were no longer ennobled or enriched by the immigrant experience, their lives became richer and more secure socially. By 1950 the consolidation of Jewish suburbia was still in flux. In the next two decades there would be many changes, silencing much of the criticism directed toward their communities by other Jews. Peter I. Rose perhaps best describes the suburban dilemma: "Jews may no longer be very Jewish, but they are still Jews. And most not only want to remain so but wish their children to remain so, too."

As Carriers of the Culture

In 1976 a television "special" honored John Wayne for his long, illustrious career in films. Wayne had become an American paragon, a symbol of the American legend, the epitome of rural virtue, the strong man of action, his speech laconic and simple, his screen persona that of the old Protestant America.

It was a sentimental evening. Scenes from many of his films were shown, and old friends and stars made brief appearances to pay homage to Wayne with homilies and pieties in keeping with the screen image. Toward the end of the program, however, there was a significant, sudden switch in the tone. Making a special presentation to Wayne was Henry Winkler, the fabled "Fonz" of TV fame. Winkler, out of deference to the guest of honor, was in formal dress and conducted himself with dignity, obviously awed.

He stood side by side with Wayne, who towered over him by almost a foot. It was a kind of graphic shorthand, the two-man tableau symbolizing the change in American culture, the change in American taste and values: Wayne, the old and idealistic and, in a profound sense, the naïve and homespun America that had disappeared, and Winkler/"Fonz" as the new and iconoclastic and obstreperous and mildly sardonic urban figure. Winkler—as TV's Italian "Fonz" or in real life a middle-class Jewish New Yorker with a degree from Yale—the tide of the American arts that swelled in post-World War II America, the entrance of the ethnic, particularly the Jew, as carriers of the culture, the new folk heroes and the new interpreters of America.

For the Jew, wrote Arthur Miller in his short story "Monte Sant'Angelo," "the whole history is packing bundles and getting away." But by the 1940s this had changed. Jews, never more secure in any country than they were in America, never more integrated into the life of a nation, entered what has been called a "golden age"—and it changed the Jewish artist, his perception of all the world as alien and himself as the stranger and outcast. He was no longer involved with the immigrant experience, the alienation of a strange land and customs, the ghetto, and the working-class movement. Violent anti-Semitism was no longer a concern. Miller's *Focus,* Laura Z. Hobson's *Gentleman's Agreement,* and Saul Bellow's *The Victim,* all written in the 1940s, were the last of the novels to be concerned with anti-Semitism in the old-fashioned sense: the Jew who looked Jewish and suffered merely because of that.

By the 1950s, the best of the young Jewish writers—Saul Bellow, Philip Roth, Bernard Malamud, Norman Mailer, Stanley Elkin, Harvey Swados—had come a long way from that dream of full assimilation, the desire to become thoroughly Americanized, that obsessed a previous generation. They rejected the Judaism and the tainted (because it was foreign) Jewishness of their parents or grandparents. The central theme of most American Jewish writing became the passage from the enclosed Jewish family to the larger, secular America—from the high tragedy of Jewish persistence in the face of persecution to the absurdity and pathos of the dissolution of Jewish identity in the midst of prosperity. There were to be no more grandfathers with Talmudic wisdom who still contained the essence of Jewish life. Jewish writers rejected the questions: What is it to be a Jew? What is it to be a Jew in America? But as gates opened wide for the Jewish writer in America, poet Karl Shapiro felt it necessary to pose this striking definition: "An American Jewish writer is a Jew who is a writer. Everybody knows what an American is; everybody knows what a writer is; but few people seem to know what a Jew is, including Jews and including American Jewish writers."

Now, like all Americans in what W. H. Auden called "The Age of Anxiety," the Jew tried to identify and locate his position in America as an American, his alienation *as an American*. Herbert Gold, in the *Commentary* Symposium of 1961, insisted that "Chicken soup and Yiddish jokes will tarry awhile. But the history of the Jews from now on will be one with the history of everybody else." In the ensuing years, they were to be at the center of American literature, speaking for America to their fellow Jews, to their gentile compatriots and to the whole world. So encompassing was their influence, poet Robert Lowell stated that "Jewishness is the theme of our literary culture in somewhat the same fashion that Midwestern and Southern writing occupied this position in earlier decades."

If the Jew emerged as something of a culture hero in a Christian world during the years 1950–70, he did so because in much of his literature he was not an expert in alienation as a Jew—that was the province of earlier writers—but an expert about a world that was morally grotesque, a world of denial and estrangement, the spokesman for all Americans about the deepest needs of our times. The Jew *is* the urban man, and he was able to create portraits of contemporary Americans, and the way Americans live, because by the 1950s the rest of the country began to lead urban lives more and more like the Jew's. And in a period in our history when the arts became increasingly trivialized, Jewish writers were still concerned with the verities. "A hundred years from today," said a gentile history professor at an eastern university, "when we wish to find out what it was like to be an American in the middle of the twentieth century, we very well might be able to find the truth only by reading Jewish writers of the period."

For a time, the recognition of certain Jewish writers seemed less an event in literary or cultural history than an incident in the development of middle-class taste. Irwin Shaw, Herman Wouk, Leon Uris, and Irving Stone were best-selling authors who occasionally dealt with Jewish themes. Critic Alfred Kazin deplored these writers for "the use, without real understanding, of the set materials of Jewish fiction: the dramatic seasoning of Jewish family bitterness, the Jewish joke, the classic *J'accuse* of Jewish experiences throughout the ages." Their work, in fact, represented a disguised form of assimilation—the attempt of certain Jews to be accepted by the bourgeois gentile community on the grounds, perhaps, that despite not being Christian they are even *more* bourgeois.

Marjorie Morningstar, by Wouk, is the exemplar of the assimilationist novel. Marjorie (née Morgenstern) is a middle-class girl with Bovary-like yearnings. Her affair with a Greenwich Village type ends unhappily, and Wouk nails down his thesis that middle-class domesticity is better than romantic love. Marjorie marries a solid citizen and settles down to the life of a suburban Jewish matron, "a regular synagogue goer, active in the Jewish organizations of the town. . . ."

Once, when Wouk was introduced at a Hadassah convention, the presiding officer said, "Mr. Wouk, meet two thousand Marjorie Morningstars." But he could have been introduced the same way to a convention of American women of any faith. Marjorie Morningstar, for the 1950s, was the perfect stereotype of the American female of her class. Wouk's book completed the long process of persuading America that the Jew was just like everyone else.

But the best Jewish writers of the postwar period had more-grievous fates for their Jews. These writers weren't self-conscious about their Judaism or Jewish characters—they played it warts and all. Philip Roth, the writer most hated by Jews for his unsparing honesty about the sterility and spiritual poverty of suburban life, castigated Jews and Jewish character in *Goodbye Columbus*. Of the writers a generation younger than Bellow or Mailer, Roth is the most talented, the most controversial, and the most sensitive to the complexities of assimilation, his work the deepest and most honest insight into the dilemma of the American Jew and his duality. He desentimentalizes Jewish suffering by his perception that the Jew is nothing more than an *arriviste* hungering after the rewards—financial, social, and sensual—of American culture.

Saul Bellow is ranked by many critics as the foremost American novelist of our times, a writer who seeks to move beyond that impoverishment that Roth chronicles. He explores the marginal man situated somewhere between the old and new, haunted by the memory of the Jewish past—irrational, premodern, pre-Western, precultural—and the modern Jew, who is soft, compromising, interested only in adjustment. He can write with great humor, is more optimistic than Roth, and through one of his characters, Herzog, he sets himself against the hopelessness of many modern Jewish intellectuals: "Let us set aside the fact that such convictions in the mouths of safe, comfortable people playing at crisis, alienation, apocalypse and desperation, make me sick. We must get it out of our heads that this is a doomed time, that we are waiting for the end, and the rest of it, mere junk, from fashionable publications. Things are grim enough without these shivery games."

Like Bellow, groping for a purpose in life, is Norman Mailer, ironically the greatest hedonist among Jewish writers as well as the greatest radical. Unlike Bellow, Mailer reinforces the apocalyptic thinking of much modern intellectual revolt. As a novelist, he is an activist who says, "The sour truth is that I am imprisoned with a perception which will settle for nothing less than making a revolution in the consciousness of our time." He has rejected everything Jewish and describes himself as a non-Jewish Jew, for whom the customs and beliefs of conventional Jews matter little. "He is," says critic Allen Guttmann, "the Jew released from his ethnic identity and invited to act out whatever roles are now within reach of his imagination." Indeed, Mailer's preoccupation in recent books has been with gentile characters, that mythical *goy* who fills Jewish thinking. "Part of Norman's problem," says a fellow Jewish writer, "is that he sees himself as the great muscular conqueror of women, the aging athlete gone to flab but who dreams of glory, the Protestant—when, in reality, he is the small Jew, Sam Slabovda, the main character in a long novel he planned but never wrote." Mailer's career has become "public"; he is a personality whose reportage is better received than his novels. "His is a career full of twists and turns," says Guttmann, "instructive rather than representative, awesome and perhaps even frightening."

Bernard Malamud is the closest of all the writers to the old Jewish traditions. His people are earthbound *schnorrers;* his best novel, *The Assistant,* is more like a novel of the 1930s, a last expression of all those Jewish fears and hope for a Messiah, a book which reminds Jews of the world of their forebears rather than the complexity of today. Malamud comes to grips with the problems of Jewish identity, giving his humble, suffering Jews a poignancy. They choose other people over political systems, life over death. "Our life is hard enough," says Morris Bober, in *The Assistant*. "Why should we hurt somebody else? For everybody should be the best, not only for you and me. We ain't animals . . . that is what a Jew believes."

The popular and critical success of Bellow, Malamud, and Philip Roth was followed by a new generation of writers. As the children of parents born in the United States, they came of age after World War II rather than during the Depression. Bruce Friedman, Burt Blechman, Jeremy Larner, Stanley Elkin, Irvin Faust, Wallace Markfield, and Jerome Charyn are fabulists, savage satirists of American life and customs, all using Jewish material and with a tendency toward the grotesque. Their books possess a nervousness, a tempo, a near-hysterical beat, a punishing isolation and loneliness of a strange, frenzied new kind. Some of them are destructive jokesters, wry, rueful, ironic, attacking their Jewish characters, but their real assault is upon the body of America. They employ satiric distortion as a means of focusing attention on human experience, and if previous generations of Jewish writers were ambivalent, these are simply repelled and disgusted by contemporary America.

Burt Blechman is a writer without mercy. His first novel, *How Much?* is about people obsessed with buying useless objects, the heroine a madwoman who goes about crying, "How much? How much?" and who buys "bargains" at any price, observing her mother's death by rushing off to a sale. In *The War of Camp Omongo*, a Jewish summer camp is a metaphor for the world, filled with precociously cunning children, as well as hypocrisy, stupidity, lechery, savagery, snobbery, knavery, violence, and blasphemy. This is Blechman's sour commentary on American life.

Bruce Friedman is funnier, deeper, and gentler than Blechman, who too often reduces his characters to caricatures by his terrible scorn. Friedman writes with a feeling that the abyss is at hand. His characters are upwardly mobile New York Jews in a time of social transition, when the old cultural identity is being withdrawn and the new is baffling and malign.

Friedman's two best novels, *Stern* and *A Mother's Kisses*, concentrate absurdly, surrealistically, on two facets of Jewishness: anti-Semitism and the phenomenon of the Jewish mother. Stern is an introverted, neurotic Jew whose wife is insulted by a Jew-baiting neighbor who calls the Sterns kikes. Stern's idea of bravery is to send his wife to ask the man not to torment them. His ulcers become worse, he suffers a nervous breakdown, and goes to a rest home, where he finds companionship and sexual adventures. He returns to find his wife cheerful (she might be having an affair with a dance instructor), remonstrates with the neighbor, and gets punched in return. In the end there is no victory, but there is a prospect for barely moderate happiness. Suburbia is all Stern has now; he is desperate to prove he is nice. It is a novel of social cruelty and comic distortion, imaginative, and a hallucination of Jewish anxiety.

In *A Mother's Kisses,* seventeen-year-old Joseph's mother, who accompanies him from New York to Kansas Land Grant Agriculture College, prides herself on not being like other mothers, the joke being that she is the archetypal Jewish mother and even more so. She is flauntingly sexual, overprotective, a vulgarian with furious energy, a schemer who presents a real Oedipal conflict to her son: " 'Did your mother ever let you down?' She gave him an ear kiss that seemed overly wet and said, 'Will you please learn to put your last buck down on this baby?' " She is a striking creation, possibly the classic portrait of the Jewish mother drawn by monstrous exaggeration, as are so many of the novel's characters.

Another gifted practitioner of black humor is Stanley Elkin, who, like Friedman, is capable of seriousness while seeming to write only marvelous comedy, his world filled with comic characters of fantastic proportions. Two other Jewish writers worthy of note are Edward Lewis Wallant and Norman Fruchter, more similar to Malamud and Bellow in their concerns and the worlds they created than to the black humorists. Wallant's death, at thirty-six, in 1962, was a great loss. A writer of great humanity, his novels were bold yet hopeless attempts to bridge the chasm between the solitary individual and the humanity outside (thereby giving the individual reason to live). Perhaps his most famous book is *The Pawnbroker*.

Fruchter's hero in *Coat upon a Stick* is an aged, pious Jew—an old man with few virtues, with a warped view of his suburban son and his fellow Jews. He is the sexton of a small New York synagogue, ritually observant, looked after by his son and cronies, yet haunted by his sins in Europe as a young man and his petty thievery, which continues to the present (tea and crackers from a supermarket, his Yiddish paper from a newsstand). He has tricked and seduced and lied and cheated; yet he is angry with his son for not being exact in the observance of all Jewish rituals in the education of the grandson. We do not see the old man as a scheming hypocrite but as Fruchter's metaphor for the vital question: What is the connection between religious ritual and morality?

Other Jewish writers, critics, and intellectuals prominent in the postwar period are Grace Paley, Myron Kaufmann, Joseph Heller, J. D. Salinger, Meyer Schapiro, Norman Podhoretz, Paul Goodman, Allen Ginsberg, John Hollander, Hilton Kramer, Delmore Schwartz, Leonard Kriegel, Harold Rosenberg, Jerome Weidman, Budd Schulberg, Clement Greenberg, Irving Howe, Philip Rahv, and Irving Kristol.

So encompassing is the Jewish presence in literature, there was the inevitable backlash. Gore Vidal and Truman Capote, certifiable Wasp writers, objected to the Jewish domination. Capote was especially bitter, speaking of "the rise of what I call the Jewish Mafia in American letters," which controls "much of the literary scene through the influence of the quarterlies and intellectual magazines. . . . I don't think there is any conspiracy on their part, just a determination to see that members of their particular group rise to the top. . . . It is fine to write about specifically Jewish problems, and it often makes valid and exciting literature—but the people who have other messages to convey should also be given a chance. Today, because of the Jewish Mafia, they're not being given that opportunity. This is something everyone in the literary world knows but never writes about."

George Elliot, author and critic, used a review of Malamud's *The Fixer* to remark that "Jewishness in a lot of recent American fiction seems to be neither Judaism nor Jewry, neither a definable religion nor a historical people, but a vague quality pretending to mystical virtue but delivering little more than sentimental smugness—tradition deteriorated into props. . . . 'Jewishness' has become what is left when Jews no longer are sure who chose them or for what, but continue, nevertheless, to act as though they had been chosen for a superior destiny."

More or less, from various perspectives, that is what the Jewish American writer was preoccupied with. But there was no denying that the years after World War II witnessed a flowering of the Jew as a new kind of urban American culture hero. As a form of philo-Semitism, this mood may not have lasted into the 1970s. But in all its manifestations, said Alfred Kazin, "I don't think that there has been anywhere in the history of the Jewish people anything quite like the influence that Jewish intellectuals have exerted on American culture. In that sense, America has really been a very great success for the Jew."

For Jews in the popular and performing arts, the postwar period proved just as bountiful and significant. Films had always been Jewish-dominated as regards ownership, but now the new Hollywood became, in some ways, even more Jewish than before: "A Semitic renaissance *sans* Talmud and rabbi," according to Tom Tugend, the West Coast correspondent for the Jerusalem *Post*. "Even black actors know more Yiddish than the average middle-class American Jew, and comedian Bob Hope cracked recently that 'Hollywood is the only place where Catholics give up matzoh balls for Lent.'" As the structure of the movie industry crumbled before TV, the top posts at the old studios were filled with a new breed of Jew, less instinctively creative than the founding generation. Bland and cautious, they generally came from the ranks of agents, or in once-classic reprise, a "rise" from the garment industry to films. Robert Evans had been a partner in Evans-Picone, a successful women's-apparel line. He did some acting, then joined Paramount as one of its creative producers, responsible for such blockbuster films as *The Godfather, Love Story,* and, as an independent, *Chinatown, Marathon Man,* and *Black Sunday*.

Jeff Chandler, Kirk Douglas, and Tony Curtis, the first of the postwar Jewish stars, assumed Anglo-Saxon names; the old studio chiefs still prevailed and refused to believe that audiences would accept Ira Grossel, Isadore Damsky, and Bernard Schwartz. In the 1950s Tony Randall and Walter Matthau had had to change their names. Betty Perske became Lauren Bacall. But with the loosening of social mores, and new definitions of sexual attractiveness, Jewish actors were increasingly accepted as Jews. Many refused to change their names or noses, George Segal probably the first to insist on keeping his name and rejecting any suggestions that he submit to surgery. He was followed by a generation of actors who, while rarely portraying identifiable Jews, were clearly urban and Jewish in their speech and attitudes and looks: Elliot Gould, Mel Brooks, Dustin Hoffman, Gene Wilder, Richard Benjamin, Martin Balsam, Judy Holliday (Tuvim). Others, like Goldie Hawn, who is Jewish, portrayed that classic American figure, the dumb but lovable blonde; Paul Newman, half-Jewish, became the all-purpose Wasp.

Barbra Streisand is, perhaps, the most telling clue to America's changing taste. Blatantly Jewish and Brooklyn in origin, she became the greatest screen idol of the postwar period, a phenomenal blend of talent, *chutzpah,* and big-city exotica that captured the American soul. The way had been prepared for her by a generation of Jewish TV comedians—Milton Berle, Jerry Lewis, Sid Caesar, Red Buttons, Phil Silvers—who made Jewish locutions part of American speech. The classy prewar Wasp heroine with her elegant clothes, hauteur, noble suffering, and restrained sexiness was out. Streisand, in her "kooky" ways and dress, her Yiddishness, her Semitic profile and ripe figure, became the contemporary heroine, the idol of teen-agers and females who hungered for liberation, and possibly the secret fantasy of American males bored with their homogenized beauties. It seemed that the only segment of the population who rejected her were Jewish men with long racial memories who grew up in Brooklyn. They spoke of Streisand as "the kind of pest you saw every day in a high school cafeteria and had to chase away from your table . . . pushy little girls you didn't want around. I don't understand what the hell people see in her." Streisand was the ugly ethnic duckling who got her revenge.

Jewish directors came to the fore, alternately creating and satirizing American myths. Arthur Penn told the story of Billy the Kid in *The Left-handed Gun* and of the Indian wars in *Little Big Man,* and in *Bonnie and Clyde,* one of the ground-breaking films of the era, he gave a remarkably vivid picture of American violence. Sydney Pollack, in *They Shoot Horses, Don't They?* re-created the world of the 1930s dance marathons. Mel Brooks lovingly destroyed such standard movie genres as the Western (*Blazing Saddles*), the horror film (*Young Frankenstein*), and slapstick comedy (*Silent Movie*). Bob Rafaelson chronicled American alienation in *Five Easy Pieces* and *The King of Marvin Gardens.* Paul Mazursky the urban Jew in *I Love You, Alice B. Toklas* and *Next Stop, Greenwich Village.* Mike Nichols and Sidney Lumet are quality, all-purpose directors, particularly adept with actors, and Alan Pakula is a master of suspense, with *All the President's Men.* Woody Allen, both actor and director, makes marvelous comedies that poke fun at revolution, science fiction, and the Humphrey Bogart cult; he has raised the portrayal of the *nebbish* to high art.

Many Jews hated and feared the films of Jewish life that appeared in the 1960s and 1970s: *Goodbye Columbus, Portnoy's Complaint, I Love You, Alice B. Toklas, The Heartbreak Kid, The Apprenticeship of Duddy Kravitz,* were films about Jewish vulgarity and neuroses, that disturbed the Jewish community. Hollywood's defense was that the artistic creators of the films—writers, producers, directors, and actors—were exclusively Jewish, but it hardly quieted the critics. The filmmakers were accused of self-hate, much as many of the Jewish writers had been vilified.

"We cannot afford this outpouring of pictures showing the Jews, warts and all," said Allen Rivkin of the Jewish Film Advisory Board, "these caricatures which are brutal without being penetrating. Whatever we may like to think, we are not solid enough, not secure enough in this country or anywhere else to strip ourselves bare on the screen."

Irving Blacker, professor of cinema at the University of Southern California concurred: "What may be funny or revealing to film people or to fifty thousand Jewish readers who can make a Philip Roth book a best-seller, is not the right fare for millions of moviegoers in small towns across the world. And with all its sophistication and freedom, Hollywood is still afraid to touch a powerful Jewish theme. When will a Jewish producer give us the story of the Holocaust?"

"The Hollywood movie industry has made little advance in probing the Jewish experience," adds another close observer. "Hollywood still cannot deal honestly with the cultural roots of the people who created it."

Milton Berle was the first great TV star, his four hundred successive stand-up comedy shows still a television record. He changed the viewing habits of the nation, making Tuesday a night when nobody expected friends for dinner, made plans for the theater, went out to a movie—indeed, many movies, faced with empty houses, closed up when Berle appeared. He was followed by the perennial Jack Benny, Red Buttons, Phil Silvers, Jerry Lewis, and Sid Caesar, one of the most innovative with his satires of movies and domestic life and a mostly Jewish company of Carl Reiner and Howard Morris, who both became important producers and directors in TV.

Robert Alan Aurthur and Reginald Rose wrote some of the best dramas in the days of live television. While the daytime world of soap operas was still concerned with the Protestant middle-class ethos and all its attendant miseries, Jewish performers and creators were prominent in prime time: Henry Winkler, Jack Albertson, Louise Lasser, Norman Lear and Bud Yorkin, Jack Klugman, Tony Randall, Gabriel Kaplan, Beatrice Arthur, Peter Falk, Linda Lavin, Jack Carter, Dinah Shore, Harvey Korman, Mort Sahl, George Burns, Henry Morgan, Dr. Joyce Brothers, Louis Nye, Alan King, Don Adams, Bert Parks, Steve Lawrence and Eydie Gormé, Robert Klein.

The "Mary Tyler Moore Show" introduced one of the first recognizable, authentic Jewish characters in TV, Rhoda Morganstern, that nice, bright, funny, once-fat Jewish girl from the Bronx (admirably played by non-Jewish Valerie Harper) who would spin off to become "Rhoda." Three of the better young Jewish actors on TV are Judd Hirsch, Barry Newman, and Ron Liebman, who, in a perverse twist, starred in shows called "Del Vecchio," "Petrocelli," and "Martinelli."

"I guess," said one Jewish TV writer, "that no matter how good things seem for us, the powers don't think America is ready yet for a series called Feinschreiber, Ginsberg, or Schlansky." "Maude," ostensibly a suburban Protestant, is Jewish in her sardonic wit and liberalism.

On Broadway, Lillian Hellman, one of the giants of the 1930s and 1940s theater, was still writing trenchant drama in the 1960s. Arthur Miller's *Death of a Salesman* was hailed as a great American play, and although the protagonist, Willy Loman, is not identified as Jewish, many Jewish men insisted that Miller "must have had a pipe-line into my kitchen, that was my father he's talking about, those were the kind of frustrating talks I had with my father." Perhaps the measure of Miller's accomplishment is that he made the Jew synonymous with middle-class longings and desperations, without the need for labels, at a time when Jews were merging into the American mainstream. Younger Playwrights include Jack Gelber, Israel Horovitz, Arthur Kopit, David Mamet, and Jules Feiffer. Joseph Papp became the most powerful and daring theatrical entrepreneur of the generation with his New York Shakespeare Festival, which does much to encourage the best experimental work in the theater besides putting on excellent (and free) productions of Shakespeare.

The musical theater had Robert Goulet, Comden and Green, Richard Adler and Jerry Ross, Jule Styne, Sheldon Harnick and Jerry Bock, Bobby Van, Frank Loesser, Bette Midler, Michael Bennett, Alan Jay Lerner and Frederick Loewe, Richard Rodgers and Oscar Hammerstein II, Harold Arlen, Steve Sondheim, Burton Lane, Leonard Bernstein, and Jerome Robbins.

The last two are rare in that they attained greater fame as composer-conductor of classical music in Bernstein's case, and Robbins as one of the great ballet choreographers. Beverly Sills, who would also become a TV star, was a star of the Metropolitan Opera. Robert Merrill, Jan Peerce, and the late Richard Tucker and Leonard Warren virtually monopolized the Met's male starring roles for years. Performing virtuosos include Isaac Stern, Daniel Barenboim, Misha Dichter, Pinchas Zuckerman, Gary Graffman, and Lorin Hollander. Among the old guard, Yehudi Menuhin and Vladimir Horowitz still sell out concert halls in rare appearances. James Levine, the conductor of the Metropolitan Opera orchestra, puts a new gloss on many productions that have grown old and cliché-ridden. Melissa Hayden and Nora Kaye were the foremost ballet dancers of the early postwar period. One of the best of the new ballet masters is Elliot Feld, whose own company approaches the mastery of the older, established groups. David Amram and David Diamond lead avant-garde composers.

Benny Goodman was one of the few big-band leaders to continue successfully into the postwar period. Buddy Morrow (Moe Zudecoff), Buddy Rich, and Les Elgart carried on the tradition for a time into the 1950s, but with the explosion of rock and folk music, the big band died. Jazz figures Allan Eager, Al Cohen, Stan Getz, and Lee Konitz are among the great of the bop and progressive-jazz era.

It was in the music of the "youth revolution" that Jews made their biggest impact, influencing an entire generation of Americans. Apostles of the counterculture, their music was in the American mold, with none of the Tin Pan Alley vulgarity and sentiment of many prewar Jewish songwriters. They catered to youth's hunger for new experience, for destruction of sacred cows, for an ambience of love, and a bitter cynicism toward all that had gone before them. Such composer-performers as Bob Dylan, Simon and Garfunkel, Janis Ian, Barry Manilow, Carly Simon, Phil Ochs, Neil Diamond, and Neil Sedaka provided touchstones for that inchoate protest of the 1960s. But it was, in the end, merely a different kind of sentimentality and pandering to an audience for whom the music was itself the revolution instead of a mere artifact. They were, in the words of one record company producer's figure of speech, "kids who would go to the barricades, if they could go in sports cars and with a $3,000 hi-fi unit." What was remarkable and telling was that Jewish artists were so integrated into America, so much a part of the contemporary nervousness, that many of them, grandchildren of despised immigrants, became the bards who, almost singlehanded, created the inner life of millions of young Americans.

RECENT TRENDS

In a 1961 article, "Jewish Teen-age Culture," sociologist David Boroff argued "that the student movement, which in the 1930s and 1940s had a good deal of Jewish leadership, no longer has a Jewish complexion."

> As the doors of American society swing open hospitably to talented Jews, the impulse to castigate and criticize becomes attenuated. It is possible that if some of the disharmonies in American life become exacerbated, Jewish teen-age intellectuals will again display the insurgency and critical fervor that once charac-

terized them. But it is more likely that, as Jews increasingly become part of the "Establishment," intellectual teen-agers will see themselves as apprentices rather than as critics.

The turbulent decade of the 1960s proved Boroff's prediction wrong, as Jewish involvement in the New Left became the Jewish Establishment's worst-kept secret. The participation of the Jerry Rubins, Abbie Hoffmans, and Mark Rudds emphasized the strong Jewish presence in the new radical student movement.

Jewish leaders dismissed the radicals-who-happened-to-be-Jewish as the self-hating children of overly permissive parents. Frightened by the possibility of an anti-Semitic backlash, they assured Christian America that the Jewish radical was overblown by the media. To support this contention, Norman Podhoretz, editor of *Commentary,* reminded his readers that

> David Dellinger is not Jewish; Tom Hayden is not Jewish; Staughton Lynd is not Jewish; Carl Oglesby is not Jewish; Timothy Leary is not Jewish; Kate Millet is not Jewish; and neither, it somehow seems necessary to add, is Stokely Carmichael Jewish, nor Huey Newton, nor Angela Davis.

Though the Jewish Establishment portrayed the Jewish activist as simply a part of an estranged minority, some radicals refused to deny their Jewish roots. "We've been messed over," asserted an SDS organizer, "but I feel it's been more sharp for American Jews. What we detest about the lives of our parents, what we could talk about as emptiness, hypocrisy, and materialism . . . is the behavior that comes out of those insecurities, plus our own experiences of those insecurities. We see a way of getting beyond that . . . a possibility of the liberation from that."

Jerry Rubin put it this way:

> I personally feel very torn about being Jewish. I know it made me feel like a minority or outsider in Amerika from my birth and helped me become a revolutionary. I am shocked at Julius Hoffman and Richard Schultz [Chicago Seven judge and prosecutor] 'cause they try to be so Amerikan. Don't they know they're still "Jewish" no matter how much "power" or "security" in Amerika they have? . . .
>
> But despite this . . . Judaism no longer means much to us because the Judeo-Christian tradition has died of hypocrisy, Jews have become landlords, businessmen, and prosecutors in Amerika.

By the end of the decade many Jewish activists questioned their involvement in the radical movement. Stokely Carmichael's crusade in the South brought black power to the fore at the 1967 Conference on New Politics in Chicago. Tension grew between black and white, and white radicals were told to organize among their own.

"I was stunned by the sudden hostility toward the Jews," recalled an SDS delegate to the Chicago convention. "It was suddenly evident that 300 years of black oppression was being blamed on the Jews. It was happening all around us and I felt threatened, perhaps for the first time in my life, as a Jew."

Some would have called this reaction paranoid, but the evidence was all too clear. In December 1968 the *Forum,* the journal of the African American Teachers Association, accused Jewish teachers in New York City of committing "educational genocide" on "the minds and souls of black children." The charge, frequently repeated during the racially tense teachers' strike in the fall of 1968, convinced many Jewish activists that their alliance with the black militants was over. "The Jew," declared the *Forum* in still another racist assault, "our great liberal friend of yesterday, whose cries of anguish still resound from the steppes of Russia to the tennis courts of Forest Hills, is now our exploiter!" Such statements became commonplace.

At a large metropolitan junior high school black militant Robert "Sonny" Carson denounced the "Weinsteins and Goldbergs as boobies' who teach black children other people's culture." In late December 1968, over radio station WBAI's "Julius Lester Program," Leslie Campbell, a controversial New York City teacher, "dedicated" an anti-Semitic poem, purportedly written by a fifteen-year-old girl, to Albert Shanker, the Jewish president of the United Federation of Teachers. In part it read:

> Hey, Jew boy, with that yarmulke on your head
> You pale-faced Jew boy—I wish you were dead;
> I can see you Jew boy—no you can't hide,
> I got a scoop on you—yeh, you gonna die.

Campbell called the girl's poetry "beautiful," saying that it had "a tremendous sense of truth," and the station's manager, Frank Millspaugh, added that the anti-Semitic tone on many Lester programs was merely the moderator's intent to inform the public about "the strong and growing hostility and resentment of Jewish whites among ghetto blacks." To make matters worse, insensitive WBAI officials again helped fan the fires of racism by permitting Tyrone Woods, also affiliated with the African American Teachers Association, to air more anti-Semitic rhetoric: "As far as I'm concerned," he told Julius Lester's radio audience, "more power to Hitler. He didn't make enough lampshades out of them. He didn't make enough belts out of them."

In the midst of the controversy, another incident made tempers flare. In January 1969, a photographic exhibit called "Harlem on My Mind" was held at the Metropolitan Museum of Art. Like the WBAI affair, the controversy grew out of a statement written by a black teen-ager. In the introductory essay to the exhibits catalog, Candice Van Ellison, a New York City high school student, wrote: "Behind every hurdle that the Afro-American has yet to jump stands the Jew who has already cleared it. Jewish shopkeepers are the only 'survivors' in the expanding black ghettos. The lack of competition allows the already exploited Blacks to be further exploited by Jews."

Immediately, the Jewish defense agencies protested to Thomas Hoving, director of the museum and a former aide to Mayor John V. Lindsay. Hoving, however, found "nothing inflammatory" about the statement. "If the truth hurts," he purportedly told a reporter, "so be it."

Besieged with similar, and at times more threatening, gestures of black anti-Semitism, the bewildered New York Jewish community directed its anger at Mayor Lindsay for appeasing the black militants.

"Outside the East Midwood Jewish Center," reported Samuel Klein, a passer-by, "were pickets—their signs called for Lindsay's removal." Inside, the rabbi of the Brooklyn synagogue sharply rebuked the crowd, who booed and jeered as the mayor tried to address the audience on the dispute between the largely Jewish United Federation of Teachers and the predominantly black Ocean Hill-Brownsville school district. The mayor was shouted down when he said he believed that both sides in the dispute were guilty of vigilante acts.

Rabbi Harry Halpern quickly stepped to the microphone. "As Jews you have no right to be in this synagogue acting the way you are acting. Is this the exemplification of the Jewish faith?"

"Yes! Yes!" the audience roared back.

Amid the tense racial atmosphere came the sudden eruption of Israel's Six Day War. Activist Jews, many of whom had defended the Palestinian people's right to self-determination, suddenly felt a heightened awareness of their Jewish identity. "I was gripped with the realization that Israel could be destroyed," said one Wisconsin SDS leader, "and I was also frightened by my own Jewish chauvinism." Another member of the radical left added, "I couldn't believe how Jewish I suddenly felt. When I heard the anti-Zionist remarks of my non-Jewish comrades, blacks and whites, I was ready to give up my pacifism. Judaism became meaningful to me."

In the aftermath of Israel's victory, militant black anti-Zionism was everywhere. In Newark, New Jersey, handbills affixed to telephone poles warned Jews to get out of Palestine. One read, "It's not your home anyway, Moses was the first traitor, and Hitler was the Messiah!!!" In New York City, teachers were called "Middle East Murderers of Colored People," and many found leaflets stuffed in their mailboxes warning them that "Your Relatives in the Middle East Will Find Themselves Giving Benefits to Raise Money to Help You Get Out from the Terrible Weight of an Enraged Black Community." In another flyer, Jesse Gray, leader of the Tenants Rights Party in Harlem, wrote, "Zionists kill black people in their own land in the Middle East. They run the people out of their communities." And in California, the *Black Panther* reminded its readers to "keep in mind the great similarity between the conditions under which the Black people live in the United States and those under which the Palestinian Arabs live in Israel."

The fires of anti-Israel sentiment were also fed by Stokely Carmichael's Student Non-Violent Coordinating Committee (SNCC). Indeed, the organization's program director, Ralph Featherstone, freely admitted that SNCC distributed anti-Israel and anti-Semitic material obtained from Arab sources. SNCC supported the Arab cause, said Featherstone, because blacks and Arabs were working for a "Third World alliance of oppressed people all over the world."

In the wake of SNCC's pro-Arab position, many Jewish members, some prominent in their respective fields, immediately resigned. Theodore Bikel, for instance, an early SNCC activist, openly condemned the new anti-Jewish policy:

> I am an American. I am a Jew. Thus I have a commitment doubly reinforced by historical and moral commitment. I am determined to make equality and freedom a reality in this country, no matter what the setbacks. I am equally determined to honor the bonds to my ethnic and religious background. . . . You have this day attempted to violate both my commitments. The violation of one alone would have been enough.

"How do you think a cry of black power would be met in Riyadh or Mecca?" he asked. "How would poor power sound in Baghdad?"

The young Jews of the New Left were also faced with a dilemma:

Was Israel's victory a barrier to Palestinian liberation? Was Israel, victorious beyond anyone's dreams, now the enemy of the Third World? Shortly after the war, the New Politics Conference in Chicago passed, at the urging of the black caucus, a resolution condemning Israel as "an imperialist lackey of the United States." As in the case of Bikel, there was a feeling among Jews that they had been betrayed. Many Jewish activists now reconsidered their place in the radical movement, pondering the urgent question: How could assimilated Jews, never steeped in Judaism, Zionism, or "old left" Jewish radicalism, reconcile being both radical and Jewish? The answer, for many, would be Jewish liberation.

Many activists found their way to the Jewish liberation, or Jewish counterculture, movement. Unlike the general New Left, which still included Jews, the "Jewish New Left" differed in its emphasis: the Jewish radicals were primarily concerned with Jewish problems. "The Radical Jewish movement," wrote Arthur Waskow, a principal voice of the new movement, "believes . . . the American crisis will require and include a liberated Jewish people." His message was carried to the college campus as an abundance of new underground Jewish radical newspapers appeared: *Jewish Liberation Journal, Jewish Radical, Chutzpah,* and *Jewish Urban Guerilla.* All concentrated on the four basic issues of the counterculture movement: the "Uncle Jakes" who sold out to the system, the plight of Soviet Jewry, the assault on the "Goodbye Columbus" culture, and Israel.

They continued to be critical of the "self-hating" Jews who remained in the anti-Israel New Left. A political cartoon in *Hashofar* expressed their contempt:

> Hey Gang! Here's a riddle for ya!! If a liberal is someone who supports other people's fights for liberation. . . . And a Radical is someone who supports his people's fight for liberation. . . . And a Pig is someone who puts down his people's fight for liberation. . . . Then what would you call [radicals of Jewish background such as] Abby Hoffman, Jerry Rubin, and William Kunstler? (Hint: Oink, Oink, Oink.)

M. Jay Rosenberg, another movement voice, called the New Left Jew "today's Uncle Tom" and a "ludicrous figure. It is becoming increasingly fashionable in certain left-wing Jewish circles

> to put down everything Jewish. These Jewish leftists, still hung up because they were not born Protestant, find that they can glibly resort to anti-Jewish stereotypes today without being referred to a

good psychiatrist. It is now quite acceptable for the Jew to attempt to ingratiate himself with the goyim by condemning what he has always been ashamed of. Its a sad sight.

The issue is one of Jewish pride. The Jewish professor who makes a point of teaching on Yom Kippur with subtle mockery of those students who stay home, the Jewish kids who lower their heads when a Philip Roth story is up for discussion in their literature course, the Jewish radicals who are prepared to fight for Czechs, the Greeks, and the Biafrans and yet reject Israel; these are our Uncle Toms and our shame. The Jew must accept his identity; and, like it or not, his Judaism is his destiny. Hermann Goering was not far from the point when he said that, "I determine who is a Jew."

"You who are so trapped in your Long Island split-level childhood," concluded Rosenberg, "that you can't see straight. You who fight everything that you are—and against the one element that gave you your goddam social consciousness: your Jewish social idealism. In the aftermath of the crematoriums, you are flippant. After Auschwitz, you are embarrassed. Thirty years after the holocaust, you have learned nothing and forgotten everything. Ghetto Jew, you'd better do some fast thinking."

Not spared from the attack of the radical Jews was the condition of American Judaism. "To be a Jew on America's terms is not to be a Jew at all," shouted a student radical picketing a fashionable suburban synagogue in Washington, D.C.

"To be a Jew on America's terms is to say *oy vey* once in a while and eat kreplach, matzo balls, and lox and bagels," the student shouted, even louder.

"To be a Jew on America's terms is to build temples with bigger stained-glass windows than the Catholic Church next door and trade in the historical and religious ethics of social justice for a $60,000 home, . . ." cried a second student.

"To be a Jew on America's terms is to forget two thousand years of oppression because of twenty years of prosperity . . . to say Judaism is a religion and not a national and cultural entity," he shouted.

To reverse this trend, Jewish activists carried their protest to the college campus, demanding Jewish-studies programs: courses in Jewish history, Yiddish, theology, and Hebrew culture. One of the first such institutions, Hebrew House, was established at Oberlin. It was a place of residence and study created by Jewish students and became integral to the credit curriculum. Students in other parts of the country also organized Jewish "free universities" offering a variety of courses: "The Shtetl

Culture," "Jewish Cooking," "Jewish Mysticism, Chassidism, and Radical Theology," "The Oppression of Jewish Women," and "Marxism, Anarchism, and Judaism." At Columbia, Yiddish was added to language study, and at Brandeis, students held a Jewish Arts Festival, which featured poetry readings, choral and dance groups, original stage productions of Yiddish and Hebrew plays, and exhibitions by Jewish filmmakers, artists, and photographers.

The most controversial of Jewish radical activities held on campus was the "Freedom Seder," originated by Arthur Waskow at Cornell University. Thousands of students, Jews and non-Jews, attended; one of the guests was Rev. Daniel Berrigan, at the time a fugitive from the FBI. The seder ritual tried to draw parallels between the Exodus from Egypt and the modern Jewish liberation movement. The Jewish Establishment was hostile to such innovation. Norman Podhoretz lashed out at Waskow as a "wicked son" and characterized the "Freedom Seder" as a "document of self-loathing and self-abasement masquerading as a document of self-affirmation."

Another prime target of the liberation movement was the Jewish Establishment. "The Uncle Jakes have sold out to the system," declared a college student. "They have become *WASH's,* white Anglo-Saxon Hebrews, and get their positions because of their bankbooks and not their integrity." To the Jewish radical, the "Pig Establishment" included the community centers, the philanthropic federations, the United Jewish Appeal, the synagogue, the Israeli Government, and all other bodies that controlled Jewish life. Jerry Kirschen, one of the movement's better satirists, in an article entitled "Pig City Follies," poked some "serious fun" at what he called Establishment "Fat Pigs."

> Oh I'm an "official" Zionist leader and I stand so proud and tall . . . and I'll never move to Israel, no I never will at all—I'm a pompous righteous leader and I look with sharp disdain at the activists for Soviet Jews who fight in freedom's name. Oh we looked away in Hitler's time and ignored the ones who cried . . . 'cause to march and shout and raise the fist is too undignified!—We're the marching Jewish liberals and we march for all the others but we're much too busy for the causes of our brothers—we're the happy Jewish ladies who sing the Zionist tune and we're sure to say kibbutz but never say it means commune!

To bring their protest to the doorstep of the Establishment, several activists invaded the offices of New York's Federation of Jewish Philanthropies and demanded the "democratization" of the agency. The students were promptly arrested and quickly dubbed the "Federation 45." The most telling incident took place in Boston in 1969, where "radical" rabbinical students picketed the annual meeting of the Council of Jewish Federations and Welfare Funds. Frightened by this unprecedented challenge to establishment goals, council officials allowed a young rabbi, Hillel Levine, to speak.

"We don't want commissions to explore the problems of youth," he said. "We do want to convert alienation into participation, acrimony into joy—the joy of being the possessors of a great legacy—a legacy which has meaning for today. This renewal can be accomplished only through a massive and personal rededication to Jewish study and meaningful Jewish existence.

> It is inconceivable for a Jewish community to be guided by Jewish principles and values if its leaders are ignorant of them. Surely some knowledge of Hebrew, of Jewish history and traditions, should be a prerequisite. Leaders of Jewish philanthropies should not only solicit funds but educate benefactors to the needs of the community. This requires Jewish knowledge. . . . Rabbis, people involved in Jewish education, Jewish scholars, students, concerned Jews should participate on all levels of decision making and allocations. Our philanthropic organizations must again become *tzedakah*. . . . The operation may not be as streamlined but it will itself be a source of spiritual renewal.

"Identities are based on ideologies and experiences," he added, "and neither can be offered by Jewish swimming pools and game rooms.

"Your response to us could be," declared Levine, " 'You pampered kids, if you want things done differently, why don't you do it yourselves and leave us alone? This is the way *we* want the Jewish community.'

"If that would be your response," he told council officials, "then with much pain and disappointment we would indeed be forced to do it ourselves."

In the end, the council promised to consider the demands: more money for educational enterprises, less for hospitals and community centers. "To insure that these priorities are honored," noted a reporter, the demonstrators "insisted that students, rabbis, and scholars be put on the boards of local fund-raising organizations." And, in a direct challenge to the fund raisers' religious integrity, they demanded a new policy requiring all organizational leaders to prove their commitment to Judaism by participating in Jewish studies.

Many of the officials saw the students as ingrates. "I know what it means to picket," fumed Benjamin Hanft, public-relations director for the council. "My father died of tuberculosis in a sweatshop, and I was a Wobbly [I.W.W.]. But Rabbi Levine is picketing some of the most generous and most concerned philanthropies in the world. That is plain ingratitude."

One student sharply disagreed with Hanft. He related a remark of a New York Jewish Federation leader: "We have 256 agencies in New York where a Jewish student can have his appendix removed, and a mental hospital where he can be committed." The student told Hanft that the federation official missed the point. "It is not our neuroses nor our ruptured appendixes we wish to share with them, it's our vision."

While confronting the philanthropies, Jewish activists also took on the American Zionists. "One of the reasons that so many of us came together," noted the first issue of *Jewish Radical,* "was a growing concern with our radical communities' increasingly anti-Israel position." This statement was by no means to be interpreted as a blanket approval of American Zionist or even Israeli policy. When, for instance, Jacques Torczyner, president of the ZOA, declared that he would support the Vietnam War in return for U.S. aid to Israel, *Jewish Liberation* assailed him as "Nixon's hatchet man in the Jewish community" and called for a rally in front of ZOA's Park Ave., New York City office. "As long as there are *gooks,*" noted a demonstrator, "there will be *kikes.*"

Again, when Abba Eban, Israel's Foreign Minister, presented an award to conservative California Governor Ronald Reagan, five hundred Jewish pickets charged that Reagan "through his welfare and education program . . . has consistently ignored the desperate needs of the poor and minorities" in California. "It is time," read their leaflet, "for the Jewish community to cease linking the Jewish homeland to the names and actions of men who perpetuate injustice in the United States."

While radical Jews were bringing their protest to the doorstep of the Jewish Establishment, the Student Struggle for Soviet Jewry (SSSJ), organized long before the Jewish Defense League (JDL), made America aware of the plight of their three and a half million coreligionists in the Soviet Union.

"Protest the Russian persecution of Jews," exhorted an SSSJ activist to crowds arriving for a concert by Russian pianist Grigory Sokolov at Philadelphia's Academy of Music. "Do not buy tickets. If you have tickets, don't use them." Other activists, including blue-shirted members of the JDL, held placards that read, "Let My People Go," "Off the Bear," and "Nazi Russian Pig Bears Beware."

At one point, a woman passer-by engaged in a shouting match with the pickets. "You must bring these facts to the public," she said, "but I think the cultural-exchange program is a great way to bring people together. This is music, not politics. How can the performer do a good concert with this going on outside?"

As she spoke, two young Jewish activists appeared dressed in striped convict uniforms with plastic balls and chains on their legs. "This is to signify the enslavement of Russia's three and a half million Jews," said one.

"There is nothing personal in this protest, nothing against the performer," noted a spokesman holding a bullhorn. "The Jews in Russia are unfortunately being deceived. But the word is getting to them. Abandon the cultural-exchange program." He raised his bullhorn and continued to urge people to turn away.

"Don't forget: when you buy tickets, you're contributing to the money that helped drop bombs on Israel," he shouted. "Why is it that the only people in Russia who have to identify themselves are the Jews —who must carry identification stating that they are Jews?"

In Washington, D.C., before the Moiseyev Dance Company performed, activists interupted the Soviet National Anthem by sounding a shofar, (ram's horn) and in New York, the SSSJ took credit for an opening-night stink bomb that disrupted a performance of the Siberian Singers and Dancers. The following evening, police searched pocketbooks and briefcases of the two thousand concertgoers and the performance came off without incident.

Soviet violinist Leonid Kogan, on a concert tour of the United States, was disturbed by the antics of the Jewish activists. "I think it is time to put an end to the Zionist outrages and to take the most resolute measures against their allies so that they do not hinder the cultural exchange between the American and Soviet peoples," he said.

At another Soviet-American cultural event, an SSSJ member spoke to a crowd about Kogan's remark. "Russia is going to know that Jewish blood does not come cheap. We cannot watch as the American Government builds bridges over the bodies of Russian Jews. There will be no SALT talks, no space talks, no trade, no cultural exchange, until Russian Jews are free. American Jewry is prepared to rush the barricades, to get arrested until Jews are free everywhere." The crowd responded, almost in unison, with an approving "Right on!"

In addition to disrupting cultural events, demonstrating at the United Nations, and harassing Russian business offices such as Tass and Aeroflot with telephone calls and broken windows, the SSSJ, now joined by the JDL and thousands of other concerned Jews, took their protest to Washington, D.C. Chanting, "Freedom now," for the 3.5 million Soviet Jews, five thousand people demonstrated midway between the White House and the Soviet Embassy. "We are going to make the life of Russians hell all over the country," shouted Yossi Templeman, an SSSJ activist. "Every single day during World War II, ten thousand Jews were gassed and turned into soap and lampshades and nobody did anything. We stand guilty and condemned for doing nothing. Never again!"

"Before the sun sets tonight," he said, "it's going to be a Nixon problem. It's going to be an American problem."

Also addressing the rally was Rabbi Meir Kahane of the JDL and a dozen other Jewish leaders, including two officials of the Italian-American Civil Rights League, who expressed their solidarity with the demonstrators, declaring that sixty members of their organization were present. David Solomon, a black Jew, was cheered when he told the crowd, "We are all of the same family, and for this—our house—I will die." Yosef Schneider, a twenty-four-year-old Soviet émigré on a seven-day hunger strike, left his "prison cage" outside the White House to tell the crowd that his permit to demonstrate ended at midnight but that he would continue his hunger strike, as he was "prepared to be arrested on behalf of Soviet Jewry."

As the demonstrators chanted "Am Yisroel Chai," several police wagons appeared. The pickets were warned that they were violating the law and would be arrested if they continued their sit-down. The singing grew louder. "It was a protest," noted a reporter, "but there was an almost festive air among those waiting to be arrested." As those arrested filed into the police vans, they began to chant, "We are Jews, we couldn't be prouder. If the Russians can't hear us we'll shout a little louder." Soon Nixon's name was substituted for "the Russians."

Directing the orderly march into the police vans, an SSSJ leader shouted encouragement. "When the papers say tomorrow that five thousand Jews were arrested, next week we'll have five thousand more." Rabbi Kahane moved through the crowd with a megaphone. "We Jews thirty years ago . . . sat on our apathy. Today we are sitting in Washington. We want to show by our actions our desperation. . . . President Nixon will have to change his policy. . . . No violence . . . no violence. . . . Do not resist at all . . . stand up and go with the police

. . . do not be afraid . . . they sat down in Moscow . . . don't be afraid to sit in Washington . . . no violence."

Suddenly, nineteen-year-old Sharon Karst ran along Sixteenth Street toward the mass sit-down blocking traffic between the White House and the Soviet Embassy, shouting, "It's O.K. I'm going back to sit down. I called my father. He said I can get arrested." A long-distance call to her parents in New Jersey had cleared the way. Holding hands with Michael Snitzer, a twenty-one-year-old student at the University of Maryland, she walked to the police bus to be photographed, searched, and charged with disorderly conduct. Together with 812 other demonstrators, she helped establish a record: the largest mass arrest for civil disobedience in the history of Washington, D.C.

"It was worth it," said Shira Finkelstein, a seventeen-year-old from Brooklyn, one of the last to be placed in a police bus. "They wanted to know how it feels to be arrested," she said. "Now they will know." As the police buses rode off, there could still be heard the prisoners' chant: "Never again! Never again! Never again!"

"Never again" was the battle cry of the Jewish Defense League, the vigilante-like organization trying to change the image of the Jews as "patsies." The group's militant stance was reflected long before the Washington demonstration in a New York *Times* ad seeking financial support. It showed JDL members brandishing baseball bats and chains and asked: "Is this any way for nice Jewish boys to behave?" The JDL's answer was, "We are *not* nice Jewish boys!"

According to JDL philosophy, there would no longer be any Talmudic discourse or Jewish humility. Shouting, "Never again," they invaded the New York office of Amtorg, the Soviet-American Trading Company, to protest the arrest of Russian Jews; battled police in front of a precinct house while protesting the harassment of Hasidic Jews by groups of blacks and Puerto Ricans in the Williamsburg section of Brooklyn; tangled with members of a pro-Nazi group; and picketed the New York Mets baseball team, satirically demanding that the Jewish population of the team equal that of the State of New York (26.2 per cent) in rebuttal to attempts to impose racial quotas at the City University of New York.

Fran Fein, a Hunter College student, was a typical JDL member, trim and pretty with long brown hair and little of the appearance of a street fighter. She was arrested, on several occasions for JDL activities and was a master of karate and a graduate of Jedel, the JDL's paramilitary camp in the Catskill Mountains.

"I grew up in East New York, where there is unbelievable anti-Semitism," she said. "My brother was mugged repeatedly, and when he almost lost an eye, I decided I should fight anti-Semitism. That's why I joined JDL."

On Halloween Eve, 1968, Rabbi Meir Kahane's "troops" were ready to show America that they were *real* Jews, Jews reminiscent of the Warsaw uprising, of Masada, of the Irgun. The place was Montefiore Cemetery in the Bronx, where anti-Semitic youths had destroyed Jewish gravestones. At midnight, JDL militants, armed with clubs and chains and wearing yamulkes, ambushed the vandals and taught them what 'never again" really meant.

Several months later, Kahane's organization again made headlines when forty members showed up at New York's prestigious Temple Emanu-El, their purpose to prevent James Foreman, a black militant, from presenting a demand for reparations for alleged Jewish exploitation of blacks. Earlier in the week, the JDL called Foreman and warned, "We'll break your legs if you show up!"

"It was raining that Friday afternoon," said Sy Polsky, a high school teacher and JDL member. "Two police cars were parked across the street, and foot patrolmen gathered in twos and threes in front of the building." Passers-by were puzzled by the appearance of a group carrying bats and chains and stopped to ask what was going on.

"Who are you and whom do you represent?" asked a temple official. The young Jewish militants brandishing weapons remained silent. Several minutes later, Kahane instructed his "troops" to split and line up at either side of the temple's entrance.

"What the hell is going on?" someone shouted. Still the question was ignored. Kahane then nodded to his followers. As though they could read his thoughts, each of them began to pin their identification onto their lapels: large white-and-blue buttons displaying a clenched fist on a background of the Star of David and the emblazoned words: "NEVER AGAIN."

"That's the most outrageous sight I ever saw," said a woman.

"It's about time the Jews stood up for themselves," said a man standing alongside her.

"You approve of vigilantes?"

"Listen, lady, my parents were killed in a concentration camp. It started there just because of people like Foreman."

"It started there," she exclaimed, "just because of hoodlums like these."

Someone else joined in, "In Germany, nobody lifted a finger when the Nazis started. Not even Jews. We've finally learned. That's why they're here."

"And their chains and bats—are they a symbol of Judaism?"

"Damn right," someone answered.

James Foreman never showed up to make his demands. Perhaps the threat to "break his legs" did it. "We knew he wasn't coming," noted Bertram Zweibon, JDL's vice-chairman, "but we went ahead because we wanted TV and the press to carry pictures of Jews standing in front of a house of worship with chains, bats, and clubs to defend it, to deter Foreman and all the other Foremans, white and black; to tell them there's a new kind of Jew."

The incident appeared on national TV and in the press, and evoked an immediate response; the JDL offices were flooded with letters. A resident of Chicago, Illinois, wrote: "We'll say it is the way for nice Jewish boys to behave. Liquidated are the meek. Our Jewish leaders say don't overreact, it will be vigilantism. Is it humaneness or sheer cowardness that our temple remains much in the fore of insults, threats, and demands for reparations. We commend your action."

A Canadian M.D.: "I would like very much to become a campaigner for your cause here in Toronto. Please carry on your excellent work."

A Californian asked, "Do you have a chapter in Los Angeles? A large number of Jewish doctors and small businesses in the Los Angeles black neighborhoods have been wiped out by militant black organizations such as the Black Panthers and CORE by methods of extortion, fire and savage beatings."

From New Bedford, Massachusetts, came a check for ten dollars: "In support of the holy task you have undertaken, to defend the lives and honor of the Jewish people of New York City. Never again!"

A Phoenix, Arizona, man wanted Kahane "to know that Jews should have organizations like JDL all over the USA" and asked, "Do you need help? Will sure collect from a lot of my Jewish friends in Phoenix and I know they are for your ideas."

Not every Jew, however, rushed to the JDL's support. The Jewish Establishment unanimously censured the JDL for carrying weapons and acting like "goons" in front of synagogues. The president of the American Hebrew Congregations declared, "They are no less offensive than whites wearing robes and hoods . . . standing in front of burning crosses." The Anti-Defamation League found "the Jewish Defense League's paramilitary operations and sensationalist appeals to raw emotion a potential danger and completely outside the Jewish tradition." The American Jewish Conference on Soviet Jewry, commenting on the JDL's "alleged" bombing of Aeroflot and Tass, said, "The act was one of barbarous terrorism. It is especially repugnant that it would be presented to the public as a form of Jewish reprisal for the Soviet Government's outrageous oppression of Jewish life . . . and the denial of basic human rights to Soviet Jews."

Other Jewish leaders dubbed the JDL "vigilantes," "goon squads," "roughnecks," and "Jewish Panthers." The latter brought this retort from Rabbi Kahane: "We are not Jewish Panthers. But when we are called Jewish Panthers we don't deny it."

To counter the Establishment's attacks, Kahane spoke in temples, on college campuses and street corners, wherever he could find an audience, insisting that only "action in the streets will bring to a halt the abuses suffered by Jews in the United States." At one elegant suburban synagogue, he told a Jewish group that they and their children "must get into the streets and get arrested. We must awaken the world and shake up the Jews."

As he spoke, he rocked back and forth before the microphone almost in the manner of orthodox prayer, hesitating at times either for emphasis or to control his stammer, and his hand frequently patted his skull cap. Two blue-shirted JDL guards flanked him on the stage, and other members stood at the back of the auditorium soliciting donations and handing out prepared literature. They wore World War II-style army combat boots and berets with the JDL emblem. Someone quipped, "They're kids playing at Irgun."

"We Jews are told to give a damn," said Kahane, referring to help sought for other ethnic groups. He paused, then asked, "But who gives a Jewish damn? No one gives a Jewish damn . . . especially most Jews."

A favorite theme of the rabbi was that the JDL is out to change the traditional image of the Jew as a "patsy." He stressed that Jews were too worried about what other groups might think about their actions. He used a favorite anecdote to make his point. Two Jews face a firing squad. "Moishe, Moishe," one whispers to the other, "the blindfold . . . it's too tight; it hurts. I must ask the officer to loosen it." Moishe turns to him sternly and admonishes, "Chaim, please, don't make trouble."

"We're not out to win friends and influence people," Kahane continued. "Our actions produce an overwhelming surge of blessings from the trapped Jew. . . . We're called un-Jewish, but if you think the concept of turning the other cheek is in our Bible—you're reading the wrong Bible."

Kahane was very critical of Jews involved in the New Left movement. "Jerry Rubin is a fraud . . . and Abbie Hoffman is a sick fraud," he explains. "Where were the SDS kids, the Jewish kids, when we marched for Soviet Jewry?" he asks.

> They're frauds, full of self-hatred and masochism. They are the products of the kind of American life that the Jewish Establishment planned, executed, and succeeded in bringing to fruition. The drugs they crave because their life is so meaningless is the fruit of the Jewish organizations that run our communities. The radicalism they espouse is the result of what our leaders created. All the Rubins and Hoffmans, all the addicts and the Portnoys, all the emotionally disturbed and, above all, all the Jews who do not know and do not care about being Jewish. All these we must take in our arms and bring to the doors of the American Jewish Committee, the American Jewish Congress, the B'nai B'rith, the Anti-Defamation League, the federations throughout the country. All these we must lay at their doorsteps and say: Here! This is yours. This is what you have created. . . . Let it be shouted from the rooftops. Our secular Jewish leaders are the enemies of the Jewish people.

Kahane injected still another divisive note in his attacks on the Jewish Establishment. He charged that the assimilated, successful Jew, "the pipe smokers in fancy Manhattan offices," had forgotten the old and the poor. Kahane saw himself as the spokesman for those abandoned in the old Jewish enclaves of New York, Chicago, Philadelphia, and South Miami Beach.

On April 22, 1971, the editors of *Jewish Week* alerted the American Jewish community to the fact that "we have swept the Jewish poor out of sight and acted as though they didn't exist." Ironically, the gaudy splendor of Miami Beach perhaps contains the most dramatic example of problems faced by Jewish old and poor. The warm climate drew the old and retired to Florida in the hope of a comfortable and secure old age. Miami, however, for many, did not turn out to be a land of milk and honey but a land of despair and loneliness. In the section of South Beach, described as an "invisible slum," thousands sometimes go hungry trying to survive on less than twenty-eight dollars a week. Eighty-five per cent of these people are over sixty-five and Jewish.

Many who congregate on Washington Avenue, Miami Beach's version of New York's Delancey Street, are in involuntary exile, "sent South" by children who had "no room" in their suburban life-style for an aging parent. "My son sends his check like clockwork," explained a seventy-five-year-old ex-garmentworker, "but he has yet to come visit me. I once called him to ask if I could come North for a short visit. I wanted to see the grandchildren. He told me I couldn't, that there was no room. That his wife, my *hachtgemachtern* daughter-in-law, would have a conniption. I remained in Florida and he sent pictures of the kids and a few dollars. What my sonny-boy forgot were the dollars that my wife and I saved to send him to school, to put clothes on his back, and to make him a success. For *him,* everything was for *him.*"

Others, however, were drawn to South Beach by the same sense of independence that sparked their emigration to America. "If I live to be a hundred," pined an eighty-five-year-old ex-leatherworker living in a one-room efficiency, "thank God I will not be a burden on my children." His three sons were successful professionals in Chicago.

"What you have here," said a social worker who has tended to Miami's elderly for fifteen years, "are lonely human beings who must stand alone despite the fact that they have children and grandchildren. They are proud of their son the doctor or their son the lawyer despite the fact that he doesn't bother to write them, and if he does, it's every six months and a postcard."

"The most desperate," says Mel Ziegler, a journalist, "do nothing but . . . struggle to keep themselves alive." He quotes a painter from New York, trapped by his failing health, and brooding: "I am not a man. Nothing. Nothing. Look at me. I am not a man." Only those, adds Ziegler, "not limited by the normal deterioration of old age—failing eyesight, failing hearing, diabetes—are not as hopeless. Still, the more docile of them (like the non-productives) spend morning, afternoon and evening, spliced only by occasional naps, on the beach or on their porches. Sometimes they are with others. Sometimes, if they can, they read. Mostly they are alone and staring blankly."

Like the elderly of South Beach, the approximately three hundred thousand poor Jews who live in New York City are also forgotten people. Many live, in constant fear of attack, behind heavily bolted doors —alone, without adequate food, medical attention, or companionship. A few have relatives that care; others have only a TV set and four walls. In their youth, noted Mark Effron, "New York symbolized the American dream. Now, for many, the city is the American Urban Nightmare."

According to Paul Cowan, "the poverty among the poor Jews who live on New York's Lower East Side compares to the poverty . . . anywhere in America—in Mississippi, the South Bronx, East Los Angeles. Most people think of the Jewish immigration as the most spectacularly successful one in American history, but the fifty-year journey from the Shtetl to the Space Age left many casualties in its wake. An estimated 250,000 Jews in New York City live below the poverty level of $3500; an estimated 150,000 more earn less than $4000 a year. Most of them are over 65 . . . and live all over New York City: in Far Rockaway, in Coney Island, . . . in Borough Park, and on the Upper West Side." Like their Miami counterparts, the poverty-stricken Jews of New York also feel left behind, "abandoned by uptown Jewish intellectuals, politicians and philanthropists who, they think, care more about blacks and Puerto Ricans than about the nagging problems of Jewish slums. And worse than that, abandoned by their own children . . . who have escaped the [old] neighborhood."

Noah Greenspan, seventy-six, recalls the glow and confidence of the Lower East Side many years ago, really speaking of what happened to all the once-prospering Jewish communities of the big cities. "That's all finished now. When a family stayed together, like in the old days, there was no unhappiness. But the kids left home and we were left behind. The children didn't visit us enough. It isn't close like the old days. Life in America loosened the family." Suddenly the old man smiled. "But I'm sure things will get better. This country was a miracle for us."

The passage of the Jew into American life is a saga of the deepest human experience. It afforded dignity and safety and psychological space to a homeless, embattled people who had been strangers in many lands for much of their history. America changed the Jew, as it changed every immigrant, but America was more profound than the process of acculturation. The Jew in America could become human and various in all the ways that Walt Whitman sang. Identity cards, restrictive laws, the murderous passion of mobs, the rights of lords—the old fears and humiliations remained, then receded, like some dark legend that loses its potency in the telling, vestiges of suffering no longer valid. The Jew spans the whole of American existence, sharing the marvelous incongruity of each citizen: his pride in his origins, his success as an American, and his simultaneous worship of Jehovah, Lincoln, and Babe Ruth.

SELECTED BIBLIOGRAPHY*

BIBLIOGRAPHICAL AIDS

Marcus, Jacob R. *An Index to Scientific Articles on American Jewish History.* Cincinnati, 1971.

————. "A Selected Bibliography of American Jewish History," *Publications of the American Jewish Historical Society,* 51 (December 1961), 97.

Rischin, Moses. *An Inventory of American Jewish History.* Cambridge, Mass., 1954.

Rosenbach, A. S. W. *An American Jewish Bibliography: Being a List of Books and Pamphlets by Jews or Relating to Them Printed in the United States from the Establishment of the Press in the Colonies Until 1850.* New York, 1926.

Rosenbloom, Joseph. *A Biographical Dictionary of Early American Jews: Colonial Times Through 1800.* Lexington, Ky., 1960.

CHAPTER I

BOOKS

Birmingham, Stephen. *The Grandees: America's Sephardic Elite.* New York, 1971.

Blau, Joseph L.; and Baron, Salo W. (eds.). *The Jews in United States, 1790–1840: A Documentary History,* 3 vols. Philadelphia, 1963.

* KEY TO PERIODICALS: AJA—American Jewish Archives AJHQ—American Jewish Historical Quarterly AJYB—American Jewish Yearbook JSS —Jewish Social Studies PAJHS—Publications of the American Jewish Historical Society RIJHN—Rhode Island Jewish Historical Notes YAJSS —Yivo Annual of Jewish Social Science

Broches, S. *Jews in New England:* Part I: *Historical Study of the Jews in Massachusetts (1650–1750)*; Part II: *Jewish Merchants in Colonial Rhode Island.* New York, 1942.

Chyet, Stanely F. *Lopez of Newport, Colonial American Merchant Prince.* Detroit, 1970.

Elzas, Barnett A. *The Jews of South Carolina: From the Earliest Times to the Present Day.* Philadelphia, 1905.

Ezekiel, Herbert T.; and Lichtenstein, Gaston. *The History of the Jews of Richmond, from 1769 to 1917.* Richmond, Va., 1917.

Fish, Sidney M. *Aaron Levy: Founder of Aaronsburg.* New York, 1951.

Freund, Miriam K. *Jewish Merchants in Colonial America: Their Achievements and Their Contributions to the Development of America.* New York, 1939.

Friedman, Lee M. *Early American Jews.* Cambridge, 1934.

──────. *Jewish Pioneers and Patriots.* Philadelphia, 1942.

──────. *Pilgrims in a New Land.* Philadelphia, 1948.

Goodman, Abram V. *American Overture.* Philadelphia, 1947.

Grinstein, Hyman B. *The Rise of the Jewish Community of New York, 1654–1860.* Philadelphia, 1945.

Gutstein, Morris A. *Aaron Lopez and Judah Touro: A Refugee and a Son of a Refugee.* New York, 1939.

──────. *To Bigotry No Sanction: A Jewish Shrine in America, 1658–1958.* New York, 1958.

──────. *The Story of the Jews of Newport.* New York, 1936.

Karp, Abraham J. *The Jewish Experience in America: The Colonial Period, Selected Studies from the Publications of the American Jewish Historical Society,* Vol. 1. Waltham, Mass., 1969.

Korn, Bertram W. *The Early Jews of New Orleans.* Waltham, Mass., 1969.

Lebeson, Anita L. *Jewish Pioneers in America, 1492–1848.* New York, 1931.

Marcus, Jacob R. *American Jewry, Documents, Eighteenth Century: Primarily Hitherto Unpublished Manuscripts.* Cincinnati, 1959.

──────. *The Colonial American Jew, 1492–1776,* 3 vols. Detroit, 1970.

──────. *Early American Jewry:* Vol. I: *The Jews of New York, New England, and Canada, 1649–1794.* Philadelphia, 1951. Vol. II: *The Jews of Pennsylvania and the South, 1655–1790.* Philadelphia, 1953.

————. *Memoirs of American Jews, 1775–1865,* 3 vols. Philadelphia, 1955–56.

Philipson, David (ed.). *The Letters of Rebecca Gratz.* Philadelphia, 1929.

Pool, David de Sola. *Portraits Etched in Stone: Early Jewish Settlers, 1682–1831.* New York, 1952.

————; and Pool, Tamar de Sola. *An Old Faith in the New World: Portrait of Shearith Israel, 1654–1954.* New York, 1955.

Rezneck, Samuel. *Unrecognized Patriots: The Jews in the American Revolution.* Westport, Conn., 1975.

Reznikoff, Charles; and Engelman, Uriah Z. *The Jews of Charleston: A History of an American Jewish Community.* Philadelphia, 1950.

Schappes, Morris U. (ed.). *A Documentary History of the Jews in the United States, 1654–1875,* 3rd ed. New York, 1971.

Silverman, Morris. *Hartford Jews, 1659–1970.* Hartford, Conn., 1970.

Simonhoff, Harry. *Jewish Notables in America, 1776–1865: Links in an Endless Chain.* New York, 1956.

Stern, Malcolm H. *Americans of Jewish Descent: A Compendium of Genealogy.* Cincinnati, 1960.

Trachtenberg, Joshua. *Consider the Years: The Story of the Jewish Community of Easton, 1752–1942.* Easton, Pa., 1944.

Wolf, Edwin; and Whiteman, Maxwell. *The History of the Jews of Philadelphia from Colonial Times to the Age of Jackson.* Philadelphia, 1957.

ARTICLES

Adelman, David C. "Strangers: Civil Rights of Jews in the Colony of Rhode Island," *RIJHN,* 1 (December 1954), 104.

Bigelow, Bruce. "Aaron Lopez: Merchant of Newport," *RIJHN,* 2 (June 1956), 4.

Blau, Joseph L. "The Spiritual Life of American Jewry, 1654–1954," *AJYB,* 56 (1955), 99.

Chiel, Arthur A. "The Rabbis and Ezra Stiles," *AJHQ,* 61 (June 1972), 294.

Chyet, Stanley F. "The Political Rights of the Jews in the United States: 1776–1840," *AJA,* 10 (April 1958), 14.

Eitches, Edward. "Maryland's 'Jew Bill,'" *AJHQ,* 60 (March 1971), 258.

Fein, Isaac M. *"Niles' Weekly Register* on the Jews," *PAJHS,* 50 (September 1960), 3.

Friedenberg, Albert M. "The Jews of America, 1654–1787: With Special Reference to the Revolution," *AJYB,* 28 (1926–27), 193.

Friedman, Lee M. "Cotton Mather and the Jews," *PAJHS,* 26 (1918), 201.

———. "Jewish Colonial Privateersmen," *PAJHS,* 40 (September 1950), 75.

Glazer, Nathan. "Social Characteristics of American Jews, 1654–1954," *AJYB,* 56 (1955), 3.

Goodman, Abram V. "A German Mercenary Observes Russian Jews During the Revolution," *PAJHS,* 59 (December 1969), 227.

Gutmann, Joseph. "Jewish Participation in the Visual Arts of Eighteenth- and Nineteenth-Century America," *AJA,* 15 (April 1963), 21.

Handlin, Oscar; and Handlin, Mary F. "The Acquisition of Political and Social Rights by the Jews in the United States, 1654–1954," *AJYB,* 56 (1955), 43.

Harap, Louis. "Image of the Jew in American Drama, 1794–1823," *AJHQ,* 60 (March 1971), 242.

Hollander, J. H. "The Naturalization of Jews in the American Colonies Under the Act of 1740," *PAJHS,* 5–6 (1897), 103.

Huehner, Leon. "Jews in the War of 1812," *PAJHS,* 26 (1918), 173.

"Jews and the American Revolution: A Bicentennial Documentary," *AJA,* 27 (November 1975), 103.

Jones, Charles C. "The Settlement of the Jews in Georgia," *PAJHS,* 1–2 (1892–1893), 5.

Kanof, Abram. "Uriah Phillips Levy: The Story of a Pugnacious Commodore," *PAJHS,* 39 (September 1949), 1.

Klein, Rose S. "Washington's Thanksgiving Proclamation," *AJA,* 20 (November 1968), 156.

Kohler, Max J. "Jewish Activity in American Colonial Commerce," *PAJHS,* 10 (1902), 47.

———. "Some Jewish Factors in the Settlement of the West," *PAJHS,* 16 (1907), 23.

Morris, Maxwell H. "Roger Williams and the Jews," *AJA,* 3 (January 1951), 24.

Morris, Richard B. "Civil Liberties and the Jewish Tradition in Early America," *PAJHS,* 46 (September 1956), 20.

Necarsulmer, Henry. "The Early Jewish Settlement at Lancaster, Pennsylvania," *PAJHS,* 9–10 (1901), 29.

Oppenheim, Samuel. "Benjamin Franks, Merchant, and Captain Kidd, Pirate," *PAJHS,* 31 (1928), 229.

Peskin, Allan. "England's Jewish Naturalization Bill of 1753," *Historia Judaica, 19* (April 1957), 3.

Rischin, Moses, "The Jews and the Liberal Tradition in America," *AJHQ,* 51 (September 1961), 4.

Schappes, Morris U. "Anti-Semitism and Reaction, 1795–1800," *PAJHS,* 38 (December 1948), 109.

——. "Jews in the American Revolution," *Jewish Life,* 8 (March 1954), 21.

——. "Jews and the Jeffersonians," *Jewish Life,* 8 (April 1954), 21.

Sherbow, Joseph. "The Impact of the American Constitution upon the Jews of the United States," *PAJHS,* 43 (June 1954), 159.

Silver, Louis. "The Jews in Albany, N.Y., 1655–1914," *YAJSS,* 9 (1954), 212.

Simonhoff, Harry. "Tolerance in Carolina in 1697," *The Chicago Jewish Forum,* 25 (Winter 1966–67), 147.

——. "Civil and Religious Liberty in Colonial Rhode Island," *The Chicago Jewish Forum,* 22 (Summer 1964), 286.

Stern, Malcolm H. "Jewish Marriage and Intermarriage in the Federal Period, 1776–1840," *AJA,* 19 (November 1967), 142.

Wiznitzer, Arnold. "The Exodus from Brazil and Arrival in New Amsterdam of the Jewish Pilgrim Fathers, 1654," *PAJHS,* 44 (December 1954), 80.

CHAPTER II

BOOKS

Alder, Cyrus; and Margalith, Aaron M. *With Firmness in the Right: American Diplomatic Action Affecting Jews, 1840–1945.* New York, 1946.

Benjamin, I. J. *My Three Years in America, 1859–1862,* 2 vols. Philadelphia, 1956.

Birmingham, Stephen. *Our Crowd: The Great Jewish Families of New York.* New York, 1967.

Breck, Allen D. *A Centennial History of the Jews of Colorado, 1859–1959*. Denver, 1960.

Bregstone, Philip P. *Chicago and Its Jews: A cultural History*. Chicago, 1933.

Brooks, Juanita. *History of the Jews of Utah and Idaho*. Salt Lake City, 1973.

Chyet, Stanley F. (ed.). *Lives and Voices: A Collection of American Jewish Memoirs*. Philadelphia, 1972.

Davidson, Gabriel. *Our Jewish Farmers and the Story of the Jewish Agricultural Society*. New York, 1943.

Davis, Moshe. *The Emergence of Conservative Judaism: The Historical School in the 19th Century America*. Philadelphia, 1963.

Fierman, Floyd S. *Some Early Jewish Settlers on the Southwestern Frontier*. El Paso, 1960.

Fitzpatrick, Donovan; and Saphire, Saul. *Navy Maverick: Uriah Phillips Levy*. New York, 1963.

Glanz, Rudolf. *The Jews in American Alaska, 1867–1880*. New York, 1953.

———. *The Jews of California: From the Discovery of Gold Until 1880*. New York, 1960.

———. *Jews in Relation to the Cultural Milieu of the Germans in America*. New York, 1947.

———. *Studies in Judaica Americana*. New York, 1970.

Glazer, Nathan. *American Judaism,* rev. ed. Chicago, 1972.

Goldberg, I. *Major Noah, American Jewish Pioneer*. Philadelphia, 1936.

Goldmann, Jack B. *A History of Pioneer Jews in California, 1849–1870*. San Francisco, 1971.

Grusd, Edward E. *B'nai B'rith: The Story of a Covenant*. New York, 1966.

Gutstein, Morris A. *Priceless Heritage: The Epic Growth of Nineteenth Century Chicago Jewry*. New York, 1953.

Heller, James G. *Isaac M. Wise, His Life, Work and Thought*. New York, 1965.

Higham, John. *Strangers in the Land: Patterns of American Nativism, 1860–1925*. New York, 1968.

Hirshler, Eric E. (ed.). *Jews from Germany in the United States*. New York, 1955.

Karp, Abraham J. *The Jewish Experience in America: In the Early Republic, Selected Studies from the Publications of the American Jewish Historical Society,* Vol. 2. Waltham, Mass., 1969.

Katz, Irving. *August Belmont, A Political Biography*. New York, 1968.

————. *The Beth El Story, with a History of the Jews in Michigan Before 1850; and, Three Hundred Years in America, by Dr. Jacob R. Marcus*. Detroit, 1955.

Korn, Bertram W. *American Jewry and the Civil War*. Philadelphia, 1951.

————. *The American Reaction to the Mortara Case: 1850–1859*. Cincinnati, 1957.

————. *Eventful Years and Experiences*. Cincinnati, 1954.

Levin, Alexandra Lee. *The Szolds of Lombard Street: A Baltimore Family, 1859–1909*. Philadelphia, 1960.

Mahoney, Tom. *The Great Merchants: The Stories of Twenty Famous Retail Operations and the People Who Made Them Great*. New York, 1955.

Marcus, Jacob R. *The Americanization of Isaac Mayer Wise*. Cincinnati, 1931.

————. *Memoirs of American Jews, 1775–1865*, 3 vols. Philadelphia, 1955–56.

Meade, R. D. *Judah P. Benjamin*. New York, 1943.

Parzen, Herbert. *Architects of Conservative Judaism*. New York, 1964.

Philipson, David. *The Reform Movement in Judaism*. New York, 1931.

Plaut, W. Gunther. *The Jews in Minnesota: The First Seventy-five Years*. New York, 1959.

Porter, G.; and Livesay, H. C. *Merchants and Manufacturers, Studies in the Changing Structure of 19th-Century Marketing*. Baltimore, 1971.

Rabinowitz, Benjamin. *The Young Men's Hebrew Association, 1854–1913*. New York, 1948.

Rosenthal, Frank. *The Jews of Des Moines: The First Century*. Des Moines, 1957.

Shinedling, Abraham I. *West Virginia Jewry: Origins and History—1850–1958*, 3 vols. Philadelphia, 1961.

Simonhoff, Harry. *Jewish Participants in the Civil War*. New York, 1963.

————. *Saga of American Jewry, 1865–1914: Links of an Endless Chain*. New York, 1959.

Suhl, Yuri. *Eloquent Crusader, Ernestine Rose*. New York, 1970.

Swichkow, Louis J.; and Gartner, Lloyd P. *The History of the Jews of Milwaukee*. Philadelphia, 1963.

Uchill, Ida L. *Pioneers, Peddlers, and Tsadikim*. Denver, 1957.

Vorspan, Max; and Gartner, Lloyd P. *History of the Jews of Los Angeles*. Philadelphia, 1970.

Watters, Leon L. *The Pioneer Jews of Utah*. New York, 1952.

Wischnitzer, Mark. *To Dwell in Safety: The Story of Jewish Migration Since 1800*. Philadelphia, 1948.

Wise, Isaac M. *Reminiscences*. New York, 1901.

Wolf, Simon. *The Presidents I Have Known from 1860 to 1918*. Washington, D.C., 1918.

Zarchin, Michael M. *Glimpses of Jewish Life in San Francisco: History of San Francisco Jewry*. San Francisco, 1952.

ARTICLES

"Anti-Jewish Sentiment in California—1855," *AJA*, 12 (April 1960), 15.

Appel, John J. "The *Trefa* Banquet," *Commentary*, 41 (February 1966), 75.

Berg, Louis. "Peddlers in Eldorado," *Commentary*, 40 (July 1965).

Cohen, Henry, "The Jews in Texas," *PAJHS*, 4 (1896), 9.

Cowen, E. D. "Moses Elias Levy's Agricultural Colony in Florida," *PAJHS*, 25 (1917), 132.

Feldman, Egal. "Jews in the Early Growth of New York City's Men's Clothing Trade," *AJA*, 12 (April 1960), 3.

Fierman, Floyd S. "Peddlers and Merchants—The Jewish Businessman on the Southwest Frontier: 1850–1880," *The El Paso Historical Society*, 8 (Spring 1963), 43.

Glanz, Rudolf, "The German Jewish Mass Emigration: 1820–1880," *AJA*, 22 (April 1970), 49.

———. "The Spread of Jewish Communities Through America Before the Civil War," *YAJSS*, 15 (1974), 7.

Goodman, Abram V. "A Jewish Peddler's Diary, 1842–1843," *AJA*, 3 (June 1951), 81.

Jacobs, Joseph. "Damascus Affair of 1840 and the Jews of America," *PAJHS*, 10 (1902), 119.

Kisch, Guido. *"Israels Herold:* The First Jewish Weekly in New York," *Historia Judaica*, 2 (October 1940), 65.

———. "The Revolution of 1848 and the Jewish 'On to America' Movement," *PAJHS*, 38 (March 1948), 185.

Korn, Bertram W. "Jewish 48'ers in America," *AJA*, 2 (June 1949), 3.

————. "The Jews of the Confederacy," *AJA,* 13 (April 1961), 3.

————. "Jews and Negro Slavery in the Old South, 1789–1865," *AJHQ,* 50 (March 1961), 151.

————. "The Jews of the Union," *AJA,* 13 (October 1961), 131.

Kramer, William M.; and Stern, Norton B. "Early California Associations of Michael Goldwater and His Family," *Western States Jewish Historical Quarterly,* 4 (July 1972), 173.

Parish, William J. "The German Jew and the Commercial Revolution in Territorial New Mexico, 1850–1900," *New Mexico Historical Review,* 35 (January 1960), 1.

Pool, David de Sola. "Jewish Colony of Sholam, Ulster County, New York, 1838," *PAJHS,* 23 (1915), 178.

Rosenbloom, Joseph R. "Rebecca Gratz and the Jewish Sunday School Movement in Philadelphia," *AJHQ,* 48 (December 1958), 71.

Ruchames, Louis. "The Abolitionists and the Jews," *PAJHS,* 42 (December 1952), 131.

————. "Jewish Radicalism in the United States." In Peter I. Rose (ed.), *The Ghetto and Beyond: Essays on Jewish Life in America,* p. 231. New York, 1969.

Ryback, Martin. "The East-West Conflict in American Reform Judaism," *AJA,* 4 (January 1952), 3.

Schappes, Morris U. "The Jews and American Slavery," *Jewish Life,* 8 (May 1954), 15.

Stern, Norton B.; and Kramer, William M. "Anti-Semitism and the Jewish Image in the Early West," *Western States Jewish Historical Quarterly,* 6 (January 1974), 129.

Supple, Barry E. "A Business Elite: German-Jewish Financiers in Nineteenth Century New York," *The Business History Review,* 21 (1957), 176.

Tarshish, Allan. "The Board of Delegates of American Israelites (1859–1878)," *PAJHS,* 49 (September 1959), 16.

"Trail Blazers of the Trans-Mississippi West," *AJA,* 8 (October 1956), 59.

Weinryb, Bernard D. "Noah's Ararat Jewish State in Its Historical Setting," *PAJHS,* 43 (March 1954), 170.

Wilson, Don W. "Pioneer Jews in California and Arizona," *Journal of the West,* 6 (April 1967), 226.

Winter, Carl G. "The Influence of the Russo-American Treaty of 1832 on the Rights of American Jewish Citizens," *PAJHS,* 41 (December 1951), 163.

CHAPTER III

BOOKS

Antin, Mary. *The Promised Land*. New York, 1912.

Bernheimer, Charles S. (ed.). *The Russian Jew in the United States: Studies of Social Conditions in New York, Philadelphia, and Chicago, with a Description of Rural Settlements*. Philadelphia, 1905.

Howe, Irving. *World of Our Fathers: The Journey of the East Europeans to America and the Life They Found and Made*. New York, 1976.

————; and Greenberg, Eliezer (eds.). *Voices from the Yiddish*. Ann Arbor, 1972.

Joseph, Samuel. *History of the Baron de Hirsch Fund: The Americanization of the Jewish Immigrant*. Philadelphia, 1935.

Karp, Abraham J. *The Jewish Experience in America: The Era of Immigration, Selected Studies from the Publications of the American Jewish Historical Society*, Vol. 4. Waltham, Mass., 1969.

Lee, Samuel J. *Moses of the New World: The Work of Baron de Hirsch*. New York, 1970.

Rawidowicz, Simon (ed.). *The Chicago Pinkas*. Chicago, 1952.

Riis, Jacob. *How the Other Half Lives*. New York, 1890.

————. *The Battle with the Slums*. New York, 1902.

Rischin, Moses. *The Promised City, New York's Jews 1870–1914*. New York, 1962.

Schoener, Allon (ed.). *Portal to America: The Lower East Side, 1870–1925*. New York, 1969.

Shiloh, Ailon (ed.). *By Myself I'm a Book: An Oral History of the Immigrant Jewish Experience in Pittsburgh*. Waltham, Mass., 1972.

Wieder, Arnold A. *The Early Jewish Community of Boston's North End*. Waltham, Mass., 1962.

Wirth, Louis. *The Ghetto*. Chicago, 1928.

Wischnitzer, Mark. *Visas to Freedom: The History of HIAS*. Cleveland, 1956.

ARTICLES

Applebaum, Emanuel. "The Palestine Colony—An Agricultural Endeavor," *Michigan Jewish History,* 4 (May 1964), 14.

Cooley, Everett L. "Clarion, Utah: Jewish Colony in Zion," *Utah Historical Quarterly,* 36 (Spring 1968), 113.

Fauman, Joseph S. "The Jews in the Waste Industry in Detroit," *JSS,* 3 (January 1941), 41.

Greenfeld, Judith. "The Role of the Jews in the Development of the Clothing Industry in the United States," *YAJSS,* 2–3 (1947–48), 180.

Handlin, Oscar. "American Views of the Jew at the Opening of the Twentieth Century," *PAJHQ,* 40 (June 1951), 323.

"Jewish Immigrant Life in Philadelphia," *AJA,* 60 (April 1957), 32.

Kligsberg, Moses. "Jewish Immigrants in Business," *AJHQ,* 56 (March 1967), 283.

Mandel, Irving A. "Attitude of the American Jewish Community Toward East-European Immigration as Reflected in the Anglo-Jewish Press," *AJA,* 3 (June 1950), 11.

Osofsky, Gilbert. "The Hebrew Emigrant Aid Society of the United States, 1881–1883," *PAJHS,* 49 (December 1959), 1973.

Panitz, Esther. "The Polarity of American Jewish Attitudes Towards Immigration, 1870–1891," *AJHQ,* 53 (December 1963), 99.

Roberts, Dorothy. "The Jewish Colony at Cotopaxi," *Colorado Magazine,* (July 1941), 124.

Rudin, James. "Beersheba, Kan.: God's Pure Air on Government Land," *Kansas Historical Quarterly,* 34 (Autumn 1968), 282.

Sapinsley, Elbert L. "Jewish Agricultural Colonies in the West: The Kansas Example," *Western States Jewish Historical Quarterly,* 3 (April 1971), 157.

Schwartz, Lois F. "Early Jewish Agricultural Colonies in North Dakota," *North Dakota History,* 32 (October 1965), 217.

Shpall, Leo. "Jewish Agricultural Colonies in the United States," *Agricultural History,* 24 (July 1950), 120.

———. "A Jewish Agricultural Colony in Louisiana," *Louisiana Historical Quarterly* (July 1937), 821.

Swichkow, Louis J. "The Jewish Agricultural Colony of Arpin, Wisconsin," *AJHQ,* 54 (September 1964), 82.

Szajkowski, Zosa. "The Attitude of American Jews to East European Immigration, 1881–1893," *PAJHS,* 40 (March 1951), 221.

———. "Emigration to America or Reconstruction in Europe," *PAJHS,* 42 (December 1952), 157.

Tcherikower, Elias. "Jewish Immigrants to the United States," *YAJSS,* 6 (1951), 157.

Waldman, Morris D. "The Galveston Movement," *The Jewish Social Science Quarterly,* (March 1928), 197.

CHAPTER IV

BOOKS

Bookbinder, Hyman H. et. al. *To Promote the General Welfare: The Story of the Amalgamated.* New York, 1950.

Cahan, Abraham. *The Education of Abraham Cahan,* trans. Leon Stein et al. Philadelphia, 1969.

———. *The Rise of David Levinsky.* New York, 1917.

Carpenter, Jesse Thomas. *Competition and Collective Bargaining in the Needle Trades, 1910–1967.* Ithaca, N.Y., 1972.

Cohen, Julius H. *They Builded Better Than They Knew.* New York, 1946.

Cohen, Morris R. *A Dreamer's Journey.* Boston, 1949.

Cowen, Philip. *Memories of an American Jew.* New York, 1932.

Epstein, Melech. *Jewish Labor in U.S.A.: An Industrial, Political and Cultural History of the Jewish Labor Movement, 1882–1952,* 2 vols. New York, 1950–53.

———. *Profiles of Eleven.* Detroit, 1965.

Feinstein, Marnin. *American Zionism, 1884–1904.* New York, 1965.

Gompers, Samuel. *Seventy Years of Life and Labor.* New York, 1925.

Goren, Arthur A. *New York Jews and the Quest for Community: The Kehillah Experiment, 1908–1922.* New York, 1970.

Green, Charles H. *The Headwear Workers: A Century of Trade Unionism.* New York, 1944.

Hapgood, Hutchins. *The Spirit of the Ghetto.* New York, 1902.

Hillquit, Morris. *Loose Leaves from a Busy Life.* New York, 1934.

Hurwitz, Maximilian. *The Workmen's Circle: Its History, Ideals, Organization and Institutions.* New York, 1936.

Landesman, Alter F. *Brownsville: The Birth, Development and Passing of a Jewish Community in New York*. New York, 1969.

Levine, Louis. *The Women's Garment Workers: A History of the International Ladies' Garment Workers' Union*. New York, 1924.

Lifson, David S. *The Yiddish Theatre in America*. New York, 1965.

Lipsky, Louis. *Thirty Years of American Zionism*. New York, 1927.

Liptzin, Solomon. *The Jew in American Literature*. New York, 1966.

Metzker, Isaac (ed.). *A Bintel Brief: Sixty Years of Letters from the Lower East Side to the Jewish Daily Forward*. New York, 1972.

Ravage, Marcus E. *An American in the Making*. New York, 1917.

Sanders, Ronald. *The Downtown Jews, Portraits of an Immigrant Generation*. New York, 1969.

Seidman, Joel. *The Needle Trades*. New York, 1942.

Shapiro, Judah. *The Friendly Society: History of the Workmen's Circle*. New York, 1971.

Soltes, Mordecai. *The Yiddish Press: An Americanizing Agency*. New York, 1925.

Stein, Leon. *The Triangle Fire*. Philadelphia, 1967.

————— (ed.). *Out of the Sweatshops: The Struggle for Industrial Democracy*. New York, 1977.

Stolberg, Benjamin. *Tailor's Progress*. New York, 1944.

Szajkowski, Zosa. *Jews, Wars and Communism—Vol. I: The Attitude of American Jews to World War I, the Russian Revolutions of 1917, and Communism*. New York, 1972.

Urofsky, Melvin I. *American Zionism from Herzl to the Holocaust*. New York, 1975.

Waxman, Meyer. *A History of Jewish Literature, Vol. IV, Part Two: From 1880 to 1935; Vol. V: From 1945 to 1960*. New York, 1960.

Yivo Institute for Jewish Research. *The Early Jewish Labor Movement in the United States*. Trans. and rev. Aaron Antonovsky, ed. Elias Tcherikower. New York, 1961.

ARTICLES

Bloom, Bernard. "Yiddish-Speaking Socialists in America: 1892–1905," *AJA*, 12 (April 1960), 34.

Cohen, Naomi W. "The Maccabaean's Message: A Study in American Zionism Until World War I," *JSS*, 18 (July 1956), 163.

————. "The Reaction of Reform Judaism in America to Political Zionism, 1897–1922," *PAJHS,* 40 (June 1951), 361.

Elazar, Daniel. "Working Conditions in Chicago in the Early 20th Century: Testimony Before the Illinois Senatorial Vice Committee, 1913," *AJA*, 21 (November 1969), 113.

Geller, Stuart M. "Why Did Louis D. Brandeis Choose Zionism?" *AJHQ,* 62 (June 1973), 383.

Goldblatt, Charles I. "The Impact of the Balfour Declaration in America," *AJHQ,* 57 (June 1968), 455.

Gorenstein, Arthur. "The Commissioner and the Community: The Beginnings of the New York City 'Kehillah' (1908–1909)," *YAJSS,* 13 (1965), 187.

Herberg, Will. "The Jewish Labor Movement in the United States," *AJYB,* 53 (1952), 3.

Karp, Abraham J. "New York Chooses a Chief Rabbi," *PAJHS,* 44 (March 1955), 129.

Liptzin, Sol. "Yiddish Drama: A Century's Survey," *Jewish Book Annual,* 18 (1960–61), 12.

Neusner, Jacob. "The Impact of Immigration and Philanthropy upon the Boston Jewish Community, 1880–1914," *AJHQ,* 46 (December 1956), 71.

Rappaport, Joseph. "The American Yiddish Press and the European Conflict in 1914," *JSS,* 19 (July–October 1957), 113.

Rischin, Moses. "Abraham Cahan and the New York *Commercial Advertiser:* A Study in Acculturation," *PAJHS,* 43 (September 1953), 10.

————. "The Early Attitude of the American Jewish Committee to Zionism," *PAJHS,* 49 (March 1960), 188.

Rockaway, Robert. "Ethnic Conflict in an Urban Environment: The German and Russian Jew in Detroit, 1881–1914," *AJHQ,* 60 (December 1970), 133.

Rubinow, Isaac M. "The Jewish Question in New York City, 1902–1903," *PAJHS,* 49 (December 1959), 90.

Schoenberg, Philip E. "The American Reaction to the Kishinev Pogrom of 1903," *AJHQ,* 63 (March 1974), 262.

Selavan, Ida C. "The Education of Jewish Immigrants in Pittsburgh, 1862–1932," *YAJSS,* 15 (1974), 126.

Seller, Maxine S. "Isaac Lesser's Views on the Restoration of a Jewish Palestine," *AJHQ,* 58 (September 1968), 118.

Zunser, Miriam S. "The Jewish Literary Scene in New York at the Beginning of the Century," *YAJSS,* 7 (1952), 277.

CHAPTER V

BOOKS

Adler, Cyrus. *I Have Considered the Days*. Philadelphia, 1941.

Bernstein, Herman. *The Truth About the Protocols of Zion*. New York, 1971.

Davies, Rosemary R. *The Rosenbluth Case: Federal Justice on Trial*. Ames, Ia., 1970.

Dinnerstein, Leonard (ed.). *Anti-Semitism in the United States*. New York, 1971.

———. *The Leo Frank Case*. New York, 1968.

Freeman, Joseph. *An American Testament: A Narrative of Rebels and Romantics*. New York, 1936.

Golden, Harry. *A Little Girl Is Dead*. Cleveland, 1965.

———. *Our Southern Landsman*. New York, 1974.

Goldman, Emma. *Living My Life,* 2 vols. New York, 1931.

Goldmann, Nahum. *Sixty Years of Jewish Life*. New York, 1969.

Mason, Alpheus T. *Brandeis: A Free Man's Life*. New York, 1946.

Meyers, Gustavus. *History of Bigotry in the United States*. New York, 1960.

Murray, Robert K. *Red Scare: A Study of National Hysteria, 1919–1920*. New York, 1955.

Rabinowitz, Ezekiel. *Justice Louis D. Brandeis: The Zionist Chapter of His Life*. New York, 1968.

Reznikoff, Charles (ed.). *Louis Marshall, Champion of Liberty: Selected Papers and Addresses,* 2 vols. Philadelphia, 1957.

Ribalow, Harold U. (ed.). *Autobiographies of American Jews*. Philadelphia, 1965.

Rosenstock, Morton. *Louis Marshall, Defender of Jewish Rights*. Detroit, 1965.

Shapiro, Yonathan. *Leadership of the American Zionist Organization, 1897–1930*. Urbana, Ill., 1971.

Silverberg, Robert. *If I Forget Thee, O Jerusalem: The Dramatic Story of How American Jews and the United States Helped Create Israel*. New York, 1970.

Szajkowski, Zosa. *Jews, Wars and Communism—Vol. II: The Impact of the 1919–1920 Red Scare on American Jewish Life*. New York, 1974.

Teller, Judd. *Strangers and Natives: The Evolution of the American Jew from 1921 to the Present.* New York, 1968.

Urofsky, Melvin I. *A Mind of One Piece: Brandeis and American Reform.* New York, 1971.

Waldman, Louis. *Albany: The Crisis in Government.* New York, 1920.

Weizmann, Chaim. *Trial and Error.* New York, 1949.

ARTICLES

Berlin, George L. "The Brandeis-Weizmann Dispute," *AJHQ,* 60 (September 1970), 37.

Hareven, Tamara K. "Un-American America and the Jewish Daily Forward," *YAJSS,* 14 (1969), 234.

Higham, John. "Social Discrimination Against Jews in America, 1830–1930," *PAJHS,* 47 (September 1957), 1.

Leonard, Henry B. "Louis Marshall and Immigration Restriction, 1906–1924," *AJA,* 24 (April 1972), 6.

Moseley, Clement C. "The Case of Leo M. Frank, 1913–1915," *The Georgia Historical Quarterly,* 51 (March 1967), 42.

Panitz, Esther. "In Defense of the Jewish Immigrant, 1891–1924," *AJHQ,* 55 (September 1965), 57.

Rockaway, Robert A. "The Eastern European Jewish Community of Detroit, 1881–1914," *YAJSS,* 15 (1974), 82.

Russell, Francis. "The Coming of the Jews," *Antioch Review,* 15 (Spring 1955), 19.

Schappes, Morris U. "The Jews and the Post-War Reaction After 1918," *Jewish Life,* 9 (April 1955), 23.

Steinberg, Stephen. "How Jewish Quotas Began," *Commentary,* 52 (September 1971), 67.

Szajkowski, Zosa. "Double Jeopardy—The Abrams Case of 1919," *AJA,* 23 (April 1971), 6.

CHAPTER VI

BOOKS

Aaron, Daniel. *Writers on the Left: Episodes in American Literary Communism.* New York, 1961.

Crowther, Bosley. *The Lion's Share: The Story of an Entertainment Empire*. New York, 1957.

Davidson, Jo. *Between Sittings*. New York, 1951.

Elovitz, Mark H. *A Century of Jewish Life in Dixie: The Birmingham Experience*. Birmingham, 1974.

Epstein, Jacob. *An Autobiography*. London, 1963.

Epstein, Melech. *The Jew and Communism: The Story of Early Communist Victories and Ultimate Defeats in the Jewish Community, U.S.A., 1919–1941*. New York, 1959.

Foner, Philip S. *The Fur and Leather Workers Union: A Story of Dramatic Struggles and Achievements*. Newark, N.J., 1950.

Fuchs, Lawrence H. *The Political Behavior of American Jews*. New York, 1973.

Guttmann, Allen. *The Jewish Writer in America: Assimilation and the Crisis of Identity*. New York, 1971.

Jews in America. By the editors of *Fortune*. New York, 1936.

Josephson, Matthew. *Sidney Hillman, American Statesman of Labor*. New York, 1952.

Karp, Abraham J. (ed.). *The Jewish Experience in America: At Home in America, Selected Studies from the Publications of the American Jewish Historical Society*, Vol. 5. Waltham, Mass., 1969.

Kazin, Alfred. *Starting Out in the Thirties*. New York, 1962.

Kent, Donald P. *The Refugee Intellectual: The Americanization of the Immigrants of 1930–1941*. New York, 1953.

Marcus, Sheldon. *Father Coughlin: The Tumultuous Life of the Priest of the Little Flower*. Boston, 1973.

Mayer, Arthur. *Merely Colossal: The Story of the Movies from the Long Chase to the Chaise Longue*. New York, 1953.

Ribalow, Harold U. (ed.). *The Jew in American Sports*. New York, 1959.

———. *Mid-Century: An Anthology of Jewish Life and Culture in Our Times*. New York, 1955.

Rosten, Leo. *Hollywood: The Movie Colony—the Movie Makers*. New York, 1941.

Sterne, Maurice. *Shadow and Light: The Life, Friends, and Opinions of Maurice Sterne*. New York, 1955.

Strong, Donald S. *Organized Anti-Semitism in America: The Rise of Group Prejudice During the Decade 1930–1940*. Washington, D.C., 1941.

Turkus, Burton; and Feder, Sid. *Murder, Inc.: The Inside Story of the Mob.* New York, 1951.

Walden, Daniel (ed.). *On Being Jewish: American Jewish Writers from Cahan to Bellow.* Greenwich, Conn., 1974.

ARTICLES

Coleman, McAlester. "The Rise of David Dubinsky," *The Nation,* 14 (May 1938), 538.

Herberg, Will. "Old-Timers and Newcomers: Ethnic Group Relations in a Needle Trades Union," *Jewish Frontier,* 20 (November 1953), 24.

Kanin, Josh. "Jews in Early Moving Pictures," *Davka Magazine* (Volume 5, Winter 1975), 9.

Krug, Mark M. "The Yiddish Schools in Chicago," *YAJSS,* 9 (1954), 276.

Raskin, A. H. "Dubinsky: Herald of Change," *Labor History,* 9 (Spring 1968), 23.

Reich, Nathan. "The Role of Jews in the American Economy," *YAJSS,* 5 (1950), 197.

Rich, J. C. "David Dubinsky: The Young Years," *Labor History,* 9 (Spring 1968), 43.

Rideout, Walter B. "O Workers' Revolution . . . The True Messiah: The Jew as Author and Subject in the American Radical Novel," *AJA,* 2 (October 1959), 157.

Rischin, Moses. "The Jewish Labor Movement in America: A Social Interpretation," *Labor History,* 5 (Fall 1964), 227.

Werner, Alfred. "Ben Zion, Jewish Painter," *Midstream,* 19 (November 1973), 24.

———. "Ghetto Graduates," *American Art Journal,* 5 (November 1973), 71.

———. "Self-Revelations: Some Autobiographies of American Jewish Artists," *Jewish Book Annual,* 31 (1973–74), 37.

Winograd, Leonard. "Double Jeopardy," *AJA,* 28 (April 1976), 3.

Yedwab, Stanley. "The Jew as Portrayed in American Jewish Novels of the 1930's," *AJA,* 2 (October 1959), 148.

CHAPTER VII

BOOKS

Barnard, Harry. *The Forging of an American Jew: The Life and Times of Judge Julian W. Mack.* New York, 1974.

Cohen, Naomi W. *American Jews and the Zionist Idea.* New York, 1975.

————. *Not Free to Desist: The American Jewish Committee, 1906–1966.* Philadelphia, 1972.

Duggan, Stephen; and Drury, Betty. *The Rescue of Science and Learning.* New York, 1948.

Feingold, Henry L. *The Politics of Rescue: The Roosevelt Administration and the Holocaust, 1938–1945.* Detroit, 1973.

Halpern, Ben. *The American Jew: A Zionist Analysis.* New York, 1956.

Kent, Donald P. *The Refugee Intellectual: The Americanization of the Immigrants of 1933–41.* New York, 1953.

Morse, Arthur. *While Six Million Died.* New York, 1968.

Mosesson, Gloria A. *The Jewish War Veterans Story.* Washington, D.C., 1971.

Schechtman, Joseph B. *The United States and the Jewish State Movement.* New York, 1966.

Thomas, Gordon; and Witts, Max M. *Voyage of the Damned.* New York, 1974.

Wise, Stephen. *Challenging Years: An Autobiography of Stephen S. Wise.* New York, 1949.

Wyman, David S. *Paper Walls: America and the Refugee Crisis, 1938–1941.* Amherst, Mass., 1969.

ARTICLES

Brody, David. "American Jewry, the Refugees and Immigration Restriction, 1932–1942," *PAJHS,* 45 (June 1956), 219.

Diamond, Sander A. "The *Kristallnacht* and the Reaction in America," *YAJSS,* 14 (1969), 196.

———. "The Years of Waiting: National Socialism in the United States, 1922–1933," *AJHQ*, 59 (March 1970), 256.

Feuer, Leon. "The Birth of the Jewish Lobby: A Reminiscence," *AJA*, 38 (November 1976), 107.

Gellman, Irwin F. "The St. Louis Tragedy," *AJHQ*, 61 (December 1971), 144.

Gottlieb, Moshe. "The American Controversy over the Olympic Games," *AJHQ*, 61 (March 1972), 181.

———. "The Anti-Nazi Boycott Movement in the United States: An Ideological and Sociological Appreciation," *JSS*, 35 (July–October 1973), 198.

———. "The Berlin Riots of 1935 and Their Repercussions in America," *AJHQ*, 59 (March 1970), 302.

Parzen, Herbert. "American Zionism and the Quest for a Jewish State, 1939–43," *Herzl Year Book*, 4 (1961–62), 345.

———. "The Roosevelt Palestine Policy, 1943–45," *AJA*, 26 (April 1974), 31.

Stock, Ernest. "Washington Heights' 'Fourth Reich,'" *Commentary*, 2 (June 1951), 581.

Szajkowski, Zosa. "The Attitude of American Jews to Refugees from Germany in the 1930's," *AJHQ*, 61 (December 1971), 101.

CHAPTER VIII

BOOKS

American Jewish Committee. *Jews in College and University Administration.* New York, 1966.

———. *Patterns of Exclusion from the Executive Suite.* New York, 1966.

Berkman, Ted. *Cast a Giant Shadow: The Story of Mickey Marcus.* New York, 1962.

Finkelstein, Louis (ed.). *The Jews: Their History, Culture, and Religion,* 2 vols. Philadelphia, 1966.

Halpern, Ben. *The American Jew: A Zionist Analysis.* New York, 1956.

Handlin, Oscar; and Handlin, Mary. *Danger in Discord: Origins of Anti-Semitism in the United States,* 3rd ed. New York, 1964.

Heckelman, A. Joseph. *American Volunteers and Israel's War of Independence*. New York, 1974.

Hecht, Ben. *A Child of the Century*. New York, 1954.

Isaacs, Harold R. *American Jews in Israel*. New York, 1967.

Kaplan, Mordecai. *Judaism as a Civilization*. New York, 1957.

―――. *A New Zionism*, 2nd ed. New York, 1959.

Levitan, Tina. *Jews in American Life*. New York, 1969.

McWilliams, Carey. *A Mask for Privilege: Anti-Semitism in America*. Boston, 1948.

Postal, Bernard; and Levy, Henry W. *And the Hills Shouted for Joy: The Day Israel Was Born*. Philadelphia, 1973.

Ringer, Benjamin. *The Edge of Friendliness: A Study of Jewish-Gentile Relations*. New York, 1967.

Rosenberg, Stuart. *The Search for Jewish Identity in America*. New York, 1965.

Sherman, C. Bezalel. *The Jew Within American Society*. Detroit, 1961.

Silver, Abba Hillel. *Vision and Victory: A Collection of Addresses, 1942–1948*. New York, 1949.

Snetsinger, John. *Truman, the Jewish Vote, and the Creation of Israel*. Stanford, Calif., 1974.

Stember, Charles; et al. *Jew in the Mind of America*. New York, 1966.

Wolfe, Ann. *Why the Swastika? A Story of Young American Vandals*. New York, 1962.

Zaar, Isaac. *Rescue and Liberation: America's Part in the Birth of Israel*. New York, 1954.

ARTICLES

Bickerton, Ian J. "President Truman's Recognition of Israel," *AJHQ,* 58 (December 1968), 1973.

Burton, William L. "Protestant America and the Rebirth of Israel," *JSS,* 26 (October 1964), 203.

―――. "Some Aspects of Israel's Impact on Identification and Cultural Patterns," *JSS,* 21 (January 1959), 25.

Hertzberg, Arthur. "Israel and American Jewry," *Commentary,* 44 (August 1967), 69.

Karp, Abraham J. "Reaction to Zionism and to the State of Israel in the American Jewish Religious Community," *Jewish Journal of Sociology,* 8 (December 1966), 150.

Marker, Jeffrey M. "The Jewish Community and the Case of Julius and Ethel Rosenberg," *The Maryland Historian,* 3 (Fall 1972), 105.

Parzen, Herbert. "President Truman and the Palestine Quandary: His Initial Experience, April–December, 1945," *JSS,* 35 (January 1973), 42.

Peretz, Martin. "The American Left and Israel," *Commentary,* 44 (November 1967), 27.

Syrkin, Marie. "How Israel Affects American Jews," *Midstream,* 19 (May 1973), 29.

Tugend, Tom. "The Hollywood Jews," *Davka Magazine,* 5 (Winter 1975), 4.

"Two Presidents and a Haberdasher—1948," *AJA,* 20 (April 1968), 3.

Weiser, Benno. "Ben Gurion's Dispute with American Zionists," *Commentary,* 18 (August 1954), 93.

CHAPTER IX

BOOKS

Berson, Lenora E. *The Negroes and the Jews.* New York, 1971.

Blau, Joseph L. *The Spiritual Life of American Jewry.* New York, 1965.

Chertoff, Mordecai S. (ed.). *The New Left and the Jews.* New York, 1971.

Cohen, Bernard. *Sociocultural Changes in American Jewish Life as Reflected in Selected Jewish Literature.* Rutherford, N.J., 1972.

Dinnerstein, Leonard; and Palsson, Mary Dale (eds.). *Jews in the South.* Baton Rouge, 1973.

Forster, Arnold; and Epstein, Benjamin R. *The New Anti-Semitism.* New York, 1974.

Friedman, Theodore; and Gordis, Robert. *Jewish Life in America.* New York, 1955.

Fuchs, Lawrence H. *The Political Behavior of American Jews.* Glencoe, Ill., 1956.

Gans, Herbert J. *The Levittowners.* New York, 1967.

Geltman, Max. *The Confrontation: Black Power, Anti-Semitism and the Myth of Integration.* Englewood Cliffs, N.J., 1970.

Ginsberg, Yona. *Jews in a Changing Neighborhood: The Study of Mattapan*. New York, 1975.

Glazer, Nathan; and Moynihan, Daniel P. *Beyond the Melting Pot*. Cambridge, Mass., 1970.

Goldstein, Sidney; and Goldscheider, Calvin. *Jewish Americans: Three Generations in a Jewish Community*. Englewood Cliffs, N.J., 1968.

Gordon, Albert L. *Jews in Suburbia*. Boston, 1959.

——. *Jews in Transition*. Minneapolis, 1949.

Gordon, Whitney H. *A Community in Stress*. New York, 1964.

Harris, Louis; and Swanson, Bert H. *Black-Jewish Relations in New York City*. New York, 1970.

Hentoff, Nat (ed.). *Black Anti-Semitism and Jewish Racism*. New York, 1970.

Herberg, Will. *Protestant-Catholic-Jew: An Essay in American Religious Sociology*. New York, 1955.

Himmelfarb, Milton. *The Jews of Modernity*. New York, 1973.

Isaacs, Stephen. *Jews and American Politics*. New York, 1974.

Janowsky, Oscar I. (ed.). *The American Jew: A Reappraisal*. Philadelphia, 1964.

Kahane, Meir. *The Story of the Jewish Defense League*. Radnor, Pa., 1968.

Kahn, Roger. *The Passionate People: What It Means to Be a Jew in America*. New York, 1968.

Kertzer, Morris. *Today's American Jew*. New York, 1967.

Kramer, Judith R.; and Leventman, Seymour. *Children of the Gilded Ghetto: Conflict Resolutions of Three Generations of American Jews*. New Haven, 1961.

Madison, Charles A. *Jewish Publishing in America*. New York, 1976.

Poll, Solomon. *The Hasidic Community of Williamsburg*. New York, 1969.

Porter, Jack N.; and Dreier, Peter (eds.). *Jewish Radicalism: A Selected Anthology*. New York, 1973.

Postal, Bernard; et al. *Encyclopedia of Jews in Sports*. New York, 1965.

Rabinowitz, Dorothy. *The Other Jews: Portraits in Poverty*. New York, 1972.

Rose, Peter I. (ed.). *The Ghetto and Beyond: Essays on Jewish Life in America*. New York, 1969.

Seeley, John R.; et al. *Crestwood Heights: A Study of the Culture of Suburban Life*. New York, 1956.

Sklare, Marshall. *Conservative Judaism: An American Religious Movement.* Glencoe, Ill., 1955.

———; and Greenblum, Joseph. *Jewish Identity on the Suburban Frontier.* New York, 1967.

———; and Vosk, Marc. *The Riverton Study: How Jews Look at Themselves.* New York, 1957.

Vorspan, Albert. *So the Kids Are Revolting . . . ?* New York, 1970.

Waskow, Arthur. *The Freedom Seder: A New Haggadah for Passover.* New York, 1970.

Weisbord, Robert G.; and Stein, Arthur. *Bitter-Sweet Encounter: The Afro-American and the American Jew.* New York, 1972.

Weyl, Nathaniel. *The Jew in American Politics.* New York, 1968.

ARTICLES

Bernstein, Melvin H. "Jewishness, Judaism and the American-Jewish Novelist," *Chicago Jewish Forum,* 23 (Summer 1965), 275.

Chyet, Stanley F. "Three Generations: An Account of American Jewish Fiction, 1896–1969," *JSS,* 34 (January 1972), 31.

Clark, Kenneth. "Candor About Negro-Jewish Relations," *Commentary,* I (February 1946), 8.

Cowan, Paul. "Jews Without Money Revisited," *Village Voice* (September 21, 28, 1972).

Dinnerstein, Leonard. "Southern Jewry and the Desegregation Crisis, 1954–1970," *AJHQ,* 62 (March 1973), 231.

Dreiser, Peter; and Porter, Jack N. "Jewish Radicalism in Transition," *Society,* 12 (January/February 1975), 34.

Duker, Abraham G. "Emerging Cultural Patterns in American Jewish Life," *PAJHS,* 39 (June 1950), 351.

———. "On Religious Trends in American Jewish Life," *YAJSS,* 4 (1949), 51.

Effron, Mark. "Left Behind, Left Alone," *National Jewish Monthly,* 89 (April 1974), 14.

Frankel, Theodore. "Suburban Jewish Sunday School," *Commentary,* 25 (January 1958), 481.

Gans, Herbert J. "Forest Park: Birth of a Jewish Community," *Commentary,* 2 (April 1951), 330.

——— "Progress of a Suburban Jewish Community: Forest Park Revisited," *Commentary,* 23 (February 1957), 113.

Gersh, Harry. "The New Suburbanites of the '50s," *Commentary,* 17 (March 1954), 209.

Glazer, Nathan. "The New Left and the Jews," *Jewish Journal of Sociology,* 2 (December 1969), 121.

Glickstein, Gary A. "Religion and the Jewish New Left," *AJA,* 26 (April 1974), 23.

Goldberg, Irving L. "The Changing Jewish Community of Dallas," *AJA,* 2 (April 1959), 82.

Gordon, Whitney H. "Jews and Gentiles in Middletown—1961," *AJA,* 18 (April 1966), 41.

Guttmann, Allan. "The Changing American Rabbinate," *Midstream,* 12 (January 1966), 16.

————. "Jewish Radicals, Jewish Writers," *American Scholar,* 32 (Autumn 1963), 563.

"The Jew in American Culture: A Symposium," *Ramparts,* 2 (Autumn 1963), 6.

Kogan, Lawrence A. "The Jewish Conception of Negroes in the North: An Historical Approach," *Phylon,* 28 (Winter 1967), 376.

Krause, Allen. "Rabbis and Negro Rights in the South, 1954–1967," *AJA,* 21 (April 1969), 20.

Lehrer, Leibush. "Reactions of Second Generation Secularist Jews to Problems of Jewish Living," *YAJSS,* 13 (1965), 79.

Meisler, Stanley. "The Southern Segregationist and His Anti-Semitism," *Chicago Jewish Forum,* 16 (Spring 1958), 171.

Polos, Nicholas C. "Black Anti-Semitism in Twentieth-Century America: Historical Myth or Reality?" *AJA,* 27 (April 1975), 8.

Porter, Jack N.; Rackovsky, Boris; and Agrillo, Anita Bach. "The Jewish Student: A Comparative Analysis of Religious and Secular Attitudes," *YAJSS,* 15 (1974), 297.

Reddick, L. D. "Anti-Semitism Among Negroes," *Negro Quarterly,* I (Summer 1942), 112.

Shankman, Arnold. "A Temple Is Bombed—Atlanta, 1958," *AJA,* 23 (November 1971), 125.

Suber, Howard. "Hollywood's Closet Jews," *Davka Magazine,* 5 (Winter 1975), 12.

Wolfe, Anne G. "The Invisible Jewish Poor," presentation to the Chicago chapter of the *American Jewish Committee,* June 8, 1971.

Ziegler, Mel. "Jewish Poverty amid Jewish Affluence: Journey's End in Miami Beach," *Jewish Digest,* 15 (March 1969), 9.

INDEX